C

Speech Communication in the 20th Century

Speech Communication in the

20th

Century

Edited by

Thomas W. Benson

• Southern Illinois University Press • Carbondale and Edwardsville •

To Everett Lee Hunt

Tables 10.1, Characteristics of Selected Technologies, and 10.2, New Technologies in Traditional Contexts, are from *The New Communications*, by Frederick Williams. © 1984 by Wadsworth, Inc. Reprinted by permission of Wadsworth Publishing Company, Belmont, California 94002.

Library of Congress Cataloging in Publication Data
Main entry under title:

Speech communication in the 20th century.

Bibliography: p.
Includes index.
1. Oral communication—History—20th century.
I. Benson, Thomas W.   II. Title: Speech communication in the twentieth century.
P95.S63   1985   302.2   84–20247
ISBN 0–8093–1196–8

88 87 86 85   4 3 2 1

Contents

PART TWO

BUILDING AN ACADEMIC DISCIPLINE: OVERVIEWS OF ORGANIZATIONAL AND CONCEPTUAL ISSUES

Illustrations

TABLES

FIGURES

Preface

ACADEMIC TEACHERS AND university departments of speech communication trace their distant ancestry to the origins of rhetoric in the fifth century, B.C.. Our earliest surviving texts were written by Plato (*Gorgias* and *Phaedrus*) and by Aristotle (*Rhetoric*). Over the centuries since the work of Plato and Aristotle, the study of rhetoric, of speech, and of human communication generally, has waxed and waned. At the beginning of the 20th century the academic study of communication in American colleges and universities was reestablished with the founding of departments and regional and national professional associations. The first regional association, which has evolved into the Eastern Communication Association, was formed in 1910 (Wichelns, 1959). Soon a national organization and other regional organizations emerged, and a modern academic discipline began to take shape.

This book was commissioned by the Eastern Communication Association to celebrate its 75th anniversary. When the Executive Council of the Association asked me to edit a volume examining the academic study of speech and communication, they gave me a free hand. Through the good offices of the Executive Council, several presidents of ECA, Gerald M. Phillips (then the editor of *Communication Quarterly*), and others, a conception began to emerge, and Southern Illinois University agreed to publish the manuscript.

With unhesitating generosity of spirit, the Executive Council and the Diamond Anniversary Committee (acting under the leadership of John F. Wilson) agreed with my proposal that our book should not be confined in subject matter or authorship to the eastern region of the country from which ECA draws its members. And the leaders of ECA agreed that the volume would be most useful if it went beyond mere celebration to provide a critical self-assessment of our professional practices and accomplishments.

This book is conceived as a successor to Karl Wallace's a *History of Speech Education in America* (1954) and Robert T. Oliver and Marvin G.

Bauer's *Re-Establishing the Speech Profession: The First Fifty Years* (1959). Authors of individual chapters were invited to assess critically the history and prospects of a major area of the field, or, in some cases, to address general problems of academic organization or endeavor. Authors were instructed to write with two audiences primarily in mind. First, we have tried to write to fellow academics in a spirit of critical self-assessment. Second, we have addressed ourselves to those who might be considering or beginning graduate study in speech communication, and who seek a general introduction to the major currents in the field. But to both of these audiences, and to others interested in the volume, including academic administrators or historians, we offer some cautions. This book is not a comprehensive history of speech communication, nor is it a recommendation about the appropriate cluster of subfields that should constitute every college or university department of speech communication. We have, with regret, not included chapters on many areas of communication study that are thriving in association with areas that are represented here. Among the missing are chapters on theatre, communication disorders, speech science, radio and television production, film, intercollegiate debate, language studies, and several other areas. Nor, because of accidents of availability of authors and limitations of space in the volume, have we been able to represent comprehensively the full scope of research methods and results that engage scholars in our field. We ask that readers be sympathetic about our omissions, taking account of what we do provide rather than taking us to task for unavoidable gaps.

The book is organized into two major parts. In the first part are reviews of major areas of inquiry within speech communication, with primary attention to the development of theory and research. I have resisted the urge to further subdivide Part One for several reasons. On purely theoretical grounds, the dialectics that describe the relations of our subfields are, luckily, mixed, and so to group subfields according to one set of distinctions is necessarily to slight other relations. It is by no means clear that we can best understand communication by settling firmly on a definition that etches in stone a single distinction, as with public vs. private, expressive vs. pragmatic, humanistic vs. scientific, oral vs. written vs. electronic, or individual vs. group. Such distinctions may all be useful as tools for analysis, but any one of them alone is inadequate as the basis for describing our objects of study, our academic literature, or the organization of our schools. If the research and theory in any of our subfields becomes sealed off from other areas, all will suffer. And so the organization of Part One has been designed to suggest both the rewards of differentiation and specialization within subfields and the desirability of stimulating cross-fertilization across traditional boundaries.

Part Two has a different design. In this section, scholars address organizational and developmental questions that go beyond any single subfield of communication studies, looking at the ways we have sought to define ourselves as a field and to prosper in and contribute to a system of higher education. The report is mixed and may hold some surprises for readers, as it did for me. For example, these chapters raise again questions that I had thought were settled—questions that go to the root of our legitimacy and as academic discipline and our mission in the academy.

Readers will find grounds to disagree with the views of some of our authors. We have not sought disagreement for its own sake, and have sought, through the review process, to guard against factionalism. Still, the book is intended to provoke debate. Authors have been encouraged to provide materials that would stimulate reexamination of our methods and commitments, not because we believe the field is in trouble but because it has reached its diamond jubilee in good health and is ready to seek new challenges. We know that we are not beginning the debate, nor do we wish to conclude it.

Acknowledgments

THIS BOOK OWES its existence to the generosity of a great many scholars. The chapter authors took time away from other commitments to prepare their materials for a deadline and along the way responded with grace to a series of independent reviews. Many other scholars helped with advice and support. Among those who reviewed individual chapters or provided other advice and support are Carroll C. Arnold (The Pennsylvania State University), Molefi Asante (State University of New York at Buffalo), Arthur P. Bochner (Temple University), John Waite Bowers (The University of Iowa), Karlyn Kohrs Campbell (University of Kansas), Herman Cohen (The Pennsylvania State University), Thomas Conley (University of Illinois), Elizabeth Fine (Virginia Polytechnic Institute and State University), Kenneth D. Frandsen (University of New Mexico), Rodcrick P. Hart (The University of Texas at Austin), William R. Haushalter (Central Michigan University), Dean E. Hewes (University of Illinois), Randy Y. Hirokawa (The University of Iowa), David L. Jamison (University of Akron), Richard L. Johannesen (Northern Illinois University), Richard Katula (University of Rhode Island), Mark L. Knapp (State University of New York, College at New Paltz), Dorothy L. Krueger (University of California, Santa Barbara), Tony Lentz (The Pennsylvania State University), James C. McCroskey (West Virginia University), Stanley E. McKenzie (Rochester Institute of Technology), Mary S. Mander (The Pennsylvania State University), Martin J. Medhurst (University of California at Davis), Michael M. Osborn (Memphis State University), Ronald J. Pelias (Southern Illinois University), Thomas M. Scheidel (The University of Washington), Jean Haskell Speer (Virginia Polytechnic Institute and State University), and John F. Wilson (Lehman College).

The Department of Speech Communication at The Pennsylvania State University has been generous in providing support for postage, telephone, photocopying, and other services. The office staff, Rita Munchinski, Joyce Diehl, Linda Harer, and Diane Roan, have been unfailingly prompt, accurate, and helpful. Dean Stanley Paulson of the College of Liberal Arts, and Robert S. Brubaker, Head of the Department of Speech, have provided years of stable leadership and personal encouragement. Colleagues and students in the department have joined to form a happy blend of personal good will, intellectual challenge, and respect for independence that continue to astonish.

Kenney Withers, director of Southern Illinois University Press, has been a model of patience, trust, and good judgment through a complicated and protracted editorial process. Joyce Atwood copy edited the manuscript with a diligence, firmness, and grace that have earned her the gratitude of editor and authors.

All royalties for this book are assigned to the Eastern Communication Association.

Part One

Contexts of Communication

Review of Theory and Research

1

Rhetorical Theory in Speech Communication

MICHAEL C. LEFF AND
MARGARET ORGAN PROCARIO

R hetorical theory is one of the oldest and most familiar of the divisions of scholarship within speech communication. Strangely enough, however, it is a difficult subject to locate. Over a period of 75 years, our literature evidences a concerted effort to chart its history, to define its nature and scope, to determine its relationship with other domains of learning, and to conceive the foundations on which it might rest. Yet, in respect to the *content* of rhetorical theory, the center from which these other efforts might be assumed to radiate, our literature is somewhat sparse and uncoordinated. During this same period, scholars in other disciplines have made notable contributions to the corpus of theory. They have refined and newly conceived such traditional elements of the art as topical invention, the theory of tropes, and the strategies of disposition. They have also introduced sophisticated constructs to account for the structure and operation of rhetorical discourse (for example, Burke's conception of the rhetorical function of the scapegoat or Perelman's analysis of the interaction between person and act in argument). Speech communication has made some contribution to this renaissance of rhetorical theory, but for the most part it has been content merely to annex its results. Preoccupied with fundamental questions of definition and placement, our literature has neither produced nor integrated a significant body of scholarship devoted to rhetorical theory *per se.*

As a consequence, a review of the literature—if it is to follow the main contour of its sources—must concentrate on the successive efforts to establish the foundations of the subject. This entails a basically historical rather than topical approach to the subject. Nevertheless, as we proceed, we intend development and to suggest reasons why they do not assume a more central and independent status. In fact, we believe that a historical analysis is the best means to uncover the obstacles preventing the discipline from moving beyond its first principles. And although it is now rarely studied, the early history of the discipline seems especially important to us. For it is here that certain fundamental problems emerge most clearly. Moreover, in the incipient stages, trends are set in motion that have lingering effects, some of them much more subtle and persistent than is usually recognized. Most important, certain attitudes concerning the mission and status of the discipline appear almost at its point of origin, and these exert a powerful influence on the work of subsequent generations.

The origins of Speech communication set it apart from most other modern disciplines. "Speech" did not emerge as a discrete academic entity until 1910, when a group of teachers of public speaking broke from the National Council of Teachers of English and formed a professional organization of their own (Rarig & Greaves, 1954, pp. 496–500). This event occurred relatively late in the history of the organization of American universities into departmental units. Consequently, the new discipline had to force its way into an already established pattern. Matters were further complicated by the need to distinguish Departments of Speech from the English departments, which previously had controlled the public speaking curriculum (Smith, 1954, pp. 449–456) and by the need to distinguish public speaking from elocution, with which it was associated (Gray, 1954, p. 424). In the early 20th century, academics had come to regard elocution as cosmetic technique totally devoid of substance. In American universities, increasingly devoted to scientific research, elocution could survive, if at all, only as a pariah. The founders of academic speech, then, had to declare their autonomy from English, but do so in a way that avoided the odium attached to the elocutionists. This endeavor required a research program generically similar to but specifically different from the work done in established departments, and this task proved difficult since speech had yet to evolve a research tradition of its own. These circumstances virtually forced an immediate effort to turn chaos into order. They also encouraged an almost neurotic concern for respectability.

Speech communication, therefore, originated with this most basic of questions: What is it that we have to study? The answer is not obvious, and the question is sometimes posed in a way that suggests nagging doubts about the possibility of a good answer. James Winans, for example, expresses shock bordering on inarticulate rage when he hears the contention that public speaking is too simple to require research (1915, pp. 18–19). The intensity of his reaction is perhaps less significant than the fact that he acknowledges and feels compelled to respond to this allegation. (Indeed, the speech teacher's speechless reaction may be a measure of the strength of the anathematized view.) Moreover, a related and equally basic problem compounds the difficulty in creating a research program for speech. The very nature of public speaking as a discipline creates a serious tension between research and teaching. A similar tension exists in most other academic fields, but rarely is it located at the conceptual center of the discipline. Unlike most other disciplines in colleges of letters and science, speech (at least as conceived in 1915) is clearly a practical art; it culminates in a performance, not in the amassing of objective knowledge or in the generation of purely abstract theory. Hence, the received conventions governing research do not fit squarely with the mission of the speech teacher. Yet, it is pedagogy that provides the most obvious and direct resource for locating the coherence of the discipline. How, then, are speech teachers to study their subject while at the same time preserving the integrity of their profession?

These issues were attacked directly, although perhaps not very subtly, in the first issue of the *Quarterly Journal of Public Speaking*. Reporting for the organizers of the National Association of Academic Teachers of Public Speaking, James O'Neill announced that the association's primary purpose was to encourage those who would "undertake *scientific investigation* to discover the *true answer* to certain problems" (1915, pp. 56–57, emphasis added). James Winans, in his article "The Need for Research," provided a more detailed account of the project. Winans issued a call for intensive, rigorous research such as had been lacking in public speaking. Such research alone could "make us orthodox." It offered the "standard way into the sheepfold." The field needed to develop a more systematic approach to its work, an approach that would allow for "a sufficiently scientific frame of mind." Moreover, he argued, research would benefit teachers by giving them a "better understanding of fundamentals and training in the methods which test and determine truth." Finally, Winans indicated some topics that might reward study. Here he was anything but rigorous or systematic. What he provided was a mere list whose items ranged from scientific study of the voice, to the psychology of speech, to the historical analysis of orators. No hint appeared concerning basic issues that might animate or unify these disparate research problems. And Winans said nothing about method, except that it might be borrowed from other disciplines. (In this respect, Winans noted that since public speaking touched on so many fields, it was possible to begin by adapting research from another field and then address questions in which others were not interested.) The "research program," in short, consisted of a call to conform with the then prevailing academic pieties and an almost random list of *things* toward which such pieties could be exercised.

In the next issue of the journal, Everett Lee Hunt (1915) made a pointed response to Winans. Hunt doubted the wisdom of being driven into the sheepfold. He protested against the "worship of scientific research as the to indicate the main theoretical topics that hover at the margins of the summum bonum of the profession" (p.185), for he believed that public speaking was essentially different from the rest of the college curriculum and that scientific research embodied an ideal antithetical to the enthusiasm and inspiration needed in public speaking. The teacher of oratory, he argued, should not be expert in a single specialized form of knowledge, but should be expert in combining various aspects of knowledge, in making associations relevant to the case at hand. The end of such instruction was to impart "personal power" and not "impersonal knowledge" (pp. 187–188). Thus, it was a grave error to center the curriculum "upon material, impersonal objects, instead of encouraging the free expression" of individuality.

This exchange between O'Neill and Winans, on one side, and Hunt, on the other, establishes (or at least foreshadows) two fundamental issues. The first has to do with the conception of the discipline. For O'Neill and Winans, the term "speaking" is crucial. They define the field in reference to the physical act of speaking and incorporate into the discipline anything that bears on that act (as, for example, voice and diction or speech science). For Hunt, the emphasis falls on *public* speaking (that is, oratory). This is a conceptual rather than objective definition, based on a historical tradition and the paradigm of the Fundamentals of Speech course. Hunt implicitly associates the discipline with the effort to develop the faculty of intelligent and articulate speech on matters of public concern.

In principle, these two positions are not opposed. The former, in fact, has a long history as an administrative definition for the field as a whole (Wallace, 1954). The latter is more specifically relevant to the rhetorical division of the field and can be folded into the more general definition. Nevertheless, in the early years of the discipline there is a fairly clear sense of rivalry between the two orientations. Moreover, the competitive urge is exacerbated because of the second major issue in the exchange—the question of the proper philosophical foundation for the discipline.

O'Neill, Winans, and Hunt initiate the debate between "science" and "humanism" in speech communication. The controversy is still with us, for like Shelley's cloud, it seems to change but not to die. In this opening salvo, Winans and O'Neill, though terribly vague on matters of detail, assume a clear general position. They advocate the standards of positivistic science. Hunt's position is more complex, for his argument incorporates two rather different strands of thought. Hunt's romanticism reveals itself in his reverence for "inspiration" and "enthusiasm" and in his strong distaste for any kind of dispassionate knowledge. At the same time, Hunt is equally influenced by the classical rhetorical tradition. He freely quotes classical authorities, and he virtually paraphrases the ideals of Isocrates, Cicero, and Quintilian in presenting his views about the goals of instruction in public speaking. This mixture of romanticism and classical rhetoric yields a peculiar result. The romantic cult of spontaneity does not accord well the highly structured rhetorics of antiquity and the studied eloquence they cultivate. More important, rhetorical humanism relies heavily on the concept of civic knowledge, knowledge conveyed by tradition and conserved by the institutions of society. The romantic commitment to inspiration works as forcefully against this concept as does the positivist ideal of unequivocal truth (Ong, 1971, pp. 7–8). For this reason, Hunt's statement of the humanist's case obscures the primary source of "content" as conceived in classical systems of invention.

The problem of locating content within the field developed into a persistent and stubborn issue. One clear manifestation of the problem occurred in a second exchange between Hunt and O'Neill. In 1922, Hunt authored an article entitled "Adding Substance to Form in Public Speaking." Hunt expressed concern that public speaking classes lacked "course content," and he proposed a remedy. Speech teachers, he maintained, should prescribe the subjects for student speeches and instruct students about those subjects. Furthermore, class discussions ought to focus on *what* students should talk about rather than on *how* they should talk about it. O'Neill (1923) took strong exception to this position. The subjects of speeches, he argued, were not the proper content for courses in public speaking. Instruction in those matters was the concern of other departments. Public speaking courses were designed to give students proficiency in the business of making speeches. In other words, they ought to deal with form.

The pedagogical issue raised here is interesting in its own right, but a far more basic problem lurks just below the surface of this debate, and it entangles both parties equally. For Hunt the content of public speaking consists in the subjects addressed. Content, therefore, must be added to public speaking courses, since it is not a property of the art of speaking. In this way, public speaking acquires content, but only at the expense of weakening its autonomy as an area of study. For O'Neill public speaking courses ought not to have any content except that which is proper to the discipline. But this proves to be either technique or material derived from other "substantive" disciplines, such as psychology or physiology. Thus, for both Hunt and O'Neill public speaking *per se* has no content.

While this exchange becomes memorialized as the form/content debate, the real issue appears to be at what level and from which sources the field should borrow its content. Neither side can break through the form/content dichotomy, since neither can imagine content without reference to an objective subject. But public speaking does not possess any distinct and exclusive subject of this type. Its subject is a process, and if process is alienated from content, then it follows that the discipline can have no substance. Thus, the disagreement between Hunt and O'Neill proves less important than their implicit agreement that subjects and processes are distinct. The dilemma crystallized here haunts the field for generations to come.

The differences between the "humanistic" and "scientific" approaches rapidly solidified into what is sometimes described as a division between two rival "schools." The Midwestern school, associated with such scholars as James O'Neill and Charles Woolbert, used spoken language as the organizing principle for the discipline and promoted specialized, scientific research. The new social sciences, psychology in particular, became the model for research (Windt, 1982, pp. 188–191). On the other side was the Cornell school. Adherents of this school explicitly linked the humanistic approach to public speaking with the term rhetoric and located the center of the discipline in relation to the rhetorical tradition. During the twenties, they established the pattern for rhetorical scholarship in the field.

In 1920, the Cornell faculty included Alexander Drummond and Everett Hunt, and among the graduate students there were such future noteworthies as Harry Caplan, Herbert Wichelns, and Hoyt Hudson. These men regarded themselves as pioneers whose chief task was to develop a disciplinary basis for rhetorical studies. They evolved the first curriculum for Ph.D. studies, one that featured seminars in rhetorical theory, divided along chronological lines, and seminars in British and American public address (Windt, 1982, pp. 196–197). This program served for decades as the dominant model for graduate education, and it has remained the core of the curriculum at some institutions. The Cornell group also produced a series of articles designed to establish the intellectual foundations of their enterprise. The most important of these were Wichelns' "Literary Criticism of Oratory" (1925) and Hudson's articles, "The Field of Rhetoric" (1923) and "Rhetoric and Poetry" (1924). Wichelns' essay proved the single most influential work of the period, but since it was devoted to speech criticism, it falls outside our present focus. We should note, however, that the perspective Hudson adopted for rhetoric in general was closely related to the argument Wichelns advanced with respect to criticism in particular.

Hudson identifies rhetoric with persuasion. He justifies this view on the basis of the historic association of the two terms, and he uses it to attack certain conventional distinctions. His first point is directed at the Midwestern school: As an art of persuasion, rhetoric applies to both oral and written communication. It subsumes such forms as pamphlets, editorials, and advertisements as well as spoken discourse. His second point touches a more fundamental matter. He asserts that, the authority of Aristotle notwithstanding, no categorical distinction between the theory and the practice of persuasion is tenable. The means of persuasion available in a given case are particular to that case. Rhetoric, then, exists primarily as a product, as a discursive response to a particular occasion. Its end consists in neither an analysis of a subject nor an analysis of a speech, but rather in a "piece of rhetorical discourse" (1923, pp. 168–171).

This subversion of the theory/practice distinction implies a radical particularism, each rhetorical act being a unique whole. To balance this view, Hudson conceives of rhetorical discourse as a discrete genre and defines its special characteristics by contrast with the poetic. As with Wichelns, the basis of this contrast rests on a distinction between fine and applied art. Thus, "the student of rhetoric investigates eloquence not for its graces and ornaments, and not with regard to its effect upon him as he reads it; our admiration may be excited by a splendid figure in Burke or Canning; we may gain considerable pleasure from perceiving the skill with which words have been joined euphoniously and rhythmically,—but such admiration and pleasure are incidental and shared by the student of literature or the general reader. The student of rhetoric looks upon each oration as an effort in persuasion; he must learn what he can of the audience to which it was addressed" (1923, p. 174). Note here how the instrumental character of rhetoric is assumed to bind it entirely to a specific audience and situation. As Hudson explains the matter, "the writer in pure literature has his eye on the subject. . . . His task is expression; his form and style are organic with his subject. The writer of rhetorical discourse has his eye upon the audience and occasion; his task is persuasion; his form and style are organic with the occasion" (1923, p. 177). Or, to round out the terminology in a tidier fashion, "poetry is for the sake of expression," while "rhetoric is for the sake of impression" (1924, p. 146). Hudson acknowledges that the line of demarcation is not absolute. Poetic objectives and strategies may enter into rhetorical discourse and vice versa. Nevertheless, in principle, the two belong to different classes of things; for poets, in exercising the essence of their craft, address a general and vague audience with the desire of pleasing. But the orator, qua orator, remains in bondage to a particular audience and a particular persuasive goal. There is an interesting ironic twist to this argument, for the radical particularity of rhetorical discourse emerges as the means of arriving at the general characteristics of the rhetorical genre. In the process of making this argument, and consistent with his basic orientation, Hudson leaves little room for a "theory" of rhetoric, since the grounds for his generic classification militate against generalization within the genre.

One of the informing principles of the Cornell school is that instruction in public speaking must have substance. As Hudson puts the point, "eloquence is organic and not an embellishment or flourish added from without" (1923, p. 179). The quotation echoes Cicero's *De oratore*, and this is probably no accident. The Cornell movement's commitment to substance stems from a determination to refurbish classical rhetoric and from a strong conviction that invention occupies the central position in classical rhetoric (Windt, pp. 192–193). All of these considerations lead to an analysis of topics, the main component in the inventional systems of antiquity. And, in Hudson's effort to "modernize the theory of invention" (1921), the topics play a central role. The topics, he maintains, allow the speaker to grasp ideas and discover the starting points of argument. Nevertheless, the classical lore on the matter cannot be appropriated without some modification. Thus, Hudson argues that the topics of modern discourse ought to be apprehended through the study of American oratory. The speaker confronted by a question of public policy can go "to certain commonplaces, from them" draw arguments, and by them select "materials for the speech. Are there not topics of popular government—principles of Americanism— which are the places from which a speaker like Webster, Lincoln, and Roosevelt will quickly derive arguments?" (1921, p. 8).

Once again Hudson displays considerable dexterity as he attributes substance to rhetoric even as he avoids commitment to notions that transcend the particular. A revived classical rhetoric demands a theory of invention, but, as we have observed, Hudson holds that theory is not separable from practice. Consequently, Hudson draws his "theory" from practice. The internal consistency of his approach is admirable, but in this instance, his position entails serious problems. If certain argumentative materials work repeatedly in different contexts, that fact would indicate significant points of interconnection among particular rhetorical acts. Do these points of interconnection not call for an explanation? And must not such an explanation rise at least to some degree beyond the realm of practice? An adherent of Hudson's position might acknowledge that such questions are of interest but not necessarily of interest to a rhetorician. For a rhetorician (in Hudson's sense of the term) it is enough to read widely, note and store in memory recurrent themes, and use them in a particular case when appropriate. The rationale for these themes arises from the political, historical, and social conventions of the culture. The explanation of why and how they work is the concern of political scientists, historians, and sociologists. But this response is self-defeating, since it implies that Hudson's topics are not really materials of rhetorical invention at all. They are instead materials derived from sources extrinsic to the art, which the rhetorician borrows for use in forming an argument. Thus, the curve of the argument circles back to the heresy attributed to the rival Midwestern school—rhetoric is purely form or technique.

Much of the problem here results from a simplistic and rhetorically inert conception of "matter." Hudson's topics are purely material; that is, they refer directly to the content of the subject, and they are discrete bits of data whose use requires no artistic effort. They are part of the scene, not of the art. Material topics of this type appear in the classical rhetorics, but they do not represent the only approach to the concept. Another tradition stresses the role of topics as modes of generating inferential connectives or warrants in rhetorical argument (Leff, 1978; 1983; Leff and Hewes, 1981; Conley, 1978; 1982). Since these connectives may be conceived as differrent from those of strictly logical inference and as deriving their characteristics from the special circumstances of rhetorical discourse, they suggest a "content" for the art of rhetoric *per se*. On this view, the "substance" of rhetoric consists in the tissue of connectives that structures the fabric of public knowledge and allows it to expand and change through the medium of persuasive discourse. On the other hand, to place the topics in the center of the inventional process and then to regard them as attributes of the subject under discussion encourages a purely managerial view of rhetoric and confounds the effort to locate a theory of invention.

To sum up, the Cornell school's effort to establish rhetoric as a discipline placed theory at the margins of the enterprise. In the long run, however, the most serious barrier to the development of theory probably did not arise from the school's overt and general scepticism about theory. To have no theory of rhetoric was and always has been a defensible response to the problem of rhetorical theory. Under other circumstances, the formulation of this position might have invited a counterstatement and provoked a useful debate. But an unacknowledged assumption about the relationship between form and content undercut the conceptual ground on which such an exchange might have occurred. So long as the notion of content was wedded to an objective subject, a "substantive" theory of rhetoric was inconceivable. At an abstract level, rhetoric was splintered between its presentational forms and the substantive materials it derived from extrinsic sources. And, under the regime of the prevailing form/content dichotomy, no theoretical construct could bridge this gap. Rhetoric engaged substance only as a concrete act of performance or as a specific critical response. Hence, the radical particularism of the Cornell school did not appear as one among a number of options for rhetorical scholarship; it seemed the only means of avoiding a descent to vacuous formalism. But it was not quite possible to rest content with the particular. The impulse to fashion a substantive rhetoric also entailed an attempt to revivify the theory of invention. The effort in this direction ran counter to the unrecognized but fundamental assumptions of those who engaged in it. The resulting confusion rendered invention an amorphous and unwieldy concept through most of the history of our literature. A comment by Karl Wallace in 1972 unwittingly demonstrated the depth and breadth of the problem. He wrote: "A significant result of the National Developmental Conference on Rhetoric was a call for a rhetorical theory which emphasized the content and substance of discourse rather than techniques and structures" (p. 387). Significant, indeed, as an index of frustration, was this call for precisely the same thing that Hunt and Hudson had demanded 50 years earlier. As the scholarship of the last decade has demonstrated, progress toward a more coherent approach to invention depended on the discovery of means to soften or to collapse the distinctions between content and technique, between substance and structure.*

From the mid-1920s to the mid-1950s, rhetorical scholarship displayed little innovation. Although studies of the history of rhetoric multiplied and became more sophisticated, rhetorical theory received only passing attention. By far the greatest activity centered on the study of public address, which gradually became standardized in terms of what came to be known as "neo-Aristotelian" criticism. In fact, most studies of this type contained little criticism, for they were dominated by historical and biographical concerns. Nevertheless, to the extent that a critical theory existed, it came from neo-Aristotelian doctrine, which focused on the influence of speeches on an immediate audience and which derived its critical apparatus from certain taxonomic divisions of classical lore, such as the modes of proof and the "canons" of the art.

The period produced one important work devoted to the conception of rhetoric, Donald Bryant's essay, "Rhetoric: Its Functions and Its Scope" (1953). Bryant's purpose was to reexplore the territory covered in 1923 and 1925 by Hudson and Wichelns. The essay was careful and thorough, and it proved to have considerable influence. For a decade and more, it was required reading in most graduate programs, and it was widely regarded as a definitive statement concerning the state of the art. Consequently, the essay provides a useful measure of how the field had progressed since the time of its origin as well as a bench mark by which to gauge the changes that would occur during the next three decades.

Bryant, like Hudson before him, began with a review of well known definitions of rhetoric. He then stated his own definition of rhetoric as "the rationale of informative and suasory discourse" (p. 404). This formulation signaled a number of important departures from Hudson. First, and most obviously, Bryant extended the scope of rhetoric to include informative as well as persuasive discourse. Second, the word rationale suggested a more abstract or theoretical conception of the art than Hudson had entertained. Later in the essay, Bryant explained that he used the term rhetoric in three senses: (1) as he defined it—a rationale or body of principles, (2) as a quality that characterized rhetorical discourse, and (3) as a study of informative and suasory discourse. Here Bryant separated what Hudson had attempted to hold in solution. More than that, the use of the first sense in his initial

---

*Another noteworthy attempt to establish a theory of invention devolved from the studies of argumentation conducted mainly by adherents of the Midwestern school. That literature is of some importance to our subject, but it moves along a different track than we are now pursuing, and it is already well summarized by Cox and Willard (1982, pp. xv–xxii).

definition indicated a significant change in priorities. And perhaps most important, Bryant did not even include "rhetorical discourse" among his senses of rhetoric; instead he referred to a "quality" that characterized such discourse. Thus, he altered the conception of the material cause of the art and pushed it to a higher level of abstraction. The force of his position became more readily apparent when he emended his definition to read that rhetoric was the "rationale of the informative and suasory in discourse" (1973, p. 14). Rhetoric was not a discrete genre of discourse; it was not to be indentified with any kind of thing, but with a quality or dimension that, in varying degrees of intensity, inhered in all kinds of discourse.

Bryant gave separate attention to the question of the function of rhetoric, which he defined as that "of adjusting ideas to people and people to ideas" (1953, p. 413). The notion of adjustment was crucial, since Bryant regarded rhetoric as predominantly an instrument, a mediator between what was known and what was accessible for belief. Rhetoric, from this perspective, dealt with appearance—not instead of reality, but rather to reinforce reality and make truth appear as truth. It played a managerial role among the arts of learning, organizing what they had discovered and shaping their findings so as to set them in "harmonious movement towards the listener as the end, towards what [happened] in him and to him" (1953, p. 412). Rhetoric, in short, guided knowledge for the "wielding of public opinion" (1953, p. 415).

Bryant's functionalism largely displaced the emphasis on substance found in the early work of the Cornell school. The contrast was not absolute, since the earlier writers had attended to the functional properties of rhetoric, and Bryant himself retained their interest in developing a system of topical invention (1953, p. 418). Moreover, like Hudson and Wichelns, he maintained a strong commitment to the genius of the particular in criticism, a commitment that led him to warn against dependence on abstract categories (1957, p. 110).

Nevertheless, at least in respect to theory, Bryant's shift in orientation was significant and indicated a general change within the field. The conception of the art had become more systematic; it was less tied to the synthesizing moment of performance. The scholarship had turned decisively toward abstract principles. In this respect, Bryant articulated a tendency reflected in the development of the literature. The articles appearing in the early issues of the *Quarterly Journal of Speech* usually centered on pedagogical issues. In the 1930s, a call for more theoretical or scientific research emerged; and in the 1950s, pedagogy served largely as an introductory or concluding topos. This tendency accelerated until, by the 1970s, pedagogy disappeared from the literature almost without a trace (Leff, 1978, p. 90). We would note, however, that this movement was neither sudden nor final in its results. At the time Bryant wrote "Rhetoric: Its Functions and Its Scope," rhetoric remained a practical art, though the emphasis had shifted from the word "practical" to the word "art." And the convoluted development of the theoretical impulse led scholars in the present decade to reopen the question of the relationship between theory and practice and to connect again the pedagogical and the theoretical (Brummett, 1984).

Before turning from Bryant's essay, we should attend to his version of "Aristotelian rationalism," since it is important as background for later developments. The most immediate source of Bryant's functionalist orientation, as he himself notes (1953, p. 414), is Bacon's conception of rhetoric as a coordinator among the various mental faculties. Nevertheless, this view fits comfortably with the then prevailing Aristotelian hegemony. The *Rhetoric* is interpreted as the organon of public opinion on the analogy of the role played by the *Topica* and the *Analytics* as the organon of scientific knowledge. Thus, the instrumental approach to rhetoric is intimately connected with Aristotle's authority. Furthermore, the Aristotelian modes of proof are lined up more or less in the order of Bacon's faculties. On this view, reason (or logic) has primacy in rhetoric, for it ought to control the process of adjusting knowledge to the interests of an audience. But since rhetoric involves matters of value, and since it is a near relative of poetry, appeals to the emotions and the imagination must sometimes support or even transcend reason. All told, then, rational process has replaced substance as the ground for respectable scholarship in the field. And the firm belief that rhetoric is a primarily rational tool for translating knowledge into opinion accounts for Bryant's conviction that Aristotle's theory "must stand as the broad background for any sensible rhetorical system" (1953, p. 404). That conviction certainly represents the consensus in 1953. Over the next 20 years matters would change dramatically.

The impulse toward change, however, originated less from a specific reaction against neo-Aristotelianism than from the apparent slack between expectations and achievements. Rhetoricians had come to conceive their work as theoretical, but in fact theory had made little progress, and speech criticism, the main arm of the field, still languished in biographical and historical detail. As Charles Stewart (1973) has demonstrated, currents of protest lurked below the placid neo-Aristotelian surface of the 1930s and 1940s. In the 1950s, these forces erupted into the open, and by the end of the decade, isolated complaint gave way to a general clamor for revision. The attack centered on scholarship in public address. Existing studies were regarded as "undistinguished" and "unimaginative" (Baskerville, 1957, p. 117); they were dismissed as "stereotyped" and "banal" (Clark, 1957, p. 84); they were attacked because their focus on extrinsic details moved critics out of, rather than more deeply into, their own subject (Redding, 1957); and they were condemned as responsive to only one critical approach, which often was applied in a sterile and mechanical way (Hochmuth, 1957, p. 89). These objections hardened into a systematic assault on the foundations of neo-Aristotelianism, and the movement reached its culmination with the publication of Black's *Rhetorical Criticism: A Study in Method* (1965), a book that in one stroke entitled and dethroned neo-Aristotelian criticism. At the same time, this unfolding drama moved quickly from discovery to diagnosis: the problem, it appeared, stemmed from the tyranny of a single, unproductive theoretical perspective. The cure, then, was obvious—more and better theories were required. Thus, the revisionist impulse in public address ended by turning to theory. By the mid-1960s, the field was once again searching for its foundations.

Early efforts to strengthen the theoretical base of the field generally sought to expand rather than overturn the existing foundations. Most frequently, the search for alternatives concentrated on the theory of a single author from outside the discipline. The process began with the attempt to incorporate the work of Kenneth Burke (Hochmuth, 1952; Holland, 1959) and I. A. Richards (Hochmuth, 1958; 1963). Rhetoricians also searched for theoretical direction in the writings of such figures as Stephen Toulmin (Brockreide & Ehninger, 1960; Trent, 1968), Richard Weaver (Johannesen, 1966), Chaim Perelman (Dearin, 1969; Arnold, 1970), and Marshall McLuhan (Sloan, 1968; Bridwell, 1970). This enterprise caused a significant expansion in the basic reading list for rhetorical theory and a more gradual expansion in the horizons of the field. Nevertheless, the attempt to extract a tidy and prefabricated "theory" from any outside source proved futile. As the application of Burke's theory illustrates, the progression of studies normally moved from general synopsis and summary to more concrete applications, with the later work proving more significant. Compare, for example, Hochmuth & Holland to the recent work of Heath (1979) & Brummett (1984). Of all the authorities listed above, Burke has had the greatest and most profound influence on our field. The corpus of his work constitutes the basic text for contemporary rhetorical theory (Burke, 1931; 1935; 1937; 1941; 1945; 1950; 1961); among the more important books about Burke are Rueckert (1982) and Lentricchia (1983). The development of his influence and the significance of his ideas mark a crucially important chapter in the history of rhetoric. To tell that story, however, would require another essay much longer than this one.

Other approaches to the problem of theory aimed at more revolutionary results. The proliferation of theoretical perspectives opened the way to a critical examination of traditional theory and encouraged philosophical analysis of competing rhetorical paradigms. This philosophical turn expressed itself in the course of a debate between Wayne Thompson and Otis Walter in 1963.

Thompson argued that the "dead hand" of classical rhetoric had suppressed theoretical innovation, since the precepts of the old rhetoric were handed down from one generation of scholars to the next without significant change or expansion. Thompson, however, was no revolutionary. He acknowledged that classical lore contained an abundance of wisdom that should not be neglected. His goal was to invigorate the old rhetoric by opening it to the methods of experimental research and the concepts of the nascent communication sciences. He would use the classical precepts as hypotheses for experimental study. In this way, they might be tested and refined rather than merely stored. Moreover, he thought rhetoricians ought to study cybernetics, general systems theory, information theory, semantics, and linguistics as sources for a new rhetoric.

Part of Walter's response was a predictable warning against borrowing from the "white rat" mentality of the social sciences. His main argument, however, was far less predictable and entailed a major shift in the balance of rhetorical studies. Thompson's fundamental error, he maintained, was to regard the precepts of persuasion as the major interest of rhetorical theory. Walter contended that they were actually trivial. The significance of classical rhetoric did not consist in the enumeration of techniques, but in the articulation of starting points, basic philosophical perspectives, for the generation of theory. Rhetoricians ought to study such starting points, flesh out those that were not fully developed, compare, contrast, and critique them, and devise new ones. Like Thompson, Walter believed that contemporary rhetorical theory was unproductive, but he insisted that the problem stemmed precisely from the Aristotelian bias that Thompson sought to preserve. An instrumental conception of rhetoric as the art of persuasion yielded "a strangely distorted view of things" that often provoked "irrelevant questions" and distracted rhetoricians from their genuine philosophical mission (p. 375).

Bryant, we might recall, specified three senses of rhetoric, which roughly translated designated theoretical, artifactual, and critical dimensions of the art. Walter transcended these categories by defining and giving privilege to a metatheoretical perspective. He thus responded to Maurice Natanson's call for a philosophy of rhetoric based on the "critique of the rationale of rhetoric which inquires into the underlying assumptions, the philosophical grounds, of all the elements of rhetoric" (1955, p. 139). And Walter clearly anticipated the main trend of later scholarship. Over the past two decades, rhetoricians have become increasingly concerned with the basic suppositions that inform their subject and have demonstrated a greater inclination to use the critique of those suppositions as the basis for their theorizing (Oravec, 1982). As these tendencies accelerated, the alignment between rhetoric and poetic, which set the bearings for earlier rhetorical scholarship, gave way to an alignment between rhetoric and philosophy.

We are still in the midst of this metatheoretical revolution, and it is always difficult to chart the history of a movement while it is in progress.

Moreover, the progress of recent scholarship is complex; it has shifted momentum several times and has incorporated a bewildering number of different strands. Consequently, we cannot hope to produce a comprehensive or wholly coherent synopsis of these developments. We can only make a tentative assessment of features that seem most significant when judged against the overall history of the field. With these qualifications in mind, two developments appear especially noteworthy: (1) efforts to revive a strong connection between rhetoric and communal values, and (2) efforts to reevaluate the connection between rhetoric and knowledge. These categories are not mutually exclusive, for much of the scholarship cuts across their unstable boundaries. Nevertheless, we believe that they represent generally different avenues of study and that they are sufficiently clear to provide the landmarks needed to direct our inquiry. [We should also note that our categories bear no relation to those used by Christine Oravec (1982) in her review of the most recent literature. This is not to suggest a critique. We have sliced the cheese at different angles partially because we deal with a longer time period and partially because we approach matters on a more synoptic and less synthetic level than she does. Oravec's essay should be read as a supplement to what follows here.]

Eubanks and Baker (1962) were the first to call for a rhetorical theory centered on values. Twentieth-century society, they contended, suffered from a value crisis, and rhetorical studies had done little to redeem the situation. This was a grievous fault, since considered from either a historical or a theoretical perspective, rhetoric's prime goal was the "enhancement of human values" (p. 160). In fact, they maintained, if rhetoric had any special subject matter of its own, it consisted in "the popular and probable value axioms related to the civil decision-making of a free society" (p. 161). Pursuing the same line of thought, Wallace (1963) complained that rhetoricians had expended far too much effort on the form of discourse and far too little on its substance (that is, the content, subject matter, ideas, and materials in discourse). Rhetoric did indeed have a substance, for its proper, though not sole, concern was "the appearance and use of value judgments in practical discourse" (p. 241). The terms "appearance," "use," and "practical" distinguished rhetoric from ethics. The special and technical analysis of value belonged within the domain of ethics, while the observation of the linguistic behavior of men engaged in making choices fell within the ambit of rhetorical studies. Ethics dealt with moral principles in the abstract; rhetoric encountered them in particular contexts. The process of making decisions required arguments that justified ethical preferences. Such justifications Wallace termed "good reasons," and he defined good reasons as "a number of statements, consistent with each other, in support of an ought proposition or a value statement" (p. 248).

Like Eubanks and Baker, Wallace was reacting against the pure instrumentalism implied in neo-Aristotelian doctrine. In both cases, this reaction involved a reinterpretation of Aristotle and other classical authorities, since these value theorists drew their inspiration from a perceived connection between ethical substance and rhetorical argument in the traditional literature. Wallace, however, pushed the implications of this concept of rhetorical substance in a systematic and especially forceful manner. In this respect, he seemed to look past Bryant to Hudson's original vision of the integrity of the field. Wallace again asserted that rhetoric was a substantive art, linked to a distinctive phenomenon. Wallace, of course, presented a much more theoretical rationale for this position than had Hudson, and he located the essence of rhetoric not in a type of discourse but in a certain kind of statement.

Fisher's essay, "Toward a Logic of Good Reasons" (1978), attempted a further refinement of value theory in rhetorical argument. The essay responded not only to the work of Eubanks and Baker and Wallace, but also to Wayne Booth's *Modern Dogma and the Rhetoric of Assent* (1974), a book that included an extended analysis of the concept of good reasons. Fisher found Booth's work lacking because it failed to distinguish the merits of competing good reasons. To rectify this problem he offered an amended definition of good reasons as "those elements that provide warrants for accepting or adhering to the advice fostered by any form of communication that can be considered rhetorical" (p. 378). The definition allowed for a contrast among good reasons and encouraged extension of the concept into forms of communication that did not have a clear-cut inferential structure, such as film, drama, and literature. And in order to make this concept operational as a logic, Fisher developed five criteria for evaluating good reasons: What were the implicit and explicit values invoked? Were they relevant? What consequences followed from adherence to these values? Were these values consistent with personal experience, with the utterances and behavior of the speaker, and with the standards of an ideal audience? Were these values superceded by other, higher values?

The logic of good reasons serves as a mechanism for judging particular value arguments in the public sphere. Yet, it does little to account for the way that such arguments are generated or the way that they accumulate and interconnect within larger patterns of discourse. Furthermore, the type of inferential discourse upon which this logic is founded may seem remote from the most frequently used and most powerful vehicles for presenting moral argument. Well aware of these and other problems, Fisher recently has shifted his emphasis from the logic of good reasons to the "narrative paradigm" (1984). The narrative paradigm arises from the conviction that man is essentially a story-telling animal and hence the narrative frame offers the most accessible and most fundamental means of structuring communication about public values. Moreover, Fisher maintains that public moral argument occurs in all forms of symbolic action, not merely in the inferential sequences of oratorical and analytical prose. Moral argument is at once product and process, a merger of form and substance, and thus the narrative coherence, reliability, and probability of stories present rational grounds for moral inducement.

W. Lance Bennett's studies of decision making by juries (1978; 1979) offer support for Fisher's view concerning the power of narrative in framing and interconnecting the elements of argument. Bennett holds that the remarkable skill with which ordinary people both present and interpret complex evidence in a formal trial stems from their capacity to process narrative forms. The elements of narrative organize information, guide interpretation, and direct judgment. Thus, the credibility of arguments does not rest on the objective status of independent facts but on the status of the evidence as a network of "symbols within the structure of a story" (1979, p. 319).

The contemporary literature on narrative is immense and complex, and in our field, we have just begun to explore the issue. The potential for rhetorical application is obviously great, but the tendency toward distraction in the face of such an awesome subject is also very real. For this reason, we believe it important to recognize that narrative theory has strong roots in the classical tradition and that it entered our current literature in conjunction with and as a near relative to the impulse to develop a rhetoric of public values. This recognition might help focus and guide our research efforts.

A rather different approach to the problem of rhetoric and public values emerges from Lloyd Bitzer's application of pragmatic rationalism to rhetorical theory. The arc of Bitzer's thought moves from the concept of situation to a concept of the public. The first phase of this movement identifies situation as the "source and ground of rhetorical activity" (1968, pp. 5–6). Bitzer asserts that while the presence of a situation is a necessary condition for the presence of rhetorical discourse, previous theory either omits reference to situation or relegates it to a peripheral role. Yet, as distinct from context, setting, occasion, or persuasive potential, rhetorical situation is what imparts to discourse its "character as rhetorical" (1968, p. 3). Thus, past theories that locate the essence of rhetoric in respect to the orator, the discourse, or the methods of the art fail to encompass what is, from a pragmatic stand point, its first cause—the situation to which all else must respond.

Bitzer defines a rhetorical situation as "a complex of persons, events, objects and relations presenting an actual or potential exigence which can be completely or partially removed if discourse, introduced into the situation, can so constrain human decision or action as to bring about a significant modification of the exigence" (1968, p. 6). An exigence, for Bitzer, is "an imperfection marked by urgency" (1968, p. 6); it is something that requires doing or correcting. An exigence is rhetorical to the degree that it can be modified by discourse addressed to a rhetorical audience. And an audience is rhetorical if it has the capacity to mediate change in respect to the exigence and if it is open to influence through discourse. We should note that this theory of the rhetorical situation has provoked a storm of controversy, most of it centered on the epistemological status of Bitzer's claim that situations determine rhetorical responses (Vatz, 1973; Consigny, 1974; Patton, 1979; Brinton, 1982). We shall deal with issues related to this controversy presently. For the moment, we wish to emphasize that an understanding of Bitzer's position, as it now exists, requires a reading of "Rhetoric and Public Knowledge" (1978) in conjunction with the earlier essay.

Following John Dewey, Bitzer holds that the public is generated. It is not a timeless, immutable phenomenon, but one that arises out of and changes with contextual circumstances. And so the public, like rhetorical discourse, emerges in response to exigencies. But, unlike rhetorical discourse, the public responds only to those exigencies that have serious, extensive, and enduring consequences. As publics originate, grow, and change, they build up a common fund of shared personal facts—a repertoire of collectively experienced terms, values, and truths. Bitzer calls this public knowledge, and he maintains that the public alone properly authorizes the ground of such knowledge. It follows, then, that the public is the legitimate source of rhetorical discourse and constitutes the ground for authorizing "discourse and action on its behalf" (1978, p. 77).

For Bitzer, the relationship between audience and public is roughly parallel to the relationship between the particular audience and the universal audience for Perelman (1969, pp. 31–35). The parallel consists in the fact that Bitzer regards the public both as more general than any particular audience and as a normative standard for discourse addressed to any particular audience. But it is only a rough parallel, since Perelman's universal audience is a construct, while Bitzer insists that "there is . . . no public-in-the-abstract: publics are real, concrete entities" (1978, p. 78). Because the public is actual and concrete, and because it has an on-going history, the public is itself open to the influence of rhetorical discourse.

This position, we believe, allows an interesting interplay between the substance and the function of rhetoric. In other cases, we have noted how these two notions remain in a symmetrical but separate relationship. Bitzer, however, implies a rather complex interaction between them. Based on our own analysis of Bitzer's text, we conclude that three forms of interaction are possible. The first occurs in what we can call normal rhetorical discourse, where both speaker and audience are representative of public knowledge. Under this condition, the rhetor uses the substance of discourse (i.e., public knowledge) in order to discharge the function of the discourse (that is, a fitting response in respect to the particular audience). This relationship is much the same as in Bryant's instrumental theory. Certain conditions, however, demand what we can call corrective rhetorical discourse. A corrective response occurs in a situation where the audience is not representative of the public. In that case, the substance of rhetoric directly informs its function, since, gauged by the sole authorizing ground for discourse, the only fitting response is for the speaker to mediate change in the audience such that it becomes representative, or at least more representative, of the public. Finally, there is what we can call generative rhetorical discourse. This occurs under the condition that the speaker finds not the audience but the public itself wanting, finds its public knowledge so impoverished or misguided that the public is incompetent. In this situation, the speaker uses the function of rhetoric to change its substance, i.e., effects a change in public knowledge. This range of options is possible because the substance of rhetoric arises from a self-regulative public. The norms that inform rhetorical discourse are the product of collective intersubjective agreements, and hence the substance of rhetoric evolves out of a process that generally resembles the way rhetoric functions.

In surveying the literature concerning rhetoric and public values, we have observed a number of interesting claims about the basis of rhetorical knowledge. We have noted the contention that rhetorical argument merges product and process, the argument that narrative coherence and reliability present a ground for knowing, and the implied conclusion that rhetorical knowledge is the product of an evolving public consensus. These positions differ markedly from the commitment to knowledge based on the objective subject that characterizes earlier scholarship in the field. They also reflect a dramatic change in the general intellectual environment, for one of the dominant movements in recent philosophy is a rejection of rigid, perspectively neutral standards of knowledge and the development of more pliable, socially conditioned criteria. As Thomas Farrell puts the point, "contemporary philosophy has now moved away from the detached derivation of criteria for knowledge and toward the more inclusive study of human activity in all its forms." (1976, p. 3). This shift in the philosophic wind has obvious and profound implications for rhetorical theory, and much of recent scholarship involves the attempt to chart its course and follow its direction.

The conscious attempt to reformulate the connection between rhetoric and knowledge begins with Robert Scott's seminal essay, "On Viewing Rhetoric as Epistemic" (1967). Since that time, the work of Scott and others has accumulated and given impulse to a rhetoric-as-epistemic movement. The movement has recruited adherents, spawned critics (e.g. Croasman & Cherwitz, 1982), and developed its own inevitable schisms. It is, in short, a complex phenomenon, and since the issues associated with it are broad and basic, most of the recent scholarship seems either relevant to or influenced by it. A comprehensive survey is impossible in this essay, and there already exist a number of detailed analyses of its development (Leff, 1978; Brinton, 1982, pp. 158–162; Railsback, 1983, pp. 352–353). Our present purpose, therefore, is simply to summarize the essential features of the rhetoric-as-epistemic position and to indicate the possible consequences of its major schism with reference to the larger sweep of the field's history.

The concept of rhetoric as epistemic is most easily understood by contrasting it with managerial theories of rhetoric. Such theories limit the function of rhetoric to the coordination and transmission of knowledge. On this view, rhetoric may translate knowledge gained elsewhere into persuasive form; it may appeal to the irrational elements of the psyche, and it may embellish the truth. But, in principle, rhetoric and knowledge belong to different domains, and rhetorical discourse cannot produce knowledge. Simply stated, the essence of the epistemic theory is that rhetoric is capable not only of reflecting knowledge but also of generating it. Three closely related corollaries follow from this defining proposition: (1) The intersubjective agreement of a community counts as a valid ground for truth; (2) reason and emotion are not mutually exclusive; human interests and desires cannot be excluded from the process by which humans come to know; (3) the act of communication and the contact of minds it involves influence the content of human knowledge.

All of these premises are susceptible to important qualifications or extensions, and hence the theory of epistemic rhetoric can take shape in a variety of different forms (Leff, 1978, p. 78). In our literature, however, two major versions of this doctrine have evolved. They differ primarily in their range of application. One version, represented by Farrell (1976; 1978), attaches the epistemic view mainly to the domain of public life. The other version, represented by Brummett (1976; 1982) and Carleton (1978), extends the concept to all domains of knowledge and regards it as the ultimate ground of human knowledge. Thus, for Brummett, even our knowledge of physical objects derives from an intersubjective consensus: "Consensus theorists do not argue that people perceive the sun, the earth, rocks and trees, etc., and *then* coat them with meaning; rather for humans, meaning shapes the manifestation of the world in the first place" (1982, p. 426). "Objects come into existence for humans through the same rhetorical process by which they are known" (1982, p. 428). We believe that this dispute is important, not so much because of the philosophical content of the argument, but because of its implications for the future direction of research. In some respects, it seems similar to the debate between the Cornell and Midwestern schools concerning the possibility of conceptual boundaries for the field.

The position Farrell assumes more or less follows traditions within the field both in respect to the kinds of discourse that seem to occupy his attention and in respect to the kinds of issues he finds significant. In "Knowledge, Consensus, and Rhetorical Theory" his main interest is not epistemological *per se*, but rather grows out of concerns about the substance of rhetoric and the place of values in rhetorical theory. This outlook is revealed clearly in what we regard as the crystallizing moment of the essay: "Rhetoric, whatever its own attributed status, is not purely a formalistic enterprise. There is something which this art is about. That 'something' is a kind of knowledge which is attributed, audience-dependent, potential in state, generative, and normative in implication" (1978, p. 11). Thus, Farrell seeks to locate the substance of rhetoric in social knowledge and to show that such knowledge is both generated by rhetorical discourse and inherently ethical in character. In the process, he contrasts social with technical knowledge and holds that the two are different in principle. His goal, however, is not to establish epistemological categories but to understand how rhetorical discourse engages knowledge in public transactions. His conception of rhetoric is informed by an implicit association of that term with a certain broad but still rather definite kind of discourse.

Carleton and Brummett, however, approach rhetoric at an almost entirely philosophical and conceptual level. Their attention centers on rhetoric as a function of language and mind that orders the phenomena of human consciousness. No specific form of action serves as a dominant referent or paradigm for the rhetorical process, since the process itself is the dominant concern. And since, by the very definition of this position, the process is everywhere, the scope of rhetoric becomes universal.

This debate, then, raises once again the issue of process and substance, though in a variant form. It is not the case here that one side advocates process and the other substance, for both would probably agree that process and substance coalesce in the texture of the rhetorical act and that theory cannot separate them categorically. Rather, the difference is one of basic orientation. Adherents of consensus theory conceive rhetoric from the perspective of a universal process applicable indifferently to any class of subjects. Adherents of the social knowledge perspective anchor their conception of rhetoric in the ground of the particular subjects of public discourse. The theoretical difference arises from a dispute about the reality of human perceptions. Practically, however, the choice between them involves concrete decisions about programs of research and curricula for graduate education. Is the field better served by expanding its effort to the whole range of rhetorical phenomena or by concentrating its focus on the public sphere where the rhetorical process manifests itself most clearly?

As we have suggested above, the effort to reconstruct the grounds of knowledge in rhetoric extends beyond the rhetoric-as-epistemic movement *per se*. One particularly important illustration of this point comes from the emerging literature devoted to the nexus between rhetoric and ideology. Although systematic study of this topic has just begun, its significance seems established beyond reasonable doubt (McKerrow, 1983). The study of ideology leads to a consideration of social theory and an attempt to comprehend basic structures that inform the social world. From the ideological perspective, these structures are the primitive units of social and political consciousness. Thus, the way that they are constructed and used within rhetorical transactions becomes a central issue in the effort to account for social knowledge. Moreover, the ideological approach encompasses the theorist, for theoretical work occurs in the matrix of the social world and falls under the influence of the same structures that govern other forms of social activity. Thus, ideological analysis applies not only to our understanding of how people come to know through rhetoric but also to our understanding of how we know about rhetoric. In a series of essays, Michael McGee energetically pursues these issues (1975; 1978; 1980; 1982).

The concept of ideology informs McGee's general stance in respect to rhetorical studies. Following Marx, McGee maintains that whereas idealism starts with a commitment to consciousness, ideology starts with the "real living individual" (1982, p. 25). From this orientation, McGee derives a materialist conception of rhetoric, which must stay in contact with the "brute reality of persuasion as a daily social phenomenon" (1982, p.25). Thus, materialist theory breaks with the tradition of studying theoretical treatises and artistic precepts and draws its substance instead from the study of actual rhetorical transactions. This approach seeks to exploit "the organic conception of human existence presupposed in nearly all rhetorical documents" (1975, p. 236). Theorists must extract their conclusions from the matter that they study. And rhetoric literally is matter, "an object, as material and omnipresent as air and water" (1982, p. 26). McGee does not mean that rhetoric is an object in the sense of so many marks on sheets of paper but rather that it is a "gestalt of relationships" (1982, p. 34). Rhetoric is a phenomenal reality that emerges when the elements of speaker, speech, audience, occasion, and change combine to form a pragmatic presence, a lived experience that cannot be ignored at the moment of impact. In sum, rhetoric is a material phenomenon that requires a primary commitment to a body of data, not a "corpus of philosophical speculations and prescriptions" (1982, p. 42). To define rhetoric as an "art or as a genre of literature," therefore, is to "distort our own sociality" (1982, p. 46).

This position marks a clear and self-conscious protest against mainstream theory in the field. If there is any significant connection with the earlier tradition, it is with the romantically tinged conceptions of Hunt and Hudson. McGee's definition of rhetoric as an object and his commitment to the genius of the particular speech event bring his thought into some relation with the early Cornell school. Yet, he certainly denies the centrality of performance in rhetoric, a basic principle of both Hunt and Hudson. And in respect to the relationship between rhetoric and knowledge, McGee's thought runs along an entirely different course.

For McGee, truth in politics is always an illusion. The sociopolitical world is coordinated according to interests, not rational laws or objective facts: "That world is a distorted structure of facts and inferences selected not for their reliable representation of the objective world, but rather for their salience to the satisfaction of intersubjective desires" (1982, p. 43). Thus, the notion that political decisions hinge on rational assessment of issues proves false: "It is easy to fool ourselves into believing . . . that we understand the measures which we are asked to ratify, that we are making a 'logical' choice among potential leaders. This conception, however, is inherently unreasonable, for there is little to be gained in believing that our choices are or ought to be based 'on the issues' when such decisions are in fact impossible" (1978, p. 153). Rhetoric, then, is the creative management of distortion and illusion, and its function is to effect social control.

In his essay, "The 'Ideograph': A Link Between Rhetoric and Ideology" (1980), McGee develops a theoretical framework for understanding the mechanisms by which rhetoric exerts social control. Ideology, he contends, is a political language characterized by certain key terms or slogans. These slogans, or "ideographs," define a particular collectivity, since they condense its ideology in a symbol system. The repertoire of ideographs includes such items as "property," "right of privacy," "rule of law," and "liberty"— these are the primitive units of ideology, and hence the most fundamental instruments of social control. Moreover, ideographs possess their own internal form that allows them to evoke subtle symbolic nuances and provoke a complex wholistic response. Consequently, since ideographs cannot suffer translation into propositional form without losing their unique force, the rhetoric of social control ought not to be viewed as a species of argumentation. The ideograph itself is the basic unit of analysis, and it must be studied in respect to its usage, not its alleged idea content. Finally, ideographs display a structural relationship to each other, both in their synchronic arrangement at any particular moment in time and in their diachronic movement through time.

McGee's ideograph represents an important theoretical construct, and its existence mitigates our introductory claim that speech communication has not made a significant contribution to the corpus of rhetorical theory. Other studies, which we do not have the space to review in detail, further attenuate this claim. In this connection, we must at least mention Michael Osborn's exacting research on archetypal metaphors as they function in rhetorical texts (1967; 1977), and Lawrence Rosenfield's fascinating effort to reconstruct the genre of epideictic oratory (1980). Significantly, these studies arise from an interest in particular kinds of rhetorical phenomena rather than from the impulse to construct grand theories. Thus, even those of us who are skeptical about McGee's materialist program should acknowledge the force of his demand for grounded theory. Perhaps, as Brummett has argued recently, the time has come for us to rethink our conception of rhetorical theory. We agree with Brummett that much of what is now classified under the heading of theory might better be regarded as rhetorical philosophy, and we believe his revised definition of the term merits wide and serious attention: "By rhetorical theory I mean essays that systematically assert propositions about how rhetoric works in the world, essays that identify some rhetorical tactic, strategy, device, etc., and attempt to account for its effectiveness in general" (1984, p. 97).

The history of rhetorical scholarship in speech communication is, for the most part, a story of repeated efforts at self-discovery. This persistent concern about basic definitional issues arises in part from the amorphous nature of the subject we study. But it is also a product of the enduring identity crisis characteristic of the field as a whole. The fact that the organization now known as the Speech Communication Association, and which might soon become the American Communication Association, has four times changed its name in 70 years surely testifies to the literal reality of that crisis. The resulting Willie Loman complex, the neurotic fear of not knowing who we are, is one of the few consistent strands stretching through the history of the field. One common response to neurotic anxiety is to identify with someone else, and that has been a typical strategy among scholars in the field. In this process of importing models for rhetorical scholarship, we have progressively complicated and broadened the scope of this small enterprise. What began as the study of public speaking has evolved into a study of the universal processes undergirding thought and language. These developments have not been entirely negative. In our judgment, current scholarship is generally better than it was 50 years ago. Nevertheless, the expansion of interests does threaten to alienate us from each other as we identify with other scholarly areas and isolate our work in increasingly disparate content areas.

We have no cure to offer for this malady and realize that advice on the matter is largely futile. The direction of research in a field follows its own momentum. It is difficult enough to chart the course of scholarship after the fact, impossible to control it before the event. One modest suggestion, however, seems appropriate as the conclusion for this essay. We might turn our gaze back toward our origins. We might once again give serious attention to the history of rhetorical scholarship in our discipline. That history is our common possession; and if it does not provide solutions to many current problems, it does seem to put them in a useful context. At any rate, it is an interesting history, and in this chapter we have only brushed its surface. We have omitted much that is interesting; we have not exhausted the subjects covered, and we have hardly touched what might be the most important concern—the place of the discipline within the life of our society. These matters, and many others as well, call for reflection.

2

The History of Rhetoric:
The Reconstruction of Progress

RICHARD LEO ENOS

INTRODUCTION

As a humanistic enterprise, historical research in rhetoric has sought to explain how individuals have structured thoughts and sentiments and conveyed meaning to others. Research in the history of rhetoric is based on the presumption that the discovery, clarification, and reinterpretation of artifacts of rhetoric will provide evidence leading to greater knowledge of communication. This quest for meaning through historical study covers several specific objectives, topics, and methodologies. The intent here is to synthesize major pedagogical and research efforts in order to review past efforts and direct readers to needed areas of inquiry. Because the present discussion focuses only on significant, representative work in the history of rhetoric by speech communication researchers, a large and distinguished body of scholarly contributions from other disciplines must go unmentioned except as a point of contrast or comparison.

A SYNTHESIS

The development and direction of research in the history of rhetoric by speech communication scholars is rooted in pedagogical and humanistic concerns. Research interests in the history of rhetoric were driven by educational objectives. Pioneers in speech communication sought to understand the nature of their study in a historical context in order to help shape the boundaries of speech communication. Early members of speech communication, particularly from eastern sections of the United States, came from departments of English and were well grounded in traditional, humanistic methods of research and a liberal arts orientation to teaching. Understandably, early scholars naturally viewed rhetoric as a humanistic enterprise that contributed to the advancement of a liberal arts education. Essays such as Hoyt H. Hudson's "Field of Rhetoric" (1923), J.P. Ryan's "Quintilian's Message" (1929), and Wayland Maxfield Parrish's "Tradition of Rhetoric" (1947) used historical rhetoric as a foundation for speech communication.

No single essay, however, had as profound an influence on the historical and humanistic emphasis of speech communication as Everett Lee Hunt's "Plato on Rhetoric and Rhetoricians" and his revision, "Plato and Aristotle on Rhetoric and Rhetoricians" (1920). Hunt's essay(s) not only provided a lucid statement about the rich history of rhetoric but also indirectly argued for the liberalizing value of speech communication in higher education—a belief that he continued to expound throughout his distinguished career. In the years to follow his landmark essay, Hunt played a major role in articulating the place of rhetoric in general education, figuring prominently in symposia on the subject (1949, 1950). In fact, scholars such as Donald C. Bryant (1950, 1953) and Donald Lemen Clark (1950) continued to discuss the place of rhetoric and its tradition in speech communication after the symposia issues were completed. Essays such as Hunt's and Bryant's not only established a humanistic perspective on education but subsequently encouraged an agenda for research. Thus a pedagogical perspective within a liberal arts orientation served as a basis for research and education in the history of rhetoric.

Other researchers complemented Hunt's efforts at arguing for a liberal-humanistic base for speech communication, particularly those educators who comprised the "Cornell School of Rhetoric," succinctly and eloquently captured in Raymond F. Howes' *Notes on the Cornell School of Rhetoric* (1976). There is little doubt that in addition to the early scholarly contributions of such individuals as Lane Cooper, Harry Caplan, Everett Lee Hunt, Hoyt Hudson, and Herbert A. Wichelns, research in the history of rhetoric was transmitted by such students of Cornell as Helen North (1956) and Wilbur Samuel Howell. In fact, even the Cornell University Press was a force in the transmission of scholarship in historical rhetoric, most noticeably demonstrated in such excellent works as *Studies in Speech and Drama in Honor of Alexander M. Drummond* (Ed. Herbert A. Wichelns, 1944), *Historical Studies of Rhetoric and Rhetoricians* (Ed. Raymond F. Howes, 1961), *Sophrosyne: Self-Knowledge and Self-Restraint in Greek Literature* (Helen North, 1966), *Of Eloquence: Studies in Ancient and Medieval Rhetoric in Honor of Harry Caplan* (Eds. Anne King & Helen North, 1970), and *Poetics, Rhetoric and Logic: Studies in the Basic Disciplines of Criticism* (Wilbur Samuel Howell, 1975).

The use of historical studies in rhetoric as a grounding for a liberal arts education in speech communication evolved from pedagogical issues to the establishment of disciplinary boundaries. In a manner not unlike the classical emphasis influenced by Hunt's perspective on rhetoric, Douglas Ehninger, Donald C. Bryant, and Wilbur Samuel Howell used their research expertise in British and Continental rhetoric to offer influential interpretations on the nature and scope of historical rhetoric. Such interpretations are particularly evident in Ehninger's "On Systems of Rhetoric" (1968; "Colloquy," with Robert L. Scott, 1975), Bryant's landmark essay "Rhetoric: Its Function and Its Scope" (1953); Karl Wallace's "Substance of Rhetoric: Good Reasons" (1963); Howell's award-winning volume, *Poetics, Rhetoric, and Logic: Studies in the Basic Disciplines of Criticism* (1975); and Howell's classic confrontation and response to Burke in their 1976 *QJS* "Colloquy." These efforts helped to establish a "philosophical" orientation through a historical assessment of rhetorical theory.

The pedagogical commitment of the speech communication discipline through historical rhetoric and its evolution to a research enterprise are evident in the training reflected in graduate programs. In his recently published collection, *Doctoral Dissertations on Rhetoric and Rhetorical Criticism*, James J. Murphy indicated that his compilation of 443 dissertation titles actually was drawn for a list of 1,280 titles that dealt with rhetoric in some form across various disciplines. Similarly, the Richard Leo Enos and Jeanne L. McClaran edition, *A Guide to Doctoral Dissertations in Communication Studies and Theatre* (1978), also lists an extensive collection of dissertations in rhetorical theory that were done out of speech communication departments. While it would be impossible to account for all the dissertations done in historical rhetoric within speech communication, it is apparent that many of the authors who established distinguished careers in historical rhetoric had extensive doctoral work in departments of speech communication. Most evident in this category are the students from the University of Iowa, several of whom established research careers that are reflected in their doctoral dissertations. Herman Cohen's dissertation on Hugh Blair (1954), Lloyd F. Bitzer's research on Hume's influence on George Campbell (1962), James R. McNally's study of Rudolph Agricola (1966), Donovan J. Och's contributions to the understanding of Aristotelian *topoi* (1966), and Ray E. McKerrow's study of Richard Whately (1974) are examples of the doctoral work at Iowa that grew out of a liberal arts orientation and has served these researchers in their subsequent careers in the history of rhetoric.

Other doctoral programs can also make claims about their distinguished students pursuing careers in historical rhetoric. Douglas Ehninger's Ohio State University dissertation on invention in British rhetorical theory (1949); Dominic A. LaRusso's Northwestern dissertation on rhetoric in

Renaissance Italy (1956); Vincent Bevilacqua's doctoral dissertation at the University of Illinois on Henry Home, Lord Kames (1961); Gerard A. Hauser's University of Wisconsin dissertation of 18th-century British rhetorical and aesthetic theory (1970); Michael C. Leff's University of California, Los Angeles, dissertation on Sulpicius Victor (1972); Keith V. Erickson's dissertation on Aristotle's *Rhetoric* at the University of Michigan (1972); and Richard Leo Enos' Indiana University dissertation on Cicero's theory and practice of forensic rhetoric (1973) are representative samples of research from various doctoral programs in speech communication committed to the history of rhetoric.

In another respect, speech communication emphasis in pedagogy shifted to research through various forms of support for study in the history of rhetoric. Sponsorship of two doctoral honors seminars in historical rhetoric (1978, 1979), cosponsored and convening first at the University of Michigan and then at Indiana University, were two of the most widely attended doctoral honors seminars since the inception of such programs in the early 1970s. The University of Michigan seminar was represented by 19 institutions, and the Indiana seminar by 12. Subsequent attention to historical studies in rhetoric among graduate programs in speech communication is evident in the essays of Gerard A. Hauser and Walter M. Carleton (1979). In sum, the pedagogical concerns of pioneers in speech communication centered on emphasizing the history of rhetoic as a dominant concern of the discipline. This emphasis not only served as a foundation upon which to construct a liberal arts education but also as a cogent justification for research to refine the understanding of the history of rhetoric and thus the nature of speech communication. Increasing specialization in historical studies evolved to the point that emphases in theory and methodology were pursued not as a means of establishing a new discipline's parameters but as a research enterprise whose scholarly concerns were of intrinsic worth.

The evolution of the history of rhetoric into a research enterprise is best realized through a discussion of topics. Three areas initially dominated the research interests of historians of rhetoric in speech communication: classical, British, and American rhetorical theory. The reasons for this initial focus are understandable. Rhetoric was understood to have been "invented" in Greece and synonymous with oral composition; its roots were apparent if not well known. Similarly, early members of speech communication often came out of departments of English and were well grounded in traditional, humanistic methods of research. The shift of emphasis to historical studies in British and American rhetoric was most likely an easy and welcome transition for these early scholars. Bromley Smith's essays on Protagoras, Prodicus, Corax, Gorgias, Hippias, and Thrasymachus from 1918 through 1927 (1918, 1920, 1921, 1926, 1927) introduced important historical figures to the discipline and were often used as a means for discussing contemporary issues in speech education. Similarly, early efforts such as Harry Caplan's "Latin Panegyrics of the Empire" (1924) and Lane Cooper's "Rhetoric of Aristotle" (1935) established the history of rhetoric as a respected study in speech communication and across other disciplines.

Research in British and American theory paralleled studies in classical rhetoric and reinforced humanistic issues and historiographic methods. Essays such as "Whately on Elocution" by James Winans (1945); Donald C. Bryant's "Earl of Chesterfield's Advice on Speaking" (1945); Horace G. Rahskopf's "John Quincy Adams: Speaker and Rhetorician" (1946); Ray Nadeau's "Thomas Farnaby: Schoolmaster and Rhetorician of the English Renaissance" (1950); and Karl Wallace's "Aspects of Modern Rhetoric in Francis Bacon" (1956) exemplify the increased attention to British and American rhetorical theory. Moreover, excellent efforts to extend the boundaries of historical rhetoric to the Continent were made by Douglas Ehninger in "Bernard Lami's L'Art de Parler: A Critical Analysis" (1946) and Wilbur Samuel Howell's "Oratory and Poetry in Fenelon's Literary Theory" (1951).

Out of these areas essays in the history of rhetoric began to stress theoretical issues. Three examples of such studies that stress theory but duplicate topics found in classical, British and American rhetorical theory are: Karl Wallace's "Bacon's Conception of Rhetoric" (1936), James H. McBurney's "Place of the Enthymeme in Rhetorical Theory" (1936), and Kenneth Hance's "Elements of the Rhetorical Theory of Phillips Brooks" (1938). Frequently, such theoretical work in the history of rhetoric concentrated on explicating complex concepts or heuristic procedures. While James H. McBurney's essay on the enthymeme in rhetorical theory (1936) is an excellent illustration of a seminal work in historical research, no article better illustrates the impact such research can have on a discipline than Otto Alvin Loeb Dieter's "Stasis" (1950), a monograph so detailed and comprehensive that it remains required reading for historians of rhetoric. There is little doubt that the popular reception of these works encouraged and prompted such other specialized studies as Prentice A. Meador, Jr.'s, discussion of epicheiremes (1964), Ray Nadeau's discussion of "Stock Issues" (1958), and Donovan J. Ochs' excellent essay on Aristotle's formal topics (1969). In fact, the specialization of scholarly inquiry in classical rhetoric was even extended to the translation and commentary of ancient treatises, as illustrated by the research of Ray Nadeau's essays on the *Rhetorica ad Herennium* (1949), Aphthonius (1952), and Hermogenes' *On Stases* (1964); Richard Leo Enos' essay on Suetonius' account of Roman rhetoric (1972); Michael C. Leff's discussion of Latin stylistic rhetorics (1973); and Keith V. Erickson's essay, "The Lost Rhetorics of Aristotle" (1976).

Research growing out of this historical/humanistic perspective had the latitude to extend its inquiries to the relationship between the structuring of thought and the structuring of discourse. Essays such as Karl Wallace's "Aspects of Modern Rhetoric in Francis Bacon" (1956), Edwin Black's "Plato's View of Rhetoric" (1958), Lloyd Bitzer's "Aristotle's Enthymeme Revisited" (1959), Otis Walter's "On Views of Rhetoric, Whether Conservative or Progressive" (1963), Wayne Brockride's "Toward a Contemporary Aristotelian Theory of Rhetoric" (1966), Wilbur Samuel Howell's "John Locke and the New Rhetoric" (1967), David Kaufer's "Influence of Plato's Developing Psychology on His Views of Rhetoric" (1978), William Lyon Benoit's "Aristotle's Example: The Rhetorical Induction" (1980), and Paul G. Bator's "'Principle of Sympathy' in Campbell's *Philosophy of Rhetoric*" (1982) all illustrate the utility of historical rhetoric in addressing issues on the relationship of the structuring of knowledge and the structuring of discourse. More recent research has also emphasized the study of invention and epistemology: James A. Berlin's "Transformation of Invention in Nineteenth Century American Rhetoric" (1981), James W. Hikins' "Plato's Rhetorical Theory: Old Perspectives on the Epistemology of the New Rhetoric" (1981), Dennis Bormann's "Two Faculty Psychologists on the 'Ends' of Speaking: George Campbell and Johann Sulzer" (1982), and James Benjamin's "Eristic, Dialectic, and Rhetoric" (1983). The impact of using historical methods to restructure epistemological processes became both a lively area in historical rhetoric and a clear bridge with researchers in communication theory.

Current research illustrates that the canon of style also merits closer examination, particularly as it relates to the expression and structuring of thought. Articles discussing the importance of style in the composition of rhetorical discourse include: Thomas M. Conley's essay, "Ancient Rhetoric and Modern Generic Criticism" (1979); Bruce W. Weaver's study on cultural determination of rhetorical styles in Greek oratory (1979); Richard L. Street's article on lexical diversity in Ciceronian oratory (1979), William Wiethoff's essays on obscurantism (1979, 1980); Donald C. Bryant's study of persuasion in the satires of Jonathan Swift (1981); and Donovan J. Ochs' essay, "Rhetorical Detailing in Cicero's Verrine Orations" (1982).

Work in historical rhetoric has been extended not only to the refinement of concepts but also to the understanding of periods. The Middle Ages and the Renaissance have been the focus of considerable attention, as exemplified by the work of such scholars as James J. Murphy (1960, 1962, 1966, 1967), James R. McNally (1967), Vincent M. Bevilacqua (1972), Kathleen Hall Jamieson (1976), Luke M. Reinsma (1977), Don Abbott (1978, 1983), Barbara Warnick (1978, 1982), William Wiethoff (1978), and Dennis R. Bormann (1980). Notable efforts in this direction can be seen in the two symposia issues of the *Western Journal of Speech Communication* on the rhetoric of the English Renaissance (Spring 1964) and the rhetorical theory of George Campbell (Spring 1968). Yet, even these developments in historical rhetoric are grounded in a tradition forged early in speech communication, a humanistic approach in the reconstruction of rhetorical thought and discourse in a public context.

Work in the history of rhetoric has also concentrated on more specialized topics, such as Michael C. McGee's "Fall of Wellington: A Case Study of the Relationship Between Theory, Practice, and Rhetoric in History" (1977). Frequently, innovative topics in historical rhetoric have established a base through the regional journals. Such articles as Michael C. Leff's studies on Boethius and fifth-century Latin rhetorical theory (1974, 1976), Ray E. McKerrow's "Probable Argument and Proof in Whately's Theory of Rhetoric" (1975), Richard Leo Enos' study of rhetoric in the Athenian Second Sophistic (1977), and Michael Volpe's "A Practical Platonic Rhetoric: A Study of the Argumentation of the *Apology*" (1977) have been made possible because regional journals have had an editioral policy encouraging receptiveness to various and innovative approaches to historical rhetoric. In fact, even reflective essays such as Marie Hochmuth Nichol's "When You Set out for Ithaka . . ." (1977) and Michael C. Leff's "In Search of Ariadne's Thread: A Review of the Recent Literature on Rhetorical Theory" (1978) have served both to analyze and direct studies in rhetoric. In short, research in historical rhetoric often served to provide a forum for traditional and exploratory topics and approaches. This receptiveness to varying approaches in turn serves as a compatible and welcome transition for scholars who share an interest in historical rhetoric but who do not come out of speech communication. Numerous articles, bibliographies, and reviews offered in such journals as *Philosophy & Rhetoric, Rhetoric Society Quarterly, College Composition and Communication,* and the journal of the International Society for the History of Rhetoric, *Rhetorica,* are contributed by members of the speech communication discipline.

Major research efforts by historians of rhetoric have resulted in some book-length studies. Several such "histories" of rhetoric have provided macroscopic accounts chronicling the major periods in the history of rhetoric. George Kennedy's *The Art of Persuasion in Greece* (1963); *The Art of Rhetoric in the Roman World: 300 B.C–A.D. 300* (1972); *Classical Rhetoric and Its Christian and Secular Tradition from Ancient to Modern Times* (1980); and his most recent effort, *Greek Rhetoric Under Christian Emperors* (1983) have provided a firm foundation for education and further research in classical rhetoric. Similarly, James J. Murphy's *Rhetoric in the Middle Ages: A History of Rhetorical Theory from Saint Augustine to the Renaissance* (1974), and Robert W. Smith's *The Art of Rhetoric in Alexandria: Its Theory and Practice in the Ancient World* (1974) have provided contexts for subsequent research. Wilbur Samuel Howell's *Logic and Rhetoric in England, 1500–1700* (1956) and his later contribution, *Eighteenth-*

Century British Logic and Rhetoric (1971) are excellent examples of how a thorough study of rhetorical theory can be treated within an accounting of a social and intellectual context. Other such works, however, often provide little detail on rhetorical theory but emphasize the social and intellectual contexts in which rhetoric occurs.

Of course, anthologies have also provided comprehensive discussion of rhetorical theory, but few theme or "period" collections exist. Keith V. Erickson's two collections *Aristotle: The Classical Heritage of Rhetoric* (1974) and *Plato: True and Sophistic Rhetoric* (1979), and James J. Murphy's *Medieval Eloquence: Studies in the Theory and Practice of Medieval Rhetoric* (1978) are representative of thorough treatments of a specific theme. Coherent collections in Roman, Byzantine, and Renaissance rhetoric are only a few areas where similar anthologies are needed. More general anthologies have provided opportunities for specific research, however. *History of Speech Education in America* (Ed. Karl R. Wallace, 1954) and the discussions of rhetorical theory included in the three-volume collection, *History and Criticism of American Public Address* (Eds. William Norwood Brigance & Marie Hochmuth [Nichols], 1943/1960, 1955) are two of the earlier, and best, examples of cooperative efforts within the discipline. The cooperative effort of scholars has not been limited to a particular period; in fact, *Historical Studies of Rhetoric and Rhetoricians* (Ed. Raymond F. Howes, 1961), *The Province of Rhetoric* (Eds. Joseph Schwartz & John A. Rycenga, 1965), and *Readings in Rhetoric* (Eds. Lionel Crocker & Paul A. Carmack, 1965) are examples of anthologies that survey various topics and periods in the history of rhetoric.

Often general anthologies appear in the form of *Festschriften*. Notable examples of these early collections include *Studies in Speech and Drama in Honor of Alexander M. Drummond* (Ed. Herbert A. Wichelns, 1944) and *The Rhetorical Idiom: Essays in Rhetoric, Oratory, Language, and Drama, Presented to Herbert A. Wichelns* (Ed. Donald C. Bryant, 1958). Other examples of such collections—frequently compiled by former students and colleagues—include: *Rhetoric and Communication: Studies in the University of Illinois Tradition* (Eds. Jane Blankenship & Hermann G. Stelzner, 1976); *Rhetoric in Transition: Studies in the Nature and Uses of Rhetoric* (Ed. Eugene E. White, 1980), dedicated to Carroll C. Arnold; and *Explorations in Rhetoric: Studies in Honor of Douglas Ehninger* (Ed. Ray E. McKerrow, 1982). Special collections of research by individuals throughout a career have also been used as a means of honoring distinguished scholars in historical rhetoric, most noticeable of which are the selected works of Harry Caplan in *Of Eloquence: Studies in Ancient and Medieval Rhetoric* (Eds. Anne King & Helen North, 1970) and Wilbur Samuel Howell's *Poetics, Rhetoric, and Logic: Studies in the Basic Disciplines of Criticism* (1975). This commendable tradition has simultaneously encouraged research by the next generation of scholars while honoring those individuals who served as models throughout their careers.

A REVIEW

The preceding synthesis of research in speech communication on the history of rhetoric provides a prologue for both assessment of, and recommendations for, scholarly study. First, and perhaps foremost, research in the history of rhetoric over the last 75 years has resulted in few scholarly texts of primary material. Outside of the translations and bibliographies of primary sources in *Communication Monographs*, few publications of seminal sources exist in speech communication. Southern Illinois University Press, however, has distinguished itself with the Landmarks in Rhetoric and Public Address series. To discuss all the contributions of the editors of these volumes would push this essay far beyond its present limits. Yet, it is not too much to say that the editing of and introductions by such individuals as Lloyd Bitzer (1963), Douglas Ehninger (1963), Harold F. Harding (1965), and Vincent M. Bevilacqua and Richard Murphy (1965) to the works of George Campbell, Hugh Blair, Richard Whately, and Joseph Priestly have been significant contributions to understanding some of the most important primary sources in the history of rhetoric. Yet, a significant amount of work at libraries and even archaeological sites is needed to uncover literary and epigraphical evidence. Warren Guthrie's monographs on the development of American rhetorical theory (1946, 1947, 1948, 1949, 1951) and the essays on Italian, Spanish, Dutch, and German treatises on preaching by Harry Caplan and Henry H. King (1949, 1950, 1954, 1956) are invaluable in retrieving and organizing primary information on important periods in the history of rhetoric. Unfortunately, however, relatively little research is done in speech communication that does not depend on non-rhetoricians for translations of primary and secondary source material. Careful philological analysis of primary sources such as William M. A. Grimaldi's *Aristotle, "Rhetoric I": A Commentary* (1980) are scarce. Yet, analyses of theories and artifacts depend on the knowledge translators bring to the sources. A historian of rhetoric who initiates inquiries without an evaluation of material in its original form risks a false start in the analytic process. Moreover, isolation from non-English sources often results in a delay in acquiring information, a delay that compels such researchers to follow rather than lead other disciplines in the explication of evidence. Textual editing, criticism, and commentary are essential for research in the history of rhetoric to flourish.

Second, macroscopic approaches that have chronicled the history of rhetoric are often better characterized as the transmission of stories rather than the advancement of historical scholarship. Sweeping histories of rhetoric that cover both centuries and cultures in their wake can do little more than provide an introduction to the discipline. That is, careful, detailed analysis of rhetorical theories is sacrificed for the transmission of historical anecdotes that chronicle rather than synthesize and analyze theory. Howell's *Logic and Rhetoric in England: 1500–1700* is an excellent example of a genuine history of rhetorical theory in a social and intellectual context. Too few such volumes exist within speech communication. Howell's analysis is based on meticulous and controlled mastery of primary sources—qualities that researchers in speech communication should emulate and not merely depend upon. Similarly, despite scores of article-length studies on prominent theoreticians, few book-length studies exist. Wilbur Samuel Howell's *Rhetoric of Alcuin and Charlemagne* (1941/1965) and *Fenelon's Dialogues on Eloquence* (1951); Karl R. Wallace's *Francis Bacon on Communication and Rhetoric* (1943); Walter J. Ong's *Ramus, Method, and the Decay of Dialogue: From the Art of Discourse to the Art of Reason* (rept. 1958) and his *Ramus and Talon Inventory* (1958); George Kennedy's *Quintilian* (1969); Dennis R. Bormann and Elisabeth Leinfellner's *Adam Müller's Twelve Lectures of Rhetoric* (1978) are illustrations of thorough treatments of individuals who have shaped rhetoric's history.

Third, specific and specialized attention to concepts, theories, and methodologies must be encouraged. Studies such as Otto A. L. Dieter's "Stasis" should be less exceptional than they are. The refinement of methodologies for understanding the cognitive processes that shape discourse will enhance both retrieval methods and analysis because such work, in turn, should (and must) call for greater attention to cognitve processes in the invention and composition of discourse. This attention should result in a closer relation between theory and practice, but relatively little work in the history of rhetoric has been done to sharpen or develop methodologies for such analysis and synthesis. New historiographic procedures and theoretical approaches seem almost nonexistent. In contrast, where the development of new statistical procedures often seems to be a *raison d'ête* for social sciences, historical studies in rhetoric lag behind in developing sensitive methodologies for the collection and examination of evidence. For example, relatively little is done in using the computer in author-attribution research, the formulaic structuring of composition, and the recurrence of themes. While the computer is currently being used in the compilation and organization of Renaissance texts under the direction of James J. Murphy, such use is more organizational than analytical. Rather, programs to aid in analysis could reach a level of sophistication that would enable theoreticians to reconstruct heuristic processes artificially and thus unlock the secrets of eloquent and effective expression of prominent rhetors. Thus, for example, it is entirely possible for historians of rhetoric to use a theory that would be the basis on which a program could be created to re-invent "Homeric" discourse or "Ciceronian" prose. Such procedures are already within our grasp, but historians of rhetoric will be little more than spectators if these procedures are not attended to and integrated within rhetorical studies.

Fourth, and as a corollary to the previous point, research directions that stress reconstruction of cognitive processes of discourse mandate a closer attention to epistemology than has been given. The history of rhetoric has often been less the history of ideas about discourse than the social consequences of rhetoric's use. As a result, relatively little attention has been paid to the relationship between the structuring of thought and the structuring of discourse. Consequently, the analysis of rhetorical theory is only rarely based upon a careful inquiry into the conceptual processes shaping discourse; instead, explications of theory are predicated upon cognitive processes that are either assumed or ignored by the historian of rhetoric. Yet without a knowledge of cognition, inquiries into invention, style, and general heuristic procedures are little more than meaningless. A fine illustration of the importance of recognizing the cognitive processes directing rhetorical discourse is seen in Donovan J. Ochs' "Cicero's *Topica:* A Process View of Invention" (1982).

To assume that a plea for greater attention to cognition in historical research signals the end to macroscopic approaches and diachronic methods is erroneous and even antithetical to the view expressed here. Historians of rhetoric who wish to make interesting links with the past through such macroscopic approaches as "systems," public knowledge, and social context must ultimately base ethnographic analyses on the conceptual notions and sentiments that tie the social fabric. Failure to account for the modalities of thought that bind a social situation risks a glib rendering of the curious, primarily because the processes of consciousness would be unconscious to the historian. Dated but sterling examples illustrating the centrality of cognitive processes are evident in works such as Eric A. Havelock's *Preface to Plato* (1963/1982) and Susanne K. Langer's *Philosophy in an New Key* (3rd ed., 1976). Yet, similar to the status of research on primary material, historians of rhetoric in speech communication are often dependent upon scholars from other disciplines to map out the conceptual terrain for their understanding of a society's use of thought and language. We are only beginning to understand the Hellenic or Renaissance mind; and until we do, little knowledge can be advanced about the rhetoric they produced or, in several cases, the inventive process upon which their discourse was based. Certainly, Michael McGee's essay "The Fall of Wellington: A Case Study of the Relationship Between Theory, Practice, and Rhetoric in History" (1977) dramatizes this need for historians of rhetoric. The merit of historical rhetoric is that it not only provides knowledge of intrinsic importance but that it also reconstructs evidence and retrieves wisdom across time that can be applied for further study. In this respect the notion of "context" is one that is extended beyond the immediate moment to include all social and intellectual forces that have shaped the structuring of thought and discourse, and thus have the potential to help to discover and synthesize knowledge about speech communication.

Fifth, relatively few reference works have been published in speech communication and, as a result, limited sources for subsequent work in the history of rhetoric are available. *Ancient Greek and Roman Rhetoricians: A Bibliographical Dictionary* (ed. D. C. Bryant, R. W. Smith, P. D. Arnott, E. B. Holtsmark & G. O. Rowe, 1968) was one effort to provide lucid accounts for students of the history of rhetoric. Similarly, Winifred Bryan Horner's edited volumes, *Historical Rhetoric: An Annotated Bibliography of Selected Sources in English* (1980) and *The Present State of Scholarship in Historical and Contemporary Rhetoric* (1983) have been made possible by efforts of scholars across disciplines but involved in historical research in rhetoric. Additional encyclopedic material, equivalent to *The Oxford Classical Dictionary*, is essential for further study and research.

Sixth, advancements in these five areas of historical rhetoric within speech communication can be sooner attained through cooperation across disciplines, with European colleagues, and in the publications of our journals. Such contributions, however, should never be seen as disharmonious with the liberal/humanistic approaches that motivated early work in rhetoric and particularly the spirit of the Cornell Tradition. Rather, a rigorous, scholarly standard for research in the history of rhetoric will advance knowledge about discourse and its centrality to the human condition. Knowledge resulting from such high expectations and standards will in turn provide the most "liberal" approach called for by such pioneers as Everett Lee Hunt, for it will provide a freedom of thought that was the promise driving the Cornell Tradition. Further efforts will promise a renaissance and fulfillment of that progressive spirit. This reawakening of the Cornell Tradition should help historians of rhetoric in speech communication to appreciate both the fine contributions of our earlier scholars and the bright future of continued studies. Yet, it would be good for scholars of speech communication to benefit from their own history in another respect. The recommendations on the importance of historical rhetoric seen in *The Prospect of Rhetoric* (1971, pp. 235–236) should be remembered and even reexamined now that a significant amount of time has passed since the Wingspread Conference. Of equal importance, eloquent statements, such as Marie Hochmuth Nichols' 1969 presidential address, "The Tyranny of Relevance" (1970), and "When You Set Out for Ithaka . . . " (1977), and Charles W. Kneupper and Floyd D. Anderson's "Uniting Wisdom and Eloquence: The Need for Rhetorical Invention" (1980) should be reread for the positive value they hold for the history of rhetoric. The great and obvious lesson of history is that it retrieves and synthesizes wisdom from the past that can be analyzed and applied for the present and future. Clearly, historical scholarship in rhetoric has provided that benefit to speech communication in two respects: one, the better understanding of the rich history of rhetoric, including its theories and heuristic procedures; and two, a historical lesson within speech communication of how such a study can benefit the temperament and direction of kindred spirits questing to know about communication from any perspective and approach that will enrich our knowledge.

CONCLUSION

On the eve of the 50th anniversary of the founding of the Speech Association of America, Lionel Crocker and Paul A. Carmack wrote in their Preface to *Readings in Rhetoric* (1965) of the growth of the discipline and that "this growth has been accomplished by a searching of the past for usable ideas in the field of rhetoric and public address" (p. viii). It is fitting to note, some 20 years after these words were penned, that Crocker and Carmack were more than optimistic—they were prophetic. The task of the retrieval of knowledge about rhetoric lost, or in need of refinement, has been a central and lively concern of the association in the last two decades. Shortly before his death, Douglas Ehninger wrote to the graduate students at the 1978 Michigan-Indiana Doctoral Honors Seminar of his belief in the value of historical rhetoric. "In the absence of history," Ehninger warned, "we always would have to be starting afresh" (1978, p. 9). Professor Ehninger's career is testimony to the maxim that the past is prologue, and his retrospective view of the future was both based on the scholars who preceded him and directed toward the young researchers whom he saw as taking up the responsibility he passed on. Many of those scholars in Professor Ehninger's past and future have been acknowleged in this chapter. In a sense, Professor Ehninger was himself echoing the past, for his testimony is itself an acknowledgement to a discipline's commitment to rigorous scholarship in a humane tradition and a fitting conclusion to recognizing its past excellence and promising future. It is clear that individuals such as Douglas Ehninger and Everett Lee Hunt—who personally experienced the growth of the history of rhetoric in speech communication—would approve of the early and subsequent efforts to reexamine rhetoric's past for future progress.

3

The Criticism of Symbolic Inducement: A Critical-Theoretical Connection

RICHARD B. GREGG

A quarter of a century ago, the Speech Association of the Eastern States published a collection of essays surveying the previous fifty years of the speech profession in America (Oliver & Bauer, 1959). The collection includes an essay, not about scholarly rhetorical criticism, but about lay criticism (Wilson, 1959, pp. 8–11). Wilson concluded that no clear and consistent approach to the criticism of public speeches could be discerned in the work of lay critics. In another essay, Arnold remarked that such a finding should not be surprising. "The 'scholarly critics' still struggle to refine their perceptions and methods in search of the way, finally, to capture the essence of a speech or a speaking career" (Arnold, 1959, p. 5).

Six years later, Black perceived three distinct critical orientations to have emerged from the struggle: an approach to the analysis of the rhetoric of movements that did not have a well-defined critical method and seemed to offer more to the study of history than rhetoric (Black, 1965, pp. 19–22); a "psychological" orientation that had to be employed with great caution, and that seemed better able to account for factors engendering a discourse than the discourse itself (pp. 22–27); and the much more fully developed neo-Aristotelian approach that was unnecessarily limiting and rigid (pp. 27–35). Black concluded "that variety is wanting in the methods of rhetoric, that the options available to the critic need to be multiplied, and above all, that the prevailing mode of rhetorical criticism is profoundly mistaken" (p. viii).

In the last two decades we have experienced a proliferation of new orientations and approaches to the analysis of rhetorical messages. As Leff put it, "By the early seventies, the monism of the fifties dissolves into a kaleidoscope of theoretical patterns" (Leff, 1980, p. 340). In view of this fecundity of critical activity, it is understandable that in the past several years rhetorical scholars have begun to take stock of the diversity, to delineate what the major lines of development have been, and to determine what it all adds up to, or whether it adds up at all.

Studies have been undertaken that attempt to group the plethora of critical studies in terms of the similarities and differences of their orientations or methods (Stewart, Ochs & Mohrmann, 1973; Brock & Scott, 1980; *The Western Journal of Speech Communication*, Fall 1980; *Central States Speech Journal*, Winter 1980). In a different vein, Swanson, in two definitive essays, examined the kinds of data rhetorical critics select to support the conclusions they draw and the ensuing claims they are constrained to make because of the particular epistemological stance they choose to adopt (Swanson, 1977a, 1977b). There is, however, one summative question that has not received much attention, and that is the question of whether, if at all, the explorations of rhetorical critics have contributed to our theoretical understanding of human rhetorical behavior.

Leff points out that for years the relationship of theory and criticism has been unclear (Leff, p. 340). But rhetorical criticism inevitably traffics in theory. A critic intent upon accounting for the inte   ion of rhetorical elements in a situation, the audience response to rhetorical messages, or the rhetorical potential of messages must make some assumptions about human behavior and symbolic meaning no matter what critical approach is being taken. Whether or not critics are conscious of the assumptions being employed, assumptions are always operative, functioning to constrain and shape the analytical process.

Generally speaking, critics are intent upon searching out certain patterns of symbolic experiencing in the rhetorical phenomena they investigate and drawing conclusions about those patterns concerning their meanings and causative or relational implications. The transformation of rhetorical behaviors into patterns will, in effect, re-present those behaviors. In some cases the transformations will re-present them in a more microscopic form than was actually experienced by those participating in the interaction who were not explicitly aware of the connections, subtleties, or implications discovered through critical analysis. In other cases, the behaviors may be re-presented in a more macroscopic form as critics strive to perceive general patterns beyond the event in order to reach conclusions with more sweeping power. In either case, it is at the points of transformation, and in the conclusions drawn about them, that theoretical concepts become activated.

Often the relationship of criticism to theory is seen in a conservative light; knowingly or unknowingly the critic calls upon theory or aspects of theory to provide the substance from which questions or analytical topoi may be drawn to illuminate rhetorical transactions. But the relationship can be the other way around. Through analysis, critical insight can lead to new or modified conclusions pertaining to human rhetorical behavior.

We should note at the outset that rhetorical criticism need not always claim to contribute to theoretical understanding in order to justify its existence as a valuable scholarly enterprise. As members of the human species, we share a great many similarities of neurological and cognitive activity. Indeed, it is the very existence of such similarities that makes communication and common understanding possible. But humans engage in rhetorical behaviors in concrete and particular situations. In many situations, the possibilities for variety and diversity of action and response are extensive. While our behaviors are constrained by species-specific characteristics, they are not determined in a manner that some other forms of life seem to be. Consequently, we may choose to respond in a wide variety of ways to the same phenomenon, depending upon the circumstances of the case. For this reason, in order to arrive at sensitive and accurate accounts of rhetorical situations, rhetorical critics must often pay close attention to the singular particularities involved, rather than engage in the kind of generalizing that distorts through selective attention. If we are to have a full understanding of human behavior, we must have accountings of particularity as well as of generality.

On the other hand, the existence of commonly shared characteristics provides opportunity for the work of rhetorical critics to achieve fresh theoretical insights into human behavior, even when critics are not striving for generality. The findings of rhetorical critics working on individual projects can be summative in effect. By adopting a metacritical perspective, we can search the works of rhetorical critics to ask whether there seem to be points of shared assumption and discovery that sum up in theoretical insight. I propose to undertake such a metacritical task here.

The approach has been inductive and the report shall be selective. The sample considered includes contemporary critical essays that seem to burrow deeply enough into human behavior and meaning to afford theoretical insight. The report selects representative critical works, and focuses on what seems to be a major developing trend. To provide some comparative context, it will be helpful to survey briefly major trends in the historical development of American rhetorical criticism.

There is general agreement that the outlines for what was to become the neo-Aristotelian, or "traditional," approach to rhetorical criticism were first sketched by Herbert Wichelns in 1925 (Wichelns, 1980, pp. 40–73). The title of his essay, "The Literary Criticism of Oratory," is instructive. Wichelns' intent was to differentiate biographical and historical criticism from criticism that was specifically rhetorical. His intention reflects the fact that the early founders of the speech communication discipline broke away from departments of literature, acting on the conviction that there were important differences between discourse written for the ages and expressing universal values and the kinds of spoken discourse produced in response to particular exigencies to affect particular audiences. Their struggle to affirm their scholarly identity as a separate and legitimate field of study, while understandable, led to the drawing of dubious distinctions. Thus, Wichelns wrote, "If we now turn to rhetorical criticism as we found it exemplified in the preceding section, we find that its point of view is patently single. It is not concerned with permanence, nor yet with beauty. It is concerned with effect. It regards a speech as a communication to a specific audience, and holds its business to be the analysis and appreciation of the orator's method of imparting his ideas to his hearers" (p. 67). Wichelns' statement is a reiteration of the idea expressed two years earlier by Hoyt Hudson, who tried to differentiate rhetoric from poetry. In the pure case, wrote Hudson, the rhetor stood at the opposite end of the spectrum from the poet. The poet composed primarily for the sake of expression and without a specific audience in mind, whereas the rhetor prepared messages with particular audiences in mind and with every intention of affecting them in quite specific ways (Hudson, 1923, pp. 144–145). Even then, the distinction as formulated was in trouble. Hudson himself admitted that pure cases were rare, and described some rhetorical aspects that could be found in poetry and some poetic aspects that occasionally crept into rhetoric. Nonetheless, the distinction hardened in the years that immediately followed, as scholars of speech discovered and elaborated what they interpreted to be their classical heritage.

The phenomenon that most typically identified the neo-Aristotelian approach to criticism was the tendency to impose classical categories on rhetorical messages and situations to describe and explain them. Wichelns, in his essay, briefly adumbrates the orientation:

> Rhetorical criticism is necessarily analytical. The scheme of a rhetorical study includes the element of the speaker's personality as a conditioning factor; it includes also the public character of the man—not what he was but what he was thought to be. It requires a description of the speaker's audience, and of the leading ideas with which he plied his hearers—his topics, the motives to which he appealed, the nature of proofs he offered. These will reveal his own judgment of human nature in his audiences, and also his judgment on the questions which he discussed. Nor can rhetorical criticism omit the speaker's mode of arrangement and his mode of expression, nor his habit of preparation and his manner of delivery from the platform; though the last two are perhaps less significant. "Style"—in the sense which corresponds to diction and sentence movement—must receive attention, but only as

one among various means that secure for the speaker ready access to the minds of his auditors. Finally, the effect of the discourse on its immediate hearers is not to be ignored, neither in the testing of witnesses, nor in the record of events. And throughout such a study one must conceive of the public man as influencing the men of his own times by the power of his discourse (Wichelns, pp. 69, 70).

Following Wichelns' direction, rhetorical critics engaged in historical reconstruction of the rhetorical situations they wished to examine; discussed the appeals of rhetorical messages in terms of ethos, pathos, and logos, with the latter often receiving the most attention; and described the characteristics of messages in light of the categories of invention, arrangement, style, and delivery. The neo-Aristotelian critical orientation led to several significant consequences that, though not necessarily entailed by the approach, did occur and did constrain the work of critics. For instance, for the most part critics tended to focus on speakers and speeches. In addition to narrowing the scope of their study to speaking, critics usually restricted themselves to formal speaking occasions, such as those of the law court, the pulpit, legislative assemblies, and other public forums. Thus, one could as easily slip into the habit of identifying rhetorical critics by the kind of discourse they examined as by their methods or purposes. A further narrowing resulted from the typical adoption of what one can term an "instrumental" point of view toward rhetorical situations. In other words, critics conceived rhetorical situations to be occasions when speakers, acting in light of purpose, situation, and audience, selected those strategies of presentation that they believed would present their case in the strongest possible light. The criterion for critical judgment tended to become an assessment of how closely the speaker came to accomplishing what could have been achieved given the circumstances.

The early critics, then, following what they believed to be Aristotle's lead, disregarded many manifestations of symbolic meaning that were nonverbal and non-oral as being irrelevant to their concerns, and they further disregarded those oral modes of discourse that did not appear to exhibit patterns of reasoning and invitations to considered judgment in a clear fashion. The shortcoming of limiting critical efforts only to those rhetorical situations that invited judgment was emphatically underlined by Black (1965):

We must be careful to distinguish between the process of coming to hold a belief and the way in which the belief would be justified. A belief can be justified quite apart from the procedure followed in coming to hold it; but it seems to be a requirement in the justification of a judgment that the right procedure was followed in forming it. It

follows that insofar as Aristotle composed the *Rhetoric* with the judgmental process in view, the scope of this theory would be limited to
those forms of discourse that bear some relation to the judgmental
process, and rhetorical discourse that finds its end in any state of mind
or mental act different from judgment would be excluded from consideration in the *Rhetoric* (pp. 112–113).

Black concludes, "Here we come upon perhaps the most severe limitation in
the scope of Aristotelian rhetoric, a limitation that is most acutely manifested in the Aristotelian doctrine of emotional appeals and in the Aristotelian typology. This limitation consists of a narrow view of human behavior"
(p. 114).

In a related fashion, students of criticism came to see how easily the
neo-Aristotelian orientation led to the unimaginative application of critical
categories so that critiques became self-fulfilling, wooden, and sometimes
irrelevant to the rhetorical dynamics being examined. One of the obviously
questionable assumptions raised by a mechanical application of the neo-
Aristotelian orientation is that there are unchanging categories into which
rhetorical messages and the elements of rhetorical situations inevitably fall.
A corresponding assumption is that discourse and situational characteristics that fall outside the range of the categories are either not rhetorical or
are not worthy of the critic's attention because they do not closely approximate what is properly rhetorical. Both of these assumptions can be seriously
questioned in light of what we have come to know about human behavior.
The shapes of discourses can be as flexible as the minds that conceive them,
and human minds are very flexible instruments indeed.

Further, there are grounds to question that what people take to be
"reasons" can be confined within the neo-Aristotelian perspective and its
notions concerning what properly constitutes reasons. The apparently dis-
connected rantings and ravings of a lunatic zealot can possess suasory
potential, and there is surely something operating as reason in the heads of
those swayed by the rantings of the zealot. Consequently, the rhetorical
appeals of the zealot fall properly within the purview of rhetorical critics.

In order to provide viable interpretations of rhetorical situations,
rhetorical critics must deal with the perceptual and experiential worlds of
the participants in those situations. For if there is a correspondence among
the intentions of a rhetor, the reactions of an audience, and the characteristics of a message, it is rhetor intentions and audience reactions that make of
the message characteristics whatever is made of them. Human intentions
and reactions reside, not autonomously in message characteristics or
situational elements, but in the perceptual and experiential worlds of humans in interaction with those characteristics and elements. The major

charge against neo-Aristotelian criticism was, in effect, that it did not properly account for the diversity of human rhetorical behavior. In other words, it could not properly account for human symbolic processing in all of its multitudinous forms.

Recognition that a critical stodginess had settled in over the rhetorical landscape led to a growing feeling of discontent during the decade of the 1950s. In 1957, in a special issue of *Western Speech* later to be expanded into a book, judgment was firmly delivered. "A glance at our critical works," wrote Marie Hochmuth Nichols, "would indicate an overwhelming number solidly established in conventional aspects of the Aristotelian tradition, with a stress upon the functional and dynamic character of rhetoric" (Nichols, pp. 75–84). A bit further on, Nichols expressed her concern about the limits of the tradition. "Rhetoric as technique designed to secure effects, not rhetoric as an art sustained in and through dialectic, has been our concern, and our lack of equipment to deal with rhetoric in its philosophical aspects has manifested itself in our criticism. The Aristotelian rationale has, of course, made easy the practice of seizing upon the mechanical aspects of the lore" (p. 24).

Robert Clark referred to "the production of a criticism which adheres too closely to the formal *topoi*; it is frequently stereotyped, occasionally banal" (Clark, 1968, p. 65). And again, "We have too much of unimaginative word counting, the pedestrian assemblage of arguments, the methodological and generalized commentary laid out on the Aristotelian pattern" (pp. 71–72). Mark Klynn adds his sense of limitation to those of Nichols. "The most important result of the monistic attitude is that conventional rhetorical critics have tended to delimit the meaning and consequence of rhetoric in a special, very narrow way. This, in turn, had led them to erect the deceptive and confining standard of 'effect' as the ultimate test of critical judgment" (Klynn, 1968, pp. 146–157).

The perceived need to broaden the practices of criticism led the writers of these essays to encourage critics to examine more closely the intellectual component of public address (Blau, 1968, pp. 18–28), to pay more attention to style (Bryant, 1968, pp. 50–63), to incorporate some aspects of literary criticism (Clark, pp. 64–73), to adopt the ideas of Kenneth Burke (Nichols, pp. 75–85), to attend to the philosophical aspects of speeches (Nilsen, 1968, pp. 86–97), and to give greater attention to the intrinsic content of speeches (Redding, 1968, pp. 98–125).

It is clear that rhetorical critics were being urged to develop criteria for judgment other than just that of the effects of discourse on audiences and to become more imaginative in their analysis. The critics cited immediately above assumed that a growing variety of critical approaches would lead to more complete critiques of rhetorical situations and messages. Over the next few years, a number of new approaches were suggested; there were, in fact, more metacritical writings outlining new critical roads to follow than there were analytical essays in which critics attempted the new directions.

The diversity of criticism itself blossomed in the late 1960s, at least partly and importantly as a result of two happenings. The first was the publication of Edwin Black's book, *Rhetorical Criticism: A Study in Method*, of which Ehninger wrote: "If Wichelns' landmark essay of 1925 gave neo-Aristotelianism its birth, this book published exactly 40 years later may well deal the school its death blow" (Ehninger, 1965, p. 230). The second happening was the growing social protest, first over black rights, then the student protest that grew into the anti-Vietnam protest, and along with it the emergent movement for women's liberation. These protest movements employed some rhetoric in the conventional sense of the term, but much rhetoric of protest appeared to be unconventional. First, protestors employed not only words, but marches, sit-ins, songs, sloganeerings, and chants. It became obvious that demonstrative acts like these were intended to function symbolically and rhetorically (Haiman, 1967). They served as ritualistic acts of affirmation for the protesters themselves and demanded the attention of non-protesters, sometimes evoking strong negative reaction. Rhetorical critics undertook analytical investigations of the rhetoric of dissent and protest, realizing that the conventional critical approach, which placed an emphasis on reasoning and common ground, was inadequate to the task. In addition to having to examine nonconventional forms, then, critics had to comprehend rhetorical functions serving purposes of coercion, confrontation, and divisiveness (Andrews, 1969; Burgess, 1968; Brooks, 1970; Scott & Smith, 1969; Scott & Brockriede, 1969; Gregg, 1971; Campbell, 1973).

The rhetoric of the social protest movements exerted influence and provoked thought beyond their own immediate concerns. The decade of the 1960s and beyond into the 1970s became a time when intellectual modes of thought and practice were questioned in addition to personal and political lifestyles. Just as political activists rebelled against "establishment" institutions, rhetorical critics rebelled against the established traditional mode of criticism. Thus, the rhetoric of social protest helped nourish the exploration of new approaches to rhetorical criticism that in their own way constituted a kind of intellectual protest.*

In 1970, the Speech Communication Association sponsored the National Developmental Project on Rhetoric. The purpose of the project participants was to examine the state of rhetorical study generally and to make recommendations for future work. Three committees were estab-

---

*I am indebted to Michael Osborn for the insight that the criticism of protest rhetoric could, itself, be understood as protest.

lished for the second meeting of the conference, and each committee issued a report following its deliberations. It is noteworthy that two of the committees not only further encouraged the study of the rhetoric of social protest but directly urged rhetorical scholars to undertake the investigation of many "nonconventional" rhetorical forms. The committee discussing the scope of rhetoric suggested the expansion of research in "the theory and practice of forms of communication which have not been investigated as thoroughly as public address" (Bitzer and Black, 1971, p. 217). The committee on rhetorical criticism was even more directive: "Rhetorical criticism must broaden its scope to examine the full range of rhetorical transactions; that is informal conversations, group settings, mass media messages, picketing, sloganeering, chanting, singing, marching, gesturing, ritual, institutional and cultural symbols, cross cultural transactions, and so forth" (p. 225).

It seemed, in the years following the committee reports, that critics were just waiting to spring from their blocks, and spring they did in many different directions. Investigative forays were made in the area of film (Rushing & Frentz, 1978; Medhurst & Benson, 1981; Medhurst, 1982) and television (Gregg, 1977; Gronbeck, n.d.). Music was analyzed for its rhetorical potential (Mohrmann & Scott, 1976; Gonzalez & Makay, 1983), as was painting (Scott, 1977; Olsen, 1983) and architecture (Stuart, 1973). Martin Luther King's famous "Letter from Birmingham Jail" caught one critic's eye (Fulkerson, 1979), and the prayers delivered at presidential inaugurals another (Medhurst, 1977). The rhetorical aspects of formal science were examined (Weimer, 1977), ideological systems were discussed in terms of their rhetorical functions (Brown, 1978), and rhetorical critics turned to the analysis of symbolic messages seemingly even more esoteric than the ones just enumerated. Cartoons (Medhurst and DeSousa, 1981), the human malady of sickness (Chesebro, 1982), the practices of psychotherapy (Makay, 1980), the nuances of pornography (Rosenfield, 1973), and the suasory potential of sugar (Mechling & Mechling, 1983) all received attention.

Is there, amidst all this diversity, any strand of similarity that has implications for theory? The question was difficult to answer when the neo-Aristotelian orientation was the predominant approach employed by critics. The difficulty was created by the fact that while the categories of data gathered in neo-Aristotelian critiques tended to be the same, the particular mix of rhetorical generalizations were warranted. Is it the case that in our time, with critics examining more and different kinds of symbolic actions than ever before and applying a wider variety of critical orientations than was previously done, it is easier to discover implications for theory?

I believe it is, and the reason is just because of such critical diversity and the broader gauged view of human rhetorical behavior that most rhetorical critics have adopted. If critics can examine human response to and the suasory potential evoked by not only formally delivered speeches but films, art, music, architecture, and a myriad of other symbolic artifacts, then clearly we seem to be assuming that there are similarities of human behavior whenever we use terms like "suasory potential" or "rhetorical response." The similarities do not lie solely in message characteristics or in the symbol systems or codes that structure them. The similarities reside importantly in the human responses to those messages and codes; in other words, they reside in what humans choose to do with symbolic messages.

Those of us in communication studies have been saying for some years that meanings are in people, not in messages, though we have not always fully appreciated the implications of the statement. But contemporary rhetorical critics demonstrate a much more complete grasp of the subtleties, sophistication, and complexity of human rhetorical-symbolic response to symbolic messages and acts in their environment than was previously the case. The work of a number of critics points the way toward the theoretical grounding needed for a complete theory of rhetoric.

Such groundings can be discovered by examining the work of just a few representative critics. The examination demonstrates that important critical similarities emerge, not from the nature of messages examined, nor from the categories of data analyzed, but rather in the critic's interpretation of the data examined.

Let us turn first to a sensititve piece of neo-Aristotelian criticism, Forbes Hill's analysis of President Richard Nixon's November 3, 1969, address concerning Vietnam (Hill, 1972). Hill's essay is an appropriate choice because he is a scholar of Aristotle's work, and his critique of the Nixon speech is an avowed and clear example of conventional criticism.

Early in his essay, Hill provides a description of the neo-Aristotelian critic's task. "Neo-Aristotelian criticism compares the means of persuasion used by a speaker with a comprehensive inventory given in Aristotle's *Rhetoric*. Its end is to discover whether the speaker makes the best choices from the inventory to get a favorable decision from a specified group of auditors in a specific situation" (p. 374). The description is revealing. The phrases, "means of persuasion" and "comprehensive inventory" allude to the categories of rhetorical situation and rhetorical message provided in Aristotle's work, which in turn reflect the characteristic Greek concern for systematization in all areas of knowledge (Lloyd, 1979; Havelock, 1976; Kennedy, 1963). Hill's descriptive statement also indicates that the critic is to focus on the rhetorical transaction between specific rhetor and specific audience as it occurs within a bound situation. The implications of Hill's phrasing are important. The rhetorical transaction is not unidirectional but involves action on the part of both rhetor and audience. It is generally agreed that in Aristotle's view a rhetor must encourage or provoke a process of judgment in the minds of the audience. The situation, then, is not one in which the rhetor selects instruments to mold and modify audience judgments at will, but rather one in which the minds of audience members must be engaged in particular ways. We shall keep a close eye on Hill's explication and discussion of this process of engagement.

Hill suggests that "the primary target was those Americans not driven by a clearly defined ideological commitment to oppose or support the war at any cost. Resentment of the sacrifice in money and lives, bewilderment at the stalemate, longing for some movement in a clearly marked direction— these were the principle aspects of their state of mind assumed by Nixon" (p. 374). This brief description of audience requires some further comment. In this situation, the process of engaging the minds of audience members in order to achieve a favorable response cannot occur in a straightforward manner. As Hill points out, those audiences with firmly held convictions regarding the Vietnam War, whether pro or con, do not figure prominently in Nixon's rhetorical effort. Hill characterizes the mind sets of members of the target audience with such terms as "resentment," "bewilderment," and "longing." These are terms that refer to phenomena of the mind best thought of as states of anxiety, frustration, and fear that emanate from more fundamentally grounded experiential values. Given these characteristics, the rhetor cannot simply marshall and order premises and issues to evoke similar movements and arrangements in the auditor's minds; the latter are presumed to be in a more ambiguous and inchoate state. Consequently, as Hill explicates the structure, premises, and style of Nixon's message, he has his eye on the kind of technical and artistic maneuvering and shaping that will invite and encourage members of the audience to experience their anxieties in ways that move them toward acceptance of Nixon's position. Hill's general assessment of the craftmanship that went into the making of the message once again contains phraseology of specific interest. "Neo-Aristotelian criticism tells a great deal about Nixon's message. It reveals the speech writer as a superior technician. It permits us to predict that given this target group the message should be successful in leading to a decision to support the Administration policies" (p. 384). Our interest is in the phrase, "leading to a decision"; we shall try to observe closely as Hill explicates the process.

Hill's analysis specifies those technical aspects of speechcraft that are used to good effect: the speech writer's artful employment of structure to reveal what is being recommended in the most favorable light while concealing questions and concerns that would be embarrassing; the selection of those premises that would make the argumentative structure of the message seem plausible; the use of evidence and language so that supportive "feeling states" would be evoked.

By following Hill's lead one can gain an appreciation of the symbolic inducements at work in the first portion of the speech. Nixon begins by setting a "historical scene" within which subsequent judgments will be arranged. The "scene" is notable for its apparent facticity. Statements of factlike assertion or statements that include specific numerical figures are perceptual promontories that shape other statements placed among them. This particular pattern of focus is strongly encouraged by two lists that Nixon enunciates very early in the speech. The first is a list of straightforward questions regarding the history of U.S. involvement in Vietnam; the second is a list of factual and declarative statements that purport to describe the past. The two lists operate to draw attention to certain "realities" and cast others into shadow. Settled into this perceptual landscape are several propositions that pertain to the origin and nature of past involvement. The first proposition is that American leaders were correct in their decision to intervene in Vietnam; the second is that their mistake was to rely too heavily on United States' combat forces. Either proposition could be questioned by portions of the target audience, but Hill concludes that the force of such questions was probably dulled or negated by the larger cognitive scene in which they were experienced.

From Hill's critique of the finer structures in Nixon's speech, from his examination of the selection and placement of claims and premises of Nixon's arguments, one gains a more comprehensive understanding of the interaction between rhetor and audience. The target audience has a fundamental "world view" structured by beliefs and emotions that are not fully articulated intellectually. The speech writer can be guided by this assorted framework in the process of selecting and shaping the message. Because the fundamental premises of the speech are located within structures of meaning already established they do not tend to be open to serious dispute. The effect is to render the target audience conducive to the acceptance of more questionable assertions. Thus, we find Hill describing the premises as resting "on what experience from the sandbox up shows to be probable" (p. 379), or as constituing a "commonplace of bargaining for virtually everyone" (p. 380), or as being perceived as a "commonplace of legislation and not likely to be questioned by anyone" (p. 381). The speech writer's task now becomes one of developing questionable claims in such a way that the audience may nestle them in among already acceptable and activated premises. From Hill's account, the Nixon speech seems to encourage such a settling motion in several ways: by introducing supporting evidence which, if believed, will induce an auditor to complete an argumentative structure by arriving at the implied claim (p. 380); by relating or attaching incentives to an accepted premise (p. 381); by promoting states of feeling such as fear or anger that will induce cognitive movement toward a claim (pp. 379 and 381). In the Nixon speech all of the cognitive activity is encouraged by invoking long-held American values and employing a style that enhances the rhetor's ethos.

In Hill's neo-Aristotelian critique, the interrelationship of rhetoric and audience belief and feeling appears to be a process of the artistic maneuvering of various structures of argument, statements intended to evoke emotions in ways that bear upon the argumentative structures, and statements intended to enhance the credibility of the advocate. The grounding for this rhetorical maneuvering consists of beliefs already held by the audience in a relatively unquestioned state.

In addition to employing such logical or quasi-logical phenomena as a "residue-like structure," the rhetor tries to "reinforce" appropriate feelings, to bring the minds of auditors into "precisely the right set," to create "controlled states" of fear or anger that will invite favorable audience perception. The purpose of all this is to induce the audience to join in those cognitive processes that will lead to desired decisions and judgments. The key is the correct positioning of audience mind set so that audience members move themselves cognitively to judgment. Thus, as Hill describes, "if the auditor believes the evidence, he finds it difficult to avoid making his own enthymeme with the conclusion that negotiated settlement will never work" (p. 380).

Following Hill's critique, we can begin to see interesting implications in the neo-Aristotelian critical approach that bear on theoretical understandings of rhetorical behavior. The critic appears to focus on certain demonstrative processes and argumentative structures that are intended to secure persuasive effect. A careful reading of Hill's essay leads us to perceive the symbolic inducements that inhere in the various structures of Nixon's speech. For example, we see the lure of consistency, the searching for and fastening on similarity, the satisfaction in the forming of system, the drive for the unfolding of implication and relatedness and completion of structure. Even the "rationalizing" of emotion occurs in structured ways. We are led by Hill's analytical interpretations to raise questions regarding the relationship of discursive systems to the larger range of cognitive activity. Hill's analysis does not stop with a description of the types of evidence employed or the argumentative strategies used or the structures of relationship developed. Rather, he goes on to talk about the feelings of probability or certainty that come with the recognition of structure or pattern. It is *structured* proof that induces those feelings of certainty or probability. We are led to suspect that the symbolic inducements inherent in these demonstrative systems, when effective, may enjoy success precisely because they are inherent in fundamental modes of perceiving and experiencing.

Hill has demonstrated the neo-Aristotelian orientation as he examines a rhetorical situation ready made for such a critical approach. His analysis is far from pedestrian. He has pushed through analytical categories to consider human perception, human experiencing, human feeling, and human knowing. He has followed, in thorough fashion, the assumption that Black says every critic must make—he has explicated the relationship of the intentions of the speechmaker through the characteristics of the message to the intentional responses of auditors. And in so doing, he has lodged his conclusions in the workings of the human mind.

Consider next a critical examination of Frederick Wiseman's film, *High School*, undertaken by Thomas W. Benson. Benson's compelling question is made clear early in the essay: "How does Wiseman draw upon the skills and contexts of his viewers to invite them to experience a particular complex of meanings as they view *High School*?" (1980, p. 234). A short time later the question is restated in a slightly different way: "This essay is an inquiry into the states of thought and feeling an audience is invited to experience" (p. 235). The important term here is "invited." Benson is aware that in a potentially rhetorical situation, the crucial action will be initiated in the thoughts and feelings of audience members. What a rhetor does in message construction is put together a set of "invitations" to respond in particular ways. And the rhetor can know some things about general audience experience to help in formulating and shaping the invitations. But the actual response will be in the heads of the audience.

The audience is not in a vacuum, however. It has considerable experience that will constrain the interpretations of audience members. And, of course, the elements of Wiseman's film are an essential part of the environment to be responded to. Benson places the impetus for rhetorical response where it belongs, in the audience itself, but the impetus is located within the complicated nexus of the larger symbolic environment. "*High School* is a created reality. But for the audience of *High School* the characters may seem quite real, their behaviors quite significant. It is into this seeming reality that we are inquiring. Our perspective is, then, an audience perspective. But the evidence for the audience's responses, as well as the evidence for the filmmakers' designs, will be sought in the film itself. . . . What I hope to do is to develop the presence and the function of . . . thematic elements in more detail than have previous writers, to show how the details of the film relate to one another to form a structure, and to offer an account of how the structure may invite a rhetorical response" (p. 435). Having explained his analytical perspective, Benson provides an overview summary of the way the elements of the film work to offer their "invitations." "An audience is invited to perceive the institution's exercise of its power as absurd and hurtful. Wiseman reveals his theme and invites us to share in a bitter laughter about the packaging of American adolescence through a remarkable filmic structure built upon accumulation, comparison, and contradiction. This seemingly simple, episodic film can be seen, upon close examination, to exhibit a startling coherence, based upon a series of dialectical relations that gain force with each additional sequence" (p. 236).

As Benson makes clear, the audience members are likely to understand what Wiseman is trying to say about the institution of the American high school because they, themselves, have been in school. He then turns to more minute analysis of the film. I do not have the space here, nor do I intend, to reproduce the entirety of his analysis. Rather, I want to refer only to a few of his comments, to indicate the way he accounts for the suasory potential in messages, and the sophisticated nature of audience response to such potential.

The film, as Benson tells us, is about institutional power. But, he writes, what has been missed by the critics who have commented on the film, is the fact that sexuality is the primary vehicle through which the power of the institution is evoked in the minds of viewers. "I will argue," he says, "that the repetition of sexual elements, and the way they are placed in context, is likely to predispose the viewer to decode them in something like the way I am describing" (p. 241).

Let us follow Benson's explication of the initial sequence in the film. Early on, he points out, Wiseman invites viewers to focus on the human body. What viewers see, beginning with the second sequence in the film, is a high school girl grooming herself in a hallway. The grooming scene, in and of itself, might be innocuous, but it flows into other filmic images to incrementally project the tone of sexuality that is important to the invited message of the film. For example, following the scene of the grooming girl, the audience is focused on the physical movements of a Spanish teacher as she conducts a lesson in class. Placed in the overall context of the film, a context that will build throughout, the gestures can be interpreted sexually. But, Benson points out, such an interpretation will be more indirectly than directly made. "Surely the film viewer would not be likely to think that the teacher was actually trying to seduce her students. But possibly the teacher's behavior does at least cross into an ambiguous area of sexual awareness. As film viewers, we have been trained by all of our film watching to look for the signs of sexual involvement on the screen" (p. 243). Further, as Benson points out, the sexuality need not be direct in its appeal. It can be indirect, through the audience's perception of behaviors associated with sexuality: "as film viewers we have been trained to be aware of the signs of courtship" (p. 243). In fact, the special power of the filmic invitations, Benson explains, may be realized through the continuous sexual imagery that does not quite come squarely into the purview of consciousness. "I will argue that the repetition of sexual elements, and the way they are placed in context, is likely to predispose the viewer to decode them in something like the way I am describing. But I must strain the reader's credulity further by arguing that the sexual material works on the viewer of the film much as it works on the student in the school: for the student, it exists as part of the double-bind that reinforces the school's power while remaining just at the edge of consciousness. And for the film viewer the sexual material is also usually just out of conscious awareness, inviting us to feel angry about the power of the school without quite realizing why we feel so angry" (p. 241).

Such images do, as Benson suggests, "guide our awareness" (p. 242). They guide, but they do not dictate. They call upon the experience of audience members. They evoke memories of the past to invite the interpretation of combinations of images and the incremental building of images in one particular way rather than in other possible ways. And always, the images of the message enjoy no more success in their invitation than they are successful in evoking the requisite audience response. Benson is fully aware of the characteristic of human symbolic behavior I am discussing. For instance, he explains that in Wiseman's film, the high school can be perceived to exercise control through a series of double-bind situations, in which a person is placed in an environment full of inconsistent messages but in which the individual may not notice the inconsistent and contradictory nature of the messages. Thus, no response is "proper," and the result can be a kind of schizophrenic behavior. But, he makes clear in a footnote, the invited response will come because of the symbolic experiencing of the audience members who participate in the familiar nuances of the film. "I am not arguing that Wiseman imposes the double-bind theory on his material. In fact, in describing his working methods, Wiseman has often said he makes little use of social science. But Wiseman has discovered a structure in his material that is remarkabley similar to the double-bind. Wiseman's structure and the double-bind hypothesis are thus not only confirming to one another but are also likely to exercise a forceful appeal to audiences whose own experience of social institutions has been double-binding" (p. 238).

Benson's close filmic analysis follows the guidelines I have portrayed in the above quotes. I would again highlight certain of his descriptive terms. The audience, he notes, is "invited" to respond. The audience, therefore, initiates response, but such response is initiated in light of message characteristics presented to it, and in light of prior experience that provides the larger context in which the perceptions of audience will be invited. The message characteristics are "structured images." The phrase, "structured images," refers to message characteristics that elicit not only explicitly stated "reasons" but feelings, emotions, values, subjective reactions—all of which comprise holistic experiencing. A part of the relevant experiencing is "out of awareness"; in other words, audience choice making occurs without a fully conscious realization that the choice making has occurred. The important summary here is that audience members have been invited to engage their own "experience" with message elements and context to respond in their own individual ways. It so happens that those ways may overlap, because they are humans together, sharing common experiencing. And, Benson's critical analysis places the important rhetorical activity in the "minds" of audience members. He is referring to complex cognitive operations that can be characterized as responses to symbolic meanings by creatures who inherently and habitually create and respond to symbolic meanings. The engagement is fully reciprocal; that is, there is interaction between rhetor, audience, and context. But it is the cognitive activity of the audience, *as humans who have the cognitive capacity to symbolize*, that determines the outcome of the rhetorical interaction. Thus it is that Benson can turn to the end of the film, where the high school principal reads a letter from a graduate who is about to parachute behind enemy lines in the Vietnam War, and who has willed his life insurance to a scholarship fund for the high school, and conclude, "In this way the film becomes an experience before it becomes evidence. And when the letter scene is finally presented, the audience can gasp at the revelation that the school meant, all along, to produce 'good soldiers.' And the audience can clinch the job of persuasion it has been allowed to perform upon itself by congratulating itself that its theory about the school is confirmed by the principal's reading of the letter" (pp. 256–257).

There are obvious similarities between Benson's interpretations of rhetorical action and the interpretation of Forbes Hill described earlier. Both place emphasis on the engagement of certain symbolic or cognitive capacities of the audience with the symbolic structuring of messages; both indicate that the meanings evoked exceed the literal structures in messages. In other words, audiences tend to make more of messages than is literally there. The "more than" comes from the larger world of the personal experience of audience members. And both Benson and Hill assume that a most important ingredient in the symbolic processing evoked in the minds of the audience is that of self-persuasion. There are profound implications here that I will turn to shortly. But first, let me briefly refer to similar critical interpretations, interpretations that seem to operate with similar assumptions, in the work of several other critics.

In "The Second Persona," Edwin Black makes direct reference to the message-mind relationship. "Discourses contain tokens of their authors. Discourses are, directly or in transmuted form, the external signs of internal states. In short, we accept it as true that a discourse implies an author, and we mean by that more than the tautology that an act entails an agent. We mean, more specifically, that certain features of a linguistic act entail certain characteristics of the language user" (Black, 1970, p. 110). By looking at message characteristics, then, we glimpse the workings of the minds of two personae, the producer of the message and the audience. Black is even more specific. "Especially must we note what is important in characterizing personae. It is not age or temperament or even discrete attitude. It is ideology—ideology in the sense that Marx used the term; the network of interconnected convictions that functions in a man epistemically and that shapes his identity by determining how he views the world" (p. 112).

To illustrate his claim, Black explicates the meaning he perceives in the recurring metaphorical pattern, the "cancer-of-communism," found in the discourse of the radical Right. A look at two of his critical interpretations reveals the mileage he gets from his perspective. "If an obsessive fear of cancer were the symptom of an acknowledged and recognizable psychological condition, the tendency of Rightist discourse to cultivate this fear may work to induce in its auditors some form of that psychological condition" (p. 115). "Because one's attitude toward one's body is bound up with one's attitude toward cancer, we may suggest that a metaphor that employed cancer as its vehicle would have a particular resonance for an auditor who was ambivalent about his own body. We may suspect, in fact, that the metaphor would strike a special fire with a congeries of more generally puritanical attitudes" (p. 116).

The term, "induce," employed by Black to refer to audience interaction with the symbolic formings in messages is appropriately chosen. It refers to the subtlety of symbolic interaction that occurs when messages invite audiences to respond in certain ways through engaging the symbolic processes of audience members. We are reminded of similar phrasing used by Hill and Benson when they describe the rhetorical processes of symbolic interaction. Hill, for instance, talks of the rhetorical function as being one of "leading to a decision," and as the attempt to "bring the minds of auditors into precisely the right set." Benson is interested in the "states of thought and feeling an audience is invited to experience," the experiences the audience is "invited to perceive" rhetorically, and to rhetorical structures that "predispose the viewer to decode" in certain ways. Each of these phrases can be taken as a reference to processes of rhetorical or symbolic inducement, that is, to those symbolic processes that invite, or entice, or in some way constrain the perceptions and experiences of those who interact with messages. The phenomena of inducement work by provoking or engaging cognitive activity in certain ways.

It is just such engagement that Hermann Stelzner appears to have in mind in his critique of the famous address John F. Kennedy presented to the Houston Ministerial Alliance during his campaign for the presidency in 1960. Stelzner notes that Kennedy's speech employs a ritualistic form well known to those familiar with Protestant sermons. He points out that "to the extent that Kennedy enters into a union with form, he reflects commitment. To the extent that the form of a sermon invites, and even immerses, the worshipper into the text, the form becomes a fundamental dynamic in the search for meaning and understanding. The truth of anything is known only so far as we enter into union with it" (Stelzner, 1976, p. 228). The invitation to identify with form and through the form to become immersed in the meaning of a text, indeed to enter into a union with it, is an example of symbolic inducement at work.

Campbell and Jamieson make essentially the same point in their discussion of the rhetoric of generic form. "That forms are phenomena has persuasive and critical significance because, as a result, forms can induce participation by others" (Campbell & Jamieson, n.d., p. 19). Their interpretation of the meaning of generic forms comports with the kind of critical interpretation we have been examining. "Recurrence of a combination of forms into a generically identifiable form over time suggests that certain constants in human action are manifest rhetorically. One may argue the recurrence arises out of comparable rhetorical situations, out of the influence of conventions on the responses of rhetors, out of universal and cultural archetypes ingrained in human consciousness, out of fundamental human needs or out of a finite number of rhetorical options or commonplaces. Whatever the explanation, the existence of the recurrent provides insight into the human condition" (pp. 26–27).

In their brief listing of the factors that can evoke recurrent rhetorical behaviors, it is the phrase, "ingrained in human consciousness," that easily finds common ground with other critical phrases of interpretation noted in the work of critics cited earlier, such as "conscious awareness," "psychological condition," and "interconnected convictions." And in addition to arriving at interpretations of rhetorical behavior that are consistent with those made by the critics discussed earlier, Campbell and Jamieson suggest that some forms of symbolic inducement may be constant across human behavior when operative in conditions of similarity, and in light of similar human expectancies. There are occasions, then, when it becomes relevant to talk of certain universals of symbolic forming and inducement.

Osborn's analysis of archetypal sea imagery in rhetoric and poetry further supports the suggestion of universality in some forms of symbolizing. "People would always have a sense of being surrounded by dark and threatening forces, whether real or imaginary. Along with fear would remain the need for symbols to express fear, symbols which could raise its salience, and motivate listeners to attitudes or actions which promised avoidance or deliverance. The great destructive power of the sea had been etched too deeply for too many centuries into human imagination to be suddenly obliterated or even significantly dulled" (Osborn, pp. 355–356). It seems fair to say that when critics discover constancies in the processes of symbolic processing and inducement, they are examining fundamentally significant aspects of human behavior.

At the outset of this essay, we asked what could be gleaned from the work of rhetorical critics that offered contributions to the theoretical understanding of human rhetorical behavior. We noted that critics need not consciously set out to contribute to theory; it is often enough to gain a thorough understanding of a rhetorical event for its own sake. On the other hand we noted that critical interpretations always imply theoretical positions, whether consciously articulated or not. Consequently, our best criticism ought to be both particular and summative. That is, it ought to illuminate particular situations and at the same time suggest hypotheses regarding human rhetorical behavior that, when added to the insights of other critics, provide generalizable understandings of the human rhetorical condition.

As Leff points out, we suffer no dearth of theories from which to borrow, if that is our desire. "We no longer lack theories; yet, we still lack secure footing in the territory that lies between the regularity of abstract patterns and the idiosyncracies of particular rhetorical events. And this situation is especially troublesome, since the gap concerns the most fundamental step in the critical process—the act of interpretation by which the critic attempts to account for and assign meaning to the rhetorical dimensions of a given phenomenon" (Leff, p. 342). After noting this difficulty, Leff undertakes to sketch the orientation for a positive theory-criticism relationship. "Theoretical principles enter at the intersection between the object and the assignment of meaning to it, but such principles are so closely connected with the object of study that they are not easily isolated in abstract form. Consequently, theory does not progress in terms of a hierarchical arrangement of abstract principles. Hypotheses move laterally as they are drawn by intuition and analogy from one case to another, and since the objective is diagnosis rather than prediction, an hypothesis assumes a different form each time it is instantiated in a given case" (Leff, pp. 348–349).

In this essay, we have examined the works of selected critics with a special focus on just such intersections, and we conducted our examination laterally rather than hierarchically. We have, I believe, discovered theoretical insights of genuine consequence. There may be a sense that what we have discerned does not appear to be radically new. However, if we fully understand the implications of the critical interpretations cited above, we get a sense of the coherent theoretical position being offered and a realization that the position offers new possibilities for the grounding of critical practice.

Earlier, we noted that contemporary criticism does not limit itself to the analysis of only certain forms of symbolic messages or symbolic interactions or symbolic situations. Rather, from the variety of their efforts, critics have demonstrated their potential for examining nearly any act or transaction where human symbolic processing is involved. It is symbolic processing that is the constant wherever rhetorical behaviors manifest themselves. And within the larger context of symbolic processing, there occur the phenomena of symbolic inducement. These phenomena should be the target of the critical enterprise; it is insight into the characteristically human cognitive action of symbolic inducement that critical interpretations can provide. The theoretical grounding just identified begins to become clear when we look at several clusters of terms that emerge from the critical essays we examined.

The first cluster can be characterized by the following phrases that refer to meanings evoked in the minds of audiences by the rhetorical characteristics of messages: "render conducive," "lead to a decision," "create states of feeling," "invite experience," "predispose the viewer," and "induce." The term "induce" is a good covering term for this cluster because the phrasings all refer to the action of symbolically inducing audiences to adopt certain perspectives, or points of view. The action of inducement, as the critics above view it, is not a passive matter of rhetorical elements manipulating audience minds, but an active matter of engaging the minds of audience members in ways that encourage them, on their own, to complete the suasory process.

That these human symbolic or cognitive processes lie at the center of critical concern can be seen from a second cluster of terms that emerge from the critical essays: "awareness," "out of conscious awareness," "past experience," "ideology," "interconnected convictions," "psychological condition," "epistemic," "ingrained in human consciousness," and "human imagination." Such phrasings of interpretation further lead us to understand that the phenomena that can engage such cognitive processes are not limited only to certain judgmental patterns but include the whole panoply of human experiencing.

While aware of the abstract nature of general cognitive processes, the critic always deals with concrete, external, and specific manifestations of those processes. They are not identified and discussed *in vacuo* or for their own sake, but as they are instantiated within rhetorical contexts. All humans operate meaningfully on the basis of similar cognitive principles just because they are all human. But such cognitive principles are capable of a very broad range of specific manifestations. Whether fully and consciously realized or not, the critics noted above are working from perspectives that are consistent with the realities of human cognitive operation.

One more observation must be made. Leff notes that a common complaint against much criticism is that it loses sight of the actual texts of messages (Leff, p. 338). Such a charge is not valid with regard to the critics I have referred to above. For while it is certain workings of the human mind that are at the center of their focus, they do pay particularly close attention to the texts of rhetorical messages. In fact, it is the characteristics and structures of such texts that serve as primary data for critical interpretation.

For these critics, textual characteristics are as real as any other physical phenomena in the external environment, and are "there" to be interacted with by audiences. Consequently, we have a critical perspective that transcends the old idealist-realist dispute about whether reality is "out there" in the external world or all "in the head," for the critical orientation described here assumes that symbolic meaning is always the result of human cognition operating in interaction with an environment.

What has emerged from the work of contemporary critics selected for discussion in this essay is clear indication of productive theoretical grounding for understanding rhetorical behavior. Such grounding lies in an understanding of how human cognition functions, and how symbolic or rhetorical inducement occurs in the larger cognitive context. Working from such a perspective, the interpretive findings of rhetorical criticism are not limited just to certain kinds of communicative behaviors, but rather they provide insight into characteristics of symbolic processing that are fundamental to all aspects of human comprehension and experience.

4

Communication and Human Rights: The Symbolic Structures of Racism and Sexism

DIANE HOPE

INTRODUCTION

Human rights discourse in the United States is characterized by the tension generated between declared ideals of human rights and the abridgement of human rights for specific groups. Historically, arguments for natural human rights and American civil rights have been intertwined in public debate, protest movement, and response. In the last quarter of the 20th century, however, the crucial distinctions between human rights and civil rights generate demanding analytical tasks of special concern to communication scholars and rhetorical critics. The issue of human rights is fraught with complex symbolic confrontations.

While guarantees specified in the Constitution and the Bill of Rights establish *civil* rights and protections for citizens, it is the "unalienable Rights of life, liberty and the pursuit of happiness" proclaimed in the Declaration of Independence that inform contemporary *human rights* communication. The original exclusion of nonwhite and female Americans from rights of citizenship reinforced legal and social conventions that worked to place both groups somehow outside the category of full human beings.

The 13th, 14th, and 15th Amendments to the Constitution finally established the Negro as citizen with the civil right of franchise. Women were specifically excluded from these reforms in 1874 and were not granted the right to vote until passage of the 19th Amendment in 1920 (Norton, 1945). Legal argument, speeches, essays, literature and art, and the nondiscursive protest activities of 19th- and 20th-century social movements are the communicative acts that have slowly advanced civil rights for nonwhites and women. They are a primary source of data for the communication scholar concerned with both civil and human rights discourse. However, sources of human rights offenses, claims, and counter arguments are also located in illusive social mythology generally masked by the dominant culture. In the last half of the 20th century, even as advances in civil rights are made, nonwhites and women continue to claim that, as groups, their natural human right to life—secure, unviolated, and safe from potential excesses of state and society—is routinely abridged through the dominant ideologies of racism and sexism.

These claims charge society with enormous hypocrisy. The ensuing response from authority and public reveals a value conflict in symbolic structures of reality central to the work of communication scholars. Although disciplinary scholarship on human rights and communication is a scant 20 years old, research methods and findings have enlarged and altered traditional assumptions concerning public persuasion and social change. Consequently, scholarly work in human rights communication has added to the troubling debate about the proper function and province of rhetorical criticism.

PURPOSE

The manifold purpose of this chapter is (1) to review briefly the similar claims of human rights abridgement made by nonwhites and women; (2) to suggest that social myths are "speech" acts proper to the work of rhetorical critics, and (3) to offer, as example, a brief exploratory sketch of one myth that connects blacks and women and acts as a rhetorical constraint to human rights; and (4) to review the major ways communication scholars have investigated human rights in the 20th century.

FINDINGS

Nonwhites and women argue that racism and sexism are the causes of human rights offenses. Both groups make three general claims: through institutionalized racism and sexism the dominant American culture defines nonwhites and women as nonpersons; they are born into groups marked by high risk of violence; as groups, both suffer disproportionately high rates of poverty. Since the mid 1960s, communication scholars have primarily investigated human rights through studies of individual agitators and studies of social movements. Although important insights have been reached, both kinds of studies have been charged with ideological biases or methodological weaknesses or both. Further, except for a very few publications, most research in the field fails to attend to the existence of racism and sexism as powerfully constricting symbolic structures. Semiological work on social myth as a form of speech is offered as an additional source of theory and method for examining the symbolic structures of racism and sexism. The particular social mythology that opposes "bad black men" and "good white women" as archetypal sexual antagonists will be sketched as one such symbolic structure. A tentative conclusion made in this exploration is that hidden sexual myths dehumanize all nonwhites and all women and are, perhaps, central to the collective power of the white male political structure. Although seldom articulated as justification for discriminatory practices in housing, jobs, law enforcement, education, welfare programs, and political opportunity, social mythology may yet be a significant rhetorical factor in the continued resistance to full human rights for all people.

HUMAN RIGHTS AND CIVIL RIGHTS: THE DISTINCTIONS

Three documents provide historic and working definitions of human rights for contemporary America: the Declaration of Independence, the Constitution with its Bill of Rights, and the United Nations Universal Declaration of Human Rights. Although it is difficult to distinguish between what are perceived as human rights and American civil rights, the argument for natural human rights found its "first and fullest expression" (Costello, 1976, p. 118), at least in the Western world, in the simple phrases contained in the Declaration: "We hold these truths to be self evident, that all men are created equal, that they are endowed by their Creator with certain unalienable Rights, that among these are Life, Liberty and the Pursuit of Happiness."

The Universal Declaration of Human Rights, adopted by the General Assembly of the United Nations on December 10, 1948, although not binding on individual nations, was strongly advocated by Eleanor Roosevelt, who chaired the drafting commission. It proclaims that "Everyone has the right to life, liberty and the security of person" (Article 3). Liberties detailed in the Bill of Rights are to be exercised without fear of "unreasonable searches and seizures" (Article IV), or "cruel and unusual punishments" (Article VIII). "Torture [Article 5], "arbitrary arrest, . . . or exile [Article 9]" are condemned in the Universal Declaration. Clearly, the motivating source for human rights codes is fear of state and societal violence: loss of life, loss of liberty, and unjust constraints against the pursuit of happiness, sanctioned oppresion, are the measures of human rights violations.

In the United States, human rights offenses stem from two general sources. One source is political agitation for social change by individuals and groups choosing to exercise and often to test the limits of civil liberties. The civil rights of franchise, free speech, and assembly, in particular, have often generated claims of repression and loss of life. The major concern of this chapter is the second source of human rights violations: claims of institutionalized oppression such as the disproportionate numbers of poor nonwhites and women voiced by both groups.

Racism and sexism are claimed to be institutionalized ideologies generated and sustained through social myths that are directly contrary to human rights ideals. As they continue to reinforce human rights offenses, myths about color and sex limit the strategic choices of members of both oppressed groups and the dominant culture. Nonwhites and women claim that the prevailing culture denies them basic human rights because they are born into stigmatized groups.

It is of course impossible to separate absolutely the communicative activities of those oppressed by reason of race and sex from groups whose human rights have been violated because they have chosen to agitate for social change. Obviously, they are often the same people. Robert Justin Goldstein, in his unique and massive study (1978) of political repression in modern America, makes the following distinction: political repression is defined as "violation of first amendment type rights and violation of due process in the enforcement and adjudication of law, related to the perceived political views of the targets of such violations" (Goldstein, p. xviii). Excluded from his study is "discrimination based on factors *other* than political belief: e.g. sex, skin color, national origin, sexual preferences" (Goldstein, p. xxi). To attempt a further distinction may constitute an unnecessary distortion of emphasis. Yet, only the factors of sex and skin color share the singular characteristic of visible, biological stigmas. Although twists of sexism oppress homosexuals, they are not visibly marked as members of a stigmatized group. The Gay Liberation movement constitutes a political choice to go public with sexual preferences in order to reverse the severely restricting social and psychological effects of hidden identities (Chesebro, Cragan & McCullough, 1973). Nonwhites and women, however, have no closets to hide in, however confining.

Similarly, white ethnic groups have been able to pass into the mainstream culture. Second-, third-, and fourth-generation ethnic groups have usually chosen to do so, and today they constitute power blocks within the dominant political structure. The severe ethnocentricism of the 19th and early 20th century was compounded by the political activism of some immigrants. European immigrants were the largest group promoting radical social change. Bringing a leftist analysis to American politics, immigrant Socialists, anarchists, and Communists bore the brunt of the severe Alien and Sedition acts of 1917, 1921, and 1927 (Goldstein, pp. 137–158). The anarchist and feminist Emma Goldman, for instance, was deported for her political views, as distinct from her feminism (Rich & Smith [Asante] 1968). Both world wars brought violent reprisal to ethnic Americans. German-Americans, Italian-Americans, and Japanese-Americans suffered extreme violations of human rights. The anarchists Nicola Sacco and Bartolomeo Vanzetti, executed in 1927, tested the limits of free speech and lost their lives. Although their "crime" is still debated, scores of Italian-Americans fell victim to both state and mob violence during the execution protests (Goldstein, p. 169). The potency of ethnocentricity weakened as white ethnic groups absorbed the culture and were absorbed by it, but it is clear that human rights violations occurred. One of the most flagrant cases of human rights violations in modern America was the internment of 112,000 Japanese Americans in camps mandated by President Franklin D. Roosevelt (Costello, p. 119). Racism as a factor in that decision, as well as in the decision to use the atomic bomb in the war against Japan, must be considered. These cases make evident the difficulty in separating the mesh of political repression, war fervor, ethnocentrism, and racism as causes of oppression.

The second half of the 20th century has produced a similar mixture of motives, protests, and responses on the part of nonwhites and women. They have been major speakers and participants in the civil rights, antiwar, student, and New Left movements. The rhetoric of human rights voiced by nonwhites and women is often, but not always, linked to specific radical or revolutionary programs for social change. Distinctions between political agitators and groups demanding full human rights are further blurred by the rhetorical strategies of authorities responding to the demands for radical change. The devil term "communism" and the god term "national security" have been used throughout the century by agents of power to link together as common enemies those seeking redress of grievances based on color and sex with political activists seeking specific changes in the power structure. The simplest establishment explanation for severe social protest is the notion of the "outside agitator," a term that mythologizes the strength of foreign agents and denies power and legitimacy to the oppressed.

American Indian movement spokesman Russell Means, for instance, is one of many voices that reject Marxism as a solution for oppression (Means, 1980). Nevertheless, because some nonwhites and some women do link their oppression to the exploitations they perceive as inherent in capitalism, all minority advocates are easily vilified by charges of anti-Americanism. Further complicating the issue are Socialist and Communist groups that rely heavily on the evidence of racism and sexism to justify demands for revolutionary change.

Despite those confusions, a basic distinction must be made between (1) groups claiming human rights offenses while exercising their civil rights in pursuit of political goals, and (2) nonwhites and women who claim they are traditionally denied the primary human right of an unviolated life because of racism and sexism.

MYTH AS SPEECH

In his book *Mythologies* (1972), Roland Barthes presents an analysis for understanding the persuasive power of the unacknowledged messages of a culture. Barthes isolates the central function of myth as "the task of giving an historical intention a natural justification, and making contingency appear eternal" (p. 142). In the case of blacks, for instance, slavery; intentional family breakups; state-sanctioned violence; and legal, economic, educational, and political discrimination have severely restricted opportunities for material gain and self worth. Myth, however, creates an "alibi" by asserting that blacks are naturally lazy. Centuries of legal, religious, economic, educational, and political restraints have forced women to be dependent on men. Myth asserts that women are naturally dependent. Myth presents an idealized vision of the world in which everything remains the same. The intent of myth, as Waldo Braden (1975) summarizes, is to "confirm, intensify, and amplify sentiments and attitudes. It acts upon beliefs already possessed. For those who cannot or do not wish to face reality, it suggests rationalizations, escapes and fantasy" (p. 122). Because it pretends to describe an eternal condition and is motivated by the desire for security, myth militates against change.

Myth is a "form of speech" that deprives its message of politics, history, and experience. Because myth mixes fact with fiction, and motive with cause, the primary activity of myth is distortion (Barthes, p. 121). Neither a blatant lie nor an obvious fairy tale, the distortion presented by myth allows an audience of "myth-readers" the security of facile identification. Because myth "transforms a meaning into a form," (Barthes, p. 109) each myth reader can reconstitute meaning from a personal supply of experience, illusion, or fantasy. "In many instances the myth is like a blank check into which the listener may fill in any meaning or feeling that he abstracts from what is pleasant while he ignores or forgets what is disturbing" (Braden, p. 122).

The major distortion of meaning into form is the transformation of political history into nature. As Barthes insists, "Myth is always depoliticized speech" (p. 143). When the history of purposeful or accidental human activity is presented as natural fact, we are in the presence of myth. Robert L. Scott (1973) remarks on the process as it occurs in argument:

An especially revealing phenomenon is the category of argument that tends to arise when proposals (or demands) are made to open certain categories of employment to women. Sooner or later someone will argue that to do so will be to act contrary to legal limitations protecting employed women. Immediately economic exploitation, either real or potential, comes sharply into focus, and, no matter how one argues, male domination is clear. This is to say, that men are superior, either wiser, stronger or more privileged, and that women are better off recognizing the fact.

Since few persons or groups are willing to admit that their dominant position is simply wanton, there is a strong tendency to legitimate the divisions upon which it rests. "That is the way things are" is apt to be the basic appeal, and, even though that appeal may find all sorts of legal sanctions, more deeply it is apt to reflect what people take to be historic, scientific, or moral laws (pp. 124–125).

In short, myth is a kind of speech whose semiological pattern constructs a message whereby reality is distorted in order to justify prevailing ideologies.

By a semiological transformation of meaning into form, myth strips away history, experience, and politics to present a specific social order as "natural." Although every use of myth can be understood as rhetorical in a broad sense, racist and sexist myths are particular distortions that compel human beings to argue for their own humanness. Because myth is so pervasive a part of cultural symbol systems, its power as a rhetorical form is limitless. Myth needs no logic, no argument, no evidence. Myth presents itself as both justification and explanation for "the way things are." Because they are symbolic structures, myths cannot be vilified, accused, banished, or held accountable. Racist and sexist myths are so deeply embedded in legal, educational, religious, political, psychological, and economic institutions that attempts to identify mythmakers as the enemy often generate paranoid and conspiratorial analyses of society.

For the oppressed, dominant myths are powerful, ghostly enemies. There are, Barthes maintains, only two general ways to combat the effects of cultural mythology, and they serve as accurate descriptions of the forms human rights rhetoric takes (p. 128). The first, demythologization, is the attempt to expose the distortions of myth: to insist on politics, history, and experience as explanations of the social order; and to demonstrate by argument and evidence that the conditions of society are not the result of nature but are the result of historical accident or political intention. As racist and sexist myths work to provide alibis for economic disparities between the races and between the sexes, human rights discourse seeks to discover intentions; as myth works to provide natural justification for the experienced violence of hierarchical order, human rights discourse seeks political and psychological causation; and, finally, as myth treats racial and sexual relationships as eternal, fixed in God or biology, human rights advocates argue that relationships are based upon power and are therefore open to change.

In addition to demythologizing, one can fight the effects of cultural myth by creating countermyths, a strategy most apparent in but not limited to art, theater, literature, and song. Martin Luther King's crusade of moral superiority, voiced as the power of love and Christian nonviolence, offered a countermyth to white racism. The Nation of Islam presents a white-skinned, blue-eyed devil as the source of racism's evils in its creation myth. In feminist countermyth, one finds celebrations of the natural superiority of women with messages that speak of women's eternal strength, beauty, and life-giving powers, plus depictions of men as genetically inferior.

Studies have explored a variety of rhetorical dimensions in the claims of nonwhites and women that attempt to combat confining cultural mythologies and redefine themselves as fully human agents of change. When the dominant culture's defining myths are internalized by the oppressed, the task of redefinition is especially difficult and often painful. Scott (1973) explores "the conservative voice" in radical rhetoric and concludes, "People experience division as oppression, seek fresh identifications, and find dominant groups hypocritical, and in responding to hypocrisy, sound a conservative voice" (pp. 123–124). Explaining the ego function of the rhetoric of protest, Gregg remarks, "In each case the rhetoric contains statements which express a sense of guilt about inadequacy, stronger perhaps among blacks and women." (p. 77). Less explored, however, are how the two false identities are linked together in, at least, one social myth, and how that myth affects the rhetoric of human rights.

AN EXPLORATORY SKETCH OF THE BLACK-WHITE SEXUAL MYTHOLOGY

Examination of the symbolic structures of racism and sexism reveals that the two ideologies are joined in sexual mythology. At its most extreme, the mythogical drama evidenced in locker room jokes, written and visual pornography, and pulp media depicts the black man as animalistic, in-humanly driven by lust for white women; the white woman is object, property to be protected from the sexual power of the black male and from her own sexual amorality. The myth speaks a cultural message that is at once, both titilating and threatening. The degradation of both blacks and women in the myth has also greatly contributed to the difficulty the two groups exhibit in attempts to work together. Although studies of feminism and gay liberation have broken through many taboos surrounding sexually rooted issues, communication scholars have been more timid about exploring the cultural myth that degrades blacks and women together.

American myths, which separately define blacks and women as nonhuman, collectively oppose the black man and the white woman in fixed images of badness and goodness: he is bad; she is good. Racist mythology defines the stereotypic black male as lazy, irresponsible toward work and family, hedonistic, violent, criminal, immoral, irrational, and dangerously endowed with sexual prowess and a lust for white women. At the opposite extreme, the white woman is pure, virginal or motherly, supportive, gentle, childlike, passive, and dependent.

> In America they share the unhappy lot of being cast together as lesser beings. It is hardly coincidence that the most aggressively racist regions are the most rigidly insistent upon keeping women in their place, even if that place is that of ornament, toy or statue. Of the ten states that refused to ratify the nineteenth amendment, giving women the vote, nine were Southern (Stimpson, 1971, p. 623).

Although sexual fears and fantasies present only one myth that reinforces racist and sexist mythology, their impact cannot be overlooked.

> In fact and fantasy, they [white men] have violently segregated black men and white women. The most notorious fantasy claims that the black man is sexually evil, low, subhuman; the white woman sexually pure, elevated, superhuman. Together they dramatize the polarities of excrement and disembodied spirituality. Blacks and women have been sexual victims, often cruelly so: the black man castrated, the woman raped (Stimpson, 1979, p. 624).

When radical or rebellious white males enact fascination with and imitation of black cool, the attraction is rooted in myths of violent black machismo.

In his essay "The White Negro" (1959), Norman Mailer voices a predominant myth of his generation's rebellion; his essay serves as a telling example of the intellectual mythology that rebels of the 1960s claimed as heritage. Mailer attempts to explain "hip" and the hipster's idealization of the "psychopathetic Negro." There are no women in Mailer's scenario, black or white, only objects of sexual conquest. In Mailer's myth, the essence of the hipster's existential struggle is imitation of the Negro's "rage" and his "powerful . . . disbelief in the socially monolithic ideas of the single mate, the solid family, and the respectable love life" (p. 10). Woman's restricted but socially valued roles of wife, mother, and mate are rejected, and she exists only as interchangeable partner in the raging search for orgasm (p. 11). The mythological "Negro" epitomizes courageous manhood.

> Indeed if one is to be a man, almost any kind of unconventional action often takes disproportionate courage. So it is no accident that the source of hip is the Negro for he has been living on the margin between totalitarianism and democracy for two centuries. . . .
>
> Any Negro who wishes to live must live with danger from his first day, and no experience can ever be casual to him; no Negro can saunter down a street with any real certainty that violence will not visit him on his walk. The cameos of security for the average white: mother and the home, job and the family, are not even a mockery to millions of Negroes; they are impossible. The Negro has the simplest of alternatives: live a life of constant humility or ever-threatening danger (pp. 10–11).

The rebel myths of the fifties defined black males as sexual, violent men who stand in symbolic opposition to the standard bearers of the square culture—white women. The myths were shared by the dominant culture. What the dominant culture feared in the mythical black, the rebel culture romanticized; what the dominant culture valued in its mythical good woman, the rebel culture derided as the ultimate objects of conquest. Detailed examination of the diverse meanings generated by the intertwined myths can perhaps add insight to the force of response when blacks and women proclaim new definitions of self.

It is, for instance, in light of the myth of the immoral, violent, sexually aggressive black male that Martin Luther King's appeal to white America can be understood as a tempting countermyth of redefinition. If the black could be redefined as morally superior, committed to nonviolence and to asexual Christian love, the deepest fears of white America might be overcome. Bad myth would be fought with a good new myth. However, the appeal was ineffective for many young blacks, convinced by their experience that the myth of the good, nonviolent, Christian black man was an inappropriate response to a racist power structure. As early as 1959, Robert Williams was insisting that the experience of white violence necessitated the right of self-defense for blacks. By 1960 his *Crusader* pamphlets consistently equated nonviolence with defeat. "The whites of America's Dixie . . . are much too brutal and savage to respond to mere words. They are too insensate to heed the words of faint-hearted liberalism. Non-violence is a scheme of suicide for Black men trying to break the chains of bondage of white oppressive brutes. It is tantamount to bedding down with a lion and relying on the goodness of his beastly sensibilities for protection" (p. 1).

Some young black power advocates denied the effectiveness of nonviolence and in varying degrees appealed directly to the potency of the "bad black" mythology. Defining their bid for black power as traditional self-determinism, they also implied, both in language and in style, that violence was possible. Insisting, for instance, that the disorders erupting in black communities were not riots, but early stages of rebellion, black power advocates said, in effect, "We can be what you fear we are!" Descriptions of the public speaking of Stokely Carmichael almost always include remarks about his sexual charisma. Pat Jefferson's work (1967), for instance, takes pains to describe the "handsome, virile" Carmichael.

> As Carmichael approached the speaker's platform with the characteristic looseness that prompted his associates to dub him "the Magnificent Barbarian," the fourteen SNCC members stood in unison. Dressed in a tight blue-gray suit and vest, blue shirt, striped tie, Italian boots, sunglasses, and an identification bracelet on his left wrist, he "generated sex." Six-foot-one and built like a "basketball guard," he resembled the sculptor's ideal model for the "statue of a Nubian god." He possessed a "disciplined wildness," an "electrifying personality." His smile, candid and warm, "dazzled" (p. 79).

The Black Panthers consciously carried the image of the bad black macho male one step further. Eldridge Cleaver (1967), soon to emerge as hero of the "revolutionaries" of the late sixties, described the impact of his first contact with the Panthers.

> From the tension showing on the faces of the people before me, I thought the cops were invading the meeting, but there was a deep female gleam leaping out of one of the women's eyes that no cop who ever lived could elicit. I recognized that gleam out of the recesses of my soul, even though I had never seen it before in my life; the total admiration of a black woman for a black man. I spun round in my seat and saw the most beautiful sight I had ever seen: four black men wearing black berets, powder blue shirts, black leather jackets, black trousers, shiny black shoes—and each with a gun! (p. 83).

Before his conversion to black radicalism (and his subsequent conversions to American capitalism and to fundamentalist religion), Cleaver was an admitted rapist and convicted felon who claimed to have practiced rape on black women before raping white women in his efforts to revenge himself on white male society (Cleaver, 1969; Hope, 1973). His rapid rise to stardom with white and black male revolutionaries indicates the depth of attraction in the "bad black" myth.

It is no wonder that the severest critics of the sexual drama portrayed by black radicals were white feminists. Schulamith Firestone (1970) rages at length about Cleaver's sexism and concludes, "The same old trick in revolutionary guise: the male defining himself negatively as man-strong by distinguishing himself from woman weak, through his control of her" (p. 122). Catherine Stimpson objects to the myths about white women described in some black male literature: "Being 'cleanly, viciously popped' which LeRoi Jones says that I want, but which my culture provides for me only in the 'fantasies' of evil, is in fact, evil" (p. 651). The bitterness of feminist charges of sexism only deepen the distrust between the two movements. Primarily white, the feminist movement generates accusations of racism from black women and men. The history of sexual exploitation of black female slaves by white men is absent from the myth. Black women are made invisible, their experience, humiliating. Excluded from the "good woman" mythology of the dominant culture, black women are denied both personhood and womanhood, making sisterhood between blacks and whites especially difficult. As Campbell (1983) states, "Because feminism is grounded in the concept of womanhood, the contemporary movement, like its earlier counterpart, is predominantly white and middle class, and feminism in both periods is vulnerable to charges of racism and classism. Because womanhood is an unattainable ideal for poor women, 'sisterhood' has been limited to middle class whites, and liberation has had diametrically opposed meanings for women of different classes" (p. 107).

Racism feeds sexism; sexism feeds racism. The two movements for human rights share a common enemy, a common myth, and common symptoms of oppression: The women's movement has extensively imitated rhetorical strategies of the black movement, yet success at joint action has been sporadic. Public address scholars have a rich source in which to explore the obstacles involved in overcoming rhetorical problems created by interdependent oppressive ideologies in the careers of Jesse Jackson and Geraldine Ferraro. Past studies of confrontational movements and movement speakers provide rhetorical insight into contemporary human rights discourse and indicate additional social myths central to racist and sexist ideologies.

SIMILAR CLAIMS OF NONWHITES AND WOMEN

Racism and Sexism: The Myths of Nonpersons

Beginning in the late 1960s, the rhetorics of both black power and women's liberation claim denial of their personhood by the dominant culture, which defines them as something less than human. The terms "racism" and its subsequent imitation "sexism" name the ideologies that define the majority of our citizens as innately inferior—less intelligent, less capable, less rational, and less moral; in short, less than full human beings. Human rights research in speech communication highlights the rhetorical task of redefining the self that is central to the rhetoric of oppression. Molefi Asante (1969) writes, "Specifically the black revolutionists are concerned with identity, black identity in a white world. . . . The rhetoric seeks to deliver the black man from the humiliating image he has had of himself" (pp. 7, 18). Wayne Brockriede and Robert L. Scott (1969) comment that the foremost implication of Stokely Carmichael's ideology is "his insistence that black people, as a matter of personal pride, must assume the right to define their own identity" (p. 118). Likewise, Karlyn Kohrs Campbell (1983) concludes that feminist rhetoric must transform womanhood into personhood. Indeed, feminist literature is dominated by the claim typified by an early WITCH pamphlet (1970): "A woman is trained from infancy that her only real goal in life is to fulfill the role of wife and mother of male heirs. She is allowed an identity only as an appendage to man" (p. 544). Although I have written elsewhere of the many differences between black and women's rhetorics (Hope 1975), the symbolic structures of racism and sexism share two primary characteristics. Each describes oppression based on unalterable marks of biology—skin color and sex—necessitating the rhetorical task of redefining identity. The second similarity is that while the dominant culture denies or masks racism and sexism, both of these ideologies are reinforced through dominant social myths. For black and female speakers, the rhetorical task begins with naming the experienced realities of racism and sexism by unmasking the pervasive, but unacknowledged, social myths.

The terms "racism" and "sexism" are at the heart of human rights discourse by the oppressed; however, because the terms are generally unspoken by authorities, separate and divisive symbolic realities are communicated. When one's personhood is the center of political crisis and the ultimate terms of that crisis are masked, symbolic confrontation reveals a social order in wild disarray. Professor Robert S. Browne's address before the 59th annual convention of the Speech Association of the Eastern States (1968) provided particularly fitting insight into the use of the term "racism" and its place in human rights communication. At the center of his admittedly "bleak" review of black-white communication he discussed implications of the term:

> Even the [Kerner] Commission report itself revealed the near hopelessness of the situation, for although it courageously identified the basic cause of racial tension as being white racism—a charge which only a year earlier had been ridiculed and characterized as sensationalism and extremism when it was made by black spokesmen such as Stokely

Carmichael—as I say, the Commission, after pointing the finger of white racism as the basic illness of the society, failed to present recommendations for destroying this vicious disease, probably because it couldn't think of any remedies. Rather, after identifying white racism as the cause of the problem, it focused its recommendations on schemes to improve the economic plight of the Negro, apparently on the assumption that once the Negro is scrubbed clean, adequately educated, and well-housed and employed, the whites will accept him and white racism will evaporate. Unfortunately, most blacks do not believe this. (p. 7)

The commission's failure was to confuse cause and consequence. As Browne implies, black rhetoric names racism as the cause of black poverty. To treat the symptom, poverty, without serious attention to the cause, racism, constitutes a basic hypocrisy. The Kerner Commission was "courageous" in naming racism because it is an ultimate term that incorporates a truly radical analysis of America's power structure.

Unlike the terms "racial prejudice" or "racial discrimination," which describe symptoms that can be treated by changes in law or special programs, "racism" presumes an institutionalized national ideology of white superiority that is denied by the dominant culture. If, as Richard Weaver concluded in 1953, the mild term "prejudice" is tainted with un-Americanism, "racism" sharpens and reveals a more severe problem. The term angers, frustrates, and alienates white America. "The black revolutionists are saying that racism is America's basic hypocrisy, because it contradicts all of the myths handed down from the founding fathers" (Asante, 1972, p. 222). For white America, to be told of racism is a total indictment, creating guilt and entailing the painful unease of cultural disillusion. If the United States is racist, then it is not the land of the free. If it is un-American to be a racist, then those who make the charge, in a perfect example of doublethink, are the most un-American of all because they unmask an invisible America for public spectacle.

Hubert Humphrey's response to the black power slogan is one of the few places in establishment rhetoric that the term "racism" appears at all. Humphrey uses it as a classic devil term. "Yes, racism is racism—and there is no room in America for racism of any color. And we must reject calls for racism, whether they come from a throat that is white or one that is black" (1968). Scott and Brockriede make the important point that "the essence of the Humphrey message was that Black Power adherents are racist, an accusation certain to alienate such people" (pp. 80–81). The accusation is alienating not only because it fails to interpret the call to black power as a justified response to white racism but also because it attempts a rhetorical cover-up, resorting to a mythical America where powers of whites and blacks are equally balanced.

The term "sexism" developed as a conscious imitation of "racism." For women intent on naming their relationship to the power structure in the late 1960s, the similarities between the oppression of blacks and women provided appropriate rhetorical symbols and strategies. "In the 1960's the Negro Problem became racism; from there to Black Power was only a very short distance to travel. In 1970, the Women Question . . . became sexism. For as it is in psychoanalysis, so it is in social-political life: to name the thing by its rightful name is instantly to begin to alter its power" (Gornick and Moran, 1972, p. xviii). Sexism, like racism, best names the totality of cultural messages that define women as nonpersons. "Certainly there is nothing in the great structural myth of our common life to indicate that woman is indeed fully human" (Gornick and Moran, p. xvi). The effects of myths that structure racism and sexism are prominently described by non-whites and women. It is striking that scholarship on myth as rhetorical constraint is only beginning to emerge. Herbert Simons (1970), for example, investigates the complex "incompatible demands" faced by movement leaders. "Unless it is understood that the leader is subjected to incompatible demands, a great many of his rhetorical acts must seem counterproductive" (p. 4). One unexplored "unproductive" rhetorical act is the deliberate exposure of great public myths. The public must either believe itself to have been duped by its culture or deny the reality of the speaker's claims, often by resorting to additional myths.

Michael McGee (1980) develops the concept of ideographs in an effort to distinguish between a "philosophy of myth" and "ideology" as explanations for "public" or "mass" consciousness (p. 1). Suggesting that ideology is a "political language" characterized by "a vocabulary of ideographs" with "the capacity to dictate decision and control public belief and behavior," McGee cites grammar school history as the "truly influential manifestation" of vertically structured ideographs "whose meanings have evolved over time" (p. 5). McGee's conclusion that social control is maintained by communities who carefully record and preserve their ideographs in popular history and in schools raises especially disturbing questions in conjunction with Browne's remarks. "Parenthetically, I would like to say that I am speaking of the black point of view. Whites may have always assumed, unthinkingly or because they had been taught it in school, that there was 'one nation, indivisible, with liberty and justice for all.' But blacks had never attached any importance to these clichés. Reality to them was something quite different" (p. 5). The ideographs "liberty" and "justice" become clichés for Browne, exposing the distance between myth and reality endured by many citizens.

Parke Burgess (1968) investigates black power as the legitimate response to the civic culture and isolates "the racist moral issue" as the center of the rhetorical realities experienced by blacks. His insistence that black power rhetoric "brings to the surface and loudly proclaims what heretofore had been fearfully hidden and yet silently worked its effects" (p. 52) indicates the major unmasking function of human rights discourse. Campbell (1973) notes an intensification of the same process in the rhetoric of women's liberation. "And the reason is simply that the rhetoric of women's liberation appeals to *what are said to be* shared moral values, but forces recognition that those values are *not* shared, thereby creating the most intense of moral conflicts" (p. 85). Robert L. Scott and Donald K. Smith in their seminal essay "The Rhetoric of Confrontation" (1969) highlight the need for communication theory that focuses on the masking function of traditional norms of discourse. "Even if the presuppositions of civility and rationality underlying the old rhetoric are sound, they can no longer be treated as self-evident. A rhetorical theory suitable to our age must take into account the charge that civility and decorum serve as masks for the preservation of injustice, that they condemn the dispossessed to non-being, and that as transmitted in a technological society they become the instrumentalities of power for those who 'have'" (p. 187). Cultural survival strategies shared by nonwhites and women is language use at variance with traditional linguistic and rhetorical theories. Black English, style, and audience participation are marks of black culture essential for the identification of a black speaker with a black audience. The remarkable ability of Stokely Carmichael, for instance, to switch linguistic structure, style, tone, cadence, metaphor, and appeal as he moved from black to white audiences demonstrates the limitations of traditional theory (Jefferson 1967; Scott & Brockriede, 1969; Asante, 1969). Russell Means (1980), a major figure in the American Indian movement, opens a printed address with the following complex charge:

> The only possible opening for a statement of this kind is that I detest writing. The process itself epitomizes the European concept of "legitimate" thinking; what is written has an importance that is denied the spoken. My culture, the Lakota culture, has an oral tradition, so I ordinarily reject writing. It is one of the white world's ways of destroying the cultures of non-European peoples, the imposing of an abstraction over the spoken relationship of a people. (p. 25)

Randall A. Lake (1983), in his study of the American Indian movement, maintains that movement theory and rhetorical theory in general cannot account for the "consummatory function" of Indian protest, partly because language itself is not considered an agent of change by American Indian cultures (p. 133). Ossie Davis (1967) considers English to be the prime carrier of racism and, thus, his enemy. Likewise, Robin Lakoff (1975) isolates sex-discrimination patterns implicit in the language women are taught to use. Campbell (1973; 1983) argues that consciousness raising is a rhetorical style and strategy peculiar to feminism and characteristic of the rhetoric that must transform womanhood into personhood. Richard Gregg (1971) concludes, "All of this points to a need for stylistic distance from the opposition in order to enhance one's self-hood. If one perceives that the linguistic devices of others are factors that reduce self concept, it becomes imperative to reject those linguistic devices" (p. 80).

Jesse Jackson's speech to the Democratic convention in San Francisco, July 17, 1983, suggests additional study of changing linguistic devices in human rights rhetoric. Rapidly altering his language, rhythm, style, and structure, Jackson publicly presents a complex persona to a large and mixed audience. Moving through carefully evidenced traditional argument, he ends in the voice of the black preacher, a tactic that implicitly demands that each separate audience recognize and acknowledge the validity of diverse rhetorical strategies as sources of power.

When human rights advocates attempt to unmask the hidden mythology that supports *civil* discourse, public confrontation with racism or sexism is demanded. Thomas Benson's study of the *Autobiography of Malcolm X* (1974) explores the symbolic power of racism as it affected Malcolm's changes in self-identity. "As Malcolm came to understand that racism had caused him to act as he had, its power to control his actions passed over to him. Motive, previously located in his condition, was now in the hands of a conscious agent. With the *Autobiography*, Malcolm shares that motive with his readers, giving them a principle of action they can carry into the confrontation with racism as it conditions their own lives" (p. 9). Discussing racism as the force which first "confined" Malcolm's actions and then as the force against which Malcolm's "enlargement" was won, Benson presents the terms "confinement" and "enlargement" as the "symbolic vehicles" that "stand as the symbols for Malcolm's discovery of himself through the act of addressing his fellow men" (p. 13). Benson's insightful analysis provides an especially useful model to examine the symbolic structures that shape the lives and rhetoric of those who must conquer the myths of nonbeing. In human rights rhetoric racism and sexism are claimed as the causes of nonwhite and female oppression. Poverty and violence are cited as the most evident symptoms.

POVERTY AND VIOLENCE: THE SYMPTOMS OF HUMAN RIGHTS OFFENSES

Both nonwhites and women claim they are born into groups marked by a disproportionate rate of poverty and a high risk of violence. Both groups cite the evidence of poverty and violence as the major symptoms of racism and sexism.

POVERTY

The evidence of poverty as a symptom of human rights abridgement marking the lives of nonwhites and women has been well documented. Even given the success of black voting blocks, poverty statistics show the non-white to have made little economic advance since the 1960s. Sidney Will-heim (1983), in his book *Black in a White America*, reports:

> Furthermore, the Urban League's study, "The Widening Economic Gap," released in July, 1979, reports that during 1976 and 1977 the median income from all Black families increased 3.5 percent (rising from $9,242 to $9,563) while White income expanded twice as much, increasing 7.7 percent (from $15,537 to $16,740); the Black-to-White income ratio for families consequently dropped from 59 percent to 57 percent. . . .
> The unemployment picture for Blacks is absolutely abominable. In 1948, the official unemployment rate for non-whites stood at 5.9 percent and 3.2 percent for whites; . . . by October of 1979, 7.6 percent of the nation's workforce was out of work; the figure for Blacks stood at 14.3 percent. (pp. 8–9)

Black speakers insist that as a group, regardless of affirmative action programs and civil rights laws, economic opportunities for blacks continue to decrease. Vernon E. Jordon, Jr. (1981), is only one of many black speakers who cites the dismal statistics. In a speech to the Urban League, responding to President Ronald Reagan's proposed budget, Jordon itemizes proposed cuts in social security, food stamps, public service jobs, medicaid, legal service, welfare and education, and concludes, "Defenders of that budget will tell us black people are not being singled out; that's true, it's only poor people who are being victimized. And we are twelve percent of the population but a third of the poor—so we are the main victims. . . . We know that if you're a black in America, you are in trouble; you are not safe, you are always in danger of losing the little you have" (pp. 611–612). For Jordon, being black means living in risk. For women, and for black women especially, economic conditions are equally tenuous.

Aid to Families with Dependent Children is the largest percentage of the welfare budget. In 1979 AFDC took 47.6 percent of the budget for over 3 million families. The families are almost totally women and their 7.5 million children (*Statistical Abstracts*, U.S. Census, 1979, p. 352). Women—black, white, and old—are the major recipients of welfare. They are the nation's poor (Hess, Markson & Stein, 1982). Feminists, although often accused of representing only middle-class women, cite economic statistics to substantiate their claim that as a group, all women suffer from sanctioned oppression. "In 1979, women full-time workers still had median earnings that were approximately 60 percent of the median earnings of men. . . . Within any given household, the difference is apt to be larger, with wives earning less than one-half their spouse's income. The saying that the more things change the more they stay the same seems to fit women's earnings in comparison to men's; there has been little change in the ratio of women's to men's earnings since 1939" (Hess et al., p. 221).

Given the facts of poverty and economic discrimination, nonwhites and women claim there are no good reasons for a rhetoric that denies the existence of institutionalized oppression. The masked reasons for this rhetoric are racism and sexism—not reasons at all, but entrenched ideologies justified by myth.

Violence

The claim that nonwhites and women risk undue violence in their lives is central to human rights rhetoric. The study of human rights communication in 20th century America requires an analysis of violence, which has been traditionally defined as falling outside the concerns of students of discourse. Violence enters the discussion of human rights communication in three ways: (1) Oppressed groups define their oppression by the quantity and kind of violence experienced; it is therefore a primary topic of their rhetoric. (2) Speech scholars have made a sharp distinction between "rational" disagreement, "coercion," and "violence" and have used such labels to condemn the styles and strategies of protesting groups. (3) The reaction to agitation for human rights often takes the form of institutional or individual acts of violence.

For these reasons violence is a proper object of study for communication scholars, yet violence is not indexed as a subject of study in communication journals through 1979 (Matlon, 1980). Although "Violence in Print" and "Violence in Television" appear, the absence of violence as a rhetorical category may indicate the confused state of academic debate over the relationship between violence and communication. Thomas Benson (1969) concludes that communication has been viewed as an alternative to violence, a cause of violence, and a form of violence; conversely, violence is also sometimes seen as a "form of communication" (p. 40). In American democracy especially, the right to bear arms and the right of assembly infuse the potential for violence into any public dispute (Neiburg, 1962).

The black male especially has been victim to both white mob and police violence. Armed agents of control, maintained by city, state, and federal government, as attested by two separate commissions to study violence in America, have been responsible for the vast majority of incidents of violence in racial disorders since World War II (Kerner, 1968; Walker, 1968).

Violence against women is a prime concern of human rights advocates. This violence, unlike that experienced by black males, is private, not public. Like most violence it is committed by men: husbands, lovers, fathers, and strangers. Rape and wife beating continue to increase as the most common violent crimes in America. Problems in gathering accurate data are additional indicators of societal tolerance of violence against women. "It is said that every year 2 million women are beaten by their husbands, and it is also said that nearly 6 million are. Pick your figure. A Justice Department survey counted 178,000 rapes during 1981, but for every woman who reported a rape to the police, perhaps nine or maybe 25 did not. It is beyond dispute, however, that extraordinary numbers of women and children are being brutalized by those closest to them" (Anderson, 1983). Feminists argue that both crimes, whether committed by individual men or groups, are sanctioned by the state. The low incidence of law enforcement and conviction works to establish a collective threat in women's lives. Susan Brownmiller (1975) has published the most extensive research on rape from a feminist perspective and concludes, "From prehistoric times to the present, I believe, rape has played a critical function. It is nothing more or less than a conscious process of intimidation by which *all* men keep *all* women in a state of fear" (p. 15). Fear of state-sanctioned male violence is one theme of feminist rhetoric that has generated only limited investigation by speech scholars (Krouse & Peters, 1975; Smith, 1976). The messages, meanings, and effects generated by myths about rape and wife beating need to be explored.

Finally, war, the epitome of state violence, must be explored in terms of its relationship to the communication of human rights. Sociologists have noted the correlation between war, repression, and domestic violence. The evidence merits our serious attention. Warren Schaich (1975) correlated incidents of collective racial violence with war from 1900 through 1969 (Table 4.1) and found that with the exception of the Korean War, the vast majority of instances of racial violence occurred during war years. Schaich's conclusions raise serious questions for communication scholars. "In each violent period, war seems to produce a state of mind whereby whites and blacks get caught up in collectively defining each other in violent terms as internal enemies at war. . . . Police violence has become more noticeable with each war involvement" (p. 390). How is the collective "state of mind" produced? How do the myths and language of war and war propaganda effect domestic violence?

Brownmiller presents a great deal of historical evidence in which the rape of the enemy's women is sanctioned as a prize of war victory (chap. 3). Has this message changed? Do the myths of soldiering continue to justify violence to women, in spite of military law, as Brownmiller asserts? Theodore Roszack (1969) in a historical investigation of the relationship between early feminism and World War I notes the rise of fanatic misogynist language in war talk. He cites Filippo Marinetti's *Futurist Manifesto* of 1909 as the extreme example:

Table 4.1
Collective Racial Violence in the United States
(1900–1967)[a]

Five-Year Periods	Number of Disturbances
1900–1904	1
1905–1909	2
1910–1914	0
1915–1919[a]	22
1920–1924	4
1925–1929	1
1930–1934	0
1935–1939	1
1940–1944[a]	18
1945–1949	0
1950–1954	0
1955–1959	0
1960–1964	11
1965–1969[a]	150

Note: Estimates of riot frequency vary. Lieberson et al., using the *New York Times* for their primary source, came up with 72 riots between the years 1913–1963 (Lieberson & Silberman, collective violence responsible for large-scale destruction of life and property. Consequently, Grimshaw identifies only 33 major interracial disturbances between 1905 and 1949 of which he lists 18 riots between 1915 and 1919 (Grimshaw, 1959: 179). Waskow, on the other hand, lists over 20 riots of minor and major importance for the year 1919. Other authors, such as W. E. B. DuBois, support the latter estimate. Waskow (1966:174) adds that "some of the so-called minor riots could not . . . qualify as riots—some were expanded lynchings, others brief clashes of sullen crowds which quickly dispersed" (1966: 174). The type of disturbance cited by Waskow as expanded lynchings or brief clashes of sullen crowds are omitted in the table presented here. Only collective racial violence resulting in personal injury, loss of life, arrests or property damage, or all four are included in Table 6.

Sources: U.S. *News and World Report*, 1964: August 28–29, 34; 1966: September 34–35; Grimshaw, 1959: 179; Waskow, 1967: 304–307; Murray, 1940: 82–87, 219–222, 32 and 4; Murray, 1944: 82–93; Franklin, 1965: 433; Osotsky, 1963: 16–24.

[a]Designated periods in which war and collective racial violence occurred.

We are out to glorify war:
The only health-giver of the world!
Militarism! Patriotism!
The Destructive Arm of the Anarchist!
Ideas that Kill!
Contempt for Women! (p. 91)

The rhetoric of war needs to be examined for its effect on the oppression of nonwhites and women.

In conclusion, poverty and violence are symptoms of human rights offenses caused by racism and sexism. Thus the effect and power of racist and sexist myths about work, poverty, welfare, marriage, violence, and war as persuasive symbolic structures that support sanctioned oppression is an important area of research for communication scholars.

COMMUNICATION SCHOLARSHIP AND HUMAN RIGHTS

Serious scholarly work in the field of speech concerning human rights did not really emerge until the 1960s. Except for a few isolated monographs, the first half of the century was marked by general silence about American oppression. Modern America, when presented at all in communication journals from the 1930s through the late 1950s, is strangely free of protest, committed to traditional "rational" discourse, and innocent of injustice. It is worth quoting a few passages from the rare publications that did address communication and racism, however obliquely, for a sense of the field's history. The first study to focus directly on Negro oratory, "Old Time Negro Preaching" (Pipes), appeared in the *Quarterly Journal of Speech* in 1945. It analyzes the topics and style of eight different sermons given in Macon, Georgia, in 1942. On style, Pipes summarizes: "Beneath all, however, is the Negro's unconscious desire and need to escape from 'an impossible world,' and the emotional outbursts, shouting, laughing and crying serve this purpose" (p. 19). Booker T. Washington, Marcus Garvey's mass movement, the police/black riots of the 1920s, the black renaissance in literature and music, and the legal and political decisions regarding black servicemen during World War II all disappear. The author's "Negro" is "unconscious" of his own oppression.

Yet Pipes is not himself unconscious of changes in social power. His concluding remarks are revealing, offering two basic explanations for the importance of old-time preaching among Negroes:

(1) The Negro today, as during the days of slavery, possesses an emotional, superstitious nature which traces its origin back to the jungles of Africa, and this emotional nature has always been one that must have an outward expression; (2) the Negro has found himself without normal outward expression because of domination by powers above his control. He was dominated in Africa by the jungle and tribal custom; in America before the Civil War, by slavery; in the "black belt" (and to a lesser degree in other parts of the United States) by the plantation system and "divine white right." But education and enlightenment are bringing into this preaching new ideas, which are at variance with the ideas of old-fashioned Negro preaching. The outcome promises to be the death of this type of preaching. Old time Negro preaching today is still a vital part of the Negroes' existence; it is preaching that is still the soul-expression of a frustrated people. But because doors to education and doors to new opportunities of normal expression are being opened wider and wider to the black man in the United States, the degree of frustration is being lowered; the result of this process, if it continues, is to be oratory's complete loss of one of the most peculiar types of public speaking that perhaps the world has ever known. (p. 21)

In an attitude similar to that of contemporary writers who view the nondiscursive acts of march, sit-in, singing, and slogan as extremely irrational and abnormal responses to public apathy (Corbett, 1969), for Pipes "emotional outbursts, shouting, laughing and crying" are not "normal expressions" of public oratory. The passage is depressing in that nothing, it seems, in Pipes' training—his undergraduate work at Tuskeegee Institute, his obvious interest and work in black preaching, and his own courage—enabled him to predict either the severity of American racism or the power of black preaching as a source of political redress.

Pipes' lament for "oratory's loss" is similar to the concluding section of another early study. Examining the speaking of James K. Vardaman, a Mississippi senator and successful candidate for governor in 1903, Eugene White (1946) concludes:

Of far more importance, however, than his skill in delivery was his interpretation of the prevailing attitudes of the people. Many Mississippians were convinced that Roosevelt was attempting to force social equality upon the South, and Vardaman capitalized the opportunity to harness the resultant forces of mass emotion and made the Negro the scapegoat for the white man's passion. . . . He was a spell binder and not a constructive builder; his basic premises were made on unstable mass prejudices and were deficient in logical proof. But there are those today in Mississippi who yet remember his personal appeal and the magnetism of his oratory, and to them he will always be Mississippi's Great White Chief. (p. 446)

The flavor of speech scholarship indicated in these two quotations is partly a function of the classical approach to speech criticism and partly a function of the past absence of academic concern with the voices of dissent in America.

Communication scholars concerned with questions of liberty, rights, and injustice focused their work upon teaching speech in a democracy, questions of propaganda arising from World War II, and individual British and American orators historically acknowledged as great public figures. In an early review of civil rights oratory and the new black power, Donald H. Smith (1967) succinctly voiced the limitations of the "famous speaker" approach. "But I can say to you that teachers of speech have a special obligation to teach students the true meaning of democracy and liberty and justice. As long as we delude ourselves that Lincoln and Jefferson and Wilson and Patrick Henry were speaking for the dignity and rights of all men, so much longer do we bury our heads in the sand, hoping the thing will go away, which it will not. You must tell your students the truth so that together we can save our nation by making it the democracy it was intended to be" (p. 448). Smith's address, delivered to the annual convention of the Speech Association of the Eastern States, is one of many exhortations from black scholars that the field must begin to pay attention to the failures of democracy. The 1954 Supreme Court decision to limit segregation precipitated an interest in civil rights speeches as sociopolitical facts of American public life. The profusion of protest movements from the late 1950s to the present also coincided with the development of "new rhetorics" and "new criticism." Many communicative acts, both discursive and nondiscursive, were obvious and legitimate areas of study. Yet in reviewing the literature, there is the disturbing sense that only when protest, long part of the public scene, spilled into the middle class and upset the academic order did a flurry of publications emerge.

AGITATIVE STUDIES

Two ways of examining the rhetoric of oppression dominated the field of communication in the late 1960s and through the 1970s. The first was a renewed interest in agitative rhetoric, and the second was the study of social movements. Agitative studies tended to focus on individual speakers, while movement studies attempted to analyze and theorize about the communication of large collections of speakers and diverse persuasive forms. Each type of study has added significantly to our understanding of protest and dissent. However, agitative studies and movement studies have some inherent limitations when applied specifically to the rhetoric of nonwhites and women.

When it does not directly explore the symbolic and mythical structures of racism and sexism as informing sources of human rights discourse, communication scholarship properly falls prey to accusations of irrelevance and inappropriateness. Molefi Asante, in the keynote speech to the Third World Congress on Black Communication (1983), includes his own early work on black rhetoric in the following charge:

> The third "revolution" in rhetoric was initiated by the civil rights movement of the 60's and maintained by student led campaigns against the Viet Nam war. . . . The intrinsic problems in Western rhetorical theory revealed themselves to be systemic because even those of us who were sympathetic to "civil rights" used a eurocentric framework to speak of "agitative rhetoric," "agitation," "protest rhetoric," etc., when in fact we should never have been forced to take that position. Thus even in that situation the European center assumed the presumption and the burden of proof rested with the dissenters, dissidents, oppressed, the disturbers of the myths. (p. 3)

The standard definitions of agitative rhetoric, when applied to nonwhites and women, impose the burden of effecting change on those whose culture recognizes only those of the oppressed who deny their own personhood. Charles Lomas (1968) defines agitation as "a persistent and uncompromising statement and restatement of grievances through all available communication channels, with the aim of creating public opinion favorable to a change in some condition" (p. 2). When the conditions are racism or sexism and the persistence of grievance continues through three centuries, the usefulness of the agitation label is weakened.

Studies of agitation presuppose as normal a condition of stability. From the point of view of the dominant culture, agitation disturbs the status quo through revelations of disorder previously made invisible by the myths of social control. "Agitation is a dirty word in our modern world" (McEdwards, 1968, p. 36). Like the "radical" and the "militant," the agitator is dismissed; all claims, no matter how well warranted, are illegitimate. For the nonwhite or female rhetor, however, speaking from a culture symbolically structured by racism and sexism, public articulation of grievances and demands creates an order that is liberating; discourse demanding full human rights must be defined as a legitimate and appropriate response to a degrading, insecure, and often threatening environment. Communication scholars must give attention to the persistent rhetorical forces at work in resistance to agitation for human rights.

MOVEMENT STUDIES

The major limitation of agitation studies in explaining confrontational social movements was voiced by Robert S. Cathcart (1983): "What is important is to distinguish those agitators who are seeking reform within the system from those who confront the system, those who produce a dialectical enjoinment by calling into question the moral legitimacy of the existing order" (p. 73). Cathcart's insistence on the study of countermovements and on counterrhetoric within movements focuses attention on the "essence" of rhetorical realities for speakers and their audiences rather than on "means and ends" (p. 72). Unfortunately, most movement theories are inadequate to explain rhetorical strategies when the essence of claim is "personhood," as it is for both nonwhites and women, and when the ensuing confrontation, no matter how masked, is a result of the culture's reluctance or inability to perceive nonwhites or women as fully human.

Major reviews of movement studies (Riches & Sillars, 1980) and special journal editions (*Central States Speech Journal*, 1980; 1983) attest to a lively and necessary debate among speech scholars about theory and terms of research. Much of the work centers on theory, less on detailed investigation of specific movements, and still less on comparisons of similar movements. Karlyn Kohrs Campbell (1983) compares the feminist movements of the nineteenth and twentieth centuries and concludes that they are one movement typified by an ideological conflict between the concepts of womanhood and personhood. Since sexism, like racism, is entrenched in centuries of traditions, values, laws, and myths, the collective identity of the dominant culture and often of individual members of that culture is intrinsically sustained by dominance over nonwhites and women. As members of powerless groups push forward to create new identities with the potential for power, demands are forced upon those with power to redefine and justify their dominance and, thus, their very identities. Only in those "social movements" whose proponents' humanity is the central claim is the crisis of public confrontation so radically tied to the psychological as well as the political reality, to social as well as economic change. Although movements to preserve the environment, eliminate nuclear weapons, end war, and so forth, may confront the public with moral dilemmas, the movements generated by racism and sexism are unique.

CONCLUSION

Human rights declarations, as well as the discourse that explains and develops them, stem from the experience of state-sanctioned violence and oppression. Nonwhites and women stand alone as groups marked by visible biological stigmas, traditionally denied human rights no matter what their political beliefs. In the ideologies of racism and sexism, both nonwhites and women are defined as nonpersons, nonwhite males as subhuman, all women as objects. The myths of social control conceal and justify the major symptoms of oppression: poverty and violence. Further, social myths such as the sexual myth explored earlier, reinforce the ideologies of racism and sexism. When unmasked by demythologization or challenged by the creation of countermyths, a severe moral confrontation arises for all members of society.

I am urging that communication scholars continue to explore the full significance of discourse that examines the ugly realities that the dominant culture tends to deny. Excellent work has emerged from the field, but scholars must also grapple head-on with the rhetorical forces, issues, symbols, and myths that reinforce racist and sexist ideologies. To do less is to deny the value of our expertise in the culture's search for full humanity for all its citizens.

5

The Paradigm of Unfulfilled Promise:
A Critical Examination of the
History of Research on Small Groups
in Speech Communication

DENNIS S. GOURAN

INTRODUCTION

R esearch on communication in the small group is a relatively recent development in the history of speech communication. In fact, for all practical purposes, the subject did not exist as an academic concern until the publication of A. Craig Baird's influential *Public Discussion and Debate* (1927, 1937). Moreover, from the 1930s, when scholars in the field began writing about the performance of groups, to the mid-1950s, attention focused almost exclusively on pedagogical issues. In spite of this emphasis, early scholarship on communication in groups had an important bearing on subsequent inquiry.

Stimulated by possibilities for the development of a science of human problem solving implied by Dewey's notions about rationality and reflective thinking, Baird and others (for example, Ewbank & Auer, 1941; Haiman, 1950; McBurney & Hance, 1939; Sattler & Miller, 1954) raised many questions about the functioning of groups that helped define the agenda for much of the quantitatively oriented scholarship that has been conducted. As interest in discussion as a problem-solving tool grew, the pedagogical focus, so pervasive throughout the period 1940-1955, began to give way to empirical investigations of claims about the performance of groups. The shift in emphasis followed the rise of controlled inquiry into social phenomena evident in such cognate disciplines as psychology, sociology, and anthropology.

By the time the study of group dynamics had entered its so-called golden age in psychology and sociology, many students of group discussion were no longer content to view effective performance as a training outcome. They had come to appreciate the complexities of collective judgment and understood the need to examine the role of the numerous personal and contextual influences that shape it. From this realization emerged a general perspective, or paradigm. In its simplest form, the paradigm can be portrayed in the following manner:

Viewing the performance of groups in the manner suggested by Figure 5.1 fostered the expectation that scholarship would lead to the identification of variables accounting for the success members experience in achieving desired objectives. Central to this thinking was the belief that the ways in which individuals interact determines their outcomes.* That the behavior essential to the achievement of any particular objective would necessarily surface, however, was not something on which one could depend. Its occurrence, researchers soon recognized, was a function of the attributes of individuals and the groups into which they form. Effort in much early quantitative work, therefore, was directed toward understanding effects of member and group traits on interaction.

As the concept of "process" gained prominence in the years following Berlo's publication of *The Process of Communication* (1960), a less simplistic representation of the paradigm shown in Figure 5.1 evolved. Direct effects of interaction and indirect effects of member-and-group characteristics were now seen as substantially more complex in their interrelationships. A more nearly cybernetic view of group performance began to emerge.

Under the leadership of process oriented scholars, instances of group interaction were increasingly regarded as the result of a confluence of factors determining at any given point what is said, how it is said, who is

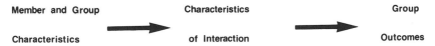

Member and Group	Characteristics	Group
Characteristics	of Interaction	Outcomes

Figure 5.1. An illustration of the basic paradigm guiding small-group research in speech communication. (Arrows should be read as "affects".)

---

*Some students of group process in other disciplines have consistently viewed the characteristics of interaction as noncentral to understanding group outcomes. Poole, McPhee, and Seibold (1982), however, recently presented a convincing case to the contrary in a study of the predictive accuracy of an interaction model and another relating decisional outcomes only to the distribution of initial member preferences.

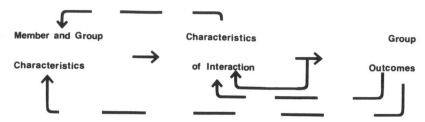

Figure 5.2. A revised version of the basic paradigm guiding small-group research in speech communication that reflects the processual nature of communication in groups.

saying it, and how participants relate to one another. In this conception, member/group characteristics and outcomes, as well as communicative behavior, are fluid phenomena in continuous states of change. A version of the paradigm better capturing this view is illustrated in Figure 5.2.

Despite the increased sophistication of those studying communicative behavior in groups, adequate descriptions of the processes involved have not as yet materialized. In that respect, the paradigm that has evolved remains one of unfulfilled promise. To date, research has tended to focus either on member and group characteristics/interaction relationships, interaction/outcome relationships, or member and group characteristics/outcome relationships.

The limited focus does not imply that past scholarship on groups done in speech communication is without merit—although one might draw such an inference from published critiques (for example, Becker, 1980; Bormann, 1970, 1980; Gouran, 1970; 1973a; Hirokawa, 1982a; Mortensen, 1970). In fact, the purpose of this review, in part, is to identify some of the potentially promising avenues of inquiry that have been opened. Unfortunately, a summary of this type does not permit a complete synthesis of the hundreds of studies that have accumulated. Still, the selection included is a good sample of previous efforts to illuminate the functions of communication in groups.

Although the boundaries are permeable, and although others have imposed a different classification scheme (see, for example, Cragan & Wright, 1980; Larson, 1971), group studies in speech communication fit two major categories: those predominately concerned with effects of member and group characteristics on group performance and those dealing with communication effects. Some research has been conducted as a result of methodological concerns and, hence, fits neither of these categories. Such scholarship, when cited, serves to illustrate developments that have facilitated inquiry into substantive issues.

EFFECTS OF MEMBER AND
GROUP CHARACTERISTICS

Researchers concerned with member and group characteristics have usually focused on a single independent variable and assessed corresponding variation in either some aspect of communication or some set of outcomes. A large number of these studies have developed; however, relatively few focus on the same variables. For this reason, the research is frequently subject to the charge of being fragmentary. Nevertheless, this volume of scholarship has yielded some useful insights into the antecedents of group performance.

REFLECTIVE-THINKING ABILITY

Given the pervasive influence of Dewey's *How We Think* on discussion pedagogy, it is not surprising that one variable receiving attention in research has been reflective thinking ability. With the development of a measure of this trait by Johnson (1943) came several investigations of its effects on different group outcomes. Among the relationships uncovered were Pyron and Sharp's (1963) and Pyron's (1964) findings of differences in perceived influence of discussion group members favoring those high in reflective-thinking ability and Sharp and Milliken's (1964) discovery of a positive association between such ability and the quality of solutions proposed by members of problem-solving groups. Whether the quality of ideas is responsible for differences in perceived influence remains to be determined.

ROLE-RELATED ATTITUDES

The attitude that one has toward his or her role in a discussion is another personal characteristic appearing to affect an individual's communicative behavior. As one illustration, Sargent and Miller (1971) studied the discussion behavior of group leaders expressing a preference for either an autocratic or a democratic style. The results demonstrated that one's stylistic predilections have clearly discernible behavioral manifestations. Autocratically inclined leaders were higher on measures of total communication, negative comments, and attempted answers to questions. Those preferring a democratic style asked more questions, did more to encourage participation, and generated more alternatives for their groups to consider.

Such differences as Miller and Sargent observed apparently stem from a cluster of personality attributes that distinguish between group members having different attitudes toward the leadership role. In support, Rosenfeld and Plax (1975) reported an investigation showing that democratically inclined leaders exceeded their autocratic counterparts favorably on nurturance, achievement, independence, intraception, abasement, and social values. In the case of the democratic style, these qualities were linked to gender, with females surpassing males. Rosenfeld and Fowler (1976) also found that democratic male leaders were comparatively high in forcefulness, whereas females preferring the same style were more open-minded and nurturant.

COMMUNICATION ANXIETY

If one's disposition toward his or her role in a discussion has consequences for performance, a possibly even more important influence is the individual's feelings about being involved at all. This has been the concern of a number of different researchers studying personality factors that inhibit participation. Lustig and Grove (1975), for instance, observed differences in communicative behavior attributable to the reticence of members of problem-solving groups. Groups containing reticent members were more task-oriented and less social in their interactions than groups consisting of non reticent participants only. Sorenson and McCroskey (1977), using a measure of interaction developed by McCroskey and Wright (1971), also reported a relationship between members' apprehension about communication and tension in both ad hoc and intact groups.

Working with the related concept of "unwillingness to communicate," Burgoon (1976) detected other consequences of one's predisposition toward participation. She noted that unwillingness to communicate was inversely related to satisfaction, attractiveness of group membership, perceived coordination of discussion tasks, amount of participation, and levels of both information-seeking and giving. This research is consistent with a study by Arntson, Mortensen, and Lustig (1980) producing evidence that those favorably disposed toward participation talk more, interrupt less, initiate more ideas, have higher credibility, and are perceived as having greater influence than less favorably disposed group members.

SELF-CONCEPT

Participants concerned about the images they project in groups tend to engage in a great deal of self-monitoring. Supportive of this hypothesis is an investigation by Rarick, Soldow, and Geizer (1976) that revealed that high self-monitors have a correspondingly higher susceptibility to pressure for uniformity than low self-monitors. Those having a strong enough self-concept not to worry about their images are able to function much more independently in groups. This was also the implication of earlier research by Crowell, Katcher, and Miyamoto (1955) showing that those with positive self-images tend to see themselves as exercising rather than responding to social influence.

ATTRIBUTION TENDENCIES

A trait only recently beginning to attract attention in research on communication in groups is locus of control. The tendency to conceive of one's own and others' behavior as predominately under the control of either external or internal influences, among other things, has implications for the judgments members of groups make. In one study, Alderton (1980) determined that internalizers sanction deviant behavior more severely than externalizers when information concerning that behavior is ambiguous. Analysis of the communication acts of groups that varied in respect to their members' locus of control was consistent with their sanctioning behavior. Internalizers attributed deviance more to internal causes, whereas externalizers focused more on circumstantial influences.

A follow-up investigation (Alderton, 1982) supported the previous findings. Comparing shifts between pre- and post-discussion judgments about the degree of personal responsibility involved in a deviant act, Alderton found that they paralleled the communicative behavior of the groups. Internalizers shifted toward the assignment of personal responsibility and concentrated on the relationship of the deviant's personal characteristics to the act. Externalizers did just the opposite.

That attribution tendencies affect communicative behavior was further demonstrated in research by Gouran, Ketrow, Spear, and Brown (1984) and by Gouran and Andrews (in press). In the first study, the investigators discovered in a case involving serious deviation that group members sanctioned a high-status offender much less severely than they did one of low status. The same difference, although less pronounced, obtained in the case of a moderately deviant act. Low-status offenders were the objects of more communication assigning personal responsibility to their acts compared with those of high status. In the investigation by Gouran and Andrews, severity of group sanctions correlated significantly with group members' attributions of personal responsibility. If such tendencies consistently contribute to differences in the perception and judgment of social behavior, the possible ramifications are disturbing. For that reason, the attribution/communication/group decision relationship is one worthy of further inquiry.

GENDER

In addition to the personal attributes that influence the communicative behavior and performance of groups, gender has surfaced as a variable of interest. Frequently considered to reflect inherent personality differences, gender effects are increasingly being viewed as a function of underlying processes of socialization that contribute both to the manner in which males and females function in groups and the ways in which others respond to them. This is evident in the previously mentioned research by Rosenfeld and Plax (1975) and Rosenfeld and Fowler (1976).

Summarizing gender-oriented group research, Baird (1976) suggested that compared with female participants, males are more task-oriented, active, aggressive, interested in problem solving, risk prone, resistant to social influence, and likely to emerge as leaders. In contrast, females appear to be more self-disclosing, expressive of their emotional states, perceptive of others' emotional states, and sensitive to nonverbal cues. Marr (1974) additionally noted that in decisional situations involving threat, female group participants may behave more rationally than males.

The differences suggested by Baird and Marr are consistent in many respects with stereotypic views of males and females in general. Recent research by Ellis and McCallister (1980), however, indicates that distinctions break down when one considers the individual's gender orientation. In comparison to traditional males and females, androgynous group members manifested significantly less stereotyped patterns of interaction.

A group member's race may also interact with gender to affect communicative behavior. Lumsden, Brown, Lumsden, and Hill (1974) varied the racial and gender composition of task groups and identified several differences in their discussions. Of interest in the present analysis were findings showing white females to be significantly less opinionated than the other three types of participants and black females to be significantly less abstract than the other three types.

That responses to male and female participation in groups vary, at least in respect to leadership, was demonstrated by Alderton and Jurma (1980). These researchers discovered that male followers expressed significantly more disagreement with male leaders than with female leaders. Female followers expressed more disagreement with female leaders.

Factors supplemental to the gender of other group members can affect one's responses to male and female participants in group discussions. Bradley (1980), for instance, varied the apparent competence of male and female opinion deviates. Analysis of the communicative behavior directed toward them indicated that hostility following the comments of females was significantly greater in the low-competence condition than in any of the remaining three. Responses to female deviates were also more reasonable when they displayed a high level of competence.

Although not directly concerned with responses to male and female discussants, Jordan and McLaughlin (1976) found that role ambiguity affects perceptions of role occupants. When a given group role is not clearly gender-linked, responses to one's suitability for performing it favors neither males nor females.

The stereotypic view that males typically evoke more favorable responses from group members than do females is increasingly doubtful. At least, that is the judgment toward which studies like those of Bradley and Jordan and McLaughlin are currently pointing. Changes in our thinking about the gender/communication relationship in discussion groups has opened a potentially fruitful area for future research.

COOPERATIVE AND COMPETITIVE TENDENCIES

Noting in a pedagogically oriented essay (Harnack, 1951) that the goal commitments (individual versus group) discussants make influences their performance, Harnack (1955) subsequently tested his suspicion that cooperativeness can be developed through training. His effort to confirm this hypothesis revealed that trained groups were significantly more cooperative than untrained groups in later discussions and that a positive correlation existed between the amount of goal-oriented behavior displayed by individual participants and their observed level of cooperative behavior.

Saine and Bock's (1973a) research supports that of Harnack. Their data revealed that group members seeking individual rewards were more argumentative than group-centered participants. In addition, argumentative contributions were more frequently followed in kind among individual-centered participants.

TASK ORIENTATION

Just as one's commitment to an individual or group goal affects communicative behavior, so too does his or her task orientation. In some cases, task demands are such that they define the appropriate manner of behaving (Wood, 1977). In other instances, however, individuals vary considerably in the ways they are disposed to approach a task. Some people require clarity and order; others do not. Burgoon (1971) tested the interaction between tolerance for ambiguity and the amount of conflicting information group members were given on perceptions of task attractiveness in decision-making discussions. Those having a high tolerance for ambiguity were most satisfied when they worked with conflicting information. The reverse was true for individuals having a low tolerance for ambiguity.

Paralleling tolerance for ambiguity is a concept that Putnam (1979) has called "preference for procedural order." Her research showed clear effects of this variable on the communicative behavior of groups divided into categories of high- and low-procedural order preferences. Participants in the high category presumably would resemble those having a low tolerance for ambiguity, and vice versa. Putnam found that groups consisting of such individuals made more summaries, goal-related statements, and procedural clarifications than did groups whose members rated low in their preferences for procedural order. In addition, they introduced more general headings as a way of signaling changes in topic. In contrast, groups consisting of individuals low in their expressed preferences for procedural order vacillated more between task-related and social-emotional issues, displayed more interruptions, and carried on more simultaneous conversations.

MANIPULATIVE TENDENCIES

The degree to which communication is distributed throughout the membership of a group and the extent to which it is focused on task activities is, in part, a function of whether manipulative individuals are present. Working with a measure of Machiavellianism, Bochner and Bochner (1972) detected an inverse relationship between the number of participants scoring high on the measure and the amount of task-directed communication occurring. As the proportion of low Machiavellians increases in a group, there also appears to be a better distribution of task-related activity.

PSYCHOLOGICAL SIMILARITIES

The extent to which the members of a group are psychologically similar has implications for the manner in which they will perform a task. In a case study of the Watergate transcripts, Gouran (1976) established a link between the psychological makeup of the conspirators most centrally involved in the cover-up and their tendencies to reinforce one another's misjudgments. Similarity, it seems, can function to promote communicative activity that interferes with a group's ability to see issues clearly and to engage in the sort of critical testing that Irving Janis (1982) considers crucial to effective decision making. A laboratory investigation of the groupthink hypothesis by Courtright (1976) was not especially supportive of this position. However, Porter's (1976) analysis of fantasy themes in the Watergate transcripts suggests that groups do share in the construction of scenarios of sometimes unrealistic porportions and that these products bear a relationship to the kinds of action taken.

EFFECTS OF INTERACTION CHARACTERISTICS

Within the body of scholarship examining the effects of the characteristics of group interaction, one line has focused on communication/outcome relationships, with communication usually being the independent variable. Often, however, this body of research starts with an outcome difference and treats communication as a dependent variable. The other line of research has reflected more of a concern with the manner in which interaction evolves in the course of group discussion.

COMMUNICATION/GROUP OUTCOME RELATIONSHIP

Common in speech communication research on small groups are investigations in which message properties or broader classes of communicative behavior are manipulated to assess a suspected corresponding variation in such outcomes as consensus, group member satisfaction, leadership emergence, source credibility, and quality of discussion. Occasionally, the manipulation of communication variables is accompanied by variation in another member, group, or contextual variable, but more often than not, the characteristics of interaction that are the focus of inquiry are examined in relative isolation.

EVIDENCE AND ORDER OF ARGUMENT. Three studies serve to illustrate the way in which evidence and the effects of the organization of information have been examined in the past. In one investigation, Stone (1969) attempted to determine whether the order in which group members are exposed to evidence affects their decisions. Decisions were based on facts presented in a legal case. He found that final judgments tended to reflect the information to which mock jurors were initially exposed, regardless of the side of the case.

McCroskey, Young, and Scott (1972) varied both message sideness and the amount of information given to discussants in an effort to test certain assumptions about which of the two factors most effectively contributes to resistance to counter-persuasion. Their results indicated that two-sided messages and messages bolstered by evidence had greater impact than those lacking supporting evidence and others presenting only one side of an issue.

Rather than focusing on information to which discussants are exposed,

Hill (1976) was concerned with the content of information. He determined that group members whose assertions are based on factual knowledge are more effective than highly opinionated discussants in contributing to group consensus. In addition, such individuals achieve a higher degree of credibility than their opinionated colleagues.

The dearth of research on the effects of information in decision-making and problem-solving discussions is probably attributable to the fact that most research has been done in laboratory settings with volunteers deliberately chosen for the lack of knowledge and information they bring to the discussion setting. Future inquiries might profit from sacrificing this element of control in the interest of better illuminating the relationship of various dimensions of information and its use to group outcomes.

CONFLICT PRODUCING AND REDUCING COMMUNICATION. Because of the controversial nature of the issues that many problem-solving and decision-making groups discuss, conflict is an almost inevitable fact of group life. Some researchers, therefore, have understandably attempted to identify those behaviors that enter into both the reduction and the production of conflict. Lumsden (1974) studied both agreement and disagreement as they relate to leadership maintenance. Her expectation that appointed leaders who express frequent agreement would receive more reinforcement, be perceived higher in credibility, and contribute more to consensus than appointed leaders expressing disagreement received substantial empirical support.

Conflict-producing communication of the kind suggested by Lumsden's work with disagreement has been the object of attention in several investigations. Harnack (1963) found that dissenters in decision-making discussions were able to influence the judgment of others, especially when they had become the targets of abusive communication. Bradley, Hamon, and Harris (1976) also noted evidence of deviant influence when expressions of disagreement with a majority position were grounded in knowledge of the issues and specific factual information. Contributing further to the notion that conflict-producing communication per se is not necessarily damaging is research by Schultz (1982) showing that discussants trained to be argumentative emerged more frequently as leaders than untrained participants.

The species of communication that Valentine and Fisher (1974) refer to as "innovative deviance" may account for the kinds of effects noted above. Innovative deviance has a constructive dimension that focuses attention on issues. Hence, it, and the cluster of behaviors that serve to define it, is likely to induce what Guetzkow and Gyr (1954) originally called "substantive conflict," that is, differences in positions deriving from a group's agenda. Bell (1974) discovered that statements capable of creating such issue-oriented conflict tend to stimulate other substantive contributions in decision-making discussions. Knutson and Kowitz (1977), moreover, produced evidence establishing that substantive conflict has a facilitative effect on group consensus, particularly when it is accompanied by orientation behavior.

ORIENTATION BEHAVIOR. According to Cragan and Wright (1980), during the 1970s, the communication variable receiving the most concentrated attention in research on groups in speech communication was orientation behavior. Individuals who make a conscious effort to keep a group oriented in the direction of its goal appear to have considerable impact on goal achievement, not to mention others' perceptions of their contributions.

Originally identified by Gouran (1969) as a potential causal factor in the achievement of group consensus, orientation soon thereafter became the object of several inquiries. Studies by Kline (1972), Kline and Hullinger (1973), Knutson (1972), and Knutson and Holdridge (1975) all were generally supportive of the orientation/consensus relationship. McCroskey, Hamilton, and Weiner (1974) additionally detected relationships of orientation to source credibility, homophily, and interpersonal attraction.

LEADERSHIP STYLE. In attempting to provide orientation in a group discussion, to some extent, one helps structure interaction into a meaningful pattern of assault upon issues. The extent to which this sort of structuring style of leadership exists has consequences for the outcomes a group achieves.

Jurma (1978, 1979) conducted two experiments aimed at more precise identification of these effects. In the first, he varied both style and task clarity. The results indicated that group members were more satisfied with a structuring style of leadership than they were with a nonstructuring style, regardless of the clarity of the task. The investigator presumed that satisfaction would be relatively low under the structuring style when a group's task requirements were clear and relatively high when they were ambiguous.

In his more recent study, Jurma tested both the structuring and the nonstructuring styles of leadership when group members differed in terms of task orientation. For highly task-oriented group members, the style of leadership to which they were subjected made little difference on either their performance or their reported levels of satisfaction. In the case of participants low in task orientation, however, the structuring style proved superior on measures of both quality and satisfaction.

Downs and Pickett (1977) further remind us of the situational nature of the effects of leadership style in a study showing that the compatibility of group members, in part, determines whether a structuring or a nonstructuring style of leadership is appropriate. Their data revealed that groups compatible in respect to "overpersonal" members were more productive and better satisfied under the structuring style. In the case of "underpersonal"/compatible and "underpersonal"/incompatible groups, style of leadership showed no relationship to either productivity or satisfaction.

PROBLEM-SOLVING AGENDAS AND FORMATS. Whereas most of the research involving the structuring of interaction has dealt with situations in which the manner of structuring has been left to confederates, a small portion has been concerned with the consequences of prescribed approaches to discussion. In one case, Bayless (1967) compared groups following a reflective-thinking model, brainstorming, and the program evaluation and review technique. Although the three types of groups did not differ in terms of the quality of their solutions, brainstorming conditions resulted in more ideas than did the reflective-thinking conditions. Brainstorming groups also produced a higher frequency of good ideas than either reflective-thinking or PERT groups.

In a similar inquiry, Larson (1969) compared groups using four different problem-solving patterns: no pattern, single question form, ideal solution form, and reflective-thinking form. Of these, the "single question" and "ideal solution" formats yielded the highest percentages of correct solutions to an industrial relations problem.

Dealing with creative problem-solving techniques exclusively, Jablin, Seibold, and Sorenson (1977) compared brainstorming with nominal groups that were also varied in respect to their members' levels of communication apprehension. Presumably, interacting groups have an inhibiting influence on creative problem-solving, yet these researchers' results did little to substantiate this claim. There was no significant difference between the two types of groups in the number of ideas generated. In the brainstorming condition, however, participants low in communication apprehension produced more ideas than those with high apprehension.

In a follow-up study, Jablin (1981) found nominal groups to be superior to brainstorming groups in idea generation. This time, communication apprehension showed no effect. Philipsen, Mulac, and Dietrich (1979) also reported finding evidence of detrimental effects of interaction in brainstorming groups. Since the time allotted for idea generation was not equivalent in the brainstorming and nominal group conditions, however, one cannot attribute the difference in idea production exclusively to the inhibiting effects of interaction.

Using a different approach to the investigation of problem-solving patterns, Hirokawa (1982b) developed instructions for "vigilant" information processing on the basis of Janis and Mann's (1977) discussion of the concept. For instructed groups, the correlation between consensus and quality of decisions was significantly higher than it was among uninstructed groups.

Outcome Based Research

The research on communication/outcome relationships reviewed to this point has varied communication characteristics or mechanisms designed to produce variation in communication in the interest of examining concomitant differences in group outcomes. Another group of scholars began with differences in group outcomes and then looked for variations in the communication of the participants. Several classes of variables have been studied in this manner.

Leadership Emergence. One of the first investigations in speech communication reflecting the outcome-based approach was conducted by Geier (1967). Working with 16 continuing task-oriented groups, he was able to distinguish emergent leaders from unsuccessful contenders in a number of respects. Those who failed to survive the process of elimination had a history of hindering goal achievement, engaging in offensive verbalizations, being rigid and authoritarian, and talking incessantly.

Gouran and Geonetta (1977a) were also interested in leadership emergence under conditions in which the acknowledged leader was the individual perceived by other group members as having exercised the most influence in a decision-making discussion. Comparing such groups with others in which influence was evenly distributed revealed that groups in the emergent condition engaged in more amplification of ideas, made more requests for amplification, did more to acknowledge their understanding of what members were saying, provided less information, and made fewer multi-functional statements.

Discussion Quality and Effectiveness. In one of several studies stimulated by an interest in the quality of decision making, Gouran, Brown, and Henry (1978) observed strong positive relationships between a measure of perceived quality and several behavioral attributes that included addressing relevant issues, analysis of issues, amplification of contributions, making goal-directed statements, using and testing evidence, performing necessary leadership functions, promoting interpersonal relations, and maintaining an even distribution of participation. Later research by Harper and Askling was supportive of some of these findings. In their study, groups with high-quality products had a higher quality of leadership, more open communication, and a higher proportion of active participants than groups whose task products were judged to be of low quality.

Hirokawa (1980) pursued the question of what distinguishes groups that make effective decisions by focusing on instrumental functions of communication. His analysis revealed that in effective groups procedural statements providing direction were followed by agreement with greater than chance frequency. The pattern was not evident in the communicative behavior of ineffective groups.

In another study, Hirokawa (1983) correlated ratings of the quality of solutions generated by decision-making groups with the occurrence of five communication functions. Quality correlated positively with the category "analysis of the problem" and negatively with "operating procedures." Apparently, the more energy a group must invest in the procedures it will follow, the less it expends on other functions necessary for reaching effective decisions.

CONSENSUS. Identifying difference in the communicative behavior of groups achieving and failing to achieve consensus was the objective in research by Gouran (1969) and Gouran and Geonetta (1977b). Although the behavior of these two types of groups was not consistently distinguishable, when it was, Gouran's analysis indicated that groups reaching consensus made statements that were more informative, provocative, and objective than those of non-consensus groups. Consensus groups were also less opinionated and provided more orientation.

Gouran and Geonetta discovered that the contributions made by members of consensus and non-consensus groups do not differ as much in kind as in the ways they are related. Sequences of statements in non-consensus groups reflected a nearly random pattern. At least, they failed to differ from the pattern suggested by the overall distribution of comments. Groups achieving consensus, on the other hand, exhibited predictability among various categories of interaction. This was especially true in the case of statements amplifying themes and those providing information.

CHOICE SHIFT. Following in the mode of the two preceding studies, Cline and Cline (1980) investigated differences between groups shifting to risk and to caution in discussions of choice dilemma problems. They were interested in testing the plausibility of the diffusion of responsibility explanation. Support would be reflected in the amount of self-referential language, with less occurring in the groups shifting toward risk. The difference was significant and in the expected direction.

GROUP MEMBER SATISFACTION. Gouran (1973b) attempted to identify sources of variation in the levels of satisfaction reported by members of decision-making groups. Significant correlates included members' perceptions of the quality of their own performance, perceptions of the quality of other members' performance, and the frequency of one's contributions.

The Evolution of Communication in Groups

Before the 1960s, nearly all research on groups done in speech communication was based on an input-output model that ignored the fact that what is being said at any given point in a discussion is both a partial consequence of what has previously transpired and a partial determinant of what follows. With the pioneering work of Scheidel and Crowell (1964) on idea development, a newer view began to gain currency.

In their research, Scheidel and Crowell attempted to determine how the characteristics of thought units expressed in a discussion influence the probability that thought units of the same or other kinds will follow. In the groups studied, a recurrent ideational pattern emerged. The pattern was identified as clarification-acceptance-further clarification; substantiation-acceptance-further substantiation. To Scheidel and Crowell, such recurrences suggested a helixlike process by which group consensus develops.

As more scholars became interested in the contingent nature of communication in groups, different lines of inquiry began to appear. The most conspicuous ones reflect concerns about three topics: phases of group development, feedback effects, and interaction sequences.

PHASES OF GROUP DEVELOPMENT. Fisher (1970a) appears to have been the first person in speech communication to deal with the phases through which groups pass in their efforts to reach decisions. In his original research on this question, Fisher observed that decision-making groups rather consistently exhibit a pattern of (1) getting acquainted and clarifying and expressing attitudes; (2) dispute over decision proposals; (3) dissipation of conflict and argument and the emergence of an acceptable decision proposal; and (4) reinforcement of the group choice. In further analyses of the same data (see Fisher, 1970b, 1979), communication revealed that groups do not progress steadily toward final decisions and that the four content dimensions originally identified appear to be distinguishable in terms of the relationship dimensions of a group's interaction.

Following Fisher's research and the development of the "Interact System Model" (see Fisher & Hawes, 1971) came a series of reports demonstrating phasic development in group communication. Among these was a case study of a consciousness-raising group by Chesebro, Cragan, and McCullough (1973) showing four stages: (1) acceptance of a new identity; (2) recognition of an antagonistic relationship to the establishment; (3) rejection of establishment values; and (4) identification with a larger community. Ellis and Fisher (1975) pointed to a three-phase development of conflict in decision-making groups, including an interpersonal, confrontation, and substantive stage. Mabry's (1975a) work with task-oriented groups yielded a four-phase model consisting of latency, adaptation, integration, and goal attainment. In encounter groups, recurrent phases are represented by boundary-seeking, ambivalence, and actualization (see Mabry, 1975b).

As research in this area continued, the notion that groups consistently exhibit the same phasic structure started to undergo challenge. In the case of consciousness raising particularly, Ellis (1979) questioned the generalizability of the research by Chesebro, Cragan, and McCullough (1974) when the same phases identified failed to surface in another similar case study. Poole (1981), moreover, produced evidence supporting a multiple-phase model by applying it and the then dominant unitary-phase model to the same data. The groups included did not for the most part manifest the same phasic patterns.

FEEDBACK EFFECTS. As an outgrowth of their 1964 study, Scheidel and Crowell (1966) became interested in feedback, which they defined as "that event in which any participant (X) initiates a comment which is followed by a comment from any other participant (Y) which in turn is followed immediately by a further comment from the first participant (X)" (p. 274). Concern with this variable lay primarily in discovering the frequency of the sequence (35 percent of all discussion activity in the sample), what its content features are in decision-making discussions (clarification in early stages and agreement in later stages), and its primary function (making consensus explicit before turning to new issues).

Other scholars subsequently began to examine additional characteristics of feedback and its effects. Leathers (1969), for example, focused on disruptive contributions. Responses to high-level abstractions were confused, tense, and withdrawn. Responses to implicit inferences Leathers found to be signal, irrelevant, and digressive. Finally, responses to the class of disruptions called facetious interpolations were personal and inflexible.

In a later study, Leathers (1970) examined the effects of trust-destroying behavior on feedback. Using a specially developed feedback rating instrument (see Leathers, 1971), he detected marked alterations in responses to group participants who had been trained to make trust-destroying statements after having spent half a discussion engaged in trust-building. Significant decreases occurred in the extent to which feedback reflected the properties of deliberateness, relevancy, atomization, fidelity, tension, ideation, flexibility, and involvement. With the same data, Prentice (1975) detected a marked increase in non-fluencies following the initiation of trust-destroying behavior.

INTERACTION SEQUENCES. The final body of scholarship reviewed in this essay reflects an interest in the degree of structure present in the interaction of discussion groups. Structure in this context is an evolutionary product of the ways in which group members' contributions shape and are shaped by one another. Following the method first introduced by Scheidel and Crowell (1964), Stech (1970) drew on information theory statistics and determined that the classification of any utterance in a problem-solving discussion has better than chance predictability—at least, in the case of the ranking task employed.

Building on Stech's effort, other researchers (some of whom have already been cited in other connections) attempted to assess the predictability of interaction sequences in different species of discussion groups. Gouran and Baird (1972) compared informal group discussions with the problem-solving variety and observed more sequential structure among informal groups. Saine and Bock (1973b), while uncovering evidence of sequential structure in both high and low consensus groups, nevertheless obtained differences in the relative predictability of particular types of sequences. Baird's (1974) findings revealed more structure in the communication of cooperatively oriented groups than in competitive groups. Finally, Donohue, Hawes, and Mabee (1981) employed Baird's results and developed a predictive model of the most-to-least-probable interact relationships one could expect in cooperative groups seeking consensus. Their data revealed a substantial correlation between expected and observed rank orderings.

A serious problem with much of the research on interaction structure has been the idiosyncratic character of the classification schemes. Stech (1975, 1977) has further suggested that the degree of predictability of interaction sequences varies as a function of the number and type of content categories, interactant roles, and the nature of a group's task. Most serious is Hewes' (1979) observation that virtually all of the research done with the sequential analysis of social interaction has lacked a theoretical foundation from which to determine the sort of structuring one should anticipate. For these reasons, our ability to draw meaningful conclusions about the manner in which communication in groups evolves is limited.

FULFILLING THE PROMISE

As this review shows, research on groups in speech communication has followed many paths. And although individual studies have each helped illuminate the determinants and effects of communicative behavior, the intricacies of overall processes remain to be unraveled. Of all the scholarship surveyed, that dealing with the evolution of communication perhaps is closest in spirit to the description of the paradigm in Figure 6.2. Nevertheless, researchers working in this area appear to be singularly unconcerned with member and group factors and with differences in outcomes that groups achieve.

The paradigm that has developed is potentially very useful. Fulfilling its promise, however, will require theorizing at a level to which researchers in our field are not accustomed. Until those designing studies begin reflecting more thoughtfully on the ways in which all classes of variables affecting group processes are interconnected, the prospects for accumulating integratable knowledge will remain more a hope than a reality.

To this point in our history, the challenge of enlarging our understanding of communication in groups has been addressed on a methodological level. But the application of sophisticated research tools does not strike at the basic problem, which is that we have simply not worked hard enough to develop the necessary theoretical premises from which to derive the consequences that become the objects of our research. Such premises would consist of statements identifying the manner in which particular sets of member and group characteristics contribute to the content and form of utterances, how these utterances shape larger patterns of interaction, and how the resulting patterns, in turn, affect the end states at which groups arrive.

In the past, it was possible to argue that we did not have sufficient empirical grounding for theoretical speculation to be useful. At present, however, that position seems to be less well justified. To the extent that this chapter has produced an inventory of some of the more significant empirical findings, the difficulty of generating more theoretically well-founded inquiries, I hope, has been reduced.

6

Stalking Interpersonal Communication Effectiveness: Social, Individual, or Situational Integration?

WILLIAM K. RAWLINS

Of concern here is the development of interpersonal communication as a subdiscipline of the speech communication field. In order to identify developmental trends in interpersonal communication scholarship, I perused every issue of each journal published by the Speech Communication Association, the International Communication Association, and the four regional communication associations. The investigation was then necessarily narrowed. Though work on conversation began to appear in the late 1920s (Howes, 1928; Oliver, 1932), much of the impetus for the speech field's interest in interpersonal communication arose during the 1930s from the human relations movement out of the Harvard Graduate School of Business Administration and the general semantics movement started by Alfred Korzybski (1933). Both movements emphasized the practical utility and psychological significance of spoken language in everyday interactions between people.

Consequently, one issue of generic importance in speech journals that emerges in the 1940s and continues to the present is what constitutes effective face-to-face communication. I studied the theoretical essays addressing this topic over the past four decades from programmatic, conceptual, and pedagogical points of view. Thus, what will be presented here is an examination of how the concept of interpersonal communication effectiveness has changed since the 1940s in the field of speech communication.

The notion of "communication effectiveness" implies that someone successfully accomplishes interpersonal objectives by employing interactional means. After surveying the literature on the subject, it became clear that authors had various views regarding what the proper goals, or ends, of interpersonal communication should be; and what means, or methods, were appropriate for conducting face-to-face interaction. Several themes regarding the preferred means and ends of interpersonal communication were common to most of the essays, though the authors disagreed widely on these issues. The most prevalent themes have been systematized here as dimensions for examining differing formulations of the appropriate means and goals of effective interpersonal communication.

I have used three major dimensions to distinguish the conceptions of communicative goals: Should we employ interpersonal interaction primarily to achieve communal or individual objectives? Should we use interpersonal communication principally to influence other persons or to achieve understanding? And, a final consideration based on authors' implied earmark of effective communication, What is the characteristic quality of an effective converser?

The recommended means for interaction comprise three continua. Should interpersonal interaction follow social conventions or idiosyncratic rules? Should communicators employ communication skills (technique) or appropriate attitudes toward communication? Should people engage in persuasion or promote each other's individual freedom?

The authors' characteristic positions on the above dimensions changed over time in the journals. The varying conceptions of these goals and means can be clustered thematically in three distinguishable, yet overlapping, developmental periods of thinking about interpersonal effectiveness that may be termed the eras of social integration, individual integration, and situational integration.

The boundaries between these periods are somewhat arbitrary. Each era is not necessarily a "specific and unitary form" which encompasses all the writings in its respective time frame (Feldman & Toulmin, 1976). Rather, I argue that the positions on fundamental issues in conceptualizing communication effectiveness are connected by "overlapping sets of resemblances" during the eras discussed (Feldman & Toulmin, 1976). We intend for the three periods to provide a basis for recognizing these "overlapping sets of resemblances" that document the qualitative changes in patterns of theorizing about effective interpersonal communication.

I recognize limitations in presenting this report. First, it is virtually impossible to trace how ideas circulate in society. The precise interplay between scholarly acceptance of a conception of communicating and its widespread social adoption is difficult to pin down. Second, only the scholarly journals of the associations already indicated comprise the text for this analysis. This is admittedly an arbitrarily closed system since important publications are consequently ignored. Nevertheless, these journals serve as primary outlets for articles regarding effective interpersonal communication and therefore provide a reasonable sample for investigating the growth of the interpersonal communication subfield. Third, the description provided here constitutes a "reconstructed logic" that synthesizes in ideal-typical fashion the "logics-in-use" (Kaplan, 1964) of many different authors. I do not intend to imply that these writers necessarily or consciously theorized in the manner specified but that their efforts can be so ordered in retrospect. Even so, the attempt to characterize anything as complex and encompassing as scholarly eras is likely to resemble a caricature in some respects.

The *social integration* era ranges from the early 1940s to the dawning 1960s. Its rubric is conformism, and a synoptic question for effective communicators in this period is, What communicative practices serve society, or the group, primarily and individuals secondarily? The *individual integration* era begins in the mid-1950s and remains influential in the 1980s. Its rubric is one of idealism/humanism and a summary question for this period is, What communicative practices liberate individuals for personal growth? The *situational integration* era commences in the early 1970s, and its favored means and ends increasingly characterize discussions of effective interpersonal communication in the 1980s. This emerging epoch's rubric appears to be pragmatism, and its representative question is, What communicative practices prosper the self primarily while acknowledging social requirements?

I shall evaluate each period's particular conception of goals by examining its communal versus individual emphasis and its stress upon influence versus understanding. I shall also consider each era's distinctive earmark of effective communication. The favored means of an era will be assessed by analyzing its emphasis upon social conventions versus idiosyncratic rules, communication skills versus attitudes towards communication, and persuasion versus individual freedom. I shall then discuss a tendency for compensatory theorizing noted in the literature and consider the issue of interactional control as an indepth example. Finally, I shall draw my conclusions regarding the perceived relativism in conceptions of interpersonal effectiveness. Let us now survey how emphasizing various goals for communication differentiates the scholarly eras.

CHANGING GOALS FOR EFFECTIVE INTERPERSONAL COMMUNICATION

COMMUNAL VERSUS INDIVIDUAL INTERESTS

Since the 1940s specific ends have been prescribed or implied by people assessing communicative effectiveness. A gradient of socially, then individually, then situationally justified outcomes appears in the literature. We can track these conceptual changes by focusing on the issue of whether communication should serve primarily communal or individual interests. Although early general semanticists initially discussed public speaking, they soon shifted their attention to interpersonal discourse and its purposes. In either case, however, efficacious communicators were seen as those who achieved social, not personal, goals. Murray (1940, p. 75) stated forcefully, "To the extent which any phase of speech facilitates social integration the speech is correct speech and good speech; to the extent that any phase of the speech interferes with social integration, regardless of its technical perfection in other phases, it is poor speech."

Murray's position was consistent with Follett's (1924) arguments for integration of transcendent social goals in decision-making and the speech field's near infatuation with the "discussional attitude." The ideal discussant was seen as a person motivated to agree, ready to relinquish personal preferences for the group's welfare, and prepared to submit individual goals to group goals (Rawlins, 1984). A larger specter loomed, however, that advanced the cause of social integration among students of communication. Several writers equated individual effectiveness with manipulation and demogoguery. In journals of communication this was apparently a reaction to Adolf Hitler (Lee, 1940; Schlauch, 1942; Murray, 1944, 1951; Lillywhite, 1952). Ironically, an abhorrent individual led the writers to promulgate standards evaluating adroit, self-serving speech as always socially undesirable. The favored communicative end in this era was promoting social goals.

The communal focus, with its attendant concern for social justifications, diminshed sharply in the era of *individual integration*. The goal for communicators now was portrayed as supporting each other in personal quests for integration of selves (Barnlund, 1962; Johannesen, 1971; Williams, 1973; Stewart, 1978; Ritter, 1977; Pearce, 1977). By providing mutual supportiveness, interactants could establish communicative contexts within which each participant would find enhancement and development of his/her creative, individualized self (Poulakos, 1974; Wise, 1972). The "special worth" of individuals was a prevalent concern in this era (Gibb, 1961); writers conceived of effective communication as a "humanizing force" (Ilardo, 1972).

The emphasis on supportiveness dwindles in the *situational integration* period. Within the perspectives of this period the skilled interactant accomplishes his/her individual purposes in changing and constraining communal circumstances. Social considerations are treated as largely regulatory. For example, Cegala (1981, p. 110) observes, "The competent communicator is able to achieve personal objectives and to do so within socially acceptable parameters." Wiemann, in turn, describes proficient speech in the relational context. "The competent communicator is the person who can have his way in the relationship while maintaining a mutually acceptable definition of that relationship. This notion of competence becomes especially meaningful when the temporal aspects of relationships are considered" (1977, p. 198). In short, in this era effective communication is seen as mediating individual and social concerns within specific situations, with consequences for each party involved being of primary interest to a participant or an observer of interpersonal exchanges.

INFLUENCE VERSUS UNDERSTANDING

A second dimension of differential emphasis involves the extent to which scholars perceive the function of interpersonal communication as influencing other persons or facilitating understanding between people. Though these are not mutually exclusive consequences of speaking, they have received neither uniform nor balanced stress across the three eras.

Scholars disagreed on this influence/understanding issue during the *social integration* era. Those under the spell of Korzybski spoke adamantly of a world where clarity of communication, not suasion, would produce social betterment. Lee (1940, p. 601) argued, "Hitler-Aristotle would teach you how to use words skillfully for 'effect'—Korzybski would teach you how to use words carefully for their *fitness with facts*." The salutory product of communication for Murray was a "meeting of minds." He stipulated, "the function of speech, its true function, and perhaps its only justifiable function. That function is that speech should serve as a social integrator; as the tools which enable attention to be obtained, comprehending and understanding to result, experience to be shared in this meeting of minds mentioned" (1940, p. 75).

Hellman (1945), however, in an argument directed against "the discussional attitude," maintained that speech teachers must continue to teach the ethical forms of persuasion. He maintained that these skills usually achieved results in a real democracy. Thus, while promoting understanding and facilitating proper evaluation (Murray, 1944) were clearly gaining recognition during this era, using speech to influence remained an important objective. Even so, there was widespread agreement that whether one aimed to influence or produce understanding via speech, the ultimate result should benefit society.

To share meanings and thereby engender understanding was of cardinal importance in the *individual integration* era (Gibb, 1961; Ilardo, 1972; Johannesen, 1971). Ilardo (1972, p. 5), for example, in his rationale for interpersonal communication stressed "understanding rather than control, sensitivity rather than influence, [and] interaction rather than one-way communication." Effective interpersonal influence was downplayed as it was associated with manipulation of others or with hidden motivations, both of which were negatively perceived (Gibb, 1961). Gorman (1967, p. 45) summed up the characteristic attitude toward influence in this era, stating, "Perhaps true communication is really sharing of perceptions in which both communicators spend more time in being open to each other than in trying to persuade each other. This may change the notion of rhetoric and the art of persuasion." Such an outlook did undermine the notion of interpersonal influence, but only temporarily.

A pragmatic concern with a given communicator purposefully influencing others in his/her social surroundings and reconciling individual and social objectives in the given case seems to characterize the emerging *situational integration* era (Hart & Burks, 1972; Phillips, 1976). Bochner and Kelly (1974) asserted effectance motivation as an important human attribute. They argued that "every human being is motivated to interact effectively with his environment; the drive to be interpersonally competent is the drive to produce effects on or to influence one's world" (1974, pp. 286–287). This view clearly challenges the passive or muted rhetorical stance of the previous era. Indeed, an individual's goals may include establishing an understanding with another person, but such comprehension may also be a functional part of influencing him/her. Deciding to influence someone in the situational era is viewed as a practical, circumstantially based choice, and accomplishing this goal frequently serves as a reason for attributing competence to a person (Wiemann, 1977; Cronen, Pearce & Harris, 1979; Cegala, 1981).

EARMARKS OF EFFECTIVE COMMUNICATION

Each period's earmark of effective communication corresponds closely to its particular emphasis regarding communal versus individual goals and influence versus understanding as communicative objectives. Thus, health was the stamp of the able communicator during the social integration era; but it was a normative, social conception (Kidd, 1975). Perhaps the root sources of this health metaphor in the speech field were Korzybski's preoccupations in *Science and Sanity* and Murray's concern with the normality of the speaker (1937). In any event, health in this period meant personal adjustment and adaptation to society's expectations accomplished through capable communication.

Health also characterized the effective conversant in the era of individual integration, but the specific conception differed. To be healthy was to aspire to, if not achieve, self-actualization (Wise, 1972; Poulakos, 1974; Macklin & Rossiter, 1976; Ritter, 1977; Pearce, 1977). The social adjuster of the prior era was transformed into a super-individual. The period's notions of effective interpersonal communication were the means for attaining this goal and presumably what its accomplishment represented. These means will be considered below.

The earmark of the situational integration era is competence. The competent communicator appropriately and effectively uses speech in various situations (Bochner & Kelly, 1974; Wiemann, 1977; McCroskey, 1982). In a competence conception the communicator's personal goals are highlighted but their fulfillment is regulated and judged by social strictures. Though the health metaphor has been abandoned for more practical terminology, competence still retains a normative quality. For a summary of the three eras' views on the goals of effective interpersonal communication, see Table 6.1.

CHANGING MEANS FOR EFFECTIVE INTERPERSONAL COMMUNICATION

In addition to their favored goals for interaction, the three eras under consideration can be distinguished according to their specified means for achieving interpersonal communication effectiveness. The pertinent dimensions for analysis include social conventions vs. idiosyncratic rules; communication skills vs. attitudes toward communication, and its complement, public speaking vs. personal speaking; and persuasion vs. individual freedom.

Table 6.1
Changing Goals for Effective Interpersonal Communication

Goals	Social Integration Era	Individual Integration Era	Situational Integration Era
Communal vs. Individual	Promote social goals	Provide mutual supportiveness	Mediate individual and social concerns
Influence vs. Understanding	Socially justified influence/ understanding	Understanding	Personally justified influence/ understanding
Earmark of effective communication	"Health," defined as personal adjustment	"Health," defined as self-actualization	"Competence" defined as appropriate achievement of goals

SOCIAL CONVENTIONS VERSUS IDIOSYNCRATIC RULES

Adherence to social conventions was celebrated both as a means for and as a desirable goal of interpersonal communication during the social integration era. Cooperating, having a conciliatory attitude, adapting to, and adjusting to others in a civil society were favored practices that were felt to produce positive results (Oliver, 1932; Murray, 1938; Allison, 1939; Snidecor, 1942; Lebo, 1959). Since cultural norms and conventions provided consensually shared bases for conversational coherence and social integration, then, for the most part, to communicate effectively was to use appropriate and customary forms. This position began to change during the era, however, because of increasing scholarly interchange between human relations theorists and general semanticists in the speech field (Tompkins, 1965).

A credo stressing the uniqueness of persons heralded the *individual integration* era (Oliver, 1957; Gibb, 1961; Johannesen, 1971; Stewart, 1972). Consequently, those cultural norms previously thought so necessary for preserving social order were now viewed as excessively controlling and stifling individual growth and self-expression (Gibb, 1961). Many social conventions governing interaction were rejected, and idiosyncratic rules became suitable guides for communicative behavior. According to these scholars, individuals could transcend the hollow roles and faceless impersonality of middle-class, post-industrial America by developing their own practices and standards for communicating in open, supportive, understanding, and truly personal relationships (Gibb, 1961; Johannesen, 1971; Stewart, 1972; Ilardo, 1972; Keller & Brown, 1968; Poulakos, 1974). Such a negotiated, communicative context would best facilitate the development of self (Kidd, 1975).

The situational integration era's stand on the present dimension emerged rather gradually but is now quite distinct. Effective communicators should observe situational requirements; both social conventions and idiosyncratic rules bear on every encounter between people (Hart & Burks, 1972; Bochner & Kelly, 1974; Sillars, 1974; Wiemann, 1977, Johnson, 1979; Cronen, Pearce & Harris, 1979). To a degree, individuals in a relationship arrange permitted conversational forms and content between particular individuals, but they are also unavoidably contextualized by an encompassing social order and historical precedents. For example, Johnson (1979, p. 14) quotes Wood's definition of communicative competence as "the mastery of an underlying set of appropriateness rules—which are determined by culture and situation—that affect the verbal and nonverbal choices in communication events." Accordingly, the proficient converser must have a sense of both the emergent and the conventional factors shaping his/her interaction with others and produce messages in light of this awareness.

A burgeoning interest in the developmental patterns of communication in enduring relationships also characterizes the transition to the situational integration era (Berger & Calabrese, 1975; Bochner, 1978; Miller, 1978; Wood, 1982). This emphasis appears to synthesize the individual integration era's stress upon communicating in personal, growth-producing relationships and the later period's concern with a given communicator monitoring the social conventions and idiosyncratic rules guiding specific interactions. Examining communication in the developmental stages of a relationship therefore fuses preoccupations of both eras into a conception with implications for situationally appropriate and effective communication in an abiding relationship with a significant other.

COMMUNICATION SKILLS VERSUS ATTITUDES TOWARD COMMUNICATION

An artificial distinction inheres in the dimension communication skills (technique) versus attitudes toward communication. While various communicative techniques constitute the embodiment of attitudes (e.g. empathizing), certain attitudes toward communicating can also function as techniques (e.g. flexibility). We contrast the two concepts, however, for purposes of analysis. Closely associated with this dimension are the three eras' particular views on public speaking in relation to personal speaking. This issue will be considered in conjunction with the skills vs. attitudes question across the periods.

Both speaking skills and attitudes toward the process were stressed in the *social integration* period insofar as they furthered social cohesion. During this era public speaking, according to time-honored rhetorical principles, served as a presupposed "first affirmative" against which a case developed for accentuating more genuine and open attitudes toward speaking in a variety of situations (Murray, 1940, 1944; Paul, Sorensen & Murray, 1946; Rarig, 1948). However, writers did not uniformly support this emphasis upon attitudes. For example, while agreeing with the superordinate goal of social integration, Snidecor (1942, p. 5) vigorously questioned stressing attitudes to the neglect of "the older, thorough approach to skills." He argued that "in shifting to the more important human values of speech, the adjusters and integrators had their eye on the ball, but they tended to forget that acquisition of even the simpler speech skills constituted an *adaptive* and *integrative* process (1942, p. 3). . . . Any technique for increased adaptation is *adjustive* whether that technique is towards the acquisition of insight into one's attitudes or the development of one's fundamental skills" (1942, p. 6). Thus, he still considered basic speaking skills essential.

Even so, the human relations movement out of the Harvard School of Business Administration along with its concern for assuaging individuals' "ego-needs" (Tompkins, 1965) spurred interest in personal interaction as opposed to public speaking. Murray (1940, p. 76) argued, "If speech is to serve human relations and social integration the common everyday conversation in the ordinary living of the student must be the point of chief emphasis of speech teaching and the speech teacher." Later in the period Holm (1960, p. 19) stated the need for an interpersonal focus and a rejection of traditional speech principles in favor of human relations. "Teachers of speech face a challenge to teach effective speaking in interpersonal, face-to-face situations, wherein the normal doctrines of rhetoric do not fully apply. They face a challenge to teach good human relations in action."

Overall, a shift from a preoccupation with public speaking guided by traditional rhetorical principles and general semantics to a growing fascination with conversation in face-to-face circumstances informed by both general semantics and the personalized attitudes of human relations occurred during the social integration era.

Humanistic and personalized attitudes toward communication were the watchwords of the *individual integration* era. By and large, writers downplayed techniques for interacting with people unless they embodied these attitudes. They viewed the "technique for communicating" orientation as highly impersonal in origin, as objectifying persons, and as reducing potentially creative encounters with human beings to a pat array of guidelines. Ogle (1955, p. 108) reported that a participant returned from the National Training Laboratory at Bethel, Maine, with "certain techniques and information he did not have before, but their importance is minimal compared to the new feelings, attitudes, and social orientations he acquires. The point made there is that these personality traits are of greater value in working with and leading other people than the most logically developed structure of do-and-don't rules and procedures for manipulating people." Much more important than techniques were attitudes toward communicating, such as genuineness, spontaneity, openness, and mutuality (Gibb, 1961; Gorman, 1967; Johannesen, 1971; Ilardo, 1972; Stewart, 1972; Flynn & Williams, 1976). Later on, Mehrley and Backes (1972, p. 208) suggested that if someone possessed suitable attitudes toward communicating, then he/she may make worthwhile use of technique. "But," they stated, "one's skills and techniques are rarely any more effective than his understanding of and attitudes toward the basic process."

Public speaking, associated with age-old techniques, a specific type of impersonal context, one-way communication, and influence on listeners, lost its luster in the individual integration era. As an embodiment of a formalized approach to communicating, public speaking was considered out of step with the preferred means and ends of the period and was contrasted with interpersonal communication (Ilardo, 1972). Observed Ilardo, "Moreover, public speaking places somewhat more emphasis on technique and method than does interpersonal communication. Such technique, while providing some hope for personal integration ("if I exert control over others by employing such-and-such a method, I will achieve a sense of self-hood"), is ultimately empty" (1972, p. 5).

Personalized speaking as opposed to public speaking became the order of the day. Keller and Brown (1968, p. 76) advanced an interpersonal ethic for communication the essence of which was that "the ethics of communication may have more to do with signs concerning the attitude of the speaker and the listener toward each other than with the elements of the message or channel involved. It may be that the central question in ethics does not concern so much one's loyalty to rationality, or cosmic truth, as it does loyalty to the person with whom one is in communication."

Basing an ethic of communication on loyalty to the other person was consistent with concerns held during the individual integration era that caring human beings promote each other's growth. Effective interpersonal communication was to conform to this ethic. Presumably, people could fulfill this ethical standard underpinning communication effectiveness in ongoing personal relationships away from the impersonal constraints of role-based interactions. Johannesen (1971, p. 381) wrote of dialogue, the epitome of the ethic in question. "One might speculate that dialogue is most likely in private, two-person, face-to-face, oral communication situations that extend, even intermittently, over lengthy periods of time." Indeed, these conditions seem requisite for such loyalty to be functional.

Grounding an ethic of communication on loyalty to the other person thoroughly personalized the process of face-to-face interaction and is quite reflective of the period. This position was consistent with a pervasive orientation that siphoned off attention from many of the diverse and necessary interactions between individuals in the public realm where such personal loyalty may be an unrealistic expectation or an unjustifiable risk or both. Nonetheless, emphasizing appropriately humanistic attitudes and communication in personal relationships remains a prevalent orientation today.

The *situational integration* era stresses communication skills along with an astute attitude of situationally appropriate communication. One of the clearest harbingers of the situational outlook was Hart and Burks' article on rhetorical sensitivity with its argument for circumstantially adept communicative technique. The authors (1972, p. 81) state that "interpersonal relationships seem to be most productive when situationally-based rhetorical strategies are employed rather than approaches which result from a rigid mind-set." In a later footnote they add, "In some cases it is probably a matter of poor technique which causes some of us to incur censure for attempting to make our views socially palatable" (1972, p. 85). Effective communication for Hart and Burks stems from knowing "the how," from being able to identify various ways of producing telling messages in every circumstance.

More recently, Rubin defines communication competence as "the ability to use language to communicate within a specific situation," and adds that "in educational systems the concept is a relatively new way of describing old concepts—basic skills" (1982, p. 19). Whether the term used is technique, competence, or skills, the stigma previously associated with employing rhetorically grounded principles in interpersonal communication is rapidly dissipating in the current period.

Accompanying this shift back to an emphasis on technique is the attitude of communicating appropriately in the given case. It is a socially realistic appropriateness, however, in contrast to the idealistic and unhampered caring for and supportiveness of the other comprising humanistic attitudes toward interaction. Thus, if a lofty, perhaps naive, connotation for proper attitudes toward communication characterized the prior epoch, the emerging usage contains a mundane, even shrewd suggestion.

An interplay of traditional rhetorical principles and personalized speaking occurs in the present epoch. In response to the piece by Ilardo quoted earlier, Jandt (1974) asserted that interpersonal communication complemented public speaking in a "traditional speech communication discipline." This view of public and private speaking as counterparts seems to be achieving wider acceptance. Several writers advocate using patently rhetorical techniques to accomplish goals in a variety of interpersonal settings, including intimacy (Hart & Burks, 1972; Sillars, 1974; Jandt, 1974; Phillips, 1976; Rawlins, 1983).

PERSUASION VERSUS INDIVIDUAL FREEDOM

A fundamental property of human communication is that what may serve as communicative means in one context often may be the desired goal in another, and vice versa. Such is the case with the dimension persuasion-individual freedom. We have already considered influence or persuasion as a potential objective for speakers in the three eras; here we will consider its obvious function as a means for attaining goals. Likewise, people frequently speak with the aim of furthering human freedom, whereas one's individual freedom is also a resource for accomplishing many personal ends.

Interpersonal communication theorists in the *social integration* era *deemphasized persuasion* as a means for aiding society. Influenced by Korzybski, they recommended an extensional orientation toward speaking which attempted to match one's use of language with the "facts" or "reality" being described (Carhart, 1942; Murray, 1944; Hillbruner, 1959). Carhart (1942, p. 335) maintained that "many problems would not arise if men habitually went to facts first and abided by them." Through proper evaluation, speakers were to avoid confusing their emotional and subjective orientations with the "facts" and foisting their resultant conclusions on their listeners (Murray, 1944).

Ideally, social motives superseded individual ones in employing speech. Proficient speaking resulted from fidelity, not strategy, and contributed to the listener's capacity to make informed evaluations and choices. In contrast to prior rhetorical theory's persuasive rudiments, Hillbruner (1959, p. 196) argued that "it might enhance the repute of our times if this generation and those coming after would, in the best sense of the word, be known as the ones who looked to the facts and spoke *truth* to the world."

The means of speaking in the *individual integration* era sustained and reflected individual freedom, growth, and transcendence of social strictures. Gibb's (1961) famous distinctions between supportive and defensive communicative climates characterize the age. Effective conversers were to be descriptive, not evaluative; problem-oriented, not controlling; spontaneous, not strategic; empathizing, not neutral; equal, not superior; and provisional, not certain. Barnlund (1962) also argued for mutual facilitation instead of manipulation. Liberated and liberating communicative practices were favored.

In their interpersonal ethic already mentioned, Keller and Brown (1968, p. 76) argued that "behavior which enhances the basic freedom of response in the individual is more ethical; behavior which either overtly or covertly attacks it is less ethical." If individuals would communicate in a manner enhancing the freedom of each, they would be much more likely to fulfill their potential as people (Keller & Brown, 1968). Thus, respecting and preserving each other's individuality and capacity for choice were essential qualities of communication in this period; persuasion as a means of structuring, prioritizing, and thereby controlling another's perceived options took a pronounced back seat (Barnlund, 1962; Gorman, 1967; Keller & Brown, 1968; Johannesen, 1971).

In contrast, *persuasion* comes to the fore in the *situational integration* era. The effective communicator has goals and frequently needs to change the emotions, beliefs, attitudes, or behaviors of other individuals to achieve them (Hart & Burks, 1972; Bochner & Kelly, 1974). But, in so doing, he/she must recognize and adapt to situational constraints that include the issue, the nature of the relationship, and the makeup of the other persons involved (Rawlins, 1983; Miller, Boster, Roloff & Seibold, 1977). Such persuasive efforts recently have been termed "compliance-gaining" (Miller, Boster, Roloff & Seibold, 1977) and also figure significantly in Wiemann's model of communicative competence. In discussing the "competent person's interaction management skills," Wiemann (1977, p. 197) states that "in spite of this other-orientation, he is successful in accomplishing his own goals in any given interaction. This notion of mutual satisfaction with the self/situation definition leaves open the possibility that one interactant may be able to persuade the other to accept a specific definition—such persuasion is well within the bounds of competent communication *if* the outcome is functional for the long-term maintenance of the social relationship."

Rhetoric and persuasion are central concerns in the developing era's conceptions of interpersonal communication effectiveness. Noting Aristotle's well-known definition of rhetoric as "the faculty of discovering in a particular case what are the available means of persuasion," McCroskey (1982, p. 1) comments that it "could almost pass as a contemporary definition of 'communication competence.'" Whereas the individual integration era accentuated protecting the other individual's choice in communicating, the situational integration era emphasizes using one's own. The ability to select from a situationally appropriate repertoire of communicative behaviors and attain positive outcomes is the mark of a competent communicator (Wiemann, 1977; Pearce, 1977; Hart & Burks, 1972). Table 6.2 presents a summary of outlooks on the means of effective interpersonal communication held during the three periods.

ON COMPENSATORY THEORIZING ABOUT INTERPERSONAL COMMUNICATION EFFECTIVENESS

There has always been a civic quality associated with public speaking. The concerned citizen's freedom to voice opinions and to gather support for them in the polis remains a bulwark of democracy. Our legacy as a field draws deeply from and contributes continuously to the democratic privileges and practices of free speech. Moreover, ours is a pragmatic field whose heritage is effects oriented; we teach the individual and social benefits potentially derived from "the good person speaking well." As an American academic discipline, therefore, we embody and shape cultural mores; we are culturally programmed and programmatic.

Our sensitivity to the interplay between communication customs and societal currents seems particularly evident in the development of the speech field's highly successful subdiscipline, interpersonal communication. In fact, the three eras we have considered suggest a dialectical and compensatory pattern of theorizing about interpersonal effectiveness.

The prevailing conceptions of effective interpersonal communication in these periods seem to compensate for over- and under-emphasized attri-

Table 6.2
Changing Means for Effective Interpersonal Communication

Means	Social Integration Era	Individual Integration Era	Situational Integration Era
Social conventions vs. Idiosyncratic rules	Social conventions guide effective speech.	Idiosyncratic rules guide effective speech.	Social conventions and Idiosyncratic rules (situational requirements) guide effective speech.
Communication Skills (technique) vs. Attitudes toward communication	Emphasis on traditional speech skills shifting to genuine and open attitudes toward interaction.	Emphasis on attitudes toward communication: genuineness, openness, mutual supportiveness	Emphasis on communication skills and attitude of situational appropriateness
Public Speaking vs. Personal Speaking	Public speaking (rhetoric) shifting to human relations	Personalized speaking	Interplay of rhetorical and personal speaking
Persuasion vs. Individual freedom	Promote appropriate evaluation, "fitness with facts."	Promote individual freedom.	Persuade according to situational constraints.
Individual Choice	Should reflect social purposes, enhance listener's.	Preserve other's.	Use one's own.

butes of and orientations toward communication in preceding eras. Each new emphasis addresses perceived shortcomings of communication practices in society and in the scholarly theorizing about such activities. We will now consider two illustrations of compensatory conceptualizing. The first is a brief review of the three periods already examined. The second is a thorough examination of how formulations of interactional control have fluctuated across the developmental eras.

OVERVIEW OF THE THREE ERAS

If judged by the journal space devoted to it, the general semantics movement had significant impact on the speech field in the 1940s. Its proponents argued strenuously against the violence done to society by a persuasive individual like Adolf Hitler. Accordingly, in the social integration era, adjusting to society, promoting social goals, and helping listeners to achieve proper evaluation were stressed. Presumably, such public-spirited communication would redress the unprincipled, self-serving, and manipulative excesses of an individual speaker like Hitler.

Over time, however, critics began to view the conventions and overarching social emphasis of this era as sponsoring extreme conformity and suppressing creative individuality. Scholars began stressing the uniqueness of persons but retained the previous era's disdain for persuasion and manipulation, since a premium was accorded individual freedom. They advocated openness to others to heighten the experience and understanding of the self. The compensatory quality of the new era seems nowhere clearer than in the contrast between the two periods' conceptions of the "healthy" communicator. In the social integration era the "healthy" person is well-adjusted to a democratic society's expectations and contributes to its further integration. The "healthy" person in the individual integration era, conversely, achieves self-actualization by communicating with other individuals in personalized and often private relationships.

Writers in the situational integration era compensate for the perceived naïveté and idealism of the individual integration era by affirming more practical means and ends for speaking. Openness with others may make one too vulnerable and persuasion may be necessary in the workaday world away from intimate associates, if not in dealing with them. Each individual's capacity for innovation is important, but prevailing theoretical conceptions place him/her once again in contexts guided by social conventions and responsibilities as well. Neither social dictates nor individualistic prerogatives alone will suffice in this situational era for justifying effective interpersonal communication. Communicants must mediate individual and social concerns. Thus, the situational era synthesizes contrasting points of view of the preceding periods.

NOTIONS OF INTERACTIONAL CONTROL

The appropriate blend of initiative versus acquiescence by communicators has been a salient issue across these periods in determining how interaction should be controlled. As a result, implicit in each era's conception of this issue is a position regarding persuasion versus compliance as communicative modes. Even the earliest writings acknowledged the necessity for conversational coherence or appropriately connected discourse, and so some blend of cooperation and control was deemed necessary (Riley, 1928). Oliver (1961, p. 21) wrote that "an occasional conversation may drift along successfully with no special guidance; but as a general rule, a conversation can no more steer itself than can a ship. A skillful control, firm but unobtrusive, is essential." Intentional or not, the cybernetic imagery is unmistakable; to be connected via communication is to control and to be controlled (Beer, 1959; Ashby, 1956).

Polar attitudes toward interactional control would stress individual initiative and strategy on one hand and acquiescence and collaboration on the other. The strategic view pictures conversation primarily as a vehicle for attaining individual goals and asks: To what extent does interaction embody a given individual's purposes? A tension between personal responsibility and selfishness inheres in this conception. Where does legitimate protection of one's interests end and greed begin? According to the strategic view, a person takes initiative, makes choices, and can be held accountable for his/her actions and, to varying degrees, their consequences (Rawlins, 1983).

In contrast, the vision stressing collaboration conceives of interaction basically as a vehicle for mutual achievement. The issue is the extent to which conversation embodies community purposes. The tension is between social responsibility and selflessness. Where does legitimate support of an encompassing social entity end and an abdication of self begin? With a collaborative outlook a person shares in creating a social process that, in turn, distributes benefits and detriments and the responsibility for producing either. Though few theorists adopt either extreme position, when they accentuate one view over the other, or when a given era appears to, the associated issues pertain.

Scholars in the *social integration* era mostly downplayed individual strategy and primarily sanctioned it when it furthered social ends (Hager, 1946). Collaboration and cooperation served as the favored bases for conversational control. Responsible and effective communicators meshed individual ambitions to promote socially integrative results, and their efforts could be appraised according to widely accepted guidelines for appropriate behavior (Kidd, 1975).

The *individual integration* era extended this endorsement of mutuality but with ironic twists. The new era did not share the previous period's enthusiasm for social integration since individual freedom and self actualization assumed prime importance. Accordingly, writers denounced persuasion and calculated strategies as limiting the other's freedom. Intentional, individual attempts to control conversation fell into disrepute, replaced by faith in the emergent properties of interaction, given appropriate attitudes by the participants. Spontaneity and mutual supportiveness would best shape dialogue, enhance self-expression, and facilitate understanding. The vitality and to some extent the implicit contradictions of such a view were stated by Keller and Brown (1968, p. 79). "Communication is, in its best sense, communion. It involves . . . 'mutual appreciative understanding.' And even though this sort of mutuality leads . . . to mutual control, the mutual control is of a sort built on a positive ethic: to bring to their finest fulfillment the purposes of each party to the communicative act."

Indeed, such mutuality implies inherent ironies. Many of this period's authors presented mutuality as a collaboration for achieving individual rather than social objectives. Facilitating another's goal attainment was encouraged but consciously pursuing a personal plan was not. The result was a conception of interaction that devalued self-serving motivations and strategies with the ultimate aim of furthering self-actualization. Moreover, the emergent nature of such conversation was accomplished by preserving each other's freedom only to be controlled by the nature of the transaction. Witness, for example, the famed "dyadic effect" in studies of self-disclosure wherein a norm tacitly develops between conversants to match each other's personal revelations. Yet, to the extent that a person surrenders conscious control over his/her communication and blends unreflectively with emerging interactions, that person renounces responsibility for his/her messages (Rawlins, 1983). The major incongruity of this conception of effective interpersonal communication is that having private motivations, designing persuasive messages, and assuming individual responsibility for both were deemphasized in the interests of unfettered personal growth.

Instead of facilitating the other's options in communicating, writers in the *situational integration* era advocate employing one's own (Wiemann, 1977; Pearce, 1977; Hart & Burks, 1972). Effective interactants plan and monitor their messages to achieve predetermined and emergent goals. Early on, Hart and Burks (1972, p. 90) asked: "Is it so shameful in an ordinary human encounter to attempt *effortfully* to make the interaction 'come off,' to achieve practical gain, or to strengthen an interpersonal bond? Is it inappropriate to choose carefully among alternate strategies so that my words have the greatest social impact possible?" More recently, Wiemann (1977, p. 210) adduced "the centrality of interaction management in the communicative competence model."

This emphasis on conscious strategy partially compensates for the incongruities regarding the role of individual intentions in guiding interaction in the individual integration era. Thus, the field has migrated from collaboration for primarily social purposes, through emergent interaction for individual purposes, to individual strategy for chiefly personal purposes in its formulations of conversational control. Matters are not necessarily resolved permanently, however; warnings regarding concern for others and social propriety accompany the present endorsement of individual strategy. Yet, many of the original writings on open communication recommended analogous limitations that were largely unheeded in the spirit of the period (Sillars, 1974). However, situational conceptions of interpersonal communication effectiveness without due regard for formal sanctions or humanistic attitudes could lead at best to an ethic of convenience and at worst to an invidious brand of interpersonal fascism that uses situational choices as stepping stones to wholesale manipulation. Perhaps the necessity for countervailing conceptions is already evident.

CONCLUSION

To slice changing conceptions of interpersonal communication effectiveness into three developmental eras distorts partially a complex process. It presents to a degree an illusion of agreement among scholars regarding crucial issues during a given period and thereby obscures diverse debates that may have thrived. Indeed, the dominant orientations of one era may be powerfully latent in another. Highlighting the present rise of situationalism, for example, deemphasizes existing alternative conceptions of effective communication. Many tenets of the other eras persist as influential positions.

Even so, the compensatory quality of various conceptual shifts in these eras is noteworthy. These changing perspectives on interpersonal communication effectiveness suggest that the concepts are not the product of immutable principles. Rather, the development of this subdiscipline involves factors that inhere in its subject matter, in the reflexive position of its theorists, and in the connection between communication theory and sociocultural evolution.

Interpersonal communication is intrinsically contradictory and unavoidably provokes the question of what constitutes the appropriate measure of personal assertion versus communal impulse. Face-to-face society exists only through communication between individuals. Such interaction, however, violates each person's subjectivity. As Barnlund (1962, p. 204) notes, "Meaning, in my opinion, is a private preserve and trespassers always run a risk. To speak of personal integrity at all is to acknowledge this. Any exchange of words is an invasion of the privacy of the listener which is aimed at preventing, restricting, or stimulating the cultivation of meaning."

On the other hand, individuality develops meaningfully only in relation to other human beings (Wolff, 1950; Mead, 1934). In a root sense, then, to assert one's personhood is to interfere with another's subjectivity. In contrast, one must renounce to a degree personal integrity to exist in a social sense. This tension between personal agency and communion (Bakan, 1966) has engendered notable dilemmas for interpersonal communication theorists. Thus far in discussions of interpersonal communication effectiveness, stressing one impulse over the other or attempting conceptual reconciliation has meant that each scholarly era contains the seeds of its own uprooting.

The compensatory appearance of much interpersonal scholarship also stems from alternatively emphasizing or theoretically resolving other interpenetrating qualities of the communication process, such as means versus ends, skills versus attitudes, and influence versus understanding. For example, communicative means like persuasion can become ends in themselves and interactional goals like social adjustment can be transformed into means. Because of the nature of the phenomena we study, our field's historical concern with specifying appropriate methods for achieving social effects almost imperceptibly converts into a focus upon stipulating proper objectives.

In addition to studying the process, interpersonal communication theorists communicate with other people. There is unavoidable interplay between theorizing about social concerns and existing in society. Yet, the typical theorist's notions about effective communication probably do not shape interaction in society as much as the responses of the people he or she encounters everyday shape his or her theorizing. Gergen (1980) further argues that scholars themselves, in reviewing each other's work, insist that theoretical statements be consistent with the common sense of the day. Thus, scholarly conceptions reflect the preoccupations and preferences of people living in a given historical moment.

However, Gergen (1973) also describes how some innovative theoretical ideas do eventually reach members of society and may alter their behavior. Thus, revisions in social practice and academic theorizing are mutually influential, though it is difficult to determine the precise nature of the process. Both activities occur by and large as responses to events of the time. Consider, for example, the parallels between the societal emphasis on democratic participation and conformity following World War II and tenets of the social integration era; the personal growth movement during the sixties and the individual integration era; and the "look out for number one" attitude and focus upon skills training currently associated with constricted employment opportunities and the Situational Integration era. Thus, there are correlations between cultural currents, developments in other fields, and these scholarly eras.

In short, interpersonal inquiry does not occur in a vacuum. An historical view of the subdiscipline reveals a relative quality to theorizing about communication effectiveness that methodological advancements or the social phenomenon being studied may not eliminate. No period is necessarily wrong; communication theorists respond to the relevant problems and variables of their circumstances, to societal trends, as well as to prior conceptions in the field. Acknowledging these factors should make us more accepting of different approaches to the subject of interpersonal communication. It also cautions against being overly prescriptive about what constitutes the right intentions or methods in communicating interpersonally.

It may not be possible to transcend the debates of one's own scholarly era. Since its early discussions of the conversational basis of public speaking, the speech communication field has generated various theoretical descriptions of proficient interpersonal communication. The emerging formulation involves a rhetoric of conversation which blends ancient principles with modern predicaments. The field, of course, will not remain static and continually faces the challenge of developing responsible theories of interpersonal communication effectiveness.

7

Organizational Communication: Historical Development and Future Directions

LINDA L. PUTNAM AND GEORGE CHENEY

Organizational communication as a specialized area of speech communication has experienced rapid growth in the past decade. Most colleges and universities with speech communication programs offer at least one course in this area. A master's degree in organizational communication can be obtained at approximately 75 institutions and 35 of these schools offer the Ph.D. Despite its growing popularity, however, organizational communication is a relative newcomer to the discipline. Its departmental roots date back to the early 1950s with the work of P. E. Lull at Purdue University; its origins can be traced to speech training for corporate executives in the 1920s. Its emergence in the field of speech communication parallels the entrance of speech communication into the mainstream of social science research.

The growth of organizational communication is concomitant with the development of industrial psychology, social psychology, organizational behavior, and administrative science; hence, experts in these fields have shaped the dominant theories, concepts, and issues that organizational communication scholars typically raise. Redding (1979b) acknowledges and laments this "wholesale transporting (borrowing? stealing?) of concepts and variables from our academic cousins" (p. 321). Recent breakthroughs, however, reflect the influence of a wider array of disciplines; namely, sociology, rhetoric, anthropology, philosophy, political science, and linguistics.

Organizational communication grew out of three main speech communication traditions: public address; persuasion; and social science research on interpersonal, small group, and mass communication. Definitions of both communication and organization were as diverse as the traditions that shaped research topics. Moreover, because definitions reflected various theoretical assumptions and concepts (Cusella, in press; Putnam, 1982a), it was unlikely that any one definition would gain wide acceptance (Porter & Roberts, 1976). In the early writings, definitions of communication had a distinctly "media-oriented" focus, shaping research on the accuracy and clarity of message composition (McMurray, 1965). Communication, in this sense, was the "process of sending and receiving messages" (Sanborn, 1964, p. 3). The publication of Lee Thayer's (1961) *Administrative Communication* and W. C. Redding's (1972) *Communication Within the Organization* shifted the focus of organizational communication from sender to receiver models. Communication referred to "those behaviors of human beings . . . which result in messages being received by one or more persons" (Redding, 1972, p. 25). This definition dismissed the notion that messages were literally transmitted from one person to another. Instead, it stressed that the message received was the one that mattered.

Recent studies have moved away from these conceptions to one of interaction, or the social creation of message and meaning (Hawes, 1974). *Process* assumes a central role in the interactive orientation, and organizational communication is broadly defined as "the processing and interpreting of messages, information, meaning, and symbolic activity within and between organizations" (Putnam, 1983a, p. 1). Definitions of *organization* have also shifted from a preoccupation with bureaucratic models to a focus on aggregates of persons arranged in patterned relationships (Barnard, 1938; Redding, 1972). Organizations are seen as involving dynamic activities rather than static collections of people; these activities are integrated through role coordination, interdependence, and interlocked behaviors (Redding, 1972; Weick, 1979).

This chapter traces the evolution of organizational communication— its major topics and research developments. In particular, it reviews the key research domains, breakpoints in new lines of work, and the interface between research and application from 1920 to 1980. Spatial limitations preclude a thorough synthesis of research findings in organizational communication. The reader is urged to consult Guetzkow (1965), Redding (1972), and Porter and Roberts (1976) for detailed state-of-the-art reviews. Other articles provide a definitive historical treatment of organizational communication (Hay, 1974; Porterfield, 1974; Redding, 1966; Richetto, 1977; Tompkins, 1967; Van Voorhis, 1974). Our chapter draws from these summaries to highlight historical developments.

Spatial limitations also preclude a review of major theorists and methodological developments in the study of organizational communication. Interested readers are directed to Tompkins (1984) and Pietri (1974) for a review of the contributions of such major theorists as Barnard, Fayol, Follett, Simon, Taylor, and Weber. Other review chapters focus on premises and metatheoretical assumptions that underlie research traditions (Putnam, 1982a; Redding, 1979b); ways of transforming traditional research into alternative approaches (Putnam, 1983b; Putnam & Cheney, 1983); research methodologies used to study organizational communication (Dennis, Goldhaber & Yates, 1978); and new models for research on systems theory and communication structure (Farace & MacDonald, 1974; Monge, 1982; Roberts, O'Reilly, Bretton & Porter, 1974; Thayer, 1967); hence, these topics will not be reviewed.

Instead, this essay reviews five areas of "traditional" organizational communication research—communication media, communication channels, networks, organizational climate, and superior-subordinate communication—and four emerging approaches: information-processing, rhetorical, cultural, and political orientations. It concludes with an overview of the practical side of organizational communication, its history, and its impact on training and consulting.

EARLY ORGANIZATIONAL COMMUNICATION RESEARCH: THE STUDY OF COMMUNICATION MEDIA

Topics covered in an introductory course on organizational communication typically begin with the research of the 1950s (Jablin, 1978b). But in actuality, one offshoot of industrial communication, business and professional speaking, dates back to the late 1920s. This section reviews publications on industrial public speaking, communication media, and the semantics of organizational messages. The first visible sign of courtship between the American business community and the speech-communication field occurred in the late 1920s. Encouraged by the popularity of Dale Carnegie's writings and courses, business began to link managerial effectiveness with communication skills (Sanborn, 1964). Even though academicians regarded Carnegie's courses as "gimmickry," they followed his lead in providing prescriptive texts for managerial success. Two textbooks that gained a widespread appeal were Hoffman's (1923) *Speaking for Business Men* and Sanford and Yeager's (1929) *Business and Professional Speaking*. These books adapted public speaking to the business scene by introducing briefs, reports, and presentational speeches as forms of public address. Most of the business speaking texts published before 1950 "provide no evidence to support their huge numbers of prescriptions" and treat communication as "speaker-centered, and success-oriented, manipulative, and simplistic" (Redding, 1966, p. 52).

Although Collins (1924) conducted a survey of public speaking courses in business administration and YMCA schools, systematic research on business speakers did not surface until the surveys of industrial training programs at Pennsylvania State University in the 1950s (Knapp, 1968; Zelko, 1951) and the studies of business rhetoric at the University of Missouri in the 1960s (Fisher, 1965). Fisher (1965) analyzed the persuasive strategies of 500 speeches delivered by top management officials. The speeches relied on a common enemy and used stylized platitudes and recurrent symbols as persuasive techniques. Shifting from content to speech preparation, Knapp (1970) reported that middle managers had very little preparation time before delivery, feared being misquoted, and relied heavily on prepared manuscripts for their delivery. A few academicians extended this work by studying audience responses to business rhetoric (Derry, 1969; Irwin & Brockhaus, 1963; Williams & Sundene, 1965). This early work on public speaking in industry laid the foundation for a plethora of courses and texts on business and professional speaking (see, for example, Bradley & Baird, 1980; Downs, Berg & Linkugel, 1977; Howell & Bormann, 1971; Zelko & Dance, 1965).

Public speaking was only one medium of communication that gained popularity in the early days of organizational research. Academicians also focused on written communication, particularly employee handbooks, company newsletters, memoranda, and information racks (Mahoney, 1954; Zelko, 1953). To understand what "information should be transmitted to whom in what media" (Van Voorhis, 1974, p. 14), studies centered on the accuracy (Beach, 1950), the readability (Paterson & Jenkins, 1948), and the functions (Dover, 1959) of written information. The few employee newsletters that existed before World War II contained mostly chitchat and notices of social events, but the number of company newsletters tripled in the 1940s, with their content shifting to information about company plans, operations, and policies (Dover, 1959). In the 1950s company publications became an arm of management, complete with persuasive appeals for action and with managerial interpretations of company events. Axley's (1983) recent study of employee publications echoed Dover's (1959) earlier observation that managerial philosophy influenced the amount of space devoted to information-giving news, status-conferring activities, and the language that depicted these events.

Typically, research in this vein compared the effectiveness of and preferences for particular types of media. Although management preferred written communiques, employees opted for supervisor conferences and group meetings as their preferred forms of communication (Peters, 1950). This finding in conjunction with Dahle's (1954) experimental comparison of five modes of communication led to the conclusion that a combination of written and oral media constituted the most effective means of communication (Sanborn, 1961), especially when message content and media use were adapted to particular audiences (Thayer, 1961). But when the sender and the receiver differed in vocabularies and problem orientations, written was more effective than oral communication. If the message required feedback or clarification, oral communication surpassed written media (O'Reilly & Pondy, 1979).

Research on communication media in organizations adopted a very narrow and often mechanical view of communication. With a zeal to improve routine practices, organizational researchers treated communications as a one-way, downwardly directed conduit for transmitting messages. Even studies that developed taxonomies of messages (Eilon, 1968) took a distinctly "media" focus; messages and media were treated as synonymous. Organizational communication consisted of "speech" media, often cast in simplistic, prescriptive principles that were devoid of any basic understanding of the complexities of communication (Redding, 1966).

A major breakpoint in this preoccupation with media came through the application of communication theory to organizational behavior. The focus of organizational communication shifted to message distortion, as characterized by two distinct lines of work—perceptual or semantic distortion and blockage in information flow. Both research strains questioned how misunderstanding occurred in organizations; one focused on the meanings of messages, and the other centered on transmission problems in message flow. Inspired by the general semanticists and under the leadership of Irving Lee at Northwestern University, perceptual distortion studies examined the effect of words and language on interpretations of organizational events. Haney (1973) discussed problems that resulted from equating inferences with observed behavior. Weaver (1958) tested the impact of labor-management semantic profiles on message flow. Triandis (1959a, 1959b) uncovered "cognitive disparity" between supervisory and work groups in making judgments about organizational events. Schwartz, Stark, and Schiffman (1970) found that concepts such as "strike," "solidarity," and "management" triggered different interpretations among union officers. Tompkins (1962) assessed what he termed "semantic information distance" between and among different levels of a nationwide trade union. Studies on semantic distance, while few in number, served as the forerunners for later work on organizational symbols. The second strain of research, message distortion, emerged in studies of upward communication, a subdivision of one of the four "traditional" domains of organizational communication.

TRADITIONAL DOMAINS OF ORGANIZATIONAL COMMUNICATION RESEARCH

From an early interest in the downward flow of information, four research "traditions" developed at roughly the same time. The four traditions—communication channels, communication climate, network analysis, and superior-subordinate communication—"represent our discipline's struggle to establish the boundaries of organizational communication" (Putnam & Cheney, 1983, p. 213). These approaches date back to the human relations movement in the 1940s, when social scientists began systematic observations of information flow in collectivities.

COMMUNICATION CHANNELS

Channel research addresses the flow of information as it relates to organizational structure; that is, upward, downward, and horizontal. Although the majority of practitioners' books in the 1940s stressed one-way, downward communication, Given (1949), Heron (1942), and Pigors (1949) emphasized the two-way nature of information flow between lower and upper levels. At the same time, Lazarsfeld, Berelson, and Gaudet (1948) initiated research on "gatekeeping" and the "two-step flow" of information.

In the 1950s and 1960s channel research attracted great interest. A number of studies revealed that lower-level employees tended to distort messages they sent upward (Planty & Machaver, 1952; Read, 1962). This research interest has continued to be pursued. Athanassiades (1973) found that a sense of security reduced upward distortion, and high achievement drive increased the tendency to distort. Through extensive research on upward distortion, Roberts and O'Reilly concluded that trust, job satisfaction, and job performance reduced upward distortion (O'Reilly, 1978; O'Reilly & Roberts, 1974; Roberts & O'Reilly, 1974a). Moreover, positive feedback from one's superior also decreased the amount of upward distortion (Jablin, 1979). Following the work of Festinger (1950) and Cohen (1959), Bradley (1978) noted that the content of upwardly-directed messages was determined by the perceived power rather than the status of receivers. In a related vein, the term "Pelz Effect" emerged from studies showing that subordinates would initiate more upward messages if they believed their superiors had upward influence (Pelz, 1952). Examination of the "Pelz Effect" continued, but it became concerned exclusively with the dyadic relationship of superior-subordinate (Jablin, 1980b).

Davis (1953), following Jacobson and Seashore (1951), developed a research technique, ECCO: Episodic Communication Channels in Organizations, to examine the spread of rumors through informal channels or the "grapevine." This body of research grew, but Davis (1978), the major analyst of informal channels, contended it was rather small. Informal communication was frequently linked with formal channels. Specifically, in effective organizations, informal and formal communication showed a positive relationship (Katz & Kahn, 1978). Tompkins's (1977, 1978) study of NASA's Marshall Space Flight Center reinforced this finding in his observation that the practices of managing and communicating fused through an emphasis on both formal and informal communication channels.

Message overload and information adequacy were also linked to frequency of message flow across different channels. Miller (1960) and O'Reilly (1980) observed the effects of "information overload" on organizational members. Miller (1960) described seven possible responses to overload conditions, including omission, error, delaying, filtering, and escaping. O'Reilly (1980) reported that perceived information overload was associated with higher satisfaction, but with lower decision-making performance. This overload, however, resulted from excess vertical rather than horizontal communication. Specifically, managers spent about two-thirds of their communication time on vertical messages to their superiors and subordinates and only one-third of their time on horizontal messages (Porter & Roberts, 1976). Perhaps as Goldhaber, Yates, Porter & Lesniak (1978) reported, horizontal coordinating functions in organizations typically occurred "on a rather informal, impromptu basis" (p. 86), rather than through formal communication channels. Several researchers extended work on communication channels by suggesting a link between perceived information adequacy and such organizational outcomes as communication satisfaction, job performance, and organizational effectiveness (Spiker & Daniels, 1981; Daly, McCroskey & Falcione, 1976; Downs & Hazen, 1977). In particular, O'Reilly and Pondy (1979) showed that relevant and accurate information contributed to individual job performance and to organizational effectiveness.

Guided by the metaphor of information flow, channel studies have treated messages and structures with misplaced concreteness; they have emphasized the "channel" through which messages are transmitted, rather than the nature or content of messages. In this perspective, communication becomes the accuracy of transmitting a message, a way of "getting information across" rather than a way of interpreting and giving feedback on the meaning of a message. Katz and Kahn (1978), while offering their own explanations for the types of messages that "move" in particular directions, bemoan the lack of empirical attention to message interpretation.

COMMUNICATION CLIMATE

In the 1960s channel research was applied to the study of communication "climate," communication that contributes to "the spirit or philosophy" responsible for organizational relationships (Koehler, Anatol, & Applbaum, 1981, p. 123). Thus, climate research incorporated communication channels into a framework of organizational relationships. The first studies of psychological or social climate were inspired by field theory (Lewin, 1951). Barnard (1938) and Roethlisberger and Dickson (1939) treated climates as implicit features of organizations; but as Jablin (1980a) noted, the first explicit linkage of psychological climate to organizational behavior appeared in McGregor's (1960) book. McGregor contended that "many subtle behavioral manifestations of managerial attitude create what is often referred to as the 'psychological climate' of the relationship" (p. 134).

"Organizational climate" differed from communication climate in its focus on organizational structure (e.g., rules, constraints), individual responsibility, rewards, job challenge, warmth, and tolerance (Litwin & Stringer, 1968). "Communication climate" became associated with such concepts as trust and openness (see Ireland, Van Auken & Lewis, 1978). Even though researchers characterized climate as a product of shared meanings among organizational members, they persisted in treating climate as having an existence of its own, one that could be approximated through summary measures of individual perceptions.

Specifically, researchers employed questionnaires that measured individual perceptions; then they inappropriately applied summary statistics to indicate how organizational members felt on the average about climate factors (see the review by Falcione & Werner, 1978). Climate factors, then, became atmospheric or meteorological elements located in the organizational environment. For example, Roberts and O'Reilly (1974b) developed a climate-type measure of 16 "atmospheric conditions" of organizational communication, including trust, influence, accuracy, overload, percent of time spent communicating in different directions, and time spent on different communication media. Muchinsky (1977), in an assessment of the Roberts and O'Reilly questionnaire, concluded that it discriminated well among organizations on the basis of individual perceptions, but it was conceptually similar to job satisfaction.

Shifting the focus of climate to leadership functions, Redding (1972) offered a holistic prescriptive model for managers known as the "Ideal Managerial Climate" (IMC). The five components of the IMC consisted of supportiveness, participative decision making, trust, openness, and emphasis on high performance goals. The IMC represented an important attempt to bridge theory and practice in organizational communication, although it was limited by its managerial view of organizational effectiveness. During the 1970s, many organizational researchers adopted an applied interest in communication climate, linking it to job satisfaction. In a detailed review, Falcione and Werner (1978) discussed empirical support for this connection. Even though Redding (1972) acknowledged the "slippery" nature of this construct, he contended that climate was more important than were communication skills "in creating an effective organization" (p. 111).

In 1983 communication climate research took a dramatic shift from previous approaches. Poole and McPhee (1983) treated climate on the *intersubjective* level, based on members' beliefs, attitudes, values, and interpretations. This conceptualization introduced an intermediate level of analysis—one between objective and subjective variables. Further, Poole and McPhee employed a "structurational" model (Giddens, 1979) to examine "the production and reproduction" of organizational climates through the use of generative rules and interaction resources. This conceptualization moved communication climate out of the confines of its meteorological metaphor by examining the way climate is produced through values and beliefs, rather than through "atmospheric" elements external to individuals.

NETWORK ANALYSIS

Climate research represented one attempt to characterize, understand, and explain communication patterns in the organization; another was network analysis. Jablin (1980a, p. 341) noted parallels between the two "schools," but argued that a major reason they developed distinct traditions was that climate focused on communication consequences while network research concentrated on communication antecedents and determinants. In addition, the two approaches became associated with different speech-communication programs—climate work with Purdue University and network analysis with Michigan State and Stanford universities.

The origins of network analysis can be traced to (1) early sociometric studies (Moreno, 1953); (2) small-group studies (Bavelas, 1950; Leavitt, 1951; Shaw, 1964); (3) information diffusion (Rogers, 1962); and (4) the mass communication work of Lazarsfeld, Berelson, and Gaudet (1948). Simply put, "a network consists of interconnected individuals who are linked by patterned communication flows" (Rogers & Agarwala-Rogers, 1976, p. 110). Network analysis, which became popular both inside and outside the speech communication field, used data about communication flow to analyze interpersonal linkages and to identify the communication structure of a larger system (Rogers & Agarwala-Rogers, 1976). The earliest network studies were the 1950s' small-group laboratory experiments that contrasted different network structures, such as circle, wheel, and chain. They found that (1) centralization, as in the wheel network, contributed to rapid performance, especially of simple tasks; (2) decentralization, as in the circle network, was associated with high satisfaction among members; (3) network structures affected leader emergence; and (4) persons in key network positions often experienced information overload (Rogers & Agarwala-Rogers, 1976).

In the 1970s organizational network research employed a systems model by treating linkages among all organizational members as "nodes" in a larger set of dyadic relationships (Farace, Monge & Russell, 1977; Monge, Edwards & Kiriste, 1978). Richards (1974b) suggested four key characteristics of linkages: (1) symmetry, (2) strength, (3) specificity, or the uniqueness of linkage function, and (4) transitivity, or consistency of linkages. Properties of network systems included centrality, connectedness, reachability, density, and range (Farace, Monge & Russell, 1977; Tichy, Tushman & Fombrun, 1979).

Research revealed that organizations were composed of a number of interrelated and often overlapping networks (Rogers & Agarwala-Rogers, 1976). In a study of three military organizations, Roberts and O'Reilly (1978) found that members rarely followed formal authority networks; rather they communicated in task-focused clusters. Moreover, the task network was larger and better developed than was the social one, but the two were closely related. Treating the group as the unit of analysis, Danowski (1980) found that production and innovation networks had stronger connectivity and greater uniformity in attitudes between groups than did maintenance networks. Researchers also investigated roles that individuals assumed in organizational networks. MacDonald (1976) observed that liaisons (persons who linked groups but were not necessarily members of them) were more satisfied with managerial messages and perceived themselves as more influential than did nonliaisons. Albrecht (1979) discovered that "key" communicators in a network identified more with management and with their jobs than did members who were not in key positions.

One type of communication role that attracted interest during the 1970s was boundary spanning. Boundary spanners are members who excel within their own work units and who also span the boundaries of work groups, departments, or organizations, or all three (Tushman & Scanlan, 1981a, 1981b). Boundary spanners, like liaisons and linking pins (members of two or more overlapping groups) perform essential integrative functions.

Early studies by Blau (1954) and Erbe (1962) linked activity across organizational boundaries with professional relationships inside the company. Similarly, Tushman and his colleagues at Columbia University noted that professional employees typically assumed boundary-spanning roles and that roughly 40% of them were also "stars" within their own work groups (Tushman & Scanlan, 1981b). Thus, boundary spanning became fertile terrain for examining multiple roles in communication networks.

In the 1980s, as organizations became reliant on advanced technology, researchers began to examine the impact of computers on communication networks (Danowski, 1983; Fowler & Wackerbarth, 1980; Hintz & Couch, 1978; Plain, 1980; Rice, 1982a). In a dissertation completed at Stanford University, Rice (1982b), who gathered two years of computer-monitored conferencing data among 800 researchers, reported that group members typically exhibited reciprocal relationships and that nontask groups occupied more information-rich roles than did task groups. Computer-based network analysis might become even more prevalent as computers perform essential information processing functions for all employees.

Most network studies gathered data with self-report instruments and analyzed it with sociograms, matrix methods, and multidimensional scaling. In speech communication, the most popular data analysis technique was Richards' (1974a, 1974b) NEGOPY, developed at Stanford University. NEGOPY, designed to analyze an entire set of system relationships, accounted for indirect and direct communication links (Rogers & Agarwala-Rogers, 1976). Techniques such as NEGOPY, although useful for characterizing communication structures at particular points in time, overemphasized the frequency of communication and gave little or no attention to the content and meanings of interaction (Putnam, 1982b). Albrecht and Ropp (1982) at the University of Washington suggested using nondirective interviews and ethnography to examine content and interpretations of network context and quantitative techniques to assess the frequency and configuration of communication systems.

SUPERIOR-SUBORDINATE COMMUNICATION

Similar to channel and climate research, the "tradition" known as superior-subordinate communication centered on information flow between subordinates and their supervisors. Jablin (1979) defined superior-subordinate communication as "exchanges of information and influence between organizational members, at least one of whom has formal . . . authority to direct and evaluate the activities of other organizational members" (p. 1202). Two key figures in research on superior-subordinate communication were W. C. Redding (1972) at Purdue University and Fredric Jablin (1979) at the University of Texas. Their reviews clustered this "tradition" into seven areas: (1) perceptions of the amount, frequency, and mode of interaction; (2) upward distortion; (3) upward influence; (4) openness; (5) feedback; (6) communicator style; and (7) effectiveness of superior-subordinate relationships. Because researchers found it natural in the 1960s and 1970s to apply concepts from channel and climate to the superior-subordinate dyad, most of the above research foci were borrowed from other "traditions." Three of the areas, however, accounted for specific task-oriented aspects of dyadic relationships: feedback, perceptual congruence, and communicator style. Studies on feedback noted that it was a multidimensional concept and that the quantity of feedback was less important than its relevance and accuracy (O'Reilly & Anderson, 1980). Cusella (1982) observed that a subordinate's intrinsic motivation increased with positive task-related feedback given by expert sources. But he posited that the timing, specificity, and rules for communicating the feedback would mitigate this effect (Cusella, 1980).

"Perceptual congruence," a concept similar to semantic information distance, referred to agreements between superiors and subordinates about aspects of their work life. Research concluded that superiors and subordinates generally disagreed about the requirements of their jobs (Boyd & Jensen, 1972), the amount of communication between them (Webber, 1970), and the personality traits of each other (Infante & Gorden, 1979). Effective supervisors were able to bridge these gaps through a relaxed, attentive communicator style (Bradley & Baird, 1977) and through asking, persuading, and passing along information (Redding, 1972). Also, supervisors who exhibited an employee-centered communication style, tolerance for disagreement, and innovativeness achieved higher employee satisfaction scores than did other supervisors (Richmond & McCroskey, 1979; Richmond, McCroskey & Davis, 1982).

Because most studies highlighted task-related messages, a significant break occurred with research that emphasized the relational dimensions of superior-subordinate interaction. Jablin (1978a) demonstrated that subordinates who perceived an "open" relationship with their superior viewed certain types of superior-subordinate interaction as more appropriate than did subordinates who perceived a "closed" relationship, thus extending climate research on trust and openness. Openness, in this sense, referred to "candid disclosure of feelings" and "a willingness to listen to discomforting information" (Redding, 1972, p. 330). Jablin (1978a) also suggested that over time different norms and communication patterns developed for "open" as opposed to "closed" superior-subordinate dyads. In two recent studies Watson (1982a, 1982b(applied RELCOM, a coding scheme for relational control (Ellis, 1979), to an analysis of superior-subordinate interaction. She reported that superiors showed resistance to and subordinates showed compliance with each other's attempts to control the relationship.

Most superior-subordinate studies employ questionnaires, rarely matched for dyadic analysis. Smircich and Chesser (1981) address this failure to assess reciprocal influences directly. Other researchers are beginning to expand and enrich the literature by emphasizing how superior-subordinate relationships create and share symbolic realities (Pfeffer, 1981a; Trujillo, 1983). In their comprehensive reviews of this literature, Jablin (1979) and Kelly (1982) lament the relative lack of attention to systemic variables that affect a dyadic relationship and urge researchers to consider situational and developmental approaches to superior-subordinate communication. In a pioneering effort to place superior-subordinate openness within an organizational system, Jablin (1982) reports that organizational size reduces openness while a supervisory position, especially at lower levels, tends to increase it.

NEW DIRECTIONS IN ORGANIZATIONAL COMMUNICATION RESEARCH

The emergence of any discipline or subdiscipline must be understood within a sociopolitical context. So it is with organizational communication. The research priorities of the first four decades are colored by (1) the human relations approach, which was quite popular until recently; (2) a related preoccupation with effective management; (3) treatment of communication either in terms of the visible, easily measured aspects of information flow or in terms of simple perceptions; and (4) an accompanying bias toward positivistic research methodologies. In an informative essay, Jablin (1978b) crystallizes the priorities and concerns of organizational communication researchers during each decade. We reprint his table (see Table 7.1) to help visualize the progress of the field.

In the 1980s the study of organizational communication is rapidly expanding to include a variety of theoretical and methodological approaches. For ease of presentation, we identify four "families" of related, but not necessarily compatible, research efforts. In each case, the "family resemblance" is based on a shared general conception of how to look at organizations; yet members of the same family may be oriented toward different methods and goals. Thus, we urge the reader to consider the family names as heuristics, or perhaps as loosely-defined perspectives. The four families of emerging research are (1) the information-processing, (2) the rhetorical, (3) the cultural, and (4) the political perspectives. Each is discussed in terms of its actual and potential contribution to organizational communication research.

Table 7.1
Past Research Priorities in Organizational Communication

Era	Predominant Research Questions
1940s	What effects do downward directed mass media communications have upon employees?
	Is an informed employee a productive one?
1950s	How do small-group communication networks affect organizational performance and members' attitudes and behaviors?
	What are the relationships between organizational members' attitudes and perceptions of their communication behavior (primarily upward and downward communication) and their on-the-job performance?
	What is the relationship between the attitudes and performance of workers and the feedback they receive?
	Is a well-informed employee a satisfied employee?
1960s	What do organizational members perceive to be the communication correlates of "good" supervision?
	In what ways do actual and perceived communicative behaviors of liaison and nonliaison roles within organizational communication networks differ?
	What is the relationship between subordinates' job-related attitudes and productivity and the extent to which they perceive they participate in decision-making?
1970s	What are the communicative components and correlates of organizational communication climates?
	What are the characteristics and distribution of "key" communication roles within organizational networks?

Reprinted by permission from Fredric M. Jablin, "Past, Present, and Future Research Priorities in Organizational Communication." Revision of a paper presented at the annual convention of the Speech Communication Association, Minneapolis, Minnesota, November 1978.

THE INFORMATION-PROCESSING PERSPECTIVE

Treating organizations as information-processing systems has gained widespread appeal outside the speech-communication field. The essence of organizing, in this perspective, is the gathering, transmitting, storing, and using of information (Galbraith, 1973; O'Reilly & Pondy, 1979). Information refers to messages and data, often treated as energy that reduces uncertainty and aids predictability. Consistent with a systemic view of organizations, information processing pervades all activities, from decision making and control to organizational design and conflict management (Huber, 1982). Initiated by organizational design theorists (Galbraith, 1973), studies of information processing center on microlevel activities, such as communication between work groups, coordination among group members, and the impact of task structure on information flow and on macro-issues, such as decision making and adaptation to organizational environments.

Information-processing research examines the impact of structural variables on communication networks, channel usage, and amount of information flow. Studies at the microlevel reveal that task uncertainty (Van de ven, Delbeque & Koenig, 1976), work flow interdependence (Tushman, 1978; Stech, 1980), and decentralized decision making lead to higher frequencies of interaction between work units. When the task is uncertain, work units coordinate their efforts through horizontal meetings (Van de ven et al., 1976), tightly connected contacts outside the group, and loosely structured ones inside the group (Connolly, 1977). In contrast, task complexity (March & Simon, 1958; Tushman, 1978); task routineness (Bacharach & Aiken, 1977); and task specialization across work groups (O'Reilly & Pondy, 1979) restrict the flow of communication between subunits. Other studies seek to determine whether information-processing requirements match work group capacities by examining type of information; information adequacy (Penley, 1982); and the routing, delaying, and modifying of messages (Huber, 1982).

At the macrolevel, information processing influences adaptation to external environments and organizational decision making. In rapidly changing environments, organizations typically increase their information flow to cope with uncertainty (Tushman & Nadler, 1978). Information flow is also critical for effective decision making at both the individual and the systemic levels. Research on individual decision makers centers on the cognitive aspects of information processing—the way managers make choices with imperfect information and within bounded rationality (March & Simon, 1958). Connolly (1977) argues that important decisions are typically made on ill-structured problems through a diffuse, multiperson process. Critical components of this process are decision networks and the effects that decisions have on relevant constituents (Ungson, Braunstein & Hall, 1981). In the decision network, credibility, accessibility, and quality of information sources assume important roles (Cusella, 1984). O'Reilly (1982) reports that organizational members use accessible sources more frequently than they do timely, relevant, or accurate ones.

Most information-processing studies adopt a mechanistic view of communication, emphasizing the amount, direction, structure, and type of information flow while ignoring message reception and interpretation. However, one theorist, Karl Weick (1979), offers an alternative information-processing model based on the formation and processing of "enactments" or meanings of organizational events. In Weick's theory the context and the degree of equivocality affect the interpretation of information. Equivocality refers to conditions that evoke multiple meanings. Weick's (1979) model posits a complex explanation for the way organizational members select, interpret, and retain equivocal information. Three published communication studies test Weick's model. Bantz and Smith (1977) examine the number of adjectives deemed necessary to reduce equivocal literary passages. Kreps (1980) assesses the number of double interacts used to process equivocal motions during faculty senate deliberations; Putnam and Sorenson (1982) test for the number of individuals, the type and number of rules, and the content of written and oral messages used to process equivocal messages in two simulated organizations. Even though these studies report different results, they attest to the importance of adding message characteristics (equivocality) and meaning to tradition models of information processing (see Eisenberg, 1983). Daft and Macintosh (1981) echo this appeal and report that work units seek out less information when message cues are equivocal. They surmise that organizations condense information into symbol systems that capture the rich meanings of organizational experiences. Indeed, "information" may serve more of a symbolic than a pragmatic function in organizations. Reacting to rational views of decision making, Feldman and March (1981) conclude that information is often misrepresented, serves a surveillance rather than a decision mode, and symbolizes social efficiency. Perhaps this is why organizational participants gather more information than they can use, act first and examine information later, and find value in data that lacks decision relevance.

The Rhetorical Perspective

The study of symbolic influence, while only of recent concern to information-processing researchers, has its roots in ancient Greco-Roman writings on rhetoric and persuasion. Today, communication scholars are applying classical and modern rhetorical theory to the study of complex organizations. This section reviews four lines of rhetorically informed organizational research. The first approach, known as "symbolic convergence theory," is being carved out by Ernest G. Bormann (1972, 1982, 1983) and his colleagues at the University of Minnesota. Symbolic convergence theory derives from "fantasy theme" analysis, a form of rhetorical criticism that highlights the way groups construct shared symbolic realities. Fantasy themes are creative and imaginative interpretations of events that are "chained out" in social settings. When a number of fantasy themes merge, they form a "rhetorical vision" that sustains formal and informal groups. Symbolic convergence theory attends to the dramatic aspects—for example, sagas, narratives, heroes, villains, inside jokes—that foster common understandings within work groups, departments, and entire organizations (Cragan & Shields, 1981). Most importantly, fantasy themes and rhetorical visions aid organizational members in making sense of the past, acting in the present, and anticipating the future (Bormann, 1983). For instance, in a study of a zero-history organization, Bormann, Pratt, and Putnam (1978) show how shared fantasies of organizational members serve as symbolic reactions to power, authority, and male-female leadership and thereby guide group behavior.

A second rhetorically grounded program, under the direction of Phillip K. Tompkins at Purdue University (Cheney, 1983; Tompkins & Cheney, 1982; P. K. Tompkins, Fisher, Infante & Tompkins, 1975) is tentatively labeled "communication and unobtrusive organizational control." This approach attempts to blend Aristotle's (1954) "enthymeme" and Kenneth Burke's (1969) "identification" to interpret, explain, and critique how organizational members are influenced and controlled. The theory posits two "enthymemic" models: enthymeme[1], which resembles Aristotle's rhetorical syllogism in that members bring with them to the organization the major premises necessary for making "appropriate" responses through organizationally desired decisions; and enthymeme[2], where conclusions are drawn from premises inculcated by controlling members of the organization (Tompkins & Cheney, 1982). The process of identification complements the two enthymemes; it is a highly "internal" means of organizational control that is often encouraged and initiated by organizational messages (Cheney, 1983). In this sense, identification serves as a motivating and often emotionally charged master premise, "Do what's best for the organization" (Simon 1976).

A third area, the study of "corporate issue advocacy," has attracted interest at the University of Houston and at Purdue University. Corporate advocacy aims to introduce, change, or reinforce public attitudes on issues of importance to organizations. As a form of purposive "external" organizational communication, corporate advocacy is amenable to analysis through traditional sender-oriented argumentation methods and through contemporary process-oriented approaches. Two types of corporate advocacy programs have emerged: an applied one at Houston and a theoretical one at Purdue. The Houston program investigates communication efforts aimed at advancing the policies of business, educational, governmental, and nonprofit organizations (Heath, 1980; Judd, 1979). Such research aids in the development of effective advocacy campaigns designed to meet organizational needs, especially ones created by external pressures. The Purdue program under the direction of Richard Crable aims to understand the rhetorical and ethical implications of organizational advocacy campaigns. Crable and Vibbert (1983), for example, examine Mobil Corporation's olios in Sunday newpaper magazines as epideictic rhetoric that reinforces particular American values.

A final area of rhetorically oriented research draws from the public address literature, but applies it to organizational settings. As businesses increase their participation in public affairs, Knapp (1970) argues for a concomitant growth in the study of "business rhetoric," that is, field research on the public speeches of business executives. Knapp recommends the blending of qualitative and quantitative methodologies in order to develop "a reliable profile of rhetorical themes, topics, and arguments for business speakers" (pp. 254–255). Organizational communication researchers are beginning to respond to this plea. In a study of an Exxon executive's speech, Geist (1982) illustrates how corporate rhetoric reestablishes a "hierarchy" of values that has been challenged through a loss of public credibility. Focusing on a religious organization, McMillan (1982) examines rhetorical adaptation in an analysis of a formal position paper prepared by officials of the Presbyterian Church. Through these and similar efforts, the scope of public address can be broadened beyond its traditional focus on political leaders.

THE CULTURAL PERSPECTIVE

A more popular approach to the study of organizational communication is known by the catchwords, "organizational cultures." The diversity of ways that organizational culture is examined is not surprising given the ambiguities that surround "culture" itself. Thus, we view the concept's usefulness to organizational study as "a family of concepts" (Pettigrew, 1979, p. 574), rather than as a unitary perspective. As an anthropological concept, culture refers to a social unit's collective sense of what reality is, what it means to be a member of a group, and how a member ought to act. Although students of "organizational culture" approach their subject in a variety of ways, most of them stress the achievement of intersubjective meaning, understanding, and common pursuits among organizational members. Smircich (1983a) offers a useful five-part schema for classifying research approaches to the study of culture.

The first approach, "culture and comparative management," treats culture as a background variable that frames different organizational structures and managerial practices across countries. Much of this research as it appears in the popular press compares U.S., Japanese, and Western European organizations (Ouchi, 1981; Pascale & Athos, 1981). The second approach, "corporate culture," treats culture as a collection of symbols, ceremonies, and practices that are produced internally through organizational interaction ("Corporate Cultures," 1980; Martin & Powers, 1983; Whorton & Worthley, 1981). Cultural research with this conception displays a systems framework. An organization's culture emerges as a response to environmental demands (Pfeffer, 1981a). Thus, it becomes appropriate to speak of "strong" and "weak" organizational cultures, the "strong" being more fitted to organizational survival than the "weak" cultures (Deal & Kennedy, 1982; Peters & Waterman, 1982). In this perspective the manifestations of culture include symbols and symbolism (Dandridge, Mitroff & Joyce, 1980; Johnson, 1977), stories (Martin & Powers, 1983; Mitroff & Kilmann, 1976); myths (Boje, Fedor & Rowland, 1982; Smith, 1973); sagas (Clark, 1972); rituals (Deal & Kennedy, 1982); folklore (Kreps, 1983); rules and norms (Shull & Del Beque, 1965), and specialized language (Hirsch & Andrews, 1983).

In the first two approaches, culture is treated as a variable—as part of a system of patterns that can be discovered and to some extent controlled for managerial improvement (Smircich, 1983b). The following three programs use culture as a *root metaphor* for understanding organizations; they view culture as something an organization is, rather than merely something an organization has (Smircich, 1983a). However, while the latter three approaches share a general concern, they differ in the anthropological base from which they borrow. The third, labeled as the "cognitive perspective," is tied to Goodenough's (1971) ethnoscience and treats culture as a system of shared cognitions, knowledge, and beliefs (Rossi, 1974). In this vein, Harris and Cronen (1979), at the University of Massachusetts, outline and apply a rules-based theory that treats "an organization [as] analogous to a culture and that . . . can be analyzed by identifying its collectively defined master contract" (p. 12). Within this framework, researchers examine member competence in "coorienting" to the master contract and in following the constitutive and regulative rules of the organization.

The fourth approach, labeled the "symbolic perspective," is grounded in the work of anthropologist Clifford Geertz (1973), who views societies as elaborate systems of shared symbols and meanings. From this view, an organization is conceived of as discourse; communication, as the process of organizing (Hawes, 1974). Organizational scripts thus need to be interpreted (Manning, 1979), read (S. P. Turner, 1983), deciphered (Van Maanen, 1973), and thematically discerned (Smith, 1973). This approach has attracted a speech communication following, particularly at the universities of Utah, Texas, and Southern Illinois. At Utah, Pacanowsky and his colleagues (Pacanowsky & O'Donnell-Trujillo, 1982, 1983) articulate a comprehensive view of organizations as cultures. The spirit of this work is captured by Pacanowsky and O'Donnell-Trujillo (1983): "Anthropologically considered, communication is not information transfer, but language use. And organizations are not to be seen as computer-like machines, but rather more like tribes" (p. 127). Along these lines, they identify and examine crucial characteristics of organizational performances. Deetz and his colleagues at Southern Illinois University (Deetz, 1984; Koch & Deetz, 1981) have developed a "metaphor analysis" of organizations as a means of describing how an organization's reality is produced and reproduced through language use and dominant metaphors. Following Lakoff and Johnson's (1980) work, Koch and Deetz (1981) identified metaphors that show "not only the current reality of the organization but also the other possibilities open to it" (p. 13). Finally, under the direction of Browning (Brown, McMillan & Blackman, 1981; Browning, 1978; Henderson, 1981; Whitfill, 1981; Browning & Hopper, 1979), researchers at Texas are conducting detailed case studies of reality construction in a variety of organizations. Browning and Hopper (1979) argue that through such descriptive research, "the reader gets a feel for characters, their relationships, and their responses to the stream of events with which they have contact" (p. 8).

The fifth and final approach to the study of organizational culture, "structural and psychodynamic perspectives," is the visible expression of unconscious psychological processes (Levi-Strauss, 1963). The analysis of structure as ordered relations that turns "parts" into a coherent, meaningful whole is central to this view (B. A. Turner, 1971). This approach to culture can reveal structures that direct behavior and that exist below the level of conscious awareness. Very few organizational analysts adopt the structural-psychodynamic approach (a few who have are McSwain & White, 1982; Walter, 1980). In an interesting structural-semiotic study, Broms and Gahmberg (1982) examine the "deep structure" of myths surrounding the "Chrysler Crisis" and report that the crisis is not the Japanese or small-car problem, but the preservation of the American Dream.

THE POLITICAL PERSPECTIVE

The political perspective, as developed in this essay, subsumes a number of diverse yet related orientations to organizational communication; namely, studies of power, politics, conflict, bargaining, and deviance. Drawing from Cyert and March's (1963) view of organizations as political coalitions, this perspective treats organizations as sets of different interest groups, "fractured by subcultures" (Baldridge, 1971, p. 25). In this view decisions emerge through an influence process frequently characterized by compromise and bargaining among groups with competing interests. However, one school within this perspective, critical theory, contends that this competition is not among equals because "dominant coalitions" or power groups control most organizational actions. This section focuses on communicative approaches to the study of organizational power, politics, conflict, and control. Communication, in this sense, refers to overt or covert means of exercising power, signaling control, or manifesting conflict.

"Power," like conflict, is a frequently used and often abused construct. This abuse stems in part from equating it with coercion, manipulation, leadership, and authority. Moreover, power is seen paradoxically as static and dynamic, actual and potential, moral and immoral, intentional and unintentional. Yet, despite this confusion, power is defined in general terms as influencing another person's behaviors to produce a desired outcome (Pettigrew, 1973; Schein, 1977). Theorists differ, however, in treating power more specifically as an individual drive (McLelland, 1975), as an interpersonal influence process (Emerson, 1962), as a resource (French & Raven, 1968), or as a characteristic of a bureaucracy—for example, technology or ideology (Bendix, 1970; Salaman & Thompson, 1980). In light of these disagreements, Goldberg, Cavanaugh, and Larson (1983) at the University of Denver survey organizational members for their meanings of power. Their study uncovers six dimensions: power as (1) instinctive drive, (2) personal charisma, (3) influence, (4) politics, (5) resource dependence, and (6) a good force (an exciting, desirable action).

Organizational scholars concentrate primarily on three of these: resource dependence, influence, and politics, with a special emphasis on resource control (Salancik & Pfeffer, 1974), work-unit centrality, dependability (Crozier, 1964), and ability to cope with uncertainty (Hickson, Hinings, Lee, Schneck & Pennings, 1971). From a communicative view these dimensions translate into influence, information control, politicking, and symbolic power. Influence models treat power as an interpersonal process defined by access to critical resources and the use of persuasive tactics. Resources typically derive from French and Raven's (1968) classic bases of power: reward, coercive, legitimate, referent, and expert power. Research on influence tactics examines the effects of goals and targets (superiors or subordinates) on the choice of particular strategies (Kipnis, Schmidt & Wilkinson, 1980; Patchen, 1968; Wilkinson & Kipnis, 1978). Other studies treat influence as a strategic maneuver for gaining power; for example, forming alliances, maintaining flexibility, neutralizing the opposition (Izraeli, 1975; Kanter, 1977).

One strategic maneuver often cited as a means of gaining power is manipulating information flow (Du Brin, 1972; Martin & Sims, 1956). Information, then, becomes a resource or a power base, controlled through accessing, withholding, distributing, or evaluating specific messages. Mechanic (1962) notes that lower-level members gain organizational power through control of complex technological information that is unavailable to high-ranking officials. A work unit's ability to generate and supply others with information becomes a source of power and autonomy (Poole, 1978). For example, work units, in their desire to be autonomous, often withhold information from and consciously ignore messages sent from other departments (Pfeffer & Salancik, 1977).

Especially important are gatekeepers who control message flow between critical sources and decision-making bodies (Pettigrew, 1972). But, such information control signifies powerlessness as well as power in that organizational members who lack access to critical resources—for example, first-line supervisors and clerical staff—frequently grasp for power through protecting their turf and blocking information flow (Kanter, 1977). The distinction between powerholders and the powerless, however, may reside in the types and practices of information control. The political approach adopts influence models of power but examines them in terms of individual versus organizational needs. Thus, political behavior often represents actions directed toward self-aggrandizement, instead of company goals (Du Brin, 1972). In a communication study of organizational politics, Jablin (1981) reports that subordinates are less open and less satisfied with superiors who are highly involved in organizational politics, as compared with those who are only minimally or moderately political.

A final approach to the study of power stems from interpreting organizational information and events. In the symbolic approach power accrues to individuals who, through the use of political language and symbolic ceremony, give meanings to both physical referents, such as budgets and products, and organizational events (Johnson, 1977; Pfeffer, 1981b). Influence, in this perspective, is the ability to use symbols, stories, and myths to promote consensus on the interpretation of events. In a provocative essay, Conrad (1983a), at the University of North Carolina, recasts traditional approaches to organizational power by placing argument at the surface level and myth and metaphor at the deeper levels that ultimately shape decisional processes. In a parallel manner, Lukes (1974) proposes a three-dimensional model of power with the third dimension based on keeping decisions out of politics through inaction and latent conflict.

Another area closely related to power and politics is organizational conflict. "Conflict" is often confounded with such concepts as "misunderstanding," "hostility," and "competition"; however, it is usually defined as the interaction between interdependent parties who perceive incompatible goals or values (Mack & Snyder, 1957). Literature on the role of communication and organizational conflict is beginning to grow as researchers link conflict to intrapersonal role dilemmas (Baird & Diebolt, 1976; Barker, 1982; Van Sell, Brief & Schuler, 1981); superior-subordinate relationships

(R. J. Burke, 1970); and boundary spanning between departments, line-staff personnel, and organizations (Adams, 1976; Lawrence & Lorsch, 1967). Although a number of typologies exist for the study of organizational conflict, communication researchers focus primarily on distinguishing constructive from destructive conflicts (Folger & Poole, 1983), on the dimensions and assumptions of conflict (Hawes & Smith, 1973), and on process or stage development models of conflict (Pondy, 1967). This review employs Pondy's (1967) typology of bureaucratic, system, and bargaining conflicts to organize research trends in this emerging area.

Bureaucratic conflict focuses on incompatibilities between superiors and subordinates, particularly those that relate to autonomy and control. Following models developed by Blake, Shepard, and Mouton (1964) and Kilmann and Thomas (1977), studies conducted at Purdue University (Bullis, Cox & Bokeno, 1982; Putnam & Wilson, 1982), at Ohio University (Ross & DeWine, 1982), and at the University of Wisconsin (Riggs, 1983; Sillars, 1980) have developed scales and coding schemes for analysis of superior-subordinate conflict strategies. These studies report that conflict between superiors and subordinates is inevitable and often a constructive force (Sussman, 1975). Tests of these scales reveal that managers typically use forcing strategies with subordinates; but supervisory level, skill, and sense of self-confidence affect the choice of conflict strategies (Conrad, 1983b; Putnam & Wilson, 1982). In a study that combines bases of power with conflict management, Richmond, Wagner, and McCroskey (1983) observe that active conflict strategies, referent power, and employee-centered leadership are linked to increased communication satisfaction and decreased communication anxiety.

Conflicts with organizational peers in the same departments are frequently managed through avoidance tactics (Putnam & Wilson, 1982). In a study on attitudes toward conflict, P. K. Tompkins, Fisher, Infante, and E. Tompkins (1974) report that individuals at upper levels with high organizational identification scores respond more favorably to organizational conflicts than do lower-level employees. System conflicts differ from bureaucratic ones in that they focus on horizontal communication and coordination across organizational levels. Putnam & Wilson (1982) report that interdepartmental conflicts are typically managed through forcing strategies. Because managers often serve as liaisons or integrators between departments, their influence often facilitates effective horizontal conflict management (Lawrence & Lorsch, 1967).

Bargaining research differs from studies of bureaucratic and system conflicts by focusing on struggles over scarce resources between interest groups. Game theoretical models with a focus on the characteristics of labor-management negotiators, availability of communication, and bargaining outcomes typify early work on bargaining (see Donohue, 1978; Smith, 1969; Steinfatt & Miller, 1974). More recent studies, however, test for the effects of message strategies on negotiated outcomes (Bednar & Glauser, 1981; Donohue, 1981b; Putnam & Jones, 1982a; Theye & Seller, 1979). (For a detailed review of the literature on the role of communication in bargaining, the reader is referred to Putnam & Jones, 1982b.) Two lines of work, however, merit special attention. Research at Purdue University under the direction of Linda Putnam (Keough, 1983; Putnam & Jones, 1982a) is exploring bargaining as the social construction of meanings through interaction between and within bargaining groups. With a micro-level orientation, work at Michigan State (Donohue, 1981a, 1981b; Dono-hue, Diez & Stahle, 1983) explores the conversational rule-structure of bargaining interaction. Both the Purdue and the Michigan State programs extend earlier research on intergroup relationships, information management, issue development, and argumentation in negotiations (Reiches & Harral, 1974; Walton & McKersie, 1965).

Research on bargaining and conflict typically assumes that organizational subgroups participate equally in competition for resources. Critical theorists, however, contend that unequal distribution of power constrains and represses many participants in organizations (Deetz, 1982). Technical rationality and the impersonal practices of bureaucracy often disguise this oppression (Deetz & Kersten, 1983). The goal of critical research is emancipation, realized through exposing the irrationality of organizational behavior, the way structure is taken for granted and embedded in organizational talk, and the way ideology and technology control belief systems (Deetz & Kersten, 1983; Zey-Ferrell & Aiken, 1981). Individuals and groups become emancipated through contradictions, the driving force of change (Benson, 1977); direct and indirect social intervention (Deetz & Kersten, 1983); and organizational deviance (Stanley, 1981). Stewart (1980), in her study of "whistle blowing" of scientists and engineers, illustrates a direct form of member dissent. Putnam's (1984) investigation of message patterns that can produce paradoxes and contradictions offers suggestions for "getting out" of organizational traps. The political perspective, through its focus on power and conflict, provides organizational communication scholars an opportunity to uncover subtle factors that constrain a person's work life.

PRACTICAL APPLICATIONS OF ORGANIZATIONAL COMMUNICATION RESEARCH

Social scientists and organizational practitioners exist in an inseparable bond that stems from the bridge between theory and practice and from the dual roles of researcher and consultant (Albrow, 1980; Zey-Ferrell & Aiken, 1981). Just as academicians shape practice with theoretical models and research findings, practitioners influence research through sharing their "personal theories" of organizational life. This section examines the links between research and practice with special attention to the history of this relationship, communication training and consulting, organizational communication audits, and implications of the emerging approaches for communication practice.

Organizational communication grew out of a concern for developing managerial skills, improving the effectiveness of various media, and discovering why communication fails (Sexton & Staudt, 1959). Early efforts to address these issues applied simple solutions to complex problems and virtually ignored developments in communication theory (Redding, 1966; Van Voorhis, 1974). In the 1950s communication training, evaluation, and consulting began to flourish. To ascertain the need for these programs, researchers surveyed employees on the amount of time they spent communicating (Klemmer & Snyder, 1972) and on the importance of such skills as listening, persuading, and interviewing for different organizational roles (DiSalvo, Larsen & Seiler, 1976; Hanna, 1978). To understand the nature and extent of organizational training programs, researchers investigated the frequency, content, and materials used in public speaking training (Hicks, 1955; Knapp, 1968, 1969; Zelko, 1951); the importance, goals, and attitudes toward communication training (Wasylik, Sussman, & Leri, 1976); the frequency, targets, and methods of training (Meister & Reinsch, 1978); and the role functions and conflicts of communication trainers and consultants (Putnam, 1979).

Training activities and problem-solving consultation are often combined in practice by organizational trainers. External consultants, who are not members of the organization, serve primarily as "trouble shooters" to diagnose problems and determine appropriate intervention techniques. Redding (1979a) defines communication consulting as a broad-ranged "helping" activity and indicates that the role requires "a thorough grounding" in rhetorical, interpersonal, and mass communication theories. Approximately one-third of 200 respondents in a survey on communication consulting employ intervention techniques associated with organizational development, a system of planned organizational change (Eich, 1977). In a literature review on the role of communication in organizational development, Axley (1980) concludes that the goals of such techniques as team building, process consultation, T-groups, and participatory decision making include improving communication, without careful attention to the repercussions these improvements will have on other organizational behaviors.

The organizational communication audit, as a type of consulting, provides an evaluation of a corporation's entire communication system. Initiated by Odiorne (1954) as a concept for the study of information flow, the communication audit now refers to a multi-instrument procedure for collecting, analyzing, and feeding back data on communication climate, networks, media usage, information flow, and communication satisfaction (Goldhaber et al., 1978; Goldhaber & Rogers, 1979). Audit systems provide standardized data-gathering techniques and a normative data bank for comparison of research results. The International Communication Audit represents a joint effort of over 100 scholars "to provide organizations with reliable, factual data about their internal communication" (Greenbaum, Hellweg & Falcione, 1983, p. 89). Richetto (1977) recaps the history of this process, and Greenbaum et al. (1983) present a very comprehensive review of studies that evaluate organizational communication systems, including research that employs the ICA Audit and the Organizational Communication Development audit developed in Finland under the leadership of Osmo Wiio (Wiio, Goldhaber & Yates, 1980). As of 1979 researchers and practitioners had administered the ICA Audit to over 5,000 employees in 19 organizations.

In many respects, theory and practice in organizational communication have taken diverse turns. Emerging areas of theory and research appear less concerned with problems that managers face and more concerned with understanding the complexities of organizational life. Communication trainers who adhere to emerging approaches might concentrate less on media usage and presentational skills and more on developing problem-solving skills for analyzing messages and organizational symbols (Smircich, 1983b). As Johnson and Shaw (1978) propose, "consultant-heroes," as opposed to "trainer technicians," deal in ideas, inspire clients to think, strive for impartiality, and have a vision for what is being done and why. From the political perspective, organizational members would need to intensify their training in bargaining and strategic decision making (Tushman, 1977).

Communication consulting, while primarily a tool of management, might be used for organizational reflection to expose repressive actions and unnecessary bureaucratic controls. While it is unlikely that consultants will become critical theorists, they might increase their awareness of the political implications of their interventions (Tushman, 1977; Browning, 1977); the value and ethical dilemmas of consulting (Redding, 1979a); and the managerial bias inherent in projects commissioned and directed by "elite" organizational members (Zey-Ferrell & Aiken, 1981).

CONCLUSION

What we have tried to do in this review is to paint, with broad strokes, a "mural" of organizational communication as a subunit of the speech communication field. We have depicted the emergence of "organizational communication" as an identifiable area of study—how it has borrowed from other fields and how its research foci have shifted during its short history. Because of the nature of this effort, we have had to organize and "color" bodies of research in ways that may make them seem too sharply distinguished; indeed a "true" painting of organizational communication would be rather impressionistic. Nevertheless, we have offered what we think is a useful schema for viewing the field now.

As organizational communication progresses, we expect it to follow the strong lines already being sketched in the 1980s. Organizational communication researchers will probably emphasize message content and process even more, striving to capture meaning, context, and changes in symbolic activity among organizational actors. We see researchers continuing to explore to a much greater extent the multiple perspectives of organizational actors, rather than looking at the world solely through a managerial lens. Third, and along similar lines, we anticipate that the meaning of "practice" or "application" will continue to broaden, as researchers attempt not only to help "the organization" (that is, upper management) but also individuals and groups within it, often through critique of the existing order. Fourth, we expect that researchers will continue to employ a pluralism of methods in order to view organizational life from a variety of angles. Finally, and perhaps most important for the student of organizational communication, we anticipate that the field will eventually move toward a clearer image of itself, a coherent identity embracing preferred concepts, theories, methods, and interventions.

8

Oral Interpretation: Twentieth-Century Theory and Practice

JILL TAFT-KAUFMAN

Perspectives on the oral performance of literature in this century have been broad in scope. Scholars in interpretation have assumed their discipline to be a performing art, literary study, a communicative act, self-development, or often some combination of these processes (Whitaker, 1969). Varying views take shape based upon which element or elements of the interpretative act are thought to be the most significant: the performer, the text, or the audience. As oral performance of literature achieves maturity in this century, the delineation between performer, text, and audience is, however, no longer clear-cut. New definitions of what constitutes a text and who audiences for interpretation might be have dramatically altered the nature of oral interpretation, forging new notions of what oral performance of literature is and what it can do. In this essay I shall trace those major currents in scholarship, pedagogy, and performance that have influenced academic oral interpretation in this century. While I cannot hope to be all inclusive in an essay of this length, I shall discuss representative thought and practice and indicate how these trends have helped to shape what oral interpretation has been, currently is, and promises to be in the immediate future.

Oral interpretation in the early years of this century was characterized by narrow theory and practice that delineated interpretation from acting. The oral performance of literature was studied primarily as a distinct style of performing art and as a communicative act between performer and audience. A shift of focus to the text, a surge in critical theory, and the corresponding rise of interpretation as literary study occurred during the

1950s and early 1960s, and a growing interest in critical theory both within and outside of the speech communication field occurred during the 1970s and early 1980s. Stimulated by theories in anthropology, sociology, sociolinguistics, and reader-response criticism, and by research done in the areas of social cognition and oral history, interpreters significantly broadened performance theory and practice.

EARLY TRENDS IN ORAL INTERPRETATION

The drive to differentiate itself from English departments and establish a unique academic identity influenced the entire speech field in the early years of this century. In keeping with this impetus, oral interpretation had to "develop an academic discipline that would resemble existing disciplines enough to justify its place within the academic community, while staking out a body of theory unique enough to avoid appropriation by similar disciplines" (Gray, 1979). The thrust toward demonstrating credentials with both academic commonality and uniqueness produced, according to Paul Gray, two significant emphases for early academic interpreters: (1) "a radical de-emphasis of emotion" in the performance of literature, with a consequent emphasis on cognitive factors, and (2) an effort to delineate clearly oral interpretation from its "closest competitor," acting.

S. H. Clark's influential *Interpretation of the Printed Page* (1915) reflected the shift away from emotion. Clark avoided discussing emotional content in literature until the fifteenth of the book's sixteen chapters (Gray, 1979). In concert with this focus, Clark attempted to distance interpretation from the negative image of elocution by downplaying the entire concept of delivery. Appropriate physical technique, Clark assumed, evolves when the reader understands the logical thought units of a text.

Oral interpretation's pursuit of academic uniqueness reinforced the attempt to distinguish clearly interpretation from acting. The debate over this distinction was not new with early 20th century academic interpreters. Elocutionists as well as the expressionists at the end of the nineteenth and beginning of the twentieth centuries had attempted to delineate the two forms. S. S. Curry, the prime spokesman for the expressionist school, had taken a strong stand on the issue in his popular *The Province of Expression* (1891). Curry clearly viewed the oral performance of literature as essentially different from and of a higher order than acting. Delicate suggestion of action was advocated as a guard against the "violent gesticulation" of the actors of the day (Edwards, 1983).

As the desire for academic viability grew, the acting versus interpretation debate appeared highly pertinent and soon found its way into early scholarly meetings and journals of this century. At the first conference of the newly formed National Association of Academic Teachers of Public Speaking in 1915, Maude May Babcock delivered a paper on "Interpretative Presentation Versus Impersonative Presentation" that was monumental in its attempts to define and delimit the characteristics of interpretation as different from those of acting. Babcock's essay was published the following year in *The Quarterly Journal of Public Speaking*. Her thesis was that interpretation is based upon a specific style of performance that does not permit literal vocal or bodily characterization. That is, impersonation, by which a performer uses overt physicalization to portray character and action, is not in keeping with interpretation, which should suggest character and action through only minimal use of body and vocal techniques. In a paper that voiced opposition to Babcock's limited scope for the performer, Rollo Anson Tallcott maintained that certain types of literature that project strong characterization might best be conveyed by impersonation. This controversy culminated in a series of articles by Babcock and Tallcott (Babcock, 1916a, 1916b; Tallcott, 1916, 1923) marking the first scholarly journal debate within the interpretation field. Explicitly it was an argument over method. Their inability to agree on definitions for the concepts of interpretation, impersonation, personation, and acting never became an explicit issue (Williams, 1977). Implicitly, however, the debate sought to establish a crucial early academic definition for the performance of literature. Babcock's assumptions about the priority of suggestion over impersonation won favor over Tallcott's notions that the arts of delivery can be classified according to their proportions of realism and suggestion and that the nature of the literature ought to dictate one's delivery method. Paul Edwards maintains that Tallcott's comprehensive classification system described in his 1922 text suggests that even Tallcott, a defender of acting, was "interested in preserving the distinction" between the two forms (p. 542).

Although Babcock's argument in favor of suggestion prevailed, the debate over the dichotomy did not die. Nearly 25 years later, Gertrude Johnson included the Babcock-Tallcott articles in the first book of collected essays on interpretation (1940). Johnson extended the debate by adding several new essays, including her own, on the question of interpretation versus impersonation. The distinction, as we shall see, would not lose its sharp edges until much later in the century.

Implicit in Babcock's idea that oral performance of literature should be based upon a set style of delivery was the premise that interpretation was both a performing art and a communicative act between performer and audience. Early textbook writers, such as Clark, Charles Woolbert and Severina Nelson (1927), and Wayland Maxfield Parrish (1932), advocated this view. Supporting the idea of interpretation as communicative act,

Woolbert, who was an early advocate of experimental research in audience psychology, elevated the role of the audience to a status commensurate with performer and text.

The perspective of oral interpretation as performing art and communicative act was nurtured early in this century by Edward Bullough's essay on "'Psychical Distance' as a Factor in Art and an Aesthetic Principle" (1912). According to Beverly Whitaker Long (1983), Bullough formulated ideas that helped shape interpreters' discussions of the process of perception during oral interpretation. Long summarizes Bullough's theory by stating that people do "not take practical scientific, or ethical attitudes towards art" as they do "toward matters in the real, workaday world." Instead, they take a "special attitude, one characterized by simultaneous separation and involvement" (p. 568). Bullough called this dual state "distance." The idea of aesthetic distance underscored for interpreters the notion that art and reality significantly differ. "In maintaining the separation of these worlds, readers do not present an imaginative world; they clearly retain their own identity in the same world of reality as that of the listener, inviting an audience to participate imaginatively in the fictive world of the text" (Long, p. 573). Such imaginative participation is elicited in performance through suggestion. Long points out that this theory, which first appeared in print in relationship to oral interpretation in 1928 (Dolman), held sway in interpretation textbooks well into the mid-century. In fact, its legacy can still be seen in a number of contemporary textbooks that call for the use of suggestion as the way to allow the audience to participate imaginatively in the experience of literature.

Although most early theorists advocated that the main function of oral interpretation was to communicate literature to an audience, a minority view was already taking shape in the 1920s. This view, which had its roots in early 20th-century expressive theory (Gray, 1979), focused upon interpretation as a method by which a reader might come to know a text through intrinsic study. Both views sought to increase literary understanding for audience and performer, but the focus on text emphasized oral reading as a critical tool for conceptual understanding. Algernon Tassin took this premise as the basis for his 1923 book *The Oral Study of Literature*. According to Thomas Sloan (1966), "Tassin saw oral reading as an instrument—both a pedagogical and a critical instrument—useful in all respects and necessary in some, for the intrinsic approach to the study of literature" (p. 6). This text-centered approach to the oral performance of literature was given credence by writers in the 1940s, such as Frank Rarig (1940), C. C. Cunningham (1941), and Sara Lowrey and Gertrude Johnson (1942). Yet the idea of oral interpretation as literary study did not achieve significant status in the field until the 1950s.

THE DOMINANCE OF TEXT-CENTERED STUDIES

By the late 1940s the status of oral interpretation was secure in academia. The early trend toward journal articles that justified the use of oral interpretation to teach reading diminished and was replaced by more diverse scholarly concerns, such as questions of prosody and discussions of historical figures and periods in oral interpretation. At approximately the same time, from 1946 to 1957, oral interpretation enrollments in colleges and universities increased almost 50% (Brooks, 1960). Graduate work in interpretation, which had begun in 1918, had proceeded at a steady, though slow pace, with 200 masters and 36 doctorates having been awarded from 1918 to 1950 (Heston, 1983). By 1938, at Northwestern, a student could elect graduate study in interpretation, a change from the undifferentiated course of study that characterized early graduate education for interpreters (Heston). Ten years later, Northwestern's Ph.D. program in interpretation had been joined by doctoral programs at the University of Wisconsin, the University of Michigan, Columbia, and Louisiana State University.

Wallace Bacon's admonition about curriculum in 1949 suggests the shift in definition that was emerging among interpretation scholars during the period. "No graduate student in Interpretation should be permitted to go forth without having some understanding of the problems of literary form and its relation to content, without having directed his attention to such matters as style, point of view, tone, structure, prosody, vocabulary, emotional appeals and meaning" (p. 317). At midcentury, the literary text was becoming the primary focus of interpretation study. The idea of oral interpretation as a way of studying and experiencing literary texts was based upon earlier currents in literary theory. The "New Criticism," which officially began in 1934 with the publication of John Crowe Ransom's "Poetry: A Note in Ontology," was influenced by I. A. Richards and T. S. Eliot, who provided the foundation upon which the New Critics had built. From Richards the New Critics extracted an intrinsic method for understanding a text. Rather than stressing the background of the author or the social milieu in which the text was written, Richards' intrinsic analysis emphasized close internal linguistic scrutiny, with special focus on irony and metaphor. To underscore the importance of metaphor the New Critics also looked to Eliot, who believed that poetic knowledge, with its emphasis on connotation, was a higher form of knowledge than that provided by science, with its stress on denotation.

The literary theorists who adopted Richards' and Eliot's ideas were not uniform in their theories of literature. Yet the representative New Critics—Ransom, Cleanth Brooks, and Allen Tate—commonly embraced the idea of intrinsic analysis as well as the distinction between poetic and scientific knowledge and the subsequent acknowledgment that metaphor was not ornamentation but both a necessary and superior form for embodying truth. This stance suggested that elements such as paradox, irony, and ambiguity hold important, unparaphrasable aspects of a poem. Perhaps most important for oral interpretation was the concept proffered by both Brooks and Ransom (Brooks, 1934; Ransom, 1947) that poetry was a dramatic utterance with the poet creating either a fictional persona or a kind of alter ego through which to speak.

Based upon these New Critical tenets, Don Geiger began in the early 1950s to establish arguments for the literary or textual foundations of interpretation. In "Oral Interpretation and the 'New Criticism'" (1950), Geiger advanced Brooks' idea that the basic characteristic of the literary construct is that literature is a complex of attitudes. Geiger fleshed out Brooks' concept by suggesting that attitudes become significant as they are directed toward something, specifically toward a named something. "Things must be named so we know what attitude should be taken toward them" (p. 512). It is the job of the oral interpreter, Geiger maintained, to communicate these attitudes. "The oral reader, like the writer, is engaged in naming the world" (p. 512). In "A 'Dramatic' Approach to Interpretative Analysis" (1952), Geiger further advanced the idea that life is a complex of situation-attitude relationships and that literature is a representation of selected experience reflected by a dramatic use of language. We may trace these situations and attitudes or dramatic elements of the experience of a text by discovering the answers to certain specific questions. The questions, which were to become staples of intrinsic textual analysis for oral inter-preters, were similar to reference points that Kenneth Burke explored in *A Grammar of Motives* (1945). Geiger credited the similarity but did not acknowledge a direct Burkean derivation of the dramatic questions, ques-tions he pointed out, that newspaper reporters also ask: (1) Who is perform-ing what action of thought or feeling or deed? (2) Where and when is it being performed? (3) How is it being performed? (4) Why is it being performed? and (5) How do the answers relate to one another?

In the same article, Geiger reaffirmed the New Critical position that the function of the language of a poem is to establish the exact nature of experience that the poem represents. Thus, he urged oral interpreters to study the subtleties of that language embodied in irony, synecdoche, con-notation, symbol, paradox, and rhythm. In keeping with the idea that the subtleties of the experience are contained in the subtleties of the language, Geiger objected to précis writing, a practice commonly advocated in earlier textbooks, such as Parrish's *Reading Aloud: Technique in Interpretation* (1936) and Argus Tressider's *Reading to Others* (1942). Use of a précis or paraphrase to get at the author's premise does not, according to Geiger, acknowledge the exact words and order that the writer uses. One must recognize that the peculiarities represented in the work are all meaningful. Understanding the relationships among words is necessary before obtaining the meaning of a work.

While Geiger's ideas are too extensive to be thoroughly discussed here, his legacy to interpretation includes an emphasis on close textual analysis, the irreducibility of a poem, literature as a form of knowledge, and literature as dramatic experience. These ideas, which appeared in frequent articles and in monograph form throughout the 1950s, were gathered into a collection of essays aimed at advanced students in the field. In *The Sound, Sense, and Performance of Literature* (1963), Geiger explored the distinct nature of oral interpretation's literary identity. Terming oral interpretation "an unformulable amalgam of acting, public speaking, critical reaction, and sympathetic sharing" (p. 86), Geiger even addressed the longstanding issue of acting versus interpretation. Unlike earlier scholars, however, Geiger's rationale was always a conceptual rather than a practical one. Both the substance and the method by which he approached oral performance set a tone for the text-centered studies that were to come.

In keeping with the view of literature as dramatic experience and as a distinct form of knowledge, Bacon and Robert Breen's book, *Literature as Experience* (1959), significantly advanced text-centered studies in interpretation. Half of this influential study explored the nature of the reader's experience in the act of reading and the significance that act holds for the individual. Stressing the correspondence between "*actual* experience which life presents and *virtual* experience which literature presents" (p. 8), Bacon and Breen summarized the writer-text-reader relationship as one in which "a writer fashions a work of art which reveals his discoveries about life, and a reader tests the value of those discoveries by a kind of sympathetic and critical imitation of the actions and reactions found in the writer's work" (p. 9). While both silent and oral readers develop attitudes empathically induced by the writer's description of actions, it is the oral reader, Bacon and Breen stressed, whose response is fuller and more consequential. Citing George Herbert Mead (1934) and Burke (1945), Bacon and Breen discussed the value of perceiving attitudes in literature as incipient social acts. The oral reader, who is "quick to anticipate the attitudes of others because of his disposition to act (developed through his insistence on a physical expression of the literary text), is closer to the genuine act than are the substitutive attitudes of the silent reader" (p. 11).

In the second portion of their book, Bacon and Breen described in unprecedented detail how a writer uses language and structure to create the distinct experience of the text. Bacon later explained in *The Art of Interpretation* (1966) how the interpreter is to convey his or her understanding of this experience. With the concept of "matching," Bacon stressed that the interpreter establishes a congruence between the inner form of the literature and his or her inner self.*

A restoration of rhetoric to literary study complemented the text-centered emphasis that had gained dominance by the 1960s. The long and symbiotic relationship of rhetoric and poetics, which had been all but severed early in the century when speech scholars declared their independence from English departments, held new promise. Acknowledging the dominance of New Critical theory in interpretation, Sloan urged that rhetoric might "negotiate a union between New Critics who see literature as aestheticians, . . . and rhetoricians who see literature as transactional gesture—communicative shaping of an experience" (1967, p. 91). Advocating the New Critical perspective of the poem as dramatic utterance, Sloan pointed out that a dramatic analysis investigates the rhetoric *in* a poem by looking at verbal strategies within a speaking situation that is totally imaginary. Extending this New Critical perspective to include a rhetorical focus, one might examine the rhetoric *of* a poem by analyzing "the ways whereby the poet through the poem uses verbal strategies" to engage an audience (1969, p. 187). Sloan saw this latter function as similar to that used by Neo-Aristotelian rhetoricians in the art of public speaking "except that it focuses on understanding the nature of the poem rather than understanding the nature of the poet or nature of rhetoric" (1969, p. 187). Thus, the New Critical focus on the poem itself might be fused with the examination of how a communicator strategically influences an audience's perceptions.†

The fusion of New Critical theory with rhetoric invited a clear translation into performance and pedagogy. Sloan described this translation by stating that "as the oral interpreter responds to a literary work, he necessarily makes himself, or is made into, an audience of that work; his responsibility as an oral interpreter means that he has a responsibility to analyze the causes of his responses and to seek to arouse those responses in other people" (1967, p. 93). The oral interpreter thus does "not merely 'perform' a poem but makes a conscious effort to get others to join him in the dance"

---

*Bacon's *The Art of Interpretation* has been one of the most influential of contemporary interpretation texts. Through this book and Bacon's longstanding presence as chair of the Interpretation Department at Northwestern, he has disseminated a vocabulary and perspective that has dominated much of modern interpretation thought. His colleague, Charlotte Lee, has produced the most popular interpretation text of recent times, *Oral Interpretation*, which has gone through six editions since 1952.

†Sloan hoped that this fusion of rhetoric and poetic would also influence rhetorical studies in which aesthetic fulfillment was usually looked upon as separate from communication.

(1967, p. 93). In doing so, he or she uses oral delivery "to clarify the implied author's style in order to elicit the audience's response to the ethos of the work" (1967, p. 96).

The influence of intrinsic analysis developed through the metaphors of literature as dramatic or rhetorical discourse, along with the accompanying premise that oral interpretation was "a viable and valuable means of studying literature" (Maclay & Sloan, 1972) prevailed throughout the 1960s. It was reflected in increased graduate activity and new curricula that included course work in literary forms, literary periods, single authors, and literary criticism. The perspective informed textbooks, such as Robert Beloof's *Performing Voice in Literature* (1966) and climaxed with Maclay and Sloan's *Interpretation: An Approach to the Study of Literature* (1972). The need for intrinsic analysis and the idea of literature as dramatic remains vital today, with dramatic analysis still used extensively in contemporary texts, such as Long and HopKins' *Performing Literature* (1982).

NEW TYPES OF PERFORMANCES

Just as the 1950s brought the strong emergence of interpretation as literary study, so it also brought significant new forms to the actual practice of performance. Until the 1950s, the dominant type of performance practice had been the solo performance. Group performance had made a debut in the early 1930s with the introduction of choral reading to the field. This ensemble technique, which arranged readers on the basis of vocal effects, boasted the advantages of a group environment to support the shy student and to provide vocal variety for an audience. Although it was extremely popular in practice and provided the subject matter of numerous articles and books in the 1930s and 1940s, it cannot be considered a forerunner of the kind of group performance that was to emerge in the 1950s. The new group performance distinguished itself initially by performances aimed at stimulating imaginative audience involvement with the literature. Moreover, while choral reading had been emphasized for its value in building student confidence, group performance of the 1950s initially gained its impetus from a distinctly different source than the classroom.

According to Joanna Maclay (1983), most scholars in group performance attribute the growth of group performance to the influence of professional theatre productions. Paul Gregory's 1951 commercial success of the First Drama Quartette in *Don Juan in Hell*, the third act dream sequence of Shaw's *Man and Superman*, along with the subsequent production of Benet's *John Brown's Body* toured a great number of college and university campuses. The style of the popular shows left a legacy that was to dictate form for academic group performances. As the concept of group performance grew popular in the 1950s, the technique became codified based on the Gregory productions and on the notion of suggestion that was generally popular in the oral interpretation textbooks of the time. Accordingly, a readers or interpreters theatre performance stressed use of scripts, stools, formal attire, presentational delivery, and basic lighting for illumination. To distinguish it from conventional theatre, directors of the form commonly dismissed memorized lines, costumes, makeup, and nearly all movement and onstage performer interaction.

In the early 1960s, definitions and assumptions about group performance that began to appear in the journals continued to reflect the idea of interpretation as communicative act and performing art (Maclay). These assumptions were solidified by the appearance of the first book devoted to the subject of group performance (Coger and White, 1967). In it, Leslie Irene Coger and Melvin White reaffirmed Coger's earlier definition (Coger, 1963) of Readers Theatre as "theatre of the mind," a form in which scene, characters, and action are all in the minds of the audience as they hear readers who interpret the author's words (Maclay).

The strict rules which Coger's definition dictated were challenged by scholars such as Bacon, who argued that, while the form was effective, "it is the text itself—not the convention of the medium which should dictate the form" (Bacon, 1966, p. 316, as quoted in Maclay). According to Maclay, one of the biggest challenges to the concept and techniques of the new form came from Marion Kleinau and Marvin Kleinau (1965), who challenged the notion that "the scene of action . . . must be set in the abstract, or in the minds of the audience, and not in the concrete area of 'the stage'" (p. 194). Kleinau and Kleinau argued that interpreters should look to the concept of configuration in the perceptual field as a basis for questioning the possibility and desirability of always keeping the scene in Readers Theatre offstage.

As Readers Theatre grew increasingly popular in the late 1960s and the 1970s, group performance courses became pervasive, as did theses and dissertations on the subject, including production studies and empirical investigations of audience response. Between 1970 and 1975, the strong rise in pedagogical activity was accompanied by the publication of three new texts devoted solely to group performance. Of these texts, only Maclay's rejected both the practical manual approach and the concept of Readers Theatre as primarily communicative act and performing art. Instead, Maclay attempted to shape an aesthetic for the medium by abstracting from "the history of theatre practice, the history of literary structure, and the psychology of visual perception, principles of audience-text-performer relationships" (Maclay, 1971, p. 6 and quoted in Maclay, 1983, p. 406). Maclay's book drew its definition from text-centered studies, emphasizing interpretation as dramatic experience and as literary study.

The current popularity of group performance is such that most introductory textbooks in interpretation now include a section on the form. While the definition of Readers Theatre as "theatre of the mind" has not entirely been put aside, a view more in keeping with Bacon's recommendation has been gaining credence since the 1970s. It is a text-centered view, one that "places the premium on the myriad potentialities of the literature rather than on what have sometimes seemed arbitrary sets of conventions" (Long, Hudson, and Jeffrey, 1977, p. 4).

Chamber Theatre, a second type of group performance that is highly innovative in its form and ambitious in its goal, places narrative fiction on the stage. Although it began in 1947, the growth of Chamber Theatre was slow compared to that of Readers Theatre partly because of the lack of publication about the concept (Maclay, 1983). It was not until the publication of Robert Breen's book in 1978 that a detailed explanation of the form was widely available. Breen, its creator, began using Chamber Theatre in his classes at Northwestern in order to enhance students' work with narration and to provide the stage with translations of fiction that were richer than most film and theatre adaptations (Maclay, 1983).

Chamber Theatre productions make use of numerous conventional theatre techniques, such as costumes, makeup, sets, props, elaborate lighting, movement, and performer interaction. The distinction between Chamber Theatre and conventional theatre is that Chamber Theatre, which transfers novels and short stories onto the stage, does not turn those genres into the dramatic mode that contains only dialogue. Instead, Chamber Theatre retains the narrative, which is delivered directly to the audience by one or more narrators, among whom may be the characters themselves. Thus, the audience's perceptions of character dialogues may be enhanced by narrative passages that explore the inner thoughts and motivations of the characters. The medium offers numerous theatrical opportunities to clarify a director's understanding of how a writer shapes a fictive experience in a narrative work. The form is based heavily upon textual analysis and has been used extensively in connection with interpretation as literary study. Wayne Booth's *Rhetoric of Fiction* (1961) intensified directors' investigations into the complexities of narrative in Chamber Theatre. Booth provided full and compelling discussion of the way a writer develops and guides reader understanding and interpretation through the complex relationships between narrator, characters, implied author, and implied audience in a work of fiction.*

Involvement with group performance, particularly with Chamber

---

*Interest in Chamber Theatre evoked interest in the narrative mode as a distinct literary genre and vice-versa. Representative studies in narrative may be found in the reference list for this chapter.

Theatre in all its theatricality, attracted some interpreters towards the previously "forbidden" realm of theatre. Breen had set a precedent for this shift not only by using the physical accoutrements of theatre performance but also by borrowing from Bertolt Brecht's ideas on Epic Theatre. In the creation of Chamber Theatre, Breen used Brecht's concept of alienation, his emphasis on simultaneous telling and showing, and his focus on the past rather than the present.

In the 1960s and 1970s, other interpreters who were looking for ways to enhance the performance of drama and group performance began to synthesize their ideas on Readers Theatre with concepts and techniques drawn from dramatic theorists. Mathias Reitz (1966) and Robert Post (1967) both acknowledged the adaptability of Stanislavsky's ideas (e.g., character objective, through-line-of-action, spine) to oral interpretation. Another theatrical source of inspiration for group performance was the work of Polish director Jerzy Grotowski. Many notions within Grotowski's early approach to performance, as articulated in *Towards A Poor Theatre* (1969) easily fit the philosophy that interpreters already held toward Readers Theatre. Grotowski wanted to return the theatre to what he considered its essential form by stripping it of all spectacle and concentrating on the simple equation of actors plus audience. In this vein, Grotowski used large, adaptable rooms rather than a proscenium arch and only a few convertible basic properties. His performers wore no makeup and suggested changes in their roles or within their characters strictly through physical and vocal control. Leslie Abel and Post (1973) conveyed Grotowski's ideas to interpreters and suggested that the director's philosophy and practice would further enhance Readers Theatre. Yet, oral interpretation during the 1960s and early 1970s still maintained its distinctions from acting.

In the 1980s there is greater fluidity than in previous decades between interpretation and theatre performance. Many interpreters who have previously eschewed theatrical elements in the staging of group performance have discovered that well-informed use of them can enrich rather than detract from an audience's experience. The shift toward theatricality can also be seen in recent one-person shows that rely upon "impersonation." The performers of these shows convey nondramatic literature in a style that an early 20th-century interpreter would clearly label "acting." Maclay, for example, does not "present" Anne Sexton; she becomes her. Further evidence of the current appreciation of theatre practice appears in the recent textbook by Long and HopKins (1982). The authors suggest that students use a variety of theatrical techniques to flesh out and expand their understanding of the literature they are to perform. Writing an imaginative autobiography of the speaker in the work, identifying the subtext, and finding the action of a line are all devices recommended. The ideas of directors such as Stanislavsky and Meyerhold are mentioned, and students are recommended to explore texts such as Francis Hodge's book on directing. In reflecting this changing dynamic, the first issue of *Literature in Performance* (1980) featured an interview with theatre director Gerald Freedman in which Freedman was questioned extensively on his techniques for helping actors build a character.

Many theatre practitioners are not aware of these changes in interpretation thought and practice and believe that interpretation is still characterized by the nontheatrical style that previously dominated. Yet some cross currents do exist. In recent years the American Theatre Association has included programs on Chamber Theatre at their national meetings. The Royal Shakespeare Company's 1982 New York production of *Nicholas Nickleby* used a concept similar to that of Chamber Theatre and included many Chamber Theatre techniques in its staging. Some university theatres include a major Chamber Theatre production as part of their theatre seasons.

Much of the recent move away from rigid performance practice has been fostered by the demonstration of new ideas at interpretation festivals. Festivals are occasions for sharing literature in performance without the constraints of competition. Consequently, they encourage experimentation. Ted Colson suggests that "the festival experience is regarded almost universally as a vital supplement to the traditional methods employed in the oral study of literature in the classroom" (Wade, Colson, McDonnell & Crouch, 1983, p. 372).

The first festival was held in 1930, cosponsored by Mount Holyoke and Smith colleges. The festival concept was initiated as an alternative to traditional forensic contests that, according to Elbert Bowen, exploit literature "for purposes having nothing to do with literature" (1976). Contests emphasize competitive delivery based upon rules. In contrast, festivals, most of which began during the text-centered years between 1950 and 1975, highlight the literature and offer students and instructor opportunities to share constructive criticism from varied interpretation scholars and to experiment with and discuss how differing directorial techniques and choices reflect differing attitudes toward performed texts. Thus, at a festival, participants gain the opportunity for practical expression based upon and fostering theoretical discussion.

Budgetary problems in the past few years have diminished festival activity in some states. The eastern region of the country has discontinued many of its festivals. In the southern and central states, however, the festival concept continues to flourish. The western states, which offer fewer and newer festivals, maintain those that they have developed, often emphasizing a cross cultural flavor in their activities (Wade et al.).

CONCEPTUAL AND METHODOLOGICAL CHANGES: NEW THEORY AND PRACTICE

Oral Interpretation scholarship today grows increasingly diverse. The pursuit of research questions has led interpreters to perceive connections with other disciplines, particularly with those social sciences and humanities that share paradigms based on analogies drawn from cultural performance. Consequently, interpreters recently have been investigating, adopting, and synthesizing theory and practice from both inside and outside of the speech communication field. The process has broadened the perimeters of interpretation and, in some cases, has forged new definitions for the concepts and relationships involved in the triad of performer, text, and audience.

From within the speech communication field and from the related field of psychological research, interpreters have drawn upon methodology and theory that enable them to explain more fully oral interpretation as a communicative act between performer(s) and audience. The use of empirical methods and the perspective of interpretation as communicative act, as we have seen, reflect established emphases. Yet the focus has gained more attention in recent years as communication theory itself is subject to more investigation and as interpreters explore the connections between interpretation and the rest of the speech communication field.

Empirical studies in interpretation may be traced back to the 1920s when interpreters sought to measure physical aspects of delivery and their effect. These types of investigations were furthered in the 1950s and 1960s with studies, such as Kenneth Harwood's (1955), which explored rates of delivery speed in conjunction with "listenability," and Martin Corbin's (1962), which demonstrated audience preference for maintenance of strong performer-audience eye contact. The need for empirical studies such as these has been advocated by a vocal minority of scholars in recent decades (Reynolds, 1962; Klyn, 1965; Brandes, 1968; Cronkite, 1970) who have claimed that the audience has been the most neglected aspect of interpretative performance and that there "is no inherent incompatability between carefully planned science and effective art" (Brandes, p. 105). More recently, HopKins and Long (1981) have suggested that empirical studies can and should be used to demonstrate the human development potential that interpreters intuitively recognize oral performance of literature to possess. G. P. Mohrmann and Stuart Kaplan's study (1980), for example, demonstrated that oral performers formed more complex impressions of literature than those who were not performing. Claims for enriched literary competency, amplified cognitive and affective development, sharpened critical skills, and altered attitudes toward social issues could be verified increasingly as interpreters investigate communication areas.

Linking interpretation study with communication and psychological fields has led some scholars to examine theories of empathy, a concept that has long been considered important by interpreters. Through an understanding of theories of empathy, interpreters seek to explain the subtle process by which a performer becomes involved in a text and an audience becomes involved in a performance. Joyce Horton (1968), for example, attempted to describe the definition, nature, function, and use of empathy in oral interpretation, stressing Lipps' psychological research on empathy and kinesthetic theories. Three years later, Gilda Parrella (1971) sought to clarify the concept of empathy by discussing its historical origins. Most recently, Ronald Pelias (1982) presented a survey of several conceptions of empathy in social cognition research and argued that "increased definitional rigor" would aid interpreters in understanding the empathic process in performance and in the teaching of performance. At the conclusion of his essay, Pelias suggested that since empathy is basic to interpretation and social development, interpretation study might influence social behavior. That is, since the interpreter assumes the role of a narrator, persona, or character for performance, such role-taking activity might transfer to real life situations.

Interest in applying communication research to the process of oral interpretation has resulted in some texts that emphasize interpretation as communicative act. In *The Communicative Act of Oral Interpretation* (1975), for example, Keith Brooks, Eugene Bahn, and LaMont Okey described interpretation as an expressive form of communication. The authors stressed the role of the listener in the interpretation process based upon a behavioralist communication model. The model stresses stimulus-response patterns and underscores the communicative potential in literature and between performer and audience. The authors' behavioralist biases can be seen in the books they recommended to the student for further reading such as Wilbur Schramm's *Science of Human Communication* (1963) and David Berlo's *Process of Communication* (1960).*

A national Speech Communication Association (SCA) convention program on the interface between interpretation and communication study (Anaheim, 1981) produced position papers that reflect more contemporary emphases. In this program, Pelias (1981) attempted to set forth ideas by which interpretation might be linked to one of the dominant areas in communication study—constructivism. Citing both Burke and Bruce Gron-

---

*Two other texts strongly influenced by early communication models are Carolyn Gilbert's *Communicative Performance of Literature* (1977) and Donald Ecroyd and Hilda Wagner's *Communicate Through Oral Reading* (1979).

beck's study on "Dramaturgical Theory and Criticism" (1980), Dwight Conquergood (1981) chose to emphasize the "resurgence of theatre as a root metaphor for interpreting human reality" and posed this resurgence as the theoretical underpining of a "nexus between interpretation and communication studies." Mary Strine (1981) argued for an idea that I shall discuss in more detail later, a post-structuralist semiotic view of oral interpretation that would stress social meanings and values and thereby link interpretation to communication study.

The diversity of contemporary communication studies reflects a refiguration of thought in the social sciences whose impact on interpreters may be seen by their additional investigations of theory from outside of the speech communication field. Enjoying an increasing freedom to shape their work without disciplinary constraints, interpreters have recently joined diverse scholars who are unified by a common interest in perceiving social life as a system of signs whose principles we may better understand through learning how to decipher them. The phenomenon that Clifford Geertz (1980) has called "genre dispersion" is currently reflected by a strong new area of research in interpretation commonly referred to as the "ethnography of performance." Interpreters working in this area have discovered that their interest in social verbal artistry is shared by scholars in anthropology, sociology, sociolinguistics, and oral history as well as by those interested in the dramaturgical perspectives on communication of which Conquergood spoke. Research concerns within this sphere include the folklore of other cultures, American folklore, the connection between oral and literary tradition, paralinguistic and prosodic features of verbal performance in everyday life, translating performances into printed texts, theatricality in everyday life, and urban ethnography.

Impetus for including the study of the relationship of text to performance within interpretation research appeared in the early 1970s. In "Oral Interpretation in the Ages Before Sheridan and Walker" (1971), Sloan maintained that if we let our identity depend upon print, our history does not begin until about the middle of the eighteenth century. Recommending the work done on oral traditions by Milman Parry (1971) and Albert Lord (1960), Sloan suggested that interpreters seek to understand how ancient poets simultaneously created and transmitted poetry orally. Perceiving poetry from this perspective, Sloan claimed, would enable the interpreter to see a poem, not as the fixed object that is a consequence of literacy, but phenomenologically as an event. Thus, the poem's meaning is not determinate and unvarying through history but "that which comes to stand over and over in encounters with the text in time" (p. 151). While Sloan was arguing for a study of the connection between the oral tradition and the history of hermeneutics that still remains to be fully explored, his interest in the oral tradition was echoed by other scholars. Barbara Kaster (1971) examined the ancient oral tradition in the light of McLuhan's claim that we are returning to the oral tradition. David Thompson (1973) acknowledged the limitations of typical studies in the history of interpretation and suggested including the study of oral tradition as a way to expand teaching and research. Such studies, Thompson argued, might invigorate interpretation scholarship in an area that has, understandably, in the past, been preempted by scholars in rhetoric.

Momentum for an ethnography of performance also came from interpreters who emphasized the significance of cultural context for oral performance. Leland Roloff (1973) suggested that interpretation scholars investigate the relationship of literature and culture. Chester Long (1974) contended that social values are intimately connected with performance, affecting both the choice of literature and the performance style. Jean Haskell Speer (1975) argued for the symbiosis between cultural lore and interpretation, maintaining that interpreters can gain new materials for performance from the folk tale, epic, legend, ballad, and song. In turn, interpreters can play an important role in preserving these forms.

Perhaps the most significant thrust for ethnography of performance research came from the 1977 article by Speer and Elizabeth Fine, entitled "A New Look at Performance." Fine and Speer argued that interpreters should join with "other humanists and with the social and behavioral sciences in an exploration of performance in human life" (p. 375). The special contribution that interpreters can bring to such a study, the authors affirmed, will be the result of "experience in creating, participating in, evaluating, and *doing* performance, experience which is not a part of the other disciplines . . . interested in the nature of performance" (p. 375). Fine and Speer reviewed some of the major performance studies in sociolinguistics, folklore, and literary criticism in order to suggest new directions for oral interpretation. From sociolinguist Dell Hymes, Fine and Speer adopted a definition of performance as "a cultural behavior for which a person(s) assumes responsibility for presentation to an audience" (p. 375). Standards for a full performance are met "'when criteria intrinsic to the tradition in which the performance occurs are accepted and realized'" (p. 375). Fine and Speer suggested folklorist Richard Bauman's (1975) terminology for describing and organizing the performance experience. Bauman's terminology is derived partly from Gregory Bateson's idea of "framing." A performance frame "uses culturally conventionalized metacommunication devices so that all behavior that takes place within the frame is said to be understood as performance" (p. 376). Thus, the physical and social context of performance can be examined, along with the performer, the audience, the act sequence, and ground rules for performance. In short, Fine and Speer stressed investigating how sociocultural factors condition "the emergent aesthetic event." Concomitantly, an interpreter might examine how the act of performance influences the performer's perceptions of himself or herself as a social being. Quoting literary critic Richard Poirier (1971), Fine and Speer noted that "Performance . . . is a process of self discovery, self transformation, in which what the artist finds most exciting in a work is finally himself as a performer" (Fine and Speer, p. 380).

Fine and Speer's article suggests a changed and greatly broadened definition of what constitutes "performance." This enlarged scope calls for new research methods that include use of videotape to record verbal art as performance and specialized notational systems for recording the necessary contextual features that previous literary and folkloric texts have ignored. In *The Folklore Text: From Performance to Print* (1984), Fine reviews the historical developments in theory and methods of textmaking or performance notation. She examines the implications of performance theory for the text and constructs a model of an ideal performance-centered text, suggesting principles for translating performance to print. In doing so, Fine draws upon contemporary translation theory and semiotics. She defines the text as "an intersemiotic translation from the performance to the print medium." "Intersemiotic translation" refers to the transference of a message from one kind of symbolic system to another. Fine's "text" would transfer paralinguistic, kinesic, and other nonverbal performance features of an oral performance into the two-dimensional, visual symbols of the printed page.

While Fine's definition of "text" relates specifically to the performance act, Mary Strine stresses a redefinition of "text" that emphasizes "the cultural values and sociopolitical alignment implicit in literary performance as a form of social productivity" (p. 12). In "Text, Intertext, and the Space Between: Semiotic Bases of Literature in Performance" (1981), Strine borrows a semiotic perspective colored by post-structuralism, one that stresses "the purposeful and systematic deconstruction of conventionalized signifying practices so as to reveal normative structure constitutive of social life" (p. 4). Acknowledging the ideas of scholars such as Roland Barthes (1979) and Julia Kristeva (1980), Strine describes the shift of focus from "work" to "text," that is, from literature "perceived as a naturally cohesive, inherently meaningful entity," such as New Criticism dictated, "to literature interpreted as a signifying practice or conventionalized form of social productivity" (p. 4). Strine points out that the "socially-isolated formalist aesthetic that the term 'work' has come to represent" (p. 4) was "acquired at the cost of cultural relatedness, and to some extent, sociopolitical responsibility" (p. 5). The perspective of "literature-as-text" enables literature to regain "its functional status as a major signifying social force" (p. 6). Thus, Strine implicitly argues against the New Critical dictate that poetic language is distinct from other forms of language. The post-structuralist perspective, particularly deconstructionism, asserts literature as an act of power.

One of the major performance ramifications that the cultural study of verbal art and especially the post-structuralist view of "text" offers is the practice and study of performance in varied social contexts. Strine points out that "as strategic signifying practices, literary performances within varied social contexts have inherent rhetorical functions" (p. 12). Kay Ellen Capo (1983) echoes the point by stating that interpretation can involve "the successful use of an aesthetic means to achieve a rhetorical end" (p. 448). Recent recognition of oral interpretation's persuasive social potential has led interpreters to experiment with performance to emphasize shared culture and values among such groups as the elderly and ethnic minorities. These performances in social contexts emphasize what Capo has called "access" to performance for new groups of people. This access has redefined the notions of literature, performer, and audience. The "literature" performed in social contexts might be such nontraditional material as oral histories. Performers may be people without backgrounds in performance, such as the handicapped who may have had no previous performance experience. Performances, which are used to reaffirm values, inform, develop awareness, promote discussion, and alter attitudes, may be for audiences of "average" citizens, special interest groups, or even legislators.

Grant money from the National Endowment for the Arts and Humanities and state endowments has strenghtened the practice of performance in social contexts. According to Capo, "it was governmental support which crystallized notions of how interpretation could be used for social change and public awareness" (p. 440). Such support has resulted in a variety of programs, from celebrations of local histories to vivifications of the needs of the handicapped. At Virginia Polytechnic Institute and State University, for example, scholars in interpretation were awarded $270,000 by the National Endowment for the Humanities. The grant extensively used public performances of folklore and oral history to help focus community attention on the forces of continuity and change in a rural Virginia county.

The interest that interpretation in social contexts generates among scholars today is evident in the fact that a Socio-Interpretation Network has been established within the Interpretation Division of SCA. Like the Ethnography of Performance and the Aesthetics and Communication networks which were begun in 1981, members of the Socio-Interpretation Network exchange papers, bibliographies, descriptions of projects and ideas for curricula.

While post-structuralist ideas on language and literature have affected emerging trends in interpretation research, recent currents of thought have also been influenced by theories that trace their modern origins to the nineteenth century. Phenomenological theory, initially articulated by Husserl and Heidegger in the nineteenth century and contributed to by Sartre and Merleau-Ponty in the twentieth, has attracted many scholars in interpretation who see it as a compelling basis for research. Such scholars use the phenomenological perspective to describe what is relevant in the experience of reading and performance and to inform the performance process through an investigation of authorial consciousness. From the phenomenological perspective, consciousness is an act wherein the subject and object are reciprocally related and analytically inseparable. Consciousness is, therefore, a unified subject-object relation. Language from this point of view is not a sign for meaning but an embodiment and incarnation of it. Yet language, as written, say the phenomenologists, is lifeless and "must be experienced directly in order to be revitalized" (Berleant, 1973, p. 340). Through sound, which gives the spoken word the status of a physical object, the word "assumes its full and equal reality" (Berleant, p. 341). Through performance, the interpreter discovers thought and feeling *in* the speaking. "The performance of the poem *is* the poem" (Valery as quoted by Berleant, p. 341); performance *is* understanding.

Phenomenological investigation of authorial presence in a text is different from that suggested by scholars interested in New Criticism, dramatism, or rhetoric. The presumption behind this investigation of authorial consciousness is that experiential patterns are fundamental self-world relations that are the real cause of unity in an individual's enterprises, including his or her fictive constructs. These latent patterns, which are embodied linguistically, are unique for each individual author. Moreover, they are the source of a literary work's "life," or being. The phenomenological critic who examines the text seeks to expose and evaluate these patterns in an individual work (Magliola, 1972). The critic also explores how these latent experiential patterns reoccur throughout the author's collected works. By investigating Tillie Olson's works in such a manner, for example, Linda Park-Fuller (1981) concludes that Olson experiences human existence as an effort to reconcile the imbalance of forces in the lived world. Fuller finds the dominant experiential metaphor that embodies this structure of consciousness in Olson's focus on the inability to breathe. Since experiential patterns have their richest manifestation in metaphor, the phenomenologist can explore constructs that may enhance perceptions of a work in new ways. For example, one might ask how an author smells love, hears sorrow, or spaces time (Magliola). Insights gained from such discoveries may be used to add color, texture, and form to a performance.

While the phenomenological perspective has not been directly responsible for the practice of interpretation as therapy, it has shared a role in fostering the practice. Experiencing a text from a phenomenological view may lead to an understanding of one's own inner landscape as well as the recognition of the diversity of others' psyches. The performance of literature, with its rich evocation of metaphor, can become a therapeutic experience for anyone who seeks to turn inward as a refuge from a contemporary culture in which vivified and meaningful symbols may seem all too few. The use of performance as individual development formed the basis for the text by Teri Gamble and Michael Gamble, *Oral Interpretation: The Meeting of Self and Literature* (1976). Today, psychosocial benefits are argued as rationale for oral performance in such specialized institutional settings as prisons, nursing homes, retirement centers, halfway houses, recreation areas, and houses of worship.

A final area that has changed the shape of interpretation research and practice today is that of reader-response criticism. Reader-response criticism is as varied as the differing philosophies that it encompasses. Phenomenology and post-structuralism are just two of the perspectives that may inform this kind of study. The perspective that the critic takes shapes his or her conceptions of what constitutes a text and a reader. Despite the differences among reader-response critics, they share a common assumption that "a poem cannot be understood apart from its results" (Tompkins, 1980, p. ix). This idea has become so prevalent among interpreters that nearly all would agree with Geiger who, in one of his later essays, stated that the locus of poetic meaning has shifted and is "fully demonstrated in the responses of readers" (1975, p. 150). The American critic whose ideas are most often acknowledged in the development of this transactional view is Louise Rosenblatt. Rosenblatt suggests that the written text of a piece of literature only becomes a poem or other fictive contruct when a "transaction occurs between reader and text" (1978). While interpreters may disagree about the extent of reader independence involved in the process, most agree that the poem as communicative process involves the reader sufficiently to suggest that there is now a range of acceptable meanings. Some believe that this range is much broader than others, but the significant word here is "range." Few interpreters believe any more that there is only one right reading and consequently one proper performance of a text. This change has had ramifications for the teaching and evaluation of performed literature.

The multiplicity of theories that has been explored by interpreters has, upon occasion, led to charges of dilettantism from both within and outside of the discipline. It is a charge that is difficult to escape when so much application of theory from outside of the field occurs. Sensitive to this charge, most interpreters today seek to immerse themselves heavily in a field before deciding which ideas or elements of it to adopt and synthesize. With such extensive use of ideas from other fields, it is also becoming more and more important for interpreters to adopt theory that is compatible with the basic tenets of oral performance. There is, for example, some debate regarding whether the premises behind deconstructionism will foster or destroy the oral performance of literature.* Controversy over the advantages and

---

*A symposium on deconstructionist perspective and interpretation, based on two 1982 SCA convention programs presented in Louisville, is featured in *Literature in Performance*, 1983, 4.

risks involved in adopting theory from other fields is reflected in a recent journal exchange between Gray and Janet Larsen McHughes. Gray asserts that "certainly the history of performance theory demonstrates conclusively that it has thrived only with a steady transfusion of ideas from other fields . . . . But our best theorists have been . . . always remarkably immune to alien religions. . . . there is much to be learned from the critical theory of the seventies, but only if we keep a steady eye on who we are and who 'they' are" (1982, p. 104).

McHughes dismisses the need for such caution by stating, "I applaud the field's new big game hunt for 'how the mind works.' Such safaris can tell us much we need to know about literature . . . and can provide us with tools and techniques we have never before owned. Such investigations, furthermore, can clarify our role in the broad field of communication, entice the theorists among us, elevate the contribution of the adapters/directors among us and build new sturdy bridges between authors and interpreters" (1982, p. 106).

As the Gray-McHughes debate indicates, the topics for investigation that have stimulated interpretation research in this century have shifted and broadened dramatically. Initial interest in matters of performance technique and the benefits of oral interpretation reflected the early desire to firmly establish the field in academia. Topics of early decades revolved around the perception that the performer alone or the performer-audience relationship warranted the most attention. Focus upon the text marked mid-century research concerns, encouring close examination of literary criticism and emphasizing oral interpretation as a form of literary study. Recent research trends reflect new and expanded notions of what constitutes a performer, a text, and an audience. Exploring and adopting theory from outside of the interpretation field, scholars have enlarged the concept of "performer" to include such persons as those who decipher a written text, and those who interact in the "performance" of life. The notion of "text" has come to suggest a transaction between reader and work, cultural verbal lore that one passes down or exchanges, and, metaphorically, the entire system of signals and signs that comprise social life. "Audience" may now include such constructs as a person to whom one displays conventionally wielded artistic verbal skills, a group whose values may be reaffirmed or changed, or the performer him- or herself. The expanded conceptions of the components of oral interpretation suggest that the formerly clear lines of demarcation between performer, text, and audience are not as operative as they once were. Many scholars today see oral interpretation as a broad dynamic whose components—performer, text, and audience—may not be just physical, but symbolic as well. The flux generated by new definitions has resulted in more contexts for performance practice and suggests a broad scope for interpretation research in the future.

THE PRAGMATISM OF PROFESSIONAL GROWTH

Professional growth for interpretation in the remainder of this century has become synonymous with two major issues: increased visibility of its scholars through publication and increased student enrollments to boost declining undergraduate and graduate programs. The first issue might seem odd, given the diverse and substantial research interests interpreters have displayed in recent years. Questions of text, performer, audience, their constitution and interplay, create well attended convention programs. Yet, relatively little of this research has found its way into print. The dearth of published research was cited as a special problem over ten years ago when Beverly Whitaker (1973) pointed out that of the more than 100 SCA convention papers about interpretation given from 1960 to 1970, only six were published in speech journals.

The situation that Whitaker noted in 1973 was corroborated in 1980 by Conquergood. In a survey on the status of oral interpretation research in SCA journals, Conquergood discovered that *The Quarterly Journal of Speech* and *Communication Monographs* reported 0% acceptance rates during their most recent three-year terms. Interpretation scholarship in the remaining national journal, *Communication Education*, accounted for only 6% of recently published articles. Two of the regional journals reported substantially higher acceptance rates, but this increase was based upon very small numbers of submissions. Editorial suggestions to combat the problem included advocating more articles demonstrating interpretation as a communicative act, thereby appealing to a broader readership.

Whitaker aptly summed up the situation that the scarcity of published research creates when she concluded: "If the available research in interpretation is not surfaced, those in adjacent disciplines will be uninformed, researchers in other areas of departments of speech misled, and the work of scholars in interpretation severely hampered" (p. 242). Conquergood saw the problem as a vicious circle. Journals both reflect and stimulate research activity in a field. The lack of published oral interpretation research has been reinforced by a lack of models.

The 1980 emergence of *Literature in Performance*, a journal devoted entirely to the aesthetics of performed literature, has been seen as an antidote to the publication problem. The large number of initial submissions to the journal reflects an enthusiasm for a forum in which interpreters may discuss nuances of their discipline without worrying about pleasing a broader SCA audience. The focusing of oral interpretation articles in one primary source seems also to have provided much of the stimulus for further investigation that Conquergood suggests was missing earlier. Yet it remains to be seen whether this channeling of interpretation research will work toward dispelling or merely increasing the vacuum of knowledge and the distortions that researchers in other areas of speech departments may have about interpretation. Despite its success and wide circulation among interpreters, *Literature in Performance* does not have the diverse readership of the national or regional SCA journals, a readership that is needed to help dissipate disciplinary isolation.

The small publication output that has plagued interpretation is fueled, as it is in all the performing arts, by the intrinsic demands of a discipline that revolves around performance. Many interpreters are simply too busy adapting, directing, and performing to see their research through the necessary channels for a published article. They are well aware that without performance experience, their insights remain mere hypotheses. Adapting, directing, and performance form the crucial foundation for the interpreter's knowledge and art.

The problem of resolving the dual demands of publication and performance reaches a climax for each individual interpreter over the question of tenure and promotion. An informal survey of representative institutions* indicates that at some universities, major adaptations and direction of full-length works are considered equivalent only to teaching or service. At such places the criteria for evaluation of professional work revolves strictly around publication. The interpreter must either adapt and direct as an additional activity that will not substantially count toward tenure and promotion or decide to eschew such activity in favor of writing—the acceptable demonstration of professional competence. At other universities, criteria for evaluation are more flexible. "Creative contributions" for "those in the arts" are considered both as teaching *and* as "contributions to the discipline." Interpreters at some universities, have been successful at listing full-length interpretative performances for public audiences as one of the evidences of research. The small number of schools that do include major adaptation and direction in their category of "research" or "research and creative endeavor" are not standardized in how they handle such matters. At some, there is no demand for outside critical evaluation of the adaptation and direction. At others, major adaptations and direction must be assessed by an impartial outside critic.

Clarifying criteria for evaluation of an artistic endeavor has been one of the major problems involving assessment of creative work in interpretation as it has been in music and theatre. Larry Clark, head of the University and

*Among those interpreters who responded to my survey, I would like to thank the following people who were particularly helpful in supplying relevant information: Lilla Heston, Janet Larsen McHughes, Marion Kleinau, John Hollwitz, Dwight Conquergood, and Joanna Maclay.

College Division of the American Theatre Association, has addressed the problem by stating, "Actually, the evaluation of the theatrical director poses such a sticky problem because the nature of the activity negates its equivalence with research and publication.... When a research project culminates in a publication, that decision is totally outside the control of the faculty researcher. Somebody else decides whether the project should be preserved and shared with the profession. Such is not the case with the production of a play. The play goes on, whether or not it is ready and whether or not anybody else believes it should be 'published'" (1983, p. 25).

In outside evaluations of interpretative theatre productions the problem of artistic assessment is compounded by the scarcity of qualified critics. The number and geographical distribution of interpreters who might serve such a function may lead to considerable expense for the department that brings in a critic. Given the size of the field, it is also difficult to avoid the charge of "cronyism."

The creation of effective criteria for evaluation obviously would help to overcome part of the current problems. Some schools report that they would consider assessing adaptation and direction for tenure decisions if a good means of evaluation were to be developed. The problem is of such importance that a task force within the Interpretation Division of SCA has been appointed to address the question of evaluation of creative work as research. Even if this task force successfully creates a standards document, interpreters are well aware that print publication is still the favored means of demonstrating professional competence. Most interpreters report that those colleges and universities that consider adaptation and direction as scholarly endeavor now require publication as well.

The second growth issue for interpretation today revolves around the contemporary malaise of all humanities disciplines: student enrollment. Interpretation has suffered less than some fields. Graduate degrees in interpretation from 1950 to 1980 show a marked increase in both masters and doctorates awarded each decade. Nearly twice as many masters were awarded in the 1970s as in the 1950s, and nearly three times as many doctorates emerged from the 1970s as from the 1950s. Yet dwindling budgets and the proliferation of more obviously practical courses in communications have taken their toll upon interpretation. Some doctorate programs have been eliminated while others have been slashed so drastically that there remain only a handful of programs that are still viable,*

---

*A survey at the beginning of the 1970s indicated 15 institutions at which a student could pursue doctoral work in interpretation. Ten of those programs are no longer operative. For further information on this study, see Judith Espinola and Kenneth C. Crannell, "Graduate Degree Programs in Oral Interpretation."

including the most extensive at Northwestern and those at Southern Illinois, University of Illinois, University of Texas at Austin, and University of Arizona. Master's programs have also suffered, and undergraduate majors in the field have, become, like all humanities majors, an "endangered species." Response to the current dominating pragmatism of college students has filtered into Judy Yordon's new text, *Roles in Interpretation* (1982), which includes a section on career opportunities for students with a background in interpretation. The Interpretation Division within SCA is trying to address the problem by appointing a task force on oral interpretation as preparation for life and work.

Despite this state of events, interpretation remains vital for students, and consequently, for programs, at a number of colleges and universities throughout the country. At Central Michigan University, for example, Bowen succeeded in placing an introductory interpretation course among those offered as university breadth requirements and as an option for oral competency. Within one year the number of sections of the course soared from two to ten. Each semester 200 to 300 students are turned away for lack of class space. The discovery of ideas through oral performance of literature has made the course so popular that the demand for it now exceeds that for the basic course in interpersonal and public communication. This model success may suggest that interpretation as a humanities subject for the general student still holds allure and, if given administrative sanction, can survive successfully the economic vicissitudes of the last two decades of this century.

It is difficult to predict the future of any humanities discipline at a time when nearly all academic disciplinary growth is besieged by problems. Yet the expanded conceptual bases and practice that interpreters have shaped for the discipline in the last two decades point to a flexibility that may be highly compatible with the retrenchment that most academic programs are experiencing. In some programs for example, scholars have integrated interpretation courses into the general curriculum by introducing students not just to literature but to the fundamentals of the aesthetic use of language and communication in general. In other programs, interest in interpretation in social contexts stresses interdisciplinary activity that can both pay for itself through outside funding and attract students who want a sense of relevance between their studies and the outside world.

A more theoretical apect of oral interpretation's growth will be the ongoing need demanded by fields whose disciplinary demarcations have been blurred—the drive to extend a healthy theoretical pluralism while at the same time maintaining a sturdy intrinsic core. The distinct integrity of oral interpretation partakes of many areas—orality, aesthetics, communication, and culture. Other disciplines may show ways to focus upon and understand any one of these aspects. Yet interpretation must continue to assert its "identifiable strength"—the investigation of the dynamic relationships among all elements involved in the process of humans aesthetically sharing their literature and lore through performance.

*I would like to thank Elizabeth C. Fine, William R. Haushalter, Ronald J. Pelias, and Jean Haskell Speer for their comments on an earlier version of this essay.

9

Technology and Communication

FREDERICK WILLIAMS

REFLECTIONS ON A "TECHNOLOGY"

MEDIA EXTENSIONS

The long-range concerns of communications scholars who study the so-called new technologies are ultimately the same as those of any researcher or theorist of human communication (cf. Williams and Rice, 1983). All are concerned with the how and why of communications processes and the sources of effectiveness. To recoin a well-known phrase, we are all concerned with the art of "good people communicating well."

To many, the new technologies are seen in terms of their visible physical aspects, as with television, communications satellites, videotape or videodisk machines, large-screen television sets, mobile telephones, the computer, videotext or teletext. More important to researchers, though, are the functional aspects of these technologies. What do they do for us? How do they extend our natural powers of communication?

In my own view, a communications technology is generally an extension or combination of existing media (Williams, 1984; Williams and Rice, 1983). For example, the telephone is really only an extension of the transmission capabilities of the human voice. Or a videodisk is an alternative storage capability for the video and audio signals of television. The new technologies are developed mainly to augment some aspect of human communication, just as traditional media have done. From cave paintings to the latest in communication satellites, media have served a fundamental human purpose. Communication technologies allow us to extend the basic capabilities of our biologically-based "natural" media—our senses of sight and sound. After all, technology is an "applied science," invented for the purpose of serving human needs. Table 9.1, reproduced from my recent textbook (Williams, 1984), summarizes details of this point. This table also points out that communications technologies may represent extensions of message preservation methods ("Recording Basis"), transmission methods, or both. Moreover, these extensions typically accommodate different traditional media, such as text, data, graphics, sound, and their extensions in broadcast media.

After a brief review of technological applications in traditional contexts of communication, this essay explores priorities for theory and research in the next few years as communication scholars turn increasingly to the human side of the communication and technology interface.

Table 9.1
Characteristics of Selected Technologies

Type	Extensions of	Recording Basis	Transmission	Message Types
Cable TV	Sound, vision, voice	—	Wire	TV programs, music, text
Satellite	Sound, vision, voice	—	Broadcasting	TV programs, music, voice text
Video-tape	Sound, vision, voice	Electromagnetic	Transportation	TV programs, movies
Video-disk	Sound, vision, voice	Optical, binary	Transportation	TV programs, movies
Digital	Sound, vision	Electronic, digital	Wire, broadcasting	TV programs, music, voice text, data
Computer	Vision	Electromagnetic	Wire	Text, data, graphics
Video-text	Vision	—	Broadcasting	Text, graphics
Teletext	Vision	—	Wire	Text, graphics

Note: Reproduced with permission of: Frederick Williams, *The New Communications*. Belmont, California: Wadsworth Publishing Co., 1984.

The Convergence of Computing and Telecommunications Technologies

Contemporary communications are marked by the convergence of multiple technologies, but this is not a new phenomenon. Long ago, language (if we may classify it as technology) converged with writing, and later, writing with printing. The wire telegraph converged with radio to produce the wireless telegraph. Audio broadcasting converged with the transmission of video signals to provide television. Today, the newest convergence is of the computer and the telecommunications network. The result is the distribution of computing power to any point on that network, as well as the automation of many of the switching components of the network itself.

Before exploring this newest convergence, let us briefly examine the computer as a communications technology. Initially, the computer was considered a calculating machine rather than a communications device. Its uses have evolved greatly. Even without examining the computer as it enters into communications networks of all types, we can analyze it alone as a communications technology. It is a communications medium in the sense that it can store or transport messages in a physical form, as electronic binary codes. Also, a computer can link source and receiver. One fascinating point is that the computer, unlike other communications technologies, can act symbolically on our messages. It is an "intelligent" technology in the sense that we can program human decision strategies into it as the basis for acting upon information.

We can also examine the computer as a specialized component in a telecommunications systems. Probably the most common (yet invisible to the public) application of this is in modern telephone switching systems. Dial codes are "read" digitally by a computer in a switching office that then selects the best open route to the caller's destination, logs the time of the call, and automatically prepares billing (if any). If more efficient routes become available, the computer will select them during the duration of the call. Further, the computer "packs" multiple calls into the same circuits.

Increasingly visible is the use of a desk-top computer as a communications device. I refer not to the "dumb" terminal that communicates with a remote mainframe computer, but to the new breed of "personal" or "home" computers. These systems are capable of storing and acting upon information, and with the proper accessories can communicate direct messages, files, and computer programs to other computers via a telephone or direct wire connection.

The Communications "Grid"

The effects of the computer-telecommunications convergence have been explored by many writers and theorists (e.g., J. McHale, 1976; J.

Martin, 1977; Williams, 1983; Pelton, 1981; Dizard, 1982), and all have drawn a similar implication. "We are rapidly approaching an era in which small communities, larger regions, whole societies, and eventually the world, will be linked by one electronic communications network (or "grid"), just as transportation networks on land, sea, and air have inter-linked most points on our globe." Electronic communications on this network will bring to daily communication a near unfathomable array of alternatives. Services will range from personalized delivery of information and entertainment to broad opportunities for interpersonal communication.

TECHNOLOGY STUDY AS AN END IN ITSELF

Writers and researchers may seem preoccupied with new technologies, especially their physical and operational aspects. However, this is a necessary way station to proceeding with the study of how humankind communicates. The field of mass communication underwent a similar transition from a near-exclusive focus upon the medium rather than the human in the communications transaction. The proper focus in the study of communications technology, consonant with the long tradition of rhetorical theory and modern speech communications, is the human transaction.

NEW TECHNOLOGIES IN TRADITIONAL CONTEXTS

Everyday communication is changing, not so much in purpose or function as in alternatives of method. Most of these alternatives are based on the aforementioned convergence of computing and telecommunications—the develoment of the communications "grid." We can examine these applications in traditional contexts of mass, organizational, and interpersonal communication, all summarized in Table 9.2.

Note in Table 9.2 how the new technologies are mainly extensions or modifications of existing media systems. For example, broadcasting is augmented by cable or cassette distribution of programs; a teleconference extends group communications; a personal computer linkage can extend interpersonal communications.

MASS COMMUNICATIONS

In the traditional sense, "mass communications" has referred to the large-scale distribution and dissemination of communications materials not necessarily designated for a specific individual (cf. Schramm and Roberts, 1971). In our times, the audiences of mass communications are more identifiable as specific groups, or "markets." New technologies have added alternatives to the duplication and dissemination systems of mass communications. The growth of "electronic publishing" is an example. Videotape cassettes, videodisks, and videogames represent one type of new media extension for certain mass content. Though the materials are electronic, their production and distribution methods follow patterns akin to traditional publishing. That is, they are produced in quantity and disseminated by wholesale distributors for sale in retail outlets. Added to this is the rental market for videocassettes, but even that is not far removed from the retail publishing business.

Distribution of television material has been further increased by cable television networks and the arrival of the communications satellite. Program transmission is no longer limited by the shortage of broadcast spectrum space. Cable and satellite offer still further alternatives; consider, for example, the substantial growth in cable of so-called network information services (H. S. Dordick, H. G. Bradley, B. Nanus & T. H. Martin, 1980). These may consist of emergency medical or police communications links,

Table 9.2
New Technologies in Traditional Contexts

Context	Traditional Form	Technology Application
Mass Communications	Newspapers, magazines books, television, radio, films	Videotape, videodisk, cable TV, direct satellite TV, videotext, teletext, digital information system
Group and Organizational	Face-to-face	Telephone conference, teleconference, computer conference, telephone conference, electronic mail, computer-aided management information system, facsimile
	Face-to-face, memo, intercom, telephone, meetings	
Interpersonal	Face-to-face, mail, telephone	Video telephone, personal computer linkage, electronic mail, voicegrams

Note: Adapted by permission: Frederick Williams, *The New Communications*. Belmont, California: Wadsworth Publishing Co., 1984.

banking from the home or business, remote shopping, and a wide variety of "call-up" services, such as reports on the weather, the stock market, airline or theatre schedules, and even a horoscope.

Also available are information services in "videotext" and "teletext" forms. Teletext refers to information "pages" that are broadcast with television signals in the spare space between picture "frames" and captured for storage in a computer like memory adjoined to a television set. Users acquire information from this memory for display on the television screen. At regular intervals, the pages are updated in memory.

Videotext consists of services in which a computerlike device is connected to telephone lines to send and receive information, which is displayed on a television set or computer screen. Pages of information are stored in a remotely located central computer to which users have access. Videotext's advantage is that it makes far more information available to users than the limited number of pages that can be stored in a home teletext unit. Both these systems, in which information from a central source can be widely disseminated, are also referred to as "electronic publishing."

Various network services available to personal computer owners are very similar to the "text" services—for example, "Compuserve" and "The Source." Both are large information files stored in central computers to which users can "dial in" for access.

Text-type services are also in the category of the earlier mentioned "network information services" (Dordick et al., 1980). They function like "mass communications" in their potential for wide-scale distribution of information. Yet, the messages are gathered by users on a relatively personal basis. Messages are transmitted only when they are called for by the user. This increasing bias toward "personal use" is contributing to the new concept of "demassification" in large-scale communications. Two-way cable systems may increase this trend. As public information services offer vastly more alternatives and a user's specific needs are met, we can say that the services, although on a large scale, are at the same time more personalized.

As a final note, most of the foregoing services (even television and high fidelity music transmission) are possible over the telephone network, with certain restrictions or modifications. Moreover, the 1983 landmark deregulation of the telephone in the United States is enabling the development of such services.

GROUP AND ORGANIZATIONAL CONTEXTS

The convergence of communications technologies has also brought about innovations in contexts for group and organizational communications. Let us examine two of these: office automation and teleconferencing.

OFFICE AUTOMATION. Though it is variously called "the office of the future," "the integrated office," or "office automation," its communications contexts are similar (Williams and Dordick, 1983). The idea is that machines be used to accomplish routine clerical tasks, giving clerical workers easier access to information and providing managers with data they require for decision-making. The new office technologies will also improve written and voice communications links in the organizational environment.

Increasingly, the foregoing technological applications are becoming interlinked. The same network that conveys a draft memo from a manager's computer terminal to a secretary's word processor may carry voice transmissions and even facsimile images. These systems are called "broadband" (high message capacity) local communications networks. They occur within an organization or as networks in a company with many branch offices. The best-known is Xerox's "Ethernet," designed to connect all work stations for two-way transmission of voice, text, and data.

Another technological component of the new office environment (which may also be adapted for home use) is the application of computers for data-base management. In briefest terms, this application allows an individual to create information structures of considerable magnitude and flexibility. These structures can be built up from individual fragments of information, then examined as a whole to determine the types of structures being generated. Information is rapidly searched for different topics and topical combinations. Calculations are performed across categories of numerical data. Sophisticated data base management programs can also be used to generate reports. That is, a "map" of the desired report is designed, and the program retrieves and formats a printed report accordingly.

Although most research literature on data base management systems is of an applied nature, our thinking need not be. In effect, large-scale data base management is an extension of the information "holding" and "retrieving" capabilities of the human brain. Just as a communications satellite makes distance less relevant in message transmission, data base management makes limits on quantity of information less relevant in decision making.

TELECONFERENCING. This term refers to the interconnection of a group of individuals via telecommunications links. Methods may vary from simple telephone conferencing to an elaborate configuration of audio and video links, facsimile transmission, computer message, and file exchanges. Teleconferencing also includes contexts in which a group of individuals has common access to a computer messaging system, which allows a variety of textual exchanges from one-to-one simultaneous communication to "notes" or "mail" deposited and retrieved from the system, as well as general contributions to an ongoing "conference" file. As anyone who has participated can testify, conferences can proceed when participation is not simultaneous—that is, you can contribute or read messages at any time. The conference is "asynchronous" in that participants need not all communicate during the same time period.

Teleconferencing raises many questions for the communications social scientist, including the most general inquiry regarding the consequences of group communication when participants are not face to face. Another consideration, as with traditional media, is how to choose the technologies most apt for each meeting. For example, complicated numerical information may be best exchanged solely by computer-operated linkages. On the other hand, if important negotiations are undertaken over a telecommunications network, voices and televised images, perhaps including private voice channels, may be critical.

INTERPERSONAL COMMUNICATIONS

Ironically, one of the oldest and most popular technological extensions of interpersonal communication is among the least researched. This is the telephone, which except for the collection of papers produced by Pool and his colleagues (1977, 1982), has received little attention from social scientists. Among the many impending changes in telephone use are those brought about by the impact of telephone deregulation in the United States. The widely-available mobile telephone may also come to affect telephone habits. The telephone is likely to shift from a "home" or "business" based communications link to an individual, person based one. We may see telephone numbers designated for persons and applicable to all an individual's communications links, rather than present ones that refer to the location of specific telephones. Beyond the telephone and new alternatives for its use, there are additional personal communication technologies. The personal computer network referred to earlier offers one. This is the creation of digitally encoded textual messages (using possibly inexpensive microcomputers) that can be directly dispatched or left in computer "mailboxes." Such technologies can fit under the label "electronic mail," but are essentially personalized message services. Already, these services are publically available through commercial operations such as the aforementioned "Source" and "Compuserve." Many individuals have access to private links via commercial organizations, governments, or universities able to support an interactive computing system.

Although these computer-aided links lack the nonverbal and vocal dimensions of face-to-face interaction, and are not typically being used for social purposes, it is possible to envisage interpersonal relationships being developed in this medium. Serendipitous encounters can occur, personal information can be exchanged, individual needs and interests met, and relationships developed.

These are a few of the traditional contexts in which we are employing the new technologies. In these contexts, we find ourselves "doing the traditional nontraditionally." This is a point I have previously applied to other aspects of modern life (Williams, 1982). However, exploring these contexts in themselves is not our essential purpose. We must explore our communication behaviors within them. This is the challenge faced by the researcher of human communication.

RESEARCH IMPLICATIONS

We conclude with a view toward research that emphasizes the human in the technology-and-user interrelation. Such research is the particular domain of the specialist in speech communications, where there is often a focus upon the circumstances and behaviors of the individual or group communicator.

TECHNICAL VALUES AND "TRANSPARENCY"

One criticism of technologies in behavior is that we tend to confuse values of the technology itself with our intended human uses of it (Ellul, 1964). This problem carries over to communications technologies. For example, engineers and implementors may assess a system based mainly on amount of message flow ("operational capacity") and the capability to perform consistently ("reliability") and to stay within a desirable cost-benefits ratio ("productivity").

Such an evaluation, however, may overlook human factors. The automobile serves as a good example. We can assess a car in terms of its value as a mode of transportation, its dependability, and its fuel economy, and still say nothing about the joy of taking a trip, or the "feel" of the machine. Further, such an assessment omits the automobile's negative effects, such as pollution and highway deaths.

What, then, do we look for in the human use of a technology, especially one applied to communications? A fundamental quality we seek is called transparency. Briefly defined, a technology is transparent when it stands as little as possible between a user and its appointed task. For example, when we make a telephone call, technical operations, such as the route the call takes, the switching mechanisms involved, and the billing system activated, are usually invisible to us. That is, the technical operation of the system is "transparent." In an opposite example, we find that current models of personal computers are not so transparent. To accomplish our objectives, we have to load programs, know how to operate those programs, and deal with problems like inadequate directions and malfunctions.

Although transparency is a researchable quality, it has seldom been studied as an overall condition. Most studies focus on "human factors," such as improving physical and sensory contact with equipment (e.g., keyboard layout, screen tint), which do not necessarily reflect upon transparency. Research on the larger "fit" is important. We may never have optimal human/technology correlation until the psychological aspects of transparency become better known, particularly their applications in machine design, operations manuals, and training. Until then, improving the fit between computer technology, for instance, and humans may require people to become more "computer literate" than computers "people literate."

PRODUCTIVITY

Most new technologies designed for the modern organization are developed and marketed with the promise of improving productivity. The promise is the ability to maintain the quantity and quality of production with a smaller investment in resources. As applied to communications, productivity is easily defined only on the level of a "factory" analogy, for example, when considering the amount of corresondence secretaries can create with word processors as compared with traditional typewriters. Clerical applications, however, may yield the most trivial benefits. They do not promise rewards on levels where communications technology investment may be the greatest—namely, in managerial communications. This more important level includes "integrated office communications systems" that link managers and staff, data base management systems, or teleconferencing.

The organizational communications researcher can be concerned with two levels of application. First is the question of how productivity can be gauged when the variables are more abstract and less quantifiable. Second is the continuing question of whether so-called improved communication has predictable (and explainable) effects on the success of an organization.

As for productivity, the research challenge is to come to grips with usable conceptualizations of the relations of the "quality" of information with concomitant decision making. Unfortunately, quality is much more difficult to gauge than quantity, which is the basis of many productivity analyses.

New technologies, such as data base management systems, give the individual a vast command over stored information, including the ability to "scan," "synthesize," "calculate," and ask "what if?" questions. As stated earlier, data base management is truly an extension of human cognitive capacity. We lack the models, however, for evaluating the relationship of these newly found capabilities with the quality of information and decision making. We are in search of qualitative concepts of productivity.

Similarly, we need adequate and comprehensive models for relating changes in communications capabilities with organizational effectiveness. Without these, it is difficult for those who control the communications expenditures in corporations to make objective managerial decisions. Which investments should be made in new communications technologies? A relatively modest plan, such as using an existing accounting computer for an internal mail system, might have profound consequences upon organizational success.

Beyond this possibility there are the already recognized consequences of new office technologies on organizational climate, no small challenge in themselves.

SOCIAL PRESENCE

Technologies are often accused of being impersonal. No doubt this is partly owing to technical restrictions—for example, the narrower acoustic range of the telephone and its lack of a visual link. Researchers Short, Christie, and Williams (1976) have termed the psychological correlates of these restrictions "social presence." This quality is assessed by filling in semantic differential scales such as "unsociable-sociable," "insensitive-sensitive," "cold-warm," and "impersonal-personal" when evaluating a medium.

The telephone again serves as an example. Without a visual exchange, individuals lack access to the nonverbal codes that often contribute to the sharing of information necessary for the development of interpersonal communications (cf. Miller, 1976, 1978). Therefore, a telephone exchange would have less social presence than a face-to-face conversation, but more than a written memo. The memo has the further restrictions of denying the paralinguistic qualities of the vocal code and the lack of an immediate potential for interactivity.

Technical restrictions, however much we focus on them, are not the only variables of social presence. Socially based variables are also important, such as privacy, media stereotypes, and the implications of selecting a given medium from certain alternatives.

Privacy becomes an issue in selecting a medium based on the formality or informality of its proposed use. The generalization is usually that the degree to which individuals feel a medium is "private" as opposed to "public" determines how comfortable they will feel communicating personally rather than formally within it. Conversely, if an individual seems purposely to select a "formal" medium (say, writing a letter) when a more informal one is available (a face-to-face conversation), the receiver is apt to feel that the exchange is intentionally formal.

Finally, we all tend to evaluate messages in terms of our stereotypes for a medium. We may not expect to learn something important and formal via television as much as from a book on the topic, nor might we expect the content to be as personally relevant to us as something we hear from a close friend. The social presence picture becomes even more complex. As alluded by Christie et al., all the foregoing technical and social effects of media on the personal qualities of our messages are modified by the style and content of what we communicate. That is, through what we say and how we say it, we make a telephone conversation more or less formal, and give it more or less social presence.

That we can vary the personal qualities of a message through style and content, of course, is no revelation to a speech communications researcher, and yet this is a very practical definition of a current gap in research. The technological researchers, by concentrating on technical qualities of media and their implications, rather than on the message itself, are failing to conceptualize the interaction of technical parameters with traditional capabilities we humans have for stylistic adaptation. Moreover, the latter hold far more consequences than the former for success in communication.

By the same token, we still have a paucity of speech communication research or theory that examines the likely interactions between personal, group, or mass communication behavior and characteristics of the new technologies. As Rice and I have argued (Williams and Rice, 1983), the traditional distinctions are blurring. If we continue to use traditional paradigms for research, we will not gain those insights that we need in order to conceptualize that critical interaction between stylistic adaptation and technical parameters. Or put more practically, we may never realize the full benefits of the new medium.

Until the research gap between study of technologies and human capabilities for using them most effectively is closed, we will not experience the full benefits of our newest technological revolution. Nor will we be in a position to carry out the educational and training objectives for which society subsidizes so many of us who pursue academic careers in communications.

10

Mass Media and Society: The Development of Critical Perspectives

WILLIAM R. BROWN

In 1982, with authorization of *Critical Studies in Mass Communication*, rhetorical critics of media—along with other critical scholars of mass communication—savored the field's legitimation of their efforts. However, as recently as the late 1960s, as Berg (1972) tells the story, the case had often been doubtful. Then, members of editorial boards were known to wonder whether rhetoricians were poaching on the domain of mass media.

Seeking such vindication, of course, had begun in the scholarly journals not long after their founding. The search paralleled the quest for a place in the academic sun sought by the field at large during the first three-quarters of the twentieth century, with the media critics' efforts shaped as much by mainstream currents of scholarship in public address, communication theory, and mass communication as by individuals' curiosity.

This essay offers a narrative and exposition of developing categories in journals for the "effects" criticism of media. The essay acknowledges the Western mind's fascination with power, the recognition in speech communication of power in oratory and in media, the division of labor between critics and empirical researchers studying the relationships between media and society, and intellectual pressures toward specialization of critical perspectives. Attending primarily to critics indigenous to speech communication, the essay follows Benson (1978) in thinking of rhetoric as "social influence" arising not only from works "obviously structured to persuade" but others which, "regardless of intent, reflect and influence social and political norms" (Benson, 1978, pp. 242–243). Further, when aesthetic criticism explains audience response in a way conceivably promotive of social influence, its practitioners are also relevant to the story.

THE CALL TO SOCIAL CRITICISM OF MEDIA

Even without Wichelns' (1925) often-quoted dictum that rhetorical criticism is concerned with effects of messages or, more precisely, with the methods of achieving such effects, chances are good that critics would have contemplated the sources of media influence.

They would have done so, first, as participants in the Western world view, attending as it does to the possibility that human beings can master nature for their own purposes. In the world of letters, such a preoccupation has been symptomized by recurrent, ambivalent fascination with the potentiality of new media. During the emergence of the English novel, for example, fear that the new medium would control the popular mind prompted such novelists as Samuel Richardson to practice evasions by representing novels to be something else: In Richardson's case *Clarissa Harlowe* was palmed off as a manual for letter writing.

Alongside Americans who have worshipped or propitiated such engines as the telegraph, the translatlantic cable, the electric light, the telephone, and the wireless, nascent media critics have seen magic in film, radio, and television. Following in the van of generations of young persons like Albert Beveridge, who had seen during their late nineteenth-century college days that oratory was the route to preferment and the secret of personal power, critics writing near the advent of chemical and electronic media spoke of their magical powers. In early articles sometimes combining criticism with pedagogy, historical narrative, or editorializing, the talking picture was expected to develop, like the earlier silent film, "into one of the most powerful social agencies of our time" (Immel, 1929, p. 161). Radio had become "a vital force in the educational and recreational life of the entire world" by 1933 (Tyson, p. 224), maturing into "the modern substitute for the hearthstone" (Townsend, 1940, p. 582) and burgeoning into "a cultural, social, and political force whose magnitude" could be but "dimly" realized in 1940 (Ewbank, p. 283). Radio was a powerful tool for political persuasion and social cohesion: Huey Long's harangues on behalf of his Share-the-Wealth campaign demonstrated "the power of radio in building a personal political following" (Bormann, 1957, p. 257). "The magic of radio" would be seen to increase popular audiences' interest in government (Archer, 1960, p. 115). During World War II, the application of radio to the war effort depended on family listening habits: "Thirty million families owning some fifty-seven million radio sets can be reached by the familiarity and vividness of the personally spoken word, with an immediacy unknown to any other medium of communication and on a scale that defies description. Radio reaches the illiterate and the shut-in, the listener in his home and the tourist in his sedan, the corner filling station, and the Park Avenue penthouse" (Steele, 1942, p. 37).

Television, gathering popular audiences on a massive scale by the early-to-middle 1950s was, as had been also the moving picture and the radio before it, a new version of the earlier-worshipped dynamo which, Henry Adams (1918) had concluded, had replaced the Virgin as an object of reverence in Western society. "Where is the magic touch in this magic carpet? It is in sight and sound occurring together and at its best when it is happening when we view it," exulted Dunham (1955, p. 258). "The sense of immediacy is one of the strongest appeals yet known to man." The magic could be black as well as white, of course; farseeing educators not only understood the "potentialities" television offered for education but also were "aware . . . of the dangers that accompany any new instrument that may be used to influence the lives of people" (Battin, 1953, p. 242).

Germinating in the Western sense of mechanical magic, this body of critical comment was also part of the attempt by scholars in general speech to win legitimacy by proving the field itself to be a good citizen. Just as, for instance, A. Craig Baird (1956) made rhetoric a mainstay of American democracy in his work in public address, forerunners of today's media critics associated film and radio with civic virtue, improved manners, and cultural enrichment. The talking picture was "going to have a most profound influence on the popular use of the mother tongue" (Immel, 1929, p. 164). Radio announcers ("the connecting link between the stations and the listeners") played an important part in "amalgamating the tendencies of the language of three centuries and a quarter on this side of the Atlantic," culminating in a much-desired form of cultural independence, "the development of a distinctly American speech" (Tyson, 1933, pp. 219–220; Hardy, 1938, p. 464). During World War II, radio was to be the vehicle for carrying "forums, debates, interviews, speeches, and dramatizations" for the end of "informing people of the progress of the war, clarifying their knowledge of democracy's stake in this conflict, and building their morale to a level that will help bring victory" (Steele, 1942, p. 38). Hope died hard, even in postwar America, that mass media would be virtuous citizens of the republic. Why could not radio, "a powerful medium for persuading the public to purchase," be equally "as powerful in disseminating ideas of good government, of developing patriotic spirit, of educating the masses?" (Townsend, 1944, p. 157). Why could radio not take back control of its own industry from advertising agencies and provide "service" defined "as work 'performed for the benefit of another'," in this case the listeners? (Weaver, 1951, p. 274) Clearly, the responsibility of the broadcast media was social "uplift" (Haakenson, 1958, p. 18). In these and similar comments scattered through practitioners' reports, calls for research, early empirical studies, and critical pieces, students of media sought partial justification of their interests just as did public address scholars and others in general speech: Their academic field was a bastion of democracy and social solidarity.

In another way the call to social criticism of media echoed the summons to scholarship in general speech: Each searched for anchoring roots. Living in an uncertain present of economic depression, global war, and postwar dislocation, media-related scholars tended to see themselves as step-children of general speech—even as first-generation academic speech people, living through World War I and the postwar uproar of the 1920s, had tended to feel as though they were "younger sons" to English departments. Just as general speech had sought an ancestral legitimacy by reviving the study of classical, British, and Continental rhetorical theory, champions of media criticism turned to the remotest part of the past they could in a search for intellectual roots. During a time when media-related criticism was becoming more common, media historians looked to the beginnings of critical comment on radio (Smith, 1962), film (Beaver, 1972), newspapers (Hudson, 1970), and even television (Scher, 1974). Early critics and publications were praised for their social consciences, whether recognizing writers who had urged journalists toward "greater honesty" (Hudson, 1970, p. 270) or early radio magazines that had included radio criticism when bluebloods like *Harper's* and *Atlantic Monthly* had ignored the medium (Smith, 1962). However, when scholars found earlier critics who had, although granting the social significance of film, patronizingly called it "canned drama" and consigned it to permanent inferiority as dramatic art, the search for roots uncovered the equivalent of embarrassing relatives (Beaver, 1972). More common, nevertheless, was the location of earlier critics as diviners of mass-media social significance. Pioneer critics of television were found to have widened their readers' horizons by, among other lessons, helping them see that TV "extends our popular cultural traditions and uses them to reinforce widely shared values and attitudes" and "by looking at TV as an 'enveloping substance' that offers a neat institutional view of ourselves and of life" (Scher, 1974, p. 8).

At least one scholar in search of identity for broadcasting was aware of these general parallels between media study and general speech. Grover (1966), adopting a comprehensive view that included but went behind social critics of media, explained that the claims for academic legitimacy in general communication and in broadcasting had a common origin, one which should be recognized as a bond. "Communications as a composite discipline has tried to go counter to the 'splintering' tendency in higher education," Grover said (1966, pp. 111–112). "The success of this approach has been limited perhaps because the total field of communications is too inclusive. But public address, which studies momentary acts of audio-visual communication, and broadcasting, which studies a particularly important channel of such communication, could possibly do a more successful job of re-laminating the splintered areas of communication research and teaching because of their overlapping interests and methods."

Such, in general and in particular, was the call to the social criticism of media. In the largely exhortative literature devoted to it through the second third of the century, such criticism was to be the response, first, to the awesome power of the media, themselves, the modern counterparts to the burning-bush medium of Yahweh while speaking to Moses. Second, it was to be the responsible search for academic identity premised both on the relation of media to the ideal society and the relation of media to speech communication in general, a field that organized itself not by a standard unit of analysis but by its synthesis of approaches to studying the problem of what happens, once said Karl Wallace, when A and B talk to each other.

The call, however, was to be taken up slowly, for reasons which next appear.

THE EMERGENCE OF SOCIAL CRITICISM OF MEDIA

When Wallace (1954) conducted one of his periodic surveys of the field's status, he gave two paragraphs to the media, reminding researchers and critics with Wichelns-like understatement that film, radio, and television were not to be "underrated."

In molding public opinion on public questions the impact of radio, television, and motion pictures may well be as great as the word spoken face-to-face. In communicating popular information, the radio and television speaker may be doing more to raise the general level of education than the lecturer without benefit of the vacuum tube. In shaping standards of culture, artistic appreciation, and moral conduct, these media doubtless produce greater effect than would Lyceum and Chautauqua, reborn and brought up to the minute. Their audience is numbered in millions of persons. They can create audiences and meet hearers at their own convenience. Their immediacy has shriveled distance and time (1954, p. 123).

Here, from one of the leaders of mid-century speech communication, was a divining of media criticism as the natural extension of public-address study. Yet, as will appear, in speech communication the social criticism of media did not begin to flourish until the late 1960s and 1970s. Why?

First, it was as though students of social influence had listened to Wichelns with two gestalts that hardly overlapped. After he had said that rhetorical criticism was concerned with the *method* of achieving effects on audiences, critics (whether directly influenced by Wichelns or not) found themselves concentrating on the artistic proofs and on classical canons as the "available means" of producing effects, usually giving an absent-minded glance at, or tacked-on, perfunctory treatment of, the other half of Wichelns' declaration of independence from literary criticism, the half announcing that rhetorical criticism was concerned with effect, period. As though being tuned in only to the latter emphasis, other scholars abandoned or refused to enlist in the ranks of the critics, wanting not to explore plausible reasons for likely outcomes of discourse but seeking rather to gauge its obtained effects.

Interested, therefore, in the social influence of mass media, effects researchers were taking a fork in the scholarly road leading them away from commerce with critics until the 1970s and 1980s, as will appear later. In gradually increasing numbers for the greater part of fifty years these measurers of media influence ran experiments, conducted surveys, executed panel studies, and content-analyzed film, radio, and TV for purposes of understanding and improving pedagogy, devising the most "effective" means of radio-TV-film production, predicting children and adults' social behavior in relation to their mass-media experiences, and predicting political behavior in relation to mass media—whether agenda-setting or voting patterns or viewing preferences. In the process, a separate subculture of research flourished and gave rise to an array of midrange models of media influence, of which most social critics of media would later apparently be ignorant: the "hypodermic" model; the N-step flow hypothesis; the gatekeeper model; the limited effects model; the uses-and-gratifications model (Schramm, 1973); and the latter's spin-off, the life-cycle-and-uses approach (Dimmick, McCain & Bolton, 1981). Arising originally from the same interest in instrumental communication that rhetoricians followed in their analyses of public discourse, their work appeared to take no account of the critics. As a group they added no impetus to the social criticism of media, although limitations in their studies later provided a niche for its development.

Nor, for the depression and post-World War II years, did the community of rhetorical critics make much of such criticism. In the first place, their field was called "speech," and they tended to define themselves as much by the data they scrutinized as by the conceptions with which they worked. Most of what they considered to be attracting audiences, as well as what they themselves read in newspapers and magazines or saw and heard on radio, film, and television was "entertainment," not deliberative or forensic or even epideictic oratory. In the next place, they were the first- and second-generation intellectual offspring of the "fourteen who made history," the founders of what had become by mid-century the Speech Association of America. They had overlearned the distinctions drawn by those like Wichelns who in the first years of the profession had justified its existence by drawing a wide boundary between rhetoric and poetic, the precise wideness or narrowness of which in later years became a topic for a succession of articles in the journals, but with little application in them to either the rhetoric or poetic of mass communication.

But these two dynamics do not account adequately for the number of missed opportunities to write social criticism of media in an area of clear overlap between rhetoric and media studies: political speaking. From the end of World War II to the end of the Eisenhower administration, rhetorical critics often either omitted mention of media influences on political communication or considered them only in critical asides. In a time when the "radio magic" of FDR was already legend and when television sets were becoming as common as bathtubs, rhetorical critics and historians interested in political speech preparation not uncommonly gave short shrift to broadcast or telecast considerations in speech writing (Runkel, 1951; Ray, 1956; Hildebrandt, 1958; Freeley, 1958; Padrow & Richards, 1959; Windes, 1960). Not only did public-address scholars often seem uninterested in the influence of mass media on such behind-the-scenes drama as speech writing, but it was not rare for them to leave out or give scant space to the shaping influences of mass media on convention and campaign speaking itself (Sillars, 1958; Murphy, 1960a, 1960b; Berquist, 1960; Vasilew, 1960; Miles, 1960; Freeley, 1961). Even on-going communication of a president with the press could not be assured of commanding attention to media-as-media influences (Martin, 1961).

Another indication of the relative importance attached to media-related political criticism comes from the showcased symposia in *The Quarterly Journal of Speech* on national elections. Among six other contributors to the 1952 symposium on postconvention persuasion was Edward Stasheff's "Campaign on the Air" (1952). Among the five contributors (Harding, 1957; Lasch, 1957; Baskerville, 1957; Ehninger, 1957; Wrage, 1957) to the analysis of the 1956 election, no one gave major attention to the explication of media effects. In the three-author treatment of the 1960 election, two (Miller, 1960; Harding, 1960) took note of media influence, both being concerned with the Kennedy-Nixon debates—with Miller seeing them as having influenced the style of the entire postdebate campaign and with Harding praying that "we do not have to suffer them again in the same form" (1960, p. 363). In 1964, with no resumption of the televised debates, none of the six writers (Wenzel, 1964; Graham, 1964; Rosenthal, 1964; Dell, 1964; Kerr, 1964; Harding, 1964) concentrated on mediafied postconvention politics. Why did critics miss opportunities to produce social criticism of media while dealing with political speaking?

The question gains urgency when one examines the *QJS* treatment of the 1968, 1972, 1976, and 1980 elections. There, the political rhetoric of media received concentration in at least one essay in every election

(Rosenfield, 1969; Bormann, 1973; Swanson, 1977; Berquist & Golden, 1981).

In general the missing of opportunities had been a matter of critical orthodoxy. As "mainstream" critics and historians, writers in the 1950s and early 1960s were witnesses to or participants in the debate that had greeted Marie Hochmuth Nichols' introduction of Kenneth Burke to the speech field during the 1950s. Potentially an impetus to social criticism of media, Burke's conceptual widening of rhetorical influence included non-verbal as well as verbal and unconscious as well as conscious strategies of identification. Hence, Burke's followers considered as rhetorical the same range of effect that Benson was to lay out for the social critic of media. Meanwhile, however, many writers on political communication would have agreed as a matter of critical convention with Minnick's later opinion, offered as part of a symposium on critical methods: While it might be "desirable for the rhetorical critic to study . . . a variety of non-verbal communications . . . if he does so, he ought to recognize . . . that he studies non-rhetorical forms of communications (at least as rhetoric is usually defined)" (1970, p. 109). During the 1950s and early 1960s, then, even though Burke offered legitimacy to the social criticism of media, his was an alternative being addressed to a community of writers secure in a scene of rhetorical scholarship in which the direction taken by Wichelns either was continuously being refined or was being challenged mostly from those like Wrage (1947) who wanted to reverse the direction of effect to that of society's influence on oratory. It had become a comfortable dialogue, and Burke appeared to many as an interloper at worst, a sojourner at best—a refugee from the New Critics' reigning emphasis on intrinsic criticism in English departments. Like Joseph and the Children of Israel in the land of the Pharoahs, sojourners are not saviors until a time of crisis.

The turning point came between 1965 and 1968. First, the gradually-developing consensus on rhetorical criticism dissolved with Black's *Rhetorical Criticism* (1965)—dedicated to Wichelns—administering the *coup de grâce* to the critical tradition that had grown up in Wichelns' shadow (other pieces in the journals such as Croft [1956] had already begun featuring anomalies in the neoclassical practice of criticism). Too, advance scouts like Gregg (1966) were beginning to spy out such new domains as that of phenomenology for their occupancy by critics; and Marshall McLuhan shot off his skyrockets, in whose glare the staid descriptions of ethos, pathos, and logos washed out to the palest of scholarly hues.

But these influences were secondary to another, one which made Burke, with his distinction between action by choice and motion by deter-minism, a refuge and a strength for critics. The post-World War II be-havioristic revolution, which earlier had turned departments of government into departments of political science, had reached speech. The "empiricists," backed by the convictions of adherents and by the hard reality of federal soft money, commanded more and more of the positions that opened in faculties through the decade of the 1960s. Specialists in rhetoric yielded departmental chairs to those in communication theory and mass communication. Publications like *Speech Monographs* and *Journal of Broadcasting* became dominated by behaviorists, along with *Human Communication Research*, the new journal of the International Communication Association. There was talk of additional journals in the future—and behavioristic approaches penetrated all the regional ones, as well as *The Quarterly Journal of Speech* and *Speech Teacher*. The field was tentatively renamed speech communication in the report of the New Orleans Developmental Project (Kibler & Barker, 1969), and there were those at the conference who felt compromised by having to keep "speech" in the new name at all, whether understood either as noun or adjective.

In all this, the rhetoricians found themselves verging on being the Russian nobility displaced by the Bolsheviks; indeed, some of them acted like White Russians in the internecine warfare that arose in some quarters. But voices of calm and rapprochement like Brockriede (1968) helped to bring about the armistice proclaimed in what would later be the new Speech Communication Association interest group, Rhetorical and Communication Theory. It was clear to all that in the new disciplinary context, critical studies had to reestablish their credentials.

The new orthodoxy came to be the gathering up of what Burke had called rhetoric-in-dispersion, the openness to theory and critical doctrine from the quarters of literature, philosophy, jurisprudence, and semiotics; the recognition of rhetorical motives in popular culture, art, and music; in cartoons, editorials, and advertisements; in plays, documentaries, docudrama, newscasts, Hollywood films, and soap operas.

Along with others committed to the humanities-centered approach to human communication, the social critics of media found a developmental niche opening to them because of a serious conceptual gap in the empiricist program. The niche was the value-laden side of human communication. As far back as 1956, Berlo himself and a colleague had speculated that the confounding variable in their empirical study of the "impact" on a Canadian audience of a radiodrama satire was value: "It might be suggested that the present study involves a third consideration besides that of initial position and educational level; namely the values of fair play, and sympathy for the underdog, which exist in our culture" (Berlo and Kumata, 1956, p. 297). By the middle 1970s, this overlooked variable in the Berlo-Kumata design would widen into the equivalent of an uncharted dark side of the moon. According to Carey (1975), the blind side in all "mainstream" media research was its ignoring of cultural influences while it concentrated on the instrumental effects of communication. The result, Carey would say, was a "transmission" view of communication instead of a "ritual" one. It was the ritual idea of communication, paralleled in anthropology by writers of "thick description" like Clifford Geertz (1973), which accounted for the creation and maintenance of pervasive social institutions in which human beings live and move and have their beings.

The constitution of society was rhetorical effect, indeed, and of a sort hardly amenable to nonlongitudinal quantitative studies of the 1950s, 1960s, and 1970s. The social study of media promised critics a complementary role to that taken by media scientists. Too, social criticism was compatible with the emphasis on rhetoric as a way of knowing, as the genesis of social reality, and as the omnipresent motive of symboling, all of which was propagated by the humanists' response to New Orleans, *The Prospect of Rhetoric* (1971). The larger community of rhetorical critics was, like Carey, beginning to converge on cultural correlates of communication. Among and like them, the media critics were poised to draw upon categories from aesthetics, popular culture, dialectical analysis, rhetorical-vision analysis, Burkeian dramatism, structural-functionalism, ideologizing, and mythic-archetypal analysis during the long-delayed answer to the call for social criticism of media.

All along, of course, there had been precursors of that criticism. They wrote, sensing some ways in which old categories had to be stretched and somehow paradoxically adapted to account for the unaccountable—namely, the magic of the Old Testament burning bush made present again in electronic media, pervasively influencing audiences' interpretation-creation of reality in their atavistic intuiting of worlds amidst the light and shadows of millenia-long campfires. Degnan (1955) had argued that stylistic distinctiveness underlay the "personality" appeal of newscasters Lowell Thomas and Edward R. Murrow, thus making ethos the basis for broadcast newsworthiness. Bormann (1957; 1958), who later would break out of the neoclassical mold to produce his own dramatistic categories, had used the artistic proofs as a search model in order to see early that the case of Huey Long pointed to the power of electronic media in the politics of candidates' image making. Haiman, always subordinating his interest in media to his intimate subject of civil liberty, had found pathos stressed in subliminal messages "registered in the fringes of the viewer's attention" thereby generating influences for economic and political decisions in which "no thought processes intervene" (1958, p. 385). Spalding (1958) had combined neoclassical categories with content analysis to be able to see how well the radio format had earlier lent itself to the believability of a sacralizer of Ford Motor Company, William John Cameron. Through efforts like these and by others for whom the social criticism of media was either a major or incidental theme, the end of the 1960s saw harbingers of fully developed media-effects criticism. Brown (1969), for instance, found the filter of television inherently more open to the street-theatre pseudo-events which de-legitimized the 1968 Democratic convention than to the conventionalized pseudo-events inside the hall—so that the former seemed more "real" to audiences than the latter.

Created by the convergence of innovative critical practitioners who by and large worked unaware of others' efforts and who reconstructed for themselves any necessary working understanding of its genesis, the social criticism of media had these defining qualities. First, its writers understood that social and cultural consequents were sufficiently complex to require plausible explanations rather than measured and straightforward reporting of results. Such a mutation in media studies found an opportunity for growth opened by media scientists' concentration on the instrumental effects of media experience. Second, writers of such criticism understood that plausible explanations for meanings derived from the technical capabilities of media as media were fused with those aroused by conventionally construed, discursive "messages." While their emphasis on that fusion could vary widely, without some attention to it writers practiced either simply the criticism of discourse (with media rendered as nondefining attributes of messages) or else concentrated on the medium itself (with common cause thus made with those media scientists who treated discursive content as irrelevant to social effects). Third, as metacritics like Swanson (1977a) saw, the practice of criticism, including social criticism, entailed commitment by critics to some *theory* of knowing in order to explicate plausible accounts of social effects via fusion of "message" and "medium." In meeting the first two criteria, media critics formed a community of scholars. In meeting the third, they created the dynamic for specialization within their ranks. That specialization is the subject of the next section.

THE FLOWERING OF SOCIAL CRITICISM OF MEDIA IN SPEECH COMMUNICATION

As is the case with all of history writing, however, the specialization among social critics of media is clearer in retrospect than to them at the time. In America, the public stress on similarity rather than on differences among media critics follows from two commonly shared assumptions. First, as long as social critics of media remain what Berger (1969) calls a cognitive minority, these practitioners cannot, in Will Rogers' phrase, afford politically to see "what's what and who's who" that are good enough to belong to the "club" of media-effect critics. In the next place, American media critics share the cultural heritage of folk-popular pragmatism and are united in its bias that social-effects criticism has to be "good" or "useful" for something. Overall, of course, criticism is "good" for making disturbingly interesting, novel experience into cognitively comfortable, interesting experience. In regard to social criticism of media, moreover, the urgency for explication is enhanced by the ascribed social potency of print, chemical, and electronic publication.

Accordingly, depending upon the individual critic's specific version of "usable" explication, the yield from criticism may be knowledge (1) theoretically sufficient to analyze media power according to its participation in real and universal categories of communication potency, with a concomitant view of reality as corresponding to such categories or forms; (2) theoretically capable of leading to prediction or perhaps even control of mediated-communication outcomes, with a concomitant view of reality as working like a machine; (3) theoretically adequate to prepare media publics to improvise on and cope with media influence, with a concomitant view of reality as the events of everyday life; or (4) theoretically comprehensive enough to suggest interventions into—without specific outcome-control over—mediated communication, with a concomitant view of reality as being evolutionary. These four possible "uses" of critical insights are my own extensions of Pepper's four categories of knowledge-generating "world hypotheses" (1942; 1970). The "uses" correspond, respectively, to four ways of construing reality: "formism," "mechanism," "contextualism," and "organicism," (Pepper, 1970, pp. 141–150).

To write in accordance with one or the other of these, the critic assumes a certain root metaphor that, if elaborated, provides a comprehensive epistemic strategy. The root metaphor for mechanism is the Machine; for formism, Similarity; for contextualism, History; and for organicism, the Organism (Pepper, 1970, pp. 186, 151, 232, 280).

To explain social learning prompted by media, the critic makes coherent assumptions about the way the world is—that is, the nature of both reality and knowledge of it. For example, in the assumptive world of the mechanist, which is shared among behaviorist researchers, the world is predominantly a vast machine whose workings are open only to inference. As parts of the inferred machine are verified, predictions or control of the workings or both are possible. Next, to social critics who practice neoclassical or Aristotelian criticism of media, the assumptive world is primarily comprised of real *types* of events, persons, or ideas that are grouped together or apart because they do or do not share some common form. Once, then, real categories of communicative potency can be seen to include media events, the formist answer to media influence can follow. To the contextualist media critics, on the other hand, the world exists assumptively neither as machine nor as form but rather as the occurrence of everyday events rendered meaningful in some context. As *enactments* in a drama of real life, media events may be coped with or improvised on. Finally, to organicist social critics, the world is predominantly processual, developmental, evolutionary; once the dynamics of media messages become apparent, strategies for intervention into them become possible.

While few social critics of media are likely to conceive that the totality of their work neatly exemplifies any one of these assumptive worlds, the emphases in individual articles do approximate the perspective of one among the four starting points for construing reality and knowledge. That approximation greatly aids the historical interpretation of social criticism of media. So also does a brief explanation of the ways of knowing associated with each assumptive world.

Mechanists and formists similarly assume that knowledge comes in the first instance from *analysis* of the world, but they diverge on what is analyzed. The former seek the parts or inferred workings of the world machine as integrating the only real reality of concrete particulars, while the latter seek to see how particulars are examples of *types*, which they distinctively consider to be real reality.

Contextualists and organicists, on the other hand, assume that knowledge comes in the first instance from *synthesis* of the world, but they diverge from each other on the extent of that synthesis. To the contextualist, the whole that is the everyday event is nevertheless unique and cannot be seen as being necessarily or determinately related to other events (accordingly, knowledge is operationalized, experiential); to the organicist the everyday event is necessarily or determinately related to all other events, although human beings may not understand entirely how they are so related. Nevertheless, knowledge depends on awareness of such coherence.

Early neoclassical critics of media influence like Bormann and Spalding (1957; 1958) wrote formistically, enabled by formism's root metaphor of Similarity to place communication events into categories of potency that are universal across time: ethos, pathos, and logos. Viewed through formistic lenses, the artistic proofs are real categories, not hypostatizations, and are the "real" reality of communicative power. Therefore, to be able to relate Long's or Cameron's media-conditioned remarks to the artistic proofs was to make a cause-to-effect analysis of social effects. This analysis of causes, then, was the knowledge product of such formistic criticism. When seeking knowledge from within the formist community, critics had sufficiently explicated the social influence of media when they concluded, for example, that iconic media intensified the potency of one or more of the artistic proofs.

The empiricists referred to earlier, on the other hand, wrote as mechanists, inclined to treat the artistic proofs as possibly convenient constructs, depending on how well they accounted for variance observed in the only real reality, that which was residing in the particulars of communication events. Operating from the mechanistic root metaphor of the Machine, they sought to interrelate and integrate more fully than did formists the variables abstracted from analysis, even as the parts of a machine are integrated. As with Berlo and Kumata (1956), they hoped to be able to predict or eventually to control the effects of media on society. When seen through the eyes of mechanists, prediction was adequately established when the invented constructs, or variables, related beyond chance to observed outcomes, which basically was their "causal-adjustment" version of truth, premised on correlation of inferred aspects of reality with "physiological configurations [in verifiers] which are the effective structures" of attitudes and expectations (Pepper, 1970, p. 228.).

Differing in the ways just sketched, formists and mechanists nevertheless shared the conviction that adequate knowledge of media-society interrelations could be established by building, as though brick by brick, figure by figure, variable by variable, a tower of knowledge. They also shared the assumption (and ideal) that the observer and the observed were radically separable. Formist prose forbade the first-person pronoun; the passive verb was imported to eliminate the human agent at the remote controls of the Machine that is the world among mechanists.

Media critics of the 1970s and 1980s, as part of the speech communication field's shift of attention away from these postulated world views, tended to amalgamate the observer and the observed. Their criticism, of course, offered analysis—but not as the primary product, as had that produced by critics and researchers writing as formists and mechanists. Instead, their analyses were subordinate to a synthesis that in Burke's phrase "uses all there is." Varying in the extent to which their synthesis was a systemic one, these critics were "contextualist" (if less systemic) and were "organicist" (if more so). With the bulk of critical writing on media partaking of contextualism and organicism during the 1970s and early 1980s, a closer look at those critics' assumptive worlds is justified.

First, the contextualists. If American scholars sometime have been initiated into the communication field's translation of Dewey's pattern of reflective thinking, they begin to understand quickly contextualist knowledge and its potential "use" to cope with or improvise on the social effects relating to mass media. For human agents, the task of problem solving not only focuses reality on an event and on the context perceivedly connected with it but also gathers into a synthesized whole the task aspects of (1) sensing a felt difficulty, (2) searching out its sources and rehearsing scenarios for solutions, (3) all the while inferring and applying standards by which to recognize the scenario most-favored for reducing the difficulty. The synthesis of these aspects is clear to anyone who has unsuccessfully attempted to make their progression a linear one. Such a presentation of reality-as-synthesized-whole is characteristic of contextualist thinking. So also does the solution of a felt difficulty exemplify the contextualist "operational theory" of truth, by which a solution is true if "it works," that is if it alters events in ways that accord with human problem-solvers' values (Pepper, 1970, pp. 270–279).

This version of truth contrasts with analysis-stressing conceptions of truth including (1) the formists' theory of degrees of correspondence between a particular (such as a chair), on one hand, and a universally real category (the platonic idea of a chair) on the other; and with (2) the mechanists' correlational "causal-adjustment theory" (Pepper, 1970).

For social critics of media who participate in the contextualist world view, the root metaphor is History, but not history as an event that is "dead and has to be exhumed." Rather, "The real historic event, the event in its actuality, is when it is going on *now*, the dynamic dramatic active event. We may call it an 'act,' if we like, and if we take care of our use of the term. But it is not an act conceived as alone or cut off that we mean; it is an act in and with its setting, an act in its context" (Pepper, 1970, p. 232). This sense of present-as-history depends, of course, upon the interpretation or significance attached to events conceivably connected to each other as act.

Burke, with his synthesis-requiring ratios within the pentad of act, scene, agent, agency, and purpose, drew critics toward his categories in their efforts to show the significance-conferring acts of media. Also, Bormann, in his view that motives "do not *exist* to be expressed in communication but rather *arise* in the expression itself" (1972, p. 406, emphasis added), thereby made the act and its significance simultaneous and, therefore, the present-into-history. The rhetorical vision, though not itself set in the "here-and-now" (1972, p. 397), provides in its dramatic unity the sense of historic significance attaching to that which is "immediately happening in the group." In general, existentialist and phenomenological philosophers also could serve as resources for contextualist social critics of media.

With these category sets to rely on, media critics set out as though to help themselves and their readers cope with media by synthesizing act and context. They tended to show plausibly (1) how the media artifact itself was an act, or (2) how such an act invited participation in it by audiences, or (3) both. As Kallen (1975, pp. 111–112) argued in his explication of the New Journalism—and by extension, any other medium—its "experience is the important thing" to the contextualist.

When critics stressed mediated communication, itself, as act, they sometimes seemed to be aesthetic critics bordering on social critics. For instance, Perry as a contextualist viewed Antonioni's film *L'Eclisse* as one "heavily indebted to phenomenology" (1970, p. 92) with its artfulness residing in its fusing of facts and values. The rhetorical workings of such art is indicated, however, when "analysis of the interconnected motifs which form the value context indicate an overwhelming complexity and profusion in the film's use of physical objects to assign values" (Perry, 1970, p. 91).

Again, Chapel (1975), while agreeing with Gerbner's view that no didactic persuasion is required in a work of fiction, used Burkeian categories to illuminate "All in the Family," "The Jeffersons," and "Mary Tyler Moore" as acts reflecting and reacting to American culture's bigotry and gender stereotypes. Koester, applying Bormann to self-help books for women, concentrated on revealing their intrinsic Machiavellian drama, but concluded as social critic that it presented "incomplete, contradictory, and debilitating advice" (Koester, 1982, p. 165). Medhurst, relying primarily on Burke's contextualistic use of "associative clusters" to derive equations carrying across *The Exorcist*, seemed both a literary critic in his "charting the movement of key images through six dramatic episodes" and a rhetorical critic in "examining the use of ambiguity within those episodes" to present a "clear rhetoric of choice . . . as the central valuative stance" (Medhurst, 1978, p. 73). Again, drawing on the associative clusters arising from fourteen sense-image motifs in *Hiroshima, Mon Amour*, Medhurst explained how the film rhetorically invites viewers to realize and cope with the lack of "absolute validity of empirically based knowledge" (Medhurst, 1982, p. 352). Such critics make it clear that art is itself a social act and that the boundary between aesthetic and social criticism is therefore a permeable one. "Experiential" critic Robert Scott affirmed the contextualist's basis for such permeability while socially criticizing the fresco painting of Diego Rivera: "We should expect controversy to be expressed in as well as to grow out of art. A demand for aesthetic purity is fundamentally a demand simply to ignore an aspect of being human" (Scott, 1977, p. 79). With the repeatability of media acts, their happenings can be history-as-now, "literally the incidents of human life" (Pepper, 1970, p. 233).

Other critics stressed interaction-of-audiences-with-media as act, seeming therefore to offer "mainstream" examples of contextualist social criticism. Turner's fantasy-theme analysis of comic strips, while emphasizing women's gender–role depiction in comic-strip art, wished also to focus rhetorically "on the interaction of medium and audience" (Turner, 1977, p. 24). Most often treated was television news. Bormann was impressed by the "awesome power of electronic media to provide, in the form of breaking news, the dramatizations that cause history-conferring fantasies to chain through large sections of the American electorate" (Bormann, 1973, p. 143). Smith concluded, after adopting the Burkean's contextualist definition of form as the arousal and satisfaction of appetites, that television's "arranging, cutting, emphasizing, and commentary is manipulation on a sophisticated level" (Smith, 1977, p. 151). Cusella (1982) saw the *Kent State* real-fiction docudrama as the TV act of rhetorically purifying William Schroeder's image for American audiences by making the slain student into an All-American boy to be emotionally adopted by viewers. Gregg, phenomenologically pursuing his synthesis of TV news as a depoliticizer of images, envisioned its frames of reference as becoming audience "taken-for-granteds" via "dull daily reinforcement" and "trivial repetition," while at the same time its techniques of dramatic narration speed up time and obliterate space insofar as national contextualizing and regional or local decontextualizing would affect interpretation of events (Gregg, 1977, p. 223, 234). Similarly, Swanson (1977b, pp. 241, 248), relying on TV's "melodramatic imperative," found it and its audiences "ignoring some issue positions, assigning meaning to campaign events within a strategic and dramatic frame of reference, becoming preoccupied with mistakes and novel, if trivial, developments." Bormann juxtaposed TV's chaining out (1) of fantasy themes conferring history on the release of Iranian hostages with (2) the fantasy themes in service of Reagan's Inaugural's "Restoration" fantasy type, in order "to bring the tacit and seldom examined dimension of TV coverage to conscious analysis" (Bormann, 1982, p. 133). Deciding that the Iranian coverage enacted the Restoration theme of the inaugural, Bormann concluded that such "intertwining" had "worked to reinforce and amplify" for audiences the core fantasy of the speech" (Bormann, 1982, p. 134). In such essays as these, the interaction of media and audiences is the significance-filled, hence historic, act.

In general, the drama arises from seeing plausible audience response antecedent and consequent to stage prompting from media, which include magazines, newspapers, song lyrics, soap operas, and film. Here media users as real-life, history-as-now participants live out women's media-foreshortened roles of human relations adjusters (Kidd, 1975), learn the nature of human history from Wells' *War of the Worlds* novel or discover the political dangers in mass media from Welles' *War of the Worlds* broadcast (Morson, 1979), enact media-modified values of progress and success (Morello, 1980), seek media-identified scapegoats for national corruption (Willkie, 1981), create in-group solidarity for social movements through protest songs (Knupp, 1981), enact the communal ritual of newsreading (Glasser, 1982), rehearse national themes and symbolic characterization via summative song lyrics in film (Roth, 1981), learn from soap-opera's characters (who share secrets with viewers but not with each other) how people adjust to experience (Rose, 1979), and process war as a universal initiation rite (Rushing & Frentz, 1980).

In these essays, the authors deal plausibly with complex and value-centered outcomes of messages that fuse content and media characteristics. As Benson (1978) indicates, these outcomes are therefore both intended and unintended; and, following the contextualist epistemic, critics produce operational truth as though seeking the goal of readers' or themselves' coping with or improvising on the drama of history now. Such critiques enjoy the strengths of verisimilitude (the contextualist's is a world of people, not formistic categories nor mechanistic engines) and scope (the range of acts is unlimited, as the preceding catalog suggests). The price paid for these strengths, however, is a loss of precision in conceiving the concatenation of so many acts at the societal level. Such precision becomes important when the reader or media critic would serve as change agent.

To effect a gain in such precision (at some cost in verisimilitude) is to shift metaphors, as Burke himself has recognized. Drawing on the metaphor of the organism's tendency to homeostasis, he elaborates it vis-a-vis parsimonious criticism of society. "A systematic analysis of interactions among a society of agents whose individual acts variously reinforce and counter one another may best be carried out," he says, "in terms of 'equilibrium' and 'disequilibrium' " (Burke, 1962, 7, p. 449). Such a shift from History to Organism as metaphor offers a gain in precision by producing an integrated synthesis, which is analogous to the inherent integration of the organism. Accordingly, the organicist's reality is that of a growing, developing system, in which everything relates to everything (integration) but some things more than others (junctures for interventions). Because the organicist's truth is therefore a coherence theory (the amount of experience held together in an explanation), the process of reality (including communication) is one of developmental balancing within the equilibrium-disequilibrium pair. Addressing this disjunction are the categories of organicism, on which media critics implicitly drew during the 1970s and early 1980s: "(1) fragments of experience which appear with (2) *nexuses* or connections or implications, which spontaneously lead as a result of the aggravation of (3) *contradictions*, gaps, oppositions, or counteractions to resolution in (4) an *organic whole*, which is found to have been (5) *implicit* in the fragments, and to (6) *transcend* the previous contradictions by means of a coherent totality, which (7) *economizes*, saves, preserves all the original fragments of experience without any loss" (Pepper, 1970, p. 283). These categories have not only lain behind critics' patterns for synthesis but have played a large part in their concomitant evaluations. Provided the critic is committed to the developing values in question, then effects of media are praiseworthy when contradictions or gaps in values are transformed into organic wholes, blameworthy when they are not. This appears to hold, regardless of the specific model being employed—be it a version of Levi-Strauss, Jung, or others.

Under the lenses of the organicist, then, criticism of media-societal effects becomes not the naming of an act but synthesis of interventions into the developmental process of the body politic. The locus of such interventions lies in categories two and three, as just cited: connections leading fragments (made apparent by counteraction, opposition, or contradition) to resolution. For most critics in the organismic reality, this has meant in practice that mediafied communication succeeds or fails at holding cultural values in creative tension, that is, homeostatic balance.

Such evaluation is clear, for instance, in the critics who combined media aesthetics with rhetorical assessment to show media artifacts as social interventions. Schuetz, attempting to combine phenomenological and "organistic" criticism, stressed that *The Exorcist* shows "goodness and evil, doubt and faith, despair and hope, secular and sacred, physical and spiritual, not as opposites to be resolved but as realistic representations of an integrated reality" (Schuetz, 1975, pp. 100–101). As an effects critic, she found that such an integration promotes audience acceptance of filmic images, "whatever the duration of the change." At about the same time, Frentz and Farrell also discerned that the power of the *The Exorcist* resided in its synthesis of "positivistic Evil" and "Transcendent Good" by means of personifying and allegorizing their clash; the result is both a reflection and conversion of America's Consciousness (Frentz & Farrell, 1975, p. 43). Not the resolution, but the "aggravation" of gaps in American life (such as "boredom" and "alienation") explains the intrinsic structure of Wiseman's *High School*, said Benson, and also leads to "an account of how this structure may invite a rhetorical response" as its social intervention (Benson, 1980, p. 235). Earlier, Benson (1974) had seen the artistic contradictions in *Joe* as reflections of mythic tensions in society-at-large. Another critic also used structuralist aesthetics to explain both the textual nature and the rhetorical working of *Mein Kampf* (McGuire, 1977). Besides structuralism, critics have adapted Jungian psychology to organismic criticism: Davies, Farrell, and Matthews not only dealt "with a film's inner workings" but also showed how archetypes and filmic myth contribute to "society's psychic balance" (Davies, Farrell & Matthews, 1982, pp. 332–333). Still other critics have related literary conventions and Burke's society-wide drama to question the organic wholes supposedly offered in prime-time television series (Chesebro & Hamsher, 1974); and another showed that romantic literature, beyond "reaffirming a culture's traditional ideals and values," can by dissociation "purify and correct" the inconsistencies between or among them (Bass, 1981, p. 269). So, too, did Medhurst and Benson (1981) see the documentary *The City* as producing a clear thesis-antithesis-synthesis pattern that balances societal values. The film's use of rhythm creates this pattern in its movement "from past (rural and slow) to present (urban and fast) to future (suburban and moderate)," all in order to "show the desirability of 'cooperation between man, machine, and nature'" (Medhurst & Benson, 1981, pp. 58, 59). In such instances as these, when aesthetically based criticism explains audience response in a way conceivably promotive of social influence, its practitioners belong to the tribe of social-media critics.

In other organismic criticism of the 1970s and 1980s, the writers' attention fell less clearly on aesthetic categories for rhetorical purposes and more strongly on the socially systemic function performed by the resolution or intensifying of tensions in myth, values, stereotypes, and roles.

Most often, critics dealt with myth from a structural vantage point, as a shorthand way to tap into interventions in the social-media system. As precedent, Europeans like Levi-Strauss (1963) and Americans like Henry Nash Smith (1957) had treated myths as system balancers, either as transformation of cultural tensions or as channels for energy. Breen and Corcoran, while relating viewer-uses to television programming, considered persistent "mythic themes" and commented on the power which myth "gives for handling conflict" (Breen & Corcoran, 1982, pp. 129–130). Rushing (1983) saw the Western myth, a balancer of the tension between individualism and community, in danger of subversion by movies like *Urban Cowboy*. Wander decided that " 'All in the Family' . . . sustains fundamental myths of American society and contains conflicts which threatened to disrupt it" (Wander, 1974, p. 604/18), concluding as well about soap operas that they "resurrect" the nineteenth-century preindustrial myth as a way to counter "real problems" (Wander, 1979, p. 88). In "The Waltons," the same critic found the series mythically filling "out the ideal 'family' " and yet being "about the death of the Family," thereby leading audiences to be aware of the contradiction between their own lives and that of the depicted family and to "wonder what a celebration of being human, having fun, creating something worthwhile would be like in our own lives, and what we can do to make this a reality" (Wander, 1976, pp. 152, 154). Further, *Roots*, drawing its vitality from narration through victims' eyes, leaves its viewers "with a tension between hope . . . and the social and economic realities" in which they find themselves and their future hopes (Wander, 1977, p. 68). Gould, Stern, and Adams (1981) disapprovingly saw prime-time shows as balancers of the poverty-affluence tension: By intensifying some aspects of American life and downplaying others, prime-time shows offer the poor-but-happy, affluent-but-tormented resolution. In the mid-1970s, Brown concluded that by itself television's use of the rural American mythology was inadequate to encompass contradictions in American culture of "personal loneliness amidst close physical proximity to others; individual powerlessness amidst burgeoning organized efforts to cherish the individual; fragmented or specialized work roles against holistic consumer roles" (Brown, 1976, p. 397). By the beginning of the 1980s, however, Schrag, Hudson, and Bernabo (1981) announced that the medium had evolved an urban myth potentially modeling coherent life-styles for city dwellers in the "New Humane Collectivity."

The organicist's mythic analysis extended to print as well as to electronic and filmic media. Brown and Crable (1973) showed that the mythic New American Eden in mass-magazine advertisements not only resolved contradictions between economic growth and ecological damage but prepared the way for corporate innocence in the upcoming energy crisis. With the direction of influence flowing the other way, Mechling (1979) saw the unfolding newspaper story of the Patty Hearst kidnapping as reflector of the public's working through its contradictory impressions of the heiress-turned-revolutionary.

Even when critics have not invoked mythic analysis as their entry point into media as systemic interventions, the topic of contradictions and their resolution has given them leads toward developing the organicists' integrated synthesis. Ewen regretted that the "consciousness industries," such as print, telegraphy, film, and the like, have "through the production of imagery reconciled demands for a better life with the general priorities of corporate life" (Ewen, 1979, p. 18). Rushing and Frentz (1978) and Frentz and Rushing (1978) explained the appeal of *Rocky* by its synthesis of American values in tension with each other. Merritt found "bashful heroes" like the Cooper and Stewart film personae costly to American society, because while they reconcile incapability and invincibility, they also conflictingly invite role-taking audiences to mix "self-effacing charm" with "extreme aggression" (Merritt, 1975, pp. 129, 139). Such paradoxes appear also to Turner, who outlines the "competitive, yet cooperative relationship between government officials and members of the press" (Turner, 1982, p. 435).

In all of this organicist criticism, then, a parsimony of explanation arises from the topic of resolution-aggravation of tensions in cultural myths, values, roles. The emergent "strategy for strategies" of intervention, then, turns out to be either the facilitating or impeding of homeostatic balance, or creative tension, in the contradictions among, the oppositions to, or the apparent fragmentation of cultural values and taken-for-granteds. Nothing in the world viewed organismically limits critics to the topics of myths and values, however. The interest in myth and archetype has simply proven to be an attractive way for writers moving away from formist and contextualist criticism to tap into societal communication as a system. To them, the dialectical confrontation of meanings seen to be resolvable in myth has been an isomorphic way to make specific what Pepper calls the "progressive" categories—those in which apparent fragments are synthesized into a whole. If critics remain interested in the organicist root metaphor, they can be expected to find other ways of conceptualizing an organic system, whether they follow the specific lead of alternative-seekers like Brown (1978, 1982) or not.

The reason for their seeking other means of system-synthesis inheres in a contradiction within the organicist's world view itself (all construals of reality have contradictions, but others do not depend on them for the dynamics of change, as does organicism). When looking at its three categories of *implicitness, transcension,* and *economy* in the synthesis achieved via the progressive categories, the critic sees that the conception of an absolute, timeless truth is emergent. "Organicism . . . requires the progressive categories to give it scope," says Pepper, "yet the progressive categories involve time and change and finitude; yet time and change and finitude cannot be true since only the absolute is true and in the absolute is no time, nor change, nor finitude" (Pepper, 1970, p. 314). In other words, the extension of organicism ultimately metamorphoses into the universal categories of formism, which leads this discussion, finally, to consider recent formist criticism of media.

Less popular but remarkably durable and adaptive, formist criticism has demonstrated its staying power. Three tactical moves by its practitioners have kept it alive and available for a new prosperity when appropriate developmental niches open. First, critics have practiced what formism preaches (that its categories are universally real) and have shown that the triad of artistic proofs and the array of classical canons are therefore applicable to a range of data formerly thought not to concern rhetorical critics. Examples include newspaper format and news-editorial writing (Berg & Berg, 1968); political cartoons ("as Rhetorical Form") (Medhurst & Desousa, 1981); film (Hendrix & Wood, 1973); and music (Le Coat, 1975; Le Coat, 1976). Next, formist critics have imaginatively used the list of artistic proofs and the canons not as catechisms to be invoked in every essay but as leads into thorough analyses of particulars in communication events, giving formistic criticism a finely grained and coherent texture: the complexities added by television to *inventio* (Larson, 1972); the heightening of pathos in *Bonnie and Clyde* by the film's reversal of emotion by featuring latent moral values of society, which reassert themselves at the end "with an enormous impact" (Free, 1968, p. 220); the influence of talk-show format on portrayal of ethos (Hammerback, 1974); the cinematic sources of ethos of *Patton* for the Silent Majority and Richard Nixon (Carpenter & Seltzer, 1974); the influence of televised predebate publicity and televised debate formats on antecedent, intrinsic, and consequent ethos of presidential candidates (Berquist & Golden, 1981). Formists have analyzed the combinations of words and music in relation to pathos (Mohrmann & Scott, 1976) and in relation to logos as audiences' enthymematic participation in "ascription" (Gonzalez & Makay, 1983).

The third formist move, one especially interesting since practitioners of organicist criticism tend by extension toward a category of the absolute, is to develop new names for universal categories and thereby to subsume claims developed by contextualists and organicists. The effort in this direction by genre critics, including Larson (1972), is so well known as to require no elaboration here. As representative case no one, however, serves better to illustrate this third tactic than Gronbeck, who while remedying the split in

Aristotle between content and form offers a new triad of universal categories of potency for television. They are, on the part of audiences, performers, and authors, (1) *mythoi* ("knowledge of universalized sequences-of-action which can arouse fear and pity"); (2) a combination of *ethoi* and *dianoia*, ("an understanding of recognizable character types and speech patterns"); and (3) *sujets*, ("particularized stories" depending heavily "upon creative inventional habits") (Gronbeck, 1983, p. 233). Such a set of real categories provides a causal explanation for television-audience interaction: "At the mythic level [*mythoi*] the character types [*ethoi* and *dianoia*] are seen to participate in the expression of timeless truths" (Gronbeck, 1983, p. 238). Such explanation of potency by the participation of particulars in real universals is the criterial argument of formists, and it converts to subordinate status what are sometimes primary themes in contextualist and organicist criticism: "I am calling for a tri-layered approach to TV criticism, one working within what essentially have been called the artistic, sociocultural, and mythic schools of criticism, and one employing what often are termed semiotic or structuralistic tools" (Gronbeck, 1983, p. 242).

Benefiting from such formistic advocates of media criticism, formism as critical school can be expected to retain its viability. Its practitioners stand ready to take up where those of organicism leave off (just as the latter can claim to take up where the former leave off); and it balances contextualism's indeterminate synthesis with its own causal analysis. In the future, social critics of media will recognize that these root metaphors complement each other and that our understanding of media-society interactions will be enhanced thereby, just as Pepper observed of our understanding of the world that alternative hypotheses about its reality "supply us with a great deal more information on the subject than any one of them alone could have done" (Pepper, 1970, p. 331). What else needs saying about the future of media-effects criticism?

A FUTURE FOR SOCIAL CRITICISM OF MEDIA

When this survey of media-effects criticism was written in the early 1980s, the art of futurism had not developed to the point of talking about *the* future. In these brief remarks, all I honestly can say is that there are pointers from the past which give clues to *a* future. I hasten to add that dynamics not now seen as part of the future-choosing system of scholars and researchers could fundamentally alter the directions I am about to suggest.

First, once launched into the universe of discourse on media, critics will pursue extensions of media thinking into areas undeveloped so far. Already the harbingers are with us. Mechling and Mechling (1981), Gumpert

(1975), and Cathcart and Gumpert (1983) are showing the way, as physical surroundings created by theme parks become media to induce us to tell stories to ourselves and as Gumpert's idea of uni-comm is fleshed out by himself and Cathcart to make media omnipresent. Further, the marriage of computers, satellites, video, and telephones promises to move media into so many mix-and-match configurations that critics for years to come will reflect on the sporelike release of media effect to all levels of human communication and the societies of which it is constitutive—around the earth. In the criticism of such mix-and-match configurations, together with contemplation (when the time comes) of theoretically feasible innovations like implantation of computerized memory aids in the human brain, critics and theorists may be led to collapse any distinction between mediator and mediated and to join others in the intellectual arena in developing a fifth root metaphor, that of the Hologram; Schrag, Hudson, and Bernabo (1981) have already found it necessary to use the term.

But wide-ranging as such critical concerns are likely to be, they will ultimately produce only a vicious circle, no matter how much cross-fertilization occurs among academic disciplines involved in the future education of media critics—unless. Unless these critics periodically shift their attention from their present preoccupation with culture and value, they will make the same mistake in reverse that Carey has found media scientists making—criticism will be crippled by critics' overweening attention to ritual versions of communication, unaware of the learning to be gained by attending to it as instrumental transmission, as well. Those shifts will be encouraged if persons making publication decisions are open to work that highlights anomalies, nonfitting relations, between "ritual" categories for media criticism, on the one hand, and the novel aspects of media-experience, on the other. Such anomaly featuring will be constructive rather than destructive. It will be seen as constructive if referees and readers can escape the provincialism of their own subspecies of models and methods for the social criticism of media.

Such a shift will also be facilitated by work that offers a rapprochement between the empiricist and the critic. That rapprochement will contain its own creative tension between precision and sophistication of mathematical inference, on one hand, and subtlety of nuance in the qualitative mode, on the other. Again, harbingers are already present. Rhetorical-vision analysis combines with audience surveys to monitor social effects of mediated portrayals of politicians and foreign policy (Rarick, Duncan, Lee & Porter, 1977; Cragan & Shields, 1977). A variety of categories and forms of statistical inference informs a study of television network news (Bantz, 1979). Content analysis is wedded to criticism to detect either movement across time or insightful nuance at a moment of time in mass-media portrayals of crime and poverty (Mechling, 1979; Gould, Stern & Adams,

1981). Frentz and Hale (1983) gather viewer reaction before selecting a specific model for film criticism. The last initiative, in particular, along with the participant-observation example of Benson (1981), seems to promise that critics' psychological set toward either a cultural or an instrumental view of communication will be periodically shifted from the one to the other.

In such an intellectual climate, the theoretical and applied uses of media criticism are likely to multiply. Always serving the useful function of providing needed interpretations of ever-new media experience, critics will aid in society's coping with and interventions into the mediafying of the population. In addition, when criticism partakes of rule-based models (Frentz & Hale, 1983) further development of that paradigm will make possible more precise prediction of some kinds of media-social interaction.

The history of trends in the social criticism of media reminds its student of still another creative tension requiring maintenance in future scholarship. Too few of the critics surveyed in this essay have concerned themselves primarily with the shaping influence of society on media; yet Benson (1978) has issued such a call to social critics. While empirical researchers have perhaps concentrated too much on that direction of influence, critics have given it too little attention. Without that attention, critics will have an unjustifiably limited role in studies of developing media in societies around the earth.

Next, as practitioners of criticism multiply their efforts, metatheorists will build on earlier pieces that combined critical rationale, method, and practice—from the beginnings of a flowering, such as Berg (1972) and Kohrs Campbell (1974) through Frentz and Hale (1983) and beyond. Alongside them, because they as human beings have to render for themselves, as well as for any others, the disturbingly novel mediafied experience into the comfortably interesting mediafied experience, finely-tuned critics will still deal with individual communication events, at once providing anchors for metatheory and moving from magic to mythicism and beyond. Together, the metatheorists and critics of specific events will remind themselves of Max Black's comment on the enduring human dilemma: "At the margins of precision, the universe wavers." To deal with that uncertainty, there will always be critics.

NOTE: I wish to thank the following research assistants for their help: Darlene Brown, Roy Grindstaff, Rebecca Lockridge, Scott Marshall, Gary Pike, and Evette Strothers. Special thanks are due Karen Altman for her help in interpreting early trends in media-related criticism.

11

Freedom of Expression and the Study of Communication

PETER E. KANE

In the multiple subdivisions of communication studies one area of specialization that has received comparatively little attention from communication scholars has been that of freedom of expression. This fact is at the same time both surprising and explainable by the direct and intimate relationship between freedom of expression and the development of all theory of communication. One would expect that such a close relationship would result in extensive examination. On the other hand the relationship is so close that it can be overlooked. Fish apparently accept the water in which they swim as given.

The purpose of this essay is twofold. First, in order to make explicit the relationship between communication theories and freedom of expression, examples of the development of the traditional body of theory will be reviewed in terms of this relationship. The second section of this essay will sketch the development of the study of freedom of expression within the communication disciplines over the last twenty-five years.

FREEDOM OF EXPRESSION AND THEORY

In our culture almost every educated person has read at least some of the Greek epic poems. For most readers these works are attractive as great, heroic adventure stories—a kind of *Star Wars* of the ancient world. Yet for the culture that produced them they were much more. The recitation of these poems not only told stories of the mythic past—stories of the Trojan War and the travels of Odysseus—but like the materials in McGuffey's Readers, these tales were also intended to teach the customs, practices, and moral precepts of the society of those who listened.

One of the first features of the Greek epics that the analytical reader cannot fail to notice is the great value placed on the performance of a skillful rhetor. The wily Odysseus is highly regarded not just for bravery but for skillful speaking as well. One of the first evidences of Telemachus' developing maturity is his able oral presentation to King Menelaus in the fourth book of the *Odyssey*. Clearly, effective oral communication was held in high regard. But additional important and valid inferences can be drawn from this evidence. These works describe the system of freedom of expression that existed in the culture. The reader learns who can speak, under what conditions, and what can be said. There is no value in effective oral communication if there is no freedom to express oneself.

In general, in the Greek epics, freedom of expression seems to be granted to members of the nobility, the ruling class. These characters—men, women, and children—are portrayed speaking their minds. Their freedom to do so arises both from their status as rulers and from the power they command to enforce their right to speak. This simple formulation is, however, subject to a number of exceptions. For example, in spite of status and force, it is often suggested that the wise man will be cautious, diplomatic, and circumspect in what he says. While it is admirable to be outspoken, it is also admirable to avoid an unnecessary confrontation by speaking with care. The protection for expression based on status can also be shared. The guest in a noble's house, no matter what his status, is treated with deference and is invited to express himself freely. This freedom of expression is enforced by the power and status of the noble host from order of the gods. Readers of the *Odyssey* surely remember the crime of the Cyclops in Book Nine in failing to provide the hospitality to guests that the gods demand. This episode stands in marked contrast to the reception at Alcinous' court in Book Seven, where Odysseus' welcome included an uninterrupted opportunity to say what he pleased.

These observations about the views on freedom of expression in the epic poems may seem self-evident, and they are. They are noteworthy because they generally go unnoticed; they are taken for granted. Nevertheless, the epic poems were created as they were because extensive although clearly limited freedom of expression existed in the Greek society of the Homeridies.

Corax and Tisias are generally regarded as the first rhetorical theorists in Western civilization. Why were these beginnings of Western rhetorical theory in Syracuse in the fifth century before Christ? Cicero's answer was that with the expulsion of the tyrant Thrasybulus a new democratic order was established that created a special demand for instruction in oratory (Sandys, 1885). The problems of adjudicating conflicting property claims in a legal system where each person represented himself were the origins of that demand. This democratic political system in Syracuse granted to each citizen freedom of expression. While the extent of this freedom is not known, the available evidence does show that each person was allowed to plead his own case without restriction on the argument and evidence that could be presented to prove the case. The instruction offered to property claimants by Corax and Tisias could not have happened without an underlying framework of freedom of expression.

What began in Syracuse developed extensively in Athens. A system of democratic government provided a society in which freedom of expression could be practiced. In this climate the study of effective communication naturally flourished.

The writings of Plato ask questions that can only be asked meaningfully in a society where freedom of expression is recognized and practiced. He asked, what is justice? What is truth? In the *Gorgias* Plato turns his attention to one of the problems of freedom of expression: the ability of the demagogue to exploit this freedom to unworthy ends. The critique of rhetoric in the *Gorgias* is directed to the rhetoric of the demagogue. In contrast, in the *Phaedrus* Plato views the proper function of rhetoric as a tool to aid in the discovery of truth.

It must also be recognized from the writings of Plato that there were limits on expression even in Athens. In the *Republic* Plato argues for limitations on freedom of expression when he suggests that the epic poets should be banned from his ideal society. The argument for this suppression is made in the name of freedom of inquiry. The epics present revealed truth based on authority (the gods) that inhibits freedom. To promote real freedom this restriction on free inquiry must be suppressed. This argument that real freedom of inquiry and expression springs from suppression is reflected in modern thought in the writings of Herbert Marcuse (Marcuse, 1969).

A more significant example of the limits to free expression can be found in Plato's *Apology*. On the one hand Socrates was free to defend himself in an open and public trial. He was free to face and answer his accusers and to use whatever arguments he chose in an effort to persuade his jury of 501 Athenians chosen by lot to hear the case. On the other hand the accusations against Socrates are speech related. As Plato presents it, Socrates was accused of misusing his freedom of expression to corrupt youth and undermine the gods. While the real crime may have been a political conspiracy against the democratic state, in Plato's writing Socrates was found guilty, condemned, and died for exceeding the society's accepted limits of freedom of expression.

The work of Aristotle reflects the continued political liberty of Athenian society. Aristotle, the great observer, records systematically in *Rhetoric* the communication practices that surround him. From his work it is clear that the rhetors of Athens in his day were actively using a broad range of persuasive techniques to influence others in both legal and legislative bodies. Significant issues were being debated and decided in an atmosphere in which freedom of expression was accepted and practiced. A work like *Rhetoric* would not have been produced in a repressive environment.

An interesting contrast to the work of Aristotle is what little we know of the theory of Hermagoras of Temnos writing in the second century B.C. While Hermagoras, like Aristotle, apparently directed particular attention to the subject of invention in relation to political questions, the examples of illustrative material that have come down to us are substantially different from those used by Aristotle. They are hypothetical cases, such as whether Orestes murdered his mother. These illustrations suggest a concern for the form of Aristotelian rhetoric but not for the content. This shift in emphasis is readily understandable when one identifies the political realities of the time. Hermagoras wrote some 150 years after the death of Alexander. Hellenistic society had fallen into rapid decline; the empire had been fragmented; authoritarian governments replaced the old ideas of political freedom. In this environment it was neither necessary nor wise to study rhetoric to express oneself freely and effectively on significant public issues. Hermagoras' theory is understandable as the appropriate product for the climate of freedom of expression of his time (Bryant, 1968).

The Roman "republic" was never really comparable to the Greek democracies. While in the early years (fourth century B.C.) some popular assemblies of all free men were held, the logistics of such assemblies serving as deliberative bodies led to their eventual disappearance. Powers of a deliberative assembly were assumed by the Roman Senate. Originally a patrician body, the Senate became a body made up of the rich and powerful of Rome regardless of whether they were noblemen. Even though Rome was ruled by a succession of more or less absolute military dictators, the absence of total, consolidated power necessitated shared political decision-making in which the Senate was an active participant.

Just as Roman government was at best a shallow copy of the democratic systems of Greece, so Roman rhetoric for the most part lacked the vitality and creative insight found in the work of the major Athenian theorists. A large portion of Roman theory organized, systemized, and codified Greek thought. Given the political climate of Rome it is not surprising that the significant creative Roman rhetorical theory should have been produced by a rich and influential lawyer active in the affairs of the Senate—Marcus Tullius Cicero. Cicero was one of those few Roman citizens who functioned in an environment in which significant persuasive communication on meaningful issues took place. However, even for the rich and powerful the free expression of ideas was often a hazardous undertaking. Several times in his career Cicero found that his words had offended other powerful people and that political expedience and his continued good health dictated that he leave Rome for a while. In the confusion of authority that occurred after the assissination of Caesar, Cicero was able to express himself forcefully in opposition to Anthony, but once the Triumvirate had consolidated their power, the punishment for this free expression was death.

The growing and evolving Roman Empire was held together in large part by two elements—military might and the consolidation of power in the figure of the god-emperors, some of whom ruled with considerable skill. In such an absolutist environment it is not surprising that what little consideration of meaningful rhetorical transactions as had appeared in Roman rhetorical theory disappeared. The work of Hermogenes of Tarsus illustrates the nature of rhetorical study in the latter part of the second century A.D. As Ray Nadeau has observed, "If we accept Hermogenes' rhetoric for what it is, a school textbook written in the heyday of the Second Sophistic preoccupation with ornamentation and virtuosity, the emphasis on verbal machinery and mechanical classifications is readily understood" (Bryant, 1968). That instruction in Hermogenes' system was the study of form without substance can be seen in his selection of illustrations, such as the point of argument between two men with beautiful wives who discover each other leaving the other's household or the issue arising from fabricating the story that Socrates maintained a brothel (Nadeau, 1964). Since discussion of significant issues in a public forum did not take place in the latter years of the Roman Empire, there was no need for developing or maintaining a body of rhetorical theory to teach such skills.

A final example of the close interrelationship between a society's practice of freedom of expression and the rhetorical theory that the society produces can be found in the work of Saint Augustine, writing in the early Christian Era around the beginning of the fifth century A.D. Paganism had been abolished by decree and the writings of pagan authors were denounced by church fathers. However, Christianity as an aggressive, proselytizing religion needed effective rhetors, and *De Doctrina Christiana* spoke to that need. The particular characteristics of this work are understandable in terms of the clearly defined and limited scope of free expression in the culture of the early church. In contrast to Plato's theory, there is no concern for the discovery of truth. Truth was revealed in scripture. What was needed was a full understanding of the revealed truth and an ability to communicate that truth effectively to others. In the first three books of *De Doctrina Christiana* Saint Augustine deals at length with the methods of understanding scripture, including detailed discussions of the nature of language and the problems of dealing with ambiguity. The fourth and final book of *De Doctrina Christiana* contains both the argument for effective communication and instruction for achieving true eloquence through the effective communication of the meaning of scripture. In sum, Saint Augustine's rhetorical theory is an exact reflection of the extent and limits of freedom of expression in the environment in which he wrote (Murphy, 1960).

There is a close and direct relationship between the practices of freedom of expression in a given culture and the nature of the rhetorical theory that the culture produces. Thus, an essential key to an understanding of theory is an awareness of the climate for freedom of expression, the scene in which the theory is formulated. Given this demonstrated relationship, the lack of attention given to the study of freedom of expression by communication scholars requires analysis. Apparently the relationship goes unnoticed. While this lack of attention may be owing to a failure to study the historical context of theory, it may also be that the relationship is so close that it is invisible.

MODERN STUDY OF FREEDOM OF EXPRESSION

In the United States the concept of freedom of expression rests not just on social and cultural determinants. Since 1791 freedom of expression has apparently been guaranteed as a legal principle by the absolute language of the First Amendment to the Constitution of the United States. Children are taught the theory that we all have a constitutional right to speak whatever is on our mind without fear of punishment. However, in the real world this theory turns out not to be correct. People are in fact legally punished for speaking their minds (Goodell, 1973; Kutler, 1982).

The apparent conflict between the theory of freedom of expression and actual practices can be seen as the impetus for the modern study of this subject. Since the issues are at the outset legal ones, it was natural that those involved in the study of law would be the first drawn to the topic. The conviction in 1918 of Jacob Abrams for protesting the United States invasion of the Soviet Union prompted Harvard law professor Zechariah Chafee, Jr., to examine freedom of expression problems in depth. The result of his examination was two articles on the Abrams case in the *Harvard Law Review* followed by a book based on those articles (Chafee, 1919, 1920a, 1920b). For the next 35 years Chafee directed attention to the issue of freedom of expression and human rights in general through his study and extensive writing. His 1941 Harvard University Press book, *Free Speech in the United States*, remains a landmark in the literature of the field.

Chafee's view that the First Amendment was designed to expand freedom of expression and erase the old restraints has been vigorously challenged by the Brandeis University constitutional historian Leonard W. Levy. Through a detailed examination of historical documents Levy developed the argument that the First Amendment was merely a vague statement of general principle and was in no way intended to change or eliminate the old common law concept of seditious libel (Levy, 1960). As Levy saw it, those who claimed that decisions of the Supreme Court were making broad inroads in First Amendment guarantees did not understand the actual intent of those who drafted the amendment. Freedom of expression, particularly where it involved criticism of the government, was not meant to be absolute.

A third legal scholar to address himself to the question of the extent and nature of freedom of expression in the United States was Thomas I. Emerson, Lines Professor of Law at the Yale University School of Law. Emerson's special contribution was his effort to develop a broad philosophical system that could be used to establish a clear definition of the extent and limits of constitutionally guaranteed freedom of expression. Writing in *Toward a General Theory of the First Amendment* Emerson concluded, "the essence of a system of freedom of expression lies in the distinction between expression and action. The whole theory rests upon the general proposition that expression must be free and unrestrained, that the state may not seek to achieve other social objectives through control of expression, and that the attainment of such objectives can and must be secured through regulation of action" (Emerson, 1966, p. 115). This basic concept was expanded and developed at length in a later work, *The System of Freedom of Expression* (1970).

The foundation work by those in the fields of history and law—Chafee, Levy, Emerson, and others—became the base upon which those in other fields were to build. In addition to the continued interest of history, law, and political science, scholars in fields with special interest in communication, such as journalism and speech, began to explore the subject from their special perspectives. In 1961 the Speech Association of America (now the Speech Communication Association) established a free speech interest group. The four people who were the principal movers behind the creation of this interest group were two lawyers, Robert M. O'Neil and George P. Rice, and two scholars whose field of special interest had been small group communication, Alvin A. Goldberg and Franklyn S. Haiman. In this year the interest group published "Cases and Problems in Freedom of Speech," edited by Mark Klyn of the University of California, Berkeley. The following year a similar volume edited by O'Neil was recognized as an official SAA publication and has been designated as volume 1 of the *Free Speech Yearbook*.

The broad goal of the free speech interest group was to stimulate interest in both scholarship and teaching in the area. The *Yearbook* and convention programs provided an outlet for scholarship. By 1964 the group, now designated as the Committee on Freedom of Speech, had secured a prominent position in the Speech Association's annual convention. The golden anniversary convention in Chicago that year was held jointly with the American Educational Theatre Association (now the American Theatre Association) and featured a single joint general session of the two groups. That program, "Problems of Censorship in the Communicative Arts," was jointly sponsored by AETA and the Committee on Freedom of Speech. The session was chaired by Franklyn Haiman.

While the regular publication of the *Yearbook* provided a focal point for freedom of speech scholarship, a great deal of scholarly work was taking place in other contexts. This interest was in part stimulated by the social conflcts of the Vietnam War era, many of which were directly related to the First Amendment rights of people. In *The Quarterly Journal of Speech* a study by George Rice dealt with the right to be silent (Rice, 1961), and Richard J. Goodman and William I. Gorden considered the rhetoric of desecration (Goodman, 1971). Peter E. Kane examined the First Amendment rights of students (Kane, 1971). A major contribution to this literature was Franklyn Haiman's SCA's Golden Anniversary Fund monograph award winning study, "The Rhetoric of the Streets: Some Legal and Ethical Considerations" (Haiman, 1967). Evidence that these articles addressed significant, broadly held concerns can be found in the 1969 SCA convention program, "Freedom of Speech and Student Protest," in which the featured speakers were all from outside the speech communication field.

The *Yearbook* itself continued to prosper. The first four volumes were edited by Robert O'Neil, who shared the position with George Rice for volume 5 in 1966. The following year Rice began the first of the regular three-year terms for editors that have been standard since then. Rice has been succeeded in order by Thomas L. Tedford, Alton Barbour, Gregg Phifer, Peter E. Kane, and Henry L. Ewbank, Jr. Through a special gift, the Herbert A. Wichelns award was established in 1976 to recognize the work of scholars publishing in the *Yearbook*. Beginning with that issue of the *Yearbook* (volume 15), a special prize committee has selected the best article, and a plaque and cash prize have been presented to its author at the Speech Communication Association convention. The first recipient of this award was William A. Linsley who, since the 1972 issue, has prepared for the *Yearbook* an extremely valuable annual review of decisions of the United States Supreme Court dealing with freedom of speech. This and subsequent awards have helped call attention to a tradition of quality scholarship fostered by the *Yearbook*.

Support for expanded teaching of freedom of speech was provided by the 1965 publication of Franklyn Haiman's *Freedom of Speech: Issues and Cases* as part of the Random House Studies in Speech series. The following year Bobbs-Merrill added Robert O'Neil's *Free Speech: Responsible Communication under Law* to its series in Speech Communication. A third text, *The Principles and Practice of Freedom of Speech*, edited by Haig A. Bosmajian, was published by Houghton Mifflin Company in 1971. The extensive and continued use of these three works is reflected by their publication history. A second edition of O'Neil's work was published in 1972. Haiman's *Freedom of Speech* reappeared in a much enlarged form in 1976 as part of a bicentennial series on citizen rights published by National Textbook Company in conjunction with the American Civil Liberties Union. Haiman served as the general editor for this series. Bosmajian's collection was reprinted in 1983 by University Press of America. Expansion of the variety of materials available for classroom use was demonstrated in the publication of William I. Gorden's simulation game book, *Nine Men Plus: Supreme Court Opinion on Free Speech and Free Press* (Gorden, 1971). Concern for the teaching of freedom of speech was also reflected in George Rice's study of students' free speech attitudes (Rice, 1959) and Thomas L. Tedford's consideration of materials to use for effective teaching of freedom of speech (Tedford, 1967). This record of publication demonstrates the success of the interest group in encouraging the expanded teaching of freedom of speech.

Like those in other interest groups, the members of the freedom of speech group quickly discovered a need to communicate among themselves. To this end a newsletter was prepared and mailed to all who requested it. This newsletter contained not only the usual organizational information of such a publication but also summaries and comments on free speech issues and cases of current concern, particularly acts of apparent suppression in an academic setting involving speech communication teachers. For the first five years and eleven issues the newsletter was produced at Northwestern University by Franklyn Haiman. In 1967 Haiman asked to be relieved of this responsibility, and Thomas L. Tedford was appointed to replace him. Tedford gave the publication the official name by which it has been known ever since: *Free Speech*. He established a regular, three-times-a-year publication schedule and added short articles and instructional material to the newsletter's contents. With Tedford the editors of *Free Speech* began to serve three-year terms. He has been succeeded in order by Haig A. Bosmajian, Peter E. Kane, Ruth M. McGaffey, and David Jamison. Since 1973 the Speech Communication Association has provided support for the printing and distribution of *Free Speech*. The work continues to be the most ambitious of any of the newsletters published by SCA divisions, sections, commissions, or other interest groups.

In 1972 the official name of the freedom of speech interest group was changed once more to its present title, The Commission on Freedom of Speech. This designation by the Legislative Council of the Speech Communication Association was a recognition that freedom of expression concerns transcend the more narrow limits of the disciplinary divisions of the association—a recognition of the fundamental, underlying role of freedom of expression in all areas of communication study. A program at the SCA convention that same year effectively illustrates this breadth. That program, chaired by Alton Barbour, featured four papers that used a behavioral science approach to the examination of freedom of speech issues. Such studies have been a feature of graduate study in freedom of expression at the University of Denver, which along with Northwestern University, has become a center for advanced speech communication study in the field.

The breadth of freedom of expression concerns is illustrated in the variety of cooperative activities with other groups. The joint convention program with the American Educational Theatre Association has already been noted. In addition, the Commission on Freedom of Speech has sponsored joint programs with the Commission on Communication and Law, the Instructional Development Division, and the Religious Speech Communication Association. Speakers representing the American Association of University Professors, American Civil Liberties Union, American Library Association, and the National Coalition Against Censorship have appeared on commission programs. In response to the United States Supreme Court's decision on obscenity in *Miller v. California* in 1973, the Speech Communication Association joined with 38 other educational and religious organizations to establish the National Coalition Against Censorship. Daniel Ross Chandler has served as the SCA's representative to this group (he has also chaired the Commission on Freedom of Speech). Programs sponsored by the American Studies Association, Caucus on Gay and Lesbian Concern, Commission on Accountability and Responsibility in Governmental Communication, and the Mass Communication Division have also included papers dealing with freedom of expression.

Finally, the Commission on Freedom of Speech has had substantial impact on the Speech Communication Association through preparing and gaining approval of policy statements on freedom of expression. In 1963 the SCA adopted a statement that originated with the freedom of speech group dealing with the right of students to hear speakers representing a broad range of views and to deal with literature selected for its artistic rather than its ideological content. This statement was supplemented in 1967 by language that recognized the constitutional right of peaceful protest. These activities culminated in 1972 with the Legislative Assembly approval of the "Credo for Free and Responsible Communication in a Democratic Society," that remains the SCA's fundamental statement of commitment to freedom of communication.

In recent years activities in regional associations have paralleled those within the Speech Communication Association. Both the Southern and Western Speech Communication associations have established freedom of speech interest groups. The major activities of these interest groups have been to develop and sponsor programs at conventions of these associations to provide an outlet for work of scholars interested in the subject area.

Duplication of the pattern developed by the SCA Commission on Freedom of Speech can be seen in the 1971 Western Speech Communication Association convention program. The Western interest group presented a program jointly sponsored by the Western Forensic Association that featured a speaker from an outside organization (American Civil Liberties Union). In the same year the interest group began to publish a newsletter containing both organizational information and a review of current freedom of expression court cases. Issues of the newsletter have appeared from time to time ever since. Not surprisingly many of those who have been active contributors to the Western interest group are those who have also been involved on a national level in the activities of the Commission on Freedom of Speech.

In the Southern Speech Communication Association the development of an interest group was stimulated by the then president of the association, Gregg Phifer, who in January 1971 established an *ad hoc* Committee on Freedom and Responsibilities of Communication, composed of Calvin Logue, Wayne Minnick, J. W. Patterson, Edward Rogge, and the then editor of the SCA's *Free Speech Yearbook*, Thomas Tedford. The following year the Southern convention recognized the group as a regular standing committee. By 1976 the committee had achieved the status of a division of the association, placing it on the same level as interest groups like oral interpretation, rhetoric and public address, and theatre. The principle responsibility of the Division on Freedom and Responsibilities of Communication has been to sponsor programs at the annual conventions of the association. Through the formal divisional structure, convention program planning takes place more than one year before the convention. Unlike the Western Speech Communication Association, the Southern's Division on Freedom and Responsibilities of Communication has never developed a newsletter for internal communication. However, in September 1973 the Southern began publication of a semiannual journal, *Communication Law Review*, designed to keep readers informed about both current issues and controversies and historical analyses of freedom of expression problems.

Some of the earliest published studies of freedom of expression by speech communication scholars appear in the regional journals. This pioneering work includes the following studies: In 1948 the *Southern Speech Communication Journal* devoted an entire issue to freedom of expression. In *Today's Speech* (now *Communication Quarterly*) studies began to appear in the 1950s. The earliest, both by George Rice, deal with student attitudes about freedom of speech (Rice, 1955) and the legal use of loudspeakers (Rice, 1957). Even though no interest group has ever developed within the Eastern Communication Association, the association's journal has published numerous freedom of communication studies. Lionel Crocker had a short free speech essay published in *Western Speech* (now the

Western Journal of Speech Communication) in 1943, but additional work did not appear until the 1960s (Crocker, 1943). The regional interest group has successfully stimulated research and publication in *Western*. The *Central States Speech Journal* has published fewer freedom of expression studies than any of the other three regional journals. The first that did appear dealt with the relationship between speech and law and was, once again, the work of George Rice (Rice, 1961b). The absence of an interest group in this regional association may be responsible, at least in part, for scholarly inactivity. However, it should also be noted that freedom of expression scholars in the geographic area, such as William Gorden, Ruth McGaffey, George Rice, and Franklyn Haiman, have published in other journals, including *The Quarterly Journal of Speech* and, of course, the *Free Speech Yearbook*.

While the bulk of the speech communication study of freedom of expression has dealt with political speech and the limitations placed on it, other subject areas have also attracted attention, particularly those of obscenity and libel. The interest in the problems of obscenity has already been noted in Speech Communication Association activities. The joint general program with the American Educational Theatre Association at the 1964 convention was concerned with censorship based on obscenity charges. The SCA's participation in the establishment of the National Coalition Against Censorship arose from a recognition of the threat to freedom of expression inherent in the irrationalities of the United States Supreme Court's opinion in *Miller v. California*.

Two other examples of concern in this area are also worth noting. In 1976 Burt Franklin and Company published a volume entitled *Obscenity and Freedom of Expression* compiled and edited by Haig Bosmajian (Bosmajian, 1976). This volume included significant portions of 70 major obscenity opinions issued (with one exception) by courts in the United States. It brought together materials that would otherwise be available only to those with access to a well-equipped law library. The second example is a Commission on Freedom of Speech program at the 1977 Speech Communication Association convention in Washington, D.C. This session, perhaps the best attended program of the convention, was entitled "The *Hustler* Hassle" and featured Larry Flynt, the publisher of *Hustler* magazine, as a guest speaker. Clearly, in this area communication scholars have been dealing with significant issues in a timely manner.

The work dealing with libel has fallen into two categories. First, there have been studies that focus on the problems of the source of communication that might be subject to legal action for defamation. In 1965 J. Christopher Reid published a study of broadcast defamation (Reid, 1965). More recently, this topic received additional explication by David M. Hunsaker in his article, "Freedom and Responsibility in First Amendment Theory: Defamation Law and Media Credibility" (Hunsaker, 1979). A further contribution to understanding in this area was Wayne Minnick's 1982 analysis of United States Supreme Court opinions designed to clarify the significant question of the difference between a "public" and a "private" person (Minnick, 1982). A second area that has attracted attention is that of group libel. Legal action in this area is closely akin to actions to punish political speech in that it involves prosecution by the state of the alleged defamer. Ruth McGaffey explored this issue (McGaffey, 1979), while earlier Peter Kane had reviewed the arguments in support of such laws that were presented in the Canadian House of Commons (Kane, 1970).

While the work in these areas shows an expanded interest in freedom of expression, the total amount of work done is not large. *The Quarterly Journal of Speech, Communication Education*, and the four regional journals have together published only about 60 freedom of expression studies. The *Free Speech Yearbook*, publishing some 10 solid scholarly articles a year, remains the most important outlet for studies in this field.

The maturing of speech communication scholarship in the area of freedom of expression is represented by Franklyn Haiman's *Speech and Law in a Free Society* (Haiman, 1981). This volume, the culmination of years of thought and work, is one of the most important contributions to the field since the work of Zechariah Chafee, Jr., and has received numerous awards. In addition to both the SCA's Golden Anniversary Fund book award and the Winans-Wichelns Award for Distinguished Scholarship, Haiman has received an award from the Playboy Foundation and the Silver Gavel Award from the American Bar Association. The study explores a broad range of communication problems and the attempts to deal with those problems through restraints and suppressions. The failures of these policies are clearly shown. Haiman's basic conclusion is that the proper remedy for bad communication is more communication rather than punishment or suppression. He goes on to argue for a positive role for government regulation to achieve this end.

Haiman's achievement is particularly noteworthy when it is recognized that over 200 books dealing with freedom of expression have been published in the United States in the last decade. The extent of work being done in this field is reflected in the annual "Freedom of Speech Bibliography" published in the *Free Speech Yearbook*, which typically lists some 400 items (since the 1974 *Yearbook* this important resource has been prepared by David Eshelman). Whether books or journal articles, only a small fraction of this work has been done by communication scholars, and even among communication scholars those identified with speech communication are in the distinct minority. More has been published in *Journalism Quarterly* than, with the exception of the *Yearbook*, all the speech communication journals combined. While the total output may be small, no apology is needed for the quality of the work produced. Speech communication scholars have repeatedly come to grips with significant freedom of expression issues and have made important contributions to knowledge in the field.

CONCLUSION

At the outset of this study the close and direct relationship between a climate of free expression and the theoretical foundations of communication studies was explored. This examination demonstrated both the way that freedom of expression can be assumed and thus ignored and the critical importance of an understanding of this vital subject area. The importance of the subject is recognized throughout the scholarly community. While over 4,000 books and articles have been published dealing with freedom of expression in the last decade, fewer than 5% of these works have been produced by speech communication scholars. With the broad, multi-disciplinary interest in the subject these figures are not too surprising; but given the crucial role played by freedom of expression in communication theory and practice, this lack of attention is both surprising and distressing. However, those speech communication scholars who have given attention to this area have done significant work. This essay has identified some of those who have been involved in organization, scholarship, and teaching in the field. The list is far from complete. It has not been my intention to name all the important contributors to freedom of expression studies. It is encouraging to note, however, that in a field that has received a great deal of attention throughout the scholarly community, one of the most important works in recent years has been produced by a speech communication scholar.

12

Speech Communication Education in American Colleges and Universities

GUSTAV W. FRIEDRICH

In her best-selling book *Passages*, Gail Sheehy (1976) describes some of the predictable crises that confront individuals as they grow up. A sensitivity to and an understanding of these developmental rhythms, she suggests, is necessary if individuals are to be able to use each crisis to stretch to their full potential.

Like individuals, academic disciplines also confront crises in the process of going through the various stages of their development. It seems especially appropriate, therefore, on the occasion of the 75th anniversary of the Eastern Communication Association to reflect on the present status of speech communication education in American colleges and universities. In doing so, this essay will elaborate on four points: (1) speech communication education has been a contributing member of American higher education from the very beginning, (2) its current status in American higher education is relatively strong, (3) the potential for significantly enhancing that status is great, and (4) doing so will require greater dedication on the part of professionals in the communication discipline.

Before developing each of these points, however, some comments on the scope of this essay are required. Reaching conceptual agreement on what composes speech communication education is not a straightforward task. The boundaries of knowledge do not possess sharp edges, and disciplines necessarily overlap. In addition, differing value structures lead individuals to see the territory in different ways. It is not surprising, therefore, that McBath and Jeffrey (1978) found a variety of alternative definitions emerging as they attempted to generate a consensus for their speech communication taxonomy. Their eventual product defined speech communication education as "the study of speech communication in pedagogical contexts—an area of the discipline which they subdivided into three parts:

> *Oral Communication Skills.* The study of strategies for improving individual competencies in speaking and listening.
> *Instructional Communication.* The study of communicative factors involved in the teaching-learning process.
> *Communication Development.* The study of the acquisition and use of speech communication skills by normal children. (p. 188)

According to this definition, then, speech communication education is concerned with the study of three phenomena: (1) the pedagogical strategies that speech communication instructors use to facilitate the acquisition of communication competence, (2) the communication skills and compentencies used by all instructors in the process of engaging in teaching and learning, and (3) the normal developmental sequence by which children acquire communication competence.

This essay focuses primarily on the first component of the definition: instructional strategies for developing the communication competencies of individuals. The scope of the essay is further narrowed to emphasize the efforts of communication instructors to develop the communication competencies of their students within the curriculum of American colleges and universities. These limitations are imposed on the essay both for reasons of focus and because this area has been most closely aligned historically with the speech communication discipline.

OUR PAST

The first point to be made, then, is that speech communication education has been a contributing member of American higher education from the very beginning. In 1636, 16 years after the Pilgrims landed in America, the Massachusetts legislature founded Harvard University. Because—like other New England colleges soon to follow—Harvard's primary mission was to train ministers of the gospel, the curriculum followed very closely that of the medieval universities. The goal was to produce clerics able to defend the church with reason and tightly developed arguments. Because Latin was the language of educated persons, students were expected to present their arguments, whether formal or informal, in the best classical Latin.

The pedagogy for developing these presentational skills was based on the Latin syllogistic disputation—with a format rigorously specified following the divisions and dichotomies of Ramistic logic (Potter, 1954). When used as a classroom teaching and testing device, a tutor (usually the college president) selected a student to serve as disputant—to defend that side of a question from one of the arts or sciences taught in the college that the tutor believed represented truth. The selected student opened the disputation by reading a carefully worded Latin discourse that stated the thesis, defined and delimited the question, and presented the strongest logically constructed arguments supporting the thesis in the form of syllogisms. At the conclusion of the presentation, the other students in the class offered objections (also in the form of a syllogism) by either disagreeing with the disputant's definitions or by denying the major or minor premises. As objections were raised, the disputant attempted to reestablish the arguments via syllogisms that the other class members disputed until the disputant silenced their objections by the logical presentation of the "truth." At all points in this process, of course, the tutor was available to assist students should they experience difficulty in the use of either Latin or logic.

In addition to its use as a classroom exercise, the syllogistic disputation was also used as a medium for academic display at commencement and other college assemblies. For such occasions, lists of potential topics were generated by students to represent the entire college curriculum, the list was "purified" by the faculty, and the college president appointed disputants whose names and topics were printed on broadsides for distribution to members of the audience. Following the disputations (usually limited to 15 minutes per participant), the college president demonstrated his mastery of Latin as he embellished and clarified his conception of the truth of each thesis.

Time, student complaints, and a broadening of the colleges' professional training goals to include lawyers, doctors, and teachers eventually led to the replacement of the Latin syllogistic disputation with more practical, English language speech training. By the 1790s, speech pedagogy in the colleges comprised English language training in the development and presentation of orations and a form of debate labeled "forensic disputations," in which two to four persons on each side debated contemporary issues.

Over time, additional changes evolved. By the time the Eastern Communication Association was founded (1909), specialists in rhetoric, elocution, and speech had replaced college presidents and tutors as providers of speech instruction. As a part of this movement toward greater specialization, rhetorical training—once synonymous with training in oratory and debate—emphasized message criticism and composition. Textbooks and methods for teaching within this tradition focused on theory and made little distinction between the tasks of the speaker and those of the writer. As an aid to college orators and debaters, itinerant elocutionists provided training in the art of speech delivery; and a small number of academic speech teachers, housed primarily in Departments of English, taught courses in public speaking and debate.

By 1959 and the 50th anniversary of ECA, the scope of speech communication education had further expanded and divided. Specialties in theatre, communication disorders, and mass communication (radio, television, and film) formed and divided into separate departments. Departments of Speech broadened their traditional concern with formal discourse in public speaking and argumentative settings to include the study of informal discourse in interpersonal and group settings.

Although this brief, selective, and undetailed historical account ignores a great many twists and turns, it demonstrates that—while the nature and importance varied—speech communication education has, from the beginning and continuously, been a part of the education provided by American colleges and universities. Readers wishing greater detail concerning this development have many excellent resources available, including the edited works of Wallace (1954) and Oliver and Bauer (1959) and the writings listed in the annotated bibliography compiled by Friedrich (1982). The advantages to be gained by a familiarity with this material is well stated by Ehninger (1953): "Not only does a knowledge of the history of speech training provide the present-day teacher with a liberal education in the aims and ideas of [the] profession, but . . . it also makes for improved instruction in the classroom" (p. 149).

OUR PRESENT

The second point to be developed in this essay is that the status of speech communication education in American higher education is currently solid. While my focus is on speech communication education in American colleges and universities, a logical starting place for surveying current trends is the secondary school. It is at this level that most college and university students receive their first formal introduction to speech training. A study by Book and Pappas (1981) sampled speech communication education in 15 states (Georgia, Indiana, Kentucky, Maryland, Massachusetts, Michigan, Minnesota, Nebraska, North Dakota, Ohio, Oklahoma, Pennsylvania, Texas, Washington, and Wisconsin). Of 8,362 schools contacted, 4,341— or approximately 52%—responded. Seventy-six percent of the respondents offer a speech course or program, and 32% of these (range: 2.2% to 58.9%) require the course for graduation. Thus, if 76% of the schools surveyed offer speech and 32% of those require it, the maximum number of students required to take a speech course is less than 25%. Additionally, because schools that do not offer a speech course are more likely to be in the 48% of schools that did not respond to the survey, the percentage of students required to take a speech course is no doubt considerably less than 25%.

What is the nature of the basic course? Book and Pappas (1981) summarize: "The basic course was described as a semester long, offered only once each year to a combination of ninth or tenth through twelfth graders. The average section had twenty students and was generally fifty-five minutes in length. While a number of topics were taught in the basic course, public speaking dominated. The most frequently cited textbooks were published in the 1960s, and teachers used a combination of both oral and written work to evaluate their students. Finally, the speech course was usually taught as a separate course, but when combined, was most frequently taught with English" (p. 203).

Many schools, of course, offer advanced courses in addition to the basic course. In terms of frequency of offering, they include drama (59.5%), advanced speech (30.3%), debate (26.5%), radio/television and mass media (18.5%), oral interpretation (14.9%), film (11.2%), discussion (7.6%), and interpersonal communication (7.0%). Some schools also offer cocurricular speech activities: theatre, the most common (78.2%), is followed by forensics (53.5%), debate (39.6%), and discussion/student congress (17.5%). Book and Pappas (1981) conclude: "The offerings of speech communication curricula in high schools across the United States have not changed much in the past fifteen years: the same number of courses are being offered, although fewer are being required; the major focus of speech programs in the curriculum continues to be public speaking; and theatre continues to be the most frequent extracurricular offering. The only content change in the basic course is a minor integration of mass media and interpersonal communication, but no major shift from the more traditional topics is evident" (p. 206).

What happens when high school students move on to the colleges and universities? Their most likely exposure to speech communication education is in the form of an introductory, or basic, course. Gibson and several colleagues have conducted three studies of the instructional practices used in the basic speech communication course (Gibson, Gruner, Brooks & Petrie, 1970; Gibson, Kline & Gruner, 1974; Gibson, Gruner, Hanna, Smythe & Hayes, 1980). For their most recent study, 2,794 questionnaires were mailed in August of 1978 to the junior and community colleges, senior colleges, and graduate schools listed in the Speech Communication Association Directory. The result was 552 useable responses for a return rate of approximately 20%.

The authors conclude that "Basic courses in American colleges and universities in the late 1970s are healthy, are viewed in many institutions as the most significant and broadly appealing offering of their department and generally are leading a movement toward basic performance skills in oral public communication" (p. 9). They found enrollments in the course to be increasing more rapidly than enrollments in other departmental courses which were, in turn, increasing more rapidly than the average for all courses in the college or university. While the course is far from being a universal requirement for college and university students, 53% of the colleges of education, 45% of the arts and sciences colleges, and 50.3% of the business schools require their majors to take the basic course.

In terms of approach to the course, 51.3% report a public speaking orientation, while 40.3% report a combination of public, interpersonal, and group communication. Fewer than 10% report an interpersonal (4.7%), communication theory (2.5%), or group communication (0.5%) approach. Consistent with this finding, 80% of the courses require from 4 to 10 performances. To accommodate this load, average class size is within the range of 18 to 30 students. Organizationally, 86% of the instructors teach sections of the course intact rather than in a large-lecture–small-lab format, and 75% of the teaching is done by graduate assistants or junior faculty in a three-semester-hour or four- or five-quarter-hour format. While undergraduates from all four years of college take the course, the majority are freshmen and sophomores.

In terms of pedagogy, 58% report using behavioral objectives to state course goals, and 86% of these use those goals to measure student achievement. In more than half of the courses, instructors videotape and replay one to three communication performances. Teacher-prepared handouts are the most common form of supplementary materials (92%), followed by film (44%), models (38%), transparencies (32%), and slides (24%).

For oral performances, teachers provide both oral (90%) and written (93%) criticism either immediately after each individual performance (48%) or after a group of speakers (32%). Grades and other forms of evaluation are usually the sole province of teacher judgment (48%) or are based on a combination of student-and-instructor participation (51%). In only 1% of the cases is assessment based exclusively on student peer evaluation.

Most of the 2,794 departments in the Gibson et al. survey, of course, offer courses beyond the basic one. In addition, the 713 institutions listed in the 1983 SCA Directory as offering a major in one or more of the communication arts and sciences offer a diverse array of skill development and theory courses. For a recent survey, Wilson and Gray (1983) drew a random sample of 200 departments listed in the 1980 SCA Directory as located in four-year institutions. While their return rate of 25% (50 departments) is low, the reported information is consistent with other information that is available. In terms of departmental emphasis, the authors found that:

40% of the departments have a communication studies emphasis, 36% report an education emphasis, 36% a broadcasting emphasis, and 30% a traditional rhetoric emphasis. (Keep in mind that some offer more than one emphasis.) Mentioned less were theatre (26%), organizational (26%), public relations (26%), mass communication (20%), speech pathology (18%), oral interpretation (18%), journalism (16%), group process/pre-law (10% each), and business, consulting, political communication, instructional media (approximately 5% each). Several others were indicated only once. Enrollment trends in these areas suggest what is happening to these emphases. When respondents were asked where enrollments were increasing, they said the greatest increases were in: broadcasting (30%), public relations (22%), organizational communication (14%), theatre and mass communication (12% each) and communication studies and general speech (10% each). Conversely, declining enrollments were noted in speech education (22%), rhetoric (16%), and oral interpretation, general communication, and theatre (about 10% each) (p. 33).

The above data can be supplemented by examining two types of information: (1) divisional membership in the national associations (a rough indicator of the major categories of courses currently offered) and (2) employment opportunity listings for speech communication professionals (an indication of where departments would like to strengthen their offerings). The divisional memberships of our two broadest associations, then, are as follows:

Speech Communication Association (5,198 members in November of 1983; with 4,452 of those members affiliating with one of ten divisions)
Forensics: 457 individuals, or 10.3% of the total
Instructional Development: 645, or 14.5%
Interpersonal and Small Group Interaction: 1,004, or 22.5%
Interpretation: 312, or 7.0%
Mass Communication: 498, or 11.2%
Organizational Communication: 156, or 3.5%
Public Address: 519, or 11.6%
Rhetorical and Communication Theory: 546, or 12.3%
Speech and Language Sciences: 102, or 2.3%
Theatre: 213, or 4.8%
International Communication Association (2,256 members as of November 1983; with members able to pay to belong to multiple divisions, the following ten divisions report a total membership of 3,354)
Information Systems: 220, or 9.8% of the 2,256 members
Interpersonal Communication: 517, or 22.9%

Mass Communication: 637, or 28.2%
Organizational Communication: 583, or 25.8%
Political Communication: 336, or 14.9%
Intercultural Communication: 270, or 12.0%
Instructional and Developmental Communication: 214, or 9.5%
Health Communication: 218, or 9.5%
Philosophy of Communication: 202, or 9.0%
Human Communication Technology: 157, or 7.0%

Despite the fact that divisional memberships do not always directly translate into course offerings (e.g., not all college and university instructors belong to these associations, some individuals who belong are not university and college teachers, and individuals are not always fortunate enough to be able to teach in their major area of interest), they can at least serve as a rough guide to existing patterns.

Additional hints about both the present and the future can be gained via an examination of employment opportunities in the discipline. Using Bulletins of the SCA Placement Service (the only full-range placement service for the profession), Clavier, Clevenger, Khair, and Khair (1979) examined the 12-year period from August 1966 through July 1978. Using a 28-category coding scheme to label areas of specialization, the authors explored yearly as well as 6-year, 9-year, and 12-year trends. Areas with the largest growth in terms of advertised positions were, in rough order of frequency, interpersonal communication, broadcasting, mass communication, and organizational communication. While the percentages were somewhat smaller, other growth areas were special speech (e.g., speech for special groups, such as business and professional people, teachers, and health professionals), small group communication, research design, persuasion, nonverbal communication, journalism, intercultural communication, and advertising. Some areas, of course, experienced less growth. Among the areas advertising fewer positions were theatre, rhetoric, black studies, clinical, speech education, debate, oral interpretation, and voice and diction. These percentages, of course, must be interpreted in context. While theatre listings declined approximately 10% in the 12-year period, mention of theatre specializations were present in approximately 25% of the 1977–1978 listings.

While less concerned with skill development, a final arena of speech communication education is that of graduate school. The 1981–1982 Directory of Graduate Programs in Communication Arts and Sciences identifies 295 departments, located in 212 institutions, that offer a graduate degree—91 at the Ph.D. level. A faculty of 4,374 (2,702 with doctorates) are helping 11,745 masters students and 2,277 doctoral students to attain a degree. A feel for the nature of their offerings can be gained by examining their list of concentrations for graduate study:

Code Systems: M.A. level, listed by 22 graduate programs; Ph.D., 7
Intercultural Communication: M.A., 54; Ph.D., 21
Interpersonal Communication: M.A., 131; Ph.D., 37
Organizational Communication: M.A., 103; Ph.D., 32
Oral Interpretation: M.A., 52; Ph.D., 12
Pragmatic Communication: M.A., 37; Ph.D., 8
Rhetorical and Communication Theory: M.A., 135; Ph.D., 41
Speech Communication Education: M.A., 108; Ph.D., 16
Speech and Hearing Science: M.A., 88; Ph.D., 27
Theatre: M.A., 128; Ph.D., 28
Radio/TV/Film: M.A., 102; Ph.D., 26

Putting the above figures into the context of higher education, Eadie (1979) compared the number of earned degrees in communication studies between 1960 and 1976 with several cognate areas:

Communication Studies: masters = 75,786; doctoral = 6,694
Psychology: masters = 65,650; doctoral = 24,633
Sociology: masters = 23,219; doctoral = 6,993
Philosophy: masters = 9,920; doctoral = 4,534
History: masters = 65,881; doctoral = 12,832
English: masters = 106,992; doctoral = 16,131
All Fields: masters = 3,055,701; doctoral = 379,610

The above data point to a relatively healthy discipline providing speech communication education at multiple levels within higher education. The third point to be developed in this essay is that the potential for enhancing this status is currently strong.

OUR FUTURE

Our recent and on-going transition from a postindustrial society to what is now described as an information-based society has thrust upon us a new and all-pervasive awareness: true power comes from the ability to combine information into useful knowledge. While robotics and automation can displace human workers, information is needed to increase their productivity. As a result, "information workers today constitute the fastest growing and most highly compensated sector of employment in the leading industrial countries; they account for nearly 50 percent of all persons employed. The industrial sector on the other hand, the actual production, extraction, and growing of goods, now employs less than one-fourth of the American work force" (Wallin, 1983, pp. 7–8).

Consistent with this focus on information as the fundamental resource of the age, the importance of oral communication as a critical basic skill is becoming widely recognized. This consensus on the importance of communication skills is most noticeable in the area of employability and career success. Galassi and Galassi (1978), after reviewing 60 years of research on the job interview, conclude: "A number of researchers . . . consider communication and interpersonal skills as the single most important set of factors in the interview. For managerial and executive positions and to a lesser extent for clerical and technical but not manual labor positions, standard English and fluent speech . . . are important in creating favorable impressions. Nonverbal behaviors . . . such as eye contact, smiling, attentive posture, smaller interpersonal distance, and direct body orientation, are influential as well" (p. 189). Not only are communication skills an important determinant in obtaining jobs, they are equally relevant to success and promotions in those positions. A 1980 study of the graduates of the 13 degree-granting institutions that compose the University of Wisconsin system concluded that the three factors given the greatest importance in the assessment of job candidates (interpersonal skills, attitude, and oral communication skills) correspond closely to the three highest-ranked factors for successful employment (interpersonal skills, motivation, and written and oral communication skills). The importance that the responding organizations place on these communication skills is further revealed by the fact that more than 90% of them provide additional training for their employees in both oral and written communication (Page & Perelman, 1980). In addition to the two reports cited here, 25 similar studies (summarized by DiSalvo, 1980) conducted between 1972 and 1980 support the conclusion that the corporate world increasingly recognizes and values the ability to communicate and work effectively with other people.

That these views are shared by both alumni and current students is demonstrated in the studies summarized by Becker and Ekdom (1980). Illustrative of the studies they cite is a survey of the alumni of the Liberal Arts and Sciences College of the University of Kansas. When asked what changes they would recommend in the general education requirements of the college, respondents were the most positive toward English and speech. For each of these, 34% recommended increasing the requirement, while only 16% and 14% respectively recommended either a decrease or total elimination of requirements in speech and English. Interestingly, the longer respondents had been out of college, the more they tended to value speech and English requirements.

The studies of current students reviewed by Becker and Ekdom produced opinions remarkably close to those of alumni. The major difference, not surprisingly, is that undergraduates rank public speaking anxiety, job interviewing, and résumé preparation as more important than do alumni.

Perhaps more surprising than the support communication skill development receives from employers and students is the support from colleagues in other disciplines. Consider the comments of James M. Banner, Jr.

(1979), then chair of the Board of Directors, American Association for the Advancement of the Humanities: "In addition to students' deficiencies in reading, writing, analytical, and historical skills, it turns out that many of them have also lost their ability to speak well; and since this skill cannot easily be measured, its loss has gone unremarked. . . . It is time that we recognize that the much vaunted 'return to basics' must include attention to the spoken as well as the written language. Once we acknowledge the crisis in speech, we shall be able to talk about it and come up with a course of action to combat it. It will be none too soon" (pp. 2–3).

Joseph Katz (1982), professor of human development and director of research for human development and educational policy at the State University of New York at Stony Brook, makes a similar point: "The three traditional competencies are writing, speaking, and mathematical reasoning. Probably no one will dispute that these are essential skills required of anyone who wants to be a well-functioning member of our society. Of the three, speaking has been the least stressed. Yet the capacity for oral expression, whether in conversation or in more formal contexts of communication, is a skill needed for both the clarity and pleasure of communication. Our neglect of the spoken word sharply distinguishes our society from that of ancient Athens, for instance, where elegance was the rule and from some levels of French and English society today" (p. 40).

Supportive of the remarks of professors Banner and Katz is the College Boards' recently announced "Project Equality." Designed to improve high school students' preparedness for college study and to reverse the decline in SAT scores, this 10-year program is aimed at identifying and developing skill in six basic areas of academic competency: reading, writing, speaking and listening, mathematics, reasoning, and studying. Among the speaking and listening skills identified are:

*The ability to engage in discussion as both speaker and listener—interpreting, analyzing, and summarizing.
*The ability to contribute to classroom discussions in a way that is readily understood by listeners—that is, succinct and to the point.
*The ability to present an opinion persuasively.
*The ability to recognize the intention of a speaker and to be aware of the techniques a speaker is using to affect an audience.
*The ability to recognize and take notes on important points in lectures and discussions.
*The ability to question inconsistency in logic and to separate fact from opinion. (Watkins, 1983, p. 14)

A related, although more ambitious, project than that of the College Board is the Paideia Proposal—a proposal described by Mortimer J. Adler

(1982) on behalf of a 22-member group. In it, three goals of learning, each requiring different approaches to teaching, are proposed as a means of ensuring the same education for all students, K-12: (1) "acquisition of organized knowledge," (2) "development of intellectual skills, skills of learning," and (3) "enlarged understanding of ideas and values." The "skills of learning" category—foundational to the rest of the curriculum—is defined by the Paideia group to include reading, writing, speaking, listening, observing, measuring, estimating, and calculating.

In a similar project for the college and university level, Ernest L. Boyer, president of the Carnegie Foundation for the Advancement of Teaching, and Arthur Levine, a foundation senior fellow, have recently argued the necessity of a revival of general education requirements focused on six broad areas (Scully, 1981). First among these areas is the shared use of symbols: "We propose that all students, from the very first years of formal schooling, learn not only to 'read and write,' but also to read with understanding, write with clarity, and listen and speak effectively" (p. 1).

Perhaps more significant than the support of employers, students, and colleagues, is the institutionalization of support in the form of a federal mandate indentifying speech communication as a basic skill. With the strong support of our colleagues in such disciplines as English, Title II of the Elementary and Secondary Education Act of 1965 was amended in the New Title II (adopted on November 1, 1978) to include speaking and listening as important basic skills. The amendment reads as follows: "The purpose of this part is—(1) to assist Federal, State, and local educational agencies to coordinate the utilization of all available resources for elementary and secondary education to improve instruction so that all children are able to master the basic skills of reading, mathematics, and effective communication, both written and oral; (2) to encourage States to develop comprehensive and systematic plans for improving achievement in the basic skills; (3) to provide financial assistance to State and local educational agencies for the development of programs in the basic skills . . . (Public Law 95–561)" (Book, 1981, p. 24).

CURRENT BARRIERS

Despite the widespread agreement of employers, alumni, students, colleagues, and society that the skills we teach are vital, at least two barriers block the needed expansion of the communication discipline. First, a consensus that communication training should be provided by communication professionals does not exist. In fact, professionals in many areas (e.g., social work, counseling, educational psychology, business communication) currently offer coursework in communication skills. In a survey of all 111 four-year medical schools in the United States, for example, Kahn, Cohen, and Jason (1979) received replies from 79 schools, 76 (97%) of which indicated that they taught courses in interpersonal skill development in their programs. In addition, Kurtz and Marshall (1982) report that, of the 85 accredited graduate schools of social work, 78% (48 of the 61 institutions responding) offer courses in interpersonal skills.

The second barrier, however, is significantly more damaging than competition from other disciplines: that is, the communication discipline appears less than firmly committed to providing training in communication skills. And resolving this situation is prerequisite to coping with the problems posed by competition from other vendors of communication training. An important indicator of this lack of commitment is the low level of training that the profession tolerates in those individuals charged with providing the majority of basic communication skills training. The Book and Pappas (1981) study of secondary schools, for example, discovered that in only eight states (of the 15 surveyed) do the majority of speech teachers have degrees in the discipline. In fact, in four states fewer than 30% have speech degrees. Even more disturbing (and perhaps owing in part, to the foregoing) are the facts that: (1) Professional involvement in speech associations, through which teachers update both content and teaching expertise, is not a high priority for speech teachers: state speech association memberships average 25% (ranging from 10% to 62%). Membership in the regional associations average 3% (with little variability among regions) and 8% in the national association (ranging from 2.3% to 12.8%). (2) The most popular textbooks being used were written before 1969: *The Art of Speaking*, by Elson and Peck (20.2%), *Basic Speech Experiences*, by Carlisle (15.7%), and *The New American Speech*, by Hedde and Brigance (11.5%). In addition, 41% use textbooks only infrequently, and 20% of the teachers do not use textbooks at all!

That this situation is not much improved at the community college level was discovered in a random sample survey of 100 two-year colleges. With 61 responses, Hegstrom (1981) reports that: "The mean percentage of faculty without a baccalaureate degree in speech communication who teach speech communication courses in two year colleges is 20% according to our respondents. The mean percentage of faculty teaching speech communication classes for whom the highest degree in speech or communication is the Bachelor's is 12%. The mean percentage performing this work for whom the highest degree in speech or communication is the Master's is 54%. Finally, the mean percentage of speech communication doctorates teaching speech communication courses at the surveyed institutions is 8%. Thus, over 30% of the speech communication instructors at the 'average institution' in this study lack a Master's degree in the subject. In the sixteen vocational/technical/business colleges in the sample, this figure climbs to

53%" (p. 64). Compounding this problem of inadequately prepared in-structors is the two-year college's dependence on part-time instructors. Hegstrom reports that at "thirty-two (53%) of the institutions part-time instructors taught up to 24% of the courses. At fourteen (23%) of the institutions, part-time instructors taught from 25–49% of the courses. At six (10%) of the institutions part-time instructors taught from 50–74% of the courses. Five (8%) of the institutions used part-time instructors for more than 75% of the speech communication courses" (p. 64).

While one would hope (if not assume) that the problem of inadequately prepared teachers is solved at the four-year college or university level, such is not the case. The most recent study of the basic course by Gibson et al. (1980) discovered that not only is approximately 75% of the basic-course teaching done by graduate teaching assistants or junior faculty but they are also given substantial freedom in what they do in these courses. Perhaps worse, the percentage of teaching done by senior staff members is decreas-ing. Thus, much of the training in basic communication skills at the college and university level is provided by untrained or inexperienced teachers who are provided with minimum guidance and supervision.

One might, of course, argue that the communication discipline has had little choice in or responsibility for creating a situation in which the majority of its communication skill training is provided by ill-prepared instructors. This argument might be more persuasive, however, were members of the discipline more actively working to change the situation and if a larger portion of the discipline's intellectual energies were devoted to creating a solid theoretical and research-based foundation on which to develop train-ing in communication skills. Unfortunately, this is not the case.

First, despite an increasing concern with defining what it means to be communicatively competent (McCroskey, 1982), little work has been de-voted to the proper sequencing of instruction aimed at facilitating com-munication competency. As a result, currently and historically, the basic high school course is usually little more than a watered-down version of the basic college course—and upper-level college courses do little to build on the skills developed in that introductory course. In addition to the tremendous waste caused by this unnecessary redundancy, this strategy squanders the current knowledge and importance of social-cognitive de-velopment in individuals. Ritter (1981), after tracing the developmental progression for adolescents cognitively (Piaget), morally (Kohlberg), and socially (Elkind and Erickson), hypothesizes about the implications of these changes for communication instruction. Among these implications are her suggestions that communication activities at the earlier levels need to: (1) be more experiential and concrete and less theoretical (e.g., use actual models and avoid complex organizational schemas), (2) be more controlled in the content of speech performance and communication exercises (e.g., reduce levels of self-disclosure), and (3) feature group work rather than individual preparation and solo performance. In short, then, the communication discipline needs to devote energy to identifying the instructional implications of the social and cognitive development of its students.

In addition to thinking carefully through the sequencing of communication skill instruction, the discipline must, second, devote greater— and significant—efforts to researching specific instructional strategies. Currently, when communication instructors look for research data to support their choices among instructional techniques, they find that it is usually conducted by scholars in disciplines other than speech. The research on strategies for helping individuals cope with their fears of communication situations is illustrative. A survey conducted by Hoffman and Sprague (1982) identified those institutions that operate a special treatment program or curriculum for communicatively apprehensive students. In terms of treatment methods, they discovered that these programs use one of three treatment methods—systematic desensitization, rhetoritherapy, or a combination of treatment methods—with systematic desensitization by far the most common approach. Yet of the controlled outcome research studies that have examined systematic desensitization as a method for reducing communication dysfunctions (and that have been published in the journal literature), only four of 52 studies have involved communication scholars (Friedrich & Goss, 1984). Similar figures could, no doubt, be provided for other areas of instructional pedagogy research. In short, when communication instructors use research data to support their choice of instructional techniques, they must depend on researchers in other disciplines to provide them with data.

Perhaps a more serious indictment than the failure to do research, however, is that, third, the field of communication has rarely developed and articulated foundational philosophies of communication competency instruction. It is difficult, for example, to find communication equivalents of interpersonal skills training models such as Carkhuff and Truax's "systematic human relations training," Ivey's "microtraining," Egan's "integrative problem solving," Kagan's "interpersonal process recall," and Goldstein's "structured learning" (Marshall, Kurtz & Associates, 1982) or ELT approaches such as Gattegno's "Silent Way," Curran's "Community Language Learning," or Lozanov's "Suggestopedia" (Roberts, 1982). Instead, communication skill development classrooms tend to feature an eclectic collection of techniques that are applied to all members of a class independent of individual problems. Such an approach ignores the fact that, for example, a student's failure to participate in classroom discussions could be a function of (1) a conscious decision to reduce involvement in that situation, (2) fear or anxiety about the results of participating, (3) a physical disability or the lack of necessary skills, or (4) faulty perceptions of the requirements of the situation. Without knowledge of which element or elements best explains the student's difficulty, the instructor may well add to rather than reduce it. Thus, for example, someone suffering from fear or anxiety is likely to be hurt by being subjected to a regimen of forced participation, but might be helped by the administration of systematic desensitization.

While an awareness of such issues is necessary when developing a philosophy of communication instruction, a philosophy of communication instruction goes way beyond them to specify means of identifying communication skills and deficiencies, choosing among instructional techniques, and determining progress in acquiring communication competence. To demonstrate the power of such a philosophy, a contrast between two approaches is illustrative. Precursors of these positions within the belletristic conception of rhetoric are described by Arnold (1959).

The first view is labeled the skills-oriented (S-O) approach. Closely associated with the Competency-Based Education Movement of the 1970s, it is probably the dominant approach in communication education today. In clarifying the nature of this position, the basic assumptions that define it will first be indentified and then, second, a beginning public speaking course that might be developed out of this position is described.

Basic assumptions:

1. It is possible to identify a repertoire of elements that define effective communication.
2. These elements can be broken down into small units and ordered according to some logical sequence.
3. Students should be pretested to determine their mastery of the requisite elements and should then begin working at an appropriate level and unit of instruction.
4. Teachers should develop a variety of instructional strategies that can aid students' progress through the sequential acquisition of elements.
5. Criterion-referenced testing should be used to determine progress in acquiring the relevant elements.

A public speaking course developed in this fashion adopts a building-block approach to the acquisition of communication competence. Organizationally, the course might start with a unit on analyzing audience and occasion and proceed through such units as selecting topics and purposes, selecting and supporting main ideas, organizing the body of the speech, preparing the introduction, preparing the conclusion, and delivering the speech. For each unit, students would be taught and evaluated in terms of component skills. Thus, for example, the "organizing-the-body-of-the-speech" unit might require students to prepare and deliver a short speech using one of the many common patterns of organization (e.g., topical, chronological, spatial, problem solution). Success would be judged in terms of the students' ability to select and use one of the patterns. Judgments about the success of the total effort would be reserved until towards the end of the semester.

The second, contrasting approach is labeled the function-oriented (F-O) approach. While less frequently defended in print, it nevertheless guides pedagogical practice in many communication classrooms. Among the basic assumptions that define this position are:

1. The acquisition of communication skills begins with a function—a need to get something done through communication—and moves gradually toward acquiring the forms that reveal that function.
2. Students can learn to become competent communicators most efficiently by focusing on function holistically rather than by learning isolated, decontextual skills.
3. The teacher should use challenging holistic communication activities focused on function and should sequence them to move from less difficult to more difficult.
4. When students lack a specific skill, they should be assigned functional tasks to maximize the necessity of using that skill.
5. Testing should be norm-referenced.

A public speaking course developed in this fashion would include numerous holistic public presentations. Within some taxonomy of function (e.g., inform, persuade, entertain), the presentations would be sequenced to move from less difficult to more difficult. Persuasive speeches might start, for example, with those that affirm a proposition of fact and move through speeches that affirm a proposition of value, create concern for a problem, and affirm a proposition of policy. Success for each speech would be judged in terms of relative accomplishment of the specific task or function.

Having briefly described two philosophies concerning methods for facilitating the acquisition of communication competence, it is possible to sharpen the contrast between them by pairing their respective views of learning:

1. In S-O, learning should start with the smallest form; in F-O, learning should start with the least difficult function.
2. In S-O, learning should move from form to function; in F-O, learning should move from function to form.
3. In S-O, learning should be decontextual; in F-O, learning should be contextual.
4. In S-O, learning should be reductionistic; in F-O, learning should be holistic.
5. In S-O, testing should be criterion-referenced; in F-O, testing should be norm-referenced.

The S-O and F-O philosophies of how teachers might best facilitate the acquisition of communication skills for their students do not, of course, exhaust the possibilities. Additionally, many effective pedagogical programs contain elements of both. The point to be made, then, is not that there is one correct approach; but, rather, that to be maximally effective, each instructor must develop, articulate, and test an individual coherent philosophy. An eclectic program put together without benefit of such a guiding philosophy will, at best, be an inefficient approach to providing communication skill instruction.

SUMMARY

The 75th anniversary of ECA finds speech communication education alive and well in the colleges and universities of America. We have even been granted a chance at the brass ring—communication classes are overflowing with students, and both employers and academic colleagues are recommending that students receive even more such instruction. Taking advantage of the possibilities posed by this situation, however, will require a major intellectual commitment on the part of the communication discipline. Providing a sustainable program of rigorous communication training must have as its foundation a solid base of theorizing, research, and writing. It is a challenge worth meeting; it is a challenge we cannot afford to ignore.

Part Two

Building an Academic Discipline

Overviews of Organizational and Conceptual Issues

13

Scientific Research Methods in Communication Studies and Their Implications for Theory and Research

W. BARNETT PEARCE

When I accepted Tom Benson's assignment to write a chapter on this topic, I envisioned a paper markedly different from the one I finally produced.* I thought to ask, "What have been the implications of scientific methods of research for theory and knowledge?" and to answer, quickly, "Not very much, and that only recently." From this position, I expected to take as my problematic the question, "How is it that the discipline managed to avoid the use of scientific methods of research for so long?" and move to a celebration of the dawn of a new day in communication research fraught with promise.

My research led me down dusty stacks of back issues of journals and to the periodic predecessors of this 75th anniversary celebratory volume, and I found that the assumption on which my anticipated problematic rests is clearly wrong. The conventional wisdom—which I uncritically shared— holds that there were few scientific studies of communication before, say, 1960, and that these were so unsophisticated as to have little continuity with current scientific research. To the contrary, our discipline began with an—admittedly controversial—explicit call for the use of scientific methods. Winans (1916, p. 22) predicted that "Our difficulty will be in getting

*So, I suspect, did he! Also to be held blameless for this document, although it is better than it would have been without their help, are Vernon Cronen, Dean Hewes, Ken Frandsen, Jay Savereid, and Gerry Miller.

into a sufficiently scientific frame of mind." Whatever might be meant by that delightfully enigmatic phrase "a sufficiently scientific frame of mind," the discipline has never lacked enthusiastic and generally competent users of scientific research methods. The first quantitative study of speech was published in 1916; the first experimental study in 1920; the first study using inferential statistical tests in 1924; and over 1,000 quantitative studies by persons in our discipline were reported during the next 50 years (Thompson, 1964). Since materials done by persons in our field but published in journals associated with other disciplines were not included in Thompson's review, his summary figure is certainly an under-representation of the amount of quantitative research.

It is quite the fashion among the methodological sophisticates of our discipline to disparage the competency of early quantitative researchers in speech. For example, in his critique of an earlier draft of this manuscript, Dean Hewes said, "we have never had a large cadre of competent users [of scientific research methods], nor do we have such a group today." His comment apparently refers to the *number* of active researchers, but faced with this evidence of productivity throughout the history of our discipline, I think it fair to interpret the remark as a gloss over his value judgment about the *quality* of those studies. I disagree with that judgment, and argue that the technical merits of research in our discipline generally reflected the current standards and procedures of social scientific research. While the sophistication of, in Hewes' euphonious phrase, "the chi-squares and t-tests of yesteryear" pale when compared to "modern research methodologies," this is not the appropriate standard. I am not aware that any of our disciplinary progenitors made revolutionary breakthroughs in methods, and I know that there are some studies that seem a veritable catechism of methodological sins, but I suspect that from a purely methodological standpoint, our discipline would not be drastically worse than others to which it might be compared.

The correction of my ill-founded historical prejudices produced a conundrum. If the use of scientific research methods is not novel, not infrequent, and not even incompetent, then how is it that they have had such little impact on theory and knowledge, and that but recently?

My assessment of the impact of the use of scientific research methods is extremely gloomy. As a result of the research done in our field before 1960, we do not know anything that we did not think we already knew; we do know that a few things that we thought we knew are wrong; and we do not have a new perspective in which to frame what we know. These are unimpressive results from all that activity.

Let me document the dimensions of the disappointing fizzle produced by scientific research methods by citing the results in the marketplace of ideas. During the first half of this century, a highly visible community of researchers studying communication had access to policymakers and planners in business and government. They saw themselves working paradigmatically to say important and useful things about the human condition from their joint emphasis on understanding the process of communication. And no one in the then-existing national or regional associations of our discipline was included. In 1945, the Viking Fund sponsored a symposium the papers of which were published as a volume titled *The Science of Man in the World Crises*, dedicated "to all who have applied the techniques of science to the solving of human problems." For that volume, Paul Lazarsfeld and Genevieve Knupfer (1945) wrote a 31-page chapter titled "Communications Research and International Cooperation," which contained neither reference nor allusion to any research done by any member of our discipline. In 1959, Berelson (p. 1) concluded that communication research "had a distinguished past" but an inauspicious future: "the innovators have left or are leaving the field, and no ideas of comparable scope and generating power are emerging . . . as for communication research, the state is withering away." Several scholars, including David Reisman and Wilbur Schramm, took exception to Berelson's pessimistic prognosis, but—conspicuously—none cited the existence and vitality of our discipline as a source for optimistic disagreement with Berelson, nor were any members of our discipline cited as past giants or future laborers in the field of communication research. In 1959, the long history of the use of scientific research methods notwithstanding, our discipline was invisible to an existing and influential tradition of communication research.

But the marketplace is not always the fairest test of the value of ideas and data. What have scientific research methods produced of value within the discipline? In the same year that the discipline was ignored by Berelson et al., the ECA celebrated our 50th anniversary and published a volume similar in intent to the present one (Oliver and Bauer, 1959). A major section of that volume dealt with "science," but the content of those chapters dealt with matters now associated with the American Speech and Hearing Association rather than the present Eastern Communication Association. Scientific methods were referred to in two other chapters. Zelko (1959) summarized the results of studies using scientific methods in a description of "the rhetoric of discussion," but Carrino (1959, p. 23) rather bemoaned "psychological influences on communication theory" such as these. Five years later, Thompson's (1964) review of *Quantitative Research in Public Address and Communication* was more impressive as a record of the industry of our scholars than as a description of their achievements. Before 1960, scientific methods of research had overthrown no existing traditions, contributed no pivotal bits of knowledge, and drawn none of its practicioners into places of respect and influence in the discipline. Why not?

If my thesis is correct, the members of our discipline will have little difficulty in providing an answer to this question, but there will be two rather large groups who will espouse different answers. Some will say that science is inappropriately applied to the phenomena of rhetoric/speech/communication, and so the paucity of results is simply what should have been expected. Others will say that the phenomena of rhetoric/speech/communication are sufficiently complex as to require more sophisticated methods than were available to the early researchers, and that additional expertise by researchers is now providing and will in the future provide a great increment in our knowledge and theory.

My thesis is that our discipline, like any other social group, uses and is shaped by a universe of discourse* that contains a world view in which some lines of thought and argument seem reasonable and others bizarre, and that the "logical force" in this particular worldview before 1960 precluded the scientific use of scientific methods of research.

Let me confess to a rather cavalier treatment to this point of the phrase "scientific research methods." The current sensibility permits no easy dichotomization between the implements and the worldview/theories of science. In his critique of an earlier version of this paper, Hewes noted that methods and theory are related, such that the evolution of increasingly sophisticated methods affects the development of theory. In perhaps the same vein, Pearce, Cronen, and Harris (1981) argued that all methods are theory-laden and vice versa, such that metatheoretical questions are implied (if not addressed) even in such methodological decisions as the size of a sample and the choice of a statistical analysis.

My argument is that precisely this concept of the relationship between the attitude or worldview of science (what Winans meant by a "sufficiently scientific frame of mind"?) and the tools or methods which scientists use was not available within the universe of discourse that existed in the discipline before 1960. My references above to "scientific research methods" followed the conventions of the times and denote only studies that analyzed data statistically or used some form of research design. Given the contemporary view, such methods may be used "unscientifically."

The archetectonic concerns that generated this universe of discourse were those of speech teachers interested in teaching public speaking effec-

---

*The terms "universe of discourse" and "language games" are used here as functionally synonomous, and as ways of describing much the same phenomena referred to as "motives" by Burke, "paradigms" by Kuhn, and "social reality" by Pearce and Cronen. The crucial assumption states that there is a "conceptual necessity" (Canfield, 1982) or "logical force" within the game that makes it impossible to use (or avoid using) particular dimensions of judgment WHILE USING THAT LANGUAGE GAME. Following this line of reasoning, one way of writing history is to locate acts within the parameters of the language games in use. Lem (1974) has explored some of the extremes to which this procedure may be pushed.

tively. The "logic" of the system was created in the dialogue of two schools of thought, which I designate rhetoric and speech. One rejected the use of scientific research methods completely as irrelevant and inappropriate; the other emasculated them by using them "unscientifically," functioning as "rhetorical critics with some promising new TOOLS for refining some portions of an ancient inquiry" (McGuckin, 1968, p. 172). Neither group treated communication itself as problematic. The research for which members of the discipline were praised or criticized was never conceptualized as leading to the revision—much less the refutation—either of the classical rhetorical worldview or even the more substantial propositions derived from the rhetorical heritage.

The universe of discourse produced by the dialogue between speech and rhetoric still exists, but another school of thought—which I refer to as communication—has immigrated into the field. The publication of Berlo's *Process of Communication* in 1960 is a convenient historical marker for the emergence of communication as a powerful logic within the discipline, and since then the universe of discourse has been powerfully affected by it.

This telling of the story addresses two puzzles. (1) How was it possible for the discipline to use scientific research procedures for so long with such minimal contributions to theory and knowledge? (2) What happened since 1959 to change the universe of discourse so drastically?

It would be naïve to expect this story to take the line of "science triumphantly marches on," but it would be nice to look to our history for morality tales of hard won victories against the encroaching darkness, or perhaps for the shoulders of giants, standing on which would further our contemporary vision. The history of our discipline does include victories and venerable scholars, but as far as scientific research methods are concerned the story must be a "cautionary tale." The discipline has shown that it is capable of compromising so powerful an epistemology as science so that 50 years of use of its research methods produced negligible results, and the forces that impeded the effective use of these methods still exist, although not currently exerting such preemptory influence.*

---

*If my analysis of the universe of discourse is correct, this statement will be perceived as begging the question—for different reasons—by persons representing the major historical traditions in our discipline.

Those in the speech tradition will likely argue that (1) not enough "science" has been done, and (2) more rigorous applications of more powerful methods will overcome the temporary embarrassment of a paucity of results. The injunction is for "more of the same" activity with strong sanctions applied against those who question the basic "scientific" assumptions and particularly against those who employ techniques perceived as less rigorous or less powerful.

Those in the speech tradition will likely aruge that (1) not enough "science" has been done, and (2) more rigorous applications of more powerful methods will

SPEECH OR RHETORIC?

The universe of discourse during the first 50 years of our history was produced by the interaction of the language games used by what Windt (1982) called the "Cornell School of Rhetoric" and the "Midwestern School of Speech," and permitted the use of scientific research methods only at the price of cutting them off from the context in which they originated. The result was a use of methods but not of ways of thinking, producing a sterile and awkward research tradition.

At the beginning of the discipline, the intellectual situation as perceived by the founders bore more than a passing resemblance to the intellectual climate that stifled the development of social science in the 17th and 18th centuries. The Renaissance appeared to require scholars to choose between

---

overcome the temporary embarrassment of a paucity of results. The injunction is for "more of the same" activity with strong sanctions applied against those who question the basic "scientific" assumptions and particularly against those who employ techniques perceived as less rigorous or less powerful.

The resulting dialogue is far from noble. Beneath the eloquence of various statements, it can be "decomposed" into a pattern like this:

"Rhetoric":	"Speech":
Don't do "science"	
	It will be productive if we use better methods
Will not!	
	Will too!
Will not!	
	Will too!
	etc.

Such repetitive and lamentable patterns are not uncommon, and are often produced by the interaction of individuals each of whom is much more sophisticated than the pattern of interaction (Cronen, Pearce & Snavely, 1979).

My purpose is to expose the limits of this language-game, making a move comparable to Wittgenstein's (1953) or the various deconstructionists. To understand my argument, it is necessary to set aside at least for the moment one's *participation* in the game. That is, each of the statements must be seen as a "move" or "act," not as a statement (whether true or false) about the world, in order to expose game-likeness of the dialogue about "scientific research methods" and to illuminate the characteristics of that game.

From this perspective, it is not relevant whether the statement in the text to which this note is attached is "true." The statement is used to establish a problematic, the explication of which reveals the characteristics of the language-game which has comprised the world as lived in our discipline: like all statements, its meaning lies in its "use."

the richness of the newly rediscovered classics, full of humane warmth and wisdom, and the "strictly rationalistic, overwhelmingly deductive procedure of the Cartesians." Renaissance scholars of either persuasion did not lack "data," but they worked in a universe of discourse that either dismissed it as irrelevant or envisioned its use "solely as illustrative materials"—either treatment adequate to thwart the utility of science (Nisbett, 1982, p. 981).

In the 20th century, the Midwestern school unwittingly played the part of the Cartesians, using a conceptually barren set of scientific methods without the worldview of science; and the Cornell school deliberately continued the tradition of the Renaissance humanists, adulating the riches of their intellectual predecessors, with no intention of displacing them as authorities. Other alternatives for the discipline seemed limited to the "elocutionist" school on the "speech teacher" flank, and General Semantics as the embodiment of more academic (e.g., less relevant to pedagogy) concerns, neither of which forced the salience of issues involved in a scientific worldview. In this dialogue, the use of scientific research methods was attacked and defended on grounds alien to the contexts which make them meaningful and guide their use.

ALTERNATIVE CONCEPTS OF THE DISCIPLINE

The Cornell school of rhetoric can be traced to a graduate seminar dealing with the classical texts offered in 1920 by Everett Hunt and Alexander Drummond, although others came to be its primary spokespersons. In this view, the discipline should be that part of a general liberal education that focuses on the study and practice of persuasion (but not other forms of communication) wherever it occurs (in oral speech, written prose, poetry, etc.). The sources of knowledge were studies of rhetoricians and orators of the past. The model curriculum included courses in classical, medieval, British and American rhetorical theory and in British and American public address.

The Midwestern school of speech, influenced by James O'Neill of Wisconsin and Charles Woolbert of Illinois, envisioned the discipline as a distinct field of study, focusing on spoken language in all its forms, and drawing on specialized and scientific studies of speech itself. An appropriate curriculum included public speaking, drama, oral interpretation, debate, (later) radio and television, voice and diction, etcetera.

A DIALECTIC THAT PRECLUDED SCIENCE

Wichelns (1969, pp. 9–10) characterized the argument between the two schools as the "form versus content" controversy, and showed how pedagogic concerns took precedence over those of epistemology. "Involved was the speech teacher's interpretation of the range of his responsibility. O'Neill would take the student as he was and develop his ability to communicate his present thought by giving him better technical command of the resources of expression. Hunt wished to stimulate thinking, give wider perspective and deeper insight; in consequence he put less stress on technical improvement. O'Neill was concerned to find a clearly delimited departmental field. Hunt, who had come to the east from the open prairie, naturally said, 'Don't fence me in.'"

The interaction between these two language games was more disastrous for the discipline than the implications of either alone. The version of science that the Midwesterners presented as an alternative to rhetoric was a barren one, prompting the rhetoricians to castigate it as irrelevant at best and more likely harmful. The criticisms of the rhetoricians, on the other hand, put the Midwesterners on the defensive, leading them to substitute rigor in method for a scientific worldview; which of course substantiated the rhetoricians' attack, leading to an increase in defensiveness based on narrow rigor, and so on in a reciprocal, destructive sequence.

The Cornell school rejected science by fiat as inappropriate to the study of an art like rhetoric, and inherently inferior to the wisdom of the humanistic heritage. This summary rejection was warranted by the disdain many rhetoricians have for data claims expressed in the vocabulary of science, particularly in quantitative descriptions of the results of laboratory experiments. e.e. cummings expressed this repugnance well. "while you and I have lips and voices which / are for kissing and to sing with / who cares if some one-eyed son of a bitch / invents an instrument to measure spring with?" In this spirit, Brigance (1933, p. 561) castigated "the present attempt to overscientize our studies in rhetoric and oratory. I prize the rewards of science as highly as any. I am proud of the uses we are making of it in phonetics, speech pathology, and other scientific fields. Precisely for that reason, I hate to see it burlesqued by applying it to fields where it has no place."

The echoes of this argument continue. As recently as 1963, Walter (pp. 380, 377) opined that communication theory was "too meticulously quantitative to be of much value to rhetoric. Its fault is not chiefly that it is quantitative, but that only the EASY problems are immediately quantitative . . . experiments are isolated bits, testing insignificant hypotheses having little relation to each other. Even though one multiplied them a hundredfold, he would not have much that would captivate keenly intelligent minds; rather, he would be endlessly letting down the bucket into the empty well." Bleum (1966, pp. 26–27) expressed his nervousness about experimental research because the origin of the discipline is in the arts and humanities, and "while art is capable of reduction to principles, it can hardly be reduced to statistical principles. This is where we come to the point of no return . . . good research implies bad art and good art implies bad research. The better the work of art the more difficult to explain it in experimental and statistical terms." Further, Bleum found the very idea of predictability—an avowed goal of scientific research as practiced by the Midwesterners—objectionable. "Some of us may sense that every time a new bit of predictability is established on the basis of mathematical logic, something is being lost. For this reason, I think, we are afraid of experimentalists."

A recent spokesperson for the Cornell tradition found the use of scientific research methods more an effort at which to jeer than to fear. Phillips (1981, p. 361) argued that "The name 'science' may have been wrongly applied to what experts do when they study human communication." The "hard sciences seek uniform enumerative generalizations from which individual examples can be predicted and controlled." This is an inherently deficient model for studying humans, each of whom is a "completely unique object." The Cornell refrain is that "art and individual action defy scientific description" (p. 363). Phillips (p. 369) concluded his polemic against "science" by characterizing it as "trying to shoot down a mountain of marshmallow with a BB rifle" and suggesting that "our path of scientific respectability lies in the traditional study of the effects of oratory and how it is taught."

This sampling of the discourse of the Cornell school provides one part of the answer to the puzzle of how the discipline subverted the utility of scientific research methods: the rhetoric between the groups provoked what might be called "methodolotry" by researchers. Those who tried to develop a "sufficiently scientific attitude" correctly anticipated such a barrage of abuse from powerful members of the discipline that they became more practiced in the arts of apologia and debate with rhetoricians than in discussions of the philosophy of science or research methods with supportive colleagues. The result was to substitute an unthinking defense of their methodology (expressed in defensive titles such as "An experimental study of . . . " or "A path-analysis of . . . ") rather than a full involvement in the language game of science. In no other discipline with which I am familiar have so many named their method in the titles of their papers, or has "methodology" been an acceptable professional self-designation. The characteristics of the methods clearly usurped the purpose for which they were developed.

The Midwestern school was unable to respond to the criticism of the rhetoricians because they were limited by two of their assumptions, one about how to do research, and the other about their legitimate purpose. The model for research was set by Woolbert: an amalgamation of a linear, Aristotelian concept of speech and a linear, Watsonian concept of behaviorism. The product was a simple experimental paradigm in which source or message variables were manipulated and the effects on audiences measured. The concept of legitimate concerns for speech scientists was limited to oral speech, and even here the focus was on matters of performance rather than substance. The content of the speech—the old rhetorical canon of "invention"—was given attention "only incidentally," and the contexts in which speech was used was completely ignored (see O'Neill, 1923, p. 27). In this perspective, the role of quantitative studies was that of a new tool with which to garner a fact or two, certainly not to suggest new questions or to produce new theories.

Simon (1951, p. 292) articulated the role of research as subordinate to conventional wisdom: "During its long life speech has accumulated diverse beliefs and assumptions, many of them from speculative or authoritarian sources. Efficiency in speech performance and in pedagogical practice demands the scientific testing of the tenability of these accumulated traditions." Even its most ardent champion described quantitative research in the Midwestern tradition as limited to the determination of the relationships between stimuli and responses, and as a servant of "received wisdom." Under the heading "The Best That May Happen," Thompson (1964, p. 223) described "the potential—and the probable—contribution of quantitative research to rhetoric . . . First, in a few specific areas, low level generalizations will bring rhetoric to the level of a science by revealing particular combinations of circumstances in which the administration of a given stimulus will produce an invariable effect. Second, some rhetorical precepts will disappear because of the failure of attempts to verify them. Textbooks contain a great deal of prudential advice that is harmless but useless. Third, and most important, the 20th century will provide an experimental foundation for a large share of the inherited rhetoric."

The attitudes reflected in these quotations identify a second reason why scientific research methods made such minimal contributions to knowledge and theory: they were envisioned as doing rhetoric by other means. The language game of rhetoric, however, as forcefully noted by members of the Cornell school, is in many ways inimical to that of science (although not necessarily that of quantitative research methods). By using methods taken from one language game in the pursuit of goals and under the evaluative criteria generated by another, researchers produced something that, as Phillips (1981) correctly noted, was not science, and it was not very productive as a form of rhetoric.

There were other models of how to do science and concurrent programs of scientific studies of communication, but they were inaccessable to our discipline because of the logic of meaning and action embedded in the social realities of "speech" and "rhetoric." The Cornell school should have been open to the tradition of social science from Vico through Marx, Compte, Spencer, Weber, James, Freud, Mead, Lasswell, Lazarsfeld, Berelson and Schramm, but they rejected science out of hand as incommensurate with liberal education; and the Midwestern school thought it illegitimate to consider theories, data, or research methods that dealt with topics other than speech per se. Quite literally, the universe of discourse in the discipline provided no vocabulary in which persons could speak as scientists.*

The Language Game of Science

"Science" has been used so often as a way to praise or blame, to identify with or distance oneself from particular others, that it seems to have no referent. But that is a problem only if science is understood as a particular method, or collection of discipline, or line of inquiry. A better concept is that "science" is a culture, and like any culture, the members do not always agree or even understand each other, and seldom can predict exactly what others will say or do. However, they can recognize when they and others are acting or speaking "like a native."

Here are some samples of how scientists talk about themselves. Miller (1973) said that the distinguishing characteristic of scientific and humanistic scholarship is its motive. The purpose "of making factual generalizations about similar phenomena not encompassed by the observations we have made" is common to "speaking like a scientist." Delia (1981) argued that any way of knowing is defined by its "commitments," and science is definitionally and distinctively defined by a combination of three commitments: participation in a critical, public community moving toward consensus; empiricism, or arguing on the basis of ordering and accounting for observations; and a concept of knowledge as progressive, entailing the elaboration or change of conceptual frameworks to account for a greater range of observations. Hawes (1975, p. 25) defined the "scientific attitude" as "curiosity and suspicion." Harris (1980, p. 27) described science as "a unique and precious contribution of Western civilization," the only way of knowing "in the entire course of prehistory and history . . . [that] encour-

---

*Let me differentiate between individuals and the discipline. My comments do not imply that individuals in the discipline could not and did not act like scientists; only that they could not do so while using the universe of discourse which characterized the discipline. Some of the most sophisticated quantitative researchers, such as Woolbert and Knower, consistently published outside the discipline. Why? My own experience is that writing for, for example, the SCA journals requires addressing a number of issues that I perceive as irrelevant to some of my purposes and that do not have to be addressed if the manuscript is to be sent to other journals. I suspect that a careful study of editorial policies and rejection letters would provide support for my description of the universe of discourse of the rhetoric-speech debate as precluding speaking like a scientist.

aged its own practicioners to doubt their own premises and to systematically expose their own conclusions to the hostile scrutiny of nonbelievers."
Lerner (1959, pp. 6–7) agreed that "social science is a genuinely new way of
looking at the world," characterized by its irreverence toward both the
unknown and the known.

> Under the rule of Social Science, there are no eternal mysteries—in its
> proper domain of human behavior—but only phenomena that have
> not yet been adequately observed. Nothing human is unscrutable; all
> behavior is amenable to inquiry. . . . As there are no more eternal
> mysteries, in Social Science, so there are no more eternal verities. Social
> Science knows no once-for-all Truth, seeks no once-for-all Law. It
> deals, at bottom, with human values—what people want; and social
> institutions—what they receive. Values and institutions are con-
> tinuously changing in the centuries since men acquired mobility. . . .
> Social science developed largely as a way of perceiving, evaluating, and
> correcting the frictions and tensions generated by the high rate of
> individual mobility and institutional change in modern society.

In deliberately messianic tones, Harris (1980, p. 28) indicted those who
attempt to subvert science, arguing that "the real alternative to science is not
anarchy but ideology; not peaceful artists, philosophers and anthropologists, but aggressive fanatics and messiahs eager to annihilate each other
and the whole world if need be in order to prove their point." Homans
(1967, p. 4) stressed the vulnerability of ideas to data: "When the test of the
truth of the relationship lies finally in the data themselves, and the data are
not wholly manufactured—when nature, however stretched out on the
rack, still has a chance to say 'No'—then the subject is a science."

I would no more attempt to definitive list of characteristics of "real
science" than I would try a stipulative definition of any other culture, but
this does not imply that cultures cannot be differentiated. Malaysians differ
from Thais, and natives of each culture know what it means to act like a
Malaysian (or Thai), but the nature of that knowledge consists of the use of
cultural resources which themselves contain various constitutive and regulative rules rather than the performance of particular behaviors or assent
to particular propositions. To act like a native is to be recognized as using
those resources; a foreigner may act appropriately but not like a native
because the act does not occur in the context of the cultural resources. The
persons cited in the preceeding paragraph obviously disagree both in relative emphasis and in some particulars about what science "really" is, but
they recognize each other as talking "as scientists"—and, I assert, would
recognize "experimental rhetoric" as something else.

The discipline emanating from the speech or rhetoric controversy comprises a culture of its own that is fundamentally incompatible with science, in which quantitative data were used—if at all—for illustrative purposes: research reports were frequently introduced with the phrase "Miller was able to show that," followed by some maxim from inherited wisdom. This suggests the third reason for the inefficacy of research using scientific methods: the researchers were not allowed by their universe of discourse to treat their data as potentially falsifying not only specific propositions derived from the ancients, but the very world view in which rhetoric emerged. They were blocked by the logic of their universe of discourse from sufficient freedom to "play" with concepts, to question assumptions, to build and test theories and world views rather than hypotheses already implied by the content of their tradition. Those who used the universe of discourse of this discipline as their only professional language—even though they employed quantitative methods—were no more scientists than Descartes was a Roman because he said *cogito ergo sum* in Latin. For the discipline to do science, a new social reality had to be incorporated.

THE COMMUNICATION INVASION

"Communication" is a discontinuous development in the discipline, better described as an invasion rather than an evolution from either rhetoric or speech. Once in the discipline, "communication" may be viewed as outflanking speech as an even more extreme alternative to rhetoric.

The success of this invasion can be seen in the flurry of name changes in recent years. In 1959, this association was known as the Speech Association of the Eastern States, affiliated with the Speech Association of America. Our journal was titled *Today's Speech*; and as part of our golden anniversary, we published a volume titled *Re-establishing the Speech Profession* (Oliver and Bauer, 1959). On the occasion of our diamond anniversary, we are the Eastern Communication Association, affiliated with the Speech Communication Association, whose journals are the *Quarterly Journal of Speech, Communication Monographs* (formerly *Speech Monographs*), and *Communication Education* (formerly *The Speech Teacher*). Our journal is now called *Communication Quarterly*, and we have on several occasions scheduled our conventions to coincide with the International Communication Association. The title of this volume is *Speech Communication in the Twentieth Century*. Judged on the basis of the words used in the titles of journals and associations—and how else should a language game be assessed?—"communication" has a record of 5-1-2 against "speech" (scoring "speech communication" as a tie), and a win by default against "rhetoric."

"Communication" developed from three sources: the indigenous research tradition that used scientific methods; the assimilation of extradisciplinary ideas; and the migration into the discipline of large groups who originated neither in speech nor rhetoric.

THE INDIGENOUS RESEARCH TRADITION

The Midwestern school had long endorsed research using scientific methods. Beseiged by rhetoric and limited by their own assumptions, a large cadre of frustrated researchers were prepared to be "early adopters" of a language game that would permit them to use the scientific research methods with which they were familiar in a language game that fit them better. By identifying themselves with "communication," these persons gave a politically necessary but misleading semblance of continuity to the "communication" movement as it took over the field.

Knower (1966), one of the earliest and most sophisticated quantitative researchers in the discipline, called for a paradigm of "communicology" as an alternative to both rhetoric and speech. Knower assumed that the study of communication was—and should remain—a "field" rather than a "discipline," and that coordinated research programs using multiple methods and involving many disciplines were the path to progress. The implimentation of the program took the form of interdisciplinary "communication research centers" at a number of universities, mostly in the Midwest.

Knower's proposals received little attention and less consideration as a proposal for the discipline, in part because the rhetoricians saw it as simply the old Midwestern attempt to be scientific. Hunt (1970) described communicology as seeking certainty and proceeding by specialization, and invidiously contrasted it with traditional rhetoric which, at its best, is "related to ideas" (p. 5) and is based on "fundamental human values" (p. 6). In an extended metaphor, Hunt claimed that the relation of communicology to rhetoric is comparable to that between musicology and music. He concluded, "Musicology has established its place, but it will not be a dominant one in the Julliard School of Music. And my own humanistic bias leads me to believe that communicology will not dominate the traditions of rhetoric, even if it makes contributions worthy of search and discovery" (p. 7).

Within the Midwestern School of Speech, Wayne Thompson, Frank Knower, Howard Gilkinson, Walter Wilke, William Utterback, Franklyn Haiman, Samuel Becker, and others identified themselves as "speech generalists." Their interests and training encompassed several modes of research, including scientific methods (Thompson, 1964, pp. 23–24, 27). As usual, the generalists were not so general as they described themselves: the dialogue between rhetoric and speech continued to frame their thinking. And as often happens, the students of the generalists appeared radical by doing what they were taught more consistently than their mentors envisioned. Thompson (1964, p. 27) recognized that the generation of researchers including Theodore Clevenger, Jr., Thomas Scheidel, John Waite Bowers, Kenneth Frandsen, Fredrick Williams, Kenneth Anderson, Gerald Miller, David Berlo, and Gary Cronkhite were qualitatively different from any produced by the discipline previously. In my judgment, that which set them apart was an easy willingness, and trained capacity, to think beyond the parameters set by the speech-rhetoric dialectic.

However, the content of "communication" in the 1960s was a discontinuous development: it drew neither raw materials nor structure from the heritage of rhetoric or speech. The primary contributions of the discipline to the development of communication theory were personnel prepared to do something discontinuous with their heritage, and a disciplinary home for a productive synthesis of conceptual contributions from a variety of sources. (These are far from negligible contributions, as Reisman noted with considerable prescience in 1959).

Assimilation of Ideas from Outside the Discipline

Scientifically motivated research about communication had been going on throughout the century, although our discipline successfully defended itself from all but the most limited contact with it for 50 years. When the students of the generalists began reading that research, they found more than just empirical findings; they encountered a universe of discourse unquestionably applicable to their research interests that did not include the limitations of speech and rhetoric. For example, Hovland's (1953) studies of communication and persuasion could not have been better designed to influence the discipline. His topic was identical to that of the Cornell rhetoricians; his method exemplified the ideal of the Midwestern school's notion of research better than anyone in the discipline had been able to achieve; and he reported it in a universe of discourse that—unlike the Midwestern school's—was not limited to oral speech. It is not too far-fetched to assume that when the speech generalists and their students read this work, they experienced an intellectual liberation of sorts.

Other major ideas that were incorporated into the field included Newcomb's "balance model" as the basis of "An Approach to the Study of Communicative Acts." This model contrasted sharply with the linear Aristotelian/behavioral model assumed by the Midwestern school and that supported Hovland's model. Introduced to the discipline in the mid-1960s by Chaffee and McLeod as the "coorientation model," Newcomb's work required the use of relational concepts and holistic thinking. Festinger's study of "informal social communication" and later "cognitive dissonance" contrasted sharply with the traditional taxonomies of the purposes of communication, and introduced an "audience-centered" approach to communication. Osgood, Suci, and Tannenbaum's "semantic differential" provided a far too convenient way of measuring meaning, and initiated the relentless pursuit of the illusive "attitude." The contortions to which this ultimately unproductive effort drove persons in the discipline resulted in their participation in universes of discourse far removed from either speech or rhetoric.

Other important influences were George Miller's *Language and Communication*; Shannon and Weavers' *The Mathematical Theory of Communication*; Ruesch and Bateson's *Communication: the Social Matrix of Psychiatry*; Cherry's *On Human Communication*; and, somewhat later, Watzlawick, Beavin, and Jackson's *Pragmatics of Human Communication*.

"Mainstream" American social psychological research was very similar to the Midwestern ideal of "science." This similarity accounted for its appeal and easy inclusion into the discipline; it also set strict limits for its impact on the discipline. While some found these research methods a bridge to a new universe of discourse, the heirs of the Cornell school were able to subsume them into the old speech-rhetoric debate, seeing them as a continued misuse of scientific methods in service to humanistic inquiry. The demands of publication and promotion often required those who were attempting to import a new way of thinking into the discipline to express themselves in terms of the old agenda. Regrettably, those best able to speak in the frame of the rhetoric-speech dialogue received the highest accolades, and sometimes they seemed to get stuck in it, forgetting that what they were saying comprised an alternative to that universe of discourse.

A cluster of other traditions were less immediately attractive but had a more significant, longer impact on the discipline. Cybernetics, general systems theory, and Bateson's "interactional view" provided universes of discourse standing in sharp relief to both rhetoric and speech. Their introduction to the discipline was opposed less by rhetoricians than by speech generalists. Rhetoricians simply did not know how to come to grips with these approaches: they were clearly "scientific" because they were not part of the humanities and used engineering and mathematical terms, but they were impossible to dismiss (as Hunt, 1970, did communicology) as simple-minded seekers of certainty who acted as narrow specialists. Speech generalists, and those who imported the more congenial American social psychological research programs into the discipline, found these approaches threatening because they seemed to forfeit the argumentative position that had been necessary to defend against the rhetoricians' insistence that the discipline should not do science. These tensions set up the "great metatheory debate" of the 1970s.

IMMIGRATION INTO THE DISCIPLINE

The Midwestern school's concept of the discipline as distinct and including everything that pertained to oral speech opened the door to some unexpected and influential immigrants. By the late 1940s, a number of groups had developed, many of which had some claim to be included within the discipline or were entangled with a group with a clear claim for inclusion. The generic term for these groups was "communication theory."

One such area is now known as "mass communication." Radio and television obviously, and film arguably, fit into the Midwestern concept of the discipline, but these areas came in association with "print journalism," which did not. The debate at many colleges about whether to have a separate Journalism department, and if so, who gets radio and television, threatened the integrity of the Midwestern concept of speech. The issue was resolved in different ways at various places, but at the level of the associations, for whatever reason, mass communication was "in." The effect was to bring members of the discipline into contact through journals, conferences, and sometimes department meetings with a tradition with a long history of scientific study that was limited neither by the restriction to speech nor to the Aristotelian/behaviorist concept of how to do research. Scientists such as Wilbur Schramm (1954) and Bruce Westley (1958) brought with them a strong antidote to the frustrations produced by the dialectic between rhetoric and speech.

A second major immigrant was the establishment in 1950 of the National Society for the Study of Communication, later known as the International Communication Association. The NSSC originated neither in speech nor rhetoric. Its origins were (1) the academic excitement based on "information theory" and cybernetics, which many thought would provide a basis for the integration of many disciplines around the shared theme of communication; (2) the military sponsorship of research in communication, the results of which were often classified but which provided both opportunity and reason to develop a new vocabulary about communication; (3) the opportunities for consulting and organizational research in businesses, which were becoming increasingly interested in problems of communication; and (4) the research opportunities presented by the booming industry of advertising and public relations. The NSSC proved a viable organization, and provided an alternative intellectual home for those frustrated by the limiting vocabularies in the associations dominated by speech and rhetoric. The ICA and SCA are to some extent rivals as the professional home of communication theorists, although there is a large overlap in their memberships. That portion of the SCA structure that is not part of the ICA is a fair representation of the current manifestation of the schools of rhetoric and speech with which the discipline began, and that portion of the ICA that has no counterpart in the SCA description of the unacculturated portions of "communication" exclusive of that tradition. On the other hand, many communication theorists are members of both organizations.

HUMANISM AND SCIENCE: ONE WORLD OR TWO

By the 1960s, the Midwestern school of speech found itself in a "centrist" position. On one side, they were flanked by the heirs of the Cornell school, who continued to insist that the scientific approach was too narrow to be useful. "It seems clear to us that methods of discovery and proof far wider than empirical methods need to be elaborated, taught, and widely used. Only a small fraction of problems . . . admit of scientific analysis and resolution" (Bitzer & Black, 1971, p. 239). On the other side, they were flanked by the "communication theorists," energetically and often productively applying scientific procedures to a much wider array of phenomena than had ever previously been envisioned as within the purview of the discipline. The obvious move was to "bridge" rhetoric and communication theory by arguing that it really constituted "one world."

There were a number of conciliatory pronouncements. Nichols (1963) said that "the humanities without science are blind, but science without the humanities may be vicious." Miller (1965) argued that science deals with "facts" and the humanities with "values," and their efforts are complementary. Arnold (1970) explicitly endorsed the one-world vision, arguing that even if rhetoric and science are different dogs, they at least are gnawing on the same bone. He exemplified the concept by collaborating with Wilson on a textbook that combined the Midwestern focus on speech and scientific studies (in the footnotes) with the Cornell emphasis on liberal education (Wilson & Arnold, 1968), and more recently collaborating with John Waite Bowers on a *Handbook of Rhetorical and Communication Theory*.

The "one world" view succeeded more in the institutions of the discipline than intellectually. The SCA established a division called "Rhetorical and Communication Theory," but most communication theorists, who had previously made the Behavioral Sciences Interest Group their disciplinary home, switched to the "Interpersonal and Small Group Interaction Division" or the "Mass Communication Division" within SCA, or affiliated with the ICA or some other organization. The Newsletter of the SCA, SPECTRA, is an acronym for the Midwestern definition of the discipline (speech, public address, education, communication, theatre, radio-television-film and arts), and the journals supposedly represent "one world." However, a study of who cites whom clearly showed that the supposed unity exists primarily in the serial pagination of the journals, not in a shared academic enterprise (Fischer & Pearce, 1974).

MOMENTS IN THE DEVELOPMENT OF "COMMUNICATION"

Since 1959, the discipline has undergone significant changes in the direction of whatever "communication" means that "speech" and "rhetoric" do not. One aspect of this change is a freedom to go beyond the conceptual limits imposed by the earlier universe of discourse. Specifically, it was finally possible not only to use scientific research methods but also to treat them scientifically.

The belatedly achieved capacity to speak like a scientist did not necessarily provide anything worth saying. The sound of science in the discipline was at first an echo of other disciplines; then the imperative tones of researchers announcing the latest method of data collection or analysis; later the shrill harshness of abstract metatheoretical debate; and currently the softer voices of groups conducting original, indigenous, theoretically grounded programs of research. But it has always been cacophonous.

IDEAS BEGGED, BORROWED, OR STOLEN

Before our golden anniversary, and for at least a decade after, there were no indigenous theories or research programs in the discipline. We were best understood as sharks, prowling academia and consuming—or at least biting—anything that moved. Our best people assimilated into the discipline the theories and research methods being employed elsewhere. The goal seemed to be to learn how to do research well enough to be published in the higher prestige journals and to apply that work to traditional concerns. For example, the concept of "credibility" in Hovland's research was comparable to the rhetorical notion of "ethos," and our journals were filled for a while with reports of factor analytic studies of the dimensions and effects of credibility, as it interacted with such message variables as opinionated language or delivery style. Miller found the notion of "counter-attitudinal advocacy" as a means of persuasion one of the implications of Festinger's cognitive dissonance theory, and explored it in a long research program. Nebergall achieved the highest distinction: he coauthored a seminal book with psychologists.

Such "me-too" scholarship was not very satisfying, in part because of the conflict between the desire to make a contribution uniquely attributable to communication theory and the necessity to use ways of thinking and writing that were developed in the more established disciplines. By any criterion, communication research during the 1950s and 1960s was unprecedently sophisticated and voluminous, yet Sereno and Mortensen (1970, p. x) expressed a widely shared opinion that it had not produced what it sought: "Our point of view is that A communication theory does not yet exist, at least not in any singular sense; what the current literature affords is rather a core of theories related to particular phases of communicative behavior."

THE GREAT MODEL HUNT

Coinciding with the increase of communication research was a search for an acceptable model of communication. In the finest Anglo-Saxon tradition of riding to the hounds, the "great model hunt" romped all over the journals but never seriously threatened to "catch" a model that would be generally accepted.

The lack of such a model was taken to be an embarrassment and an impediment to progress. Westley and MacLean (1957) lamented the state of the field as "a jungle of unrelated concepts . . . and a mass of undigested, often sterile, empirical data." At issue was not only *how* communication should be described, but for what *purpose*. Before the 1950s, the model for "scientific" research—based on a shotgun wedding between Watson and Aristotle—was clear and so taken for granted that it was seldom stated. The great model hunt opened the question of how communication should be thought of, and made possible the incursion of many ideas—including some that seemed inimical to what "science" was thought to be. Particularly during the decade of the 1960s, those who strove for an "objective" science were confronted by those using an explicitly value-laden approach, including some who also claimed to be "scientific." Wilder (1982) described the clash between objective scientists (who talked primarily with each other at conventions) and humanistic celebrationists (who wrote best selling textbooks) as a contest between "methods" and "morals."

The great model hunt came to no conclusion, but it did engender a dialogue in which discussions of the issues became quite sophisticated, particularly in identifying the incompatibility between usually processual concepts of how communication works and usually static, linear models and research methods that guided research about it. Perhaps the major influence was Berlo's (1960) *The Process of Communication*, which presented an excellent description of communication as processual in its first chapters, then developed at length a very linear model. The inconsistency between the two parts exemplified the difficulty confronting the field, and there were several lines of response. Some developed models of bewildering complexity, such as Dance's (1967) "Helical" model or Barnland's (1970) "transactional" model. Others relentlessly pursued research from a "behavioral science" orientation, while some took personal excursions into altered states of awareness or group gropes toward increased interpersonal sensitivity.

The motivation for all of this effort was the conviction that we should be developing a communication theory and a body of research based on it, if only we knew how.

METHOD-DRIVEN INNOVATIONS

In the continuing effort to find ways of studying communication commensurate with hunches that it is a systemic, fluid phenomenon, some turned to advanced research methods. Miller (1977, p. 12) reported that many researchers adopted "the notion that, in principle, communication is a marvelously complex phenomenon, and the only way of advancing knowledge is to look for more and more complex methodologies to describe and analyze communication." The problem with this program was that the availability of new methods dictated the direction of lines of research and theorizing. The hope was that a methodological breakthrough would permit rapid conceptual progress; yearning for a "methodological fix" is well exemplified in this statement: "Today's scientific quest is, in fact, a search for procedures and instruments that will allow new explanatory concepts, principles, and theories to be tested" (Emmert & Brooks, 1970, p. viii).

The 1960s and 1970s displayed a repeated pattern: a new research technique—a form of statistical analysis, measuring technique, coding system—would be discovered and announced in messianic terms to the discipline; it would be applied to an array of relevant phenomena that could not be effectively analyzed by previously popular methods; penetrating criticisms of the method would undercut the findings of studies that used it; and another research methodology would be discovered. In this fad-ish way, the discipline endorsed and then retreated from factor analysis; adopted n-way analysis of variance as a replacement of t- and F-tests and then regression (multiple and stepwise) as superior to ANOVA; discovered multivariate designs, such as MANOVA, canonical correlation, causal modeling, path analysis, and discriminant function analysis; and stumbled on techniques for studying temporal sequences, such as Markov modeling, stochastic process analysis, and lag-sequential design. In the process, researchers developed an unprecedented sophistication. They calculated the power of their statistical tests to determine the relative probability of making a Type I or Type II error, and they eschewed the technique of simply reporting the "significance level" of the difference between mean scores in favor of describing the amont of variance accounted for by the independent variable. Studies that found significant differences were sometimes rejected because the design was too powerful and the amount of variance accounted for, although unlikely to occur by chance, was not theoretically significant.

Some lines of research were totally dependent on a given methodology. The "agenda-setting" function of mass media was conceptually tied to lag-sequential analysis; and credibility research was defined in terms of the technique of factor analysis. When problems with the method were identified, the line of research was terminated as well. Cronkhite and Liska (1976) wrote a devastating critique of factor analysis, among other things showing that there are several methods of "rotating" the factoral structure, that there is no reason to select one of these rather than another, and that the "dimensions" of credibility that are found depend on which method of rotation is used. Similarly, McCroskey and Young (1979) deliberately included obviously irrelevant information in a factor analysis of credibility, and "discovered" three new "dimensions of source credibility: size, weight and time." Because these results followed from conventional practice but are ludicrous, McCroskey and Young (1979, p. 7) concluded that:

> it is time to once and for all call a halt to the proliferation of factor analytic studies of source credibility. We believe future studies of this type will serve no useful purpose, and in fact will continue to direct our attention away from more worthwhile pursuits. Hopefully, as a field we will learn from our experiences with this decade of wasted effort. Sophisticated statistical analyses and high speed computers cannot substitute for the critical capacity of human beings. Factor analysis must be preceded by careful conceptualization and construct delineation or the product of even the most massive research effort, as we hope we have illustrated above, will lead to nothing, or worse, to inappropriate knowledge claims.

Long ago, Kurt Lewin proposed "the law of the hammer," which describes the tendency of social scientists to use whatever method they have available on all the phenomena they are interested in, whether it fits or not, and conversely to be interested in the phenomena compatible with that method. Clearly, there have been examples of the operation of the law of the hammer in communication research: "methodological conventionality has been allowed to dictate theoretical moves and observational strategies in ways which are detrimental to the study of interpersonal communication" (Hewes, 1977, p. 2). However, Hewes argued that the law of the hammer occurs not only frequently, but necessarily: "Conventional choices of methodologies introduce into the perspective additional requirements and constraints that influence observation and theory in ways not consciously chosen by the researcher" (p. 3). There is no solution. "The social sciences . . . will always find their methodologies lagging behind their theoretic structures. (If this were not the case, then we should let statisticians take over the job of theory construction.) Since we must cope with methodologies which constrain the testing of our theories, our best solutions would appear to be broad methological training coupled with a low animal cunning in contriving methological twists. The 'law of the hammer' will likely remain with us, but its effects can be moderated through constant vigilance" (Hewes, 1977, p. 19).

CONCEPTUALLY-DRIVEN INNOVATION

The consensus that no adequate communication theory existed led some to sketch models and others to search for more powerful research methods. A third response was to explore the assumptions underlying both modeling and methods; a search for more adequate concepts. Rather than asking what is communication that we may study it and develop a theory about it, this approach switched the problematic, asking "if we had a theory of communication, what would it look like?"

There was an existing answer to the question about the shape of a theory, based on the traditional form of quantitative research set by Woolbert's amalgam of Aristotle and behaviorism. In this view, a theory consisted of general, lawlike relationships among operationally defined variables. The appeal of this concept, particularly in the context of the traditional dialectic with rhetoric, is that it offers a rigorous test of knowledge claims. "Few movements have set such explicit standards for legitimate cognitive claims. . . . This demand . . . says to its adversaries: if you assert that there are other forms of knowledge and other means for testing knowledge claims, you must clearly and rigorously state what these are and provide convincing justifications of their legitimacy" (Bernstein, 1978, p. 207). One of the quickest ways to pick a nasty fight these days is to call someone a "positivist," but at least this aspect of positivism characterized the most prominent communication scientists in the 1960s and 1970s.

Not everyone found that image of theory satisfactory, in part because communication theorists had begun reading widely, and found that there was much other than rhetoric as expressed in our discipline that provided an alternative to behaviorism. The dialectic between speech and rhetoric— particularly as conducted by the "one-world" proponents—had taken the unfortunate and untenable turn of defining science as neo-behaviorism and rhetoric as everything else, specifically all the humanities. As "speech generalists" became disentangled from that dialectic, they discovered

all manner of curious theoretical animals which had not been tamed and taxonomized by the field: semiotic, structuralism, critical theory, hermeneutic . . . and other creatures great and small. Most of these ideas had been around for some time, but they were not learned in the field because, simply, they were not taught. So suddenly the question was no longer "Is this or that Science?" but "What is 'science' anyway, especially as regards human behavior?"

Thus ensued in the mid-70s the era of the great "metatheoretical debate" ("What theoretical posture is most appropriate to the objects/ relationships of our study?" and the less great "metametatheoretical debate" ("What is all this metatheoretical debate about, anyway? Let's get on with the research.") (Wilder-Mott, 1982, p. 18).

For much of the time, the agenda for the metatheoretical debate was set by the trichotomy of laws, systems, and rules as discrete types of theories (Cushman & Pearce, 1977; Benson & Pearce, 1977). That conceptualization was challenged by Cronen and Davis (1974) and by Bormann (1980), and no one rose to its defense—I think because the significance of the issue had passed.

Contemporary Scientific Theories of Communication

Like the great model hunt, the metatheoretical debate had neither a decisive moment nor a definitive winner; but it seemed to serve its purpose. The participants drew different conclusions about what a theory should look like, but they found enough clarity and enthusiasm to engage in the development of communication theories. We have finally developed a universe of discourse in the discipline that facilitates individuals in developing, as Winans hoped, a "sufficiently scientific attitude."

In 1964, Thompson claimed that listing all of the individuals in the discipline who had done a quantitative study was not feasible. In 1968 the New Orleans Conference complained that too much of that research consisted of isolated studies by graduate students done for their theses, and called for research programs by mature scholars. Seventeen years later, I am in Thompson's position: it is not feasible to identify here all of the theoretically grounded research programs employing sophisticated methodologies conducted by seasoned scholars in the discipline. Three new phenomena are most heartening, however: the appearance of book-length monographs that combine theory and research (e.g., Woelfel & Fink, 1980; Rogers & Kincaid, 1982; Pearce & Cronen, 1980; Reardon, 1978; Miller & Burgoon, 1973), new journals (such as *Communication, Communication Research, Human Communication Research, Applied Communication Research*, and *Critical Studies of Mass Communication*), and articles that summarize and often critique the substantial research in particular areas (e.g., the essays in the annual *Communication Yearbook* published by the ICA, the *Sage Annual Reviews of Communication Research*, and the series entitled *Progress in the Communication Sciences*, published by Ablex).

The contemporary period is uncharacteristically lacking a particular genre of rhetoric: heated parental polemics that tell other people that they should not do as they are doing. Perhaps this is for the best of reasons. A considerable number of persons in the discipline are turning their energies to the conduct of vigorous research programs, unfettered by the vestiges of the old universe of discourse, rather than trying to legitimate what they want to do or to define the proper province of what other people might do within the discipline. The occasional attack on "science" by rhetoricians (e.g., Phillips, 1982) seems quaint rather than a sufficient cause for a spirited defense; those who define science as inappropriate for the art of persuasion seem to be talking among themselves rather than initiating another round of polemics such as those that characterized our first 50 years.* I suspect that there will be another great metatheoretical debate in the not too distant future, but that it will differ from those in the past because it will be conducted on the basis of the products of research programs rather than arguments about the legitimacy of "starting points." As such, we will be in a position to change paradigms by scientific revolutions or evolutions rather than engage in sophistry and public relations.

CAUTIONARY TALES

The concept of communication has been one of the most exciting ideas of the 20th century. The various lines of inquiry about communication traverse the entire spectrum of academia. Ironically, the discipline that appropriated the name "communication" was in dire danger of missing it entirely and has made less of an original contribution to it than many others.

Quite unintentionally, the discipline lobotomized itself by producing a universe of discourse that defined its proper province so narrowly as to preclude contact with others dealing with communication in a more substantive manner, and to preclude the adventurousness of thought necessary to make a contribution in isolation from other disciplines. This universe of discourse, based on restrictions of interests, prefigures dialogue in which members of the discipline spend an incalculable amount of energy telling each other what not to study and how not to study it. Whatever pathological reason sustains these patterns, it is difficult to discern any laudable consequences, particularly regarding theory and knowledge.

The moral of these cautionary tales is that we should be less cautious. This is a historically situated judgment, not a categorical preference for methodological sloppiness and conceptual anarchy. Bateson (1979, p. 242) characterized "rigor and imagination" as the "two great contraries of

---

*Whups! The debate continues. See Millar (1983).

mental process," and noted that "either . . . by itself is lethal. Rigor alone is paralytic death, but imagination alone is insanity." Genius may be shown both in the detailed elaboration of given systems of thought, or in the overthrow of one system by another.

For good reasons and bad, our discipline has erred in the direction of too much rigor. We have been not nearly fundamental enough in our critique of our own assumptions, and not nearly radical enough in the construction of theories and models. At the conceptual level, we have paid too great a compliment to a single, unquestionably venerable strand of our intellectual heritage. As a result, we have *de facto* rejected other lines of thinking and have produced few of our own. Before the "communication invasion," our discipline was virtually innocent of Wittgenstein and of Marxist and other critical theories; and when people in our discipline read, e.g., Peirce, James, Mead and various Asian sages, they grappled with them in terms of the concerns of the universe of discourse in our discipline. It is at least arguable that any restatement of, e.g., Buddhism or pragmatism according to the agenda of the Cornell school of rhetoric or the Midwestern school of speech constitutes a fundamental misrepresentation. At the methodological level, we have been so concerned to be "not wrong" that we have not given ourselves the opportunity to let our data lead us far from where we began. The testing of hypotheses is an important component of the scientific culture, but it is a means to an end, not a consummatory ritual. The rigorous test and confirmation—and even more, the disconfirmation— of hypotheses is a spur to bold and imaginative thinking. Backed against the wall by the caustic criticisms of rhetoricians and hamstrung by its own concept of what science is like, the Midwestern school erred by treating methodological orthodoxy as the sole criterion of science, and rigor as the only virtue.

The "communication invasion" was more effective in breaking the stranglehold of the "rhetoric-speech" dialectic than in providing a new center to the discipline. The period since 1960 has been one of newly minted jargons and incommensurate universes of discourse employed in adjacent offices. I suspect that this cacophony is a necessary transitional period, and I note with satisfaction that pockets of clarity have developed within the din. At least some of the clatter is the noisy process of developing original ideas.

Cautionary tales should, I suspect, allude to fearsome beasts lurking in the shadows to devour the unwary, and this tale has described just such a beast: the universe of discourse produced by the "speech-rhetoric" dialogue. The freedom unintentionally acquired during the communication invasion may be forfeited by those who, for the best of reasons, attempt to address substantive concerns within the parameters of that dialogue. For this reason, neologisms masquerading as jargon and fascination with exotic perspectives if only for their novelty serve important functions.

Whether any of the new ideas behind the novel argots and disciplinary exogamy will make their mark on the larger community that deals in some way with communication remains to be seen, but we have moved past the stage of merely "promising." Members of our discipline have "delivered" monographs and research programs, some of which transcend the dialectic of the universes of discourse of "speech" and "rhetoric." In this lies the source of hope and pride.

The power of our discipline derives from its diversity and disorder. Disorder results from the simultaneous presence of incommensurate paradigms, each with a viable claim to be the legitimate frame for the discipline. As a result, there is "room" for innovation within sanctioning institutions. One need not fight overly difficult battles against the priests of peerhood to justify one's choices about topic or method; it is usually possible to find allies who will support any set of choices.

Diversity is manifested in the inability to express what we as a discipline are about in the universes of discourses used either by traditional humanities or orthodox social sciences. When talking to my colleagues, whether in the arts or sciences, I often have to use their "language" rather than my own, and I always feel that something important cannot be said. That which cannot be said differs depending on whether it is the humanists or the scientists whom I am addressing, but either omission seems equally important.

I choose to interpret disorder as a necessary enabling condition of innovation, and diversity as something more than an inconsistent mix of traditional perspectives. Because of its topic and its history, our discipline has something important to say but has not yet found a langauge in which to speak effectively. We have been more successful in developing a corpus of knowledge, capacities, and procedures than we have in crafting a universe of discourse in which to express and practice them.

In my judgment, the belated promise of our discipline will be realized as we develop—and express ourselves in—a universe of discourse capable of expressing our unique contributions. By introducing a new way of speaking as much as by saying novel things, we will, as Apel (1980) contends we should, "keep the conversation going."

14

The Development of Research in Speech Communication: A Historical Perspective

HERMAN COHEN

This essay is not intended to be a comprehensive history of a discipline or even a detailed history of a particular division of a discipline. Rather, it is my hope to place a discipline in a historical context by examining some of the more important research trends that the discipline of communication has followed. This essay will explicate the ways in which other fields have influenced research in speech communication. I will evaluate that influence and to show what effects, both beneficial and harmful, have occurred as we have redirected our focus. As various influences have been brought to bear on our research I will also indicate the choices that were available to us, those paths we chose to take, and the consequences of those choices. I will also speculate about what might have happened had alternate paths been chosen. Finally, I will show what the present characteristics of our profession are and will project what developments might occur in the near future.

The tone of this essay is somewhat personal because it is the product of experience as well as research. This work is the outcome of careful scrutiny of national and regional journals and convention programs and textbooks. I have consulted many leaders in our profession, including a number of former SCA presidents, some of whose careers began in the late 1920s. In addition I have drawn upon the perceptions produced by 35 years of professional experience as a graduate student, professor, editor, department head, and evaluator of speech communication programs. My observations, based on my experience, will inform what follows.

To undertake a historical investigation of research in speech communication is to encounter several problems. The first is the recognition that the history of the discipline is, at this time, almost completely unexplored. Little serious scholarship has been devoted to the development of an understanding of how our profession began, developed, and evolved. We must, for the present, be content with anecdotal histories of regional associations (Wichelns, 1969; Houchin, 1969) and the Karl Wallace edited *History of Speech Education in America* (1954). Although these works are useful, the association histories are largely chronological and the Wallace volume is a scholarly, pedagogical work focusing largely on the fairly distant past before speech, speech communication, and communication emerged as a distinct academic profession.

Speech communication is essentially a field without a history. To borrow a term from anthropology we are, in the main, a "deracinated" field. That is, we are a field with no clear idea of our sources and traditions and, so to speak, our ethnic heritage. We really do not know what our roots are and like deracinated peoples, we reinvent our history from time to time, often creating different ones (Turnbull, 1972). Furthermore, the histories we have are often quite short range. I may go too far to use Erik Erikson's language and say that we have an "identity crisis" (Erikson, 1968, pp. 15–19), but we are often not certain who we are. It may not be without significance that we do not offer courses in the intellectual history of our field. Courses such as the history of psychology, history of social thought, and history of philosophy are fairly standard in other fields, as are books and monographs on these subjects. We may offer courses in the history of rhetorical theory, but they do not treat the general development of the history of ideas in speech communication, and they do not provide us with the kind of time binding available to other fields (Korzybski, 1958). Although some first steps are being taken to remedy these defects, we still have no very clear idea of our time binding (Braden, 1984; Smilowitz and Sillars, 1982; Cohen, 1982a; Cohen, 1982b; Cohen, 1982c; Becker, 1982; Cohen, 1983a; Cohen, 1983b; Cohen, 1980; Cohen, 1984). Most of us are aware of the "state of the art," of the most recent research and thought, and what is being written in our field and related disciplines. Few of us, however, have a very coherent idea of how the art arrived at its present state. We are not very aware of how questions come to be posed, of the various paths we have taken, which were detours, which were dead ends, and which led to bountiful fields. We are also not very cognizant of the paths not taken— those alternate paths available to us that we chose not to travel. It may not be immediately useful to speculate what might have happened if we had chosen otherwise when we came to intellectual forks in the road, but in order to assess the values of the paths we have taken we must understand that other choices were available to us and that we might have become a different kind of field.

The history of the speech communication profession remains largely undiscovered. The development of a historical understanding requires, among other tasks, careful reading of professional journals, scrutinizing of national and regional convention programs, the study of the histories of leading departments, and the examination of the influence and careers of prominent scholars of the past. The understanding of our professional development offers a fruitful and necessary area of research for graduate students and established scholars.

A second problem that we face as we seek to develop a historical understanding of our profession is that we have not clearly specified, for ourselves and others, what the dimensions of our field are. We are not certain of our jurisdiction and our membership. It is certainly true that as knowledge expands disciplines overlap and share mutual concerns. In the case of speech communication the situation is more extreme and more confused than in other fields. We, for example, do not have an agreed upon nomenclature for our profession, for our institutional arrangements, and for our journals. Among other titles, we are variously known as speech, speech communication, communication, and communication studies. We have undergone more name changes than most other fields and our professional nomenclature is still unsettled; indeed it is still a matter of professional contention and disagreement. Clearly, we do not have the stability of titles that is found in such fields as English, history, geography, or chemistry. We are also not certain which subareas are contained within our field. Thus, our departments represent various constituencies and are unpredictable from department to department. We cannot be certain whether such areas as telecommunications, oral interpretation, theatre, film, communication disorders, or even linguistics, journalism, public relations, and advertising are represented in our departments. In some cases we are still lodged in our parental homes—departments of English. The arrangements within institutions are also not very predictable. The pattern, or lack of pattern, of our historical development has resulted in our being housed in such faculties as humanities, social science, liberal arts, fine arts, and communications. Few other fields have such heterogeneous affiliations.

An additional factor that complicates the historical study of communication is that the boundaries are not very clear. It is true, of course, that the present expansion of knowledge makes it difficult to draw firm lines between disciplines. Nonetheless, the width of our interests sometimes makes it difficult to distinguish how what we do differs from work done in other fields. Much of our work resembles, and in some cases is indistinguishable from research done in fields as diverse as sociology, psychology, English, journalism, and philosophy. Thus, the historical investigator does not always find it a simple task to determine which work is done outside the field and which inside, and more importantly, to determine where the foci of our field are. The problems in studying the history of communication research that I have enumerated are firmly based in the story of the ways in which our field developed, as I will show later in this essay.

The student of the historical development of speech communication must understand that the field has not been clear about its definition. We have not always been clear whether our field is in the humanities, the social sciences, or both. Although through most of our history the emphasis was on the humanities we have given varying importance to humanistic and behavioral perspectives. Both emphases have been present from our beginning as a profession, however. Two paths were followed. Development in the social sciences occurred at the same time as our development in the humanities. This situation is not unique. Many other fields have shown similar ambivalences. Nonetheless, this pattern is important in the study of our historical development, especially as we examine the "empirical-rhetorical" conflict of the 1960s.

Although the history of speech communication as an organized field dates only to the first or second decade of the 20th century, we must remind ourselves of developments in the 19th century that were influential in determining the form our discipline would take in its formative and later years. Most of the 19th century was characterized by the transformation, if not the decay, of the traditional study of oral communication. Our professional ancestors had been seriously concerned with the study of rhetoric and by the late 18th and early 19th centuries, they had refined their scholarship to a sophistication that was not regained until more than one century later. Progress ceased, however, as we turned from the complex and demanding study of rhetoric to the simpler, more romantic pursuit of elocution (Haberman, 1954; Hochmuth & Murphy, 1954; Robb, 1954). We became almost neo-Ramistic in our surrender of traditional rhetoric to devote our attention almost exclusively to delivery and style. No longer were teachers of speech concerned with the traditional elements of discourse. The source of ideas, the place of logic and reason, the structure of ideas, the relation of speaker to the audience, and the situation were ignored (Ong, 1958; Howell, 1956; Howell, 1951). In time even style's importance decreased and our field became one whose concern was largely, if not solely, with delivery. This development did not seem to be entirely a bad thing. Professors of oratory were appointed in colleges and universities, and textbooks complete with scholarly paraphernalia were published (Brown, 1886; Hamill, 1882; Fulton & Trueblood, 1893; Kleiser, 1906). Schools and departments of oratory were formed, as well as oral English sections of English departments. From our perspective, we seemed to be thriving.

Meanwhile, the rhetorical tradition was by no means abandoned. As concentration on oral presentation increased, the teachers of composition became the preservers of the rhetorical tradition. To be sure, these professors of English were not much concerned with orality; but such writers and teachers as Genung (1890, 1895), Hill (1895), Phelps (1883), Quackenbos (1860), and others clearly show the influence of theorists like Bacon, Blair, Campbell, and Whately as well as the classical theorists. This development was not surprising since the belletristic tradition was dominant in English faculties in the 19th century in the United States, and rhetoric was studied together with other modes of discourse in an integrated view of written and oral communication. Indeed Blair's *Lectures on Rhetoric and Belle Lettres* was the most popular textbook in American colleges and universities in the early 19th century (Schmitz, 1948, p. 96). Thus, the rhetorical heritage was kept alive but in somewhat different form, and when we returned to our tradition our history was discontinuous, as it has been through much of our professonal development. As I will point out later, we were, because of this discontinuity, constrained to begin our studies of human communication at a cruder level than that known to our colleagues in English, and even significantly below the level of 18th century rhetorical theory.

Still another characteristic of speech communication must be taken into account in studying our historical development. We are, to put it simply, a derivative field. The separation between disciplines exists only because of what is not known. When all the hiatuses are filled, the intellectual, but not the political, basis for separate disciplines should cease to exist. Unhappily, that day has not yet come and it is still instructive to examine in what ways we are derivative and what choices we made in our derivations.

As we look at our derivative history we are aware, I think, that our development resembles some fields and is quite different from others. Let me suggest a fairly rough taxonomy of derivations in order to see where we fit in these schemes.

The first derivative form is one that represents many of the most respected academic disciplines. These are the fields that have developed because of a marked need for intellectual differentiation from the parent field. These differentiations began to occur much before our time, of course. Many of the most traditional disciplines, such as psychology, sociology, political science, anthropology, and economics, developed in that way.

A second derivative form is represented by those disciplines that developed through the need to make practical applications of theoretical and conceptual formulations drawn from other disciplines. Among that group we could cite such fields as engineering, social work, and clinical psychology.

A third derivative category, and perhaps most important to us, is represented by fields that have sought to create a synthesis based on conceptualizations and theories derived from a number of other fields. The goal of this kind of development has been, through synthesis, to create a distinctive conceptual and methodological base. Fields such as human development, social psychology, and urban planning are representative of this form of derivation. Although, because of its diversity, speech communication is something of a mixed mode, it is really representative of this third category.

This taxonomy is not absolutely firm. A number of derivative fields share in more than one of the characteristics of the various forms. Also, once fields have developed their own identity they do not cease to be derivative. They continue to borrow from other disciplines, but they also become lenders of their own distinctive thought and methodology. These derivations have not been consistent, nor have they developed at the same rate. Some fields with fairly recent lineage have been effective in constructing a conceptual core and have established a clear identity both to themselves and to the world of scholarship. Other fields of more ancient descent are still experiencing problems defining themselves and explaining their mission to other professions.

The fact that speech communication is a derivative field is not, in the abstract, a deficiency. All disciplines are, to some degree, derivative. They are all dependent on each other and share theories, methodologies, and conceptualizations. The most successful derivations are characterized by interdependence and reciprocity. The derivativeness of speech communication is more dependent and less reciprocal than most other fields. The trade balance with related fields is negative. We import much more than we export. We frequently cite the work of other fields but our work is seldom cited.

The pattern of development of speech communication makes it slightly similar, in some ways, to other synthesizing fields; and yet it is radically different in many other ways. Those differences and similarities may become clearer if we remind ourselves of the circumstances under which we established ourselves as a visible academic discipline. The fact that we established ourselves by leaving The National Council of Teachers of English is significant. The causes of the departure were largely pedagogical, not scholarly. As the oral English division of the NCTE we wanted greater freedom in teaching courses in oral communication and we saw ourselves in an inferior role vis-à-vis the very much larger parent discipline. We should note also that the NCTE was then, as it is now, an association largely concerned with composition, not with literature. Thus we were really a small field stressing peformance derived from a larger field also stressing performance (Grey, 1954; Smith, 1954; Sillars, 1983). Since we began as a peformance field, we have developed, in some ways, in the reverse order of other fields. Speech began as an applied field and turned to the development of theory, research, and criticism only after it had established itself as a profession. This pattern is not at all the norm in the social sciences or the humanities. For the most part, their applications were developed after a substantial body of scholarship had already been developed. Even our presentation of self reflected our own performance and pedagogical view of ourselves. The term "public speaking" remained in the name of the national association and the title of the national journal for a long time. So strong was our oral orientation, from the very outset, that "speech" became the "umbrella" profession for all of the oral arts. We included in our membership and interests theatre, oral interpretation, and speech correction; and when it began to develop, broadcasting became one of our provinces as well.

An examination of our journals in the early period of our history is instructive in illuminating the pattern of development. Two paths are followed simultaneously, one much less visible than the other. The great bulk of the articles in the teens and early twenties deals with the very practical problems of teaching, play production, and forensics, together with descriptive articles about "how we do it at our place." Articles of this sort, although they seem naïve and primitive now, were probably essential for the development of cohesion and identity, and they parallel the early stages of other fields (Lyman, 1915; Babcock, 1915; Dennis, 1916; Weaver, 1916; Dithridge, 1915; Winans, 1917; Kay, 1917; Ryan, 1917). At the same time we find the early and faint signs of something quite different—the possibility that speech might become a research field. The very first issue of what is now the *Quarterly Journal of Speech* contains an article by James Winans (1915) on "The Need for Research" and the first four journals contain reports from the Research Committee (1915a and 1915b), and an article on "Research Problems in Voice and Speech" (Blanton, 1916). Productivity of research and scholarship was, with certain exceptions, slow in coming, however. Here and there, during our early years, we find an occasional article on Greek and Roman rhetoric, some work in speech disorders, and very significantly, the early foundational work of Charles Woolbert. For the most part, however, we were sending group maintenance messages to each other. We perceived ourselves as a performance field. Our concern with research and scholarship was secondary; its significance developed gradually. The importance of research was not really evident until almost two decades had passed.

Speech communication still displays a good deal of ambivalence about whether its primary objective is to teach skills, to advance scholarship, or somehow to combine both of these goals. In our own time, some writers have argued that we really have no business teaching performance courses in public speaking (Burgoon, 1976). Others in our profession who seem more aware of our tradition and heritage advocate the continuation and improvement of performance courses. Politically, at least, the second view seems stronger because many other fields have recognized the need for competence in public speaking, small group problem-solving, interpersonal communication, and organizational communication for their students, and that part of our enterprise seems to be thriving.

An additional insight to be derived from our origins is that although research may not really be an "add on," it was not a central objective of our establishment as a field and it did not become part of our consciousness until much later.

When we began to turn from purely pedagogical concerns in the late teens and early twenties we were not clear whence the models of our research should be drawn. We, of course, had no research tradition even in the NCTE. The interest in research began shortly after the elocutionary period, during which responsibility for rhetorical studies had been assumed by departments of English and classics. Since the separation from English was based on practical rather than intellectual motives, it was almost inevitable that we turned to directions from literary studies as the basis for our early scholarship. Moreover, we seemed almost inevitably drawn to studies in ancient rhetoric. In the late teens and early twenties, papers on various aspects and figures in classical rhetoric were produced by Everett Lee Hunt, Bromley Smith, Edwin Flemming, Hoyt Hudson, Paul Shorey, and Giles Grey, among others (Hunt, 1920; Smith, 1918; Flemming, 1918; Hudson, 1924; Shorey, 1922; Grey, 1923). That our research took this turn is not at all surprising. First, our professional development began at a time when many of our members had been educated in the late 19th and early 20th centuries; classical education was then standard in American colleges and universities. Second, if we were to find some sort of theoretical base for our field, the most visible and available sources for writers who had theorized about public speaking were the classics. It is interesting to note that it was in the 1930s, 1940s, and 1950s that the first mention is made of rhetorical theorists who wrote in English. The effort to construct a theoretical base was very little concerned with the construction of our own theories of rhetoric. We were dealing, in reality, with the history of rhetorical theory and the application of ancient theory to our work. No wonder that much early scholarship said more about Aristotelian theory than about the subjects we were studying. The pattern for our later development was set in those early days. Although few of us would choose to be called Aristotelians or Platonists or Ciceronians, we have now become Burkeans, Toulminites, and Habermassians (Burke, 1950; Toulmin, 1958; Habermas, 1979). In short, we continue to base the best of our scholarship in rhetorical theory on our derivations from writers outside our field. To be sure we have adopted some of these figures, but persons trained in speech communication have contributed precious little to theories of rhetoric. Instead, we continue to rely on theories developed by persons educated in literary, classical, and philosophical studies, including the persons mentioned earlier and other writers such as Booth, Weaver, and Perelman (Booth, 1961; Weaver, 1953; Perelman, 1969). We are certainly more sophisticated than we were half a century or more ago, but we are almost as derivative as we were early in our professional development.

At the same time that these developments in rhetoric were occurring another very interesting and significant path was being cleared. Our evolution as a behavioral science was really simultaneous with our development as a humanities based field.

In a very realistic sense, the study of human communication has been behavioral, if not scientific, from almost its inception, and behavioral science from its beginnings has been concerned with communication. Plato admonished us to be behavioral when, in the *Phaedrus*, he specified that rhetoricians must know the nature of souls and what affects them. Although it is primitive by contemporary standards, Aristotle's treatment of the emotions and of persons represents a genuine effort to describe human communication behavior. Since the impetus for the study of communication came from the need to persuade, to achieve change in human behavior, we need to recognize that our interests have been based in psychology for 2,500 years. Our first "research" was "effects research" and has continued to dominate our interests until almost the present day.

Throughout the history of our field our interest in human behavior has followed, almost in tandem, developments in the more general intellectual world. This relationship was perhaps most evident during the blossoming and development of the New Science from the late 16th through the 18th centuries. Studies in faculty and associational psychology quickly found application in the works of rhetorical theorists, perhaps most obviously developed in George Campbell's *Philosophy of Rhetoric* (Bacon, 1899; Campbell, 1855; Kames, 1871; Burke, 1836; Blair, 1836; Locke, 1813; Smith, 1963). To be sure, these works in rhetorical theory were not strictly comparable to modern behavioral research with its emphasis on experimentation and control, but they draw on contemporary investigations of human behavior.

As early as the 1920s, the influence of the behavioral sciences was evident in professional discussions, articles, and, indeed, in spirited academic debate. Our breaking away from the NCTE may be interpreted much too simply. The formation of a professional speech association was not just a "spin-off" from an English association. To be sure, speech teachers felt that insufficient attention was being paid to oral communication in English departments, but they did have their own oral English section of NCTE. Other reasons for the division are more crucial to our present concern. Many of our founders and early members were concerned with much more than questions of equity and separate identity. They actually perceived speech to be different in its orientation and its roots from the discipline of English. Their interests were much deeper and broader than the teaching of oral composition. Many of the organizers of the new profession had studied with or had been influenced by the most advanced psychological thought of the period. The influence of psychologists such as James, Munsterberg, Holt, and Watson on Winans and Woolbert is well known (Winans, 1915b, pp. 45–118; Woolbert, 1917a, 1917b, 1923, 1930). The later work of other founders, such as O'Neill, Sarrett, Gisalson, and Rarig, hardly supports the notion that we were dominantly concerned with the literary act of composition. From the very first number of the ancestor of the *QJS* the case was made, most notably by Winans and Woolbert, that our research and study must be based on an understanding of human behavior. By 1917, Mary Yost wrote on "Argument from the Point-of-View of Sociology" (1917). Although research based in the social sciences was less frequent than that based in the humanities, the foundation for a behavioral approach was being laid.

The establishment of *Speech Monographs* in 1934 represented a response to the research interests of the profession and provided an outlet for our scientific and behavioral research. To be sure, many of the articles were in what we now call "speech science." Nonetheless, they were clearly indicative of the emergent research orientation and direction of our field. In fact, the incorporation of "speech correctionists" in our early organizations was of marked assistance in providing a strong early impetus in shaping our research. The growth of behavioral research advanced at a pace rapid enough to justify an article by William Utterback in 1937 on "An Appraisal of Psychological Research in Speech" (1937).

The influence of the social sciences has, over the years, determined directions our research has taken us. As a consequence, behavioral science has exerted its force in shaping our perceptions of human communication and indeed, of human nature. Almost without examination of alternatives we chose as our model for research the hardest of the social sciences, experimental psychology, which was itself founded on the hard science model of 19th-century chemistry and physics. With that choice, we accepted the "scientific" ideology of controls, replicability, experimentation, measurement, and the laboratory. Very early on, we began using the term "science" to describe our orientation; we even used the verb form, "doing science," borrowed directly from the physical sciences, to describe our activities. We perceived ourselves as doing our business as scientists do theirs.

That such a development occurred in the early days of our development should not be surprising. Our establishment as a profession occurred during the First World War, and our initial growth took place in the 1920s and 1930s. Those were times when the term "scientific" had acquired almost magical properties. "Science," or perhaps as Robert Nisbet refers to it, "scientism" was seen as a virtual panacea to the ills of mankind and the world (Nisbet, 1976, p. 6) if only we could systematize and regularize our thought and analysis as real scientists had done. The scientific spirit pervaded the intellectual atmosphere and, almost inevitably, influenced those who were seriously studying human communication.

At this point we need to enter a reservation in order to avoid the impression that in early times we were awash in behavioral research. Most of the articles in the early issues of the *QJS* cannot, even charitably, be characterized as research, let alone behavioral research. The great bulk of the articles in the teens and twenties dealt with the very practical problems of teaching, play production, and forensics.

Productivity of research and scholarship was, with certain exceptions, slow in coming. James Winans and the Research Committee were urging us on to scholarship and prescribing the directions of our future research, and the very significant foundational work of Charles Woolbert was being published. These contributions were exceptions, however, and were over balanced by our more pedagogical concerns. Nevertheless, an important direction for our future research was being charted because of the developing interest in research and the social sciences.

In spite of the recommendations of Woolbert, Winans, and others, and the valuable work of early scholars, we were not able in our early history, or for that matter in the present, to form a conceptual core in the behavioral or social sciences. In part this failure was the result of the nature of our field. The heterogeneity of our membership and interests made the achievement of a clear identity of ourselves and of our research goals very difficult. Various constituencies of our profession saw themselves as representing the natural sciences, the social sciences, the humanities, and the arts.

The fact that research and inquiry were not central to our enterprise contributed to our failure to become the science principally concerned with human communication and that defined a conceptual core that was uniquely ours. Instead of defining our interests and staking out our research territory, we became a derivative, even a dependent research field.

Our early research attempts were, for the most part, not successful. Several reasons may be offered for this deficiency. First, our history as a performance field and our early reliance on psychology imposed limits on our research. Instead of seeking to explore the entire scope of human communication, we restricted ourselves largely to effects studies. Persuasion became our dominant focus. Perhaps because of the small number of researchers in our field, we tended not to persist in lines of inquiry, even within our limits.

Second, we were not successful because we did not become theory builders about human communication. Although we were attracted to science, we did not construct theories for ourselves. Rather, we tended toward conceptual derivation. Almost all the theories we used were derived from elsewhere and our contributions to theories of communication were all but invisible. As mentioned earlier, we ran a negative trade balance with the social sciences, and we were much more borrowers than lenders. While we cite social scientists frequently in our work, our work is rarely cited in theirs. Our contributions do not seem very central to the outside world. In order to comprehend the pattern of our development we must examine the situation between 1914 and the post-World War II period.

Sometimes we have failed, in our effort to be scientific, to integrate our social science with our earlier traditions. An interesting case in point is our work in small groups. Early in the development of our field we were attracted to a conception of group decision making based on John Dewey's work (Dewey, 1910; Baird, 1928; Ewbank & Auer, 1941; McBurney & Hance, 1950). That model was based on the assumption that groups operate most effectively in a framework of reason, conciliation, and compromise. Considerations of process, interaction, or other psychological or social factors were not only ignored, they were discouraged. Saddest of all perhaps, any applications of rhetoric and persuasion were also discouraged. We were ignoring what we knew best. When in the 1950s we discovered the work of Bales, Hare, and Homan, we made a 180-degree turn to the study of process and interaction and again ignored the rhetorical aspects of group decision making (Bales, 1950; Hare, 1976; Homan, 1950). This defect is being remedied, but years of valuable time were lost and our work in small groups does not draw very much on our rhetorical competence.

In the years between the wars we had a quiet, tranquil existence. We were an expanding field. Departments of speech, often combined with theatre and speech correction, were established; and courses in speech were introduced as components of other departments, usually English. Our graduate offerings increased and a number of departments, mostly in the Middle West, were offering Ph.D.'s. Our teaching and writing was largely concerned with public speaking, although "group discussion" was taught and written about from the late 1920s on. Most of the present subdivisions of our field were unknown, or at least not seriously considered during those years. Although some tentative, exploratory writing was done by Robert Oliver, Elwood Murray, and others, what we now call interpersonal communication was of little concern to us (Murray, 1934; Murray, 1936; Murray, 1943; Oliver, 1932; Howes, 1928). Intercultural communication, organizational communication, communication theory, discourse analysis, and other contemporary taxonomic divisions were not even thought of. Indeed, relatively little research in a field as standard as rhetorical criticism was carried on before the late 1940s.

The tranquil, if obscure, life of speech communication was severely disturbed at the end of World War II. That period represented an intellectual revolution in the social sciences. They moved very rapidly from a descriptive methodological base to a quantitative, empirical, experimental, and behavioral approach to the questions they asked. Many disciplines, such as political science, sociology, economics, anthropology, and geography, underwent radical and rapid change, and we saw considerable conflict and ferment between the traditionalists and the modernists in many disciplines. The lines between conventional fields became blurred, and a general exchange of theories, conceptualizations, and methodologies took place. Sociologists borrowed from political scientists, and geographers contributed to the work of anthropologists. Perhaps most important to us, the scope of the social scientists had broadened to include almost all aspects of human behavior, including communication.

Speech communication slumbered peacefully through the early stages of this revolution, and then we awoke to discover that while we had been tending to public speaking a number of social scientists, such as Robert Bales at Harvard, and Hovland, Janis, and Kelly, at Yale, had undertaken systematic, scientific studies of human communication (Bales, 1950; Hovland, Janis & Kelly, 1953). With our awareness came a sense of desperation and even of panic. It was not so much that someone had invaded our territory as that someone was exploring a territory we should have discovered but had not. We had lost our opportunity, but we did not know how we should react. Our response was to cast a wide net and bring in material from the social sciences that we thought might be useful to us. Since we were not well grounded in the theories of the social sciences, we tended, at least initially, to choose methodologies rather than conceptualizations. We did not inquire very carefully whether these methodologies were those suited to the questions we had to ask. Indeed, in many cases, we simply repeated the questions asked by those we regarded as our intellectual superiors.

The researchers of the 1950s and 1960s seemed to be rushing into social science. An entirely different result might have occurred if scholars had taken sufficient time to absorb the new behaviorism and to contemplate how the innovative research might be most useful in answering our questions. We did not ask how new theories and methods might best be adapted and modified. Instead, we tended to acquire materials indiscriminately and with little alteration.

Our reaction, when combined with our earlier history, created certain characteristics, some of which remain with us to the present day. Understandably, we reenacted the schism that had occurred in other fields. Traditional rhetoricians and the new "empiricists" regarded each other with disdain and sometimes even with contempt. Some of us who observed the conflict felt that the very traditional work of rhetoricians was not only outdated but irrelevant. From the perspective of the 1980s that great dispute turns out to be nothing more than a family squabble. The conflict was mostly about methodology, not conceptualization. The questions asked and the problems explored by the new scholars were not essentially different from the questions we had been asking all along. We were still largely concerned with effect studies. That emphasis was understandable in light of our history as a pedagogical and performance field. The study of persuasion was central in the days of ferment. As with other fields, in time the conflict was ameliorated and does not now occupy as much of our time.

One cannot question that behavioral science has come to communication. It came early, but it was largely derivative and governed by the positivism of early experimental psychology. We did not, until quite recently, consider alternatives from the softer social sciences. We were not very attracted to field study, qualitative research, or participant-observation that might have been better suited to the study of elusive human communication. In the recent past, we have begun to loosen some of the restrictions we imposed on ourselves, and we have reason to hope for a more flexible, adaptable, and humanistic approach to the study of communication behavior.

When we decided to become serious about being social scientists, we caused ourselves some problems. We approached our new task with few resources. Few of our scholars really had any comprehensive knowledge of science and what it means to "do science." With certain exceptions, we knew little about the philosophy of science. We were not trained to theorize about science, and we were deficient in our mastery of methodology. Our lack of competence in methodology was the easiest defect to remedy. Those were skills we could learn with relative ease, but we learned more about statistical manipulation than the underlying rationales for statistical and experimental methodology. Because of the persistent influence of experimental psychology, we chose experimental methodology as the research mode for answering our questions and eschewed methods that might have been more effective and better adapted to the examination of human communication—a behavior that is not altogether suited to controlled laboratory research.

Because of the conditions under which we began to enact our newly enhanced scientific role, we accepted the more apparent mechanisms of science almost blindly. And because we had insufficient background in science, we did not clearly understand the limitations of highly quantitative methodologies, and accepted them almost unquestioningly. We had become true believers in quantitative research.

What were the limitations that we did not fully grasp and that shaped our values? Partly because of our dependence on methodology, we perceived that science was an enterprise quite distinct from the arts and humanities. Oddly, the relationships between science and other forms of scholarship were recognized and taken into consideration more persistently by natural scientists than by social scientists. Scholars in communication accepted methodology as the equivalent of science and became victims of scientism, which Robert Nisbet defines as "science with the spirit of discovery and creation left out" (1976, p. 4). We, and other social scientists, failed to distinguish between what Nisbet called "logic of discovery" and the "logic of demonstration" (1976, p. 3). We became so concerned about being expert in the techniques of methodologies, experimental design, and measurement—the logic of demonstration—that we neglected the creative aspects of our work—the logic of discovery. We did not see clearly that "what is vital is the underlying act of discovery or illumination or invention that is the clue to all genuine creative work" (Nisbet, 1976, pp. 5, 16). Our dependence on methodology caused our awareness of the nature of discovery to lag. Our positivistic orientation contributed to our not recognizing clearly that, although demonstration is properly subject to rules and prescriptions, invention is not. We have sometimes deluded ourselves into thinking that creativity can be summoned by adherence to the purity of methodology.

Knowledge of statistics and experimental design came, in many cases, to serve as a substitute for the ability to formulate interesting questions and it inihibited insightful perception of communication phenomena. Intuition has been suppressed, and undue weight has been placed on statistical verification with the consequent blurring of the larger picture. As Nisbet puts it: "The great harm of the present consecration of method . . . is that it persuades students that a small idea abundantly verified is worth more than a large idea still insusceptible to textbook techniques of verification" (1976, p. 17). One is reminded of Francis Bacon's *Idols of the Mind* when we observe the attempt to represent our knowledge as a composite of precise rules for designing problems, arranging data, achieving hypotheses, and in verifying results.

Our positivistic posture and reliance on methodology had led us into believing that our "verification" is synonymous with "proof." But as Lord Peter Medawar, a Nobel Laureate in biology and medicine put it, "People tend to the use of the word 'proof' in the empirical sciences as if it had the same weight and connotation as it has in logic and mathematics. . . . But with the empirical sciences . . . it is not so much a question of finding 'proofs' as expanding the grounds for having confidence in them (Nisbet, 1976, p. 17).

In the process of becoming "empirical" we also lost sight of one of our governing precepts—the Aristotelian admonition that we should be concerned with the given case. We began to draw the same kind of generalizable conclusions that marked the work of those we regarded as our intellectual superiors. By relying so heavily on experimental methodology, we neglected the kind of valuable work that had been done as qualitative research, field studies, and participant-observer studies. We did not see the precedent for us in such works as Oscar Lewis's *Children of Sanchez*, Margaret Mead's numerous works, Riesman's *Lonely Crowd*, and the Lynds' *Middletown* (Lewis, 1961; Riesman, 1950; Lynd & Lynd, 1929). We made little use of what David Riesman called "empirical observation combined with reflection" (Nisbet, 1976, p. 21). As John Dewey reminded us years ago, without perception of problems there would be "no real thought at all; only musing, reverie, simple association, daydreams, and the like" (Nisbet, 1976, p. 16).

After this analysis, what hopes do we have for the future? Some hopeful signs are on the horizon. Some of us have begun to comprehend philosophy, especially the philosophy of science. A few of us have even come to understand that science itself is a rhetorical enterprise. We have generated precious few theories concerning human communication, but perhaps our new learning will motivate us. I am pessimistic, however, about the prospects of our developing a conceptual core that will give us our individual intellectual stamp. We are perhaps not as dependent on experimental psychology as we were in the earlier days of the revolution, but we continue to be dependent on other fields for our thought.

My hope is that as we mature and learn we will recognize that we may be scientists; but we must acknowledge that our roots are also in the arts and the humanities, and their methods of inquiry may give us perceptions and insights that rigid adherence to scientific methodology may not. I also hope that we will place greater value on asking important questions rather than on finding experimental answers. To quote Nisbet again, "what is statistically significant is often trivial" (1976, p. 18).

Now that we have examined the paths we followed to arrive at our present state, it is appropriate to ask what kind of field we are after 75 years of development. What is our present professional status? To our credit we have clearly matured and established ourselves. We have active national, regional, and state organizations. We publish scholarly journals, hold conferences, and, in general, behave much like other professions. We are a leaner profession than we were in our earlier days. Our former associates in theatre and communication disorders have formed their own associations and no longer meet with us or contribute much to our journals. Even the formerly tiny National Society for the Study of Communications has become the thriving International Communication Association. It is interesting that many of the groups that were formerly under the speech umbrella are larger than we are.

In spite of our professional apparatus, we have not, in 75 years, been accepted as a central discipline in the academy. The fact that we are not represented in the offerings of some of the most prestigious institutions is not without significance, although we might be tempted to attribute our absence to snobbery and ignorance. The disappearance of departments of speech communication in some private and public colleges and universities should arouse our deep concern—not our paranoia. Many administrators and faculty do not see our mission very clearly, perhaps because we do not present ourselves very clearly. To many outsiders our work seems to duplicate the work of other disciplines. In short, we do not seem to be selling a product that is different from or superior to that offered by other disciplines. In fairness, I must point out that, in these times of economic restraint, we are not alone. Other fields, such as linguistics, classics, geography, anthropology, and religious studies, have come under pressures similar to those of speech communication. Together, in contrast to disciplines such as English, psychology, and chemistry, we are seen to be not central to the academic enterprise.

We have matured greatly as a field although we retain much of our derivative character. Our research is increasingly more sophisticated and flexible. We are not as confined in our hard science, positivistic model as we were. I have no serious question that we will continue to flourish as a field; but truly to prosper, we will need to be clearer in our own minds and in our presentation of ourselves about what contributions we can make that are uniquely ours.

15

Legitimizing Speech Communication: An Examination of Coherence and Cohesion in the Development of the Discipline

ARTHUR P. BOCHNER AND ERIC M. EISENBERG

Over the course of its history, the field of speech communication has struggled to achieve recognition as a legitimate discipline. This paper attempts to place the problem of legitimation in historical and institutional context in order to clarify why speech communication seems so misunderstood by other disciplines and why its self-image is so weak. The plan is to produce a different attack on the problem than is customary, by viewing legitimation as a rhetorical problem rather than an ontological one.

The entire history of speech communication as an academic discipline spans less than eighty years. From a charter membership of 156 "academic teachers of public speaking" whose interests were largely confined to collegiate instruction in speaking, the discipline has mushroomed into a diverse profession covering all human interaction. Although a few graduate degrees in subjects related to speech were granted before 1920, the first Ph.D. in speech was not awarded until 1922; and as late as 1933 a student could do doctoral work in a speech department at only six universities (Gray, 1953; O'Neill, 1935). Presently, more than 900 college departments grant degrees in speech; about 250 of these offer graduate work, and at least 50 confer the highest degree (Edwards & Barker, 1983; Ehninger, 1968; Gray, 1953; O'Neill, 1935; Paulson, 1980). Until 1940 only a few journals solicited research on speech, but the proliferation of graduate programs over the past two decades has expanded the market for scholarly work substantially. Today there are more than one dozen journals and two annuals that regularly publish such scholarship.

Still, the prime objective, acceptance as a legitimate discipline, has not been achieved. The discipline finds itself in much the same predicament it was in when Winans fostered a scholarly ideal for the field, "not yet able to take [itself] for granted" (1915, p. 18). Within the past three years departments at Vermont, Colorado, Massachusetts, Denver, SUNY-Buffalo, Albany, Michigan, and Washington State have been eliminated or seriously threatened. While this is not the first time the survival of speech departments has been placed in doubt (Smith, 1963), it may be the most menacing challenge the discipline has ever faced. Many authorities on higher education are predicting at best slow and uncertain rates of enrollment growth (Carnegie Council on Policy Studies, 1980), and an extended period of severe decline cannot be ruled out. As universities reduce the size of their faculties and reorganize the structure of their colleges—as many are certain to do—it is reasonable to expect unrecognized disciplines to be placed on the defensive. Recent experiences single out speech communication as one of the vulnerable disciplines (Spectra, 1977).

The current besiegement raises again the vexing question of whether speech communication is a legitimate discipline. Not surprisingly, recent literature within our field has sounded a chorus of affirmative responses. The problem of disciplinary legitimacy has been addressed in three ways. The most common form of response has been to compare the "essential" qualitites of speech communication to the defining characteristics of disciplines. For example, Paulson (1980) lists six traits of disciplines identified by Heckhausen (1972) and concludes that speech communication fits the bill. Similarly, Gouran (1979) circumscribes several properties necessary for classification as a discipline and finds nothing inherent in the nature of speech communication that would prevent it from satisfying these requirements.

A second line of defense has been definitional. Writers ask what speech communication is and where it belongs in the curriculum. Marlier (1980) implies that speech communication would fare better if it were viewed as a distinct kind of discipline, a field of specialized generalists focused on process rather than content. Delia (1979) insists that the field should promote a single, unified perspective grounded in the practical tradition that is its heritage; and both Dance (1980) and Hostettler (1980) attempt to reclaim territory in the liberal arts for speech communication.

A third approach has concentrated on the future by admitting the discipline's credibility problem, rationalizing its causes, and offering a constructive program for improving its status. Speech communication is viewed as a newer and developing discipline at a time when older, established ones are favored (Paulson, 1980); and as a field that lacks a shared universe of concepts (Gouran, 1980). The field's scholarship, according to these writers, compares unfavorably to other disciplines (Delia, 1979), is shallow (Simons, 1976), and is derivative rather than original (Cohen, 1975). It is presumed that recognition will come after the field matures, unifies, develops its own theory, and toughens its scholarly standards.

None of these writers considers the possibility that speech communication cannot or will not achieve the status it seeks. Yet several factors make this possibility important to contemplate. First, some disciplines not much older than speech communication are considerably more secure; for instance, sociology, anthropology, and psychology. Second, more established disciplines also suffer from fragmentation (Koch, 1976), fractionation (House, 1977), lack of achievement (Gergen, 1982), failure to develop an endemic philosophy (Royce, 1976), crisis in confidence (Elms, 1975), questionable distinctiveness (Koch, 1981), paradigmatic pluralism (Friedrichs, 1970), and insignificance (Moscovici, 1972). Third, several disciplines that have recorded important achievements in research are less secure on some campuses than speech communication; for instance, geography and music. It is quite possible, then, that standing in the academic world is not conditioned by disciplinary consensus, theoretical distinctness, and high scholastic standards, though these commendable traits may be characteristic of disciplines that up to now have prospered.

Our point of departure here is the doubtful assumption that speech communication can achieve legitimation as a discipline by becoming coherent, independent, and more scholarly. Even if legitimation could be won in this fashion, the glaring trends in the history of speech communication point to less independence, greater fragmentation, and more incoherence. In this chapter we shall examine the field's legitimation predicament by analyzing historical evidence bearing on the institutional and academic development of speech communication. Our analysis shall proceed as follows:

1. A brief review of the events that led to departmentalization of speech in universities. This will include a consideration of factors that led to the rapid expansion of disciplines in the late 19th and early 20th centuries and the revolt that divided speech from English.

2. An analysis of the long and apparently futile struggle to define what speech (and later speech communication) is. This will include discussions of three issues: difficulties in securing a satisfying generic name for the discipline, the progressive broadening of the field's boundaries and its effect on distinctiveness, and problems of establishing coherence and cohesiveness within the discipline.

3. A look at the two-world problem, focusing not only on the controversy surrounding the division between rhetoric and communication but also on the unfortunate historical segregation of mass communications from speech communication.

4. A consideration, in light of these analyses, of what is reasonable to expect from the discipline in the future. Our conclusions shall be drawn

from a measured analysis of what the discipline has been and the constraints that bear upon what, in all probability, it can become in the future.

ORIGINS OF SPEECH DEPARTMENTS

Before the late 19th century, academic departments as we know them did not exist. The early colleges were elitist and not a central part of American life. Their role was limited mainly to supplying literate and knowledgeable ministers, lawyers, and doctors. For the most part, the colleges remained detached from the farming and shopkeeping that were the mainstream of American life. This isolation of work from education was reflected in the classical curriculum of the time. Even after the development of new knowledge made it impossible for a single tutor to teach all subjects, the tradition of a broad, unified curriculum was retained.

The character of higher education gradually began to change in the middle of the 19th century. Although a number of factors contributed to the radical transformation that was to occur, the most profound influence was the transition from an agrarian to an industrialized society. Industrialization created a need for knowledge and skills that could not be acquired at home or taught by the church. The American dream then moved from the frontier to the corporation, and the diploma replaced the apprenticeship as the principal means of gaining access to a better life.

Recognizing the educational demands brought about by rapid industrialization, the federal government prompted the expansion of higher education in 1862 by passing the Morrill Act, which established land-grant colleges. The Morrill Act shifted the focus of higher education away from the elite and toward a utilitarian function. This meant that the curriculum had to change. The classical, intellectually unified curriculum had to change in order to make room for the more practical and specialized needs of new generations of students.

Historians of higher education point to several other factors that contributed to the emergence of departments as the central structural units of universities. First, many American professors studied at German universities and transported the ideal of the research-oriented university with them when they returned from their studies (Trow, 1978). Second, the development of new fields of knowledge made it increasingly necessary to specialize. The pressure for specialization was reinforced by the commercial and industrial demand for technically skilled and pragmatically oriented graduates (Anderson, 1978). Third, the incentives provided by tax support encouraged universities to assume a regional focus. As the faculty became more diversified, decision making grew increasingly decentralized. For the sake of institutional efficiency as well as intellectual integrity, curriculum decisions were taken out of the hands of the higher administration and placed instead in the laps of departments. The emergence of new fields and the creation of departments to represent them was then more easily accomplished. In this atmosphere, an unequivocal record of achievement was less important than distinctness. A field seeking departmental status had to show mainly that it was not trying to invade the turf of an older discipline (Williams, 1976).

Finally, the remarkable achievements of 19th-century physics created an uncritical admiration for scientific research. Since techniques for analyzing social data were developing rapidly, there seemed no reason to doubt that the methods of physics could be applied successfully to the problems of humanity (Becker, 1968; Koch, 1976). The time was ripe, then, for the debut of new fields of inquiry that would extend the methods of physics to the puzzles of social life.

It was against this background that speech was launched as a discipline. In this respect it was not much different from psychology, which Koch claims "was unique in the extent to which its institutionalization preceded its content and its methods preceded its problems" (1978, p. 485). The birth of speech paralleled that of sociology, which met with little resistance, according to Williams, because "established aristocrats of academe in the 1890s and early 1900s could see no fundamental cognitive challenge in such rag-picking at the periphery of the intellectual marketplace" (1976, pp. 87–88).

Speech was not ushered into existence as a result of a rational and deliberate division of subject matter. Like other disciplines instituted at about the same time, speech was the product of social processes (Wax, 1969). While the movement toward departmentalization of an autonomous speech curriculum apparently began during the latter decades of the 19th century (Gray, 1954; Smith, 1954), the birth of the discipline is most commonly associated with the establishment of its first national organization in 1914. The National Association of Academic Teachers of Public Speaking was, according to Bryant, "conceived in discontent, gestated in rebellion, and born in secession" (1971, p. 3). The 17 dissident speech teachers who walked out on the National Council of Teachers of English and the Speech Arts Association were angry about the diminished importance assigned to instruction in speech within English departments. Smith (1954) suggests that the disenchantment of speech teachers at this time stemmed from the stubborn rejection of utilitarianism by English departments, the low prestige of oral instruction owing to the excesses of elocutionism, and the growing tendency to identify rhetoric with literature and literary criticism. The teaching of practical discourse was being suffocated by the narrow concentration on literary studies; that is, language, literature, and literary criticism.

The founding fathers of the field saw an opportunity and seized it. They recognized that the educational reforms of the period favored utilitarian subjects. English was not inclined to break loose from its classical heritage, nor could it conceal its prejudice for nonoral discourse. It would, therefore, be very difficult for English to prevent the rebellious speech faction from establishing a strong case for independence. Furthermore, if speech instruction could gain academic credibility, the justification for separation could be made even stronger. It was mainly for this reason that speech was defined originally as a scientific field. The combination of a utilitarian function and a scientific perspective would be unassailable.

The pages of the first issues of the *Quarterly Journal of Public Speaking* support this portrayal of the field's origins. We should briefly address how the pioneers of the field viewed the situation. First, all disciplines must lay claim to a special expertise and speech was no exception. The expertise claimed by speech was public speaking. This is reflected both in the first name of the national association and in the first scholarly journal. Second, and also reflected in the association's name, was the emphasis on academic subject matter. This emphasis was made mainly to distinguish public speaking from the ill-reputed elocutionism, for as Hunt (1915) admonished, "there can be no doubt of the scholastic deficiencies of many 'elocution' teachers and others who have conducted college courses as though imparting parlor accomplishments in a ladies' seminary" (p. 184). Third, the success of the field was seen as contingent on its scientific viability. Winans (1915) discouraged "dry-as-dust studies of speakers," stating the main objective of the field as "getting into a sufficiently scientific frame of mind." Instead, Woolbert went as far as to say that speech was distinct from English because "it is only by a stretch of the term that English can claim sanctuary as a science. Speech, on the other hand, claims as its ancestry disciplines that are of the elect among the sciences: physics, physiology, anatomy, psychology" (1916, p. 66). Thus, the case for speech was built on the foundation of (1) a pragmatic subject matter, (2) an academic orientation, and (3) a scientific spirit. There were high expectations but there was no visible record of achievement.

DEFINING THE FIELD

The pioneers in the field recognized that a number of obstacles stood in the way of developing a positive image of public speaking as an academic discipline. First, the field was not well understood by established members of the academy. Where it was understood, it was often not well respected, largely because the excesses of elocutionism had cast suspicion on oral subjects in general. Consequently, teachers of public speaking rarely got promoted (Graves, 1954). Second, the curriculum of public speaking was unorganized; it was not clear which subjects fit under the rubric "public speaking" (O'Neill, 1913). Third, the field aspired to an academic goal that was not shared equally by all of its members. It was determined to become scientific, though it possessed no body of scientific research and only a few of its teachers were even moderately qualified as scientists. Moreover, the fostering of a scholarly ideal created an unpleasant tension between the practical goals of teachers of public speaking and the academic objectives brought about by departmentalization.

The early developers of the field attempted to resolve these problems by offering descriptions of the discipline that would appeal to all factions without alienating any of them. The rallying point for these treatises was reproach of the enemy. Speech had to transcend "the minutiae of philology" and the "extravagance of the old-line elocutionists" (Woolbert, 1923). It was thought that this could be accomplished by devotion to the methods of science. Considerable caution had to be exercised, however, because most teachers of oral subjects were unfamiliar with science and resistant to research. As a result, there was considerable opposition to the idea of transforming the study of speaking into an entirely academic endeavor. As Hunt remarked in an important early article on the subject: "The function of teachers of public speaking is to produce public speakers, ridiculous as that may seem to university scholars. . . . Because of these fundamental differences between the work of the speaker and the work of the scientist, it seems to me both unnecessary and unwise to hold up the scientific ideal as our chief hope of salvation" (1915, pp. 186–190).

Sensing that Hunt's view was shared by many other teachers of public speaking, proponents of the scientific spirit were forced to develop a description of the field's mission accommodating this point of view. Thus, Winans (1915) admitted that the case for research may have been overstated, but he also suggested that research would secure a better position for the field and "a better position will put us into a frame of mind conducive to good teaching" (p. 200). Woolbert (1917) took a similar stand. He agreed that "research was not for everybody" and "we are a teaching branch of the educational tree and we shall always remain so" (1917, p. 12), but he also strongly encouraged investigation. It was his opinion that opportunities to expand speech instruction would be facilitated by earning respectability through research: "No research; no favor in the eyes of educators. We occupy a delightful position among disciplines, but the test of its permanence is our willingness to do in Rome what the Romans do. We may long and sigh and pine; but presidents and deans are not moved that way, sad to relate. They are becoming pretty stony-hearted toward all those who conclude not to make serious and persistent efforts to increase the kingdom of knowledge" (1917, p. 26).

In sum, the field's calling was in teaching; research was important principally because it would convince outsiders this teaching had merit. Whether one favored teaching or research, however, there was still the question of subject matter: *What* was to be taught and/or researched?

The problem of defining, naming, and delineating the boundaries of the field was a sizable one for the founding fathers. First, there was the troubling matter of identifying the field's first principles, its seminal works. Although the teaching of public speaking was grounded in the tradition of classical rhetoric, the study of rhetoric had become almost exclusively associated with the study of literature and literary criticism. Since the field's initial justification rested on a fragile distinction between oral and literary discourse, texts on rhetoric could not easily be depicted as foundational. In fact, the first serious attempt to detach rhetoric from composition did not occur until the mid-1920s (Hudson, 1923); and as late as 1931, classical texts on rhetoric still were not publicly viewed as cornerstones for the field (Hudson, 1931). Lacking its own texts and its own program statement, the field was forced to embrace psychological theory, because it was scientific, and because psychological studies of audience behavior had obvious relevance for the theory and practice of speaking.

Second, the field had to guard against overly narrow self-definition. There was no disputing the fact that teaching public speaking was the main function of the new departments, but many of the field's leaders seriously questioned whether the teaching of public speaking was a sufficiently profound basis upon which to build a discipline. Winans (1915) expressed this concern in the first issue of *The Quarterly Journal of Public Speaking* when he observed that "public speaking is the only field [one] can break into without preparation" (p. 23). Moreover, there was some doubt about whether public speaking could ever overcome its association with elocution. If the field was to grow into a secure and reputable discipline, it would have to attract bright young people. Only a broader definition of the field's scope could hope to offer such a challenge.

Third, there was the semantic problem: what should the field be called? Public speaking was the obvious choice. After all, concern over the teaching of public speaking had sparked separation from English, and there was no questioning the special expertise of teachers of speaking. But as a generic title for the new departments, public speaking soon outlived its usefulness. In fact, public speaking was never widely adopted as a departmental title (Smith, 1954). Rather, names adopted by newly formed departments were highly diverse: oratory, oral culture, science and art of expression, oral English, etcetera (Smith, 1954; Ryan, 1918). This diversity may have had a negative impact on the image of the field, for as Ryan argued: "A multitude of names does not suggest clarity and certainty in the mind of the layman, while in the mind of the college man the very multitude is taken as evidence of the unsatisfactory educational value of the work, or proofs of the inadequate scholarship of the teacher" (1918, pp. 3–4). This situation prompted the national association to form the first in a long line of committees to investigate the naming issue. In 1917 the term "speech" was "hastily adopted" (Winans, 1923) after strong objections were raised by opponents of the term "public speaking." Speech was considered desirable as a name because it had an intellectual connotation and extended the instructional domain of the field beyond the platform. But the decision to adopt "speech" was highly controversial (Winans, 1923), and as late as 1935 fewer than 50% of all departments were titled "speech." Nevertheless, the term "speech" was explicitly endorsed by the national association. In 1918 the association's organ was renamed *The Quarterly Journal of Speech Education*, and in 1923 the association dropped the terms "public speaking" and "academic" from its title, becoming the National Association of Teachers of Speech.

Finally, there was the question of what "speech" meant and where it fit among the disciplines. By the time Woolbert published "The Teaching of Speech As an Academic Discipline" in 1923, the constraints impinging upon self-definition were well understood. Orality had to be emphasized, but it could not be confined to public speaking. The field had to attract new students devoted to research, meaning that practical concerns had to be balanced by intellectual challenges. Speech was not oral English but a field in its own right. For the time being at least, it was necessary to state rhetorical principles in terms of pragmatic and behavioristic psychology. And the rules of the academy had to be honored. Speech teachers must "measure up to the academic and scholarly standards of their colleagues in other disciplines on the same faculty" (Woolbert, 1923, p. 7).

As a result, speech education was construed as "the widest of all possible academic programs" (Woolbert, 1923, p. 16). According to Woolbert, speech required study and practice; it was art and science. The field fell between the sciences of psychology, physiology, and physics on the one side and the humanistic fields of literature, criticism, and philology on the other. Nothing oral was ruled out: talk, conference, conversation, recitation, phonetics, voice science, acting. Speech as a discipline, then, was awkwardly defined as "the study and practice of such data of speech the activity as helps the student and practitioner to adjust himself to his environment and to be useful to his fellows" (Woolbert, 1923, p. 2).

Woolbert's description of the discipline diminished some problems and magnified others. As Knower (1932) observed some years later, "there are very few other fields of learning that attempt to build on such a broad foundation" (p. 48). By recasting rhetorical principles in the terms of modern psychology, speech ran the risk of being viewed as a derivative of psychology. Thus, the issue of distinctiveness did not disappear. Moreover, speech now had a new problem with which to contend: coherence. What principles tied together speaking, reading, conversation, dramatic arts and speech science? Was there a rational basis for classifying these subjects as parts of the same field, or were they really pieces of different puzzles?

This recounting of the field's infancy suggests that many of the issues we are wrestling with today were first introduced a long time ago. Rather than declining in importance or disappearing entirely, controversy over what to call our subject matter, whether it is distinctive, and how it coheres has intensified. Next, we shall briefly consider the development and current standing of these issues.

NAMING THE FIELD

No other issue has seemed at once both so absurd and so significant as the question of what to call the discipline. The national association has altered its name four times and is presently contemplating a fifth change. It has been called the National Association of Academic Teachers of Public Speaking (1914); National Association of Teachers of Speech (1923); Speech Association of America (1946); and Speech Communication Association (1970). Each of the association's journals has shifted its name at least once, and it is difficult to identify more than one or two major departments that have retained the same name throughout the course of their history.

Why has the field been so fixated on what it should be called? This question is difficult to answer. One gets the impression from the literature on this issue that leaders in the national association have assumed the field would be better understood and better accepted if a more respectable name could be found.

While it is sensible to sympathize with Carroll Arnold's conclusion that "arguments over semantics usually do not accomplish much" (1972, p. 72), and to laugh along with Fred Williams, when, in response to one heated debate over whether the term "speech communication" should be hyphenated, he observed, "the world will never believe this" (Kibler & Barker, 1969, p. 182), it is also important to understand the overall impact of these changes. By all accounts the field is no better understood or accepted today (McBath & Jeffrey, 1978) and perhaps, as Bacon argued, this is because "constant changing of name weakens and confuses the image of the Association" (1977, p. 2). Nor is there convincing evidence that the discipline's self-identity has been strengthened, or its power struggles muted, as the recent controversy over whether the national association should reorganize by splitting its scholarly function from its teaching and professional functions suggests (*Spectra*, 1983).

DISTINCTIVENESS

When the dissident leaders of the speech rebellion elbowed their way out of English, they were forced to accept some stifling consequences. Although many teachers of public speaking undoubtedly felt more at home in the world of literature and criticism, the field as a whole had little choice but to seek refuge in the sciences. But science was new and unfamiliar to these men, so it was natural for them to defer to and become dependent on psychology. Given their circumstances, it is unlikely that many of them thought it possible that speech could become an exclusive and exhaustive discipline. They wanted security and respect, but there is no reason to believe they envisioned an academic empire.

Nevertheless, one thing leads to another. In the 1920s and 1930s, articles authored by Hudson (1923) and Wichelns (1925) inspired a revival of Aristotelianism (Bryant, 1971), thereby rescuing classical rhetoric from the confines of composition. During roughly the same period, writers such as Woolbert (1917), Yost (1917), Utterback (1922), and Knower (1929) laid the foundation for quantitative research by showing how psychological and sociological theories could be applied to persuasion, conviction, and argumentation (Thompson, 1967).

Until late in the 1930s it was, as these developments suggest, perfectly acceptable—even preferable—to view the speech teacher as "the Academy's best borrower" (Woolbert, 1930, p. 9), and "the ready servant in all other fields of knowledge" (Ryan, 1918, p. 5). But when the aspirations of speech departments began to include the offering of graduate degrees, especially the Ph.D., it was no longer functional to retain this image of the field. The problem was first discussed at length by Knower, who pointed out that colleagues in other disciplines wanted to know "whether speech is an educational discipline with unifying principles which give it a status distinctive from other provinces of learning with which it is allied" (1937, p. 457). Later on, Hager (1946) observed that "more established fields wondered whether we were utilitarians, opportunists or montebanks—or all three" (1946, p. 26). Knower believed these difficulties could be overcome by showing that the study of speech belonged in speech departments, "because of the more favorable conditions for it in our discipline" (1937, p. 457). According to Knower, the solution was to stipulate a definition of speech that would clearly differentiate the study of speech within the discipline from speech inquiry in other disciplines.

But the field eventually learned that distinctiveness cannot be stipulated into existence. Whereas Knower attempted to restrict the scope of the field, the unmistakable historical trend since the 1930s has been to expand it. The 1963 SAA Committee report on "The Nature of the Field of Speech" accurately describes what has happened: "The field of speech reflects the thrust characteristic of contemporary academic disciplines—a moving out from its original center in expanding segments of specialized study. Speech also reveals, like other fields, increasing interaction with disciplines whose boundaries have widened to include aspects of speech behavior of particular interest to them" (Wallace, Smith & Weaver, 1963, p. 332).

In recent years, the scope of the field has broadened further. At the 1968 New Orleans Conference on Research and Instructional Development, behavoral scientists described the central focus of the field as "spoken symbolic interaction." While this focal point appeared to restrict inquiry to oral discourse, the authors of the conference report implied that this was not their intention. The term "central focus," they said, "does not represent an attempt to impose any rigid boundaries regarding the types or kinds of inquiry undertaken by scholars in this area of study" (Kibler & Barker, 1969, p. 19). Furthermore, the phrase "spoken symbolic interaction" "may be equivalent to symbolic interaction through speech, symbolic codes in speech interaction, or similar transformations" (Kibler & Barker, 1969, p. 19). As a result nonspoken discourse could be subsumed under the rubric of speech inquiry. Following this conference, the study of nonverbal communication by behavioral scientists in speech began to flourish, and the boundaries of the field expanded to accommodate the widespread interest in forms of symbolic interaction other than speech.

The trend toward more diffuse boundaries was further incited by the National Developmental Project on Rhetoric. At the Wingspread Conference held in January 1970, conference participants endorsed an enlarged definition of rhetorical studies. For the first time, rhetorical studies covered "all forms of human communication" and all modes of inquiry: "philosophical, historical, critical, empirical, creative, or pedagogical" (Ehninger, Benson, Ettlich, Fisher, Kerr, Larson, Nadeau & Niles, 1971). Specifically, conferees recommended that "the phrase 'rhetorical studies' be understood to include any human transaction in which symbols and/or systems of symbols influence values, attitudes, beliefs, and actions" (Ehninger et al., 1971, p. 214). The Committee on the Advancement and Refinement of Rhetorical Criticism filed a report at the Pheasant Run meeting in May 1970 that went even farther: "The effort should be made to expand the scope of rhetorical criticism to include subjects which have not traditionally fallen within the critic's purview: the non-discursive as well as the discursive, the nonverbal as well as the verbal, the event or transaction which is unintentionally as well as intentionally suasive . . . informal conversations, group settings, mass media messages, picketing, sloganeering, chanting, singing, marching, gesturing, ritual, institutional and cultural symbols, cross cultural transactions, and so forth" (Sloan et al., 1971, pp. 221, 225).

Ironically, two conferences that were convened largely for the purpose of defining the scope of the field in a manner that would decrease fragmentation and concentrate research efforts actually had the effect of blurring boundaries between speech communication and other fields. The behavioral scientists emphasized an extremely broad view of messages, while the humanists stressed persuasion without restricting the phenomena that could conceivably be viewed as persuasive. While these conferences can be credited with achieving a more attractive and socially significant vision of the field, they also had the effect of muddling distinctions between speech communication and other fields. "We are," wrote Becker shortly after the Wingspread Conference, "confounded by the lack of distinction between what we perceive to be part of our field and what others perceive to be part of the field of English, social psychology, linguistics, history, philosophy, journalism, or political science" (1974, p. 1).

COHERENCE AND COHESIVENESS

Here we shall briefly raise two questions: (1) How cohesive is the community of speech communication teachers and scholars and (2) to what extent is the field's subject matter coherent? We believe it is rather easy to establish that the field is largely noncohesive and only minimally coherent, though we do not see lack of coherence as necessarily unique or detrimental to the development of this discipline.

Cohesiveness is a measure of the amount of solidarity in the discipline, an estimate of its unity. To a certain extent all disciplines that divide their subject matter into areas of specialized focus (and we cannot think of any that do not) run the risk of losing a sense of singularity, a feeling of having more in common with associates in different areas of the same field than with colleagues in different fields. Some fields, however, seem much more adept than others at maintaining the appearance of unity even after they become highly differentiated. The American Psychological Association (APA), for example, gives its various audiences the distinct impression it represents a single field, though in reality the specialized research groups, interest groups, societies, cliques, claques, and areas represented by the APA demonstrate that the field is polymorphous and its subdivisions speak largely incommensurable languages (Koch, 1976). The APA, however, presents psychology as a monolithic field. This impression management not only enriches psychology's public image but also improves the membership's sense of identity. Most psychologists would not feel like a part of the field without belonging to the APA. Membership in the field is certified by membership in the APA, regardless of one's specialized interests.

What can be said for psychology cannot be said for speech communication. The field of speech is conspicuously noncohesive. This fact is clearly evident in the historical development of the national association. Instead of becoming an organization inspiring loyalty and certifying membership in the discipline, the national association developed a parochial focus unrepresentative of many factions of the field. Seeking a more cohesive affiliation, speech scientists and clinicians formed ASHA, teachers of theater arts formed AETA, and behavioral scientists formed NSSC, which later became ICA. Rather than remaining loyal to the national association, many members of these new organizations severed ties to it or never established them. Thus new teachers and scholars entered subareas of the discipline without identifying with the goals of the national association. As a result, the national association never established any significant political clout, and the profession was left without a single voice to speak for the discipline as a whole. Moreover, speech science, speech communication, communication, and theatre arts evolved more as segregated than as integrated fields. Subsequently, when new organizations were created, they developed without a sense of belonging to a larger, transcendent organization representative of the total spectrum of "communication study." For example, groups such as NAEB (broadcasting) and AEJ (journalism) developed autonomously and without feeling obliged to attach themselves to the national association.

This lack of cohesiveness so vividly reflected in the historical development of organizations representing the field is also evident in the way the study of speech (or communication) is structured in universities. There is very little consensus among universities about the kind of discipline this is—or even whether it is one discipline. Typically the Department of Speech is placed in the School of Liberal Arts or the College of Arts and Sciences. But in some universities it is grouped with the humanities or arts, while in others it is classified as a social or behavioral science. One can even find places in which some courses in the department fulfill humanities requirements, while other courses in the same department fulfill social science requirements. In some universities the speech science curriculum is divided from speech communication and located in a different college, usually in allied health; in others, speech science remains part of speech communication while operating autonomously. The structural relations between speech communication and theater arts reflect a similar pattern. Then there are those universities in which the study of speech or communication is not part of some other school but a college in its own right. Here again, a wide variety of structures can be identified: School of Communication, School of Communications, School of Speech, even Human Communication. Some of these schools cater almost entirely to professionally-oriented students; others exclusively focus on graduate education and research. Many of these house a Department of Speech; some do not. One can even find instances in which the Department of Speech resides outside the College of Communication(s).

These organizational patterns raise troubling questions about the field's coherence. Do the various parts of instruction and inquiry in speech communication fit together in some sensible and logical way? If so, what are the organizing principles or concepts that tie together such unique areas of inquiry as public address, dramatic arts, broadcasting, journalism, and organizational communication?

Testimony from leaders of the discipline in recent years leaves little doubt that the field yearns for coherence and is frustrated by its absence. Troubled by "growing fragmentation," Becker encouraged the field to reverse the trend by identifying the "central core of the field" by which he meant "the concepts which we perceive as fundamental" to the intellectual goals of the field, concluding that speech communication could not hope to achieve recognition as a legitimate discipline unless or until it determined what the central emphasis of the field should be (Cohen, 1975). This view was reinforced by Blankenship, who expressed uneasiness with the "lack [of] a commonly agreed upon central focus" and warned that "when the center does not hold, things fall apart" (Blankenship, 1978, pp. 1, 22). More recently, Anderson echoed the sentiments of his predecessors when he identified the search for commonalities that tie the divisions of the field together as the most pressing problem for the profession (Anderson, 1983).

The longing for coherence was fortified by sources outside the field as well, most notably Thomas Kuhn (1962). *The Structure of Scientific Revolutions*, Kuhn's tour de force, created the impression that a field of knowledge was unified (and hence coherent) to the extent it possessed a vocabulary universally applicable to the puzzles of the field. This interpretation of Kuhn's thesis inspired scholars in disciplines such as speech communication to seek a single "paradigm" capable of integrating the entire field. Since Kuhn seemed to favor "persuasion" over "proof," the search for a unifying "paradigm" became polemical and contentious. In the absence of clearly articulated criteria for arbitrating different interpretations of "the nature of man" or "the essence of communication," validity must rest almost entirely on belief. It is not surprising, then, that the pursuit of a unifying "perspective" encouraged the marketing of metatheories. Instead of unifying the field, the "paradigm-pushers," to use Koch's term, engaged in polemical research that changed few minds, and, ironically, seemed further to divide the field into polarized sects than to unify it around common goals (Bochner & Krueger, 1979).

Two questions need to be asked about this craving for coherence. First, is it realistic to strive for coherence? Can a field that defines its subject matter as all symbolic codes, all symbolic interaction, or persuasive phenomena, discursive and nondiscursive, reasonably expect to achieve coherence, eliminate fractionation, and become an integrated, unified discipline? Probably not. Koch argues that psychology, to take one example, would not suffer one crisis of confidence after another if the field would only abandon the expectation of becoming theoretically coherent and integrated. According to Koch (1976, pp. 490–491), "no large subdivision of inquiry, including physics, can [become coherent]" because coherence requires agreement on a single set of terms—a homogeneous language—by which all persons participating in the field communicate with and use to understand each other: "None of the currently institutionalized sciences form single, homogeneous language communities. Physicists in one empirical area do not necessarily fully 'understand' physicists in another; pathologists do not necessarily understand electro-physiologists, and so on. And within each scientific area, even when cut rather finely, one may distinguish disorderly 'hierarchies' of language communities: in the extreme case, there many be quite definite and unique observable properties and relations which only two men, perhaps working in the same laboratory, may be able to perceive, and denote by some linguistic expression" (Koch, 1976, p. 529).

The assumption that legitimate disciplines are or must be coherent is unfounded and chimerical. Becher's (1981) clever ethnographic study of six academic disciplines—physics, history, biology, sociology, mechanical engineering, and law—boldly exposes the illusory character of disciplinary coherence. Academics interviewed in this study were strongly committed to an ideal of "group solidarity"—what we have been calling cohesiveness—which gave them "a mystical notion of oneness" whether they were biologists, physicists, sociologists, or lawyers. At the same time, however, representative scholars in each discipline expressed concern over deep-seated divisions within their disciplines—rival factions, competing ideologies, contentiousness, extreme diversity, fragmentation, and breakdowns in communication across specialties. Becher reported that "nearly all of those interviewed were at pains to emphasize that their disciplines, even if unified, were far from being homogeneous unities. Some went out of their way to draw attention to the complexity and variety of the approaches adopted, and the lack of any simple rubric to describe the activity in which they were engaged" (1981, p. 115).

Not only is coherence an unrealistic objective but, even worse, the search for coherence militates against cohesion. Consider what happens when a discipline looks for a single framework, perspective, or paradigm capable of making the field as a whole seem coherent. Promoters of particularized points of view are given license to make outrageous claims about the range of issues to which their largely unspecified perspectives apply. Instead of achieving the consensus desired, this process facilitates polarization and antagonism. The field is divided into sects, which have the overall effect of inducing a messianic climate more appropriate to the goal of religious conversion than the objective of disciplinary unification.

It is our view that the goal of coherence facilitates a divisive process that not only fails to produce coherence but runs the very real risk of creating an atmosphere in which differences in point of view are not tolerated. To universalize a perspective is to ask that "reality-under-a-certain-description" be viewed as accommodating all possible descriptions of reality. By disavowing its relativity, such a claim assumes a privileged status that makes "all other descriptions unnecessary because it is incommensurable with them" (Rorty, 1979, p. 378). No field of knowledge has ever been able to settle on a final set of terms under which all its inquiry could be subsumed.

The study of organizations underscores the issues we are raising. For example, Etzioni (1960) has argued that it is unproductive to evaluate an organization against some "ideal" of performance that is, in principle, unreachable. The organization will always fall short and its identity will be weakened. Moreover, incomplete goal consensus is common to all organizations; a balance must be struck between coordination and consensus on the one hand and differentiation and idiosyncrasy on the other. Weick (1979) opposes consensus as an ideal for organizations because, as he sees it, the process by which consensus is achieved tends to escalate destructive conflict and limit creativity.

The position advanced here is that the development of a stronger and more respectable field rests more on cohesion than coherence. The aim should not be to arrive at a final set of terms by which the field can be understood and communicated but rather to tolerate differences and discourage privileged discourse. We turn next to a consideration of the barriers to cohesion.

ROADBLOCKS

In the previous section we attributed considerable importance to the lack of solidarity among individuals who consider themselves part of the field. We pointed out that one of the most significant barriers to the development of a sense of singularity is organizational, that is, the absence of a transcendent national organization capable of representing the discipline as a whole. Here we shall address two other barriers to cohesion. The first is principally an artifact of the historical development of speech communication: the division between humanistic (rhetorical) and scientific (communication) studies. The second stems from the autonomous and largely segregated evolution of mass communications: the division between mass communications and speech communication.

RHETORIC AND COMMUNICATION

Over the years, one of the most divisive controversies in the field has centered on the question of whether rhetorical studies and communication studies belong to one world or two (Arnold, 1972; Brockriede, 1971; Bowers, 1968; Miller, 1975; Snow, 1963; Williams, 1970). Few departments have been unaffected by this dispute. Many have experienced open hostility; some have opted for civil inattention; a few have settled for passive but peaceful disrespect. While this tussle may no longer resemble what Bryant once characterized as "a kind of warfare of new and old, of ancient and modern, of 'science and religion,' among the students of speech communication" (1971, p. 8), the rhetoric/communication schism still tends to pit one faction against the other and thereby disunite the field.

When we examine what scholars say about rhetoric and communication, we find a number of polarizing distinctions. Typically, rhetorical studies have been considered "humanistic," while communication studies have been classified as "scientific." Often rhetoric is called "traditional," while communication is referred to as "experimental." Sometimes rhetoricians are labeled "humanists," and communication researchers, "empiricists." There are even occasions when the rhetorician as "humanist" is contrasted against the communication scholar as "behaviorist."

When we look at what scholars do rather than what they say, we find that none of these maps fits the territory very well. First of all, many experimental studies were published in speech journals before the term "communication" gained widespread popularity (Thompson, 1967). Some scholars in the early years even referred to their research as "experimental rhetoric." Second, research on rhetoric often involves making inferences from observations. All such research is empirical. Critics of communication research have occasionally charged that research on communication has been carried out in the logical empiricist tradition, meaning that it adheres to the philosophical principles of positivism, particularly reductionism and the verifiability criterion of meaning. This view of communication research, however, has been forcefully debunked by Miller and Berger (1978). They showed that the terms (logical) "empiricist" and "behaviorist" cannot be meaningfully applied to any practicing communication researcher or any research program in the field. Indeed, the class of "behaviorist" communication researchers is vacant. Third, the literature presents many examples that discredit the typical distinctions drawn between rhetorical and communication studies: (1) rhetorical studies that attempt to generalize about rhetoric; (2) communication studies that do not measure variables quantitatively; (3) communication studies that are principally concerned with values; (4) rhetorical studies that employ scientific methods; and (5) communication studies that focus on "texts" of talk, conversation, or speech.

The point is that it has become increasingly difficult to erect an iron curtain between rhetorical studies and communication studies. The National Developmental Project on Rhetoric (Bitzer & Black, 1971) transformed the focus of rhetoric from a relatively static to a dynamic subject matter; from inquiry about rhetoric to inquiry about rhetorical transactions. This subtle maneuver shifted the focus of rhetorical studies to the realm of social studies. Perhaps this is why the old dichotomies seem so worn. The field has fundamentally altered and broadened what it wants to know about rhetoric.

These developments parallel what has been happening in other fields of "social" inquiry. Taxonomies of inquiry are being refigured. The humanities and social sciences are no longer inherently discontinuous—if they ever were—and this is so whether one considers method or mission. As Geertz reports, "rather than face an array of natural kinds, fixed types divided by sharp qualitative differences, we more and more see ourselves surrounded by a vast, almost continous field of variously intended and diversely constructed works we can order only practically, relationally, and as our purposes prompt us" (Geertz, 1980, p. 167). There is now, according to Geertz, a third world of inquiry resting somewhere between Snow's "two cultures" (Snow, 1963). As the definition of what it means to do scientific research has been liberalized and the conception of what a humanist is has become less certain, "third-world" scholars have been liberated from the constraints of scientific and humanistic dogma and freed to concern themselves with the methodological requirements of the particular questions they are seeking to answer.

While we can anticipate that rhetorical and communication studies will become increasingly "blurred genres" in the future, we do not expect all differences—ideological, methodological, and pedagogical to disappear. Arnold (1972) observed that scholars in rhetoric and communication seem to be "digging in the same turf," but they employ different jargon to describe what they dig up. What Arnold did not mention is that to the extent scholars in rhetoric and communication belong to different language communities, they occupy somewhat different worlds. Communication between these worlds is difficult, and it is unlikely that occupants of such different language communities can truly understand each other. The development of a third culture where the metaphors of humanistic and scientific world views merge is significant because it provides a place where tolerance can be encouraged and understanding achieved. But the field is too broad, too diverse, and too specialized to expect the entire discipline to form a homogeneous terministic culture. This variety does not mean the field is illegitimate. What it does mean is there will always be some tension, lack of understanding, and difficulty in communication among the subcultures comprising the field. All of the social studies experience these difficulties.

MASS COMMUNICATIONS AND SPEECH COMMUNICATION

In this chapter we have repeatedly referred to "the field" or "the discipline" as if there were one field or one discipline under which all the diverse inquiry on speech and communication could sensibly be placed. However, the study of communication (to use the broader term) has not evolved institutionally as a single field but as two autonomous fields: mass communications and speech communication. The two fields sprouted from different intellectual seeds. Over the years, they have maintained separate organizational structures and engaged in little, if any, cross-fertilizing interactions. Scholars socialized in mass communications programs would, with few exceptions, be unfamiliar with the events we have reviewed in this paper.

Carey's (1979) description of the haphazard development of mass communications sheds light on why the fields developed autonomously. The early departments of journalism had something in common with speech. Both were committed to the teaching of practical skills, and both were the products of rebellions within English. Until the years immediately following World War II, there was no instruction in "mass communications." The only comparable courses were in radio or broadcasting within speech and in print media within journalism.

The social problems connected with the transition from war to peace inspired a series of studies, conducted near the end of the war, that laid the foundation for mass communications as a discipline. Hovland's group at Yale (Hovland, Lumsdaine & Sheffield, 1949) and Lazarsfeld's team at Columbia (Lazarsfeld, Berelson & Gaudet, 1948) produced the memorable studies from which mass communications originated. These studies introduced a new vocabulary that emphasized and gave legitimacy to communication theory and mass communications. Within a few short years, these studies were considered the seminal works in the new field of mass communications.

Unlike speech and journalism, which began without a strong foundation of original scholarship, mass communications was formed after the publication of these pioneering studies. The problem was where to place mass communications in the curriculum. Carey contends that mass communications was absorbed by journalism because speech was more secure about its humanistic heritage. Journalism, on the other hand, needed the scientific legitimacy that mass communications could bring it. Thus, mass communications became part of journalism, ultimately the larger part, and was constituted not as an adjunct to speech but as an option: "There were now options to studying speech, or rhetoric, or drama—one could now study communications" (Carey, 1979, p. 27).

These events produced a number of unfortunate consequences. First, mass communications developed a narrow scientific orientation (Carey, 1979). Operating as an almost entirely autonomous enterprise, mass communications was unaffected by the philosophical controversies and paradigm clashes characteristic of other social sciences in the 1970s. Carey believes this isolationism stifled the development of new perspectives. As a result, the intellectual issues remain largely what they were when the field commenced (Carey, 1979). Second, the meanings of communication theory have been muddled. While both fields share an interest in and a commitment to the development of communication theory, they tend to view the content of communication theory very differently. In speech communication, mass communications is seen as a minor part of communication theory, whereas in mass communications the part often is viewed as the whole. Students drawn to communication study by an interest in mass media usually do not become concerned with theory development until or unless they are exposed to the broader views of communication theory presented in speech communication courses. Third, there is little interaction across the boundaries. Reeves and Borgman (1983) studied the citation patterns in the major journals in both fields and found that speech communication and mass communications formed discrete communication networks. In view of the growing interest in media criticism among rhetoricians and the emphasis on cultural studies among "new wave" scholars in mass communications, this finding is alarming.

The political exigencies that made it expedient for mass communications to develop within departments of journalism no longer justify—if they ever did—the seclusion of one branch of communication study from the other. Assuming speech communication has overcome its resistance to the postwar infatuation for quantitative studies, and mass communications has recognized the promise of formal and cultural studies, the time would seem right for increased interaction across the divide. Greater contact between mass communications and speech communication could result in a whole that is greater than the sum of its parts, and at the very least, would open up new vistas for communication research and provoke an enlarged sense of singularity.

PAST AND FUTURE

The main problem we have been concerned with is legitimation. How can speech communication be better understood and respected by other disciplines? And how can the field improve its own self-image? Looking over the field's development in the 20th century, we found three typical attacks on the legitimation problem. First, the field has attempted to establish its distinctness by stipulating a definition that could differentiate the study of speech communication within the field from related inquiry in other fields. Second, the field has tried to upgrade standards of scholarship so that research in speech communication would compare more favorably with scholarship in more recognized disciplines. Third, the field has searched for a core set of concepts that would tie together the fragmented divisions within the field and make the study of speech communication more coherent. These strategies have not been successful. The field is no better understood than it ever was and its self-image has not markedly improved over the years. The developments we have described strongly suggest, in fact, that the field has become less distinct and less coherent and is no more confident about the significance of its scholarship than it was in the past. If these are the paths to legitimation, the likelihood of success seems remote indeed.

We do not see these facts as cause for alarm. Placed in the context of the ways in which universities evolved during the late 19th and early 20th centuries, the difficulties encountered by speech communication become quite understandable. The disciplines that became departmentalized during this period came into existence as a result of social conflicts rather than epistemological mandates. Universities and colleges were divided into departments unsystematically and with little concern for how the new disciplines would ultimately be related or separated. The divisions separating anthropology, sociology, psychology, and later on, human relations, speech, social work, etcetera, were arbitrary and without rational foundations. As time passed, departments came to symbolize disciplines and, for all practical purposes, disciplines were seen as embodied in departments.

This chaotic organization of disciplines produced some regrettable consequences. Separated arbitrarily from each other, the new departments became rivals for possession of some of the same subject matter. Some disciplines achieved a mandate to investigate particular subjects by means of particular methods, but none of them became mutually exclusive and/or exhaustive.

The point is that none of these fields can convincingly establish its inherent distinctiveness or coherence and each one has openly expressed doubts about the significance of its scholarship. Nevertheless, some disciplines are more vulnerable than others. There is no getting around the fact that when resources become scarce and program review committees begin nominating departments for extinction, speech communication is one of the first departments threatened. We have been arguing that this vulnerability is owing more to political factors than ontological ones. All of the fields of social study are divided between humane and scientific interests and each one suffers from fragmentation, incoherence, and doubtful significance. The difference is that some disciplines have been able to create an impression that they are distinct and coherent, even though they are not. The fields that are perceived as monolithic and solitary disciplines are rarely threatened. Those that fail to manifest these impressions are never secure.

The rivalry for students, research funds, and support services has only decreased what little chance there ever was for mutual understanding and respect among the isolated tribes of the academy. With few exceptions, hardly anyone really respects disciplinary boundaries. The competition for resources and survival, however, has encouraged certain disciplines to attempt to exert control over subject matter that does not belong to any single discipline. As a result, suggests Wax (1969), the problem in the social sciences now is not too much overlap but too little. And the gaps between disciplines promoted by departmental competition only intensify this difficulty. In the long run, what could possibly be gained by making communication theory, to take one example, the sole province of one discipline? Would scholars in other disciplines who were interested in communication theory respect this decision? Would they be forced to change disciplines?

It is our contention that the field's approach to the problem of legitimation has been mistaken. Instead of trying to measure up to an ideal of what disciplines ought to be, the field should take a hard look at what disciplines really are. The established social fields are not the coherent, distinct, and scholarly enterprises they seem to be, but they do possess one characteristic that is sorely lacking in speech communication—that "mystical sense of oneness" discussed by Becher (1981).

The field should strive for greater cohesiveness because it would make communication study more politically effective, both locally and nationally. To achieve greater cohesiveness it will be necessary to create a climate in which differences will be tolerated and common goals promoted. There is a need for a single, transcendent national organization that can forcefully represent the discipline as a whole; and it would certainly help to have a covering term—preferably "communication"—that would be applied universally as the name of the discipline. We believe these are sensible goals to work toward because each segment of the field could benefit without sacrificing anything substantial. Considering what communication study in all its diversity is really about, we can find no better tactic than increased cohesiveness for strengthening the position of our discipline in the academy.

16

The Rise and Fall
of Departments

THOMAS F. MADER,
LAWRENCE W. ROSENFIELD, AND
DIANE C. MADER

One of our respondents complained about the title of this chapter: "'Rise and Fall' suggests to me the fate of the Roman Empire. . . . I refuse to encourage any inference that our departments are bound to fail." Because a number of respondents felt that such might be our inference, we want to assure the reader that we are not grim determinists. Our project was (1) to summarize briefly the spread and development of speech/communication departments in higher education,* (2) to determine those factors that contribute to the maintenance and growth of speech/communication departments and those factors that weaken and sometimes destroy departments.

In regard to our second purpose, our approach was twofold. First, we interviewed more than 60 faculty members, chairpersons, and deans throughout the country. The interviews, which were conducted either by phone or in person, lasted from 45 minutes to 4 hours and covered a wide range of topics. Before these interviews, we sent a letter to all intended interviewees explaining the purpose of our project; in addition, the letter contained a list of questions that we asked each person to ponder (see Appendix). Second, we contacted William Work and Robert Hall at the

---

*We chose "speech/communication" to represent speech departments, speech communication departments, communication departments, and departments that have both speech areas and communication areas, as well as departments with these terms in their title: communication studies, communications, communication arts, rhetoric.

national headquarters of the Speech Communication Association to gain access to the SCA archives on departmental self-examinations and studies pertaining to departments that have faced, or are facing, crises. We then analyzed what information we had accumulated from the interviews and from SCA. In regard to interviews, we chose excerpts that either represented a consensus or seemed incisive and original. The SCA material provided us with a reference point as far as it confirmed or questioned what our respondents told us. For the most part, the SCA studies and the perceptions of our respondents were consonant.

We assured our respondents that they would remain anonymous. At the same time, we do not believe we violate any confidence by noting that the people we contacted are well-known in the field, and that many of them serve or have served as chairs of departments or as college deans. In addition, the willingness of the people we contacted to speak openly and at length on a variety of issues allowed us to give structure to a project that we sometimes felt was unmanageable. In many ways, their insights guided us in determining how to develop this chapter.

We have divided the chapter into three parts, and each part deals with a question: (1) Where did we start? (2) Where are we? (3) What questions need answers?

WHERE DID WE START?

Donald K. Smith notes that "In 1900 there were no departments of speech [but] . . . after the turn of the century, separate departments of speech appeared in a majority of American institutions of higher education" (Smith, pp. 447, 449). There appear to be four reasons for the birth of speech departments. First, in the 19th century the dominant interests of English departments were compostion, literature, and language. Second, public speaking became subordinate to these new interests and therefore something of an afterthought. Third, whatever the emphasis of English departments, students demanded instruction in public speaking, argumentation, and debate. Fourth, speech professors were not happy being members of English departments that merely tolerated what they were doing (Smith, pp. 453–464). James Winans complained that "Public Speaking is made secondary to English. . . . Many heads of English departments refuse to promote teachers of public speaking" (Rarig and Greaves, p. 498). And Charles Woolbert argued that speech and English were "essentially different disciplines" (Smith, p. 456).

The Public Speaking Conference of New England and North Atlantic States on March 25, 1913, resolved that "[D]epartments of Public Speaking in American colleges should be organized entirely separate from departments of English" (Lyon, p. 46). The Conference was formed in 1910 and was the forerunner of the Eastern Communication Association. The following year, 17 professors of speech left the National Countil of Teachers of English Convention, moved to another hotel, and issued a manifesto declaring their independence from English departments (Weaver, pp. 195–199). "The decisive action of the men who framed the first charter of the association led ultimately to the present program of speech in America. The founders offered a new focus for the relatively random efforts of teachers and associations that had for twenty-five years or more striven, with occasional success, to unify, to place on a solid foundation, and to give academic stature to training in speech which was something more than elocution" (Rarig & Greaves, p. 500).

WHERE ARE WE?

The 1983 SCA Directory listed 1,620 departments of speech/communication in colleges and universities in the 50 states, the District of Columbia, Guam, Puerto Rico, the Virgin Islands, Canada, and Japan. Student interest in speech/communication seems to be at an all-time high. At least one institution has over 900 majors; any number of institutions have from 100 to 600 majors. In fact, speech/communication has become so popular that some departments of necessity have raised standards to limit the number of students majoring in the field: "We don't have sufficient staff to handle the demand. And our administration isn't giving us more money to increase staff. As a matter of survival, we have become very selective." Another respondent said, "If we raise standards any higher, we'll have the equivalent of an honors program." Two respondents reported that a large number of honors program students in their institutions major in speech/communication "because ours is the best department in the college."

Speech/communication appears to thrive in public institutions in all parts of the country. In regard to private institutions, speech/communication seems to do best in the Midwest, followed by the South and the West. In the East, speech/communication seems to lack a tradition—or has a tradition limited to a skills orientation, primarily to prepare students for teaching licenses in public schools. But in all areas of the country, the profession appears to be in a tremendously healthy state.

On the debit side, speech/communication has not done well in Ivy League colleges and colleges labeled "minor Ivy League." Harvard, Yale, and Princeton used to offer courses in speech/communication; they no longer do. Dartmouth College has a three-person department, although Dartmouth's focus is on intercollegiate debate. The University of Pennsylvania has the Annenberg School of Communication, which is limited to media studies. Cornell disbanded its Department of Speech in 1967, although there is presently a Department of Communication Arts in the College of Agriculture and Life Sciences. Amherst, Williams, and Wesleyan eliminated their departments in the 1960s. Mount Holyoke and Smith dispensed with their speech/communication staffs around the same time. Hamilton College in New York has a three-person department that seems in fine shape, yet Hamilton no longer requires students to take four years of speech, as it once did. And our respondent from Hamilton said that the program in speech/communication is not viewed enthusiastically by members of other departments. However, Hamilton maintains its tradition of offering courses in rhetoric and public speaking, and the tradition has strong support from alumni.

Staff from SCA told us that about 15 departments have been eliminated since 1968; another dozen or so departments are labeled "distressed." We talked to people who were members of departments no longer in existence, and we spoke to people who presently are in "distressed" departments (our interviewees volunteered the information that their departments were facing crises). We also spoke to people whose departments had faced the threat of annihilation and had survived. And we spoke to people whose departments are highly respected by administrators, students, and faculty—departments that are stable, successful, and rather sure of the future.

These discussions provided us with strong hints about why a department fails or becomes distressed. "Strong hints," however, do not provide us with clear cause-and-effect relationships, and so we make no claims to uncovering the mystery underlying the rise and fall of any department. But it is apparent that part of the mystery can be explained by looking at the role of administrators in determining the fate of a department.

THE INFLUENCE OF ADMINISTRATORS

Self-study reports or postmortems by disbanded or threatened departments detail negative attitudes on the part of a key administrator. These reports identify at least four reasons for an administrator's hostility or antipathy toward a department.

First, the administrator desires to place his or her mark on an institution. Generally, this means the administrator is new to the institution and is looking for ways of making the institution more efficient by eliminating "weak" departments, departments whose academic worth is questionable. For example, a study of a Department of Speech and Drama in a middle-sized university that was eventually transformed into a Department of Drama says that "In 1946 the Department of Speech and Drama . . . listed 76 courses in the catalogue and a faculty of ten. . . . By 1954 the catalogue listed some 126 courses. 40 percent of the courses were in drama, 20 percent in speech correction, [and] 20 percent in rhetoric, public speaking, and oral interpretation. / In 1956 a new dean was appointed . . . The dean came to the university . . . to make the university one of the best in the country. Departments were encouraged to seek national reputations through new appointments" (March and Romelaer, pp. 254–255). However, all new appointments in the speech program were on the instructor or acting assistant professor level, even though there was a Ph.D. program in speech. Tenured professors in the program who retired or died were not replaced. Given this situation, it is not surprising that in 1963 the program's faculty was informed by an associate dean that "the situation obtaining in the Speech program was unprecedented in University practice—namely, that work on the graduate level was being directed by a group of faculty members not one of whom had been carrying on an active program of research and publication such as is usually involved in graduate teaching and one of whom had not yet completed the work for his Ph.D. degree" (March & Romelaer, pp. 256–257). By 1964 there was no doctoral program in speech, and by 1968 there was no program in speech at all.

Second, the administrator is under pressure to cut costs. Our respondents noted cost as a significant problem. Most often when departmental costs are calculated, the budget is for classroom instruction, administration, and supplies. This kind of budgeting can work to the disadvantage of a speech/communication department. For example, a physics department may require much more extensive capital costs or support services, yet such costs may not show up as directly in the budget analysis. In addition, speech/communication departments that offer multiple sections in public speaking, voice and articulation, and small group communication, must of necessity limit enrollment in each of these sections. (Many respondents claimed that the move away from skills courses was a response to the cost factor rather than a concern for offering more academically reputable courses. As one respondent commented, "you can't teach public speaking to 400 students, but you can offer a mass lecture in some theory course.")

Third, the administrator needs to find resources to expand new areas of knowledge, such as those pertaining to technology. Few of our respondents commented on this problem, although one indicated that, in his situation, "the computer may be our undoing." However, a number of respondents expressed anxiety about the proliferation of areas of study in a host of institutions, primarily to meet the demands of students who are career-oriented. As one respondent said, "It's ironic that with the decline in student population, there has been a rise in the variety of offerings colleges make to this shrinking universe. It's difficult to see that this kind of academic smorgasbord can last."

Fourth, the administrator does not understand what speech/communication is. This lack of understanding is generally expressed in two questions: What is distinctive about speech/communication as a discipline? Whatever speech/communication is, does it not overlap what is being done in other units of the institution? Admittedly, these questions may be, as one of our respondents alleged, "more of a ploy to justify eliminating the department rather than an expression of administrative ignorance. That would seem to be the case when the department has been around for some time."

DANGER SIGNALS

While hostile or unsympathetic administrators undoubtedly play a significant role in the demise of departments, other factors seem equally significant, factors that we label "danger signals." What are the danger signals?

First, departments subject to administrative scrutiny generally have shrunk to fewer than 10 full-time faculty members. This reduction might imply that the department was attracting fewer students and thus has become vulnerable to administrative attack. Or it might mean that the department attracts as many or even more students than before but now carriers a much heavier load. Whatever the case, the department is in an impossible situation if the administration sees it as a target. A department that by choice or necessity takes on heavier loads might be viewed by the administration as not doing a quality job. Two departments whose self-studies we examined tried to provide service courses to their respective universities, an undergraduate program, and a graduate program. Both were staffed by a small faculty. The result was that in one department there was an average of 80 students in senior seminars and in the other department an average of 200 students in senior seminars. One of the departments had a 42:1 student-faculty ratio. Yet both departments, despite their incredible loads, had respectable records in research and publication.

Second, departments tempt administrative attack when faculty members engage in internecine warfare. N. Edd Miller notes that "[Intradepartmental friction] may exist simply because of mysterious interpersonal difficulties or it may be there because a department houses disparate families (rhetoric, theatre, speech therapy, radio-television) or it may result from differences in philosophy and goals of members of the department" (Miller, p. 1). Of five institutions with a history of intradepartmental friction, two no longer exist, two survived in weakened condition, and one is still regarded as "distressed." Although a number of our respondents said that there are a few outstanding departments that experience interpersonal tensions as a matter of course, most respondents agreed that "communication breakdowns" seemed inappropriate to our profession. In addition, respondents said that a number of defunct departments, or departments forever facing crises, seemed to have staff members lacking common sense, people who had a "death wish," a yearning for a way "to rationalize self-doubts by destroying everything and everyone who contributed to those feelings of personal inadequacy." On the positive side, one respondent said, "The stable departments have faculties that operate as a team, each contributing the skills needed for good teaching and superior scholarship. And all of them are granted the status and respect due one who performs well."

Third, departments that have uninspired leadership are prime targets for administrative scrutiny. One respondent said that "In the case of two major universities, the administration and/or faculty committees made weak appointments to chairs and allowed mediocrity to spread. Then they judged the departments unfit to survive. . . . The two chairs alluded to . . . alienated both colleagues and superior officers." Other respondents summed up poor leadership this way:

1. A chair who is no more than an executive secretary has no sense of mission and no sense of direction. Chairing is more than a chore; it requires imagination as well as efficiency.
2. Chairs who do no research or publication and who do not keep up with the field are in no position to explain speech/communication.
3. Chairs who construe effective leadership as blindly pacifying the demands of administrators tend to exploit and demoralize their faculties without actually satisfying administrative demands.

CONFLICT RESOLUTION

Yet despite administrative hostility or inept leadership, a number of distressed departments (the number, as far as we can tell, is not large) have survived by rising above internal bickering and uniting against the "common enemy," educating administrators about the importance of the discipline, and cultivating their constituencies.

First, the need to rise above internal bickering certainly seems evident, but our study indicates that this is not an easy accomplishment: "There is so much ego involved when people are petty. And for a professional to admit being petty seems to void one's claim to professionalism." Another respondent noted that "for staff members who believe they are secure because of tenure or reputation, the needs of the commonweal may seem beneath contempt. Sometimes you have to convince them that institutional earthquakes are no respecters of tenure, not when the survival of a department is in question."

Second, a concern for personal survival combined with an insight into one's professional commitment should enable the department to expend its energies on reports justifying the quality, cohesiveness, and significance of the discipline. This is a matter of educating administrators. This type of positive action may, as a number of respondents suggested, change the position of the department from defense to offense, because staff members themselves begin to appreciate the worth of what they are doing. In addition, the crisis may enable staff members to see beyond themselves and the department and focus on the needs of the institution. As one respondent said, "Sometimes we are so preoccupied with our survival that we don't see the whole picture. Colleges and universities are undergoing terrific stress and change. We have to adapt—we have to determine where we fit in and how we can spell this out to administrators." Equally important, crisis may force a department to discuss, criticize, and restructure its goals, procedures, and curriculum in light of the need to explain the coherence of the discipline and the staff's appreciation of how each faculty member contributes to that coherence. Educating administrators, in other words, may be a means by which departments educate themselves.

Third, a number of departments faced with crisis cultivated their constituencies. It has become a truism that departments faced with extinction abruptly discover the need to mobilize their various groups of supporters if they have any hope of averting disaster. Flourishing departments seem to identify these constituencies as a matter of course, and such departments establish a clear, enduring understanding of the relationship of a department to its supporters. Other than seeking out administrators knowledgeable about and sympathetic to speech/communication, three constituencies seem primary: current and former students, colleagues in other disciplines, and the civic community. We shall consider the significance of each of these constituencies in turn.

Although students do not generally have a formal voice in a department, their allegiance to the department obviously can be helpful. The best way of ensuring student allegiance is for the staff to do a great job of teaching. In this regard, speech/communication professors usually come off rather well; perhaps this is why student protest in a number of cases prevented dismemberment of a department (this is evident from a number of case studies). But students are, as students, not a legitimate demographic class in that they are, as one respondent put it, "merely sojourners, temporary visitors in the Academy." It is when these students become alumni that they can best be considered a constituency in a political sense.

The department's ability to maintain contact with and draw upon its alumni is a source of strength that the better-run departments capitalize upon. They serve their graduates by sending them periodic newsletters and by providing job-placement services. In addition, strong departments en-

courage students to become members of national and regional organizations and to continue their memberships as alumni. Through membership in
a professional association, alumni keep in touch with one another and with
the institution. In short, the sense of continuity and participation is a
reminder of worthwhile experiences, experiences that owe their source to a
particular department.

The speech/communication department's second constituency is faculty in other disciplines. Dealing with this constituency, as our respondents
indicate, can be a touchy issue. Faculty outside our discipline may support
us for the wrong reasons: "We teach students how to speak correctly, but
some peoples' notions of correctness are extreme. And there are faculty
members in other disciplines who have peculiar standards for effective
communication." Or faculty in other areas may support us for the right
reasons, but may be unrealistic. As one respondent complained: "[Our
institution] believes that speech is tremendously important because we
teach our students how to think, how to write, how to take notes, how to do
research, how to develop a personality, and how to speak. We do our best.
But we have over 30 students in our public speaking classes. We have money
problems. So far, no one has noticed that we're not doing quite what they
[the faculty] expect."

A number of respondents indicated that they are trying hard to deal
with the expectations of faculty in other disciplines by achieving a balance
between theory and practice, and between the need for small classes for
skills and the large classes for theory. One respondent commented, "Ideally,
all of our classes should be small. Realistically, we have to accede to budget
limitations."

Beyond their perceiving what we do in our discipline, colleagues in
other disciplines probably note what we do as members of the college
community. Do we serve on committees? Do we exert influence on what is
happening in the college? Do we communicate to people outside our department? Do we practice what we preach?

College service, however, was a debatable point. One chair said that he
tells his staff to avoid college committees "because they are a waste of time.
They should spend their time doing research and writing." He heads a
department that has done well and that achieved renown. On the other
hand, many chairs indicated that college service was "absolutely essential."
As one of them said, "We are people dedicated to communication. If we
can't communicate with our colleagues in other disciplines, or if we imply
that communication isn't important in our own community, why are we
doing what we're doing?" On the one hand, some respondents said that
teaching, writing, and research—without any other activity—are the key to
personal and departmental survival, a somewhat monastic view that has
apparently served some departments well. On the other hand, respondents

claimed that involvement in the college community was not only vital but also appropriate.

Finally, in regard to the civic community as a constituency, many of our respondents saw the civic community as a significant supportive base, yet one that we do not seem to appreciate adequately. As one respondent noted, "We simply do not make use of those people in the town or city who have high regard for the importance of speech. In fact, when people tell us how important speech is we seem embarrassed, as though we weren't convinced ourselves." Another respondent said that "Given our discipline, we have a commitment to do everything within our power to *move* people. We should be active in the academic and social community. We ought to set a standard for effective decisionmaking that others can follow. We should be models of persuasiveness. Isn't that what we profess?" But despite this concern for civic responsibility and influence, we were left with the suspicion that people in our discipline do not make much of an impact on the civic community. In fact, the civic community (which, incidentally, includes parents of students) was the one constituency that distressed departments cultivated least.

WHAT QUESTIONS NEED ANSWERS?

Departments that are under fire invariably are confronted with these two questions:

1. How do you define the discipline?
2. What significant intellectual contributions are members of your profession proud of?

In regard to defining the discipline, three subquestions primarily concerned our respondents:

a. Has the tendency to separate into departments of theatre/drama, speech correction/communication science, and speech/communication (or communication arts, communications, human communication, rhetoric) weakened or strengthened the discipline?

b. Has the evolving of "speech" into "speech communication" or "communication" helped to define the discipline more clearly?

c. Can we eliminate (rather than solve) the problem of defining the discipline by claiming to be an interdisciplinary area of study?

In regard to significant intellectual contributions, two subquestions were emphasized by our respondents:

a. What is the importance and relevance of our research and writing?

b. Has our identification with intercollegiate debate strengthened or weakened our academic reputation?

While all of these questions pertain to one's perspective on the profession, the answers provide college administrators with some idea of whether a department knows where it is going. It is for this reason that we will consider what our respondents said about our (1) identification as a discipline and (2) contributions to the academic world.

IDENTIFICATION: HOW WE SEE OURSELVES

Under this heading, there are three questions we need to consider.

1. Has the tendency to separate weakened or strengthened the discipline?

C. M. Wise noted more than 30 years ago that "the splitting, seceding, splintering, or fragmentation at the national and regional levels is being reflected at the departmental level, where the actual damage is serious" (Bagwell, p. 337). Wise's reference was to the separation of theatre from speech, and then the separation of speech into arts (rhetoric, public address) and sciences (speech correction and audiology).

Some of our respondents did not share Wise's anxiety about "fragmentation." Those who favored separation into distinct areas of study did so for the following reasons:

a. Separation is a sign that we have come to recognize what makes us distinctive from one another. This means that we have (each of us) developed a focus that enables us to specialize and avoid the pitfalls of being dilettantes. ("Dilettantes coach debate, direct two plays a year, teach three preparations, head the speech clinic, do no research, and write no articles. They are well-intentioned and energetic people who should be teaching high school students.")

b. Separation eliminates tensions that arise when staff in different areas begin to argue about allocation of resources.

c. Separation acknowledges that the language we speak is the same, but that the dialects are different. ("Speech correction is as different from rhetoric as theatre is from English, and it is useful to recognize this difference.")

Although there were more respondents who favored separation, there were nearly as many who did not favor separation, and the latter group were more emphatic in presenting their views. The case against separation is as follows:

a. Academically, separation ignores what we have in common and therefore discourages dialogue. ("Separation is similar to the blind men trying to describe the elephant, each coming up with a definition limited to the part of the elephant he could feel. The result is that each definition is a distortion, rather than a piece of the truth that collectively might give us a fairly good idea of the elephant.")

b. Administratively, "big" is more efficient and therefore less costly. Three or four separate departments means three or four chairs, each with their own administrative assistants.

c. Pragmatically, "big" is "better." A department that houses numerous areas of study will have a larger faculty, which means potentially more influence in the institution.

2. Has the evolving of "speech" into "speech communication" or "communication" helped to define the discipline more clearly?

Respondents indicted that this was a big issue in interpreting the meaning of our discipline. Since we did not do a statistical study, the best we can offer is an intuition that 45% are loyal to "speech" (variations: rhetoric, public speaking, public address, a combination of the aforementioned), 45% approve the transformation of "speech" into "speech communication" or "communication" or "communication studies," and 10% had no opinion.

Respondents who favored "speech communication" or "communication" over "speech" offered these reasons:

a. Speech implies an emphasis on skills and techniques, which are low-level matters of academic concern. Speech/communication implies that the discipline has specific content. Our inability to identify the content of our field as more than rhetoric and rhetorical theory has been one of our weaknesses.

b. "Communication" has an aura of respectability about it that "speech" does not. ("With due respect to Korzybski, the word is the thing. Speech is an activity, like eating and drinking. Communication is a field of study.").

c. Speech/communication has expanded the horizons of both scholars and students and has helped them to see the relevance of theory to practice.

d. Speech/communication allows us to incorporate media studies into the discipline.

Respondents who did not favor the shift from "speech" to "speech communication" or "communication" said the following:

a. We have moved too far away from the rhetorical tradition, one that stressed the importance of teaching students to speak well. ("Do you know there are so-called communication departments that do not offer a single course in public speaking? All they do is talk about communication. Can you imagine the Art department doing nothing more than talking about art?")

b. Rather than making clear what we really do that distinguishes us from other departments, we have confused the issue by identifying our interests with those of sociology, pyschology, political science, and anthropology. In addition, our fascination with the social sciences is moving us away from our humanistic origins and toward a behavioral orientation.

c. Speech/communication deemphasizes the importance and relevance of rhetoric at a time when scholars in English and philosophy have discovered not only the significance of rhetoric but also our contributions to maintaining the rhetorical tradition.

One respondent who was tentative about the move from "speech" to "speech/communication" said that the change has been a "mixed blessing. On the one hand, it gives us the latitude to examine speech more exhaustively. On the other hand, the term is so broad that just about everything comes under the aegis of communication." Another respondent expressed uneasiness about the proliferation of titles, which she claimed "could get embarrassing. Whatever we call ourselves, we ought to settle on one title. Speech, speech communication, communication, communication arts, human communication, communication studies, or rhetoric. But one title." Two respondents who were totally opposed to any move from "speech" said the following:

a. "[The name changing] simply continues our hollow tradition of faddishness."

b. "[Communication] doesn't point to what we do; it merely conceals what we haven't done well."

Some respondents felt that, in regard to their departments, the shift to speech communication or communication was their "salvation." Others who had made the shift to one of the new titles were satisfied that they had done so, but indicated that a number of departments on their campuses are becoming sensitive to territoriality: "Getting new courses through a divisional curriculum committee is more of an uphill battle than it ever was. All departments are concerned about shrinking enrollment and don't like the idea that they must now compete with a department that possibly overlaps their area of interest. And it increases the anxiety of these departments when they realize that we have more majors than they do."

3. Can we eliminate (rather than solve) the problem of defining the discipline by claiming to be an indisciplinary area of study?

For some respondents, "interdisciplinary" had favorable connotations because "interdisciplinary" implied that the speech discipline was thereby acknowledged. As one respondent commented, "I think it's pefectly fine if I team-teach a course with someone in psychology or philosophy—which I've done. This sort of thing suggests that I have a perspective different from a person in another discipline, and that this perspective is useful to students." For other respondents, "interdisciplinary" had less favorable connotations, primarily because they saw "interdisciplinary" as a code word suggesting that "since everyone is concerned about communication, no one can make a claim to communication as his or her field of study."

Probably the most interesting aspect of this question dealt with what our specific "contribution" is to communication. In other words, when someone in speech or speech communication is asked to partake in an interdisciplinary venture, what is the expertise of the person in speech? On the whole, the answers were (1) rhetoric (2) persuasion (3) political speaking. One respondent said that he had been asked by the classics department to teach a course in classical rhetoric because "no one in classics understood what rhetoric meant, but given that Aristotle and Plato spent their time debating about rhetoric, students in classics ought to know something about rhetoric."

The interdisciplinary question raised a side issue that for some respondents was a major issue: "Should speech or speech/communication departments hire people whose doctorates are in another field?" Most respondents felt that this practice was unwise, an indictment of the field, and "suicidal." One respondent noted that "Hiring someone from another discipline says that we don't have people in our area competent to deal with certain subject matter, even though this subject matter is pertinent to what we do. This is absurd. If we have a discipline, then we have people who are able to teach within this discipline. If not, we're asking for trouble." By contrast, another respondent said, "We tried for a long time to find someone in speech who was an expert in research methods. We couldn't find anyone, and we really bent over backwards. We hired a person in political science, the best person who applied for the job. We're pleased with him, but we're not pleased that no one in our field could compete with him."

For some respondents, hiring someone with a doctorate outside speech or speech/communication indicated an obsession with approval or legitimation: "What the department is saying is that someone in a legitimate field is willing to teach in our department. Therefore, the administration should take our field seriously." Respondents who had had experience with colleagues possessing degrees outside the field indicated (on the whole) that these people were "outstanding." One respondent said, "We tried for a long time to prove that what we were doing was worth doing. We even had a respectable publication record. But we had no star, no one who was known for doing something that caught the attention of people in other disciplines. We hired a star, but he was a sociologist, with a decent interest in communication." Our interviews indicated that hiring someone outside the field of speech or speech/communication may be justified, but such procedure should be the exception. Should it become the rule, our discipline would disappear.

CONTRIBUTIONS TO THE ACADEMIC WORLD

1. What is the importance and relevance of our research and writing?

There seemed to be general agreement that our research and writing has become more sophisticated than it was a number of years ago. Respondents were impressed with the expertise demonstrated by many of the writers in our field. Some respondents were optimistic that we would eventually arrive at a breakthrough: "We don't presently have a Chomsky or a Freud or a McLuhan, someone who originates rather than expands upon. But we won't have to wait long for a seminal thinker to arrive on the scene." (One respondent claimed Chomsky and McLuhan as members of our discipline; another made a similar claim for Kenneth Burke). Respondents especially seemed impressed with the work done in the behavioral and experimental areas: "*Communication Monographs, Human Communication Research*, and our regional journals have a coherence and a sense of professionalism that imply confidence and imagination."

Respondents who were critical of the research and writing done in the field said the following:

a. We write few books, and the ones that are written are generally explications of original research done by people in other fields.

b. Behavioral and experimental articles do not significantly advance knowledge in our field. The conclusions are usually predictable and in many cases trivial.

All respondents acknowledged the importance of writing and research to improving the reputation of the discipline and, by extension, the significance of departments. At the same time, respondents noted, with some frustration, that despite our enormous output, (1) we are not read by people in other fields and (2) we are not read by administrators "upon whom our lives depend." Again, it is difficult to tell whether these complaints are true, although as one respondent noted, "Our book reviewers ritualistically complain that the latest anthology on communication failed to include a single article by someone in our field." And a few respondents pointed to our being rejected over and over again by the American Council of Learned Societies "because presumably we do not meet their standards for research and scholarship." The overall feeling seems to be that people in our field have become enormously sensitive to the need for excellence in research and writing, that we are on the way to achieving excellence, but that we still have a distance to go. And all respondents agreed that without such excellence, our profession will lack distinction and probably more and more of our departments will face crises.

2. Has our identification with intercollegiate debate strengthened or weakened our academic reputation?

Originally, our question referred to extracurricular activities in general, but our respondents, with few exceptions, confined "activities" to debate. On the whole, respondents were sympathetic to debate, seeing it as one of our genuine contributions to academic life and one that we can be especially proud of. One respondent said, "I became interested in speech as a result of debate. Both as debater and coach, I regarded debate as a personal commitment." Others felt that debate was "the public relations arm of the department," that faculty members in other departments believed debate useful in getting students "to think on their feet," and that students attracted to debate were among the most intelligent group in the college. One respondent warned that "departments that have de-emphasized debate or have done away with it will eventually pay the price." And a number of respondents, who were former debate coaches, spoke with pride of alumni debaters who have achieved success and fame in various professions.

Other respondents were not sympathetic to debate. One said that his department no longer has responsibility for debate, nor does it want the responsibility. However, his university does have a debate program, but it is sponsored by the philosophy department. Others who were critical of debate typified it as "an embarrassment . . . sophistic . . . intellectually sterile . . . unreal . . . an index of what's wrong with us . . . deserving of the audience it gets, one judge and one timekeeper." One respondent said that she had read the final debate of the National Debate Tournament in the *Journal of the American Forensic Association* a few years ago and found it "appallingly incomprehensible." A few respondents complained about the "poor delivery" of debaters, and one said that competitive debate "virtually destroyed rational concepts of communicability. No one can keep up with the speed at which debaters speak. They don't need coaches; they need monitors." In regard to what contributions intercollegiate debate made to departments, unsympathetic respondents could see none.

A third group was sympathetic to debate but also critical of it. One said that "Debate is extremely worthwhile and has great potential, but debate coaches do little to improve upon the activity." One respondent pointed to the popularity of "off-topic" debate and said that it was ironic that it took a group of Ivy League students to introduce this alternative to orthodox debate. Another respondent felt that debate is "a wonderful exercise in research and argument, but it isn't interesting. Debate coaches should develop a structure for debate that is audience-oriented, that will actually encourage intelligent people to sit through a debate without feeling pain." In regard to what contributions debate made to departments, this group of respondents generally felt that, whatever the merits of debate, a department should continue the activity if it draws majors to the department and if the administration highly regards intercollegiate debate.

AFTERWORD

We recognize that we have presented no formula for maintaining and strengthening departments, nor have we accounted for those departments renowned in the field that seemingly will go on forever. Success is often described in clichés, as though success were its own best explanation. Departments that are effective seldom provoke analysis, nor do inept departments attract our attention. But all of us become concerned about departments that demonstrate promise and at some point disappear or become endangered. These departments make us conscious of both our strengths and our weaknesses, cautious about our immortality, and concerned about the commonwealth we call our profession. Any threat to a department performing well becomes a challenge to our profession to do better. A positive attitude is not defensive, cynical, or fatalistic. It confirms our sense of confidence in what we are doing and where we are going together with our willingness to acknowledge that we can do better.

Confidence does require that we have a sense of who we are and what we do, a sense of identity and achievement. Our study indicates to us that the profession has a better sense of identity that it had some years ago; for one thing, the profession has become less defensive. But turmoil regarding identity is apparent, and this is healthy insofar as it expresses anxiety about how our discipline is defined. In regard to achievement, there is a mixture of satisfaction and discontent that strikes us as being healthy. We have done well. We have improved. We can do better. It is this type of healthy tension that should enable more departments to rise and fewer to fall.

APPENDIX

January 8, 1983

FROM: Diane C. Mader, College of Old Westbury, New York
Larry Rosenfield, Hunter College (CUNY), New York
Tom Mader, Hunter College (CUNY), New York

TO:

Tom Benson of Penn State has asked us to write a chapter called "The Rise and Fall of Speech (or Speech Communication) Departments" for a volume commissioned by the Eastern Communication Association to commemorate its 75th anniversary. Benson hopes to have the book published by Spring 1984.

The three of us have drawn up a list of people who we believe are knowledgeable about the rise and fall of speech (or speech communication) departments. Your name is on that list. We hope that you are willing to help us in our survey and analysis.

[MORE]

WE INTEND TO CALL YOU WITHIN THE NEXT FEW WEEKS. We would like to tape our conversation, if you have no objection. The taping is a matter of convenience. We will not quote you on any point unless you give us permission to do so.

Here are some of the questions we will probably ask you:

1. Do "good" departments succeed, and "bad" departments fail? (Do some departments succeed in spite of their limitations? Do other departments fail in spite of their apparent strengths?)

2. Do speech departments succeed or fail primarily because of political considerations (the dean doesn't like the speech chairperson, a number of other departments could make use of the speech staff lines, the speech staff is not part of the "in" group, etc.) or primarily because of academic considerations (speech courses lack content, are "easy," duplicate what's being done in other departments, are superfluous, imply that the field is not a "discipline"; speech staff does not do enough research or writing, or the research and writing are not of high quality; speech staff does not take an active role in the life of the academic community, does not serve on significant college committees and shows no interest in doing so, etc.)?

3. To what extent is cost a significant factor in the failure of speech departments? (For example, is it too expensive to offer more than a few sections of public speaking, given the need to keep such sections comparatively small?)

4. Has the movement from "speech" to "communication" (or "speech communication" helped or hurt our field?

5. Has the split with theatre and/or communication sciences (pathology, audiology) weakened or strengthened speech departments? What do the splits imply?

6. How significant is the chairperson in the rise or fall of a department? What kind of chairperson tends to help departments that rise? What kind of chairperson is associated with departments that fall?

7. To what extent has the emphasis *or* de-emphasis on extra-curricular activities helped or hurt speech departments? (We are thinking especially of forensics, clinical activity, acting.)

8. Some departments seem to revolve around a bread-and-butter course, offer "the basic course." Is this healthy? Or is the tail wagging the dog?

9. To what extent is the view of speech/communication as "interdisciplinary" helpful? To what extent does it do harm?

10. Does the success or failure of a speech department depend significantly on whether speech faculty members "communicate" well?

How do we fare in regard to collegiality? Do we talk to one another enough? Are we aware of our constituencies: the students we presently teach, our alumni, and so on? Are we models for our students, not only in terms of speaking well but also in terms of "civic virtue"? Are we active in community affairs, national affairs, college affairs? Does it make any difference?

11. A number of speech departments have hired individuals with Ph.D.'s outside the speech/communication area. And there are a few departments with a rather significant number of Ph.D.'s outside the speech/communication field. Does this bode well for the future not only for the speech/communication Ph.D. but also for speech departments?

We may not be able to get to all of these questions with each person we contact; in addition, other questions may well arise in the course of a discussion with someone who sees the rise or fall of a speech department as depending upon something we haven't thought of. Whatever the case, we hope you are willing to help us out. We think we've been given an interesting project to undertake. Whether or not that project succeeds depends very much on people like you. We will be more than grateful for the information and insights you can give us.

SENT BY: _____
      Diane C. Mader

17

Keeping the Faith:
On Being a Teacher-Scholar
in the 20th Century

JANE BLANKENSHIP

Whether one dates the beginning of speech communication teachers from the time of the ancient Egyptian Ptah-ho-tep (2500 B.C.) or Zeno of Elea, the teacher of Pericles in the fifth century, we have a very long and not infrequently distinguished genealogy. Aristotle probably delivered the material in his *Rhetoric* as Lyceum lectures late in his life, and the central role of rhetorical communication, politics, and ethics in Greco-Roman education has been amply documented (Clark, 1957). Then, as now, teachers of speech communication were concerned with the construction of communities through communication. History records teachers who have viewed speech as merely a "bag of tricks" by which we are deceived or cajoled, but there have always been teachers who suggest the primacy of substance and ideas and the ethical grounding of communication. History records, of course, that there have always been teachers who have espoused partial views of their students as "thinking machines," but there have always been other teachers to remind us of a more holistic view of students, carefully acknowledging both the affective and the cognitive dimensions of their natures and the reciprocities between those dimensions.

In this chapter I shall focus on what it means to be a teacher-scholar in speech communication in the 20th century. Still, it would be useful to recall briefly our beginnings. Not until the Roman schoolmaster Quintilian (b. A.D. 45) did speech teachers teach in "public schools." Quintilian wrote the first extant major treatise on speech communication pedagogy that deals with communication training in early childhood through old age. That not inconsiderable 20th century teacher of speech communication, Andrew

Weaver (1952, p. 39) reminds us of how essentially modern his Roman predecessor was: "Quintilian believed in the integration of various fields of knowledge. He saw relationships among all subjects and was persuaded that knowledge in a given area could not be mastered successfully if separated from other areas. He saw the need to concentrate on the improvement of skills and habits, but he recommended the fixing of the skills and habits in real life situations. He not only attempted to integrate all areas within the school, but also went outside the school into the community for applications of his teaching." Further, "Quintilian pointed out the individual needs and abilities of students, and recommended that each person be treated in the manner which would best make use of his talents and aptitudes. Thus, the principle of individual differences functioned significantly in his philosophy."

It is not my purpose, here, to trace the history of speech communication education; any number of readily available books make that information accessible to anyone who would know the roots of our discipline. But it is my purpose to suggest that not to know the history of the discipline may destine one to repeat mistakes, duplicate research findings, and inflate one's own importance in a conversation which began long before we were born and which will continue long after we are gone.

For those who take the shorter view of such matters, the following early firsts on our own continent may be enlightening: In 1736, when Harvard University was founded, speech was a part of the curriculum. In the 18th century, rhetoric, the first of the areas of speech communication to be granted a place in the academy, was a part of the curriculum at the College of William and Mary, Princeton University, and the University of Pennsylvania. By 1847 public debates followed their earlier siblings, oratorical contests, into the colleges and universities. By 1862 a Department of Elocution and Rhetoric was founded at Hamilton College. By 1892 the first autonomous, continuously maintained Department of Speech was founded at the University of Michigan (D. K. Smith, 1954). By 1922, the first Ph.D. in speech was awarded.

The History of Speech Education (Wallace, ed., 1954) chronicles the subsequent growth and development of courses, departments, and professional organizations. By 1930, there were 2,083 courses in college speech, under 694 titles (Weaver, p. 55). By 1952, 7,530 M.A.'s had been granted and 621 Ph.D.'s (Weaver, p. 56).

Not only have the numbers and diversity of speech communication courses continued to grow, but a substantial body of scholarship has developed as well. Journals abound at the national and regional levels; some state organizations sponsor journals. A quick perusal of the *Index to Journals in Speech Communication, 1915–1979* (Matlon, 1980) reveals something of the large number of authors who have contributed to our journals; 6,327 different people have contributed to *Quarterly Journal of Speech, Communication Monographs, Communication Education, Communication Quarterly, Human Communication Research, Journal of Communication, Journal of Broadcasting, Central States Speech Journal, Southern Speech Communication Journal, Philosophy and Rhetoric, Western Journal of Speech Communication, Journal of the American Forensic Association,* and *Association for Communication Administration Bulletin.** Journals continue to grow in numbers; for example, in 1983 the Speech Communication Association established a new one, *Critical Studies in Mass Communication* and, of course, many speech communication scholars publish widely in interdisciplinary journals and in journals sponsored by a variety of cognate disciplines.

Conventions provide another outlet for contemporary scholarship. One only has to examine the differences between the 1940 and any recent Eastern Communication Association convention programs to see the growth in numbers and diversity of programs. In 1940, excluding business meetings and the luncheon, there were only 20 programs. The *Program* (Harding, 1940) indicates that the Speech Association of the Eastern States (ECA's predecessor), at that time, included "*all* phases of speech work (fundamentals, public speaking, debating, voice and diction, speech correction, interpretation, dramatics, theater, discussion, conference, public opinion, radio, and tests and measurements)." In addition to programs dealing with pedagogy in kindergarten-college, rhetoric, dramatics, discussion and conference, and speech correction, there were programs such as "Speech in Adult Education," "Putting the News on the Air" (news analysts and commentators from CBS, NBC, and the Mutual Broadcasting System) and "Measuring Public Opinion," (including a presentation by George Gallup, "The Method of Sampling and the Place of Polling Public Opinion in a Democracy"). About 27% of the program participants were women. As in 1983, our 1940 program contained a spectrum of established areas of study continually refreshing themselves and of newer areas at the early stages of development.

Speech communication has not only been concerned with pedagogical and scholarly matters but those professional concerns that also contribute to the quality of life in the academy. The range of such matters includes guidelines for tenure and promotion decisions, concerns for the qualitative judgments of programs and departments, affirmative action programs, and the like. Again, ECA helped lead the way; for example, in 1973, our

---

*This number excludes those who have written for *Journalism Quarterly* but for no other journal included in the *Index*. Further, it does not include those who have only contributed to journals devoted solely to film, such as *Film Quarterly, Journal of the University Film Association*, etcetera.

Executive Council initiated the Equal Opportunity Task Force on the Status of Women in the Speech Communication Profession in the Eastern States Region.

Clearly, *persons* have taught the classes, written the articles, and served on the committees. And, it is on *persons* that this chapter focuses. In this chapter I shall sketch something of what it has meant to live a career; to write one's way through a series of books and articles; to think in public; to participate in the activities of professional associations; and somehow to make room for all the other activities of life—and in doing all of this, to keep the faith as a teacher-scholar in the 20th century. I draw from five kinds of sources: journal series, such as *Speech Teacher's (Communication Education's)* "Great Teachers of Speech"; ECA's 1982 Career Paths Committee's detailed questionnaire; illustrative material from convention programs "in honor of" and *Festschriften* pointing to those characteristics most valued; audio taped and printed material by leaders in the discipline for a variety of projects; and, most especially, comprehensive interviews and conversations with six of our colleagues,* who will serve as "representatives anecdotes" (Burke, 1969, pp. 59–61).† While they are quite different in personality and life style, they share an essential cluster of personal-professional characteristics that illuminates both their individual characters and some sense of what they share with each other and with us.

One very large group of our colleagues is especially "unrepresented" in this chapter—elementary and secondary teachers. Although it is difficult to know precisely how many teach a speech communication course or direct cocurricular activities in secondary schools, we can estimate that the number must be at least 8,000-10,000 persons and may be substantially higher. A 1978–1979 survey (Book & Pappas, 1981) estimates that some 3,297 high school teachers in the 15 states surveyed teach a speech communication course or direct cocurricular activities.‡

Secondary school teachers of speech communication, according to the Book and Pappas survey, are most typically young, many multidegreed; they sustain themselves, most times, without membership in state, regional, or national professional speech associations. Still, it would be misleading to suppose that the professional communication organizations are uncon-

*My profound thanks go to the six persons whose "dialogue" constitutes much of the second half of this chapter. Their candor and trust that I would not injure their confidence is deeply moving. My profound thanks also go to my parents on the occasion of their 50th anniversary whose loving support has never wavered.

†Although I have borrowed the term "representative anecdote" from Kenneth Burke (1969, 59–61), I am bending it to my own purposes in this chapter.

‡The Book and Pappas (1981) sample included secondary school teachers in several states in the Eastern region: Pennsylvania, Maryland, and Massachusetts.

cerned about them. The Speech Communication Association, for example, has been instrumental in preparing a variety of documents of major interest to teachers and school systems, such as *Preparation of Elementary and Secondary Teachers in Speech Communication and Theatre: Competency Models* and *Program Guidelines and Standards for Effective Oral Communication Programs*. And Andrew Wolvin (1982, p. 272) reminds us that "the federal government's 'Back to Basics' program now includes (thanks to the lobbying efforts of Dr. Barbara Lieb-Brilhart and the SCA) speaking and listening skills." Each state agency "is mandated to include assessment and development funds for speech as well as for reading and writing." (Wolvin, p. 272)

Why would the professional organizations *not* care? As R. R. Allen and Kenneth Brown (1976, p. v) observe, "functional speech communication behaviors are of such crucial significance that they must be emphasized progressively and continuously throughout the school experience." Our students are often introduced to our discipline in high school and the impact of K-12 teachers on the growth and expectations who do belong to our organizations act as a constant and important reminder of the intimate links between all of us in the educational process. The child comes to kindergarten having communication experiences and that child develops not solely as a third grader, or a high school student, or a college student. The child starts somewhere and goes somewhere. And, all of us, regardless of what point in that journey we are primarily concerned with, know that the traveler on that journey is a whole person not very much concerned with our "territorial imperatives."

The largest recent growth of academic speech communication professionals has been in the community colleges. At the 1983 ECA Convention, it was estimated that approximately 50% of all speech communication teachers at the college/university levels are in the community colleges. ECA helped take the lead in acknowledging their growing importance in 1972 by establishing an Ad Hoc Committee on Community Colleges and in 1973 by establishing the Task Force to Integrate Community Colleges and Two-Year Institutions into ECA.* Those early groups helped us to identify priorities among community college teachers and the ways we could, reciprocally, help each other. There is now also a vigorous Community College Section within the Speech Communication Association.

Not only are we changing in where we teach but, increasingly, we are becoming more multicultural. ECA's Minority Voices Division, SCA's

---

*The pioneer 1972 *ad hoc* committee was chaired by Darlyn Wolvin; the pivotal 1973 Task Force was chaired by Ruth Goldfarb. ECA is indebted to them and their colleagues for informing us of the importance and potential growth of the community colleges to speech communication education.

Black Caucus and Commission on International and Intercultural Speech Communication play important roles in helping make us more mindful of our multicultural profession. Colleagues such as Brown (1975), Hawthorne (1977), Niles (1975), Edwards (1975), Daniel (1976), and Cummings (1975) have helped us better to understand the profession and how it relates to the black experience, speech communication at predominantly black colleges, the life of black professors on predominantly white campuses, and directions in black studies. Molefi Asante's work, *Contemporary Black Thought: Alternative Analysis in Social and Behavioral Science* (1980), Jack L. Daniel's *Black Communication: Dimensions of Research and Instruction* (1974), Arthur L. Smith's *Language, Communication, and Rhetoric in Black America* (1972), and Melbourne Cummings and Jack L. Daniel's "Scholarly Literature in the Black Idiom" (1980) are illustrative of how our scholarship can be enriched by examining alternative perspectives.

As with all other disciplines, whether we teach at small colleges, at medium sized or large universities makes a significant difference in our daily lives and the nuances of evaluative criteria by which we are judged. At a 1982 ECA meeting of the Career Paths Committee a colleague from a small college chided those from larger research universities: "You have to remember that most of the time I teach four or five courses, plus advising, plus committees. Time off for research? You've got to be kidding and I rarely get *any* travel money. I'm lucky to get to the regional and state conventions." A survey by Buckley (1982) reports that 67.8% of us are teaching in programs with no doctoral program. Only 6.2% of us teach where a doctoral program has graduated 1–10 Ph.D.'s in the last 10 years; 3.5%, where we have graduated 11–50; and 6.2%, graduating over 50 Ph.D.'s in that time span. Rather, two-thirds (67.4%) consider their primary responsibility to be teaching undergraduates; 28% "balance" their teaching between undergraduate and graduate students; only 4.6% consider their primary work to be teaching graduate students.

ECA's Career Paths Committee set out to find out more about who we are in the speech communication profession and how we spend our time. Buckley (1982) summarized some of those findings for us. We are 32.9%, assistant professors; 22.8%, associate professors; 29.3%, full professors. Three-fourths of us are age 50 or younger; two-thirds are 46 or younger; half are age 40 or younger. The male-female ratio is more than three-to-one (male 73.8%; female 26.2%).* "Nearly one-third" of our colleagues in speech communication have "never published an article or book and the

---

*The Buckley (1982) study also indicated some future shifts; for example, in 1981 less than 23% in the profession were women, but 50% of the graduate students were women.

total exceeds 41% for those who have published" two or fewer items during their career (p. 85).

Are we satisfied with our jobs? Most seem to be, with 32.5% expressing "above average" job satisfaction and 24.5% "extremely" satisfied; only 13.6% (total) indicated "below average satisfaction," "very dissatisfied," and "extreme dissatisfaction" (p. 154). Many of us knew we wanted to be teachers early: "Most of the members of the field formed lasting opinions as to the worthiness of teaching as a career before undergraduate graduation, and nearly one fifth considered college teaching as a profession before their junior year of college." (p. 137)

Now that we have briefly identified what many of us do, let us examine how we talk about some of those teacher-scholars whom we most admire and whom we honor by *Festchriften*. The prefatory essays to such volumes make clear that the persons so honored are of different temperaments and personalities and, to some extent, differing teaching styles and different scholarly "trademarks." Of course, the "impact an individual has on students is an amalgam of many things: personality, ideas, values, behavior, and a collection of even more intangible factors" (VanGraber, 1982, p. xi). In sorting out some of the materials in *Festchriften* and distinguished service awards into the typical personnel committee categories for evaluation—teaching, research/publication, and service—some illuminating patterns emerge. Characteristics typically cluster around rigor and high standards, requiring students to think for themselves, and accessibility. "Growth was not only possible, it was necessary. Improvement [was] expected" (VanGraber, p. xiii). Or, he "could demand, and get more and better work from a student than the student ever imagined was possible." (Nebergall & Wenzel, 1976, p. xi). Or, "he attempted to teach us *how* to think, not what to think. The maxim of this, if there is one, might be 'Do as I do, not as I say.'" (Wilder-Mott, p. 38). Another student wrote: "To be true to the liberalizing education . . . we had no choice but to pursue ideas where they led us, to make judgments as good as we could make, and to make them after the most rigorous research, thinking, and arguing we could muster. The legacy they leave us is not the positions they have taken in the course of their own productive careers, but rather the tradition of taking scholarship seriously, of grappling with ideas rigorously, of giving as much of self to students as they could, and of all the other aspects of the teacher-scholar that connote a humane but hard-headed way of dealing with people and with ideas." (Brockriede, 1976, p. xiii) Another recalled, "The door stands open at [her] office. . . . She is always available to talk to a student or a colleague, most often about that person's concerns, but sometimes too about her current work. As graduate students we all learned that if one wanted . . . a stimulating half-hour of conversation, one could always count on [her] to be caught up with some new idea and anxious to talk about it. No one can say how much the morale of a generation of graduate students came to depend on those occasions when we could entice her to leave the office and join a group for coffee and talk" (Nebergall & Wenzel, 1976, p. xii). Openness of several kinds seems to be a keynote: Openness to people (He was "always . . . willing to talk all night, sometimes after talking on [an especially interesting topic] a good share of the day") and openness to ideas (He "challenges us with what Umberto Eco terms an 'open' rather than a 'closed' text"). (Hudson, 1944, p. 5; Wilder-Mott, 1981, pp. 38–39).

Many of those honored have written texts, thereby reaching many students well beyond their own classrooms. It could be said of more than a few as was said of one: "His several textbooks . . . have contributed substance and dignity to undergraduate courses" (Bryant, 1979, p. 20).

Teaching often extends to counseling of a broader kind; for example: "Not only did he find time to counsel his students but his colleagues as well. Rarely did one find time when he was *not* poring meticulously over the manuscripts of colleagues or listening to them as they tried out ideas on him" (Blankenship, 1974, p. 188). A strong sense of colleagiality pervades such behavior: "The basis of [this] sharing with . . . students and colleagues alike was profound respect and affection. In a very real sense, these were the tangible and personal examples of his deep belief in the 'dignity and worth of the individual,' leads to a state of mind best described by the old fashioned work, *respect*" (Blankenship, 1974, pp. 188–189). A titular term for this cluster is suggested by William Reuckert (1982, p. 1) when he writes about his association with Kenneth Burke: "without exception, for me, it has been a generative relationship."

"Profound" and "meticulous" are two of the characteristic terms to describe the work of our honorees. There is talk of the quality of "research" and "publication;" more typically, "scholarship" seems the preferred term. VanGraber (p. x) describes this terminological relationship directly: "Publication, while frequently confused with scholarship, is not the same thing. . . . It is the product and demonstration of curiosity and criticism, of evaluation and judgment. Scholarship is the exercise of discipline and consistency, and of that most favorable of [his] god-terms, 'rigor.' Sometimes, scholarship culminates in publication. Always, it contributes to the continued growth and development of the scholar."

Precision, incisive analysis, and "clarity, force, and liveliness" in the communication of ideas to be sure (Barrett, 1974, p. 5); still, all are undergirded with a vital enthusiasm for learning. For example: "He *likes* ideas . . . they always suggest something for him to do (Hudson, p. 3)."

The kind of scholarship most often applauded (whether in classical rhetoric or organizational communication) is that which is forward looking. Consider these observations: "a typical conversation—a hard-headed detailed appraisal of what *is*, an exploration of the whys, the *causes* of things, and most characteristically, a concern for the possibilities toward which we should ideally, and could realistically work" (Blankenship, 1978b, p. 1). He "undertook precedent-setting experimental research in speech communication in the 1930's, thus anticipating the behavioral focus" (Howell, 1972, p. 3). "He is, as always, concerned with what needs to be done in order to understand and make communication effective, not with what has been accomplished" (Paulson, 1980, p. x).

Not only are most of those honored by *Festchriften* and distinguished service awards teachers and scholars, but they are also people frequently "called upon to speak for the good of the order" (Nebergall & Wenzel, 1976, p. ix). They are typically "involved," even "devoted" to our profession; they are, in short, "thorough and total" professionals. They "tirelessly" serve on our committees, edit our journals, hold offices. They do the tedious, continuous, and far from glamorous chores, frequently without self-advertisement, that allow our organizations to survive. "Traditionally," as Bruce Gronbeck (1980, p. 4) observes, "those who have received distinguished service awards have been more than scholars, more than placeholders"; they have embodied "general standards of conduct worth emulating. They have had a spiritual richness to their professional lives." They share the gift of giving "substance to personal and professional values" (Gronbeck, p. 4).

Frequently, on personnel committees, we hear that "we really have no way to measure effectiveness of teaching." So it may be instructive to turn our attention, in some greater detail, to that most "elusive" aspect of the publication/scholarship-teaching-service requirement placed upon many of us by colleges and universities. Certainly, those who write for the series entitled "Great Teachers of Speech" in *The Speech Teacher* (now, *Communication Education*) can "take the measure" of effective teaching.

An informal, but not casual, clustering of the characteristics most pointed to include the following, and there was no doubt about the "first among equals" of the clusters. Cluster One: integrity; honesty; rectitude; square-shooting; good. Cluster Two: dynamic; vitality; invigorating; momentum; spirit; "the dynamic energy which wells up out of her sheer joy of living"; "willing to adventure" (Weaver, 1964, p. 4; Donner, 1962, p. 218). Cluster Three: sympathy; open-door policy; "never failed to center . . . interest in the student who walked in to chat"; an "old fashioned professor . . . as much interested in his students as he is in his subject matter" (Nelson, 1955, p. 113; Nichols, 1976, p. 7). Cluster Four: rigor, best we could be. Cluster Five: free of pretense; unostentatious; modest; valued sincerity; hated sham. Cluster Six: knew what s/he wanted; unafraid.

It may be most instructive to listen to more particulars about Clusters Three and Six: Haberman (1961, p. 5) perhaps captures the essence of

Cluster Three when he talks about the "ideal teacher of speech." Although he is not specifically talking about college/university teaching, its applicability is clear when we substitute "student" for "child": "The ideal teacher of speech understands children. Not children in the abstract or children as a generalization, or children at large, but rather children the plural of one child plus another child plus another child and so on." The comments below reveal the tangibleness of such an ideal: "His strongest claim to greatness as a teacher . . . was his deep interest in the individual: his problems and potentialities" (Lilly, 1955, p. 22). "Her firm insistence upon dealing with *students* rather than with *subject matter*; she is much less concerned about what the student does to the subject matter than about what the subject matter does to the student" (Weaver, 1964, p. 2). "She knows [our] thoughts, feelings, hopes and fears, and even some of [our] dreams. . . . She deeply respects [our] individuality. . . . She regards every person as infinitely worthwhile and makes each understand that she expects [us] to live up to [our] potential" (Weaver, p. 3). "Each of us . . . can recall our individual gifts from this extraordinary teacher—for the gift of time when she was sorely taxed for it; her concern that we be ourselves while honoring with her the more general commitment to love of letters; permanence in value; excellence of craft; the gift of her affection for each, uniquely, when it embraced so many of us simultaneously" (Blankenship, 1978, p.4).

Cluster Six is also not merely an "ideal" but very "real" as observed by the students who write, "She is always frank and fearless in expressing her honest judgments" (Weaver, 1964, p. 3). "She eloquently and firmly stood her ground, always on deep-seated principles" (Smith, 1962, p. 107). "He was unafraid of his convictions" (Nelson, p. 117). "We recognized a stubborness to fight for his ideals" (Nelson, p. 117). "He knew what he wanted; he worked toward clearly conceived ends" (Okey, 1962, p. 14).

Other qualities were mentioned, such as generosity, "merriment"; concern for communication skills; "faith and enthusiasm *in* and *for* speech education" (Okey, 1962, p. 13); "conversationalist in the true sense, for he loved to talk and loved to listen"; love of the language and precision in its use; and helpfulness in teaching students to write. One student-turned-colleague (Hochmuth, 1955, p. 160) wrote, "He tried to get over the idea that a sentence was not an uninterrupted journey up the Rhine River, but that one could get off at Coblenz, or Bonn, or Cologne—and that even between points one didn't try to take in all the scenery." And, she confided: He "still calls me down for writing sentences that move across a page like freight cars about to go off the track."

Not know how to describe excellence in teaching? The writers in this *Communication Education* series do. Like most memories in such *encomia*, clarity and nostalgia blend, but the teachers talked about so vividly and so affectionately are very "real" teachers and their influence quite tangible.

One student (Lee, 1962, p. 299) wrote, "It is difficult to separate what you learned [from him] from what you have become in the years that have followed."

Now let us turn our attention to examining six of our colleagues in order to describe in greater detail "what it has meant to live a career; to write one's way through a series of books and articles, thinking in public; to participate in the activities of professional associations; and to somehow make room for all the other activities of life."* No claim is made that this sample is "representative" in the antiseptic use of that term. Half of the samples are women; a recent estimate (Buckley, 1982) is that 26.2% of speech communication professors are women. All have been "active researchers"; the same study reports that only 33.7% in our discipline are categorized that way. Still, their dialogue with us captures some of the texture of the 20th century in speech communication and sets of standard for excellence.

All six have written for our journals and have presented papers at our conventions from the early stages of their careers; all have written or edited several books; each of the six has taught several generations of students; all six have held responsible positions in our regional and national organizations and on their own campuses. Of our six, two are between 30-40; two between 42-52; and two are emeritus professors. Collectively, they can remind us about some of what they have observed about our discipline's growth and change, about our profession. They are, at once, individuals with their own unique joys and concerns and our colleagues with whom we share at least some of those joys and concerns.

How did they 'get into' speech communication? Half said they got into speech communication "by accident," or by "a series of otherwise imperceptible choices." All six engaged in a range of student activities, many with a strong performance base. Typically, they began in high school through debate, forensics, student government, and an occasional communication course. Buckley's study (1982) suggests that the growing diversity of the discipline may now lead to a somewhat broader range of entry points for those in their twenties.

Any particularly influential teachers during high school? Some. A pattern seems to emerge around a clustering of terms: evidence/support; argument; analysis; precision. Teachers cited include: "A woman in high school who observed my behavior in class and cordially required that I join the debate team; a philosophy professor whose lectures embodied brilliant evidence and argument." "Because I liked to read and analyze what I read . . . [several of my English teachers] taught me to see how-things-were-put-together rather than just to say 'I like that' or 'I don't like that.' Less

*Letter detailing this assignment from editor to author.

directly the one speech teacher who was a 'softie of sorts' but in her class I learned to make a point and support it. Less directly a chemistry teacher whom I didn't like and thought sort of 'fumbling' but who forced the issue of my being more precise."

Four of the six majored in communication (by a variety of titles) in undergraduate school. They had double majors or minors in history, political science, psychology, economics, English, and philosophy. Any particular influential teacher in undergraduate school? Almost certainly so: "A debate coach—not brilliant but thorough model of the values of hard work." "A famous visiting professor—I had no idea who he was. He had forgotten more about [the subject] than the class was likely to learn that semester. . . . That sense of a scholar who had done a lot of reading, and a lot of work, who had culled a lot of information and was able almost instantaneously to take over a bad report and just finish it for the student without anybody feeling bad about the situation." Another respondent recalled:

> Two teachers were particularly influential and to some extent for different reasons—one who had a great interest in archetypal heroes and heroines and I think that caught my young imagination. . . . Mostly, she took an interest in me. Several times took me to the first real plays I ever saw. She just seemed to care about us as people as well as students. The second teacher, my first year writing teacher. She was demanding, expected a lot of us and generally got it. She let us try our wings. And she didn't just correct papers, she taught us to write. She didn't just ooh and ah or dislike pieces of literature. . . . She analyzed them, argued with them, carried on a dialogue with them. She was the first very bright, very articulate young woman professional I ever met. I don't think I thought of it at the time this way—not until recently—but she was almost surely a role-model for me.

Several commented on the profoundness of these early relationships, for example: "They were closer than I really experienced, in a sense, before that time [the M.A. program] or after that time." At least one speculated about why so firm a bonding: "These were very vulnerable years and I needed to value and be valued—we always do, of course, but at this time we were beginning to be expected to be adults not just to be one someday. I don't know what these teachers saw in me but I am forever grateful that they helped teach me what a competent, caring teacher, competent, caring person could be."

How did they choose their graduate schools? Several ways; for example: recommendations from teachers; they received an assistantship or a fellowship; to study a particular subject with a particular professor; locale and friendship; reputation of the department and proximity to home. In graduate school, were they conscious of having a "mentor" or "role model"? Clearly so, although several were slightly uneasy with those descriptors. For example, "I don't think I thought of them as 'mentors'—that sounded too grand for a struggling grad student like me to have." "A 'role-model'? That vocabulary came in much later. But there were people I admired—people I wanted to emulate.... They taught me habits of mind . . . habits of conduct. . . . to set high standards for yourself and to do your best to live up to them . . . to do your job." Another was less uneasy about the term: "My mentors? A woman from school [who] got me a scholarship to college, then a Jesuit philosophy teacher—he insisted I could be anything I wanted; then a person who set standards I would never reach and put me on a *Quarterly Journal of Speech* editorial board; then [X and Y] who encouraged me through the rough years. I always admired [Z] from afar and figured if she could make it—there must be a chance for women. [X and Y] confirmed that. My generation was the first to benefit from affirmative action. I wouldn't have gotten my first job without it." It was not uncommon for them to have several mentors: "Many. First: In general she knew so much, was so elegantly articulate, had such passionate love of her subject, demanding, a skilled scholar, a strong sense of the obligatory, strong sense of history, close colleagial ties, respected students and learning. She cared. Second: Knowledgeable, disciplined, demanding, expected the best, high energy, very complete person, seemed tough but helpful, precision. Third: Broad reading, witty, concerned for freedom of speech and politics. Fourth: A gentle but rigorous approach to people. Willingness to work hard—long time—on major projects. Another: Urbane, demanding but patient, always wanted you to be right, grasp of subject in broad perspective, absolutely brilliant but not pompous. Kind. They didn't set out to show us how much they knew—but to help us learn."

What functions did mentors fulfill? Several, for example: "Mainly taught me what professional conduct was all about. I learned about the meaning and importance of colleagiality from them. I learned to develop a strong sense of self without becoming self-centered. I learned to argue vigorously without viciousness and how to respect the work of others often when it is substantially different from my own. I think I always wanted to observe those habits, and our teachers in grad school were not about to let us do anything else." One respondent summarizes: "Of course, I learned to develop certain research skills from them, but most important I learned attitudes and tonalities."

At what points in their careers did they begin to attend and participate in conventions? All of our six began attending conventions rather early in their careers, but the younger two started earlier than the others.

Attendance at and participation in conventions have figured sometimes vividly in our respondents' lives, but conventions have functioned in different ways at different stages of careers. In the early stages of a career, several functions were identified. For example: One respondent, who had applied for a job armed only with an M.A. from a relatively small department, talked about job hunting from two different perspectives: "The initial [reason I attended] would be job hunting and learning how to work a convention so you did not have to exist in the 'slave market.' After the Ph.D. from a Big Ten department I could go into a convention with some very direct support from the faculty at the doctoral institution that I had attended. People who came into the job market with just M.A.'s . . . for them it's a whole different convention."

Not unexpectedly our respondents also attended "to watch famous people be famous." But, there were other reasons as well. One reports: "My first job was at a small college with an even smaller department and there was little disciplinary stimulation and no shop talk. I'd come there from a Big Ten department and the corridors were filled with interesting talk. Oh, I read the journals and talked with friends in other departments about matters of mutual interest, but I really was parched to talk with people in my own discipline. And, I had to go off campus to do that." Another observed: "I had to get started somewhere, and reading papers at conventions seemed less threatening than publishing. So, that is where I first started getting feedback on my papers from other than close friends. Conventions tell us what is going on often before materials reach the journal stage."

At least one rite of passage from "Gee Whiz" reverence of "famous people" to a more mature kind of acknowledgment typically takes place at conventions. For example, one of our respondents speaks of his "overcoming the awe of the big names" in the field: "It finally hit me when a person who went through the presidency of SCA turned out to be a very close friend of mine, and I can remember standing there thinking that this was a person who had doubts about what he was doing and was concerned about certain issues and we had talked about these issues in an informal way and then see people come up and say 'Oh Dr. so and so . . . I've always wanted to meet you!' Now, I have awe in terms of respect but not 'Oh there's . . .'" Sometimes this same rite of passage is acknowledgedly humorous, as well: "One of the most marvelous moments in my own development came during the first time I ever got to be on a program with a very well known figure, whose works I had read in graduate school and whom I very much 'revered.' I was pleased, of course, to be in such company—more than a little terrified that I might not do well. Then, I happened to look over at him while he was presenting his paper and little beads of perspiration were running down the back of his neck and I knew that he was nervous, *too!* At that moment I said to myself, 'Well, maybe I can make it after all.'" By the middle of careers, our six generally agree that a dominant motive for attending conventions is "to meet colleagues, meet friends." Later, they are pleased that they have reached a point in their careers when there is "no need to hustle at conventions any more." They can "avoid smoke, noise, and booze" and spend "quiet times with friends."

Certain programs remain highlights over a whole career. Not too unexpectedly many of these are tied to excellence of quality; for example: "Every once in a while I participate in a program that is an intellectual high or I go to a program that is an intellectual high." Sometimes scholarly excellence mixes with other values: "One program in particular has stayed with me. It was a program 'in honor of' and as I sat in the room I could see my teachers and some of my teachers' teachers and some of my students. It was a very personal lesson in the history of twentieth-century speech communication education. The sense of family, the mutual respect, the profoundness of the affection, the sense of having a tradition to live up to—made a lasting impression on me. Second, the program focused mainly on papers replete with 'footnotes.' In the midst of that awesome scholarly display—someone, best known as a teacher, spoke 'On Being a Speech Teacher.' Her exceptional presence and eloquence was stunning but what really stood out was how very much that speech belonged with the others."

Many times convention highlights centered around meeting and talking with colleagues whom they had admired and around personal recollections of winning awards, offices, and the like. Three typical responses to such "rewards" seem to be: "I needed all the encouragement I could get and it was a big boost." "I had worked hard nearly three years on that piece and was pleased to have someone say 'well done.'" "An office lets you get things done that you think ought to be done. You have to move from grumbling about how things are to positively trying to do something."

Our commentators also recall the settings for our conventions. Just getting there is difficult—juggling the time, the money, being away from family at vacation times, and sometimes the "perilousness" of travel: "When the SCA conventions used to be in December just getting to New York or Chicago in the dead of winter was a hair-raising business amidst the snow and ice storms." And, occasionally, convention contexts are amid storms greater than those inevitable Christmas blizzards: "Several whole conventions I remember vividly because they occurred at times of national crises—the Central States Convention in Chicago that coincided with the assassination of Martin Luther King, Jr., and the ECA convention several years ago in Ocean City when the tragic abortive mission to rescue the hostages in Iran took place. The world outside the convention hotel and the world inside (still trying to act, at least partly, like a convention) created a profound sense of emotional and intellectual vertigo."

Do they like to teach? Unanimously so. One observes: "Watching students grow and mature. There's something that's just inherently exciting about that, that you really can't quantify and there's no way to describe it empirically except that it gives a quality to the environment that I would miss if I were not teaching." Another points to a not uncommon analogy: "Teaching is like parenting with less trauma. Despite the public conception—the rewards are very tangible—a student well taught is a piece of evidence completely communicating, etcetera. Students seem to be disproportionately grateful and indebted . . . and that is frightening." Another talks about the reciprocal nature of teaching: "I like talking with those who are opening up to new knowledge, new alternatives, new discoveries, and seeing their development is a constant wonder to behold. Quite frequently we learn a lot together. Certainly they are often teaching me. I like teaching also because I'm something like the 'true believer' that what we study in speech communication is useful. Frequently, with grad students—we write, talk on the phone, see each other at conventions, take pride in each others' accomplishments and worry together during dark days." Several believe their teaching has improved "over the years." One says, for example: "I have become more student centered in my teaching. I try to find out what the students perceive to be their needs as they relate to the particular course and try to relate the instruction to those needs. I try to create a learning environment in which students have as much opportunity to participate as I do. . . . Early in my career I was very 'professorial' and lectured at students." Another muses about his teaching in relation to that of his graduate students: "I do enjoy it but I'm a much poorer teacher of basic courses now than I was as a graduate student. I look at our own graduate students and I see the creativity—just awesome in terms of what I'm doing in *my* classes. I don't know where I lost it; perhaps in the pressures of other responsibilities."

How do they characterize the people in the discipline whom they most admire? Several spoke in a particularly detailed way; one describes four whom she admired in this way: "(1) generous in support of colleagues especially women, secure, unthreatened, bright, well read, reliable, supportive. (2) brilliant person who gets along well with noncompetitive colleagues. (3) a big brother type who always gives advice when asked plus the advice is always good, reads papers in draft without engaging in mercy-killing and is unfailingly constructive and supportive. (4) a father type who sends me long letters telling me why I should not take administrative jobs. All are well published, well respected, humane, commonsensical and generous with their time and constructive but have high standards." Another describes four other teachers:

> (1) Thoughtful, bright, caring, constructive, not ashamed to change his mind and admit "mistakes" or new directions, widely read. Good critic; he can point out problems without savaging. Generous with time and concern. Loves to pun and have fun with language. (2) Marvelously quick wit and humor. Cuts through quickly to the core of things. Takes time to reinforce graduate students. Very bright. Can be argu-

mentative and incisive without being destructive. Broadly concerned. Capacity to juggle several (lots) of projects at one time. Warm. (3) Totally secure. Doesn't feel threatened by his equally high-powered colleagues. Takes time to help graduate students. Very demanding. Prods me to be more focused and less diffuse in interests. Strong colleagial sense. Doesn't let me weasel and get away with less than my best effort. (4) Thoughtful and articulate. Sets high standards for himself and, less obviously so, for those who work for him. Strong sense of delivering on promises. Willing, always, to do his share of the job. Cares about students and the profession. Never gets ahead at others' expense. Strong sense of where he's going and how he wants to put-together-life. Low-keyed humor.

Figure 17.1 contains the *clusters* of descriptors by our six informants.

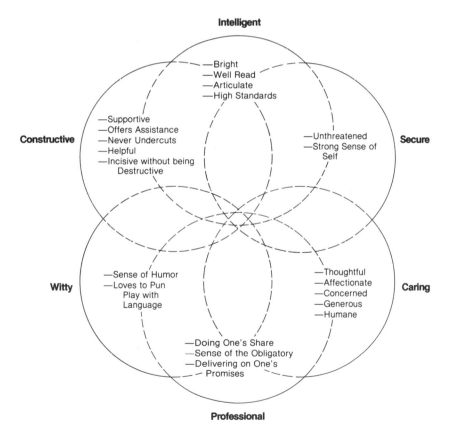

Figure 17.1. Clusters of descriptors for those most admired by our six primary informants.

What do our participants *least* admire in their colleagues? Our six are vividly clear about that; for example: "People who think they can build their own careers by destroying the reputations of good scholars. Venal, petty, small minded, insecure. I also intensely dislike women who feel that since they are threatened by other women they should undercut young careers and save their own—fortunately, these are few and the few are mediocre." "Least like? That's simple: Self-centered people—filled with self importance. Ill mannered. Dishonest." "I intensely dislike those who 'clone' in the name of 'mentoring'—who tie their students to their *works* rather than to their *habits* of mind. Such people seem to think that mentoring is more about *reflection* than about *illumination*. And I dislike those who think learning is a *combat* zone." A fourth listed, "Irresponsibility. Arrogance. Narcissism and inflated notion of importance. Selfish. Thoughtless. Dishonest."

What about their self-perceptions? When asked, "What do you see as your own strengths?" their answers most frequently were "capacity for hard work" and "tenaciousness." The list also included love of detail, sense of responsibility, willingness to see other perspectives, sense of colleagiality, commitment to professionalism, "chunking time" and using it effectively, willingness to listen to students, "some writing skills." One confided: "I developed in my career a professional tolerance of persons who I would like to strangle. . . . To do it any other way is not going to gain anything in the long run." Their self-perceived weaknesses? One stands out clearly; variations on the same theme include: "I try to do too much"; "I'm always attempting to juggle too many things at once and so I sometimes feel scattered and parcelled out"; "My desk looks like it exploded. . . . I'm easily fragmented."

How do they account for their "success"? In several ways: "By hard work. A consistent kind of an attempt to keep active." Another extends the list: "Hard work; strong support from family, teachers, colleagues; willingness to learn. Luck—maybe at some key spots in my career." And, a third extends the list further: "Good degree; reputable adviser; support from key senior colleagues; affirmative action; a supportive family; luck; vitamins." Yet another puts them all together neatly: "I always have a major project going at all times and have done this throughout my career; I always have ongoing work to do—work that's important to me. I've had a stable and loving home life. And, a lot of it depends on luck."

With any such "high energy" persons, there are costs and problems. How do they find time to do all that they do? "Physical stamina helps. I don't need much sleep." "I can sit still for long periods of time and I'm a 'speed reader'—that often keeps me from disaster!" Our youngest respondent, in her mid-30s, replied whimsically: "Actually I am 67 years old! I work grad student hours, from 11-4 a.m., the house is quiet, the phone doesn't ring. Being a nocturnal animal is very helpful." On scheduling, they observe: "There's never enough time. But I can juggle whatever at almost any hour of the day or night. Sometimes I'm saved by the capacity to relax and just forget all the rush and then pick up and work at a fast pace again." "If I'm committed to it I will find a way to get it done. What that generally means is working late nights, getting up early in the morning and working, trying to arrange a schedule to have blocks of time at home. It's just attention to scheduling and at times some surges of frenetic activity over a short period of time."

Uniformly the support of family and friends is profound: "My kids keep me sane. They know all of this academic stuff is advanced foolishness, so they keep it in perspective. My friends save me from myself often." One comment seems to capture how this works: "I find time to do it [all] because I have a very supportive family—griping at times, concerned at times, but also recognizing I'm unlivable with when I'm doing research and I'm unlivable with when I'm not doing research. . . . So [we] might as well put up with the periods of frenetic activity and enjoy the other times we have." In the end they seem to have reached a peace with all of this: "I know it is hard to unwind. I sometimes think some of us never do unwind. Oh, well. If that is the nature of the beast, so be it!"

Why do they persist? That's easy: "Because I like what I do and hope it makes some modest difference." "I persist because if I weren't doing it I probably would die professionally. I enjoy teaching, I love teaching. I think I persist simply because I enjoy what I do." Another replied "It's my profession; it's what I like to do; it's what I do and I would do this and continue to do this work even if I weren't paid for it, and I suspect that in retirement I will be involved in writing and research and will persist in publishing because that's who I am." Certainly, they seem to understand that without joy in one's work, their "career" would provide a bleak interior landscape, indeed.

The second part of the 20th century has seen unprecedented growth and change in our discipline. How have those changes affected the professional lives of our six? Their answers sketch for us not only some details of their lives but point to some of the most fundamental changes in the discipline. Most profound of the changes seem to center around increased sophistication in research, changes in research and teaching directions, reorganization of the discipline, and the impact of the Women's Movement. First, they point to "increased sophistication in the *kinds of research* we're doing and in the *kinds of questions*, more importantly, that we're asking." Further, they point to the changes of configurations within departments: "Many if not most of the departments, when I began teaching, consisted of speech pathology and audiology, rhetoric, and theatre and oral interpretation. In fact, the first department I taught in was a four-person department with *no areas* at all. I taught public speaking, oral interpretation, voice and diction—things like that. Now, there are lots of different configurations. . . . speech pathology and theatre frequently are separate. They are no longer our daily 'corridor' colleagues and that has simply changed, in major ways, who 'we talk to.'" Several also talked about matters of placement: "Years ago—or at least up until the 1960s or even later, most departments of speech communication were located in the College of Arts and Humanities. Increasing numbers particularly at large universities now are in the College of Social and Behavioral Sciences where we have to face up to being 'the new person on the block' for a long time. This has involved two changes. Where I am 'placed' in the academy (some of my colleagues feel like 'displaced' persons), and learning second and third languages." Another points out how his research has changed: "My general knowledge has grown a great deal because the general knowledge of the field has grown a great deal. . . . In my most recent research I draw from diverse disciplines that intersect with our field. . . . Changes in cognate disciplines have also had a great impact on my life, most particularly in the last few years."

With changes of such magnitude also comes the proliferation of problems as well as benefits. Here are some: "To say that the discipline now includes far more *areas* of study may be an understatement. When I was a student—the departments most typically were called English (with speech a subsection). . . . The names of the associations have gone from 'elocution' to 'public speaking' to 'speech' to 'speech communication' and some, to 'communication.' Other important changes have been afoot: our numbers have grown substantially at the university and college level; and we ask our students to engage in 'theory building' at increasingly young ages—frequently at the expense of their time for broad reading, maturing. Thus, we may have brighter 'specialists'—fewer who examine broader questions and more who, to use Boulding's term, suffer from 'specialized deafness.'" Yet another observes: "A mixed blessing has been the growing diversity of our research efforts. It has enriched the range of what we study and of the questions we ask; but too many departments try to teach everything, and frequently they don't have the capacity to do it. They would be better off doing what they do well instead of responding to every new area. Moreover, until we are able to explain the common threads within that diversity we are subject to nearly endless quarrels from within and questioning from without. How do we fit together? Surely there are persuasive alternative answers to that question—but we had better learn how to 'spell them out.' We simply do not have the resources to be all things to all people."

They worry about other things as well. One expressed her concern over "increasing demands on the young to publish earlier and to publish more. Growing cynicism about the old personnel trio: teaching, research/publication, and service. What does service get you when it's tenure time? Not much. Teaching? Well, it's always mentioned but if you don't have publications, teaching is not likely to get you a promotion. I worry about the impact of this shift on teaching and on service and on those who must live in a pressure cooker and such a limited one at that." Yet another worries: "Internecine warfare may always have existed; now it rages and has frequently wasted time and done nothing to improve our tempers. I have no illusions that my earlier colleagues didn't have their fair share of ego—but now much of the time self-advertisement seems to be the order of our day." Perhaps one person summed up much of the temper of our times with special aptness: "Increased restlessness everywhere."

Without exception, the six reflected on the impact of the Women's Movement; for example: "When I was in graduate school at most 5-10% of the students were women and even fewer blacks. Now, I teach in a department where at least half of our graduate students are women; three are blacks; two, Asian-American; and two, Hispanic-Americans." "As a result of the Women's Movement I've had to change my old consciousness—how I teach, how I relate to my colleagues, and the issues I become interested in or try to defend within a university environment or within a professional association." Not surprisingly the women speak in still greater detail. One observes: "It's easier for women now. I was the first woman in tenure track, the first pregnant women [to teach in my division], etcetera. Now women are a fixture on campus. I'm still the token woman on important university committees—but this too shall pass as the bright assistant professors move up. Departments that wouldn't admit female grad students in the 50s are now trying to hire us. Although I benefited greatly from affirmative action, I resent job offers because I am a woman. I'd rather be considered a neuter gender professional and I'd like to assume that I can treat colleagues that way."

Several point to early wounds. One, for example, recalls:

I was hired before affirmative action by an unusually enlightened chairman—he had probably never even heard of the Women's Movement but he just hired people who could do the job. I cannot tell you how annoyed I was when a new chair put me down on the affirmative action list several years later. I formally and publically requested that he take my name off the list. He was not going to get around hiring other qualified women by that game. Then, when the press really came, I would get calls offering me a job. . . . Sometimes people would flat-out say: 'We've been told we have to hire a woman, preferably a senior woman.' That kind of remark makes an unhappy frame for one of the letters I received when I was applying for jobs while still in graduate school—one, a mimeoed one at that (!) said bluntly 'We do not accept applications from women.' So much for getting a Ph.D. I guess I didn't know how much anger (perhaps, rage) I was 'entitled to' until talking out similar experiences with other women in the profession. Our psychic bonds are profound, if somewhat newly discovered on my part. I think it's somewhat better now—I hope so.

Another asks us to recall some earlier colleagues and to pause before rejoicing too much: "I don't think I was very much aware of my 'predecessors' in my early 'growing up' days in the profession but now I know enough to unabashedly admire them—Maud May Babcock who became the first woman ever on the University of Utah faculty in 1892. Just think of what that must have been like! Henrietta Prentiss became SCA's first woman president in 1932. And, did you know that the very first Ph.D. in speech was awarded to a woman? Certainly Marie Hochmuth Nichols was a major role-model for the few women in graduate school in the 50s, 60s, and 70s. Still, of course, it's useful to remember only one woman has been named editor of *Quarterly Journal of Speech* [1963–1965] and none of *Monographs*. Any of the ECA's *Communication Quarterly*? Certainly not in recent history."

Most of our six "representative anecdotes" have always set career goals and still do. Their early ones were quite particular and not at all unexpected: to get an M.A., a Ph.D., a job, tenure, and to "move up through the ranks." Future goals? Most cited a similar goal. For example, "I want to continue to learn and write my most thoughtful pieces now that I am 50." "I want to write something of substantial value—something that makes a difference." They are not unmindful of how difficult that really is. Says one: "I tend to forget how genuinely unimportant and ephemeral so-called academic contributions are. I still want to write something that will survive me. Realistically, I know I won't but I'd like to. I think that keeps a lot of us writing." Illustrative of several, however, is this comment: "I never really set career goals; I just did work that I thought important when it occurred to me that I should be doing it."

When we examine those lauded in journal articles and honored by volumes, and when we talk in depth to six who illustrate the capacity to combine teaching, scholarship, and service, a comment from one of our youngest respondents seems especially apt. When asked, "What do you most admire in your colleagues?" he replied, "They do their share." They do, indeed.

What we have not detailed about the participants in our dialogue is substantial. We have not rounded out more fully our anecdotal sketches by drawing the fuller circumferences of their lives. They swim, play chess and tennis, read novels ("I could spend the rest of my life reading fiction," one confided), garden, travel, get involved in their children's sports activities, run for town offices, listen to music both casually and by following scores, play musical instruments, like old movies (and some newer ones also), and like "sharing quiet times with family and friends . . . not doing anything in particular." Rather, in this chapter we have focused on examining them as people at work with what Polanyi (1962, p. 59) might refer to as "tools." He observes: "We pour ourselves out into them and assimilate them as part of our existence. We accept them existentially by dwelling in them." A more detailed examination of their individual ways of working, as reflected in their interviews and conversations, would reveal not only their shared habits but also how unique they are as individuals. Still, we have been able to gain some insights into what it means to be speech communication teacher-scholars in the 20th century as they and we go about "keeping the faith" with the discipline and the larger communities of which we are a part. It is to be hoped that these representative anecdotes remind us that we are a part of a continuing dialogue about permanence and change, about permanence amidst change. We share profound bonds with our teachers, colleagues, family, and students. Frequently, we are persons of "great expectations" for our discipline and ourselves, and we are not unmindful that this is often a world in which one gets what one "asks for" more directly than is sometimes supposed.

What is the state of our art? And the quality of our teacher-scholars? Perhaps only a volume on the occasion of ECA's 100th anniversary can tell us that.

Reference List

Notes on Contributors

Index

Reference List

ABBREVIATIONS COMMONLY USED IN THIS REFERENCE LIST

AJS	*American Journal of Sociology*
AMJ	*Academy of Management Journal*
AMR	*Academy of Management Review*
AP	*American Psychologist*
ASQ	*Administrative Science Quarterly*
ASR	*American Sociology Review*
CCC	*College Composition and Communication*
CE	*Communication Education*
CHE	*Chronicle of Higher Education*
CM	*Communication Monographs*
CQ	*Communication Quarterly*
CSSJ	*Central States Speech Journal*
ECA	Eastern Communication Association
HBR	*Harvard Business Review*
HCR	*Human Communication Research*
HLR	*Harvard Law Review*
HR	*Human Relations*
ICA	International Communication Association
JACR	*Journal of Applied Communication Research*
JAP	*Journal of Applied Psychology*
JBC	*Journal of Business Communication*
JC	*Journal of Communication*
JPC	*Journal of Popular Culture*
JQ	*Journalism Quarterly*
LP	*Literature in Performance*
POQ	*Public Opinion Quarterly*
PP	*Personnel Psychology*
PR	*Philosophy and Rhetoric*

QJPS   *Quarterly Journal of Public Speaking*
QJS   *Quarterly Journal of Speech*
QJSE   *Quarterly Journal of Speech Education*
SAA   Speech Association of America
SAES   Speech Association of the Eastern States
SCA   Speech Communication Association
SGB   *Small Group Behavior*
SM   *Speech Monographs*
SSCJ   *Southern Speech Communication Journal*
SSJ   *Southern Speech Journal*
ST   *Speech Teacher*
TS   *Today's Speech*
WJSC   *Western Journal of Speech Communication*
WS   *Western Speech*
WSC   *Western Speech Communication*

PREFACE

Oliver, R. T., & Bauer, M. G. (Eds.). (1959). *Reestablishing the speech profession: The first fifty years.* Mineola, NY: SAES.

Wallace, K. R. (Ed.). (1954). *History of speech education in America.* New York: Appleton.

Wichelns, H. A. (1959). *A history of the Speech Association of the Eastern States.* Mineola, NY: SAES.

1. RHETORICAL THEORY IN SPEECH COMMUNICATION

Arnold, C. C. (1970). Perelman's *New Rhetoric. QJS, 56,* 87–92.

Baskerville, B. (1957). Selected writings on the criticism of public address. *WJSC, 21,* 110–118.

Bennett, W. L. (1978). Storytelling in criminal trials: A model of social judgment. *QJS, 64,* 1–22.

Bennett, W. L. (1979). Rhetorical transformations of evidence in criminal trials: Creating grounds for legal judgment. *QJS, 65,* 311–323.

Bitzer, L. F. (1968). The rhetorical situation. *PR, 1,* 1–14.

Bitzer, L. F. (1978). Rhetoric and public knowledge. In D. M. Burks (Ed.), *Rhetoric, philosophy, and literature: An exploration.* West Lafayette; Ind., Purdue University Press.

Black, E. (1965). *Rhetorical criticism: a study in method.* New York: Macmillan.

Booth, W. C. (1974). *Modern dogma and the rhetoric of assent*. Chicago: University of Chicago Press.

Bridwell, J. H. (1970). Marshall McLuhan: An experience. *CSSJ, 21*, 154–159.

Brinton, A. (1982). William James and the epistemic view of rhetoric. *QJS, 68*, 158–169.

Brockriede, W., & Ehninger, D. (1960). Toulmin on argument: An examination and application. QJS, *46*, 44–53.

Brummett, B. (1976). Some implications of "process" or "intersubjectivity": Postmodern rhetoric. *PR, 9*, 21–54.

Brummett, B. (1982). On to rhetorical relativism. *QJS, 68*, 425–430.

Brummett, B. (1984). Rhetorical theory as heuristic and moral: A pedagogical justification. *CE, 33*, 97–108.

Bryant, D. C. (1953). Rhetoric: Its functions and its scope. *QJS, 39*, 401–424.

Bryant, D. C. (1957). On style. *WJSC, 21*, 103–110.

Bryant, D. C. (1973). *Rhetorical dimensions in criticism*. Baton Rouge: Louisiana State University Press.

Burke, K. (1931). *Counter-statement*. New York: Harcourt, Brace.

Burke, K. (1935). *Permanence and change, an anatomy of purpose*. New York: New Republic.

Burke, K. (1937). *Attitudes toward history* (2 vols.). New York: New Republic.

Burke, K. (1941). *The philosophy of literary form, studies in symbolic action*. Baton Rouge: Louisiana State University Press.

Burke, K. (1945). *A grammar of motives*. New York: Prentice-Hall.

Burke, K. (1950). *A rhetoric of motives*. New York: Prentice-Hall.

Burke, K. (1961). *The rhetoric of religion: Studies in logology*. Boston: Beacon Press.

Carleton, W. M. (1978). What is rhetorical knowledge? A response to Farrell and more. *QJS, 64*, 313–328.

Clark, R. D. (1957). Lessons from the literary critics. *WJSC, 21*, 83–89.

Conley, T. M. (1978). "Logical hylomorphism" and Aristotle's *konoi topoi*. *CSSJ, 29*, 92–97.

Conley, T. M. (1982). Pathe and pisteis: Aristotle's *Rhet*. II.2–11. *Hermes, 110*, 300–315.

Consigny, S. (1974). Rhetoric and its situations. *PR, 7*, 175–186.

Cox, J. R., & Willard, C. A. (Eds.). (1982). *Advances in argumentation theory and research*. Carbondale: Southern Illinois University Press.

Croasman, E., & Cherwitz, R. A. (1982). Beyond rhetorical relativism. *QJS, 68*, 1–14.

Dearin, R. D. (1969). The philosophical basis of Chaim Perelman's theory of rhetoric. *QJS, 55*, 213–224.

Eubanks, R. T., & Baker, V. L. (1962). Toward an axiology of rhetoric. *QJS, 48,* 157–168.

Farrell, T. B. (1976). Knowledge, consensus and rhetorical theory. *QJS, 62,* 1–14.

Farrell, T. B. (1978). Social knowledge II. *QJS, 64,* 329–334.

Fisher, W. R. (1978). Toward a logic of good reasons. *QJS, 64,* 376–384.

Fisher, W. R. (1984). Narration as a human communication paradigm: The case of public moral argument. *CM, 51,* 1–22.

Gray, G. W. (1954). Some teachers and the transition to twentieth-century speech education. In K. R. Wallace (Ed.), *A history of speech education in America.* New York: Appleton.

Heath, R. L. (1979). Kenneth Burke on form. *QJS, 65,* 392–404.

Hochmuth, M. H. (1952). Kenneth Burke and the "new rhetoric." *QJS, 38,* 133–144.

Hochmuth, M. H. (1957). Burkean criticism. *WJSC, 21,* 89–95.

Hochmuth, M. H. (1958). I. A. Richards and the "new rhetoric." *QJS, 44,* 1–16.

Hochmuth, M. H. (1963). *Rhetoric and criticism.* Baton Rouge: Louisiana State University Press.

Holland, L. V. (1959). *Counterpoint: Kenneth Burke and Aristole's theories of rhetoric.* New York: Philosophical Library.

Hudson, H. H. (1921). Can we modernize the study of invention? *QJS, 7,* 325–334.

Hudson, H. H. (1923). The field of rhetoric. *QJS, 9,* 167–180.

Hudson, H. H. (1924). Rhetoric and poetry. *QJS, 10,* 143–154.

Hunt, E. L. (1915). The scientific spirit in public speaking. *QJS, 1,* 185–193.

Hunt, E. L. (1922). Adding substance to form in public speaking. *QJS, 8,* 256–265.

Johannesen, R. L. (1966). Richard Weaver's view of rhetoric and criticism. *SSJ, 32,* 133–145.

Leff, M. C. (1978). In search of Ariadne's thread: A review of the recent literature on rhetorical theory. *CSSJ, 29,* 73–91.

Leff, M. C., & Hewes, D. E. (1981). Topical invenion and group communication: Towards a sociology of inference. In G. Ziegeimueller & Rhodes (Eds.), *Dimensions of argument: Proceedings of the second summer conference on argumentation.* Annandale, Va.: Speech Communication Association.

Leff, M. C. (1983). The topics of argumentative invention in Latin rhetorical theory from Cicero to Boethius. *Rhetorica, 1,* 23–44.

Lentricchia, F. (1983). *Criticism and social change.* Chicago: University of Chicago Press.

McGee, M. C. (1975). In search of the 'the people': A rhetorical alternative. *QJS, 61,* 235–249.

McGee, M. C. (1978). "Not men but measures": The origins and import of an ideological principle. *QJS, 64*, 141–154.

McGee, M. C. (1980). The 'ideograph': A link between rhetoric and ideology. *QJS, 66*, 1–16.

McGee, M. C. (1982). A materialist conception of rhetoric. In R. E. McKerrow (Ed.), *Explorations in rhetoric: Studies in honor of Douglas Ehninger*. Glenview, Ill.: Scott, Foresman.

McKerrow, R. E. (1983). Marxism and a rhetorical conception of ideology. *QJS, 69*, 192–205.

Natanson, M. (1955). The limits of rhetoric. *QJS, 41*, 133–139.

O'Neill, J. M. (1915). The national association. *QJS, 1*, 51–58.

O'Neill, J. M. (1923). Speech content and course content in public speaking. *QJS, 9*, 25–52.

Ong, W. J., S. J. (1971). *Rhetoric, romance, and technology*. Ithaca, N.Y.: Cornell University Press.

Oravec, C. (1982). Where theory and criticism meet: A look at contemporary rhetorical theory. *WJSC, 46*, 56–71.

Osborn, M. (1967). Archetypal metaphor in rhetoric: The light-dark family. *QJS, 53*, 115–126.

Osborn, M. (1977). The evolution of the archetypal sea in rhetoric and poetic. *QJS, 63*, 347–363.

Patton, J. H. (1979). Causation and creativity in rhetorical situations: Distinctions and implications. *QJS, 65*, 36–55.

Perelman, C., & Olbrechts-Tyteca, L. (1969). *The new rhetoric: A treatise on argumentation*. (J. Wilkinson & P. Weaver, trans.). Notre Dame, Ind.: University of Notre Dame Press.

Railsback, C. C. (1983). Beyond rhetorical relativism: A structural-material model of truth and objective reality. *QJS, 69*, 351–363.

Rarig, F. M., & Greaves, H. S. (1954). National speech organizations and speech education. In K. R. Wallace (Ed.(. *A history of speech education in America*, New York: Appleton-Century.

Redding, W. C. (1957). Extrinsic and intrinsic criticism. *WJSC, 21*, 96–102.

Rosenfield, L. R. (1980). The practical celebration of epideictic. In E. E. White (Ed.), *Rhetoric in transition: Studies in the nature and uses of rhetoric*. University Park: Pennsylvania State University Press.

Rueckert, W. H. (1982). Kenneth Burke and the drama of human relations (2nd ed.). Berkeley: University of California Press.

Scott, R. L. (1967). On viewing rhetoric as epistemic. *CSSJ, 18*, 9–17.

Sloan, J. H. (1968). Understanding McLuhan: Some implications for the speech teacher and critic. *ST, 17*, 140–144.

Smith, D. K. (1954). Origin and development of Departments of Speech. In K. R. Wallace (Ed.), *A history of speech education in America*. New York: Appleton-Century.

Stewart, C. J. (1973). Historical survey: Rhetorical criticism in twentieth-century America. In G. P. Mohrmann, C. J. Stewart, & D. J. Ochs (Eds.), *Explorations in rhetorical criticism*. University Park: Pennsylvania State University Press.

Thompson, W. N. (1963). A conservative view of progressive rhetoric, *QJS, 49*, 1–7.

Trent, J. (1968). Toulmin's model of argument: An examination and extension. *QJS, 54*, 252–259.

Vatz, R. E. (1973). The myth of the rhetorical situation. *PR, 6*, 154–161.

Wallace, K. R. (1954). The field of speech. *QJS, 40*, 117–129.

Wallace, K. R. (1963). The substance of rhetoric: Good reasons. *QJS, 49*, 239–249.

Wallace, K. R. (1972). *Topoi* and the problem of invention. *QJS, 58*, 387–395.

Walter, Otis. (1963). On views of rhetoric, whether conservative or progressive. *QJS, 49*, 367–382.

Wichelns, H. A. (1925). The literary criticism of oratory. In *Studies in rhetoric and public speaking in honor of James A. Winans*. New York: Century.

Winans, J. A. (1915). The need for research. *QJS, 1*, 17–23.

Windt, T. O., Jr. (1982). Hoyt Hudson: Spokesman for the Cornell school of rhetoric. *QJS, 68*, 186–200.

2. THE HISTORY OF RHETORIC: THE RECONSTRUCTION OF PROGRESS

Abbott, D. (1978). *Retórica e elocuencia*: The evolution of rhetorical thought in eighteenth century Spain. *QJS, 64*, 295–303.

Abbott, D. (1983). Antonio De Capmany: Human nature and the nature of rhetoric. *QJS, 69*, 75–83.

Bator, P. G. (1982). The "principle of sympathy" in Campbell's *Philosophy of rhetoric. QJS, 68*, 418–424.

Benjamin, J. (1983). Eristic, dialectic, and rhetoric. *CQ, 31*, 21–26.

Benoit, W. L. (1980). Aristotle's example: The rhetorical induction. *QJS, 66*, 182–192.

Berlin, J. A. (1981). The transformation of invention in nineteenth century American rhetoric. *SSCJ, 46*, 292–304.

Bevilacqua, V. M. (1961). The rhetorical theory of Henry Home, Lord Kames. Unpublished doctoral dissertation. University of Illinois.

Bevilacqua, V. M. (1965). Philosophical origins of George Campbell's *Philosophy of rhetoric. CM, 32*, 1–12.

Bevilacqua, V. M. (1972). Vico, rhetorical humanism, and the study methods of *Our time. QJS, 58*, 70–83.

Bevilacqua, V. M., & Murphy, R. (Eds.). (1965). *A course of lectures on oratory and criticism*. By Joseph Priestley. Carbondale: Southern Illinois University Press.

Bitzer, L. F. (1959). Aristotle's enthymeme revisited. *QJS, 45*, 399–408.

Bitzer, L. F. (1962). The lively idea: A study of Hume's influence on George Campbell's *Philosophy of rhetoric*. Unpublished doctoral dissertation, University of Iowa.

Bitzer, L. F. (Ed.). (1963). *The philosophy of rhetoric*. By George Campbell. Carbondale and Edwardsville: Southern Illinois University Press.

Bitzer, L. F., & Black, E. (Eds.). (1971). *The prospect of rhetoric: Report of the national developmental project*. Englewood Cliffs, N.J.: Prentice-Hall.

Black, E. (1958). Plato's view of rhetoric. *QJS, 44*, 361–374.

Blankenship, J., & Stelzner, H. G. (Eds.). (1976). *Rhetoric and communication: Studies in the University of Illinois tradition*. Urbana, Chicago, London: University of Illinois Press.

Bormann, D. R. (1980). Adam Müller on the dialogical nature of rhetoric. *QJS, 66*, 169–181.

Bormann, D. R. (1982). Two faculty psychologists on the "ends" of speaking: George Campbell and Johann Sulzer. *CSSJ, 33*, 299–309.

Bormann, D. R., & Leinfellner, E. (1978). *Adam Müller's twelve lectures on rhetoric: A translation with a critical essay*. Ann Arbor: University Microfilms International.

Brandes, P. (1949). Aristotle and the undergraduate. *SSCJ, 14*, 264–269.

Brigance, W. N. (Ed.). (1960). *A history and criticism of American public address* (Vols. 1–2). New York: Russell & Russell.

Brockriede, W. E. (1966). Toward a contemporary Aristotelian theory of rhetoric. *QJS, 52*, 33–40.

Bryant, D. C. (1945). The Earl of Chesterfield's advice on speaking. *QJS, 31*, 411–417.

Bryant, D. C. (1950a). Aspects of the rhetorical tradition: The intellectual foundation. *QJS, 36*, 169–176.

Bryant, D. C. (1950b). Aspects of the rhetorical tradition: Emotion, style, and literary association. *QJS, 36*, 326–332.

Bryant, D. C. (1953). Rhetoric: Its functions and its scope. *QJS, 39*, 401–424.

Bryant, D. C. (Ed.). (1958). *The rhetorical idiom: Essays in rhetoric, oratory, language, and drama, presented to Herbert A. Wichelns*. Ithaca: Cornell University Press.

Bryant, D. C. (1981). Persuasive uses of imaginative literature in certain satires of Jonathan Swift. *SSCJ, 46*, 175–183.

Bryant, D. C., Smith, R. W., Arnott, P. D., Holtsmark, E. B., & Rowe, G. O. (Eds.). (1968). *Ancient greek and roman rhetoricians: A biographical dictionary*. Columbia, Mo.: Artcraft Press.

Caplan, H. (1924). The Latin panegyrics of the empire, *QJS, 10*, 41–52.

Caplan, H. (1970). *Of eloquence: Studies in ancient and medieval rhetoric* (Eds. Anne King and Helen North). Ithaca & London: Cornell University Press.

Caplan, H., & King, H. H. (1949). Italian treatises on preaching: A book-list. *CM, 16*, 243–252.

Caplan, H., & King, H. H. (1950). Spanish treatises on preaching: A book-list. *CM, 17*, 161–170.

Caplan, H., & King, H. H. (1954). Dutch treatises on preaching: A list of books and articles. *CM, 21*, 235–247.

Caplan, H., & King, H. H. (1956). Bibliography of German studies on preaching [Special issue]. *CM, 23*.

Carleton, W. M. (1979). A rhetorical rationale for interdisciplinary graduate study in communication. *CE, 28*, 332–338.

Clark, D. L. (1950). The place of rhetoric in a liberal education. *QJS, 36*, 291–295.

Clark, D. L. (1957). *Rhetoric in Greco-Roman education.* New York: Columbia University Press.

Cohen, H. (1954). The rhetorical theory of Hugh Blair. Unpublished doctoral dissertation, University of Iowa.

Conley, T. M. (1979a). The Greekless reader and Aristotle's *Rhetoric. QJS, 65*, 74–79.

Conley, T. M. (1979b). Ancient rhetoric and modern genre criticism. *CQ, 27*, 47–53.

Cooper, L. (1935). The rhetoric of Aristotle. *QJS, 21*, 10–19.

Crocker, L., & Carmack, P. A. (Eds.). (1965). *Readings in rhetoric.* Springfield, Ill.: Charles C. Thomas.

Dieter, O. A. L. (1950). Stasis. *CM, 17*, 345–369.

Edney, C. W. (1952). Campbell's lectures on pulpit eloquence. *CM, 19*, 1–10.

Ehninger, D. (1946). Bernard Lami's *L'art de parler*: A critical analysis. *QJS, 32*, 429–434.

Ehninger, D. (1949). Selected theories of *inventio* in English rhetoric: 1759–1828. Unpublished doctoral dissertation, Ohio State University.

Ehninger, D. (Ed.). (1963). *Elements of rhetoric.* By Richard Whately. Carbondale and Edwardsville: Southern Illinois University Press.

Ehninger, D. (1968). On systems of rhetoric. *PR, 1*, 131–144.

Ehninger, D. (1975). Colloquy II. A synoptic view of systems of western rhetoric. *QJS, 61*, 448–453.

Ehninger, D. (1978). The promise of rhetoric. In R. L. Enos, W. E. Wiethoff, T. M. Lentz, & D. Salerno (Eds.). *H TEXNH: Proceedings of the speech communication association 1978 doctoral honors seminar,* "Research methods and topics for the history of rhetoric" (pp. 1–9). Ann Arbor: Privately printed.

Enos, R. L. (1972). When rhetoric was outlawed in Rome: A translation and commentary of Suetonius's treatise on early Roman rhetoricians. *CM, 39,* 37–45.

Enos, R. L. (1973). The forensic oratory of Marcus Tullius Cicero: The development and application of a practical rhetoric. Unpublished doctoral dissertation, Indiana University.

Enos, R. L. (1977). The effects of imperial patronage on the rhetorical tradition of the Athenian second sophistic. *CQ, 25,* 3–10.

Enos, R. L., & McClaran, J. L. (1978). *A guide to doctoral dissertations in communication studies and theatre.* Ann Arbor: University Microfilms International.

Enos, R. L., Wiethoff, W. E., Koch, B. J., McClaran, J. L., & Vincent, B. A. (Eds.). (1979). *H TEXNH: Proceedings of the speech communication association 1979 doctoral honors seminar,* Research methods and topics for the history of rhetoric." Ann Arbor: Privately printed.

Enos, R. L., Wiethoff, W. E., Lentz, T. M., & Salerno, D. (Eds.). (1978). *H TEXNH: Proceedings of the speech communication association 1978 doctoral honors seminar,* "Research methods and topics for the history of rhetoric." Ann Arbor: Privately, printed.

Erickson, K. V. (1972). Aristotle's *Rhetoric*: Essays and bibliography. Unpublished doctoral dissertation, University of Michigan.

Erickson, K. V. (Ed.). (1974). *Aristotle: The classical heritage of rhetoric.* Metuchen, N.J.: Scarecrow Press.

Erickson, K. V. (1976). The lost rhetorics of Aristotle. *CM, 43,* 229–237.

Erickson, K. V. (Ed.). (1979). *Plato: True and sophistic rhetoric.* Amsterdam: Editions Rodopi NV.

Grimaldi, W. M. A., S. J. (1980). *Aristotle, "Rhetoric I": A commentary.* New York: Fordham University Press.

Guthrie, W. (1946). The development of rhetorical theory in America. *CM, 13,* 14–22.

Guthrie, W. (1947). The development of rhetorical theory in America. 1635–1850. *CM, 14,* 38–54.

Guthrie, W. (1948). The development of rhetorical theory in America, 1635–1850. *CM, 15,* 61–71.

Guthrie, W. (1949). The development of rhetorical theory in America: 1635–1850. *CM, 16,* 98–113.

Guthrie, W. (1951). The development of rhetorical theory in America, 1635–1850: The elocution movement. *CM, 18,* 17–30.

Hance, K. G. (1938). The elements of the rhetorical theory of Phillips Brooks. *CM, 5,* 16–30.

Harding, H. F. (Ed.). (1965). *Lectures on rhetoric and belles lettres.* By Hugh Blair (2 vols.). Carbondale and Edwardsville: Southern Illinois University Press.

Hauser, G. A. (1970). Description in eighteenth century British rhetorical and aesthetic theories. Unpublished doctoral dissertation, University of Wisconsin-Madison.

Hauser, G. A. (1979). Searching for a bright tomorrow: Graduate education in rhetoric during the 1980s. *CE, 28,* 259–270.

Havelock, E. A. (1982). *Preface to Plato.* Cambridge, Mass.: Harvard University Press. (Originally published, 1963.)

Hinks, J. W. (1981). Plato's rhetorical theory: Old perspectives on the epistemology of the new rhetoric. *CSSJ, 32,* 160–176.

Horner, W. B. (Ed.). (1980). *Historical rhetoric: An annotated bibliography of selected sources in English.* Boston: G. K. Hall.

Horner, W. B. (Ed.). (1983). *The present state of scholarship in historical and contemporary rhetoric.* Columbia: University of Missouri Press.

Howell, W. S. (1951a). *Fenelon's dialogues on eloquence.* Princeton: Princeton University Press.

Howell, W. S. (1951b). Oratory and poetry in Fenelon's literary theory. *QJS, 37,* 1–10.

Howell, W. S. (1956). *Logic and rhetoric in England, 1500–1700.* Princeton: Princeton University Press.

Howell, W. S. (1957). Classical and European traditions of rhetoric and speech training. *SSCJ, 23,* 73–78.

Howell, W. S. (1965). *The rhetoric of Alcuin & Charlemagne: A translation, with an introduction, the Latin text, and notes.* New York: Russell & Russell.

Howell, W. S. (1967). John Locke and the new rhetoric. *QJS, 53,* 319–333.

Howell, W. S. (1969). Adam Smith's lectures on rhetoric: An historical assessment. *CM, 36,* 393–418.

Howell, W. S. (1971). *Eighteenth-century British logic and rhetoric.* Princeton: Princeton University Press.

Howell, W. S. (1975). *Poetics, rhetoric, and logic: Studies in the basic disciplines of criticism.* Ithaca & London: Cornell University Press.

Howell, W. S. (1976). Colloquy II. The two-party line: A reply to Kenneth Burke. *QJS, 62,* 69–77.

Howes, R. F. (Ed.). (1961). *Historical studies of rhetoric and rhetoricians.* Ithaca: Cornell University Press.

Howes, R. F. (Ed.). (1976). *Notes on the Cornell school of rhetoric.* Riverside, Calif.: Privately printed.

Hudson, H. H. (1923). The field of rhetoric. *QJS, 9,* 167–180.

Hunt, E. L. (1920). Plato on rhetoric and rhetoricians. *QJS, 7,* 35–56. Revised and republished (1961) under the title: Plato and Aristotle on rhetoric and rhetoricians. In R. F. Howes (Ed.), *Historical studies of rhetoric and rhetoricians.* Ithaca: Cornell University Press. (1965). In L. Crocker and P. A. Carmack (Eds.), *Readings in rhetoric.* Springfield, Ill.: Charles C. Thomas, Publisher.

Hunt, E. L. (1926). An introduction to classical rhetoric. *QJS, 12*, 201–204.

Hunt, E. L. (1949). Rhetoric and general education. *QJS, 35*, 275–279.

Jamieson, K. M. (1976). Pascal vs. Descartes: A clash over rhetoric in the seventeenth century. *CM, 43*, 44–50.

Kaufer, D. S. (1978). The influence of Plato's developing psychology on his views of rhetoric. *QJS, 64*, 63–78.

Kennedy, G. A. (1963). *The art of persuasion in Greece*. Princeton: Princeton University Press.

Kennedy, G. A. (1969). *Quintilian*. New York: Twayne.

Kennedy, G. A. (1972). *The art of rhetoric in the Roman world: 300 B.C.–A.D. 300*. Princeton: Princeton University Press.

Kennedy, G. A. (1980). *Classical rhetoric and its Christian and secular tradition from ancient to modern times*. Chapel Hill: University of North Carolina Press.

Kennedy, G. A. (1983). *Greek rhetoric under Christian emperors*. Princeton: Princeton University Press.

Klapper, P., Anderson, P. R., Emmons, L. C., Jones, H. M., Demos, R., Richards, I. A., Ulman, B. L., Forester, N., Dunkel, H. B., & Hunt, E. L. (1949). A symposium on rhetoric and general education. *QJS, 35*, 419–426.

Kneupper, C. W., & Anderson, F. D. (1980). Uniting wisdom and eloquence: The need for rhetorical invention. *QJS, 66*, 313–326.

Langer, S. K. (1976). *Philosophy in a new key* (3rd ed.). Cambridge, Mass.: Harvard University Press.

LaRusso, D. A. (1956). Rhetoric and the social order in Italy, 1450–1600. Unpublished doctoral dissertation, Northwestern University.

LaRusso, D. A. (1960). Rhetorical education: Italy, 1300–1450. *WJSC, 24*, 213–219.

Leff, M. C. (1972). The frozen image: Sulpicius Victor and the ancient rhetorical tradition. Unpublished doctoral dissertation, University of California, Los Angeles.

Leff, M. C. (1973). The latin stylistic rhetorics of antiquity. *CM, 40*, 273–279.

Leff, M. C. (1974). Boethius and the history of medieval rhetoric, *CSSJ, 25*, 135–141.

Leff, M. C. (1976). Saint Augustine and Martianus Capella: Continuity and change in fifth-century Latin rhetorical theory. *CQ, 24*, 2–9.

Leff, M. C. (1978). In search of Ariadne's thread: A review of the recent literature on rhetorical theory. *CSSJ, 29*, 73–91.

Lentz, T. M. (1982). Writing as sophistry: From perservation to persuasion. *QJS, 68*, 60–68.

McBurney, J. H. (1936). The place of the enthymeme in rhetorical theory. *CM, 3*, 49–74.

McEwen, R. W., Hollinshead, B. S., Perrin, P. G., Weaver, A. T., Brigance, W. N., Wallace, K. R. Pettet, E. B., & Leyden, R. C. (1950). Rhetoric and general education. A symposium continued. *QJS, 36,* 1–9.

McGee, M. C. (1977). The fall of Wellington: A case study of the relationship between theory, practice, and rhetoric in history. *QJS, 63,* 28–42.

McKerrow, R. E. (1974). Whately's theory of rhetoric. Unpublished doctoral dissertation, University of Iowa.

McKerrow, R. E. (1975). Probable argument and proof in Whately's theory of rhetoric. *CSSJ, 26,* 259–266.

McKerrow, R. E. (Ed.). (1982). *Explorations in rhetoric: Studies in honor of Douglas Ehninger.* Glenview, Ill.: Scott, Foresman.

McNally, J. R. (1966). An appraisal of Rudolph Agricola's *de inventione dialectica libri tres* as a philosophy of artistic discourse. Unpublished doctoral dissertation, University of Iowa.

McNally, J. R. (1967). Rudolph Agricola's *de inventione dialectica libri tres*: A translation of selected chapters. *CM, 34,* 393–422.

Meador, P. A., Jr. (1964). Minucian, *On epicheiremes*: An introduction and a translation. *CM, 31,* 54–63.

Murphy, J. J. (Ed.). (n.d.). *Doctoral dissertations on rhetoric and rhetorical criticism.* London: University Microfilms International.

Murphy, J. J. (1960). The earliest teaching of rhetoric at Oxford. *CM, 27,* 345–347.

Murphy, J. J. (1962). The medieval arts of discourse: An introductory bibliography. *CM, 29,* 71–78.

Murphy, J. J. (1966). Aristotle's *Rhetoric* in the Middle Ages. *QJS, 52,* 109–115.

Murphy, J. J. (1967). Cicero's rhetoric in the Middle Ages. *QJS, 53,* 334–341.

Murphy, J. J. (1974). *Rhetoric in hte Middle Ages: A history of rhetorical theory from Saint Augustine to the Renaissance.* Berkeley, Los Angeles & London: University of California Press.

Murphy, J. J. (Ed.). (1978). *Medieval eloquence: Studies in the theory and practice of medieval rhetoric.* Berkeley, Los Angeles, & London: University of California Press.

Nadeau, R. (1949). *Rhetorica ad herrenium*: Commentary and translation of book I. *CM, 16,* 57–68.

Nadeau, R. (1950). Thomas Farnaby: Schoolmaster and rhetorician of the English Renaissance. *QJS, 36,* 340–344.

Nadeau, R. (1952). *The progymnasmata of Apthonius* in translation. *CM, 19,* 264–285.

Nadeau, R. (1958). Hermogenes on "stock issues" in deliberative speaking. *CM, 25,* 59–66.

Nadeau, R. (1964). Hermogenes' *On stases*: A translation with an introduction and notes. *CM, 31*, 361–424.

(Nichols), M. H. (1955). *A history and criticism of American public address* (Vol. 3). New York: Russell & Russell.

Nichols, M. H. (1970, February). The tyranny of relevance. *SPECTRA, 6*, 1, 9–10.

Nichols, M. H. (1977). When you set out for Ithaka . . . *CSSJ, 28*, 145–156.

North, H. (1956). Rhetoric and historiography. *QJS, 42*, 234–242.

North, H. (1966). *Sophrosyne: Self-knowledge and self-restraint in Greek literature*. Ithaca: Cornell University Press.

Ochs, D. J. (1966). The tradition of the classical doctrines of rhetorical *topoi*. Unpublished doctoral dissertation, University of Iowa.

Ochs, D. J. (1969). Aristotle's concept of formal topics. *CM, 36*, 419–425.

Ochs, D. J. (1982a). Cicero's *Topica*: A process view of invention. In R. E. McKerrow (Ed.), *Explorations in rhetoric: Studies in honor of Douglas Ehninger*, Glenview, Ill.: Scott, Foresman.

Ochs, D. J. (1982b). Rhetorical detailing in Cicero's verrine orations. *CSSJ, 33*, 310–318.

Ong, W., J., S. J. (1958). *Ramus and Talon inventory*. Cambridge, Mass.: Harvard University Press.

Ong, W., J., S. J. (1958/1974). *Ramus, method, and the decay of dialogue: From the art of discourse to the art of reason*. New York: Octagon Books, Farrar.

Parrish, W. M. (1947). The tradition of rhetoric. *QJS, 33*, 464–467.

Rahskopf, H. G. (1946). John Quincy Adams: Speaker and rhetorician. *QJS, 32*, 435–441.

Reinsma, L. M. (1977). Rhetoric in England: The age of Ælfric. 970–1020. *CM, 44*, 390–403.

Ryan, J. P. (1929). Quintilian's message. *QJS, 15*, 171–180.

Scott, R. L. (1975). Colloquy I. A synoptic view of systems of western rhetoric. *QJS, 61*, 440–447.

Schwartz, J., & Rycenga, J. A. (Eds.). (1965). The province of rhetoric. New York: Ronald Press.

Smith, B. (1918). The father of debate: Protagoras of Abdera. *QJS, 4*, 196–215.

Smith, B. (1920). Prodicus of Ceos: The sire of synonymy. *QJS, 6*, 51–68.

Smith, B. (1921). Corax and probability, *QJS, 7*, 13–42. (a)

Smith, B. (1921). Gorgias: A study of oratorical style. *QJS, 7*, 335–359. (b)

Smith, B. (1926). Hippias and a lost canon of rhetoric. *QJS, 12*, 129–145.

Smith, B. (1927). Thrasymachus: A pioneer rhetorician. *QJS, 13*, 278–291.

Smith, R. W. (1974). *The art of rhetoric in Alexandria: Its theory and practice in the ancient world*. The Hague: Martinus Nijhoff.

Street, R. L., Jr. (1979). Lexical diversity as an indicator of audience adaptation in Ciceronian orations. *CSSJ, 30*, 286–288.

Volpe, M. (1977). A practical rhetoric: A study of the argumentation of the *Apology*. *SSCJ, 42*, 137–150.

Wallace, K. R. (1936). Bacon's conception of rhetoric. *CM, 3*, 21–48.

Wallace, K. R. (1943). *Francis Bacon on communication & rhetoric or: The art of applying reason to imagination for the better moving of the will.* Chapel Hill: University of North Carolina Press.

Wallace, K. R. (Ed.). (1954). *History of speech education in America: Background studies.* New York: Appleton-Century.

Wallace, K. R. (1956). Aspects of modern rhetoric in Francis Bacon. *QJS, 42*, 398–406.

Wallace, K. R. (1963). The substance of rhetoric: Good reasons. *QJS, 49*, 239–249.

Wallace, K. R. (1973). Francis Bacon and method: Theory and practice. *CM, 40*, 243–272.

Walter, O. M. (1963). On views of rhetoric, whether conservative or progressive. *QJS, 49*, 367–382.

Warnick, B. (1978). Fenelon's recommendations to the French academy concerning rhetoric. *CM, 25*, 75–84.

Warnick, B. (1982). The old rhetoric vs. the new rhetoric: The quarrel between the ancients and the moderns. *CM, 49*, 263–276.

Weaver, B. J. (1979). Cultural determination of rhetorical styles: A study in Greek oratory. *CQ, 27*, 12–18.

White, E. E. (Ed.). (1980). *Rhetoric in transition: Studies in the nature and uses of rhetoric.* University Park & London: The Pennsylvania State University Press.

Wichelns, H. A. (Ed.). (1944). *Studies in speech and drama in honor of Alexander M. Drummond.* Ithaca: Cornell University Press.

Wiethoff, W. E. (1978). The martial "virtue" of rhetoric in Machiavelli's *Art of War*. *QJS, 64*, 304–312.

Wiethoff, W. E. (1979). Obscurantism in a ncient hellenistic rhetoric. *CSSJ, 30*, 211–219.

Wiethoff, W. E. (1980). The obscurantist design in Saint Augustine's rhetoric. *CSSJ, 31*, 128–136.

Winans, J. S. (1945). Whately on elocution. *QJS, 31*, 1–8.

3. THE CRITICISM OF SYMBOLIC INDUCEMENT: A CRITICAL-THEORETICAL CONNECTION

Andrews, J. R. (1969. Confrontation at Columbia: A case study in coercive rhetoric. *QJS, 55*, 9–16.

Arnold, C. C. (1959). Rhetoric in America since 1900. In R.T. Oliver & M.

G. Bauer (Eds.), *The speech profession: The first fifty years*. New York: SAES.

Benson, T. W. (1980). The rhetorical structure of Frederick Wiseman's *High school*. *CM, 47*, 233–261.

Bitzer, L. F., & Black, E. (Eds.). (1971). *The prospect of rhetoric*. Englewood Cliffs, N.J.: Prentice-Hall.

Black, E. (1965). *Rhetorical criticism: A study in method*. New York: Macmillan.

Black, E. (1970). The second persona. *QJS, 56*, 109–119.

Blau, J. L. (1968). Public address as intellectual revelation. In T. R. Nilsen (Ed.), *Essays on rhetorical criticism*. New York: Random House.

Brock, B. L., & Scott, R. L. (Eds.). (1972/1980). *Methods of rhetorical criticism* (2nd ed.). Detroit: Wayne State University Press.

Brooks, R. D. (1970). Black power: The dimensions of a slogan. *WS, 34*, 108–114.

Brown, W. R. (1978). Ideology as communication process. *QJS, 64*, 123–140.

Bryant, D. C. (1968). Of style: Buffon and rhetorical criticism. In T. R. Nilsen (Ed.), *Essays on rhetorical criticism*. New York: Random House.

Burgess, P. G. (1968). The rhetoric of black power: A moral demand? *QJS, 54*, 122–133.

Campbell, K. K. (1973). The rhetoric of women's liberation: An oxymoron. *QJS, 59*, 74–86.

Campbell, K. K., & Jamieson, K. H. (n.d.). Form and genre in rhetorical criticism: An introduction. In Campbell and Jamieson (Eds.), *Form and genre: Shaping rhetorical action*. Falls Church, Va.: SCA.

Campbell, K. K., & Jamieson, K. H. (Eds.). (n.d.). *Form and genre: Shaping rhetorical action*. Falls Church, Va.: SCA.

Central States Speech Journal, 31 (1980, Winter).

Chesebro, J. W. (1982). *Illness as a rhetorical act: A cross cultural perspective. CQ, 30*, 321–331.

Clark, R. D. (1968). Literary and rhetorical criticism. In T. R. Nilsen (Ed.), *Essays on rhetorical criticism*. New York: Random House.

Ehninger, D. (1965). Rhetoric and the critic. *WS, 29*, 227–231.

Fulkerson, R. P. (1979). The public letter as a rhetorical form: Structure, logic, and style in King's "Letter from Birmingham jail." *QJS, 65*, 121–136.

Gonzalez, A., & Makay, J. K. (1983). Rhetorical ascription and the gospel according to Dylan. *QJS, 69*, 1–14.

Gregg, R. B. (1971). The ego-function of the rhetoric of protest. *PR, 4*, 71–91.

Gregg, R. B. (1977). The rhetoric of political newscasting. *CSSJ, 28*, 221–237.

Gronbeck, B. E. (n.d.). Celluloid rhetoric: On genres of documentary. In K. K. Campbell & K. H. Jamieson (Eds.), *Form and genre: Shaping rhetorical action*. Falls Church, Va.: SCA.

Haiman, F. (1967). The rhetoric of the streets: Some legal and ethical considerations. *QJS, 53*, 99–114.

Havelock, E. A. (1976). *Origins of western literacy*. Toronto, Canada: The Ontario Institute for Studies in Education.

Hill, F. (1972). Conventional wisdom—Traditional form—The president's message of November 3, 1969. *QJS, 58*, 373–386.

Hudson, H. H. (1923). Rhetoric and poetry. *QJSE, 9*, 144–145.

Kelso, J. A. (1980). Science and the rhetoric of reality. *CSSJ, 31*, 17–29.

Kennedy, G. (1963). *The art of persuasion in Greece*. Princeton: Princeton University Press.

Klynn, M. S. (1968). Toward a pluralistic rhetorical criticism. In T. Nilsen (Ed.), *Essays on rhetorical criticism*. New York: Random House.

Leff, M. (1980). Interpretation and the art of the rhetorical critic. *WJSC, 44*, 337–349.

Lloyd, G. E. R. (1979). *Magic, reason and experience*. Cambridge: Cambridge University Press.

Makay, J. J. (1980). Psychotherapy as a rhetoric for secular grace. *CSSJ, 31*, 184–196.

Mechling, E. W., & Mechling, J. (1983). Sweet talk: The moral rhetoric against sugar. *CSSJ, 34*, 19–32.

Medhurst, M. J. (1968). *Hiroshima, mon amour*: From iconography to rhetoric. *QJS, 68*, 345–370.

Medhurst, M. J. (1977). American cosmology and the rhetoric of inaugural prayer. *CSSJ, 28*, 272–282.

Medhurst, M. J., & Benson, T. W. (1981). *The city*: The rhetoric of rhythm. *CM, 48*, 54–72.

Medhurst, M. J., & DeSousa, M. A. (1981). Political cartoons as rhetorical form: A taxonomy of graphic discourse. *CM, 48*, 197–236.

Mohrmann, G. P., & Scott, F. E. (1976). Popular music and world war II: The rhetoric of continuation. *QJS, 62*, 145–156.

Nichols, M. H. (1968). Burkean criticism. In T. R. Nilsen (Ed.), *Essays on rhetorical criticism*. New York: Random House.

Nilsen, T. R., Ed. (1968). *Essays on rhetorical criticism*. New York: Random House.

Nilsen, T. R. (   ). Interpretative function of the critic. In T. R. Nilsen (Ed.), *Essays on rhetorical criticism*. New York: Random House.

Oliver, R. T., & Bauer, M. G. (Eds.). (1959). *The speech profession: The first fifty years*. New York: SAES.

Olsen, L. C. (1983). Portraits in praise of a people: A rhetorical analysis of Norman Rockwell's icons in Franklin D. Roosevelts "four freedoms" campaign. *QJS, 69*, 15–24.

Osborn, M. (1977). The evolution of the archetypal sea in rhetoric and poetic. *QJS, 63*, 347–363.

Rosenfield, L. W. (1973). Politics and pornography. *QJS, 59*, 413–422.

Rushing, J. H., & Frentz, T. S. (1978). The rhetoric of "Rocky": A social value model of criticism. *WJSC, 42*, 63–72.

Scott, R. L. (1977). Diego Rivera at Rockefeller Center: Fresco painting and rhetoric. *WJSC, 41*, 70–82.

Scott, R. L., & Brockriede, W. (1969). *The rhetoric of black power*. New York: Harper & Row.

Scott, R. L., & Smith, D. K. (1969). The rhetoric of confrontation. *QJS, 55*, 1–8.

Stewart, C. J., Ochs, D., & Mohrmann, G. P. (Eds.). (1973). *Explorations in rhetorical criticism*. University Park: Pennsylvania State University Press.

Stelzner, H. G. (1976). John F. Kennedy at Houston, Texas, September 12, 1960. In Blankenship, J., & Stelzner, H. G. (Eds.), *Rhetoric and communication: Studies in the University of Illinois tradition*. Urbana, Chicago, London: University of Illinois Press.

Stuart, C. (1973). Architecture in Nazi Germany: A rhetorical perspective. *WJSC, 37*, 253–263.

Swanson, D. L. (1977). A reflective view of the epistemology of critical inquiry. *CM, 44*, 207–219. (a)

Swanson, D. L. (1977). The requirements of critical justifications. *CM, 44*, 306–320. (b)

Western Journal of Speech Communication, The, 44 (1980, Fall).

Weimer, W. B. (1977). Science as a rhetorical transaction: Toward a nonjustificational concept of rhetoric. *PR, 10*, 1–29.

Wichelns, H. A. (1980). The literary criticism of oratory. In B. L. Brock & R. L. Scott (Eds.), *Methods of rhetorical criticism*. Detroit: Wayne State University Press.

Wilson, J. F. (1959). Rhetorical criticism by laymen. In R. T. Oliver & M. G. Bauer (Eds.), *The speech profession: The first fifty years*. New York: SAES.

4. COMMUNICATION AND HUMAN RIGHTS: THE SYMBOLIC STRUCTURES OF RACISM AND SEXISM

Asante, M. (1983). *An Afrocentric rhetoric*. Keynote address, 3rd World Conference on Black Communication, Barbados. July 23, New York: Rockefeller Foundation.

Barthes, R. (1972). *Mythologies*. (A. Lavers, Trans.). New York: Hill & Wang.

Benson, T. (1970). Violence: Communication breakdown? Focus on recent publications, *TS, 18* (Winter), 39–46.

Benson, T. (1974). Rhetoric and autobiography: The case of Malcolm X. *QJS, 55*, 1–8.

Braden, W. (1975). Myths in a rhetorical context. *SSCJ, 40*, 113–126.

Browne, R. S. (1968). Dialogue between the races—A top priority. *TS, 16*(3), 5–8.

Brownmiller, S. (1975). *Against our will: Men, women and rape.* New York: Simon & Schuster.

Burgess, P. (1968). The rhetoric of black power: A moral demand? *QJS, 54*, 122–133.

Campbell, K. K. (1973). The rhetoric of women's liberation: An oxymoron. *QJS, 56*, 74–86.

———. (1983). Femininity and feminism: To be or not to be a woman. *CQ, 44*, 275–287.

Cathcart, R. (1983). A confrontational perspective on the study of social movements. *CSSJ, 34*, 69–74.

Central States Speech Journal, (1980). *31* (4) [Winter issue].

Chesebro, J., Cragan, J., & McCullough, P. (1973). The small group technique of the radical revolutionary: A synthetic study of consciousness raising. *SM, 40*, 136–146.

Cleaver, E. (1968). A letter from jail. Reprinted in R. Fabrizio, E. Karos, & R. Menmuir. (1970). *The rhetoric of no.* New York: Holt.

Corbett, E. (1969). The rhetoric of the open hand and the rhetoric of the closed fist. *CCC, 20*, 288–296.

Costello, M. (1978). Political prisoners. The rights revolution, (S. Stencel, Ed.), Editorial Research Reports, Washington, 107–126.

Davis, O. (1967). The English language is my enemy. Reprinted in A. Smith (Ed.). (1972). *Language communication and rhetoric in black America.* New York: Harper & Row.

Firestone, S. (1970). *The dialectic of sex: The case for feminist revolution.* New York: Bantam.

Franklin, J. H. (1965). *From slavery to freedom.* New York: Knopf.

Goldstein, R. J. (1978). *Political repression in modern America: From 1870 to the present.* Cambridge, Mass.: Schenkman.

Gornick, V., & Moran, B. (Eds.). (1972). *Woman in sexist society.* New York: Signet.

Gregg, R. (1971). The ego-function of the rhetoric of protest. *PR, 4*, 71–91.

Grimshaw, A. D. (1959). A study in social violence: Urban race riots in the United States. Unpublished doctoral dissertation, University of Pennsylvania.

Hess, B., Markson, E., & Stein, P. (1982). *Sociology.* New York: Macmillan.

Hope, D. (1975). Redefinition of self: A comparison of the rhetoric of the women's liberation and black liberation movements. *TS, 23* (1), 17–25.

Humphrey, H. (1966). Address at the NAACP convention, July 6. Reprinted in R. Scott & W. Brockriede. (1969). *The rhetoric of black power.* New York: Harper & Row.

Jefferson, P. (1967). The magnificent barbarian at Nashville. *SSJ, 33,* 77–87.

Jordon, V. (1981). Back to basics for black people. *Vital Speeches, 47* (21), 659–663.

Krouse, A. N., & Peters, M. (1975). Why women kill. *JC, 25,* 98–105.

Lake, R. (1983). Enacting red power: The consummating function in Native American protest rhetoric. *QJS, 69,* 127–142.

Lakoff, R. (1975). *Language and women's place.* New York: Harper & Row.

Leiberson, S., & Silberman, R. (1965). Precipitance and underlying conditions of race riots. *ASR, 30,* 887–898.

Lomos, C. (1968). *The agitator in American society.* Englewood Cliffs, N.J.: Prentice-Hall.

Mailer, N. (1959). The white Negro: superficial reflections on the hipster. Reprinted in H. Jaffe & J. Tytell, (Eds.). (1970). *The American experience: A radical reader.* New York: Harper & Row.

Matlon, Ronald (Ed.). (1980). *Index to journals in communication studies through 1979.* Falls Church, Va.: SCA.

McEdwards, M. (1968). Agitative rhetoric: Its nature and effect. *WS, 32,* 36–43.

McGee, Michael. (1980). The ideograph: A link between rhetoric and ideology. *QJS, 66,* 1–16.

Means, R. (1980). For the world to live, "Europe" must die. *Mother Jones,* 5(10), 22–38.

Murray, F. (Ed.). (1944). *The Negro handbook.* New York: Macmillan.

Neiburg, H. L. (1962). The threat of violence and social change. *American Political Science Review, 56,* 865–873.

Norton, T. (1945). *The constitution of the United States: Its sources and its application.* New York: Nesterman.

Osotsky, G. (1963). Race riot, 1900, a study of ethnic violence. *Journal of Negro Education, 32,* 16–24.

Pipes, W. H. (1945). Old time Negro preaching: An interpretive study. *QJS,* 30, 15–21.

Report of the National Advisory Commission on Civil Disorders. (1968). (The Kerner Report). New York: Bantam.

Rich, A., & Smith, A. (Asante). (1970). *The rhetoric of revolution.* Durham, N.C.: Moore.

Riches, S., and Sillars, M. (1980). The status of movement criticism. *WJSC,* 44, 275–287.

Roszak, T. (1969). The hard and the soft: The force of feminism in modern times. In B. Roszak & T. Roszak (Eds.). (1969). *Masculine/Feminine.* New York: Harper & Row.

Schaich, W. (1975). A relationship between collective racial violence and war. *Journal of Black Studies, 5,* 374–394.

Scott, R. L. (1973). The conservative voice in radical rhetoric: A common response to division. *SM, 40,* 123–135.

Scott, R. L., & Smith, D. K. (1969). The rhetoric of confrontation. *QJS, 55,* 1–8.

Simons, H. (1970). Requirements, problems and strategies: A theory for social movements. *QJS, 56,* 1–11.

Smith, A. (Asante). (1969). *The rhetoric of black revolution.* Boston: Allyn & Bacon.

Smith, D. D. (1976). The social content of pornography. *JC, 26,* 16–24.

Smith, D. H. (1967). Social protest and the oratory of human rights. *TS, 15,* 2–8.

Stimpson, C. (1972). Thy neighbor's wife, thy neighbor's servants: Women's liberation and black civil rights. In V. Gornick & B. Moran (Eds.), *Woman in sexist society.* New York: Signet.

U.S. Census. *Statistical Abstracts,* 1980.

U.S. News and World Report. 1964, April, 28–29; 1966, September, 34–35.

Walker, D. (1968). *Rights in Conflict: A Report to the National Commission on Causes and Prevention of Violence.* New York: Bantam.

Waskow, A. I. (1967). *From race riots to sit-in, 1919 and the 1960's: A study in the connections between conflict and violence.* New York: Anchor.

Weaver, R. (1953). *The ethics of rhetoric.* Chapt. 9, Ultimate terms in contemporary rhetoric. Chicago: Henry Regner.

Willheim, S. (1983). *Black in white America.* Cambridge, Mass.: Schenkman.

Williams, Robert. (1960). South Africa: 1960. *The Crusader, 1* (41), 1–8.

5. THE PARADIGM OF UNFULFILLED PROMISE: A CRITICAL EXAMINATION OF THE HISTORY OF RESEARCH ON SMALL GROUPS IN SPEECH COMMUNICATION

Alderton, S. (1980). Attributions of responsibility for socially deviant behavior in decision-making discussions as a function of situation and locus of control of attributor. *CSSJ, 31,* 117–127.

Alderton, S. (1982). Locus of control-based argumentation as a predictor of group polarization. *CQ, 30*, 381–387.

Alderton, S. M., & Jurma, W. E. (1980). Genderless/gender related task, leader communication, and group satisfaction. *SSCJ, 46*, 48–60.

Arntson, P. H., Mortensen, C. D., & Lustig, M. W. (1980). Predispositions toward verbal behavior in task-oriented interaction. *HCR, 6*, 239–252.

Baird, A. C. (1927). *Public discussion and debate*. Boston: Ginn.

Baird, A. C. (1937). *Public discussion and debate* (2nd ed.). Boston: Ginn.

Baird, J. E., Jr. (1974). A comparison of distributional and sequential structure in group discussions. *SM, 41*, 226–232.

Baird, J. E., Jr. (1976). Sex differences in group communication: A review of relevant research. *QJS, 62*, 179–192.

Bayless, O. L. (1967). An alternate pattern for problem-solving discussion. *JC, 17*, 188–197.

Becker, S. L. (1980). Directions for small group research for the 1980s. *CSSJ, 31*, 221–224.

Bell, M. A. (1974). The effects of substantive and affective conflict in problem-solving groups. *SM, 41*, 19–23.

Berlo, D. K. (1960). *The process of communication*. New York: Holt.

Bochner, A. P., & Bochner, B. (1972). A multivariate investigation of Machiavellianism in four-man groups. *SM, 39*, 277–285.

Bormann, E. G. (1970). The paradox and promise of small group research. *SM, 37*, 211–216.

Bormann, E. G. (1980). The paradox and promise of small group research revisited. *CSSJ, 31*, 214–220.

Bradley, P. H. (1980). Sex, competence, and opinion deviation: An expectation states approach. *CM, 47*, 101–110.

Bradley, P. H., Hamon, C. M., & Harris, A. M. (1976, Autumn). Dissent in small groups. *JC, 26*, 155–159.

Burgoon, J. K. (1976). The unwillingness to communicate scale: Development and validation. *CM, 43*, 60–69.

Burgoon, M. (1971). Amount of conflicting information in a group discussion and tolerance for ambiguity as predictors of task attractiveness. *SM, 38*, 121–124.

Chesebro, J. W., Cragan, J. F., & McCullough, P. (1974). The small group technique of the radical revolutionary: A synthetic study of consciousness raising. *SM, 41*, 136–146.

Cline, R. J., & Cline, T. R. (1980, Fall). A structural analysis of risky-shift and cautious-shift discussions. *CQ, 28*, 26–36.

Courtright, J. A. (1978). A laboratory investigation of groupthink. *CM, 45*, 229–246.

Cragan, J. F., & Wright, D. W. (1980). Small group research of the 1970's: A synthesis and critique. *CSSJ, 31*, 197–213.

Crowell, L., Katcher, A., & Miyamoto, S. F. (1955). Self-concepts of communication skill and performance in small group discussions. *SM*, 22, 20–27.

Dewey, J. (1910). *How we think*. Boston: Heath.

Donohue, W. A., Hawes, L. C., & Mabee, T. (1981). Testing a structural-functional model of group decision making using Markov analysis. *HCR*, 7, 133–146.

Downs, C. W., & Pickett, T. (1977). An analysis of the effects of nine leadership-group compatibility contingencies upon productivity and member satisfaction. *CM*, 44, 220–230.

Ellis, D. G. (1979). Relational control in two group systems. *CM*, 46, 153–166.

Ellis, D. G., & Fisher, B. A. (1975). Phases of conflict in small group development: A Markov analysis. *HCR*, 1, 195–212.

Ellis, D. G., & McCallister, L. (1980). Relational control sequences in sex-typed and androgynous groups. *WJSC*, 44, 35–49.

Ewbank, H. L., & Auer, J. J. (1941). *Discussion and debate: Tools of a democratic society*. New York: Appleton-Century.

Fisher, B. A. (1970). Decision emergence: Phases in group decision-making. *SM*, 37, 53–66. (a)

Fisher, B. A. (1970). The process of decision modification in small discussion groups. *JC*, 20, 51–64. (b)

Fisher, B. A. (1979, Fall). Content and relationship dimensions of communicating in decision-making groups. *CQ*, 27, 3–11.

Fisher, B. A., & Hawes, L. (1971). An interact system model: Generating a grounded theory of small groups. *QJS*, 57, 444–453.

Geier, J. G. (1967). A trait approach to the study of leadership. *JC*, 17, 316–323.

Gouran, D. S. (1969). Variables related to consensus in group discussions of questions of policy. *SM*, 36, 387–391.

Gouran, D. S. (1970). Response to "the promise and paradox of small group research." *SM*, 37, 217–218.

Gouran, D. S. (1973). Group communication: Perspectives and priorities for future research. *QJS*, 59, 22–29. (a)

Gouran, D. S. (1973). Correlates of member satisfaction in group decision-making discussions. *CSSJ*, 24, 91–96. (b)

Gouran, D. S. (1976). The Watergate cover-up: Its dynamics and its implications. *CM*, 43, 176–186.

Gouran, D. S., & Baird, J. E., Jr. (1972). An analysis of distributional and sequential structure in problem-solving and informal group discussions. *SM*, 39, 16–22.

Gouran, D. S., & Andrews, P. H. (1984). Determinants of punitive re-

sponses to socially proscribed behavior: Seriousness, attribution of responsibility, and status of the offender. *SGB, 15, 525–543.*

Gouran, D. S., Brown, C. R., & Henry, D. R. (1978). Behavioral correlates
of perceptions of quality in decision-making discussions. *CM, 45, 51–63.*

Gouran, D. S., & Geonetta, S. C. (1977). Patterns of interaction as a
function of the degree of leadership centralization in decision-making
groups. *CSSJ, 28, 47–53.* (a)

Gouran, D. S., & Geonetta, S. C. (1977). Patterns of interaction in decision-
making groups at varying distances from consensus. *SGB, 8, 511–
524.* (b)

Gouran, D. S., Ketrow, S. M., Spear, S., & Brown, J. (1984). Communicative characteristics of groups discussing socially deviant acts of individuals varying in their occupational status. *SGB, 15, 63–86.*

Guetzkow, H., & Gyr, J. (1954). An analysis of conflict in decision-making
groups. *HR, 7, 367–382.*

Haiman, F. S. (1950). *Group leadership and democratic action.* Boston:
Houghton Mifflin.

Harnack, R. V. (1951). Competition and cooperation. *CSSJ, 3, 15–20.*

Harnack, R. V. (1955). An experimental study of the effects of training in
the recognition and formulation of goals upon intra-group cooperation.
SM, 22, 31–38.

Harnack, R. V. (1963). A study of the effects of an organized minority upon
a discussion group. *JC, 13, 12–24.*

Harper, N. L., & Askling, L. R. (1980). Group communication and quality
of task solution in a media production organization. *CM, 47, 77–100.*

Hewes, D. C. (1979). The sequential analysis of social interaction. *QJS, 65,
56–73.*

Hill, T. A. (1976). An experimental study of the relationship between
opinionated leadership and small group consensus. *CM, 43, 246–257.*

Hirokawa, R. Y. (1980). A comparative analysis of communication patterns within effective and ineffective decision-making groups. *CM, 47,
312–321.*

Hirokawa, R. Y. (1982). Group communication and problem-solving effectiveness I: A critical review of inconsistent findings. *CQ, 30, 134–141.* (a)

Hirokawa, R. Y. (1982). Consensus group decision-making, quality of
decision, and group satisfaction: An attempt to sort "fact" from
"fiction." *CSSJ, 33, 407–415.* (b)

Hirokawa, R. Y. (1983). Group communication and problem-solving effectiveness II. *WJSC, 47, 59–74.*

Jablin, F. M. (1981). Cultivating imagination: Factors that enhance and
inhibit creativity in brainstorming groups. *HCR, 7, 245–258.*

Jablin, F. M., Seibold, D. R., & Sorenson, R. L. (1977). Potential inhibitory effects of group participation on brainstorming performance. *CSSJ, 28,* 113–121.

Janis, I. L. (1982). *Groupthink* (2nd ed.). Boston: Houghton Mifflin.

Janis, I. L., & Mann, L. (1977). *Decision making.* New York: Free Press.

Johnson, A. (1943). An experimental study in the analysis and measurement of reflective thinking. *SM, 10,* 83–96.

Jordan, W. J., & McLaughlin, M. L. (1976). The effect of sex-role ambiguity on impression formation processes in individuals and groups. *WSC, 40,* 32–39.

Jurma, W. E. (1978). An experimental study of the relationship of leadership structuring style and task ambiguity to the resulting satisfaction of group members. *SGB, 9,* 124–134.

Jurma, W. E. (1979). Effects of leader structuring style and task-orientation characteristics of group members. *CM, 46,* 282–295.

Kline, J. A. (1972). Orientation and group consensus. *CSSJ, 23,* 44–47.

Knutson, T. J. (1972). An experimental study of the effects of orientation behavior on small group consensus. *SM, 39,* 159–165.

Knutson, T. J., & Holdridge, W. E. (1975). Orientation behavior, leadership, and consensus: A possible functional relationship. *SM, 42,* 107–114.

Knutson, T. J., & Kowitz, A. C. (1977). Effects of information types and level of orientation on consensus-achievement in substantive and affective small-group conflict. *CSSJ, 28,* 54–63.

Larson, C. E. (1969). Forms of analysis and small group problem-solving. *SM, 36,* 452–455.

Larson, C. E. (1971). Speech communication research on small groups. *ST, 20,* 89–107.

Leathers, D. G. (1969). Process disruption and measurement in small group communication. *QJS, 55,* 287–300.

Leathers, D. G. (1970). The effects of trust destroying behavior in the small group. *SM, 37,* 180–187.

Leathers, D. G. (1971). The feedback rating instrument: A new means of evaluating discussion. *CSSJ, 22,* 32–42.

Lumsden, G. (1974). An experimental study of the effect of verbal agreement on leadership maintenance in problem-solving discussion. *CSSJ, 25,* 270–276.

Lumsden, G., Brown, D. R., Lumsden, D., & Hill, T. A. (1974, Fall). An investigation of differences in verbal behavior between black and white informal peer group discussions. *TS, 22,* 31–36.

Lustig, M. W., & Grove, T. G. (1975). Interaction analysis of small problem-solving groups containing reticent and non-reticent members. *WSC, 39,* 155–164.

Mabry, E. A. (1975). Exploratory analysis of a developmental model for task-oriented small groups. *HCR, 2,* 66–74. (a)

Mabry, E. A. (1975). Sequential structure of interaction in encounter groups. *HCR, 1*, 302–307. (b)

Marr, T. J. (1974). Conciliation and verbal responses as a function of orientation and threat in group interaction. *SM, 41*, 6–18.

McBurney, J. H., & Hance, K. G. (1939). *Discussion in human affairs.* New York: Harper & Brothers.

McCroskey, J. C., Hamilton, P. R., & Weiner, A. N. (1974). The effect of interaction behavior on source credibility, homophily, and interpersonal attraction. *HCR, 1*, 42–52.

McCroskey, J. C., & Wright, D. W. (1971). The development of an instrument for measuring interaction behavior in small groups. *SM, 38*, 335–340.

McCroskey, J. C., Young, T. J., & Scott, M. D. (1972). The effects of message sidedness and evidence on inoculation against counter-persuasion in small group communication. *SM, 39*, 205–212.

Mortensen, C. D. (1970). The status of small group research. *QJS, 36*, 304–309.

Philipsen, G., Mulac, A., & Dietrich, D. (1979). The effects of social interaction on group generation of ideas. *CM, 46*, 119–125.

Poole, M. S. (1981). Decision development in small groups I: A comparison of two models. *CM, 48*, 1–24.

Poole, M. S., McPhee, R. D., & Seibold, D. R. (1982). A comparison of normative and interactional explanations of group decision-making: Social decision schemes versus valence. *CM, 49*, 1–19.

Porter, L. W. (1976). The White House transcripts: Group fantasy events concerning the mass media. *CSSJ, 27*, 272–279.

Prentice, D. S. (1975). The effect of trust-destroying communication on verbal fluency in the small group. *SM, 42*, 262–270.

Putnam, L. L. (1979). Preference for procedural order in task-oriented small groups. *CM, 46*, 193–218.

Pyron, H. C. (1964). An experimental study of the role of reflective thinking in business and professional conferences and discussions. *SM, 31*, 157–161.

Pyron, H. C., & Sharp, H., Jr. (1963). A quantitative study of reflective thinking and performance in problem-solving discussion. *JC, 13*, 46–53.

Rarick, D. L., Soldow, G. F., & Geizer, R. S. (1976). Self-monitoring as a mediator of conformity. *CSSJ, 27*, 267–271.

Rosenfeld, L. B., & Fowler, G. D. (1976). Personality, sex, and leadership style. *CM, 43*, 320–324.

Rosenfeld, L. B., & Plax, T. G. (1975). Personality determinants of autocratic and democratic leadership. *SM, 42*, 203–208.

Saine, T. J., & Bock, D. G. (1973). The effects of reward criteria on the structure of interaction in problem-solving groups. *SSCJ, 39*, 55–62. (a)

Saine, T. J., & Bock, D. G. (1973). A comparison of the distributional and sequential structures of interaction in high and low consensus groups. *CSSJ*, *24*, 125–130. (b)

Sargent, J. F., & Miller, G. R. (1971). Some differences in certain communication behaviors of autocratic and democratic leaders. *JC*, *21*, 233–252.

Sattler, W. E., & Miller, N. E. (1954). *Discussion and conference.* Englewood Cliffs, N.J.: Prentice-Hall.

Scheidel, T. M., & Crowell, L. (1964). Idea development in small discussion groups. *QJS*, *50*, 140–145.

Scheidel, T. M., & Crowell, L. (1966). Feedback in small group communication. *QJS*, *52*, 273–278.

Schultz, B. (1982). Argumentativeness: Its effect in group decision-making and its role in leadership perception. *CQ*, *30*, 368–375.

Sharp, H., Jr. & Milliken, J. (1964). The reflective thinking ability and the product of problem-solving discussion. *SM*, *31*, 124–127.

Sorenson, G., & McCroskey, J. C. (1977). The prediction of interaction behavior in small groups: Zero history versus intact groups. *CM*, *44*, 73–80.

Stech, E. L. (1970). An analysis of interaction structure in the discussion of a ranking task. *SM*, *37*, 249–256.

Stech, E. L. (1975). Sequential structure in human social communication. *HCR*, *1*, 168–179.

Stech, E. L. (1977). The effect of category system design on estimates of sequential and distributional structure. *CSSJ*, *28*, 64–69.

Stone, V. A. (1969). A primacy effect in decision-making by jurors. *JC*, *19*, 239–247.

Valentine, K., & Fisher, B. A. (1974). An interaction analysis of innovative deviance in small groups. *SM*, *41*, 413–420.

Wood, J. T. (1977). Leading in purposive discussions. *CM*, *44*, 152–165.

6. STALKING INTERPERSONAL COMMUNICATION EFFECTIVENESS: SOCIAL, INDIVIDUAL, OR SITUATIONAL INTEGRATION?

Allison, R. (1939). Changing concepts in the meaning and values of group discussion. *QJS*, *25*, 117–120.

Ashby, W. R. (1956). *An introduction to cybernetics.* London: Chapman & Hill.

Bakan, D. (1966). *The duality of human existence.* Chicago: Rand McNally.

Barnlund, D. C. (1962). Toward a meaning-centered philosophy of communication. *JC, 12,* 197–211.

Beer, S. (1959). *Cybernetics and management.* New York: Wiley.

Berger, C. R., & Calabrese, R. J. (1975). Some explorations in initial interaction: Toward a developmental theory of interpersonal communication. *HCR, 1,* 99–112.

Bochner, A. P. (1978). On taking ourselves seriously: An analysis of some persistent problems and promising directions in interpersonal research. *HCR, 4,* 179–191.

Bochner, A. P., & Kelly, C. W. (1974). Interpersonal competence: Rationale, philosophy and implementation of a conceptual framework. *ST, 23,* 279–301.

Carhart, R. (1942). A speech teacher looks at general semantics. *QJS, 28,* 332–338.

Cegala, D. J. (1981). Interaction involvement: A cognitive dimension of communicative competence. *CE, 30,* 109–121.

Cronen, V. E., Pearce, W. B., & Harris, L. M. (1979). The logic of the coordinated management of meaning: A rules-based approach to the first course in interpersonal communication. *CE, 28,* 22–38.

Feldman, C. F., & Toulmin, S. (1976). Logic and the theory of mind. In J. Arnold (ed.), *Nebraska symposium on motivation 1975.* Lincoln: University of Nebraska Press.

Flynn, J. H., & Williams, D. A. (1976). The unstructured group in the interpersonal communication course. *CSSJ, 28,* 36–41.

Follett, M. P. (1924). *Creative experience.* New York: Longmans.

Gergen, K. J. (1973). Social psychology as history. *Journal of Personality and Social Psychology, 26,* 309–320.

Gergen, K. J. (1980). Towards intellectual audacity in social psychology. In R. Gilmour, & S. Duck (Eds.), *The development of social psychology.* London: Academic Press.

Gibb, J. (1961). Defensive communication. *JC, 11,* 141–148.

Gorman, M. (1967). A critique of general semantics. *WS, 31,* 44–50.

Hager, C. F. (1946). Speech and effective communication: Re-examination of basic assumptions. *QJS, 32,* 26–30.

Hart, R. P., & Burks, D. M. (1972). Rhetorical sensitivity and social interaction. *SM, 39,* 75–91.

Hellman, H. E. (1945). Debating is debating—and should be. *JS, 31,* 295–300.

Hillbruner, A. (1959). Plato and Korzybski: Two views of truth in rhetorical theory. *SSJ, 24,* 185–196.

Holm, J. N. Human relations: A challenge to the teacher of speech. (1960). *TS, 8,* 17–19.

Howes, R. F. (1928). Training in conversation. *QJS, 14,* 253–259.

Ilardo, J. A. (1972). Why interpersonal communication? *ST, 21,* 1–6.

Jandt, F. D. (1974). Why interpersonal communication?—Round II. *TS, 22,* 37–39.

Johannesen, R. L. (1971). The emerging concept of communication as dialogue. *QJS, 57,* 373–382.

Johnson, F. L. (1979). Communicative competence and the Bernstein perspective. *CQ, 27,* 12–19.

Kaplan, A. (1964). *The conduct of inquiry.* Scranton: Chandler Publishing.

Keller, P. W., & Brown, C. T. (1968). An interpersonal ethic for communication. *JC, 18,* 73–81.

Kidd, V. (1975). Happily ever after and other relationship styles: Advice on interpersonal relations in popular magazines, 1951–1973. *QJS, 61,* 31–39.

Korzybski, A. (1933). *Science and sanity: An introduction to non-Aristotelian systems and general semantics.* Lancaster, Pa.: Science Press.

Lebo, J. R. (1959). Conversation spoilers. *TS, 7,* 14–15.

Lee, I. J. (1940). General semantics and public speaking. *QJS, 26,* 594–601.

Lillywhite, H. (1952). Toward a philosophy of communication. *JC, 2,* 29–32.

Macklin, T. J., & Rossiter, C. M. (1976). Interpersonal communication and self-actualization. *CQ, 24,* 45–50.

McCroskey, J. C. (1982). Communication competence and performance: A research and pedagogical perspective. *CE, 31,* 1–7.

Mead, G. H. (1934). *Mind, self and society.* Chicago: University of Chicago Press.

Mehrley, R. S., & Backes, J. G. (1972). The first course in speech: A call for revolution. *ST, 21,* 205–211.

Miller, G. R. (1978). The current status of theory and research in interpersonal communication. *HCR, 4,* 164–178.

Miller, G., Boster, F., Roloff, M., & Seibold, D. (1977). Compliance-gaining message strategies: A typology and some findings concerning effects of situational differences. *CM, 44,* 37–51.

Murray, E. (1937). *The speech personality.* New York: Lippincott.

Murray, E. (1938). What is fundamental in speech? *The Southern Speech Bulletin, 4,* 1–4.

Murray, E. (1940). Speech standards and social integration. *QJS, 26,* 73–80.

Murray, E. (1944). The semantics of rhetoric: A dialogue on public speaking in 1944. *QJS, 30,* 31–41.

Murray, E. (1951). What are the problems of communication in human relations? *JC, 1,* 23–26.

Ogle, M. F. (1955). What happened to me at Bethel. *JC, 5,* 102–109.

Oliver, R. T. (1932). Conversation in the speech curriculum. *QJS, 18,* 108–111.

Oliver, R. T. (1957). Talkers all: Our human destiny. *TS, 5,* 31–33.

Oliver, R. T. (1961). Conversational rules—their use and abuse. *TS, 9,* 19–22.

Parks, M. R. (1981). Ideology in interpersonal communication: Off the couch and into the world. In Michael Burgoon (Ed.), *Communication Yearbook 5.* Beverly Hills: Sage.

Paul, W. B., Sorensen, F., & Murray, E. (1946). A functional core for the basic communications course. *QJS, 32,* 232–244.

Pearce, W. B. (1977). Teaching interpersonal communication as a humane science: A comparative analysis. *CE, 26,* 104–112.

Phillips, G. M. (1976). Rhetoric and its alternatives as bases for examination of intimate communication. *CQ, 24,* 11–23.

Poulakos, J. (1974). The components of dialogue. *WS, 38,* 199–212.

Rarig, F. M. (1948). Our speech and our interpersonal relations. *QJS, 34,* 439–444.

Rawlins, W. K. (1983). Individual responsibility in relational communication. In M. Mander (Ed.), *Communications in transition.* New York: Praeger.

Rawlins, W. K. (1984). Consensus in decision-making groups: A conceptual history. In G. M. Phillips & J. T. Wood (Eds.), *Emergent issues in human decision making.* Carbondale: Southern Illinois University Press.

Riley, F. K. (1928). The conversational basis of public address. *QJS, 14,* 233–242.

Ritter, E. M. (1977). Accountability for interpersonal communication instruction: A curricular perspective. *CSSJ, 28,* 204–213.

Rubin, R. B. (1982). Assessing speaking and listening competence at the college level: The communication competency assessment instrument. *CE, 31,* 19–32.

Schlauch, M. (1942). Semantics as social evasion. *Science and Society, 6,* 321–330.

Sennett, R. (1977). *The fall of public man.* New York: Knopf.

Sillars, A. L. (1974). Expression and control in human interaction: Perspective on humanistic psychology. *WS, 38,* 269–277.

Snidecor, J. C. (1942). A reconsideration of training in speech skills and adjustments. *WS, 7,* 2–6.

Stewart, J. (1972). An interpersonal approach to the basic course. *ST, 21,* 7–14.

Stewart, J. (1978). Foundations of dialogic communication. *QJS, 64,* 183–201.

Tompkins, P. K. (1965). General semantics and human relations. *CSSJ, 16,* 285–289.

Wiemann, J. M. (1977). Explication and test of a model of competence. *HCR, 3,* 195–213.

Williams, K. R. (1973). Reflections on a human science of communication. *JC, 23,* 239–250.

Wise, C. N. (1972). A prolegomena to a study of the antecedents of interpersonal communication. *TS, 20,* 59–63.

Wolff, K. H. (1950). *The sociology of Georg Simmel.* Glencoe, Ill.: Free Press.

Wood, J. T. (1982). Communication and relational culture: Bases for study of human relationships. *CQ, 30,* 75–83.

7. ORGANIZATIONAL COMMUNICATION: HISTORICAL DEVELOPMENT AND FUTURE DIRECTIONS

Adams, J. S. (1976). The structure and dynamics of behavior in organizational boundary roles. In M. D. Dunnette (Ed.), *Handbook of industrial and organizational psychology.* Chicago: Rand McNally.

Albrecht, T. L. (1979). The role of communication in perceptions of organizational climate. In D. Nimmo (Ed.), *Communication yearbook 3.* New Brunswick, N.J.: ICA / Transaction Books.

Albrecht, T. L., & Ropp, V. A. (1982). The study of network structuring in organizations through the use of method triangulation. *WJSC, 46,* 162–178.

Albrow, M. (1980). The dialectic of science and values in the study of organizations. In G. Salaman and K. Thompson (Eds.), *Control and ideology in organizations.* Cambridge, Mass.: MIT Press.

Aristotle. (1954). [*The rhetoric & poetics*] (W. R. Roberts, trans.). New York: Modern Library.

Athanassiades, J. C. (1973). The distortion of upward communication in hierarchical organizations. *AMJ, 16,* 207–226.

Axley, S. R. (1980, May). *Communication's role in organizational change: A review of relevant literature.* Paper presented at the annual conference of the International Communication Association, Acapulco.

Axley, S. R. (1983, May). *Managerial philosophy in organizational house organs: Two case studies.* Paper presented at the annual conference of the ICA, Dallas.

Bacharach, S. B., & Aiken, M. (1977). *Communication in administrative bureaucracies, AMJ, 18,* 365–377.

Baird, J. E., Jr., & Diebolt, J. C. (1976). Role congruence, communication, superior-subordinate relations, and employee satisfaction in organizational hierarchies. *WSC, 40,* 260–267.

Baldridge, J. V. (1971). *Power and conflict in the university*. New York: Wiley.

Bantz, C. R., & Smith, D. H. (1977). A critique and experimental test of Weick's model of organizing. *CM, 44,* 171–184.

Barker, J. R. (1982). *An exploratory study of the role sending process and role incongruence*. Unpublished master's thesis, Purdue University.

Barnard, C. (1938). *The functions of the executive*. Cambridge, Mass.: Harvard University Press.

Bavelas, A. (1950). Communication patterns in task-oriented groups. *Acoustical Society of America Journal, 22,* 727–730.

Beach, B. (1950). Employee magazines build morale. *Personnel Journal, 29,* 216–220.

Bednar, D. A., & Glauser, M. (1981, August). Interaction analysis of collective bargaining. In K. H. Chung (Ed.), *Academy of Management Proceedings*. San Diego: Academy of Management Association.

Bendix, R. (1970). The impact of ideas on organizational structure. In O. Grusky & G. A. Miller (Eds.), *The sociology of organizations: Basic studies*. New York: Free Press.

Benedict, R. (1934). *Patterns of culture*. Boston: Houghton Mifflin.

Benson, J. K. (1977). Organizations: A dialectical view. *ASQ, 22,* 1–21.

Blake, R. R., Shepard, H. A., & Mouton, J. S. (1964). *Managing intergroup conflict in industry*. Houston: Gulf Publishing.

Blau, P. M. (1954). Patterns of interaction among a group of officials in a government agency. *HR, 7,* 337–348.

Boje, D. M., Fedor, D. B., & Rowland, K. M. (1982). Myth making: A qualitative step in OD interventions. *Journal of Applied Behavioral Science, 18,* 17–28.

Bormann, E. G. (1972). Fantasy and rhetorical vision: The rhetorical criticism of social reality. *QJS, 58,* 396–407.

Bormann, E. G. (1982). Symbolic convergence theory of communication: Applications and implications for teachers and consultants. *JACR, 10,* 50–61.

Bormann, E. G. (1983). Symbolic convergence: Organizational communication and culture. In L. L. Putnam & M. E. Pacanowsky (Eds.), *Communication and organization: An interpretive approach*. Beverly Hills: Sage.

Bormann, E. G., Pratt, J., & Putnam, L. (1978). Power, authority, and sex: Male response to female leadership. *CM, 45,* 119–155.

Boyd, B. B., & Jensen, J. M. (1972). Perceptions of the first-line supervisor's authority: A study in superior-subordinate communication. *AMJ, 15,* 331–342.

Bradley, P. H. (1978). Power, status, and upward communication in small decision-making groups. *CM, 45,* 35–43.

Bradley, P. H., & Baird, J. E., Jr. (1977). Management and communicator style: A correlational analysis. *CSSJ, 28,* 194–203.

Bradley, P. H., & Baird, J. E., Jr. (1980). *Communication for business and the professions.* Dubuque, Iowa: William C. Brown.

Broms, H., & Gahmberg, H. (1982). *Mythology in management culture.* Helsinki: School of Economics and Business Administration.

Brown, M. H., McMillian, J., & Blackman, B. (1981). Investigation into the implications of organizational myth-making in a nursing care facility. In L. L. Putnam & M. E. Pacanowsky (Eds.), *Proceedings of the first annual ICA/SCA jointly sponsored conference on interpretive approaches to organizational communication.* West Lafayette, Ind.: Purdue University.

Browning, L. (1977, December). *Applied communication within our field: The politics of change.* Paper presented at the annual meeting of the SCA, Washington, D. C.

Browning, L. D. (1978). A grounded organizational communication theory derived from qualitative data. *CM, 45,* 93–109.

Browning, L. D., & Hopper, R. (1979). *How messages get to mean— influences in a bureaucratic organization.* Unpublished manuscript, Department of Communication, University of Texas-Austin.

Bullis, C. B., Cox, M. C., & Bokeno, S. L. (1982). *Organizational conflict management: The effects of socialization, type of conflict, and sex on conflict management strategies.* Paper presented at the annual conference of the ICA, Boston.

Burke, K. (1969). *A rhetoric of motives.* Berkeley: University of California Press.

Burke, R. J. (1970). Methods of resolving superior-subordinate conflict: The constructive use of subordinate differences and disagreements. *Organizational Behavior and Human Performance, 5,* 393–411.

Cheney, G. (1983). The rhetoric of identification and the study of organizational communication. *QJS, 69,* 143–158.

Clark, B. R. (1972). The organizational saga in higher education. *ASQ, 17,* 178–184.

Cohen, A. R. (1959). Situational structure, self-esteem, and threat-oriented reactions to power. In D. Cartwright (Ed.), *Studies in social power.* Ann Arbor: Institute for Social Research.

Collins, G. R. (1924). Public speaking in colleges of Business Administration and United YMCA Schools. *QJSE, 10,* 374–379.

Connolly, T. (1977). Information processing and decision making in organizations. In B. M. Staw & G. R. Salancik (Eds.), *New directions in organizational behavior.* Chicago: St. Clair Press.

Conrad, C. (1983). Organizational power: Faces and symbolic forms. In L. L. Putnam & M. E. Pacanowsky (Eds.), *Communication and organization: An interpretive approach.* Beverly Hills: Sage. (a)

Conrad, C. (1983). Supervisors' choice of modes of managing conflict. *WJSC, 47,* 218–228. (b)

Corporate culture: The hard to change values that spell success or failure (1980, October 17). *Business Week,* pp. 148–160.

Crable, R. E., & Vibbert, S. L. (1983). Mobil's epideictic advocacy: "Observations" of Prometheus-Bound. *CM, 50,* 380–394.

Cragan, J. F., & Shields, D. C. (1981). *Applied communication research: A dramatistic approach.* Prospect Heights, Ill.: Waveland Press.

Crozier, M. (1964). *The bureaucratic phenomenon.* Chicago: University of Chicago Press.

Cusella, L. P. (1980). The effects of feedback on intrinsic motivation: A propositional extension of cognitive evaluation theory from an organizational communication perspective. In D. Nimmo (Ed.), *Communication yearbook 4.* New Brunswick, N.J.: ICA / Transaction Books.

Cusella, L. P. (1982). The effects of source expertise and feedback valence on intrinsic motivation. *HCR, 9,* 17–32.

Cusella, L. P. (1984). The effects of feedback source, message and receiver characteristics on intrinsic motivation. *CQ, 32,* 211–221.

Cusella, L. P. On the need for conceptual authenticity in organizational communication research. *CQ,* in press.

Cyert, R. M., & March, J. G. (1963). *A behavioral theory of the firm.* Englewood Cliffs, N.J.: Prentice-Hall.

Daft, R. L., & Macintosh, N. B. (1981). A tentative exploration into the amount and equivocality of information processing in organizational work units. *ASQ, 26,* 207–224.

Dahle, T. L. (1954). An objective and comparative study of five methods for transmitting information to business and industrial employees. *SM, 21,* 21–28.

Daly, J. A., McCroskey, J. C., & Falcione, R. A. (1976, April). *Communication apprehension, supervisor communication receptivity and satisfaction with supervisors.* Paper presented at the annual convention of the ECA, Philadelphia.

Dandridge, T. C., Mitroff, I., & Joyce, W. F. (1980). Organizational symbolism: A topic to expand organizational analysis. *AMR, 5,* 77–82.

Danowski, J. A. (1980). Group attitude uniformity and connectivity of organizational communication networks for production, innovation, and maintenance content. *HCR, 6,* 299–308.

Danowski, J. A. (1983, May). *Automated network analysis: A survey of different approaches to the analysis of human communication relationships.* Paper presented at the annual conference of the ICA, Dallas.

Davis, K. (1953). Management communication and the grapevine. *HBR, 31,* 43–49.

Davis, K. (1978). Methods for studying informal communication. *JC*, 28, 112–116.

Deal, T. E., & Kennedy, A. A. (1982). *Corporate culture*. Reading, Mass.: Addison-Wesley.

Deetz, S. A. (1982). Critical interpretive research in organizational communication. *WJSC*, 46, 131–149.

Deetz, S. (1984). Metaphors and the discursive production and reproduction of organization. In L. Thayer & O. Wiio, *People, communication, and organizational performance*. New York: Ablex.

Deetz, S., & Kersten, A. (1983). Critical models of interpretive research. In L. L. Putnam & M. E. Pacanowsky (Eds.), *Communication and organization: An interpretive approach*. Beverly Hills: Sage.

Dennis, H. S., Goldhaber, G. M., & Yates, M. P. (1978). Organizational communication theory and research: An overview of research methods. In B. D. Ruben (Ed.), *Communication yearbook 2*. New Brunswick, N.J.: ICA / Transaction Books.

Derry, J. O. (1969). *The effects of a public relations speech on five Chicago audiences*. Unpublished master's thesis, University of Wisconsin--Milwaukee.

DiSalvo, V., Larsen, D. C., & Seiler, W. J. (1976). Communication skills needed by persons in business organizations. *CE*, 25, 269–275.

Donohue, W. A. (1978). An empirical framework for examining negotiation processes and outcomes. *CM*, 45, 247–257.

Donohue, W. A. (1981). Analyzing negotiation tactics: Development of a negotiation interact system. *HCR*, 7, 273–287. (a)

Donohue, W. A. (1981). Development of a model of rule use in negotiation interaction. *CM*, 48, 106–120.

Donohue, W. A., Dietz, M. E., & Stahle, R. B. (1983). New directions in negotiation research. In R. Bostrom (Ed.), *Communication yearbook 7*. Beverly Hills: Sage.

Dover, C. J. (1959). The three eras of management communication. *JC*, 9, 168–172.

Downs, C., Berg, D., & Linkugel, W. (1977). *The organizational communicator*. New York: Harper & Row.

Downs, C. W., & Hazen, M. D. (1977). A factor analytic study of communication satisfaction. *JBC*, 14, 63–73.

Du Brin, A. J. (1972). *The practice of managerial psychology*. Elmsford, N.Y.: Pergamon Press.

Eich, R. K. (1977). *Organizational communication consulting: A descriptive study of consulting practices and prescriptions*. Unpublished doctoral dissertation, University of Michigan.

Eilon, S. (1968). Taxonomy of communications. *ASQ*, 13, 266–288.

Eisenberg, E. M. (1983, May). *Strategic ambiguity in organizations*. Paper presented at the annual conference of the ICA, Dallas.

Ellis, D. G. (1979). Relational control in two group systems. *CM, 46,* 153–166.

Emerson, R. M. (1962). Power-dependence relations. *ASR, 27,* 31–41.

Erbe, W. (1962). Gregariousness, group membership, and the flow of information. *AJS, 67,* 502–516.

Falcione, R. L., & Werner, E. (1978, April). *Organizational climate and communication climate: A state-of-the-art*. Paper presented at the annual conference of the ICA, Chicago.

Farace, R. V., & MacDonald, D. (1974). New directions in the study of organizational communication. *PP, 27,* 1–15.

Farace, R. V., Monge, P. R., & Russell, H. M. (1977). *Communicating and organizing*. Reading, Mass.: Addison-Wesley.

Feldman, M. S., & March, J. G. (1981). Information in organizations as signal and symbol. *ASQ, 26,* 171–186.

Ference, T. P. (1970). Organizational communications systems and the decision process. *Management Science, 17,* B-83-B-96.

Festinger, L. (1950). Informal social communication. *Psychological Review, 57,* 271–282.

Fisher, R. M. (1965). Modern business speaking: A rhetoric of conventional wisdom. *SSJ, 30,* 326–327.

Folger, J. P., & Poole, M. S. (1983). *Working through conflict*. Chicago: Scott, Foresman.

Fowler, G. D., & Wackerbarth, M. E. (1980). Audio teleconferencing versus face-to-face conferencing: A synthesis of the literature. *WJSC, 44,* 236–252.

French, J. R. P., Jr., & Raven, B. (1968). The bases of social power. In D. Cartwright & A. Zander (Eds.), *Group Dynamics: Research and Theory* (3rd ed.). New York: Harper & Row.

Galbraith, J. R. (1973). *Designing complex organizations*. Reading, Mass.: Addison-Wesley.

Geertz, C. *The interpretation of cultures*. (1973). New York: Basic Books.

Geist, P. R. (1982, November). *The transformation of a villain: The tragic form of Exxon's corporate rhetoric*. Paper presented at the annual meeting of the SCA, Louisville, Ky.

Giddens, A. (1979). *Central problems in social theory*. Berkeley: University of California Press.

Given, W. (1949). *Bottom-up management*. New York: Harper.

Goldberg, A. A., Cavanaugh, M. S., & Larson, C. E. (1983). The meaning of "power." *JACR, 11,* 89–108.

Goldhaber, G. M., & Rogers, D. P. (1979). *Auditing organizational com-*

munication systems: The ICA communication audit. Dubuque, Iowa: Kendall/Hunt.

Goldhaber, G. M., Yates, M. P., Porter, D. T., & Lesniak, R. (1978). Organizational communication: 1978 *HCR, 5,* 76–96.

Goodenough, W. H. (1971). *Culture, language and society.* Reading, Mass.: Addison-Wesley.

Greenbaum, H. M., Hellweg, S. A., & Falcione, R. L. (1983, May). *Evaluation of communication in organizations: An analysis of current and past methodologies.* Paper presented at the annual conference of the ICA, Dallas.

Guetzkow, H. (1965). Communication in organizations. In J. G. March (Ed.), *Handbook of organizations.* Chicago: Rand McNally.

Haney, W. V. (1973). *Communication and organizational behavior.* Homewood, Ill.: Richard D. Irwin.

Hanna, M. S. (1978). Speech communication training needs in the business community. *CSSJ, 29,* 163–172.

Harris, L., & Cronen, V. (1979). A rules-based model for the analysis and evaluation of organizational communication. *CQ, 27,* 12–28.

Hawes, L. C. (1974). Social collectivities as communication: Perspectives on organizational behavior. *QJS, 60,* 497–502.

Hawes, L. C., & Smith, D. H. (1973). A critique of assumptions underlying the study of communication in conflict. *QJS, 59,* 423–435.

Hay, R. D. (1974). A brief history of internal organizational communication through the 1940's. *JBC, 11,* 6–11.

Heath, R. L. (1980). Corporate advocacy: An application of speech communication perspectives and skills—and more. *CE, 29,* 370–377.

Henderson, S. (1981). Reality bargaining: The emergence of consensual validation. In L. L. Putnam & M. E. Pacanowsky (Eds.), *Proceedings of the first annual ICA/SCA jointly sponsored conference on interpretive approaches to organizational communication,* West Lafayette, Ind.: Purdue University.

Heron, A. (1942). *sharing information with employees.* Palo Alto, Calif.: Stanford University Press.

Hicks, M. A. (1955). Speech training in business and industry. *JC, 5,* 161–168.

Hickson, D. J., Hinings, C. R., Lee, C. A., Schneck, R. E., & Pennings, J. M. (1971). A strategic contingencies theory of intraorganizational power. *ASQ, 16,* 216–229.

Hintz, R. A., & Couch, C. J. (1978). Mediated messages and social coordination. *JC, 28,* 117–123.

Hirsch, P. M., & Andrews, J. A. Y. (1983). Ambushes, shootouts, and knights of the roundtable: The language of corporate takeovers. In L. R.

Pondy, P. Frost, G. Morgan, & T. Dandridge (Eds.), *Organizational Symbolism*. Greenwich, Conn.: JAI Press.

Hoffman, W. G. (1923). *Public speaking for business men*. New York: McGraw-Hill.

Howell, W. S., & Bormann, E. G. (1971). *Presentational speaking for business and the professions*. NY: Harper & Row.

Huber, G. (1982). Organizational information systems: Determinants of their performance and behavior. *Management Science, 28*, 138–155.

Infante, D. A., & Gordon, W. I. (1979). Subordinate and superior perceptions of self and one another: Relations, accuracy and reciprocity of liking. *WJSC, 43*, 212–223.

Ireland, R. D., Van Auken, P. M., & Lewis, P. V. (1978). An investigation of the relationship between organization climate and communication climate. *JBC, 16*, 3–10.

Irwin, J. V., & Brockhaus, H. H. (1963). The 'Teletalk project': A study of the effectiveness of two public relations speeches. *SM, 30*, 359–368.

Izraeli, D. N. (1975). The middle manager and the tactics of power expansion: A case study. *Sloan Management Review, 16*, 57–70.

Jablin, F. M. (1978). Message-response and "openness" in superior-subordinate communication. In B. D. Ruben (Ed.), *Communication yearbook 2*. New Brunswick, N.J.: ICA / Transaction Books. (a)

Jablin, F. M. (1978, November). *Research priorities in organizational communication*. Paper presented at the annual meeting of the SCA, Minneapolis. (b)

Jablin, F. M. (1979). Superior-subordinate communication: The state of the art. *Psychological Bulletin, 86*, 1201–1222.

Jablin, F. M. (1980). Organizational communication theory and research: An overview of communication climate and network research. In D. Nimmo (Ed.), *Communication yearbook 4*. New Brunswick, N.J.: ICA / Transaction Book. (a)

Jablin, F. M. (1980). Superior's upward influence, satisfaction, and openness in superior-subordinate communication: A reexamination of the "Pelz Effect." *HCR, 6*, 210–220. (b)

Jablin, F. M. (1981). An exploratory study of subordinates' perceptions of supervisory politics. *CQ, 29*, 269–275.

Jablin, F. M. (1982). Formal structural characteristics of organizations and superior-subordinate communication. *HCR, 8*, 338–347.

Jacobson, E., & Seashore, S. (1951). Communication practices in complex organizations. *Journal of Social Issues, 7*, 28–40.

Johnson, B. M. (1977). *Communication: The process of organizing*. Boston: Allyn & Bacon.

Johnson, B. M., & Shaw, M. R. (1978, November). *Preparing the com-*

munication consultant. Paper presented at the annual meeting of the SCA, Minneapolis.

Judd, L. R. (1979, May). *Research frontiers of corporate advocacy.* Paper presented at the annual conference of the ICA, Philadelphia.

Kanter, R. M. (1977). *Men and women of the corporation.* New York: Basic Books.

Katz, D., & Kahn, R. L. (1978). *The social psychology of organizations* (2nd ed.). New York: Wiley.

Kelly, L. (1982, May). *A critical review of the literature on superior-subordinate communication.* Paper presented at the annual conference of the ICA, Boston.

Keough, C. M. (1983). *Bargaining communication and arbitration arguments: An analysis of the collective bargaining between the Teaching Assistants Association and the University of Wisconsin-Madison.* Unpublished master's thesis, Purdue University.

Kilman, R. H., & Thomas, K. W. (1977). Developing a forced-choice measure of conflict-handling behavior: The mode instrument. *Educational and Psychological Measurement, 37,* 309–325.

Kipnis, D., Schmidt, S. M., Wilkinson, I. (1980). Intraorganizational influence tactics: Explorations in getting one's way. *JAP, 65,* 440–452.

Klemmer, E. T., & Snyder, F. W. (1972). Measurement of time spent communicating, *JC, 22,* 142–158.

Knapp, M. L. (1968). Public speaking in business and industry: Policies, publications, and publicity. *JBC, 5,* 3–10.

Knapp, M. L. (1969). Public speaking training programs in American business and industrial organizations. *ST, 18,* 129–134.

Knapp, M. L. (1970). Business rhetoric: Opportunity for research in speech. *SSJ, 35,* 244–255.

Koch, S., & Deetz, S. (1981). Metaphor analysis of social reality in organizations. *JACR, 9,* 1–15.

Koehler, J. W., Anatol, K. W. E., & Applbaum, R. L. (1981). *Organizational communication: Behavioral perspectives* (2nd ed.). New York: Holt.

Kreps, G. L. (1980). A field experimental test and revaluation of Weick's model of organizing. In D. Nimmo (Ed.), *Communication yearbook 4.* New Brunswick, N.J.: ICA / Transaction Books.

Kreps, G. (1983). Using interpretive research: The development of a socialization program at RCA. In L. L. Putnam & M. E. Pacanowsky (Eds.), *Communication and organization: An interpretive approach.* Beverly Hills: Sage.

Lakoff, G., & Johnson, M. (1980). *Metaphors we live by.* Chicago: University of Chicago Press.

Lawrence, R. R., & Lorsch, J. W. L. (1967). *Organization and environ-*

ment: Managing differentiation and integration. Cambridge, Mass.: University Press.

Lazarsfeld, P., Berelson, B., & Gaudet, H. (1948). *The people's choice.* New York: Columbia University Press.

Leavitt, H. J. (1951). Some effects of certain communication patterns on group performance. *Journal of Abnormal and Social Psychology, 46,* 38–50.

Levi-Strauss, C. (1963). *Structural anthropology* (C. Jacobson & B. G. Schoepf, trans.). New York: Basic Books.

Lewin, K. (1951). *Field theory in social science.* New York: Harper.

Litwin, G., & Stringer, R. (1968). *Motivation and organizational climate.* Cambridge, Mass.: Harvard University Press.

Lukes, S. (1974). *Power: A radical view.* London: Macmillan.

MacDonald, D. (1976). Communication roles and communication networks in a formal organization. *HCR, 2,* 365–375.

Mack, R. W., & Snyder, R. C. (1957). The analysis of social conflict—Toward an overview and synthesis. *Journal of Conflict Resolution, 1,* 212–248.

Mahoney, T. A. (1954). How management communicates with employees. *Personnel, 31,* 109–114.

Manning, P. K. (1979). Metaphors of the field: Varieties of organizational discourse. *ASQ, 24,* 660–671.

March, J. G., & Simon, H. A. (1958). *Organizations.* New York: Wiley.

Martin, J., & Powers, M. E. (1983). Truth or corporate propaganda: The value of a good war story. In L. Pondy, P. Frost, G. Morgan, & T. Dandridge (Eds.), *Organizational symbolism.* Greenwich, Conn.: JAI Press.

Martin, N. H., & Sims, J. H. (1956). Thinking ahead: Power tactics. *HBR, 34,* (6). 25–29.

McLelland, D. C. (1975). *Power: The inner experience.* New York: Irvington Publishers.

McGregor, D. (1960). *The human side of enterprise.* New York: McGraw-Hill.

McMillan, J. J. (1982, November). *Language about God in a religious organization: Changing attitudes toward women.* Paper presented at the annual meeting of the Speech Communication Association, Louisville, Ky.

McMurray, R. N. (1965). Clear communication for chief executives. *HBR, 43,* 131–147.

McSwain, C. J., & White, O. F., Jr. (1982, August). *The case for lying, cheating, and stealing—Organization development as ethos model for management practice.* Paper presented at the Academy of Management Meeting, New York.

Mechanic, D. (1962). Sources of power of lower participants in complex organizations. *ASQ, 7*, 349–364.

Meister, J. E., & Reinsch, N. L., Jr. (1978). Communication training in manufacturing firms. *CE, 27*, 235–244.

Miller, J. G. (1960). Information input, overload, and psychopathology. *American Journal of Psychiatry, 116*, 695–704.

Mintzberg, H. (1973). *The nature of managerial work*. New York: Harper & Row.

Mitroff, I. I., & Kilmann, R. H. (1976). On organizational stories: An approach to the design and analysis of organizations through myths and stories. In R. H. Kilmann, L. R. Pondy, & D. P. Slavin (Eds.), *The management of organizational design: Strategies and implementtion*. New York: Elsevier.

Monge, P. R. (1982). Systems theory and research in the study of organizational communication: The correspondence problem. *HCR, 8*, 245–261.

Monge, P. R., Edwards, J. A., & Kiriste, K. K. (1978). The determinants of communication and communication structure in large organizations: A review of research. In B. Ruben (Ed.), *Communication yearbook 2*. New Brunswick, N.J.: ICA / Transaction Books.

Moreno, J. L. (1953). *Who shall survive? Foundations of sociometry, group psychotherapy and sociodrama*. New York: Beacon House.

Morgan, G., & Smircich, L. (1980). The case for qualitative research. *AMR, 5*, 491–500.

Muchinsky, P. M. (1977). An intraorganizational analysis of the Roberts and O'Reilly organizational communication questionnaire. *JAP, 62*, 184–188.

Odiorne, G. (1954). An application of the communication audit. *PP, 1*, 235–243.

O'Reilly, C. A. (1978). The intentional distortion of information in organizational communication: A laboratory and field investigation. *HR, 31*, 173–193.

O'Reilly, C. A. (1980). Individuals and information overload in organizations: Is more necessarily better? *AMJ, 23*, 684–696.

O'Reilly, C. A. (1982). Variations in decision maker's use of information sources: The impact of quality and accessibility of information. *AMJ, 25*, 756–771.

O'Reilly, C. A., & Anderson, J. C. (1980). Trust and the communication of performance appraisal information: The effect of feedback on performance and job satisfaction. *HCR, 6*, 290–298.

O'Reilly, C. A., & Pondy, L. R. (1979). Organizational communication. In S. Kerr (Ed.), *Organizational behavior*. Columbus, Ohio: Grid.

O'Reilly, C. A., & Roberts, K. H. (1974). Information filtration in organization: Three experiments. *Organizational Behavior and Human Performance, 11*, 253–265.

Ouchi, W. G. (1981). *Theory Z*. Reading, Mass.: Addison-Wesley.

Pacanowsky, M. E., & O'Donnell-Trujillo, N. (1982). Communication and organizational cultures. *WJSC, 46*, 115–130.

Pacanowsky, M. E., & O'Donnell-Trujillo, N. (1983). Organizational communication as cultural performance. *CM, 50*, 126–147.

Pascale, R. T., & Athos, A. G. (1981). *The art of Japanese management*. New York: Warner Books.

Patchen, M. (1968). Alternative questionnaire approaches to the measurement of influence in organizations. *AJS, 69*, 41–52.

Paterson, D., & Jenkins, J. (1948). Communication between management and workers. *JAP, 32*, 71–80.

Pelz, D. C. (1952). Influence: A key to effective leadership in the first-line supervisor. *Personnel, 29*,3–11.

Penley, L. E. (1982). An investigation of the information processing framework of organizational communication. *HCR, 8*, 348–365.

Peters, R. W. (1950). *Communication within industry*. New York: Harper & Row.

Peters, T. J., & Waterman, R. H., Jr. (1982). *In search of excellence*. New York: Harper & Row.

Pettigrew, A. M. (1972). Information control as a power resource. *Sociology, 6*, 187–204.

Pettigrew, A. M. (1973). *The politics of organizational decision-making*. London: Tavistock.

Pettigrew, A. M. (1979). On studying organizational cultures. *ASQ, 24*, 570–581.

Pfeffer, J. (1981). Management as symbolic action: The creation and maintenance of organizational paradigms. In L. L. Cummings and B. M. Staw (Eds.), *Research in Organizational Behavior* (Vol. 3). Greenwich, Conn.: JAI Press. (a)

Pfeffer, J. (1981). *Power in organizations*. Marshfield, Mass.: Pittman. (b)

Pfeffer, J., & Salancik, G. R. (1977). Organizational design: The case for a coalitional model of organizations. *Organizational Dynamics, 6*(2), 15–29.

Pietri, P. H. (1974). Organizational communication: The pioneers, *JBC, 11*, 3–6.

Pigors, P. (1949). *Effective communication in industry*. New York: National Association of Manufacturers.

Plain, H. G. (1980, May). *Computer-linked memo systems, expectations and utilization: A case study*. Paper presented at the annual conference of the ICA, Acapulco.

Planty, E., & Machaver, W. (1952). Upward communications: A project in executive development using the syndicate method. *Personnel, 28,* 304–318.

Poole, M. S. (1978). An information-task approach to organizational communication. *AMR, 30,* 493–504.

Poole, M. S., & McPhee, R. D. (1983). A structurational analysis of organizational climate. In L. L. Putnam & M. E. Pacanowsky (Eds.), *Communication and organization: An interpretive approach.* Beverly Hills: Sage.

Pondy, L. R. (1967). Organizational conflict: Concepts and models. *ASQ, 12,* 296–320.

Porter, L. W., & Roberts, K. H. (1976). Communication in organizations. In M. D. Dunnette (Ed.), *Handbook of industrial and organizational psychology.* Chicago: Rand McNally.

Porterfield, C. D. (1974). Organizational communication: Developments from 1960 to the present. *JBC, 11,* 18–24.

Putnam, L. L. (1979). Role functions and role conflicts of communication trainers. *JBC, 17,* 37–52.

Putnam, L. L. (1982). Paradigms for organizational communication research: An overview and synthesis. *WJSC, 46,* 192–206. (a)

Putnam, L. L. (1982, April). *Understanding the unique characteristics of groups within organizations.* Paper presented at the Conference on Research in Small Group Communication, State College, Pa. (b)

Putnam, L. L. (1983). Organizational communication amendment. *Spectra, 19,* 1–2. (a)

Putnam, L. L. (1983). The interpretive perspective: An alternative to functionalism. In L. L. Putnam & M. E. Pacanowsky (Eds.), *Communication and organization: An interpretive approach.* Beverly Hills: Sage. (b)

Putnam, L. L. (1984). Contradictions and paradoxes in organizations. In L. Thayer and O. Wiio (Eds.), *People, communication, and organizational peformance.* New York: Ablex.

Putnam, L. L., & Cheney, G. (1983). A critical review of research traditions in organizational communication. In M. Mander (Ed.), *Communication in transition.* New York: Praeger.

Putnam, L. L., & Jones, T. S. (1982). Reciprocity in negotiations: An analysis of bargaining interaction. *CM, 49,* 171–191. (a)

Putnam, L. L., & Jones, T. S. (1982). The role of communication in bargaining. *HCR, 8,* 262–280. (b)

Putnam, L. L., & Sorenson, R. L. (1982). Equivocal messages in organizations. *HCR, 8,* 114–132.

Putnam, L. L. & Wilson, C. E. (1982). Communicative strategies in organizational conflicts: Reliability and validity of a measurement scale. In M. Burgoon (Ed.), *Communication yearbook 6.* Beverly Hills: Sage, 1982.

Read, W. H. (1962). Upward communication in industrial hierarchies. *HR*, *15*, 3–15.

Redding, W. C. (1966). The empirical study of human communication in business and industry. In P. E. Reid (Ed.), *The frontiers in speech-communication research*. Syracuse: Syracuse University Press.

Redding, W. C. (1972). *Communication within the organization: An interpretive review of theory and research*. New York: Industrial Communication Council, Inc.

Redding, W. C. (1979). Graduate education and the communication consultant: Playing God for a fee. *CE*, *28*, 346–352. (a)

Redding, W. C. (1979). Organizational communication theory and ideology: An overview. In D. Nimmo (Ed.), *Communication yearbook 3*. New Brunswick, N.J.: ICA / Transaction Books. (b)

Reiches, N. A., & Harral, H. B. (1974). Argument in negotiation: A theoretical and empirical approach. *SM*, *41*, 36–48.

Rice, R. E. (1982). Communication networking in computer-conferencing systems: A longitudinal study of group roles and system structure. In M. Burgoon (Ed.), *Communication yearbook 6*. Beverly Hills: Sage. (a)

Rice, R. E. (1982). *Human communication networking in a teleconferencing environment*. Unpublished doctoral dissertation, Stanford University. (b)

Richards, W. D. (1974, May). *Network analysis in large complex systems: Techniques and methods—tools*. Paper presented at the annual conference of the ICA, New Orleans. (a)

Richards, W. D. (1974, May). *Network analysis in large complex systems: Theoretical basis*. Paper presented at the annual conference of the ICA, New Orleans. (b)

Richetto, G. M. (1977). Organizational communication theory and research: An overview. In B. D. Ruben (Ed.), *Communication yearbook 1*. New Brunswick, N.J.: ICA / Transaction Books.

Richmond, V. P., McCroskey, J. C., & Davis, L. M. (1982). Individual differences among employees, management communication style, and emloyee satisfaction: Replication and extension. *HCR*, *8*, 170–188.

Richmond, V. P., & McCroskey, J. C. (1979). Management communication style, tolerance for disagreement, and innovativeness as predictors of employee satisfaction: A comparison of single-factor, two-factor, and multiple-factor approaches. In D. Nimmo (Ed.), *Communication yearbook 3*. New Brunswick, N.J.: ICA / Transaction Books.

Richmond, V. P., Wagner, J. P., & McCroskey, J. C. (1983). The impact of perceptions of leadership style, use of power, and conflict management style on organizational outcomes. *CQ*, *31*, 27–36.

Riggs, C. J. (1983). Communication dimensions of conflict tactics in organizational settings: A functional analysis. In R. Bostrom (Ed.), *Communication yearbook 7*. Beverly Hills: Sage.

Roberts, K. H., & O'Reilly, C. A. (1974). Failures in upward communication in organizations: Three possible culprits. *AMJ, 17,* 205–215. (a)

Roberts, K. H., & O'Reilly, C. A. (1974). Measuring organizational communication. *JAP, 59,* 321–326.

Roberts, K. H., & O'Reilly, C. A. (1978). Organizations as communication structures. *HCR, 4,* 283–293.

Roberts, K., O'Reilly, C., Bretton, G. E., & Porter, L. (1974). Organizational theory and organizational communication: A communication failure. *HR, 27,* 501–524.

Roethlisberger, F. J., & Dickson, W. J. (1939). *Management and the worker.* Cambridge, Mass.: Harvard University Press.

Rogers, E. M. (1962). *Diffusion of innovations.* New York: Free Press.

Rogers, E. M., & Agarwala-Rogers, R. (1976). *Communication in organizations.* New York: Free Press.

Ross, R., & Dewine, S. (1982, November). *Interpersonal conflict: Measurement and validation.* Paper presented at the annual meeting of SCA, Louisville, Ky.

Rossi, I. (1974). *The unconscious in culture.* New York: Dutton.

Salaman, G., & Thompson, K. (1980). Introduction. In G. Salaman & K. Thompson (Eds.), *Control and ideology in organizations.* Cambridge, Mass.: MIT Press.

Salancik, G. R., & Pfeffer, J. (1974). The bases and use of power in organizational decision making: The case of a university. *ASQ, 19,* 453–473.

Sanborn, G. A. (1961). *An analytical study of oral communication practices in a nationwide retail sales organization.* Unpublished doctoral dissertation, Purdue University.

Sanborn, G. A. (1964). Communication in business: An overview. In W. C. Redding & G. A. Sanborn (Eds.), *Business and industrial communication: A source book.* New York: Harper & Row.

Sanford, W. P. & Yeager, W. H. (1929). *Business and professional speaking.* New York: McGraw-Hill.

Schein, V. E. (1977). Individual power and political behaviors in organizations: An inadequately explored reality. *AMR, 2,* 64–72.

Schwartz, M. M., Stark, H. F., & Schiffman, H. R. (1970). Responses of union and management leaders to emotionally toned industrial relations terms. *PP, 23,* 361–367.

Sexton, R., & Staudt, V. (1959). Business communication: A survey of the literature. *Journal of Social Psychology, 50,* 101–118.

Shaw, M. (1964). Communication networks. In L. Berkowitz (Ed.), *Advances in experimental social psychology* (Vol. 1). New York: Academic Press.

Shull, F., & Delbeque, A. (1965). Norms, a feature of symbolic culture. In

W. J. Gore & J. W. Dryson (Eds.), *The making of decisions.* Glencoe, Ill.: Free Press.

Simon, H. A. (1976). *Administrative behavior* (3rd ed.). New York: Free Press.

Sillars, A. (1980). The sequential and distributional structure of conflict interactions as a function of attributions concerning the locus of responsibility and stability of conflicts. In D. Nimmo (Ed.), *Communication yearbook 4.* New Brunswick, N.J.: ICA / Transaction Books.

Smircich, L. (1983a). Concepts of culture and organizational analysis. *ASQ, 28,* 339–358.

Smircich, L. (1983b). Implications for management theory. In L. L. Putnam & M. E. Pacanowsky (Eds.), *Communication and organization: An interpretive approach.* Beverly Hills: Sage.

Smircich, L., & Chesser, R. J. (1981). Superiors' and subordinates' perceptions of performance: Beyond disagreement. *AMJ, 24,* 198–205.

Smith, D. H. (1969). Communication and negotiation outcome. *JC, 19,* 248–256.

Smith, D. H. (1973, November). *The master symbol as a key to understanding organizational communication.* Paper presented at the annual meeting of the SCA, New York.

Spiker, B. K., & Daniels, T. D. (1981). Information adequacy and communication relationships: An empirical examination of 18 organizations. *WJSC, 45,* 342–354.

Stanley, J. D. (1981). Dissent in organizations. *AMR, 6,* 13–19.

Stech, E. L. (1980, November). *Work group communication modes and assessment of contingency and situational models of leadership.* Paper presented at the annual meeting of the SCA, New York.

Steinfatt, T. M., & Miller, G. R. (1974). Communication in game theoretic models of conflict. In G. R. Miller & H. W. Simons (Eds.), *Perspectives on communication in social conflict.* Englewood Cliffs, N.J.: Prentice-Hall.

Stewart, L. P. (1980). "Whistle blowing": Implications for organizational communication. *JC, 30,* 90–101.

Sussman, L. (1975). Communication in organizational hierarchies: The fallacy of perceptual congruence. *WS, 39,* 191–199.

Taylor, F. W. (1947). *Scientific management.* New York: Harper.

Thayer, L. O. (1961). *Administrative communication.* Homewood, Ill.: Richard D. Irwin.

Thayer, L. O. (1967). Communication and organization theory. In F. Dance (Ed.), *Human communication theory.* New York: Holt.

Theye, L., & Seiler, W. (1979). Interaction analysis in collective bargaining: An alternative approach to the prediction of negotiated outcomes. In D. Nimmo (Ed.), *Communication yearbook 3.* New Brunswick, N.J.: ICA / Transaction Books.

Tichy, N. M., Tushman, M. L., & Fombrun, C. (1979). Social network analysis for organizations. *Academy of Management Review, AMR, 4,* 507–519.

Tompkins, P. K. (1962). *An analysis of communication between headquarters and selected units of a national labor union.* Unpublished doctoral dissertation, Purdue University.

Tompkins, P. K. (1967). Organizational communication: A state-of-the-art review. In G. Richetto (Ed.), *Conference on organizational communication.* Huntsville, Ala.: George C. Marshall Space Flight Center, NASA.

Tompkins, P. K. (1977). Management qua communication in rocket research and development. *CM, 44,* 1–26.

Tompkins, P. K. (1978). Organizational metamorphosis in space research and development. *CM, 45,* 110–118.

Tompkins, P. K. (1984). Functions of communication in organizations. In C. Arnold & J. W. Bowers (Eds.), *Handbook of rhetorical and communication theory.* New York: Allyn & Bacon.

Tompkins, P. K., & Cheney, G. (1982, November). *Toward a theory of unobtrusive control in contemporary organizations.* Paper presented at the annual meeting of the SCA, Louisville, Ky.

Tompkins, P. K., Fisher, J. Y., Infante, D. A., Tompkins, E. V. (1974). Conflict and communication within the university. In G. R. Miller & H. W. Simons (Eds.), *Perspectives on communication in social conflict.* Englewood Cliffs, N.J.: Prentice-Hall.

Tompkins, P. K., Fisher, J. Y., Infante, D. A., & Tompkins, E. V. (1975). Kenneth Burke and the inherent characteristics of formal organizations. *SM, 42,* 135–142.

Triandis, H. C. (1959). Categories of thought, of managers, clerks, and workers about jobs and people in an industry. *JAP, 43,* 338–344. (a)

Triandis, H. C. (1959). Cognitive similarity and interpersonal communication in industry. *JAP, 43,* 321–326. (b)

Trujillo, N. (1983). "Performing" Mintzberg's roles: The nature of managerial communication. In L. Putnam & M. Pacanowsky (Eds.), *Communication and organization: An interpretive approach.* Beverly Hills: Sage.

Turner, B. A. (1971). *Exploring the industrial subculture.* London: Macmillan.

Turner, S. P. (1983). Complex organizations as savage tribes. *Journal for the Theory of Social Behavior, 7,* 99–125.

Tushman, M. L. (1977). Special boundary roles in the innovation process. *ASQ, 22,* 587–605.

Tushman, M. L. (1978). Technical communication in R & D laboratories: The impact of project work characteristics. *AMJ, 21,* 624–645.

Tushman, M. L., & Nadler, D. A. (1978). Information processing as an integrating concept in organizational design. *AMR, 3,* 613–624.

Tushman, M. L., & Scanlan, T. J. (1981). Boundary spanning individuals: Their role in information transfer and their antecedents. *AMJ, 24,* 289–305. (a)

Tushman, M. L., & Scanlan, T. J. (1981). Characteristics and external orientations of boundary spanning individuals. *AMJ, 24,* 83–98. (b)

Ungson, G. R., Braunstein, D. N., & Hall, P. D. (1981). Managerial information processing: A research review. *ASQ, 26,* 116–134.

Van de Ven, A., Delbeque, A. L., & Koenig, R. (1976). Determinants of communication modes within organizations. *ASR, 41,* 332–338.

Van Maanen, J. (1973). Observations on the making of policemen. *Human Organization, 32,* 407–418.

Van Sell, M., Brief, A., & Schuler, R. (1981). Role conflict and role ambiguity: Integration of the literature and directions for future research. *HR, 34,* 43–71.

Van Voorhis, K. R. (1974). Organizational communication: Advances made during the period from WW II through the 1950s. *JBC, 11,* 11–18.

Walter, G. A. (1980, August). *Beneath bureaucratic anarchies: The principle abyss.* Paper presented at the Academy of Management Meetings, New York.

Walton, R. E., & McKersie, R. B. (1965). *A behavioral theory of labor negotiations: An analysis of a social interaction system.* New York: McGraw-Hill.

Wasylik, J. E., Sussman, L., & Leri, R. P. (1976). Communication training as perceived by training pesonnel. *CQ, 24,* 32–38.

Watson, K. (1982). A methodology for the study of organizational behavior at the interpersonal level of analysis. *AMR, 7,* 392–402. (a)

Watson, K. M. (1982). An analysis of communication patterns: A method for discriminating leader and subordinate roles. *AMJ, 25,* 107–120. (b)

Weaver, C. H. (1958). The quantification of the frame of reference in labor-management communication. *JAP, 42,* 1–9.

Webber, R. A. (1970). Perceptions of interactions between superiors and subordinates. *HR, 23,* 235–248.

Weick, K. (1979). *The social psychology of organizing* (2nd ed.). Reading, Mass.: Addison-Wesley.

Whitfill, J. (1981). Life in the country jail: A look at the loosely coupled system. In L. L. Putnam & M. E. Pacanowsky (Eds.), *Proceedings of the first annual ICA/SCA jointly sponsored conference on interpretive approaches to organizational communication.* West Lafayette, Ind.: Purdue University.

Whorton, J. W., & Worthley, J. A. (1981). A perspective on the challenge of public management: Environmental paradox and organizational culture. *AMR, 6,* 357–361.

Wiio, O. A., Goldhaber, G. M., & Yates, M. P. (1980). Organizational communication research: Time for reflection? In D. Nimmo (Ed.), *Communication yearbook 4.* New Brunswick, N.J.: ICA/Transaction Books.

Wilkinson, I., & Kipnis, D. (1978). Interfirm use of power. *JAP, 63,* 315–320.

Williams, F., & Sundene, B. (1965). A field study in effects of a public relations speech. *JC, 15,* 161–170.

Zelko, H. P. (1951). Adult speech training: Challenge to the speech profession. *QJS, 37,* 55–62.

Zelko, H. P. (1953). Information racks: New frontier in industrial communication. *Management Review, 42,* 75–76.

Zelko, H. P., & Dance, F. E. X. (1965). *Business and professional speech communication.* New York: Holt.

Zey-Ferrell, M., & Aiken, M. (1981). Introduction to critiques of dominant perspectives. In M. Zey-Ferrell & M. Aiken (Eds.), *Complex organizations: Critical perspectives.* Glenview, Ill.: Scott, Foresman.

8. ORAL INTERPRETATION: TWENTIETH-CENTURY THEORY AND PRACTICE

Abel, L. G., & Post, R. M. (1973). Twoards a poor readers theatre. *QJS, 59,* 436–442.

Arrington, R. M. (1975). Some American Indian voices: Resources in intercultural rhetoric and interpretation. *ST, 24,* 191–194.

Babcock, M. M. (1916). Impersonation versus interpretation. *QJPS, 2,* 340–343. (a)

Babcock, M. M. (1916). Interpretative presentation versus impersonation presentation. *QJPS, 2,* 18–25. (b)

Bacon, W. A. (1949). Graduate studies in interpretation. *QJS, 35,* 316–319.

Bacon, W. A. (1960). The dangerous shores: From elocution to interpretation. *QJS, 46,* 148–152.

Bacon, W. A. (1966). *The art of interpretation.* New York: Holt.

Bacon, W. A. (1975). The dangerous shores a decade later. In R. Haas & D. A. Williams (Eds.), *The study of oral interpretation: Theory and comment.* Indianapolis: Bobbs-Merrill.

Bacon, W. A., & Breen, R. S. (1959). *Literature as experience.* New York: McGraw-Hill.

Bahn, E., & Bahn, M. L. (1970). *A history of oral interpretation.* Minneapolis: Burgess.

Barthes, R. (1979). From work to text. In J. V. Harari (Ed.), *Textual strategies: Perspectives in post-structuralist criticism*. Ithaca: Cornell University Press.

Bauman, R. (1975). Verbal art as performance. *American Antrhopologist, 77*, 293–311.

Beloof, R. L. (1966). *The performing voice in literature*. Boston: Little, Brown.

Berleant, A. (1973). The verbal presence: An aesthetics of literary performance. *Journal of Aesthetics and Art Criticism, 31*, 339–346.

Berlo, D. K. (1960). *The process of communication*. New York: Holt.

Booth, W. C. (1961). *The rhetoric of fiction*. Chicago: University of Chicago Press.

Bowen, E. R. (1976). A quarter-century of collegiate oral interpretation festival going. *CE, 25*, 127–131.

Brandes, P. D. (1968). The research: A behavioral approach. In J. W. Gray (Ed.), *Perspectives on oral interpretation: Essays and readings*. Minneapolis: Burgess.

Breen, R. S. (1978). *Chamber theatre*. Englewood Cliffs, N.J.: Prentice-Hall.

Brooks, C. (1947). *The well-wrought urn: Studies in the structure of poetry*. New York: Harcourt.

Brooks, K. (1960). Oral interpretation in American universities. *WJSC, 24*, 142–147.

Brooks, K., Bahn, E., & Okey, L. (1975). *The communicative act of oral interpretation*. Boston: Allyn & Bacon.

Bullough, E. (1912). 'Physical distance' as a factor in art and an aesthetic principle. *The British Journal of Psychology, 5*, 87–118.

Burke, K. (1945). *A grammar of motives*. Englewood Cliffs, N.J.: Prentice-Hall.

Campbell, P. N. (1967). *The speaking and the speakers of literature*. Belmont, Calif.: Dickenson.

Capo, K. E. (1983). From academic to social-political uses of performance. In D. W. Thompson (Ed.), *Performance of literature in historical perspectives*. Lanham, Md.: University Press of America.

Clark, L. D. (1983). Evaluating theatrical directors for promotion and tenure. *Association for Communication Administration Bulletin, 43*, 24–25.

Clark, S. H. (1915). *Interpretation of the printed page*. New York: Row, Peterson.

Coger, L. I. (1963). Interpreters theatre: Theatre of the mind. *QJS, 49*, 157–164.

Coger, L. I., & White, M. R. (1967). *Readers theatre handbook*. Glenview, Ill.: Scott, Foresman.

Conquergood, D. (1980). *From manuscript to print: Interpretation research in speech communication journals.* Fact finding survey sponsored by the Interpretation Division's Research Committee.

Conquergood, D. (1981). *Communication as performance: Dramaturgical dimensions of everyday life.* Paper presented at the Speech Communication Association convention, Anaheim, Calif., November, 1981. Now in John Sisco (Ed.) (1983). *The Jensen Lectures: Contemporary Communication Studies.* Tampa: University of South Florida.

Corbin, M. T. (1962). Response to eye contact. *QJS, 48,* 415–418.

Cronkhite, G. (1970). The place of aesthetics in a paradigm of interpretation. *WJSC, 34,* 274–287.

Cunningham, C. C. (1941). *Literature as a fine art.* New York: Thomas Nelson & Sons.

Curry, S. S. (1891). *The province of expression: A search for principles underlying adequate methods of developing dramatic and oratoric delivery.* Boston: School of Expression.

Doll, H. D. (Ed.). (1982). *Oral interpretation of literature: An annotated bibliography with multimedia listings.* Metuchen, N.J.: Scarecrow Press.

Dolman, J. (1928). *The art of play production.* New York: Harper.

Doty, G. A. (1980). Interview: Gerald Freedman on building a character, *LP, 1,* 51–61.

Ecroyd, D. H., & Wagner, H. S. (1979). *Communicate through oral reading.* New York: McGraw-Hill.

Edwards, P. C. (1983). The rise of 'expression.' In D. W. Thompson (Ed.), *Performance of literature in historical perspectives.* Lanham, Md.: University Press of America.

Eliot, T. S. (1932). The metaphysical poets. In *Selected essays: 1917–1932.* New York: Harcourt.

Espinola, J. C. (1977). Narrative discourse in Virginia Woolf's *To the lighthouse.* In E. M. Doyle & V. H. Floyd (Eds.), *Studies in interpretation II.* Amsterdam: Editions Rodopi, NV.

Espinola, J. C. (1977). Oral interpretation: An act of publication. *Western Journal of Speech Communication, 2,* 90–97.

Espinola, J. C., & Crannell, K. C. (1972). Graduate degree programs in oral interpretation. *ST, 21,* 123–126.

Fine, E. C., & Speer, J. H. (1977). A new look at performance. *CM, 44,* 374–389.

Fine, E. C. (1984). *The Folklore text: From performance to print.* Bloomington: Indiana University Press.

Gamble, T., & Gamble, M. (1976). *Oral interpretation: The meeting of self and literature.* Skokie, Ill.: National Textbook Company.

Geertz, C. (1980). Blurred genres: The refiguration of social thought. *American Scholar, 49,* 165–179.

Geiger, D. (1950). Oral interpretation and the New Criticism. *QJS, 36,* 508–513.

Geiger, D. (1952). A dramatic approach to interpretative analysis. *QJS, 38,* 189–194.

Geiger, D. (1953). Modern literary thought: The consciousness of abstracting. *SM, 20,* 1–22.

Geiger, D. (1955). Pluralism in the interpreter's search for sanctions. *QJS, 41,* 43–56.

Geiger, D. (1963). *The sound, sense, and performance of literature.* Chicago: Scott, Foresman.

Geiger, D. (1967). *The dramatic impulse in modern poetics.* Baton Rouge: Louisiana State University Press.

Geiger, D. (1975). Interpretation and the locus of poetic meaning. In R. Haas & D. A. Williams (Eds.), *The study of oral interpretation: Theory and comment.* Indianapolis: Bobbs-Merrill.

Gilbert, C. A. (1977). *Communicative performance of literature.* New York: Macmillan.

Gray, P. H. (1979). My life and hard times in a speech communication department. *SSCJ, 44,* 159–166.

Gray, P. H. (1982). Readers respond. A letter to the editor. *LP, 2,* 103–105.

Gronbeck, B. (1980). Dramaturgical theory and criticism: The state of the art (or science?). *WJSC, 44,* 315–330.

Grotowski, J. (1969). *Towards a poor theatre.* New York: Simon & Schuster.

Gudas, F. (1983). Dramatism and modern theories of interpretation. In D. W. Thompson (Ed.), *Performance of literature in historical perspectives.* Lanham, Md.: University Press of America.

Haas, R. (1977). Phenomenology and the interpreter's interior distance. In E. M. Doyle, & V. H. Floyd (Eds.), *Studies in interpretation II.* Amsterdam: Editions Rodopi, NV.

Harwood, K. (1955). Listenability and readability. *SM, 22,* 49–52.

Heston, L. (1983). Early graduate education: Michigan, Northwestern, Wisconsin. In D. W. Thompson (Ed.), *Performance of literature in historical perspectives.* Lanham, Md.: University Press of America.

Hodge, F. (1982). *Play directing: Analysis, communication, and style* (2nd ed.). Englewood Cliffs, N.J.: Prentice-Hall.

HopKins, M. F. (1969). Linquistic analysis as a tool for the oral interpreter. *ST, 18,* 200–203.

HopKins, M. F. (1977). Structuralism: Its implications for the performance of prose fiction. *CM, 44,* 93–105.

HopKins, B. W., & Long, M. F. (1981). Performance as knowing and knowing performance. *CSSJ, 32,* 236–242.

Horton, J. (1968). The response: A discussion of empathy. In J. W. Gray (Ed.), *Perspectives on oral interpretation*. Minneapolis: Burgess.

Hudson, L., & Long, B. W. (1981). Teaching interpretation in the 80's. In G. W. Friedrich (Ed.), *Education in the 80's: Speech Communication*. Washington, D.C.: National Education Association.

Hymes, D. (1975). Breakthrough into performance. In D. Ben-Amos & K. Goldstein (Eds.), *Folklore: Performance and communication*. The Hague: Mouton.

Jeffrey, P. R. (1972). Resurrecting the past: Historical documents as materials for readers theatre. *ST, 21,* 310–314.

Johnson, G. E. (Ed.). (1940). *Studies in the art of interpretation*. New York: Appleton-Century.

Kaster, B. (1971). Massaging the message: Marshall McLuhan and oral interpretation. *SSJ, 37,* 195–199.

Kleinau, M. (1969). Symposium: Experimental and empirical studies in oral interpretation: the interpreter. *WJSC, 33,* 227–240.

Kleinau, M. (1981). Contexts for the future. *Issues in interpretation, 4,* 13–15.

Kleinau, M., & Isbell, T. L. (1977). Roland Barthes and the co-creation of text. In E. M. Doyle & V. H. Floyd (Eds.), *Studies in interpretation II*. Amsterdam: Editions Rodopi, NV.

Kleinau, M., & Kleinau, M. D. (1965). Scene location in readers theatre: Static or dynamic? *ST, 14,* 193–199.

Kleinau, M. L., & McHughes, J. L. (1980). *Theatres for literature*. Sherman Oaks, Calif.: Alfred.

Klyn, M. S. (1965). Potentials for research in oral interpretation. *WJSC, 29,* 108–113.

Kristeva, J. (1980). The bounded text. In L. S. Roudiez (Ed.), *Deire in language: A semiotic approach to literature and art*. New York: Columbia University Press.

Lee, C. (1952). *Oral interpretation*. Boston: Houghton Mifflin.

Long, B. W. (1977). Evaluating performed literature. In E. M. Doyle & V. H. Floyd (Eds.), *Studies in interpretation II*. Amsterdam: Editions Rodopi, NV.

Long, B. W. (1983). A "distanced" art: Interpretation at mid-century. In D. W. Thompson (Ed.), *Performance of literature in historical perspectives*. Lanham, Md.: University Press of America.

Long, B. W., & HopKins, M. F. (1982). *Performing literature*. Englewood Cliffs, N.J.: Prentice-Hall.

Long, B. W., Hudson, L., & Jeffrey, P. R. (1977). *Group performance of literature*. Englewood Cliffs, N.J.: Prentice-Hall.

Long, C. C. (1974). *The liberal art of interpretation*. New York: Harper & Row.

Lord, A. B. (1960). *Singer of tales.* Cambridge, Mass.: Harvard University Press.

Lowrey, S., & Johnson, G. E. (1942). *Interpretative reading.* New York: Appleton-Century.

Maclay, J. H. (1971). *Readers threatre: Toward a grammar of practice.* New York: Random House.

Maclay, J. H. (1977). The interpreter and modern fiction: Problems of point of view and structural tensiveness. In E. M. Doyle & V. H. Floyd (Eds.), *Studies in interpretation I.* Amsterdam: Editions Rodopi NV.

Maclay, J. H. (1983). Group performance in academic settings. In D. W. Thompson (Ed.), *Performance of literature in historical perspectives.* Lanham, Md.: University Press of America.

Maclay, J. H., & Sloan, T. O. (1972). *Interpretation: An approach to the study of literature.* New York: Random House.

Magliola, R. (1972). The phenomenological approach to literature: Its theory and methodology. *Language and Style, 5,* 79–99.

McHughes, J. L. (1982). Readers respond. Professor McHughes replies. *LP, 2,* 105–106.

McLuhan, M. (1962). *The gutenberg galaxy.* Toronto: University of Toronto Press.

Mead, G. H. (1934). *Mind, self and society.* Chicago: University of Chicago Press.

Mohrmann, G. P., & Kaplan, S. J. (1980). The effect of training on the oral interpreter's reception of a text. *CSSJ, 31,* 137–142.

Park-Fuller, L. (1981, November). *Designing a performance through an investigation of the authorial consciousness.* Paper presented at the SCA convention, Anaheim, Calif.

Parrella, G. (1971). Projection and adoption: Toward a clarification of the concept of empathy. *QJS, 57,* 204–213.

Parrish, W. M. (1932). *Reading aloud: A technique in the interpretation of literature.* New York: Thomas Nelson & Sons.

Parry, M. (1971). *The making of Homeric verse: The collected papers of Milman Parry.* Oxford: Clarendon Press.

Pearse, J. A. (1980). Beyond the narrational frame: Interpretation and metafiction. *QJS, 66,* 73–84.

Pelias, R. J. (1981, November). *Some implications of constuctivist research for oral interpretation.* Paper presented at the SCA convention, Anaheim, Calif.

Pelias, R. J. (1982). Empathy: Some implications of social cognition research for interpretation study. *CSSJ, 33,* 519–532.

Peterson, E. E., & Langellier, K. M. (1982). Creative double bind in oral interpretation. *WJSC, 3,* 242–252.

Poirier, R. (1971). *The performing self*. New York: Oxford University Press.

Post, R. M. (1967). Oral interpretation and the Stanislavsky method. *SSJ, 32*, 180–187.

Ransom, J. C. (1938). Poetry: A note on ontology. In *The world's body*. New York: Scribner's.

Rarig, F. M. (1940). Some elementary contributions of aesthetics to interpretative speech. *QJS, 26*, 527–539.

Reitz, M. (1966). The application of selected dramatic theories of Stanislavsky as a solution to disunity in readers theatre. *ST, 15*, 191–196.

Reynolds, J. (1969). Symposium: Experimental and empirical studies in oral interpretation: The audience. *WJSC, 33*, 241–249.

Richards, I. A. (1926). *Principles of literary criticism*. New York: Harcourt.

Robb, M. M. (1968). *Oral interpretation of literature in American colleges and universities: A historical study of teaching methods*. (2nd ed.). New York: Johnson Reprint.

Roloff, L. H. (1973). The field of interpretation: Instructive wonder. *Interpretation Division Newsletter*, 7–9.

Rosenblatt, L. M. (1978). *The reader, the text, the poem: The transactional theory of the literary work*. Carbondale: Southern Illinois University Press.

Schneider, R. J. (1976). The visible metaphor. *CE, 25*, 121–126.

Schramm, W. (1963). *The science of human communication*. New York: Basic Books.

Sloan, T. O. (1962). A rhetorical analysis of John Donne's "The Prohibition." *QJS, 48*, 38–45.

Sloan, T. O. (Ed.). (1966). *The oral study of literature*. New York: Random House.

Sloan, T. O. (1967). Restoration of rhetoric to literary study. *ST, 16*, 91–97.

Sloan, T. O. (1969). The oral interpreter and poetry as speech. *ST, 17*, 187–190.

Sloan, T. O. (1971). Oral interpretation in the ages before Sheridan and Walker. *WJSC, 35*, 147–154.

Speer, J. H. (1975). Folklore and interpretation: Symbiosis. *SSJ, 24*, 209–210.

Strine, M. S. (1977). Narrative strategy and communicative design in Flannery O'Connor's "The violent bear it away." In E. M. Doyle and V. H. Floyd (Eds.), *Studies in interpretation II*. Amsterdam: Editions Rodopi NV.

Strine, M. S. (1981, November). *Text, intertext, and the space between: Semiotic bases of literature in performance*. Paper presented at the SCA convention, Anaheim, Calif.

Symposium: Media and the performance of literature (1982). *LP, 2,* 1–45.

Taft-Kaufman, J. (1980). A rhetorical perspective for teaching the solo performance of Shakespearean dramatic literature. *CE, 29,* 112–124.

Taft-Kaufman, J. (1983). Deconstructing the text: Performance implications. *LP, 4,* 55–59.

Tallcott, R. A. (1916). The place for personation. *QJPS, 2,* 116–122.

Tallcott, R. A. (1922). *The art of acting and public reading.* New York: Bobbs-Merill.

Tallcott, R. A. (1923). Teaching public reading. *QJSE, 9,* 53–66.

Tassin, A. (1923). *The oral study of literature.* New York: Knopf.

Thompson, D. W. (1973). Teaching the history of interpretation. *ST, 22,* 38–40.

Tomkins, J. P. (1980). An introduction to reader-response criticism. In J. P. Tompkins (Ed.), *Reader-response criticism: From formalism to post-structuralism.* Baltimore: Johns Hopkins University Press.

Tressider, A. (1942). *Reading to others.* New York: Scott, Foresman.

Valentine, K. B. (1983). "New Criticism" and the emphasis on literature in interpretation. In D. W. Thompson (Ed.), *Performance of literature in historical perspectives.* Lanham, Md.: University Press of America.

Valentine, K. B., & Donovan, M. (1978). Rationale for communication arts in correctional institutions. *Journal of Arizona Communication & Theatre Association, 9,* 2–6.

Wade, A., Colson, T., McDonnell, W. E., & Crouch, I. M. (1983). Interpretation festivals in colleges and universities: Eastern, southern, central, and western states. In D. W. Thompson (Ed.), *Performance of literature in historical perspectives.* Lanham, Md.: University Press of America.

Whitaker, B. J. (1969). Critical reason and literature in performance. *ST, 18,* 191–193.

Whitaker, B. J. (1973). Research directions in the performance of literature. *SM, 40,* 238–242.

Williams, D. A. Impersonation: The great debate (1975). In R. Haas & D. A. Williams (Eds.), *The study of oral interpretation: Theory and comment.* Indianapolis: Bobbs-Merrill.

Williams, D. A. (1983). From academic to psycho-social uses of literature. In D. W. Thompson (Ed.), *Performance of literature in historical perspectives.* Lanham, Md.: University Press of America.

Woolbert, C. (1920). The effects of various modes of public reading. *JAP, 4,* 162–185.

Woolbert, C. H., & Nelson, S. E. (1927). *Art of interpretative speech.* New York: Appleton-Century.

Yordon, J. E. (1982). *Roles in interpretation.* Dubuque, Iowa: William C. Brown.

9. TECHNOLOGY AND COMMUNICATION

Dizard, W. P. (1982). *The coming information age.* New York: Longman.

Dordick, H. S., Bradley, H. G., Nanus, B., & Martin, T. H. (1979, September). Network information services: The emergence of an industry. *Telecommunications, 3*(3), 217–234.

Ellul, J. (1964). *The technological society.* New York: Knopf.

Martin, J. (1977). *Future developments in telecommunications.* Englewood Cliffs, N.J.: Prentice-Hall.

McHale, J. (1976). *The changing information environment.* Boulder, Colo.: Westview Press.

Pelton, J. (1981). *Global talk.* Alphen aan den Rijn, Netherlands: Sijthoff and Noordhoff.

Pool, I. de S. (Ed.). (1977). *The social impact of the telephone.* Cambridge, Mass.: MIT Press.

Pool, I. de S. (1982). *Forecasting the telephone: A restrospective technology assessment.* Norwood, N.J.: Ablex.

Schramm, W., & Roberts, D. F. (Eds.). (1971). *The process and effects of mass communication* (2nd ed.). Urbana, Ill.: University of Illinois Press.

Short, J., Williams, E., & Christie, B. (1976). *The social psychology of telecommunications.* New York: Wiley.

Williams, F. (1982). Doing the traditional nontraditionally. In H. F. Didsbury, Jr., (Ed.), *Communications and the future.* Bethesda, Md.: World Future Society.

Williams, F. (1983). *The communications revolution.* New York: New American Library.

Williams, F., & Dordick, H. (1983). *The executive's guide to information technologies.* New York: Wiley.

Williams, F. (1984). *The new communications.* Belmont, Calif.: Wadsworth.

Williams, F., & Rice, R. (1983). Communication research and the new media technologies. In R. Bostrom (Ed.), *Communication yearbook 7.* Beverly Hills: Sage.

10. MASS MEDIA AND SOCIETY: THE DEVELOPMENT OF CRITICAL PERSPECTIVES

Adams, H. (1918). *The education of Henry Adams.* Boston: Houghton Mifflin.

Archer, G. L. (1960). Conventions, campaigns, and kilocycles in 1924: The first political broadcasts. *JB, 4,* 110–118.

Baird, A. C. (1956). Introduction. In A. C. Baird (Ed.), *American public addresses: 1940–1952*. New York: McGraw-Hill.

Bantz, C. R. (1979). The critic and the computer: A multiple technique analysis of the *ABC Evening News*. *CM, 46,* 27–39.

Bass, J. D. (1981). The romance as rhetorical dissociation: The purification of imperialism in *King Solomon's mine*. *QJS, 67,* 259–69.

Battin, T. C. (1953). The implications of television in education. *SSJ, 18,* 242–247.

Beaver, F. E. (1972). Early film criticism: Some prevailing attitudes and problems. *CSSJ, 23,* 126–131.

Benson, T. W. (1974). *Joe*: An essay on the rhetorical criticism of film. *JPC, 8,* 610/24–618/32.

Benson, T. W. (1978). The senses of rhetoric: A topical system for critics. *CSSJ, 29,* 237–250.

Benson, T. W. (1980). The rhetorical structure of Frederick Wiseman's *High school*. *CM, 47,* 233–261.

Benson, T. W. (1981). Another shooting in cowtown. *QJS, 67,* 347–406.

Berg, D. M. (1972). Rhetoric, reality and mass media. *QJS, 58,* 255–263.

Berg, M. W., & Berg, D. M. (1968). The rhetoric of war preparation: The New York press in 1898. *JQ, 45,* 653–660.

Berger, P. L. (1969). *A rumor of angels*. New York: Doubleday.

Berlo, D. K., & Kumata, H. (1956). *The Investigator*: The impact of a satirical radio drama. *JQ, 33,* 287–298.

Berquist, G. F. (1960). The Kennedy-Humphrey debate. *TS, 8,* 2–3.

Berquist, G. F., & Golden, J. L. (1981). Media rhetoric, criticism and the public perception of the 1980 presidential debate. *QJS, 67,* 125–137.

Bitzer, H. F., & Black, E. (Eds.). (1971). *The prospect of rhetoric: The report of the national developmental project sponsored by the Speech Communication Association*. Englewood Cliffs, N.J.: Prentice-Hall.

Bormann, E. G. (1957). A rhetorical analysis of the national broadcast of Senator Huey Pierce Long. *SM, 24,* 244–257.

Bormann, E. G. (1958). This is Huey P. Long talking. *JB, 2,* 111–122.

Bormann, E. G. (1873). The Eagleton affair: A fantasy theme analysis. *QJS, 59,* 143–159.

Bormann, E. G. (1982). A fantasy theme analysis of the television coverage of the hostage release and the Reagan inaugural. *QJS, 68,* 133–195.

Breen, M., & Corcoran, F. (1982). Myth in the television discourse. *CM, 49,* 127–136.

Brockriede, W. (1968). Dimensions of the concept of rhetoric. *QJS, 54,* 1–12.

Brown, W. R. (1969). Television and the Democratic National Convention of 1968. *QJS, 55,* 237–246.

Brown, W. R. (1976). The prime-time television environment and emerging rhetorical visions. *QJS, 62,* 389–399.

Brown, W. R. (1978). Ideology as communication process. *QJS, 64,* 123–140.

Brown, W. R. (1982). Attention and the rhetoric of social intervention. *QJS, 68,* 17–27.

Brown, W. R., & Crable, R. E. (1973). Industry, mass magazines, and the ecology issue. *QJS, 59,* 259–272.

Burke, K. (1967). Dramatism. In D. Sills (Ed.), *Encyclopedia of social science.* New York: Macmillan.

Campbell, K. K. (1974). Criticism: Ephemeral and enduring. *ST, 23,* 9–14.

Carpenter, R. H., & Seltzer, R. V. (1974). Nixon, *Patton,* and a silent majority sentiment about the Vietnam War: The cinematographic bases of a rhetorical stance. *CSSJ, 25,* 105–110.

Cathcart, R., & Gumpert, G. (1983). Mediated interpersonal communication: Toward a new typology. *QJS, 69,* 267–277.

Carey, J. W. (1975). A cultural approach to communication. *Communication, 2,* 1–22.

Chapel, G. W. (1975). Television criticism: A rhetorical perspective. *WJSC, 39,* 81–91.

Chesebro, J. W., & Hamsher, C. D. (1974). Communication, values, and popular television series. *JPC, 8,* 589/3–603/17.

Cragan, J. F., & Shields, D. C. (1977). Foreign policy communication dramas: How mediated rhetoric played in Peoria in campaign '76. *QJS, 63,* 274–289.

Croft, A. J. (1956). The functions of rhetorical criticism. *QJS, 42,* 283–291.

Cusella, L. P. (1982). Real-fiction versus historical reality: Rhetorical purification in *Kent State*–The docudrama. *CQ, 30,* 159–164.

Davies, R. A., Farrell, J. M., & Matthews, S. S. (1982). The dream world of film: A Jungian perspective in cinematic communication. *WJSC, 46,* 326–343.

Degnan, J. M. (1955). Oratorical style and newscasting, *WS, 19,* 69–73.

Dell, G. W. (1964). Republican nominee: Barry M. Goldwater. In presidential campaign 1964: Symposium. *QJS, 50,* 399–404.

Dimmick, J. W., McCain, T. A., & Bolton, W. T. (1981). Media use and the life span: Notes on theory and method. In G. Wilhoit (Ed.), *Mass communication yearbook.* Beverly Hills: Sage.

Dunham, F. (1955). The social effect of television in the United States. *WS, 19,* 257–262.

Ewbank, H. L. (1940). Trends in research in radio speech. *QJS, 26,* 282–287.

Ewen, S. (1979). The bribe of Frankenstein. *JC, 29,* 12–19.

Foster, E. S. (1957). Radio and television. *TS, 5,* 6–7.

Freely, A. J. (1961). The presidential debates and the speech profession. *QJS, 47*, 60–64.

Free, W. J. (1968). Aesthetic and moral value in *Bonnie and Clyde*. *QJS, 54*, 220–225.

Frentz, T. S., & Farrell, T. B. (1975). Conversion of America's consciousness: The rhetoric of *The exorcist*. *QJS, 61*, 40–47.

Frentz, T. S., & Hale, M. E. (1983). Inferential model criticism of *The empire strikes back*. *QJS, 69*, 278–279.

Frentz, T. S., & Rushing, J. H. (1978). The rhetoric of *Rocky: Part two*. *WJSC, 42*, 231–240.

Geertz, C. (1973). *The interpretation of cultures*. New York: Basic Books.

Glasser, T. L. (1982). Play, pleasure and the value of newsreading. *CQ, 30*, 101–107.

Gonzales, A., & Makay, J. J. (1983). Rhetorical ascription and the gospel according to Dylan. *QJS, 69*, 1–14.

Gould, C., Stern, D., & Adams, T. D. (1981). TV's distorted vision of poverty. *CQ, 29*, 309–314.

Graham, M. W. (1964). Margaret Chase Smith. In presidential campaign 1964: Symposium. *QJS, 50*, 390–393.

Gregg, R. B. (1977). The rhetoric of political newscasting. *CSSJ, 28*, 221–237.

Gronbeck, B. E. (1983). Narrative, enactment, and television programming. *SSCJ, 48*, 229–242.

Grover, D. H. (1966). Broadcasting: A search for identity. *CSSJ, 17*, 106–112.

Gumpert, G. (1975). The rise of uni-comm. *TS, 23*, 34–38.

Haakenson, R. (1958). How much should industry practices influence our teaching of broadcasting. *CSSJ, 9*, 15–20.

Haiman, F. S. (1958). Democratic ethics and the hidden persuaders. *QJS, 44*, 385–392.

Hammerback, J. C. (1974). William F. Buckley, Jr., on *Firing Line*: A case study in confrontational dialogue. *TS, 22*, 23–30.

Harding, H. F. (1957). Rhetoric and the campaign of 1956. *QJS, 43*, 29–54.

Harding, H. R. (1960). John F. Kennedy: Campaigner. In Presidential campaign 1960: A symposium (Part II). *QJS, 46*, 362–364.

Harding, H. R. (1964). Democratic nominee: Lyndon B. Johnson. In Presidential campaign 1964: Symposium. *QJS, 50*, 409–414.

Hardy, W. G. (1938). Radio and the American language. *QJS, 24*, 453–464.

Hendrix, J. (1970). An introductory prognosis. In Rhetorical criticism: prognoses for the seventies: A symposium. *SSJ, 36*, 101–104.

Hendrix, J., & Wood, J. A. (1973). The rhetoric of film: Toward critical methodology. *SSCJ, 39*, 105–122.

Highlander, J. P. (1959). Open heart surgery on television: A case study. *QJS*, *45*, 128–133.

Hildebrant, E. V. (1958). Senator Wayne Morse on speech preparation. *TS*, *6*, 7–9.

Hudson, R. V. (1970). Will Irwin's pioneering criticism of the press. *JQ*, *47*, 263–271.

Immel, R. K. (1929). Speech and the talking pictures. *QJS*, *15*, 159–165.

Kallen, R. A. (1975). Entrance. *JPC*, *9*, 106/8–113/15.

Kerr, H. P. (1964). Democratic convention. In Presidential campaign 1964: Symposium. *QJS*, *50*, 405–408.

Kibler, R. J., & Barker, L. L. (Eds.). (1969). *Conceptual frontiers in speech-communication*. New York: Speech Association of America.

Kidd, V. (1975). Happily ever after and other relationship styles: Advice on interpersonal relations in popular magazines. *QJS*, *61*, 81–39.

Knupp, R. E. (1981). A time for every purpose under heaven: Rhetorical dimensions of protest music. *SSCJ*, *46*, 377–389.

Koester, J. (1982). The Machiavellian princess: Rhetorical dramas for women managers. *CQ*, *30*, 165–172.

Larson, B. (1972). The election eve address of Edmund Muskie: A case study of the televised public address. *CSSJ*, *23*, 78–85.

LeCoat, G. G. (1976). Music and the three appeals of classical rhetoric. *QJS*, *62*, 157–166.

LeCoat, G. G. (1975). The rhetorical element in Monteverdi's *Combat-timento*: A study in "harmonic oratory." *WJSC*, *39*, 165–174.

Levi-Strauss, C. (1963). *Structural anthropology*. New York: Basic Books.

Martin, C. L. (1961). Eisenhower before the press. *TS*, *9*, 23–25.

McGuire, M. (1977). Mythic rhetoric in *Mein Kampf*: A structuralist critique. *QJS*, *63*, 1–13.

Mechling, E. W. (1979). Patricia Hearst: Myth America 1974, 1975, 1976. *WJSC*, *43*, 168–179.

Mechling, E. W., & Mechling, J. (1981). The sale of two cities: A semiotic comparison of Disneyland with Marriott's Great America. *JPC*, *15*, 166–179.

Medhurst, M. J. (1978). Image and ambiguity: A rhetorical approach to *The exorcist*. *SSCJ*, *44*, 73–92.

Medhurst, M. J. (1982). *Hiroshima, mon amour*: From iconography to rhetoric. *QJS*, *68*, 345–370.

Medhurst, M. J., & Benson, T. W. (1981). *The city*: The rhetoric of rhythm. *CM*, *48*, 54–72.

Medhurst, M. J., & Desousa, M. A. (1981). Political cartoons as rhetorical form: A taxonomy of graphic discourse. *CM*, *48*, 197–236.

Merritt, R. L. (1975). The bashful hero in American film of the nineteen forties. *QJS*, *61*, 129–39.

Miles, E. A. (1960). Keynote speech at national nominating conventions. *QJS, 46,* 26–31.

Miller, N. E. (1960). Contest for the presidency: Overview. In presidential campaign 1960: A symposium. *QJS, 46,* 355–356.

Minnick, W. C. (1970). A prognosis in rhetorical criticism: Prognosis for the seventies—A symposium. *SSJ, 36,* 108–110.

Mohrmann, G. P., & Scott, E. E. (1976). Popular music and World War II: The rhetoric of continuation. *QJS, 62,* 145–156.

Morello, J. T. (1980). The great bull market of 1928: Investment advertising and the encouragement of stock speculation. *CSSJ, 31,* 95–105.

Morson, G. S. (1979). The war of the Well(e)s. *JC, 29,* 10–20.

Murphy, R. (1960). Adlai Stevenson: Part I. Stevenson as spokesman. *TS, 8,* 3–5.

Murphy, R. (1960). Adlai Stevenson: Part II. Stevenson and his audience. *TS, 8,* 12–14.

Padrow, B., & Richards, B. (1959). Richard Nixon . . . his speech preparation. *TS, 7,* 11–12.

Pepper, S. C. (1970). *World hypotheses: A study in evidence.* (2nd ed.). Berkeley: University of California Press.

Perry, T. (1970). A contextual study of M. Antonioni's film *L'Eclisse. SM, 37,* 79–100.

Rarick, D. L., Duncan, M. B., Lee, D. G., & Porter, L. W. (1977). The Carter persona: An empirical analysis of the rhetorical visions of campaign '76. *QJS, 63,* 258–273.

Ray, R. F. (1956). Ghostwriting in presidential campaigns. *TS, 4,* 13–15.

Rose, B. (1979). Thickening the plot. *JC, 29,* 81–84.

Rosenfield, L. W. (1969). George Wallace plays Rosemary's baby. *QJS, 55,* 36–44.

Rosenthal, P. I. (1964). Republican national convention. In presidential campaign 1964: Symposium. *QJS, 50,* 394–398.

Roth, L. (1981). Folk song lyrics as communication in John Ford's films. *SSCJ, 46,* 390–396.

Runkel, H. W. (1951). A president prepares to speak. *WS, 15,* 5–9.

Rushing, J. H. (1983). The rhetoric of the American western myth. *CM, 50,* 14–32.

Rushing, J. H., & Frentz, T. S. (1978). The rhetoric of *Rocky:* A social value model of criticism. *WJSC, 42,* 63–72.

Rushing, J. H., & Frentz, T. S. (1980). *The Deer Hunter:* Rhetoric of the warrior. *QJS, 66,* 392–406.

Scher, S. N. (1974). The role of the television critic: Four approaches. *TS, 22,* 1–6.

Schrag, R. L., Hudson, R. A., & Bernabo, L. M. (1981). Television's new humane collectivity. *WJSC, 45,* 1–12.

Schramm, W. (1973). *Men, messages, and media.* New York: Harper & Row.

Scott, R. L. (1977). Diego Rivera at Rockefeller Center: Fresco painting and rhetoric. *WJSC, 41,* 70–82.

Schuetz, J. (1975). *The exorcist:* Images of good and evil. *WJSC, 39,* 92–101.

Sillars, M. O. (1958). The presidential campaign of 1952. *WS, 22,* 94–99.

Smith, H. N. (1957). *Virgin land: The American west in symbol and myth.* New York: Vintage Books.

Spalding, J. W. (1959). The radio speaking of William John Cameron. *SM, 26,* 56–63.

Smith, C. R. (1977). Television news as rhetoric. *WJSC, 41,* 149–159.

Smith, R. L. (1962). Radio's early prospectors—The critics of the twenties. *QJS, 48,* 136–141.

Stasheff, E. (1952). The campaign on the air. In F. Haberman (Ed.), The election of 1950: A symposium. *QJS, 38,* 412–414.

Steele, R. W. (1942). Radio in a world at war. *SSJ, 8,* 37–39.

Swanson, D. L. (1973). Political information, influence, and judgment in the 1972 presidential campaign. *QJS, 59,* 130–142.

Swanson, D. L. (1977). And that's the way it was? Television covers the 1976 presidential campaign. *QJS, 43,* 239–248.

Swanson, D. L. (1977). A reflective view of the epistemology of critical inquiry. *CM, 44,* 207–219.

Townsend, H. W. (1940). Psychological aspects of radio speech. *QJS, 26,* 579–585.

Townsend, H. W. (1944). Factors of influence in radio speech. *QJS, 30,* 187–190.

Turner, K. J. (1977). Comic strips: A rhetorical perspective. *CSSJ, 28,* 24–35.

Turner, K. J. (1982). Press influence on presidential rhetoric: Lyndon Johnson at John Hopkins University, April 7, 1965. *CSSJ, 33,* 425–436.

Tyson, L. B. (1933). The radio influences of speech. *QJS, 19,* 219–224.

Vasilew, E. (1960). The real vs. the mythical campaign. *TS, 8,* 25–27.

Wallace, K. R. (1954). The field of speech, 1953: An overview. *QJS, 40,* 117–129.

Wander, P. (1974). Counters in the social drama: Some notes on *All in the Family. JPC, 8,* 604/18–609/23.

Wander, P. (1976). On the meaning of *Roots. JC, 26,* 64–69.

Wander, P. (1977). *The Waltons:* How sweet it was. *JC, 27,* 148–154.

Wander, P. (1979). The angst of the upper class. *JC, 29,* 85–88.

Weaver, J. C. (1951). Radio and the quality of living. *SSJ, 16,* 272–277.

Wenzel, J. W. (1964). Moderate republicans: Campaign for the nomination, Rockefeller, Lodge, Scranton. In presidential campaign 1964: A political symposium. *QJS, 50,* 385–414.

Wichelns, H. (1925). The literary criticism of oratory. In A. Drummond (Ed.), *Studies in rhetoric and public speaking in honor of James Albert Winans*. New York: Century.

Wilkie, C. (1981). The scapegoating of Bruno Richard Hauptmann: The rhetorical process in prejudicial publicity. *CSSJ, 32*, 100–110.

Windes, R., Jr. (1960). Adlai E. Stevenson's speech staff in the 1956 campaign. *QJS, 46*, 32–43.

Wrage, E. J. (1947). Public address: A study in social and intellectual history. *QJS, 33*, 451–457.

Yauger, J. T. (1971). Persuasive tactics of a radio politician: W. Lee O'Daniel. *SSCJ, 36*, 364–377.

11. FREEDOM OF EXPRESSION AND THE STUDY OF COMMUNICATION

Aristotle. (1946). *Rhetoric* (R. Roberts, trans.). Oxford: University Press.

Bosmajian, H. A., Ed. (1971). *The principles and practice of freedom of speech*. Boston: Houghton Mifflin.

Bosmajian, H. A. (1976). *Obscenity and freedom of expression*. New York: Burt Franklin.

Bosmajian, H. A. (1983). *The principles and practice of freedom of speech*. (2nd ed.). Washington, D.C.: University Press of American.

Bryant, D. C. et al. (1968). *Ancient Greek and Roman rhetoricians*. Columbia, Mo: Artcraft Press.

Chafee, Z., Jr. (1919). Freedom of speech in war time. *HLR, 32*, 932.

Chafee, Z., Jr. (1920). A Contemporary state trial—The United States versus Jacob Abrams *et al. HLR, 33*, 748. (a)

Chafee, Z., Jr. (1920). *Freedom of speech*. New York: Harcourt. (b)

Chafee, Z., Jr. (1941). *Free speech in the United States*. Cambridge, Mass.: Harvard University Press.

Chafee, Z., Jr. (1956). *Three human rights in the Constitution*. Lawrence: University Press of Kansas.

Cicero, M. T. (1903). *De oratore* (J. Watson, trans.) New York: Macmillan.

Cortright, R. L. (1948). The challenge we face. *SSJ, 14*, 33–39.

Courtenay, W. R. (1948). Freedom through religion. *SSJ, 14*, 22–26.

Crocker, Lionel. (1943). Training to exercise freedom of speech. *WS, 7*(2), 1–5.

Emerson, T. I. (1966). *Toward a general theory of the first amendment*. New York: Random House.

Emerson, T. I. (1970). *The system of freedom of expression*. New York: Random House.

Free speech yearbook, Vols. 1 (1962)–22 (1984).

Goodell, C. (1973). *Political prisoners in America*. New York: Random House.

Goodman, R. J., and Gordon, W. I. (1971). The rhetoric of desecration. *QJS, 57*, 23–31.

Gorden, W. I. (1971). *Nine men plus*. Dubuque, Iowa: William C. Brown.

Haiman, F. S. (1965). *Freedom of speech issues and cases*. New York: Random House.

Haiman, F. S. (1967). The rhetoric of the streets: Some legal and ethical considerations. *QJS, 53*, 99–114.

Haiman, F. S. (1976). *Freedom of speech*. Skokie, Ill.: National Textbook Company.

Haiman, F. S. (1981). *Speech and law in a free society*. Chicago: University of Chicago Press.

Hale, L. I. (1948). Freedom through speech. *SSJ, 14*, 9–15.

Hunsaker, D. M. (1979). Freedom and responsibility in first amendment theory. *QJS, 65*, 25–35.

Kane, P. E. (1970). The group libel law debate in the Canadian House of Commons. *TS, 18*(3), 21–25.

Kane, P. E. (1971). Freedom of speech for public school students. *ST, 20*, 21–28.

Klyn, M. (1961). "Cases and problems in freedom of speech." Unpublished manuscript, Freedom of Speech Interest Group, SAA, 1961.

Kutler, S. I. (1982). *The American inquisition*. New York: Hill & Wang.

Lee, I. J. (1948). Freedom from speech. *SSP, 14*, 27–32.

Levy, L. W. (1960). *Legacy of suppression*. Cambridge, Mass.: Harvard University Press.

Levy, L. W. ed. (1966). *Freedom of the press from Zenger to Jefferson*. Indianapolis: Bobbs-Merrill.

Marcuse, H. (1969). *Repressive tolerance. A critique of pure tolerance*. Boston: Beacon Press.

McGaffey, R. (1979). Group libel revisited. *QJS, 65*, 157–170.

Meeman, E. J. (1948). Freedom through the press. *SSJ, 14*, 16–21.

Minnick, W. C. (1982). The United States Supreme court on libel. *QJS, 68*, 384–396.

Murphy, J. J. (1960). Saint Augustine and the debate about a Christian rhetoric. *QJS, 46*, 400–410.

Nadeau, R. (1964). Hermogenes' *On Stases*: A translation with an introduction and notes. *SM, 31*, 361–424.

[*Odyssey*] (1961). (R. Fitzgerald, trans.). New York: Doubleday.

O'Neil, R. M. (1966). *Free speech: Responsible communication under law*. Indianapolis: Bobbs-Merrill.

O'Neil, R. M. (1972). *Free speech: Responsible communication under law* (2nd ed.). Indianapolis: Bobbs-Merrill.

Plato. (1875). [*Apology*] (B. Jowett, trans.). New York: Scribner's.

Plato. (1938). [*Gorgias*] (L. Cooper, trans.). London: Oxford University Press.

Plato. (1938). [*Phaedrus*] (L. Cooper, trans.). London: Oxford University Press.

Plato. (1945). [*The Republic*] (F. Cornford, trans.). New York: Oxford University Press.

Pullias, A. C. (1948). Freedom through education. *SSP, 14*, 4–8.

Reid, J. C. (1965). Broadcast defamation. *SSJ, 30*, 199–214.

Rice, G. P., Jr. (1955). What do students care about freedom of speech? *TS, 3* (4), 19–21.

Rice, G. P., Jr. (1957). Lawful use of loud-speaking devices. *TS, 5* (2), 28–29.

Rice, G. P., Jr. (1959). Student attitudes toward free speech and assembly. *ST, 8*, 53–57.

Rice, G. P., Jr. (1961a). The right to be silent. *QJS, 47*, 349–354.

Rice, G. P., Jr. (1961b). The meets and bounds of speech and law. *CSSJ, 13*, 7–10.

Sandys, J. E. (1885). *M. Tulli Ciceronis ad M. Brutum Orator.* Cambridge: Cambridge University Press.

Tedford, T. L. (1967). Teaching freedom of speech through the use of common materials. *ST, 16*, 269–270.

12. SPEECH COMMUNICATION EDUCATION IN AMERICAN COLLEGES AND UNIVERSITIES

Adler, M. J. (1982). *The Paideia Proposal: An educational manifesto.* New York: Macmillan.

Arnold, C. C. (1959). Rhetoric in America since 1900. In R. T. Oliver & M. G. Bauer (Eds.), *Re-establishing the speech profession: The first fifty years.* New York: SAES.

Banner, J. M., Jr. (1979). Accurate spoken English is a basic skill, too. *Humanities Report, 1*, 2–3.

Becker, S. L., & Ekdom, L. R. V. (1980). That forgotten basic skill: Oral communication. *ACA Bulletin, 33*, 12–25.

Book, C. L. (1981). Speech communication in the secondary school. In G. W. Friedrich (Ed.), *Education in the 80's: Speech Communication.* Washington, D. C.: National Education Association.

Book, C. L., & Pappas, E. J. (1981). The status of speech communication in secondary schools in the United States: An update. *CE, 30*, 199–208.

Clavier, D., Clevenger, T., Jr., Khair, S. E., & Khair, M. M. (1979).

Twelve-year employment trends for speech communication graduates. *CE, 28*, 306–313.

DiSalvo, V. S. (1980). A summary of current research identifying communication skills in various organizational contexts. *CE, 29*, 283–290.

Eadie, W. F. (1979). Earned degree trends in communication studies, 1960–1976. *CE, 28*, 294–300.

Ehninger, D. (1953) Aspects of current research in the history of speech education. *SSJ, 18*, 141–149.

Friedrich, G. W. (1982). History of American Communication Education: A selected, annotated basic bibliography. Annandale, Va.: Speech Communication Module—ERIC Clearinghouse on Reading and Communication Skills.

Friedrich, G. W., & Goss, B. (1984). Systematic desensitization. In J. A. Daly & J. C. McCroskey (Eds.), *Avoiding communication: Communication apprehension, reticence, and shyness.* Beverly Hills: Sage.

Galassi, J. P., & Galassi, M. (1978). Preparing individuals for job interviews: Suggestions from more than 60 years of research. *Personnel and Guidance Journal, 57*, 188–192.

Gibson, J. W., Gruner, C. R., Brooks, W. D., & Petrie, C. R., Jr. (1970). The first course in speech: A survey of U. S. colleges and universities. *ST, 19*, 13–20.

Gibson, J. W., Gruner, C. R., Hanna, M. S., Smythe, M., & Hayes, M. T. (1980). The basic course in speech at U. S. colleges and universities: III. *CE, 29*, 1–9.

Gibson, J. W., Kline, J. A., & Gruner, C. R. (1974). A re-examination of the first course in speech at U.S. colleges and universities. *ST, 22*, 206–214.

Hall, R. N. (Ed.). (1980). Directory of Graduate Programs: Communication Arts and Sciences 1981–1982. Annandale, Va.: SCA.

Hart, R. P. (Ed.) (1979). The status of graduate study in communication [Special issue]. *CE, 28*, 259–393.

Hegstrom, T. G. (1981). The Denver Conference recommendations: A status report. *ACA Bulletin, 35*, 62–67.

Hoffman, J., & Sprague, J. (1982). A survey of reticence and communication apprehension treatment programs at U. S. colleges and universities. *CE, 31*, 185–193.

Kahn, G. S., Cohen, B., & Jason, H. (1979). The teaching of interpersonal skills in U.S. medical schools. *Journal of Medical Education, 54*, 29–35.

Katz, J. (1982). It's time to reverse our retreat from reality in teaching college students. *CHE*, July 21, 40.

Kurtz, P. D., & Marshall, E. K. (1982). Evolution of interpersonal skills training. In E. K. Marshall, P. D. Kurtz, & Associates (Eds.), *Interpersonal helping skills: A guide to training methods, programs, and resources.* San Francisco: Jossey-Bass.

McBath, J. H., & Jeffrey, R. C. (1978). Defining speech communication. *CE, 27,* 181–188.

McCroskey, J. C. (1982). Communication competence and performance: A research and pedagogical perspective. *CE, 31,* 1–7.

Oliver, R. T., & Bauer, M. G. (Eds.). (1959). *Re-establishing the speech profession: The first fifty years.* New York: SAES.

Page, P., & Perelman, S. (1980). *Basic skills and employment: An employer survey.* University of Wisconsin System: Interagency Basic Skills Project.

Potter, D. (1954). The literary society. In K. R. Wallace (Ed.), *History of speech education in America: Background studies.* New York: Appleton.

Ritter, E. M. (1981) The social-cognitive development of adolescents: Implications for the teaching of speech. *CE, 30,* 1–10.

Roberts, J. T. (1982). Recent developments in ELT—Part I and bibliography. *Language Teaching, 15,* 94–110.

Scully, M. G. (1981). General education called a "disaster area" by Carnegie officials; Need for revival seen. *CHE,* April 13, 1.

Sheehy, G. (1976). *Passages: Predictable crises of adult life.* New York: E. P. Dutton.

Speech Communication Directory. Annandale, Va.: SCA.

Wallace, K. R. (Ed.). (1954). *History of speech education in America: Background studies.* New York: Appleton-Century.

Wallin, F. W. (1983). Universities for a small planet—A time to reconceptualize our role. *Change,* March, 7–9.

Watkins, B. T. (1983). Mastery of 6 basic subjects and 6 intellectual skills urged for college-bound students. *CHE, 26* (12), 1, 14–15.

Wilson, G. L., & Gray, P. A. (1983). A survey of practices and strategies for marketing communication majors. *ACA Bulletin, 45,* 32–35.

13. SCIENTIFIC RESEARCH METHODS IN COMMUNICATION STUDIES AND THEIR IMPLICATIONS FOR THEORY AND RESEARCH

Apel, K. O. (1980). *Towards a transformation of philosophy.* Boston: Routledge & Kegan Paul.

Arnold, C. (1970). Rhetorical and communication studies: One world or two? *CSSJ, 21,* 175–180.

Barnland, D. C. (1970). A transactional model of communication. In K. K. Sereno & C. D. Mortensen (Eds.), *Foundations of communication theory.* New York: Harper & Row.

Bateson, G. (1979). *Mind and nature: A necessary unity.* New York: Bantam.

Benson, T., & Pearce, W. B. (1977). Alternative bases for constructing communication theory: A symposium. *CQ, 25*, whole spring issue.

Berelson, B. (1959). The state of communication research. *POQ, 23*, 1–6

Berlo, D. K. (1960). *The process of communication.* New York: Holt.

Bernstein, R. (1978). *Toward a reconstruction of social & political theory.* Philadelphia: University of Pennsylvania Press.

Bitzer, L., & Black, E. (1971). *The prospect of rhetoric: Report of the national development project.* Englewood Cliffs, N.J.: Prentice-Hall.

Bleum, A. W. (1966). Remarks in response to Professor Knower. In P. E. Reid (Ed.), *The frontiers in experimental speech-communication research.* Syracuse: Syracuse University Press.

Bormann, E. G. (1980). *Communication theory.* New York: Holt.

Brigance, W. N. (1933). Wither research? *QJS, 19*, 561.

Canfield, J. W. (1981). *Wittgenstein, language and world.* Amherst: University of Massachusetts Press.

Carrino, E. D. (1959). Psychological influences on rhetoric. In R. T. Oliver & M. G. Bauer (Eds.), *Re-establishing the speech profession: The first fifty years.* New York: SAES.

Cronen, V. E., & Davis, L. K. (1978). Alternative approaches for the communication theorist: Problems in the laws-rules-systems trichotomy. *HCR, 4*, 120–128.

Cronkite, G., & Liska, J. (1976). A critique of factor analytic approaches to the study of credibility. *CM, 43*, 94–107.

Cushman, D. P., & Pearce, W. B. (1977). Generality and necessity in three kinds of theories with special attention to rules theory. *HCR, 3*, 173–182.

Dance, F. E. X. (1967). A helical model of communication. In F. E. X. Dance (Ed.), *Human communication theory.* New York: Harper.

Delia, J. (1981). Remarks made at the annual convention of the ECA, Pittsburgh.

Emmert, P., & Brooks, W. D. (1970). *Methods of research in communication.* Boston: Houghton Mifflin.

Fischer, R., & Pearce, W. B. (1974). An empirical test of the 'one world' hypothesis. *CSSJ, 25*, 142–146.

Harris, M. (1979). *Cultural materialism: The struggle for a science of culture.* New York: Random House.

Hawes, L. C. (1975). *Pragmatics of analoguing.* Reading, Mass: Addison-Wesley.

Hewes, D. E. (1977). *Current perspectives in interpersonal communication: Research methodology.* Paper presented to the ICA, Berlin.

Homans, G. C. (1967). *The nature of social science.* New York: Harcourt.

Hovland, C., Janis, I., & Kelly, H. (1953). *Communication and persuasion.* New Haven: Yale University Press.

Hunt, E. L. (1970). Classical rhetoric and modern communicology. *WS, 34*, 1–7.

Knower, F. H. (1966). The present state of experimental speech-communication research. In Paul E. Reid (Ed.), *The frontiers in experimental speech communication research*. Syracuse: Syracuse University Press.

Lem, S. (1974). *The futurological congress*. New York: Avon.

Lerner, D. (1959). Social sciences: Whence and wither? In Daniel Lerner (Ed.), *The human meaning of the social sciences*. New York: World.

McCroskey, J., & Young, T. J. (1970). *Ethos and credibility: The construct and its measurement after three decades*. Paper presented to the ECA, Philadelphia.

McGuckin, H. E., Jr. (1968). The experimentalist as critic. *WS, 32*, 167–172.

Millar, F. E. (1983). Science as criticism: The burden of assumptions. *CQ, 31*, 224–232.

Miller, G. R. (1965). *Speech communication: A behavioral approach*. Indianapolis: Bobbs-Merrill.

Miller, G. R. (1973). *Humanistic and scientific approaches to communication inquiry: Rivalry or reapprochment*. Paper presented to the SCA, New York.

Miller, G. R., & Burgoon, M. (1973). *New techniques of persuasion*. New York. Harper & Row.

Miller, G. R. (1977). *The pervasiveness and marvelous complexity of human communication: A note of skepticism*. Keynote address presented at the 4th annual Conference on Communication. California State University at Fresno.

Nichols, M. H. (1963). *Rhetoric and criticism*. Baton Rouge: Louisiana State University Press.

Nisbett, R. A. (1982). History of social sciences. *New Encyclopedia Britannia. 16*, 980–990.

Oliver, R. T., & Bauer, M. G. (Eds.). (1959). *Re-establishing the Speech profession: The first fifty years* (15th ed.). New York: SAES.

O'Neill, J. M. (1923). Speech content and course content in public speaking *QJSE, 8*, 27.

Pearce, W. B., & Cronen, V. E. (1980). *Communication, action, and meaning*. New York: Praeger.

Pearce, W. B., Cronen, V. E., & Harris, L. M. (1982). Methodological considerations in building human communication theory. In Frank E. X. Dance (Ed.), *Human Communication Theory*. New York: Harper & Row.

Phillips, G. M. (1981). Science and the study of human communication: An inquiry from the other side of the two cultures. *HCR, 7*, 361–370.

Reardon, K. K. (1978). *Persuasion: Theory and context*. Beverly Hills: Sage.

Reisman, D. (1959). Comments. *PDQ, 23*, 7–15.

Rogers, E., & Kincaid, L. (1981). *Communication networks*. New York: Free Press.

Schramm, W. (1954). *The process and effects of mass communication*. Urbana: University of Illinois Press.

Sereno, K. K., & Mortensen, C. D. (1970). *Foundations of communication theory*. New York: Harper & Row.

Simon, C. T. (1951). Speech as a science. *QJS, 37*, 292.

Thompson, W. N. (1964). *Quantitative research in public address and communication*. New York: Random House.

Walter, O. M. (1963). On views of rhetoric, whether conservative or progressive. *QJS, 49*, 367–382.

Westley, B., & MacLean, M., Jr. (1957). A conceptual model for communications research. *JQ, 34*, 31–38.

Westley, B. (1958). Journalism research and scientific method: I. *JQ, 35*, 161–169.

Wichelns, H. A. (1969). A history of the speech association of the eastern states. *TS, 17*, 3–22. (Originally published in 1959.)

Wilder-Mott, C. (1982). Rigor and imagination. In Carol Wilder-Mott and John Weakland (Eds.), *Rigor and imagination*. New York: Praeger.

Wilson, J., & Arnold, C. (1968). *Public speaking as a liberal art* (2nd ed.). Boston: Allyn & Bacon.

Winans, J. A. (1916). The need for research. *Quarterly Journal of Public Speaking, 1*, 17–23.

Windt, T. O., Jr. (1982). Hoyt H. Hudson: Spokesman for Cornell school for rhetoric. *QJS, 68*, 186–200.

Wittgenstein, L. (1953). *Philosophical Investigations*. G. H. von Wright & G. E. M. Anscombe (Eds.) (G. E. M. Anscombe, trans.). Oxford: Basil Blackwell.

Woelfel, J., & Fink, E. (1980). *The measurement of communication process: Galileo theory and method*. New York: Academic Press.

Zelko, H. P. (1959). Emergence of a rhetoric of discussion. In R. T. Oliver & M. G. Bauer (Eds.), *Re-establishing the speech profession: The first fifty years*. New York: SAES.

14. THE DEVELOPMENT OF RESEARCH IN SPEECH COMMUNICATION: A HISTORICAL PERSPECTIVE

Babcock, M. M. (1915). Teaching interpretation. *QJPS, 1*, 173–76.

Bacon, F. (1899). *Advancement of learning*. New York: Colonial Press.

Baird, A. C. (1928). *Public discussion and debate*. Boston: Ginn.

Bales, R. F. (1950). *Interaction process analysis*. Reading, Mass.: Addison-Wesley.

Becker, S. (1982). *The historical origins of Mass Communications research in our field*. Paper presented at the annual convention of the SCA, Louisville.

Blair, H. (1836). *Lectures on rhetoric and belles lettres*. London: William Sills.

Blanton, S. (1916). Research problems in voice and speech. *QJPS, 2*, 9–17.

Booth, W. C. (1961). *The rhetoric of fiction*. Chicago: University of Chicago Press.

Braden, W. W. (1984). Keeping in touch with the past. *CE, 33*, 121–24.

Brown, M. T. (1886). *The synthetic philosophy of expression*. Boston: Houghton Mifflin.

Burgoon, M. (1976). Public speaking: A hell of a way to run a railroad. *Florida Speech Journal, 10*, 3–7.

Burke, E. (1836). *The sublime and the beautiful*. New York: C. Dearborn.

Burke, K. (1950). *A rhetoric of motives*. Englewood Cliffs, N.J.: Prentice-Hall.

Campbell, G. (1855). *The philosophy of rhetoric*. New York: Harper & Brothers.

Cohen, H. (1980). *Do we have a field or are we out in left field? A history of lost opportunities*. Paper presented at the annual convention of the ECA, Ocean City.

Cohen, H. (1982). *A contemporary history of an ancient field*. Paper presented at the annual convention of the ECA, Hartford.

Cohen, H. (1982). *Behavioral science comes to communication*. Paper presented at the annual convention of the SCA, Louisville.

Cohen, H. (1982). *The dehumanization and decay of values in research in speech communication*. Paper presented at the annual convention of the SCA, Louisville.

Cohen, H. (1983). *On the state of the speech communication discipline*. Paper presented at the annual convention of the SCA, Washington.

Cohen, H. (1983). *Unterschiedliche ansätze and ströungen in der geschichte amerikanischen sprechwissenschaftlicher forschung*. Paper presented at Fachtung der Deutschen Gesellschaft für Sprechwissenschaft und Sprecherziehung, Marburg.

Cohen, H. (1984). *A historical perspective of performance in speech communication*. Paper presented at International Colloquium on Communication, Tempe, Ariz.

Dennis, R. B. (1916). The oratorical contest—A shot in the dark. *QJPS, 2*, 26–30.

Dewey, J. (1910). *How we think*. New York: Heath.

Dithridge, R. L. (1915). High school plays in New York City. *QJPS, 1*, 288–297.

Erikson, E. (1968). *Identity: Youth and crisis*. New York: Norton.

Ewbank, H. L., & Auer, J. J. (1941). *Discussion and debate*. New York: Appleton.

Flemming, E. G. (1918). A comparison of Cicero and Aristotle on style. *QJSE, 4*, 61–71.

Fulton, R. J., & Trueblood, T. C. (1893). *Practical elements of elocution*. Boston: Ginn.

Genung, J. F. (1890). *The practical elements of rhetoric*. Boston: Ginn.

Genung, J. F. (1895). *Outlines of rhetoric*. Boston: Ginn.

Grey, G. W. (1923). How much are we dependent on ancient Greeks and Romans? *QJS, 9*, 258–279.

Grey, G. W. (1954). Some teachers and the transition to twentieth-century speech education. In Karl R. Wallace (Ed.), *A history of speech education in America*. New York: Appleton-Century.

Haberman, F. W. (1954). English sources of American elocution. In Karl R. Wallace (Ed.), *A history of speech education in America*. New York: Appleton-Century.

Habermas, J. (1979). *Communication and the evolution of society*. Boston: Beacon Press.

Hamill, S. S. (1882). *The science of elocution*. New York: Phillips and Hunt.

Hare, A. P. (1976). *Handbook of small group research* (2nd ed.). New York: Free Press.

Hill, A. S. (1895). *The principles of rhetoric*. New York: American Book.

Hochmuth, M., & Murphy, R. (1954). Rhetorical and elocutionary training in nineteenth-century colleges. In Karl R. Wallace (Ed.), *A history of speech education in America*. New York: Appleton-Century.

Homan, G. C. (1950). *The human group*. New York: Harcourt.

Houchin, T. D. (1969). A history of the Speech Association of the Eastern States. *TS, 17*, 23–28.

Hovland, C., Janis, I., & Kelly, H. (1953). *Communication and persuasion*. New Haven: Yale University Press.

Howell, W. S. (1951). *Fenelon's dialogues on eloquence*. Princeton: Princeton University Press.

Howell, W. S. (1956). *Logic and rhetoric in England, 1500–1700*. Princeton: Princeton University Press.

Howes, R. F. (1928). Training in conversation. *QJS, 14*, 253–260.

Hudson, H. H. (1924). Rhetoric and poetry. *QJS, 10*, 143–154.

Hunt, E. L. (1920). Plato on rhetoric and rhetoricians. *QJS, 6*, 35–56.

Kames, H. (1871). *Elements of criticism*. New York: Barnes.

Kay, W. J. (1917). Course I in public speaking at Washington and Jefferson College. *QJPS, 3*, 242–248.

Kleiser, G. (1906). *How to speak in public*. New York: Funk & Wagnalls.

Korzybski, A. (1958). *Science and sanity* (4th ed.). Lakeville, Conn: International Non-Aristotelian Library Publishing Company.

Lewis, O. (1961). *The children of Sanchez*. New York: Random House.

Locke, J. (1813). *An essay on human understanding*. Boston: Cummings & Hilliard.

Lyman, R. L. (1915). Oral English in the high school. *QJPS, 1*, 241–259.

Lynd, R. S., & Lynd, H. M. (1929). *Middletown*. New York: Harcourt.

McBurney, J. J., & Hance, K. G. (1950). *Discussion in human affairs*. New York: Harper & Brothers.

Murray, E. (1934). Speech training as mental hygiene. *QJS, 20*, 37–47.

Murray, E. (1936). Study of factors contributing to the maldevelopment of speech personality. *SM, 2*, 95–108.

Murray, E. (1943). Studies in personal and social integration *SM, 11,* 9–27.

Nisbet, R. (1976). *Sociology as an art form*. London: Oxford University Press.

Oliver, R. T. (1932). Conversation in the speech curriculum. *QJS, 18*, 108–11.

Ong, W. J. (1958). *Ramus: Method, and the decay of dialogue*. Cambridge, Mass.: Harvard University Press.

Perelman, C., & Olbrechts-Tyteca, L. (1969). *The new rhetoric*. Notre Dame, Ind: Notre Dame University Press.

Phelps, A. (1883). *English style in public discourse*. New York: Scribner's.

Quackenbos, G. P. (1860). *Advanced course of composition and rhetoric*. New York: Appleton.

Research Committee, The. (1915). Making a start toward research work. *QJPS, 1,* 194–196.

Research Committee, The. (1915). Research in public speaking. *QJPS, 1,* 24–32.

Riesman, D. (1950). *The lonely crowd*. New Haven: Yale University Press.

Robb, M. M. (1954). The elocutionary movement and its chief figures. In Karl R. Wallace, (Ed.). *A history of speech education in America*. New York: Appleton.

Ryan, J. P. (1917). The Department of Speech at Grinell. *QJPS, 3*, 203–209.

Schmitz, R. M. (1948). *Hugh Blair*. New York: King's Crown Press.

Shorey, P. (1922). What teachers of speech may learn from the theory and practice of the Greeks. *QJS, 8*, 105–131.

Sillars, M. D. (1983). *On the state of speech communication research*. Paper presented at annual meeting of the SCA, Washington, D.C.

Smilowitz, M., & Sillars, M. O. (1982). *The research orientation of the early twentieth-century speech profession*. Paper presented at the annual convention of the SCA, Louisville.

Smith, A. (1963). *Lectures on rhetoric and belle lettres*. London: Thomas Nelson & Sons.

Smith, B. (1981). The father of debate: Protagoras of Abdera. *QJSE, 4*, 196–215.

Smith, D. K. (1954). Origin and developments of departments of speech. In Karl R. Wallace, (Ed.), *A history of speech education in America*. New York: Appleton-Century.

Toulmin, S. E. (1958). *The uses of argument*. Cambridge, Mass: Cambridge University Press.

Turnbull, C. M. (1972). *Mountain people*. New York: Simon & Schuster.

Utterback, W. E. (1937). An appraisal of psychological research in speech. *QJS, 23*, 175–182.

Wallace, K. R. (Ed.). (1954). *A history of speech education in America*. New York: Appleton-Century.

Weaver, R. M. (1953). *The ethics of rhetoric*. Chicago: Henry Regnery.

Weaver, T. A. (1916). The interschool forensic contest. *QJPS, 2*, 141–148.

Wichelns, H. A. (1969). A history of the Speech Association of the Eastern States. *TS, 17*, 3–20.

Winans, J. A. (1915). The need for research. *QJPS, 1*, 17–23.

Winans, J. A. (1915). *Public speaking*. Ithaca: Sewell Publishing.

Winans, J. A. (1917). Public Speaking I at Cornell University. *QJPS, 3*, 153–162.

Woolbert, C. H. (1917). Suggestions as to methods in research. *QJPS, 3*, 12–26.

Woolbert, C. H. (1917b). Conviction and persuasion. *QJS, 3*, 249–264.

Woolbert, C. H. (1923). The teaching of speech as an academic discipline. *QJS, 9*, 1–18.

Woolbert, C. H. (1930). Psychology from the standpoint of a speech teacher. *QJS, 16*, 9–18.

Yost, M. (1917). Argument from the point-of-view of sociology. *QJPS, 3*, 109–127.

15. LEGITIMIZING SPEECH COMMUNICATION: AN EXAMINATION OF COHERENCE AND COHESION IN THE DEVELOPMENT OF THE DISCIPLINE

Anderson, K. E. (1983). Are we ready for the 1980s? *Spectra, 19*, 1–3.

Anderson, K. I. (1977). In defense of departments. In D. E. McHenry (Ed.), *Academic departments*. San Francisco: Jossey-Bass.

Arnold, C. C. (1972). Rhetorical and communication studies: Two worlds or one? *WS, 36*, 75–81.

Becher, T. (1981). Towards a definition of disciplinary cultures. *Studies in Higher Education, 6*, 109–122.

Becker, E. (1968). *The structure of evil*. New York: Free Press.

Becker, S. L. (1974). Presidential message. *Spectra, 10*, 1–2.

Bitzer, L. F., & Black, E. (1977). *The prospect of rhetoric*. Englewood Cliffs, N.J.: Prentice-Hall.

Blankenship, J. (1978). Presidential Message. *Spectra, 14*, 1.

Bochner, A. P., & Krueger, D. (1979). Interpersonal communication theory and research: An overview. In D. Nimmo (Ed.), *Communication yearbook 3*. New Brunswick, N.J.: Transaction Books.

Bowers, J. W. (1968). The pre-scientific function of rhetorical criticism. In T. R. Nilsen (Ed.), *Essays on rhetorical criticism*. New York: Random House.

Brockriede, W. (1971). Trends in the study of rhetoric: Toward a blending of criticism and science. In L. Bitzer & E. Black (Eds.), *The prospect of rhetoric*. Englewood Cliffs, N.J.: Prentice-Hall.

Bryant, D. C. (1971). Retrospect and prospect. *QJS, 57*, 1–10.

Carey, J. (1979). Graduate education in mass communication. *CE, 28*, 282–293.

Carnegie Council on Policy Studies. (1980). *Three thousand futures: The next twenty years in higher education*. San Francisco: Jossey-Bass.

Cohen, H. (1975). Presidential message. *Spectra, 11*, 1–2.

Dance, F. E. X. (1980). Speech communication as a liberal arts discipline. *CE, 29*, 328–331.

Delia, J. (1979). The future of graduate education in speech communication. *CE, 28*, 271–281.

Edwards, R., & Barker, L. (1983). Evaluative perceptions of doctoral programs in communication. *ACA Bulletin*, 76–91.

Ehninger, D. (1968). The field of speech and the SAA. *Spectra, 4*, 1–2.

Ehninger, D., Benson, T. W., Ettlich, E. E., Fisher, W. R., Kerr, H. P., Larson, R. L., Nadeau, R. B., & Niles, L. A. (1971). Report of the committee on the scope of rhetoric and the place of rhetorical studies in higher education. In L. Bitzer & E. Black (Eds.), *The prospect of rhetoric*. Englewood Cliffs, N.J.: Prentice-Hall.

Elms, A. C. (1975). The crisis of confidence in social psychology. *AP, 30*, 967–976.

Etzioni, A. (1960). Two approaches to organizational analysis: A critique and a suggestion. *ASQ, 5*, 257–278.

Friedrichs, R. (1970). *A sociology of sociology*. New York: Free Press.

Geertz, C. (1980). Blurred genres: The refiguration of social thought. *American Scholar, 49*, 165–182.

Gergen, K. J. (1982). *Toward transformation in social knowledge*. New York: Springer-Verlag.

Gouran, D. S. (1979). Speech communication: Its conceptual foundation and disciplinary status. *CE, 28*, 1–8.

Gray, G. W. (1953, September). The development of graduate work in speech in the United States. *ST*, 173–177.

Gray, G. W. (1954). Some teachers and the transition to twentieth-century speech education. In K. P. Wallace (Ed.), *History of speech education in America*. New York: Appleton-Century.

Hager, C. F. (1946, February). Speech and effective communication: Re-examination of basic assumptions. *QJS, 26–30.*

Heckhausen, H. (1972). Discipline and interdisciplinarity. In L. Apostel (Ed.), *Interdisciplinarity*. Brussels: Organization for Economic Cooperation and Development.

Hostettler, G. F. (1980). Speech as a liberal study II. *CE, 29, 332–347.*

House, J. S. (1977). The three faces of social psychology. *Sociometry, 40,* 161–177.

Hovland, C. I., Lumsdaine, A. A., & Sheffield, F. D. (1949). *Experiments on mass communication*. Princeton: Princeton University Press.

Hudson, H. H. (1923). The field of rhetoric. *QJSE, 9,* 167–180.

Hudson, H. H. (1931). The tradition of our subject. *QJS, 17,* 320–329.

Hunt, E. L. (1915). The scientific spirit in public speaking. *QJPS, 1,* 185–193.

Kibler, R. J., & Barker, L. L. (1969). *Conceptual frontiers in speech communication*. New York: SAA.

Knower, F. H. (1929). A suggestive study of public-speaking rating scale values. *QJS, 15,* 30–41.

Knower, F. H. (1936). Some present problems and next steps in graduate work in speech. *QJS, 23,* 456–468.

Koch, S. (1976). Language communities, search cells, and the psychological studies. In W. J. Arnold (Ed.), *Nebraska symposium on motivation 1975.* Lincoln: University of Nebraska Press.

Koch, S. (1981). The nature and limits of psychological knowledge: Lessons of a century qua "science." *AP, 36,* 257–269.

Lazarsfeld, P. F., Berelson, B., & Gaudet, H. (1948). *The people's choice.* New York: Columbia University Press.

Kuhn, T. S. (1962). *The structure of scientific revolutions.* Chicago: University of Chicago Press.

Marlier, J. T. (1980). What is speech communication, anyway? *CE, 29,* 324–327.

McBath, J. H., & Jeffrey, R. C. (1978). Defining speech communication. *CE, 27,* 181–188.

Miller, G. R. (1975). Humanistic and scientific approaches to speech communication inquiry: Rivalry, redundancy, or rapprochement? *WSC, 39,* 230–239.

Miller, G. R. (1981). "'Tis the season to be jolly": A yuletide 1980 assessment of communication research. *HCR, 7,* 371–377.

Miller, G. R., & Berger, C. (1978). On keeping the faith in matters scientific. *WJSC, 42,* 44–57.

Moscovici, S. (1972). Society and theory in social psychology. In J. Israel & H. Jajfel (Eds.), *The context of social psychology: A critical assessment.* New York: Academic Press.

O'Neill, J. M. (1913). The dividing line between departments of English and public speaking. *Public Speaking Review, 3,* 231–238.

O'Neill, J. M. (1935). The professional outlook. *QJS, 21,* 60–72.

Paulson, S. F. (1980). Speech communication and the survival of academic disciplines. *CE, 29,* 319–323.

Rarig, F. M., & Greaves, H. S. (1954). National speech organizations and speech education. In K. Wallace (Ed.), *History of speech education in America.* New York: Appleton-Century.

Reeves, B., & Borgman, C. L. (1983). A bibliometric evaluation of core journals in communication research. *HCR, 10,* 119–136.

Rorty, R. (1979). *Philosophy and the mirror of nature.* Princeton: Princeton University Press.

Royce, J. R. (1976). Psychology is multi-: Methodological variate, epistemic, world view, systemic, paradigmatic, theoretic, and disciplinary. In W. J. Arnold (Ed.), *Nebraska symposium on motivation 1975.* Lincoln: University of Nebraska Press.

Ryan, J. P. (1918). Terminology: The department of speech. *QJSE, 4,* 1–11.

Simons, H. W. (1975). Dealing with disciplinary diversity. *Spectra, 11,* 1–2.

Sloan, T. O., Gregg, R. B., Nilsen, T. R., Rein, I. J., Simons, H. W., Selzner, H. G., Tompkins, P. K., & Zacharias, D. W. (1971). Report of the committee on the advancement and refinement of rhetorical criticism. In L. F. Bitzer & E. Black (Eds.), *The prospect of rhetoric.* Englewood Cliffs, N.J.: Prentice-Hall.

Smith, D. K. (1954). Origin and development of departments of speech. In K. Wallace (Ed.), *History of speech education in America.* New York: Appleton-Century.

Smith, R. G. (1963). The dignity of a profession. *CSSJ, 13,* 83–87.

Snow, C. P. (1963). *The two cultures: And a second look.* New York: Mentor Books.

Thompson, W. N. (1967). *Quantitative research in public address and communication.* New York: Random House.

Trow, M. (1977). Departments as contexts for teaching and learning. In D. E. McHenry & Associates (Eds.), *Academic departments.* San Francisco: Jossey-Bass.

Utterback, W. E. (1922). Measuring the reaction of the audience to an argumentative speech. *QJSE, 8,* 181–183.

Wallace, K. R., Smith, D. K., & Weaver, A. T. (1963). The field of speech: Its purpose and scope in education. *ST, 12,* 331–335.

Wax, M. L. (1969). Myth and interrelationship in social science: Illustrated through anthropology and sociology. In M. Sherif & C. W. Sherif (Eds.),

Interdisciplinary relationships in the social sciences. Chicago: Aldine Publishing.

Weick, K. E. (1979). *The social psychology of organizing, 2nd Edition.* Reading, Mass.: Addison-Wesley.

Wichelns, H. A. (1958). The literary criticism of oratory. In D. C. Bryant (Ed.), *The rhetorical idiom.* Ithaca: Cornell University Press.

Williams, K. R. (1970). Speech communication research: One world or two? *CSSJ, 21,* 175–180.

Williams, R. M., Jr. (1976). Sociology in America: The experience of two centuries. *Social Science Quarterly, 57,* 77–111.

Winans, J. A. (1915). The need for research. *QJPS, 1,* 17–23.

Winans, J. A. (1923). Speech. *QJSE, 9,* 223–231.

Woolbert, C. H. (1916). The organization of departments of speech science in universities. *QJPS, 2,* 64–77.

Woolbert, C. H. (1917, January). Suggestions as to methods in research. *QJPS,* 12–26.

Woolbert, C. H. (1923). The teaching of speech as an academic discipline. *QJSE, 9,* 1–18.

Woolbert, C. H. (1930). Psychology from the standpoint of a speech teacher. *QJS, 16,* 9–18.

Yost, M. (1917). Argument from the point-of-view of sociology. *QJPS, 3,* 109–127.

16. THE RISE AND FALL OF DEPARTMENTS

Arnold, C. C. (1954). The case against speech: An examination of critical viewpoints. *QJS, 40,* 165–169.

Bagwell, P. D. (1952). The Gilman plan for the reorganization of the Speech Association of America: A symposium. *QJS, 38,* 330–340.

Edwards, R., & Barker, L. (1977). A rating of doctoral programs in speech communication, 1976. *ACA Bulletin, 20,* 59–69.

Gillespie, P. P. (1979). Research and the department. *ACA Bulletin, 28,* 2–3.

Lyon, C. E. (1915). The English-public speaking situation. *QJS, 1,* 46–56.

March, J. G., & Romelaer, P. J. (1979). Position and presence in the drift of decisions. In J. G. March & J. P. Olsen (Eds.), *Ambiguity and Choice in Organizations.* Bergen: Universitetsforlaget.

Miller, N. E. (1982). Memorandum sent to the SCA National Headquarters.

Pace, R. W. (1979). Getting our share of internal resources. *ACA Bulletin, 29,* 44–47.

Rarig, F. M., & Greaves, H. S. (1954). National speech organizations and speech education. In Karl R. Wallace (Ed.), *A history of speech education in America*. New York: Appleton-Century.

Smith, D. H. (1979). Ethos, information distribution, and professionalism in higher education. *ACA Bulletin, 29*, 34–38.

Smith, D. K. (1954). Origin and development of departments of speech. In Karl R. Wallace (Ed.), *A History of Speech Education in America*. New York: Appleton-Century.

Wood, R. V. (1979) Hard times. *ACA Bulletin, 24*, 11–17.

17. KEEPING THE FAITH: ON BEING A TEACHER-SCHOLAR IN THE 20TH CENTURY

Allen, R. R., & Brown, K. L. (Eds.). (1976). *Developing communication competence in children: a report of the SCA's national project on speech communication competencies*. Skokie, Ill.: National Textbook.

Asante, M. [Smith, A. L.] (1980). *Contemporary black thought: Alternative analysis in social & behavioral science]* (A. L. Smith, Ed. and trans.). New York: Sage.

Barrett, H. (Ed.). (1974). *Rhetoric of the people*. Amsterdam: Editions Rodopi NV. Blankenship, J. (1974). Karl R. Wallace: The giver of good reasons. *ST, 23*, 183–190.

Blankenship, J. (1978, November). *In remembrance of Marie Hochmuth Nichols*. Paper presented at the annual meeting of the SCA, Minneapolis.

Blankenship, J. (1978, November). *A tribute to Robert K. Kibler*. Remarks delivered at the annual meeting of the SCA, Minneapolis.

Blankenship, J., & Stelzner, H. G. (Eds.). (1976). *Rhetoric & communication: Studies in the University of Illinois tradition*. Urbana, Chicago, London: University of Illinois Press.

Book, C. L., & Pappas, E. J. (1981). The status of speech communication in secondary schools in the United states: An update. *CE, 30*, 199–208.

Brockriede, W. (1976). Letter. In J. Blankenship & H. G. Stelzner (Eds.), *Rhetoric & communication: Studies in the University of Illinois tradition*. Urbana, Chicago, London: University of Illinois Press.

Brown, D. R. (1975). Self-disclosure & identification: Dyadic communication of the new black assistant professor on a white campus. *Association for Communication Administration Bulletin, 13*, 22–26.

Bryant, D. C. (1979). Waldo W. Braden. *Spectra, 15*, 20.

Buckley, D. C. (1982). *Faculty career paths in speech communication*. Unpublished doctoral dissertation, Southern Illinois University.

Burke, K. (1969). *A grammar of motives*. Berkeley: University of California Press. (Originally published, 1945.)

Clark, D. L. (1957). *Rhetoric in Greco-Roman education.* New York: Columbia University Press.

Cummings, M. S. (1975). The profession and how it relates to the black experience. *ACA Bulletin, 13,* 27–28.

Cummings, M. S., & Daniel, J. (1980). Scholarly literature in the black idiom. In B. E. Williams & O. Taylor (Eds.), *Working papers for the International Conference on Black Communication: August, 1979.* New York: Rockefeller Foundation.

Daniel, J. L. (1976). Black rhetoric: The power to define self in an age of world citizenship. *ACA Bulletin, 16,* 39–42.

Daniel, J. L. (1974). *Black communication: Dimensions of research and instruction.* New York: SCA.

DeVito, J. (1977). Marie Hochmuth Nichols. *Spectra, 13,* 16.

Donner, S. T. (1962). Ralph Dennis: A great teacher. *ST, 11,* 214–220.

Edwards, M. L. (1975). A reflection upon reality: Speech communication and its relationship to the black experience. *ACA Bulletin, 13,* 29–30.

Gilman, W. E. (1974, April). Eastern public speaking conference—1949. *ECA Newsletter,* p. 7.

Gronbeck, B. (1980). Douglas Ehninger. *Spectra, 16,* 4.

Gulley, H. E., & Seabury, H. F. (1954). Speech education in twentieth-century public schools. In Karl R. Wallace (Ed.), *History of speech education in America.* New York: Appleton.

Haberman, F. W. (1961). Toward the ideal teacher of speech. *ST, 10,* 1–9.

Harding, H. (Ed.). (1940). *Eastern public speaking conference: 1940.* New York: H. W. Wilson.

Hawthorne, L. S. (1977). Black studies: Where we are and where we ought to be. *ACA Bulletin, 22,* 32–33.

Hochmuth, M. K. (1955). Wayland Maxfield Parrish. *ST, 4,* 159–161.

Howell, W. S. (1972). Franklin Knower. *Spectra, 7,* 3.

Hudson, H. (1944). Alexander M. Drummond. In D. C. Bryant, B. Hewitt, K. R. Wallace, H. A. Wichelns (Eds.), *Studies in speech and drama in honor of Alexander M. Drummond.* Ithaca: Cornell University Press.

Hunt, E. L. (1965). Introductory remarks. In *Addresses delivered at the meeting honoring Professor Harry Caplan.* Remarks delivered at the annual meeting of the SCA, New York.

Konigsberg, E. (1959). Speech education in public high schools. In R. T. Oliver & M. G. Bauer, (Eds.), *Re-establishing the speech profession: The first fifty years.* New York: SAES.

Lee C. I. (1962). Cornelius Carman Cunningham. *ST, 11,* 297–299.

Lilly, E. K. (1955). The young Lew Sarett. *ST, 4,* 22–23.

McBride, Frank (1955). Rarig. *ST, 4,* 231–232.

Nebergall, R., & Wenzel, J. (1976). Preface: Professors Wallace, Nichols, Murphy, and the Illinois tradition. In J. Blankenship & H. G. Stelzner

(Eds.), *Rhetoric and communication: Studies in the University of Illinois tradition*: Urbana, Chicago, London: University of Illinois Press.

Nelson, S. E. (1955). Charles Henry Woolbert. *ST, 4*, 114–117.

Niles, L. A. (1975). Speech communication at predominantly black colleges. *ACA Bulletin, 14*, 17–18.

Nichols, M. H. (1976). Bower Aly. *Spectra, 12*, 7.

Okey, L. L. (1962). Thomas Clarkson Trueblood, pioneer, 1856–1951. *ST, 11*, 10–14.

Oliver, R. T., & Bauer, M. G. (Eds.). (1959). *Re-establishing the speech profession: The first fifty years*. New York: SAES.

Paulson, S. F. (1980). The quest of Carroll C. Arnold. In E. E. White (Ed.), *Rhetoric in transition: Studies in the nature and uses of rhetoric*. College Park: Pennsylvania State University Press.

Polanyi, M. (1962). *Personal knowledge*. Chicago: University of Chicago Press.

Rueckert, W. H. (1982). Some of the many Kenneth Burkes. In H. White & M. Brose, (Eds.), *Representing Kenneth Burke*. Baltimore: Johns Hopkins University Press.

Smith, A. L. [Asante, M.] (Ed.). (1972). *Language, communication, and rhetoric in black America*. New York: Harper & Row.

Smith, D. K. (1954). Origin and developments of departments of speech. In Karl R. Wallace (Ed.), *History of speech education in America*. New York: Appleton-Century.

Smith, J. F. (1962). Maud May Babcock, 1867–1954. *ST, 11*, 105–220.

Van Graber, M. J. (1982). Dedication. In R. E. McKerrow (Ed.), *Explorations in rhetoric: Studies in honor of Douglas Ehninger*. Glenview, Ill.: Scott, Foresman.

Wallace, K. R. (Ed.) (1954). *History of speech education in America*. New York: Appleton-Century.

Weaver, A. T. (1964). Gladys Louise Borchers—Teacher of speech. *ST, 13*, 1–5.

Weaver, A. T., & Borchers, G. L. (1952). Smith, D. K. *The teaching of speech*. New York: Prentice-Hall.

Winchelns, H. A. (1961). James Albert Winans. *ST, 10*, 259–264.

Wilder-Mott, C. (1981). Rigor and imagination. In C. Wilder-Mott & J. H. Weakland (Eds.), *Rigor and imagination: Essays from the legacy of Gregory Bateson*. New York: Praeger.

Wolvin, A. C. (1982). Speech communication education in the eastern states. *CQ, 30*, 270–273.

Notes on Contributors

THOMAS W. BENSON is Professor of Speech Communication at The Pennsylvania State University. He is a former editor of *Communication Quarterly* and a recipient of the Speech Communication Association's Robert J. Kibler Memorial Award.

JANE BLANKENSHIP is Professor of Communication Studies at the University of Massachusetts, Amherst. A former president of the Eastern Communication Association and the Speech Communication Association, she has published articles on contemporary rhetorical theory, language behavior, and political communication and is the author or editor of several books, including *A Sense of Style* and (with Hermann Stelzner) *Rhetoric and Communication*. Her essay "Influence of Mode, Sub-mode, and Speaker Predilection on Style" received an SCA Golden Anniversary Monograph Award.

ARTHUR P. BOCHNER is Professor of Communication at the University of South Florida, Tampa. He has written extensively on the dilemmas of interpersonal communication in long-term relationships and the development of modern communication theory. His recent publications appear in *The Handbook of Rhetoric and Communication* and *Rigor and Imagination: Essays from the Legacy of Gregory Bateson*.

WILLIAM R. BROWN, Professor of Communication at Ohio State University, has served on editorial boards for *Central States Speech Journal, Communication Monographs*, and *The Quarterly Journal of Speech*. His media criticism has appeared in these journals, as well as in *Imagemaker: Will Rogers and the American Dream* and three editions of *The Rhetoric of Western Thought*. He received the 1979 Golden Anniversary Award for "Ideology as Communication Process" (*QJS*, 1978).

GEORGE CHENEY is a lecturer in speech communication at the University of Illinois at Urbana-Champaign. He is currently completing his doctoral dissertation, a study of the U. S. Catholic Church organization, under Phillip K. Tompkins at Purdue University. His research and teaching center on organizational communication, specifically the ways in which organizational rhetoric shapes and is shaped by individual participation in the dominant institutions of society. He has published in *The Quarterly Journal of Speech*, *Communication Monographs*, and *Central States Speech Journal*, and has coauthored several book chapters.

HERMAN COHEN is Professor of Speech Communication at The Pennsylvania State University. His research specialty is the history of rhetorical theory. He served as president of the Speech Communication Association and as editor of *Western Speech Communication Journal*.

ERIC M. EISENBERG is Assistant Professor of Communication Arts and Sciences at the University of Southern California. His articles dealing with organizational communication and communication networks have appeared in *Human Communication Research* and *Journal of Communication*. He is the recipient of the 1982 W. Charles Redding Award for the outstanding doctoral dissertation in organizational communication.

RICHARD LEO ENOS is Associate Professor of Rhetoric and Director of Graduate Studies in English at Carnegie-Mellon University. In addition to his doctoral work in speech communication, classical studies, and ancient history at Indiana University, he has studied at the American School of Classical Studies at Athens and has been involved in research projects in Greece since 1972. He is the first recipient of the Karl R. Wallace Memorial Award for research in classical rhetoric.

GUSTAV W. FRIEDRICH is Professor and Chair of the Department of Communication at the University of Oklahoma. He has coauthored *Teaching Speech Communication in the Secondary School*, *Public Communication*, *Growing Together . . . Classroom Communication*, and has edited *Education in the 80's: Speech Communication*. He has served as editor of *Communication Education* and as president of the Central States Speech Association.

DENNIS S. GOURAN is Professor of Speech Communication and Head of the Department of Speech Communication at The Pennsylvania State University. He is the author of *Discussion: The Process of Group Decision-Making*, *Making Decisions in Groups: Choices and Consequences*, and numerous essays and research reports on communication in decision-making groups. He is a former editor of *Central States Speech Journal* and current president of the Central States Speech Association.

RICHARD B. GREGG is Professor of Speech Communication at The Pennsylvania State University. He has written articles and book chapters on rhetorical criticism, rhetorical theory, and American political rhetoric. He is coauthor of *Speech Behavior and Human Interaction* and author of *Symbolic Inducement and Knowing: A Study in the Foundations of Rhetoric.*

DIANE S. HOPE is Associate Professor of Language and Literature at the Rochester Institute of Technology. Among her publications in the rhetoric of movements are "Redefinition of Self: A Comparison of Black and Women's Liberation Rhetoric," "Intimate Communication Between Women," and with Warren L. Schaich, "The Prison Letters of Martin Sostre: Documents of Resistance." In 1979–1981 she designed and implemented an interdisciplinary major program in communication at Randolph Macon Women's College, Virginia, under a grant from the National Endowment for the Humanities.

PETER E. KANE is Professor of Communication at the State University of New York, College at Brockport, where he teaches freedom of speech and mass media law. He is a longtime member of the Speech Communication Association's Commission on Freedom of Speech and has served as editor of *Free Speech* and *Free Speech Yearbook.*

MICHAEL C. LEFF is Professor of Communication Arts at the University of Wisconsin, Madison. He is former book review editor of the *Quarterly Journal of Speech* and is a member of the editorial board of *Pre-text: Interdisciplinary Journal* and of *Rhetoric Society Quarterly.* He is a councillor of the *International Society for the History of Rhetoric* and is a frequent contributor to journals in speech communication.

DIANE C. MADER is Assistant Professor of Communications at Nassau County Community College. She has published a number of articles in *et cetera* and is presently writing a book on interpersonal communication. She has a special interest in the relationship between speech and writing and has given a number of convention papers on this topic.

THOMAS F. MADER is Associate Professor of Communications at Hunter College, City University of New York. He has published articles and reviews in *Philosophy and Rhetoric, College Composition and Communica-*

tion, Quarterly Journal of Speech, et cetera, and *Journal of Communication*. He is presently working on an analysis of William Buckley's use of words.

W. BARNETT PEARCE is Professor and Chair of Communication Studies at the University of Massachusetts, Amherst. He was president of the Eastern Communication Association in 1981–1982. He is coauthor of *Communicating Personally* (with Charles Rossiter) and *Communication, Action and Meaning: The Construction of Social Realities* (with Vernon Cronen). His forthcoming book, from SIU Press, coauthored with Uma Narula, deals with communication theory in the context of national development in India. His research in gender, intercultural communication, family therapy, conversation, international communication, and other subjects expresses the perspective of the theory of "coordinated management of meaning."

MARGARET ORGAN PROCARIO is a doctoral candidate and teaching assistant in the Department of Communication Arts, University of Wisconsin, Madison.

LINDA L. PUTNAM is Associate Professor of Communication at Purdue University. She has authored essays on conflict in organizations, bargaining, and critical approaches to organizational communication in anthologies and in *Communication Monographs; Human Communication Research; Communication Yearbooks 4, 5*, and *6*; and *Western Journal of Speech Communication*. She is coeditor of *Communication and Organization: An Interpretive Approach*, and serves on the editorial boards of several journals.

WILLIAM K. RAWLINS is Assistant Professor of Speech Communication at The Pennsylvania State University. His articles dealing with interpersonal communication and friendship have appeared in *Human Communication Research, Communication Monographs*, and *Communication Quarterly*.

LAWRENCE W. ROSENFIELD is Professor of Communications at Hunter College, City University of New York. He is the author of *Aristotle and Information Theory* and, with Laurie Hayes and Thomas Frentz, is coauthor of *The Communicative Experience*.

JILL TAFT-KAUFMAN is Associate Professor of Speech Communication and Dramatic Arts at Central Michigan University. Her articles on the theory and practice of oral interpretation have appeared in *Literature in Performance, Communication Education, Central States Speech Journal*, and *The*

Michigan Speech Association Journal. She is a contributor to the abstracts for *Literature in Performance* and has chaired the Research Committee of the Interpretation Division of SCA. Her work on rhetorical criticism of literature includes "Rhetorical Implications of Shakespeare's Changes in His Source Material for *Romeo and Juliet,*" in *Rhetorical Dimensions in Media: A Critical Casebook.*

FREDERICK WILLIAMS is Professor of Communications in the Annenberg School of Communications at the University of Southern California, where he served as founding Dean from 1972 to 1980.

Index